T0309184

INTRO

A Guide to COMMUNICATION SCIENCES *and* DISORDERS

FOURTH EDITION

INTRO

A Guide to COMMUNICATION SCIENCES *and* DISORDERS

FOURTH EDITION

Michael P. Robb, PhD

PLURAL PUBLISHING INC.

Plural Publishing Inc.

9177 Aero Drive, Suite B
San Diego, CA 92123

email: information@pluralpublishing.com
website: https://www.pluralpublishing.com

Typeset in 11/33 Palatino by Flanagan's Publishing Services, Inc.
Printed in the United States of America by Bradford & Bigelow

Library of Congress Cataloging-in-Publication Data

Names: Robb, Michael P., author.
Title: INTRO: a guide to communication sciences and disorders / Michael P. Robb.
Other titles: Guide to communication sciences and disorders
Description: Fourth edition. | San Diego, CA: Plural Publishing, Inc., [2025] | Includes bibliographical references and index.
Identifiers: LCCN 2023034413 (print) | LCCN 2023034414 (ebook) | ISBN 9781635504767 (paperback) | ISBN 1635504767 (paperback) | ISBN 9781635504385 (ebook)
Subjects: MESH: Communication Disorders | Hearing Disorders
Classification: LCC RC423 (print) | LCC RC423 (ebook) | NLM WL 340.2 | DDC 362.196/855—dc23/eng/20231011
LC record available at https://lccn.loc.gov/2023034413
LC ebook record available at https://lccn.loc.gov/2023034414

CONTENTS

SECTION 2
Developmental Communication Disorders

FOREWORD TO THE FIRST EDITION

Prior to his passing, Professor John H. Saxman (1938–2023) was intending to pen the Foreword to the fourth edition of INTRO. In memory of his contributions to the profession and support of this book, his original Foreword to the first edition is provided below.

Welcome to the fascinating and complex fields of speech and language pathology and audiology. These two professions are applied fields that draw on theory and knowledge from a variety of disciplines that support the practices devoted to prevention, assessment and evaluation, and treatment of disorders of speech, language, and hearing across the life span of human beings. This textbook provides the beginning student with an understanding of the basic conceptual and content knowledge and the vocabulary necessary to appreciate the complexity of human communication disorders. Within the crowded arena of introductory textbooks, there are a number of features of this text that make it particularly appealing, not the least of which is the sole authorship by Professor Robb. The distinct advantage of one author is that the perspective across the various topics is consistent and presented in a cohesive organization and level throughout. Capturing the right level is important for an introductory text, and Professor Robb has done so based on his years of teaching the course for which this text is intended.

There are additional features of this text that add to its appeal. These features are in its contextualization. I applaud the approach the author takes to provide a context for both speech-language pathology and audiology within the broadly defined communication sciences. The scope of practice within each profession engages activities not directly targeted at communication, such as swallowing or intraoperative auditory assessment; however, the raison d'être of these professions is situated in human communication. The inclusion of historical referents within each chapter is another appealing feature, which gives the beginning student a perspective on how the contemporary fields have evolved from the contributions of earlier scholars working in different disciplines such as physics, engineering, phonetics, psychology, medicine, and philosophy. The historical references also allow the student to appreciate the tremendous advances in technology that assist the current speech and hearing scientists and practitioners to better understand and serve individuals with communication impairments. Finally, the text is written with full recognition that students around the world are preparing for careers in speech and language pathology and in audiology. Although the education and training will follow different models and the practice requirements might be different in various countries, the core substance of the fields is essentially the same. The text limits its discussion to the English-speaking communities but clearly addresses the relevant multilingual/multicultural issues. Here the author brings his personal experience from teaching the introductory course in the United States and New Zealand.

A few observations about the communication context are in order. The overview of communication helps the reader appreciate the fundamental role of communication in all of nature. The most common definitions of communication involve some description of a mutual exchange of information or energy between two entities with varying degrees of elaboration of the process and its outcomes. A definition of this sort reminds us that communication is a universal among living entities ranging from the biochemical exchanges of unicellular organisms to complex symbolic systems such as language in humans.

The simple three-component model of communication (a sender, a communication channel, and a receiver) adapted from Shannon and Weaver has the advantage of identifying the major functional components involved in the act of communication. The model is an abstraction of the factors that influence and define the communication outcome. Applying this model to human communication and its disorders requires the specific knowledge of how the communication partners, who are both senders and receivers, acquire and use natural language abilities and what factors can impair the ability to acquire and use language for effective communication. That, of course, leads beyond the abstraction of a communication model to the primary content of this textbook. The content is an elaboration on the specifics of the human language user in a social milieu and the disorders that disrupt communication through problems that can originate anywhere within the communication dynamic. The human communicator is more than a "source code" generator and interpreter in an information system process and therein lies the nexus of communication sciences and disorders as a discipline of study.

Communicating with others is such a common experience that we give little thought to how it is accomplished. Because we are so familiar with being communicators, we generally are unaware of the learning and practice that went into developing the necessary communication skills that began as early as while still in the womb. We easily use different modes of communication available to us in our daily activities and only on occasion or in very limited circumstances do we experience the challenges of impeded communication. The situation is quite different, of course, for the person who has a communication disorder. The nature of the communication disorder and its consequences for the individual who experiences it depend on a host of interacting factors: organismic and environmental, developmental and acquired. The learning objectives stated for each chapter in this text appropriately focus on understanding the nature and consequences of the major disorders and their treatment in human beings.

Finally, it is appropriate to recognize the importance of the author 's experience in the education of students at all levels of their apprenticeship in the field. Because he has taught beginning students in a career spanning several decades, he is familiar with the changing learning culture and mode of today's student. This experience is realized in the writing style and learning aids used throughout the text. In addition to his significant contributions as a teacher, Professor Robb has maintained an active research and scholarship agenda that gives him further credibility as an authoritative escort for beginning students in their introduction to the field. On a personal note, it is a unique pleasure for me as I approach the close of my academic career to acknowledge a treasured friend and former student for his achievement in producing a book that promises to stimulate the development of many future careers in communication science and disorders.

John H. Saxman, PhD
Professor Emeritus
Speech-Language Pathology and Audiology
Teachers College, Columbia University
New York, New York

PREFACE

Since the original 2010 publication of *INTRO: A Guide to Communication Sciences and Disorder*, the book remains unique in many ways from other introductory texts. The structure of the book is consistent across chapters to assist beginning students in grasping new vocabulary and concepts. Each chapter provides a focus on "past and present." An introduction to each of the various disorders would not be complete without knowing some of the fascinating historical background surrounding each disorder, as well as current theories. A portion of each chapter is dedicated to diverse and cultural aspects of communication disorders as well as prevalence information about various communication disorders as found in English-speaking countries around the world, including Australia, Canada, the United Kingdom, the United States, and New Zealand. The chapters include a series of FYI (for your information) items, which present interesting and novel information about the topic area. Websites are listed at the end of the chapters to provide students with an opportunity to learn more about each topic. Many of these websites provide up-to-date links to streaming video examples.

This fourth edition of *INTRO* has been expanded from 13 to 15 chapters. The original chapter covering neurogenic communication disorders has been divided into separate chapters on neurogenic language disorders and motor speech disorders. A new chapter on the ever-expanding topic of autism spectrum disorder is new to this edition and provides more comprehensive coverage of the range of developmental communication disorders.

Being the sole author of this book ensures a balanced writing style that is missing from existing introductory texts. My intent is to deliver clear and concise information for students wishing to learn the fundamentals of the myriad of communication disorders that occur across the life span. For some, this information will serve as a springboard for pursuit of a professional career in audiology and speech-language pathology. For others, my hope is that you will acquire an appreciation of the gift of communication that we so often take for granted. Students and instructors alike should be pleased with this new edition of *INTRO*.

As in previous editions of the book, there are some individuals I wish to thank. I am particularly indebted to Ray Kent who encouraged me to write a book of this kind and provided valuable oversight throughout its creation. Most of the illustrations throughout the book were made possible by the tireless work of Chia Pan. My initial exposure to the field of communication sciences and disorders was provided by my mother, Mary Jo Robb, whose professional career was spent educating children. During my first year of university study, she introduced me to one of her colleagues, a school-based speech-language pathologist. After our meeting, I changed my university major to communication sciences and disorders and never looked back. Finally, there was no one more influential in shaping my career than John Saxman (1938–2023), who passed away during the final stages of this book revision. He was a soft-spoken, kind-hearted individual who was a superb mentor, good friend, and best man. Thank you, John.

—M. Robb

Communication Sciences and Disorders
Nazareth College

University of Wyoming

College of Applied Medical Sciences
King Saud University
Riyadh, Saudi Arabia

REVIEWERS OF THE FOURTH EDITION

Plural Publishing, Inc. and the author would like to thank the following reviewers for taking the time to provide their valuable feedback during the development process:

Jane Bickford, BAppSc (SpPath), PhD, CPSP
Lecturer
Speech Pathology and Audiology
Flinders University
South Australia, Australia

Angela D. Haendel, PhD Candidate, CCC-SLP
Clinic Director and Assistant Professor
Speech-Language Pathology
Concordia University Wisconsin
Mequon, Wisconsin

Melissa Johnson, PhD, CCC-SLP
Assistant Professor
Communication Sciences and Disorders
Nazareth College
Rochester, New York

Breanna Krueger, PhD, CCC-SLP
Assistant Professor
Communication Disorders
University of Wyoming
Laramie, Wyoming

Lisa Rickard, AuD, CCC-A
Assistant Clinical Professor
Department of Hearing and Speech Sciences
University of Maryland
College Park, Maryland

Carmen Larimore Russell, PhD, CCC-SLP
Professor and Chairperson
Communication Disorders and Deaf Education
Fontbonne University
Saint Louis, Missouri

Mohammed Safi, PhD, CCC-SLP
Assistant Professor
College of Applied Medical Sciences
King Saud University
Riyadh, Saudi Arabia

To Jenne

SECTION 1

Background to Communication Sciences and Disorders

1

COMMUNICATION DISORDERS AND THE PROFESSIONS

OBJECTIVES

After reading this chapter, the student should be able to:

- Recognize the different forms and types of communication.
- Demonstrate an understanding of the audiology and speech-language pathology professions.
- Describe the various work settings for audiologists and speech-language pathologists.
- Demonstrate an understanding of developmental and acquired communication disorders.
- Demonstrate an understanding of organic and functional communication disorders.
- Demonstrate an understanding of epidemiology, including prevalence and incidence.
- Demonstrate an understanding of the code of ethics.
- Describe cultural competency in audiology and speech-language pathology.

KEY TERMS

Communication Disorder	Acquired Disorder	Edward Wheeler Scripture
Encode	Etiology	Carl Seashore
Decode	Organic Disorder	Samuel Orton
Verbal Communication	Functional Disorder	Lee Edward Travis
Discussion	Idiopathic	Charles Van Riper
Dialogue	Epidemiology	Max Steer
Debate	Prevalence	Sara Stinchfield Hawk
Nonverbal Communication	Incidence	Raymond Carhart
Paralanguage	Speech-Language Pathology	Hallie Quinn Brown
Sign Language	Audiology	Itinerant Speech-Language Pathologist
Body Language	Speech-Language Pathologist	Acute Care Hospital
Tactile Communication	Audiologist	Rehabilitation Hospital
Proxemics	John Thelwall	Telehealth
Physical Appearance	Alexander Melville Bell	Ethical Behavior
Model	Alexander Graham Bell	Code of Ethics
Transmission Model	Visible Speech	Beneficence
Feedback Loops	Henry Sweet	Nonmaleficence
Speech Chain	Hermann Gutzmann	Evidence-Based Practice
Spoonerism	Logopedics	Culturally Competent
Developmental or Congenital Disorder	Wilhelm Wundt	Culturally Responsive

INTRODUCTION

Communication is any act involving the exchange of information related to a person's needs, wants, perceptions, knowledge, or feelings. At birth we are equipped with the physical attributes to communicate. Our earliest forms of communication are quite basic and revolve around fundamental needs and desires between infant and caregiver. As we grow, we learn to communicate more effectively by observing other people communicating. We model our communication on what we see, hear, and experience. Our communication skills grow in complexity and sophistication through formal education, and by practicing those skills and having them evaluated.

Most of us take communication for granted. We tacitly assume that when we speak, we will be understood, or when someone speaks to us, we will understand them. Only when a breakdown in communication occurs do we realize how special and vital this act is to our daily lives. A communication disorder is a diagnosed condition in which a person is unable to say correctly what they want to say and/or is unable to understand some or most of what is being said. Some individuals may have an isolated impairment in speech or hearing; others may have impairment in both domains. Simply put, a communication disorder is any impairment in the exchange of information that deviates from what might be considered normal. The nature of the disorder may range from mild to severe. However, the impact of the disorder upon a person's ability to communicate may be profound, regardless of the severity. The focus of this book concerns situations when the process of speaking and listening is somehow impaired. A **communication disorder** is one of the most common types of disabilities found throughout the world. When communication fails, misunderstandings occur, and sometimes people become frustrated, worried, or even angry. Some communication impairments are minor and can be easily corrected, whereas others are more severe and may require an extensive period of treatment. This first chapter is intended to introduce the nature and type of communication disorders found across the life span—from children to adults. In addition, the professions dedicated to helping individuals with communication disorders are profiled.

FYI

The most widely used language in the world is Mandarin with more than 1.2 billion speakers. Next on the list is Spanish with more than 700 million speakers. English is the third most widely used language with 500 million speakers.

TERMINOLOGY AND DEFINITIONS

As a prerequisite to understanding various communication disorders, it is important to first have a grasp of normal communication. Knowledge concerning the normal process of communication serves as the foundation for the identification and management of communication disorders. The word *communicate* is related to the word *common*. The word has its origin in the Latin verb *communicare*, which means "to share" or "to make common." When we communicate, we make things common. Communication is one of those activities that we take for granted. It seems to occur naturally, and we spend most of our living hours engaged in some form of communication. Although we tend to think of communication as talking to someone, communication also occurs in other ways, like when we watch television or send a text message. We communicate to others by the way we dress, the style of our hair, and the tattoos we choose (or choose not) to wear. At a fundamental level, communication can be defined as a two-way process in which a message is sent and received. The sender's role in the process of communication is to generate (or **encode**) a message. The receiver's role is to translate (or **decode**) this message. Communication is never a one-way process. Both the sender and the receiver need to participate. If the sender is unable to clearly encode a message, then a breakdown in communication occurs. Similarly, if the receiver is unable to successfully decode a message, then communication is likely to fail. Excellent communicators are those who have mastered the process of both sending and receiving messages. It is estimated that 75% of a person's day is spent communicating in some way. Most of our daily communication involves speaking and listening to others. The remaining portion of the day is spent communicating via reading and writing.

Verbal communication is at the core of what most of us do; it is the expression of language using spoken words. Our verbal communication varies depending on the communication act as well as the formality of communication. Acts of verbal communication include (a) discussion, (b) dialogue, and (c) debate. **Discussion** is an act of verbal communication to make decisions. Discussions are likely to involve the exchange of facts and opinions between communicating partners. **Dialogue** refers to the free-flowing conversational exchange of ideas. These ideas involve the sharing of perspectives and understandings. The act of **debate** differs from discussion and dialogue because this form of verbal communication is used to achieve agreement on a topic, which other participants of the communication may not share. We often think of debate as the verbal communication found in the political arena. One person states a point of view, which is subsequently challenged by an opposing view.

Verbal communication also varies in its formality. The level of formality can be found in the vocabulary and grammar characterizing spoken language. Formal verbal communication follows a specific code of communication that might be found in settings such as classrooms, courtrooms, job interviews, or formal parties. Alternatively, informal communication also has a specific code of communication but allows for a much-varied manner of speaking. Situations such as hanging out with friends and informal parties are likely to reflect a markedly different form of speaking compared with more formal settings.

Nonverbal communication refers to the features of communication that occur aside from what is spoken or heard. There are at least six different types of nonverbal communication that we use and experience daily. These include (a) paralanguage, (b) sign language, (c) body language, (d) tactile communication, (e) proxemics, and (f) appearance. **Paralanguage** refers to factors such as tone of voice, loudness, inflection, and pitch. By altering these various parameters of voice, the message conveyed is likewise altered. A simple example would be to communicate an identically worded message, such as "*Watch your step*," in a soft comforting voice versus a loud, alarming voice. A listener of this same message would likely interpret these messages quite differently.

Sign language is a form of expressive communication where words are replaced by gestures. Commonly used gestures include waving, pointing, and using fingers to indicate number amounts. There are also fully developed language systems that rely exclusively on signs, as are often found in the deaf community. This form of sign language is discussed further in Chapter 15.

Body language pertains to our use of facial expressions or postures to communicate information. Facial expressions are responsible for a huge proportion of nonverbal communication. One needs to simply smile or frown to communicate a clear nonverbal message. One way of concealing our communication via body language would be to put on a "poker face," which is a face that shows no emotion or change in expression. Expert card players are masters in the use of body language to prevent other card players from knowing the strength of their card hand.

Tactile communication refers to communication that occurs via touch. The use of touch can play a comforting role when paired with verbal communication such as consoling a grieving spouse. Use of touch between parent and child during the infancy period has also been shown to play an integral part in establishing social interaction. **Proxemics** concerns how space and time are used to communicate. A common example is our need for interpersonal space when communicating with others. The amount of personal space needed when having a casual conversation with another person usually varies between 18 in. and 4 ft. In contrast, the personal distance needed when speaking to a crowd of people is around 10 to 12 ft. Our **physical appearance** plays an important role in communication. Physical appearance such as clothes and hairstyle serve to convey a message regarding a person's attitude, mood, wealth, and cultural background, which subsequently affects the judgment and interpretations of others.

> **FYI**
>
> Before the development of speech, the most primitive form of human communication was likely to have been shouting. A group of primates would construe loud sounds as associated with danger.

> **FYI**
>
> The first vocalization produced by infants is a cry. Babies cry for various reasons: when they are uncomfortable, hurt, hungry, or for no reason at all. Researchers are now exploring whether the early crying of infants is language specific. For example, do German babies cry differently than Chinese babies? If so, it would seem that babies are acquiring this ability prior to birth—in their mother's womb.

MODELS OF COMMUNICATION

The term **model** has a wide range of uses. It can refer to a type of product, a person who poses for photographers, or a miniature version of an object. From an academic standpoint, a model refers to an abstract idea. The **transmission model** of communication is an idea regarding the way in which humans communicate. This classic model was proposed by Claude Shannon and Warren Weaver (1949), who were electrical engineers working for Bell Telephone Laboratories in the United States. The essence of the model is that the successful transmission of a message requires both a sender and a receiver. A simplified version of the transmission model is shown in Figure 1–1. The model depicts the process of communication as one in which a person affects the behavior or state of mind of another person. If the effect was smaller or different from what was originally intended, then a failure in communication takes place. A modification of the transmission model was proposed by Wilbur Schramm in 1954 through the inclusion of **feedback loops**. Feedback refers to the activity whereby information is sent back to the source from where the message came. As a reaction to this information, the speaker adjusts their message by strengthening, deemphasizing, or changing the content or form of the original message. The feedback can come from either the speaker or the listener. As speakers, we are constantly monitoring and evaluating our personal communication behavior. During the encoding of a message, we may revise our message mentally before speaking, or we may even choose to revise our message midstream to ensure the message is clearly presented. Feedback from the listener can take many shapes and forms. The listener may send nonverbal body language cues (e.g., eye contact, head nod) indicating that the message was understood, or the listener might simply state back to the original speaker that the message was not understood. The use of feedback is critical to the successful communication of messages. An example of the modified transmission model that includes feedback is shown in Figure 1–1.

A more detailed version of the transmission model was proposed by Denes and Pinson (1973) with specific reference to the linguistic and physiological contributions to speaking and listening. They referred to this model as the **speech chain** (Figure 1–2). According to the speech chain model, the process of encoding a message is organized across three levels: (a) linguistic, (b) physiological, and (c) acoustic. The linguistic level is the first step in the speech chain, whereby the message is organized in the brain. It is the point in the chain where we think about speaking. Once we determine the message to be spoken, the various motor nerves required to produce the sounds and words of the message send impulses from the brain to the speech musculature. Structures such as the lips, tongue, and jaw are set into motion.

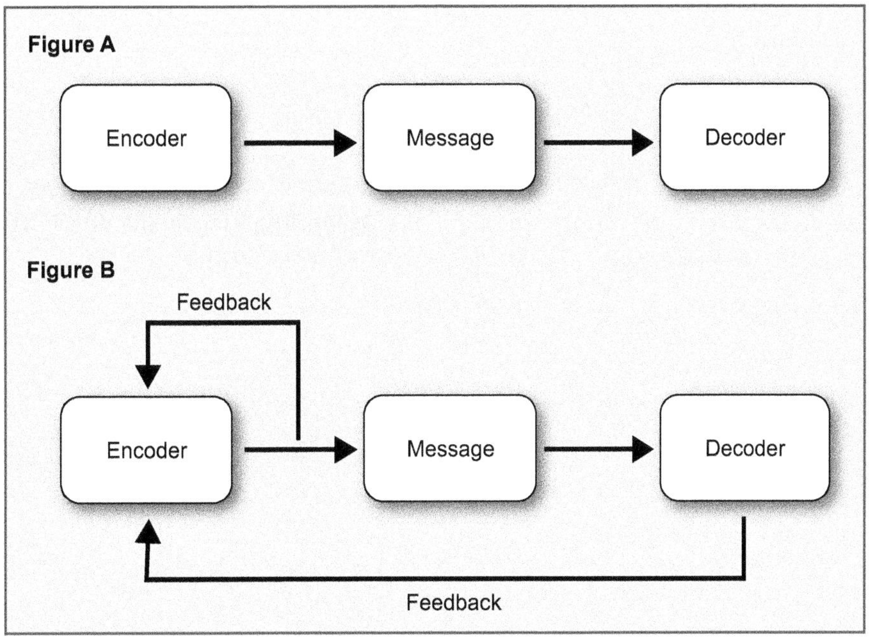

FIGURE 1–1. Models of communication. **A.** Classic transmission model of communication. **B.** Revised transmission model that includes feedback loops.

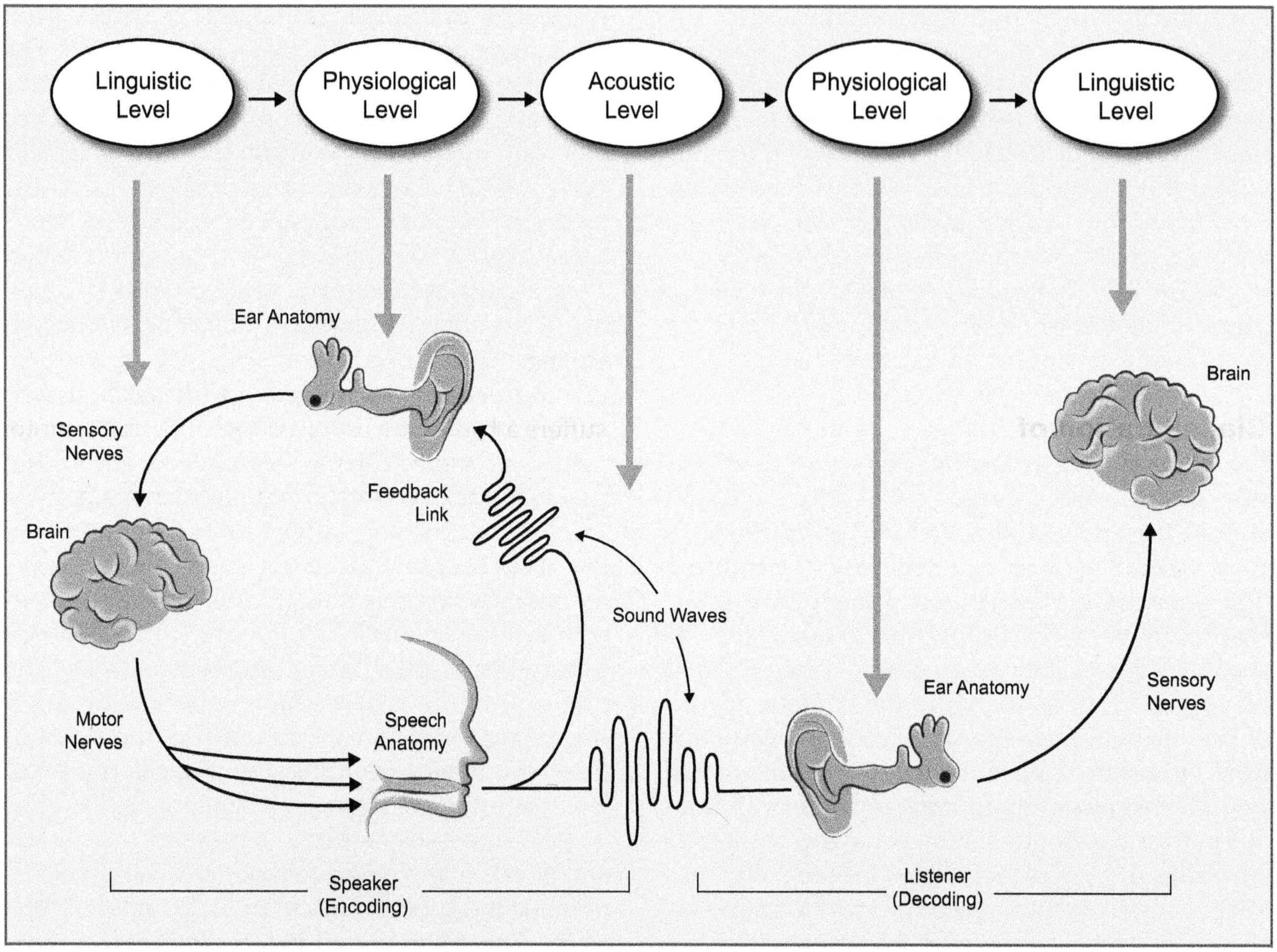

FIGURE 1–2. The process of communication depicted at linguistical, physiological, and acoustic levels.

This physiological process represents the next link in the speech chain. Once these words leave our mouth, they become an airborne acoustic signal, thus representing the third and final link in the process (chain) of speech encoding. There is also a side, or feedback, link in the process of speech encoding. We naturally listen to our own voices when talking. By doing so, the message spoken is compared with what was originally intended to be spoken. An example of this type of feedback is evident when we produce a **spoonerism** (or slip of the tongue). The phrase "mix up your words" spoken as *"wix up your mords"* is one such example. If we judge the message to be incorrectly spoken, the message can be modified and corrected. The remaining links of the speech chain are related to the process of decoding.

The steps involved in decoding the message occur in the reverse order of those just described for speech encoding. When listening to a message, our ears are exposed to the acoustic signal after it leaves the mouth of the speaker. At a physiological level, the muscles, bones, and nerves of the ear transform this acoustic signal into electrical impulses along auditory (sensory) pathways leading to the brain. Once the sensory impulses reach the brain, they are deciphered into individual sounds, words, and sentences. This deciphering of the acoustic signal into a linguistic message represents the final link in the speech chain.

The speech chain model is useful to illustrate communication disorders. Any breakdown or disruption in the process of encoding that occurs along the pathway from the brain to the actual execution of speech can result in a communication disorder. Similarly, any breakdown in the decoding process between the ear and the brain can result in a communication disorder.

> **FYI**
>
> Many of the characters from the classic Looney Tunes cartoons were developed based on a speech pattern. Porky Pig produced speech with a stutter. Daffy Duck, Tweety Bird, and Elmer Fudd all produced speech with some form of unique articulation disorder.

Classification of Communication Disorders

Communication disorders can be grouped into two general categories. The first grouping is characterized by the timing of when the disorder first occurred. Specifically, did the disorder occur before or after birth? Any medical or health condition, including a communication disorder that occurs prior to birth, during birth, or shortly after birth, is referred to as a **developmental** or **congenital disorder**. An example of a developmental communication disorder is a child who is born with a cleft of the lip or palate (Figure 1–3A). This cleft, if left unrepaired, can greatly impair speech production. The second group of communication disorders is characterized by a medical or health condition found to occur later in life (i.e., after birth); if that is the case, the disorder is referred to as an **acquired disorder**. Most often, an individual with an acquired communication disorder demonstrates normal communication prior to experiencing the disorder. An example of an acquired communication disorder is an individual who suffers a traumatic brain injury following a motor vehicle accident (Figure 1–3B). As a result of this accident, the individual may experience a marked impairment in the ability to produce or understand speech. Prior to the accident, the person's communication most likely was normal.

Communication disorders can also be classified by the cause (i.e., **etiology**) of the disorder. A medical or health condition with a known physical cause is called an **organic disorder**. In most cases, the physical condition is visible to the naked eye. Such is the case in a typical 7-year-old child

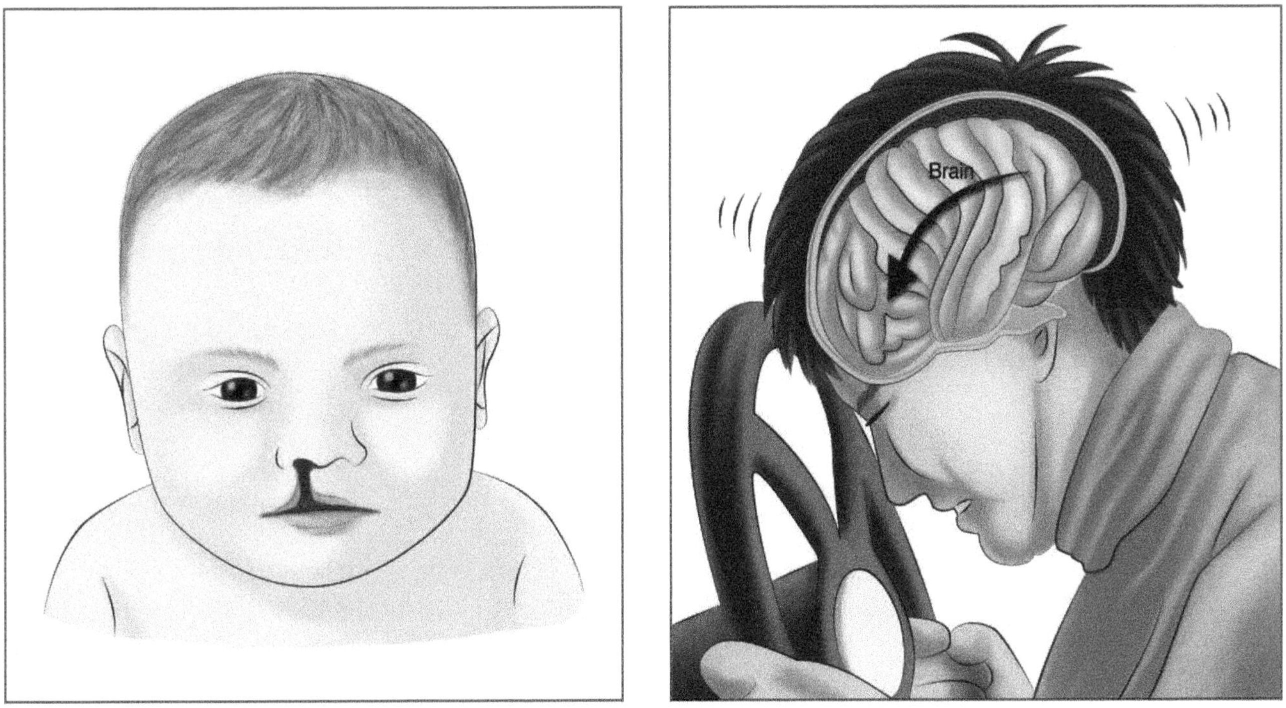

A **B**

FIGURE 1–3. Examples of developmental and acquired communication disorders. **A.** A child born with a cleft lip and palate. **B.** An individual with a head injury resulting from a motor vehicle accident.

who has lost her two front (central incisor) teeth. This condition is likely to pose a problem for the correct articulation of speech sounds that involve these physical structures (e.g., "s" and "th" sounds; Figure 1–4). An organic disorder, such as an impairment resulting from a brain abnormality (e.g., a stroke), can be invisible to the naked eye. If there is no known anatomical, physiological, or neurological basis for the observed disorder, the term **functional disorder** is used. A closely related term is **idiopathic**, which denotes a condition that has an unknown cause. School-age children who mispronounce speech sounds, such as "wabbit" for "rabbit," and who show no apparent physical problems would be classified as demonstrating a functional communication disorder. Several communication disorders have no readily identifiable cause. Although we may not know the precise cause of these functional disorders, they still can be successfully treated. An illustration of the overlap of developmental and acquired disorders that have a functional or organic basis is shown in Figure 1–5. These terms can be used collectively to refer to communication disorders. The ensuing chapters categorize each type of communication disorder according to both the timing and cause of the disorder.

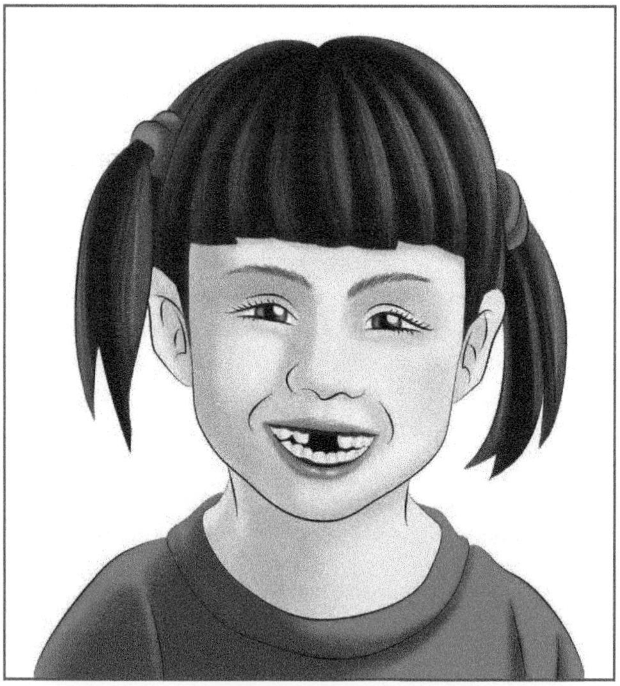

FIGURE 1–4. Example of an organic communication disorder found in most normally developing children. The absence of upper central incisors is likely to affect speech sound production, but only temporarily.

A final comment about classifying communication disorders relates to the way we may label a person who is demonstrating a disorder. In the past, it was common to reference the disorder (or label) first and the person second. For example, we might have referred to an individual as being a "cleft palate child." In other instances, an individual was simply labeled by the disorder, where we referred to the person as a "stutterer." The more appropriate manner of referring to a communication disorder is to recognize the person

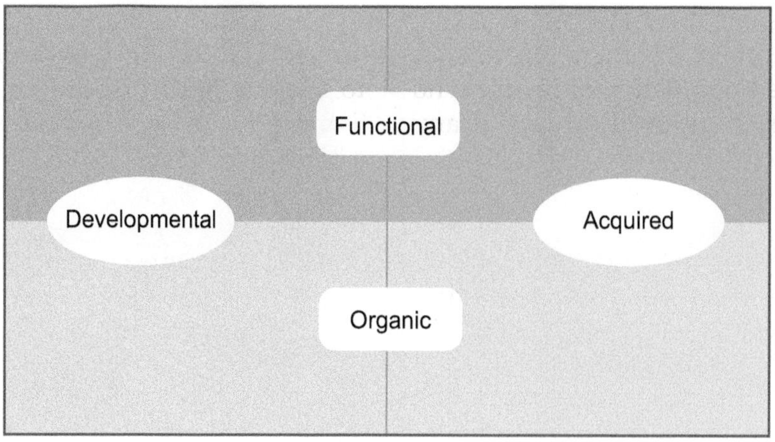

FIGURE 1–5. Categorization of communication disorders according to when the disorder occurred (developmental versus acquired) and how the disorder occurred (functional versus organic).

first and the disorder second. So as professionals in the field of communication disorders, we may encounter a child *with* a cleft palate or a person *who* stutters. Clearly, this form of labeling is not unique to communication disorders. In practice, placing the individual first should be applied when referring to any medical- or health-related condition.

Occurrence of Communication Disorders

Epidemiology refers to the study of how often diseases and conditions occur in people and why. A common way of charting the occurrence of a disorder or disease is in reference to the overall population. **Prevalence** is a frequently used epidemiological measure of how commonly a disease or condition occurs in a population at a particular point in time. The prevalence is calculated by dividing the number of persons with the disease or condition at a particular time by the number of individuals examined. Prevalence often is expressed as a percentage. The **incidence** of a disease is another epidemiological measure. Incidence measures the rate of occurrence of new cases of a disease or condition and is likewise expressed as a percentage. Incidence is calculated as the number of new cases of a disease or condition within a specified time period (usually 1 year) divided by the size of the population. So, prevalence is a measure of all the cases of a disease at a point of time, and incidence is the measure of new cases of a disease in a time period. In the context of communication disorders, prevalence refers to the estimated population of people who are managing communication disorders at any given time, whereas incidence refers to the annual diagnosis rate of new cases of communication disorders.

Most epidemiology information on communication disorders relates to prevalence. Approximately one out of every seven individuals has some form of communication disorder. This number encompasses disorders of either speech or hearing, ranging in severity from mild to profound. The prevalence of communication disorders in the United States is about 46 million people. Approximately 2.7 million Australians have a communication disorder. There are also prevalence data regarding certain types of communication disorders, which might be further categorized by age groups. Specific prevalence information for various communication disorders is presented in Chapters 3 through 14. Some types of communication disorders occur more often than others. For example, 2.5 million people in the United Kingdom are estimated to have speech and language disorders. Of this number, 800,000 have a disorder so severe that it is difficult for most people to understand them. The worldwide prevalence of communication disorders in children is approximately 25% of the population but decreases with increasing age. This lowering in prevalence presumably reflects a large number of children outgrowing or receiving treatment to alleviate the disorder.

Communication Disorders in Boys and Girls

A well-known fact is that boys tend to be more susceptible than girls for many childhood diseases. This vulnerability is evident early in life, with male infants showing significantly higher rates of premature birth and congenital abnormalities than female infants. Developmental disorders such as autism are three to four times more common in boys than girls, and behavioral disorders are at least twice as common. The same is true for communication disorders. Take, for example, the condition of stuttering; boys are three times more likely to develop a stuttering disorder than girls. The precise reason why males are more prone to various health disorders remains unknown. Some genetics experts believe there probably is a biological difference that gives females a health advantage over males. One suggestion is that males are disadvantaged by not having the second X sex chromosome found in women. Having two X chromosomes may help to protect women against disease. This vulnerability is apparent in male mammals of all species, indicating a likely evolutionary explanation. It could well be that nature provides a health advantage to females because the survival of the species depends on them. Males simply may be more expendable than females.

THE PROFESSIONS

Speech-language pathology and audiology are health professions that collectively contribute to the field of human communication sciences and disorders. The profession of **speech-language pathology**, also referred to as speech-language therapy, encompasses the study of human communication, swallowing, speech and language development, and related disorders. The profession of **audiology** encompasses the study of human communication, normal processes of hearing, and hearing loss. **A speech-language pathologist** is a professional educated in the study of human communication, swallowing, speech-language development, and related disorders. By evaluating the speech, language, and swallowing skills of children and adults, the speech-language pathologist determines what communication or swallowing problems exist and the best way to treat them. An **audiologist** is a professional educated in the study of human communication, normal hearing processes, hearing loss, balance, and other related disorders. The audiologist determines whether a person has a hearing loss, the type of loss, and the best way to treat the loss. Speech-language pathology and audiology are distinct disciplines, but they have considerable overlap. To be fully skilled in either discipline, one should be familiar with both. Each discipline deals with impairments that disrupt the ability of the individual to communicate normally.

> *FYI*
>
> Most audiologists and speech-language pathologists engage in clinical practice. They often are referred to as clinicians. The people with communication disorders seen by these professionals are referred to as clients.

The audiology and speech-language pathology professions are found worldwide but are not uniform across nations. A listing of some of the professional associations for audiologists and speech-language pathologists around the world is shown in Table 1–1. There are approximately 210,000 speech-language pathologists and 17,000 audiologists currently working in the United States. Approximately 7,000 speech-language pathologists and 3,000 audiologists work in Australia, and approximately 1,300 speech-language pathologists and 500 audiologists are found in New Zealand. The number of speech-language pathologists and audiologists currently practicing in Canada is 8,000 and 1,800, respectively. The number of speech-language pathologists and audiologists in India is approaching 5,000. Both speech-language pathologists and audiologists are in high demand, and there are insufficient numbers to meet the demand, which is likely to increase because the number of people with communication disorders is predicted to grow. Members of the baby boomer generation are now entering their retirement years, and this large population is likely to contribute to an increase in the number of communication disorders that accompany old age. In addition, medical advances are resulting in an improved survival rate for premature infants as well as for older adult stroke victims. The increase in survival rate will undoubtedly increase the number of individuals likely to require the services of a speech-language pathologist or audiologist.

A BRIEF HISTORY OF THE PROFESSIONS

The field of communication sciences and disorders has evolved over time. The first audiologists and speech-language pathologists were not given formal professional titles. They were researchers and teachers who took an interest in helping individuals with speaking and hearing difficulties. The foundation of the audiologist and speech-language pathologist professions was influenced by many disciplines, including biology, psychology, medicine, physics, linguistics, rhetoric, and education. Several individuals contributed to the field, and some of the more noteworthy contributions are highlighted here.

John Thelwall (1764–1834) is recognized as a pioneering speech scientist and therapist in the United Kingdom (Figure 1–6). Thelwall was

Table 1–1. Some of the Professional Associations in Audiology and Speech-Language Pathology

Australia	Audiology Australia/Audiological Society of Australia (ASA) Speech Pathology Australia (SPA)
Britain	British Academy of Audiology (BAA) British Society of Audiology (BSA) Royal College of Speech and Language Therapists (RCSLT)
Canada	Canadian Academy of Audiology (CAA) Speech-Language and Audiology Canada (SAC)
India	Indo-International Society of Communication and Hearing Sciences (IISCHS) Indian Speech and Hearing Association (ISHA)
Ireland	Irish Academy of Audiology Irish Association of Speech and Language Therapists (IASLT)
Malaysia	Malaysian Association of Speech-Language and Hearing (MASH)
New Zealand	New Zealand Audiological Society (NZAS) New Zealand Speech-Language Therapists' Association (NZSTA)
Singapore	Speech-Language and Hearing Association, Singapore (SHAS)
South Africa	South African Association of Audiologists (SAAA) South African Speech-Language-Hearing Association (SASLHA)
United States	American Academy of Audiology (AAA) American Speech-Language-Hearing Association (ASHA)
Worldwide	International Association of Communication Sciences and Disorders (IALP)

FIGURE 1–6. John Thelwall, a pioneering speech scientist and orator.

part of the Elocutionary Movement in the early 1800s, which stressed high standards of education and high standards in the use of language. Thelwall was well-known for giving radical political speeches. In addition to his oratory skills, he published several works dealing with elocution, the acquisition of language, the anatomy of the speech organs, and the link between speech and mental illness. Thelwall noted that some children with speech defects respond better in therapy to a female rather than a male. He also was the first to classify speech disorders as being either natural (organic) or habitual (functional).

Alexander Melville Bell (1819–1905) and **Alexander Graham Bell** (1847–1922) were father and son who were both eminent English scientists and inventors. The family eventually settled in Canada and the United States. Although most people know of the contribution made by Graham Bell to the development of the first practical telephone, few know of the contributions made by his father. Melville spent most of his life assisting others with their speech, through formal elocution lessons or correction of speech disorders (Figure 1–7). His wife Eliza was severely hearing impaired, which influenced his own work as well as that of his son. Melville developed a transcriptional system known as **visible speech** that included drawings of the head and neck showing the physical movements behind the articulation of individual speech sounds. Following his father's death, Graham published the transcription system and taught it to teachers of the deaf.

Henry Sweet (1845–1912) was a pioneer in modern transcriptional phonetics (Figure 1–8). He was an Oxford graduate and studied speech through an interest in the English language. He developed the Broad Romic symbol system that eventually led to the International Phonetic Alphabet. He established England as the birthplace of the science of phonetics. The 1913 play *Pygmalion*, written by George Bernard Shaw, which later became the theatrical musical *My Fair Lady*, is thought to be based loosely on the life of Henry Sweet (aka Henry Higgins).

One person who contributed to the development of the professions in Germany was **Hermann Gutzmann** (1865–1922). He helped to establish the field of **logopedics**, which is the science and study of dealing with speech defects in children. Gutzmann studied speech disorders from a medical point of view. He went on to create the Berlin School for Speech and Voice Therapy. The services provided by the Berlin School attained worldwide acclaim. The term logopedics is still in use today. A well-known professional society for speech-language pathologists and audiologists is the International Association of Logopedics and Phoniatrics.

Wilhelm Wundt (1832–1920) was a German medical doctor, psychologist, physiologist, and professor who attended the Leipzig School in Germany (Figure 1–9). The Leipzig School was a research center in Germany that was responsible for training the first generation of psychologists. Sigmund Freud was influenced by the Leipzig School. The school also dabbled in techniques for quantitatively measuring aspects of hearing and speech. Upon graduation, Wundt remained at the Leipzig School and developed a psychology laboratory. He is widely regarded as the "Father of Experimental Psychology." In particular, he is credited with developing the science of psychophysics, which forms the basis for the testing of hearing. Some of Wundt's students were influential in the field of communication disorders.

Edward Wheeler Scripture (1864–1945) graduated from Leipzig in 1888 under the supervision of Wundt. He was an American who developed skills in hearing measurement such as threshold testing and magnitude estimation. Scripture eventually developed a psychology laboratory at Yale University and wrote a book comparing stuttering with lisping, or "super-energetic versus subenergetic" speech production.

Carl Seashore (1866–1949), who was born in Sweden, traveled to America and studied under Scripture at Yale University (Figure 1–10). Seashore had interests in music, voice, and hearing. He built the first audiometer with the help of Scripture. He is also the individual who developed the concept of the decibel by separating loudness magnitude into units of 40 steps each. He later became the head of the psychology department at the University of Iowa.

In 1920, Seashore was approached by **Samuel Orton** (1879–1948), who was a physician interested in learning disabilities. Orton's daughter had difficulties in speaking and reading. He suggested to Seashore that someone should be specifically educated to work with individuals having these

A

FIGURE 1–7. **A.** Alexander Melville Bell. **B.** A copy of Bell's business (professional) card as published in his textbook *Visible Speech* in 1867.

PROFESSIONAL CARD.

Mr A. MELVILLE BELL, Author of 'Visible Speech' may be consulted in all Cases of Impediment or Defect of Speech, Vocal Weakness, Monotony, Oratorical Ineffectiveness, &c.

STAMMERING AND STUTTERING.

The experience of upwards of Twenty-five years' Practice enables Mr A. Melville Bell to undertake the permanent, and, in most cases, the speedy Removal of Stammering and other forms of Vocal Impediment.

References of the highest class are furnished to inquirers.

A limited number of Pupils can be accommodated as Boarders; but residence in the Establishment is not required in order to effect a Cure.

DEFECTS OF ARTICULATION.

In cases of Lisping, Burring, and other Single Elementary Defects, the entire Removal of the Faculty Habit rarely needs more than from Six to Twelve Lessons.

Children who are backward in acquiring the power of Speech are trained to the perfect use of their Vocal Organs. Parents or Governesses are invited to be present at the Lessons, and are directed in the means of carrying on the improvement, which is always rapidly commenced.

ELOCUTION.—PRONUNCIATION, READING, DELIVERY AND ACTION.

Clergymen, Barristers, Members of Parliament, and other Public Readers and Speakers, are Privately Instructed in the Principles and Practice of Effective Delivery, Oratorical Composition, &c.

Ladies and Non-professional Pupils, receive Special Lessons in the art of Reading, &c., according to individual requirements.

VISIBLE SPEECH—UNIVERSAL ALPHABETICS.

Pupils are practically initiated in the Physiology of Speech, and in the use of the Universal Alphabet, so as to be enabled to produce, and to record, all varieties of Native or Foreign Sounds.

Dialectic peculiarities are corrected; and Foreigners are taught to pronounce English with the characteristics of vernacular utterance;

TERMS.

Single Lessons in any Department, - - - - - -		- One Guinea.
Cure of Stammering, Stuttering, &c., -	(Twelve Lessons,)	- Ten Guineas.
Removal of Lisping, Burring, &c., - -	(Six Lessons,)	- Four Guineas.
Elocution, Reading, Delivery, &c., - -	(Six Lessons,)	- Three Guineas.
Visible Speech,—Vocal Physiology, &c., -	(Six Lessons,)	- Three Guineas.

The following additional Establishments for the Cure of Stammering and for Elocutionary Instruction are conducted (in Edinburgh) by Mr Mevills J. Bell; and (in Dublin) by Mr D. C. Bell.

Edinburgh: No. 13 South Charlotte Street.
Dublin: No. 1 Kildare Place.

B

FIGURE 1–8. Henry Sweet, an expert in phonetics (aka Henry Higgins).

FIGURE 1–9. Wilhelm Wundt, known as the "Father of Experimental Psychology."

FIGURE 1–10. Carl Seashore, inventor of the audiometer.

FIGURE 1–11. Lee Edward Travis, known as the "Father of Speech-Language Pathology." (Reprinted with permission from Van Riper, C. [1981]. An early history of ASHA. *ASHA Magazine*, *23*[11], 855–858.)

types of difficulties. Seashore selected the most promising student from the undergraduate psychology class at the University of Iowa and offered the chance to earn this specialized doctorate to **Lee Edward Travis** (1896–1987; Figure 1–11). Travis received his doctorate in 1924 and is recognized as the founding father of the speech-language pathology profession in the United States. Travis established himself as a particular expert in the area of stuttering and had many well-known students who went on to establish educational programs across the United States, including **Charles Van Riper** (1905–1994), who established the program at Western Michigan University, and **Max**

Steer (1931–2003), who established the program at Purdue University.

Around the same time that Travis was completing his studies, **Sara Stinchfield Hawk** (1885–1977; Figure 1–12) was awarded a master's degree in 1920 from the department of psychology at the University of Iowa. Her thesis topic pertained to the area of stuttering. In 1922, Hawk became the first person in the United States to receive a doctoral degree specifically designated in the area of speech pathology, awarded by the University of Wisconsin. Both Hawk and Travis were among the 25 founding members of the American Speech and Hearing Association established in 1925.

Raymond Carhart (1912–1975; Figure 1–13) is referred to by many as the "Father of Audiology" in the United States. He is credited with coining the word *audiology* to designate the science of hearing. Carhart was a professor of speech at Northwestern University. When World War II broke out, he was commissioned as an officer in the U.S. Army where he developed an aural rehabilitation program for individuals who were deafened because of war exposure. His wartime efforts working with thousands of hearing-impaired soldiers served as the basis for the development of a new discipline that is now audiology. Upon conclusion of the war, he returned to Northwestern and proceeded to develop a specific program in audiology.

Last, the efforts of **Hallie Quinn Brown** (1849–1949; Figure 1–14) have been overlooked by many historians in regard to her contributions to speech-language pathology in the United States. She was a renowned American elocutionist and educator in the late 19th century and a significant figure in the history of speech-language pathology in the United States. She was born the daughter of two former slaves. She taught reading and provided elocution training to children and women, most notably African Americans from plantations who had been denied the opportunity of a proper education.

EDUCATIONAL PREPARATION

People who choose to become either audiologists or speech-language pathologists are entering a clearly defined field of professional practice. So what does it mean to be a *professional*? A professional can be defined as a person who is trained

FIGURE 1–12. Sara Stinchfield Hawk, the first person to obtain a doctorate in speech-language pathology.

FIGURE 1–13. Raymond Carhart, known as the "Father of Audiology."

FIGURE 1–14. Hallie Q. Brown, American elocutionist and educator in the late 19th century.

to do a special job in exchange for payment. This often is the case when considering people in the sports world, where it is easy to distinguish a professional athlete, who is paid, from an amateur athlete, who is not. Another form of professionalism is in regard to occupations that require education or training pertinent to a specialized field, as distinguished from general education. Training for professionals who work in communication disorders has developed from different starting points and within different philosophical contexts in various countries. The educational requirements to become an audiologist or speech-language pathologist share many commonalities, but they are not identical. There also are differences between countries regarding the educational requirements for each profession. The differences between countries can be broadly categorized as reflecting an American model or British model of education. These models are presented separately.

The American Model

A primary feature of the model of education used in the United States is the emphasis on a liberal arts and sciences education at the undergraduate level followed by a period of intensive and concentrated education at the (post) graduate level. To become eligible to practice as either an audiologist or speech-language pathologist in the United States, a graduate-level education is required.

An example of the typical educational model for both degrees is provided in Table 1–2. As undergraduates, students pursue a bachelor's degree in a major usually called Communication Disorders. This major encompasses fundamental aspects of both audiology and speech-language pathology. The first 2 years of undergraduate education involve coursework covering a wide range of general education courses. These courses serve to satisfy the liberal arts and sciences foundation for the bachelor's degree. The final 2 years of undergraduate education focus more specifically on courses in audiology and speech-language pathology, which satisfy the major requirements for the degree. The bulk of this coursework centers on normal aspects of hearing and speech and an introduction to some of the more common communication disorders, such as child language disorders and phonological disorders. Upon graduation, the student holds a preprofessional bachelor's degree in communication disorders. To satisfy the educational requirements to become an audiologist or speech-language pathologist professional, the student must obtain a graduate degree. Students are allowed to choose freely whether to pursue graduate education in audiology or speech-language pathology.

> **FYI**
>
> Universities that offer educational degrees in audiology and speech-language pathology usually have their own clinic that provides diagnostic and therapeutic services to the local community and an opportunity for students to work alongside experienced clinicians as part of their clinical training.

Table 1–2. American Model for the Education of Audiologists and Speech-Language Pathologists

Audiology	*Speech-Language Pathology*
Undergraduate Education	**Undergraduate Education**
4-year bachelor's (BS or BA) degree	4-year bachelor's (BS or BA) degree
Years 1 and 2 "related" areas of study	Years 1 and 2 "related" areas of study
Years 3 and 4 "major" areas of study	Years 3 and 4 "major" areas of study
Minimal fieldwork	Minimal fieldwork
Graduate Education	**Graduate Education**
3- to 4-year Doctor of Audiology (AuD) degree	2-year master's (MS or MA) degree
Years 1 to 3 audiology coursework	Years 1 and 2 speech-language pathology coursework
1800 hr of fieldwork	400 hr of fieldwork
Year 4 externship	Three 1-semester externships
Clinical fellowship year (CFY)	Clinical fellowship year (CFY)
National examination	National examination
Obtain CCC-A	Obtain CCC-SLP

FYI

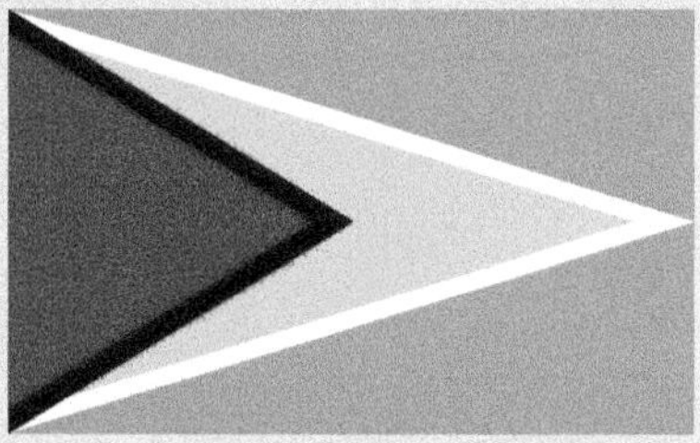

Source: Sangjinhwa, Public domain, via Wikimedia Commons.

There are hundreds of university programs worldwide that educate audiologists and speech-language pathologists. Yet, there are still many countries that offer no formal educational programs, requiring residents of those countries to travel abroad to obtain their professional qualification. One of the newest communication disorders programs can be found at the University of Guyana. The university offers a combined audiology and speech-language pathology degree. The first group of students graduating from the program entered the workforce in 2019.

To become a qualified audiologist, the requisite degree is a Doctor of Audiology (AuD), which spans 3 to 4 years of graduate study beyond the bachelor's degree. The first 2 years involve detailed coursework and on-site clinical education in audiology and hearing science. The final year involves extensive off-campus full-time clinical experience (an externship), where students acquire a considerable number of fieldwork hours. The AuD degree also requires students to complete a research project.

For those wishing to become a speech-language pathologist, the requisite degree is a master's degree, which takes 2 years of full-time study to complete. Across the 2 years of study, students complete coursework in speech, language, and swallowing disorders and engage in a mix of on-campus and off-campus clinical experiences. Students who complete either the AuD or master's degree in speech-language pathology are eligible to work after graduation. The first year of professional employment for a speech-language pathologist is referred to as the clinical fellowship year (CFY). During the CFY, the individual works in their respective profession; however, periodic oversight is provided by a work colleague who holds professional membership status in the American Speech-Language-Hearing Association (ASHA). Membership status is designated by the acronym CCC, which refers to the Certificate of Clinical Competence. Individuals who complete the 1-year clinical fellowship make a formal application to ASHA to be awarded the CCC. Audiologists may choose to obtain the CCC from ASHA or, alternatively, obtain board certification from the American Academy of Audiology. All audiologists and speech-language pathologists working in the United States generally are expected to hold national certification to practice in their respective professions. There is also an expectation that these individuals will continue to up-skill throughout their professional careers. ASHA requires audiologists and speech-language pathologists to attain a minimum of 30 hr of professional development education every 3 years. Failure to do so can result in a loss of CCC status and limits a person's ability to practice professionally.

The British Model

The British model of audiologist and speech-language pathologist education is in widespread use throughout the United Kingdom, Australia, India, Ireland, New Zealand, and South Africa. The British model places less emphasis on a liberal arts education compared with the American model. Instead, education is more concentrated on the essential coursework and clinical competencies for becoming either an audiologist or speech-language pathologist. The British model for the education of audiologists and speech-language pathologists allows for one of two paths. One path involves completion of a concentrated 4-year undergraduate degree. In the first year, university students immediately begin studying their major. By the conclusion of the 4-year degree, these students are likely to have taken the same number of courses in audiology or speech-language pathology as an American student. The second path involves completion of a 2-year master's degree in audiology or speech-language pathology. To obtain a master's degree, it is not mandatory to hold a bachelor's degree in communication disorders; this prerequisite requirement can be met by any degree that is compatible with audiology or speech-language pathology, such as psychology, health, linguistics, biology, engineering, or education. Like the United States, most countries require audiology graduates to complete a CFY as part of the first year of professional experience prior to becoming full-fledged members of their respective professional associations. This is not necessarily the case for speech-language pathology graduates. Examples of the typical British educational models for audiology and speech-language pathology degrees are provided in Table 1–3.

Qualities of an Audiologist and Speech-Language Pathologist

Individuals who work as either audiologists or speech-language pathologists interact with people of all ages and backgrounds. One of the prime attributes of becoming a successful professional is having good people skills, such as knowing how to interact effectively with others who have various disorders and a range of backgrounds. People are individuals, with as many similarities from one person to the next as there are differences. An effective audiologist or speech-language pathologist is able to relate to a wide range of clients while consistently bringing out their best performance, whether it is related to testing the hearing of an older adult or promoting language development in a young nonverbal child. The two professions are not physically demanding, but they can be emotionally and intellectually challenging. These professionals need to approach problems objectively and provide support to their clients and families. Many disorders are complex and not fully understood, so professionals should be able to tolerate challenge and uncertainty. Because a

Table 1–3. British Model for the Education of Audiologists and Speech-Language Pathologists

Audiology	*Speech-Language Pathology*
Path 1 Undergraduate Degree	**Path 1 Undergraduate Degree**
4-year bachelor's degree	4-year bachelor's degree
Year 1 "related" areas studied	Year 1 "related" areas of studied
Years 2 to 4 audiology coursework	Years 2 to 4 speech-language pathology coursework
350 hr of fieldwork	350 hr of fieldwork
Three 1-semester externships	Three 1-semester externships
Path 2 Master's Degree	**Path 2 Master's Degree**
Bachelor's degree in related areas (psychology, biology, engineering, health)	Bachelor's degree in related areas (psychology, biology, linguistics, health, education)
Years 1 and 2 audiology coursework	Years 1 and 2 speech-language pathology coursework
350 hr of fieldwork	350 hr of fieldwork
Three 1-semester externships	Three 1-semester externships
Clinical Fellowship Year	
National examination	
Obtain CCC	

client's progress may be slow, audiologists and speech-language pathologists must have patience and compassion. Another quality of being a good audiologist or speech-language pathologist is to have sharp listening skills and exceptional observational skills. These professionals also should be able to effectively communicate test results and possible treatment choices to their clients and families in a manner that is easily understood.

PROFESSIONAL WORK SETTINGS

Speech-language pathologists and audiologists can be found in a range of work settings, some of which are quite unique. Sometimes, the professionals work side by side. A description of the more common work settings is provided here.

Education

By far, the largest employers of speech-language pathologists are public and private schools, and specialized schools such as those designated for hard of hearing and deaf children. The type of work performed by a speech-language pathologist in educational settings may involve employment at a single school; in contrast, serving as an **itinerant speech-language pathologist** entails traveling between many schools and having a caseload of clients in each school. Some audiologists are employed in deaf education centers or in public school systems where they may be involved in performing routine audiological assessments on students. Higher education settings such as colleges and universities also employ audiologist and speech-language pathologist lecturers and professors to teach students pursuing a career in communication disorders. Approximately 50% of the speech-language pathologist workforce and 10% of the audiologist workforce can be found in educational settings.

Medical

Approximately 40% of speech-language pathologists and 60% of audiologists are employed in health care settings, including hospitals and residential or nonresidential health care facilities. The two primary medical settings are acute care and rehabilitation care. An **acute care hospital** is one where the patient has recently been admitted because of a planned surgery or an accident or trauma. The type of patient seen by the speech-language pathologist in an acute setting may be someone who has had their larynx removed as a result of throat cancer or possibly an individual who recently experienced a stroke or motor vehicle accident. In these situations, the speech-language pathologist often will initially visit the patient in the hospital bed shortly after the medical condition has been treated. The speech-language pathologist will diagnose whether a communication disorder exists and assess swallowing function. A patient might eventually transfer from an acute care hospital to a **rehabilitation hospital** where they are being managed on a longer-term basis. The speech-language pathologist is typically employed to provide treatment to the patient, assisting with the individual's eventual discharge from the hospital and transition to communicating in another environment. Once discharged, the individual could still have a communication disorder and likely would receive services via a residential (e.g., nursing home) or nonresidential facility. When clients and clinicians are not in the same physical location, there is a **telehealth** option, which involves the delivery of speech and language services via telecommunications (e.g., phone, Internet). The type of client seen by an audiologist in a hospital setting may be an individual who receives a hearing assessment as part of a routine physical examination. Newborn infants routinely receive a hearing assessment prior to being discharged from the hospital. Sometimes audiologists can be found in the operating room of hospitals where they may monitor a patient's hearing during a delicate operation that can affect the hearing mechanism.

Private Practice

Individuals engaged exclusively in private practice account for approximately 5% of the speech-language pathology workforce and 20% of the audiology workforce. The type of client seen by a speech-language pathologist private practitioner is generally one who is not in a medically acute condition. Rather, the speech-language pathologist may see children with mild communication disorders that typically do not qualify for therapy services in a school setting. Or the speech-language pathologist may offer a unique or specialty type of service, such as working exclusively with individuals who have voice problems or individuals who may speak English as a second language and are receiving assistance with reducing the strength of their foreign accent. Audiologists may work independently or with other private practitioners such as ear, nose, and throat physicians. A major facet of this type of job setting is the prescription and fitting of hearing aids. It is not unusual for some audiologists to hold full-time employment in another setting but also engage in a minimum level of private practice.

Research

A small percentage (approximately 5%) of speech-language pathologists and audiologist professionals work exclusively in research settings. These individuals are not engaged in clinical practice or education but rather in scientific investigations of basic and applied aspects of communication sciences and disorders. One well-known institution in the United States is the Boys Town National Research Hospital in Omaha, Nebraska, that focuses on childhood deafness, visual impairment, and related communication disorders. A well-known hearing research laboratory in Melbourne, Australia, is the Bionics Institute.

Industry

One work setting that is unique to audiologists is common when they are employed in the hearing aid industry. Around 5% of audiologists work in the industry and may serve as sales representatives for large hearing aid companies. These individuals are experts on current hearing aid devices on the market and provide consultation to practicing audiologists about the latest product advancements.

FYI

There is a severe shortage of audiologists and speech-language pathologists worldwide, including university-level lecturers and professors. In addition to this overall shortage, less than 25% of the workforce is made up of males. This gender imbalance is also found in other allied health professions such as nursing, physiotherapy, and occupational therapy.

PROFESSIONAL ETHICS

To be a professional involves behaving with dignity and in an ethical manner, and in such a way that people trust your judgment. **Ethical behavior** refers to doing the right thing and encompasses attributes such as honesty, respect, and responsibility. Being honest involves truthfulness and refraining from lying and cheating. Respect involves tolerance and openness toward others regardless of personal or cultural differences. Responsibility means taking your professional duties seriously and accepting culpability for your decisions. Many professional organizations have established a series of behavioral guidelines that govern the day-to-day activities of a professional. These guidelines are referred to as a **code of ethics**, consisting of a list of commonsense rules and regulations concerning doing the right thing when individuals are engaged in their chosen professional practice.

Most professional associations establish an ethics board that is designed to handle any complaints raised against individual members. Individuals who are found to be in violation of any of the established codes may run the risk of being sanctioned by their professional association. The level of sanctioning can range from a reprimand that could involve payment of a fine, to the temporary suspension of professional licensure, and in extreme cases, to being adjudicated by state or national law enforcement agencies.

The audiologist and speech-language pathologist professions adhere to a code of ethics, an example of which is established by ASHA. There are slight differences in the code of ethics developed by audiologist and speech-language pathologist associations worldwide, but some of the common tenets are that audiologists and speech-language pathologists should do the following:

- Safeguard the welfare of the clients they serve.
- Maintain high standards of professional competence.
- Maintain accurate and up-to-date information about the nature, management, and treatment of communication disorders.
- Uphold the dignity of the profession and accept the profession's self-imposed standards.

Professional Licensure

Whenever we try to help others, we inevitably risk harming them. Most health professions, namely medicine, are often practiced with tight regulations imposed by local and national governments. These regulations are designed to safeguard the public from potential harm, whether it is emotional, physical, or financial. They attempt to ensure that professionals work within a well-defined scope of practice in which the education and training of the professional are suited to the health problem at hand. The concepts of **beneficence** and **nonmaleficence** are used to determine whether a particular profession should be regulated. Beneficence refers to "doing good" and implies that positive steps are taken by the professional to prevent harm to the patient or remove the patient from harm. Nonmaleficence refers to an obligation by the professional "not to harm" the patient. Beneficence and nonmaleficence can be seen as two ends of the same continuum of patient care.

Health care workers are committed to helping others and should therefore consider the principles of beneficence and nonmaleficence. This has prompted many countries to license (or regulate) various health care professions in a manner like what is found in medical practice. At present, there is surprisingly little worldwide consistency regarding the regulation of the audiologist and speech-language pathologist professions by government bodies. Yet, both professions have the potential for causing patient harm. Table 1–4 provides examples of some of the harm that can occur to patients who have a communication disorder and are seen by an incompetent audiologist or speech-language pathologist. The United Kingdom and South Africa require professional licensure of all audiologists and speech-language pathologists. Australia, Canada, and the United States vary regarding the total number of states or provinces that require licensure. At present, neither profession is regulated in New Zealand, although steps are being taken to mandate licensure. Currently, a conviction for practicing as an audiologist or speech-language pathologist without a license is a minor misdemeanor in countries where no professional licensure is required.

Table 1–4. Examples of Harm That Might Be Caused by an Unqualified or Incompetent Audiologist or Speech-Language Pathologist

Audiologist Error	***Potential Harm***
Misdiagnosis of brainstem tumor	Failure to treat the problem resulting in worsening of the tumor
Misdiagnosis of newborn hearing loss	Delayed/disordered speech, cognitive, learning outcomes
Failure to identify conditions of chronic otitis media in preschool children with speech and language difficulties	Permanent sensorineural hearing loss, poor educational achievement
Failure to provide necessary environmental support for communicatively impaired patients who have demonstrated physical weakness (stroke, paralysis)	Injury due to fall
Purchase of unnecessary hearing aids	Financial harm
Speech-Language Pathologist Error	***Potential Harm***
Initiation of feeding too soon or inserting objects into the mouth during dysphagia treatment	Patient choking and/or aspirating leading to aspiration pneumonia and possible death
Providing therapeutic services to an individual with a perceived voice problem without first referring to an otolaryngologist	Overlooking possible cancer of the larynx, resulting in surgical removal of larynx and possible death
Failure to identify seizure activity in clients with speech disorder, such as those with traumatic brain injury or cerebral palsy	Permanent brain damage, coma, death
Incorrect choice of augmentative devices for nonverbal patients	Limitation of communication competence if choice is below the patient's abilities; frustration, withdrawal, decreased motivation to attempt communication; inappropriate educational and vocational placement

Evidence-Based Practice

The notion of **evidence-based practice** (EBP) has its origins in the field of medicine where it is known as evidence-based medicine. EBP is a form of clinical decision-making by the practitioner to help improve the patient's outcome. The need for EBP was driven by the desire to shift health care away from basing decisions primarily on opinion and past practices, many of which had not been sufficiently examined to determine their effectiveness. A simple way of conceptualizing EBP is based on asking the questions, *"Why am I practicing this way?"* and *"Is there evidence that can guide me to a better outcome in my practice?"* The processes of EBP can be illustrated in the shape of a triangle (Figure 1–15). Two points on the triangle represent the professional's search for best practice based on their personal experience as well as that found in the academic and research arena. The third point of the triangle represents the professional's acknowledgment of their client's needs and values. The center of the triangle is EBP, which is a collection of the three points that should guide the professional's practice.

Two types of evidence guide professional practice. The first is evidence that demonstrates effective treatment approaches (i.e., what to do). The second type of evidence demonstrates ineffective treatment approaches (i.e., what not to do). Both are equally important in helping to improve the patient's outcome. The implementation of EBP in the field of communication disorders is only just beginning, as it is in most professions. Like what has been found in medicine, audiologists and speech-language pathologists cannot rely on what they learned several years ago (e.g., as students) to carry them through a lifetime of professional practice. On average, research in any area of health can be expected to double every 10 years. Keeping this in mind, for practice to be effective, the information we base our practice on needs to be constantly updated. As expert clinicians, audiologists and speech-language pathologists should consistently seek new information to improve therapeutic effectiveness (El Amin et al., 2023). Many professional associations require their members to regularly attend professional development events, such as workshops and conferences, to keep abreast of current and best practices.

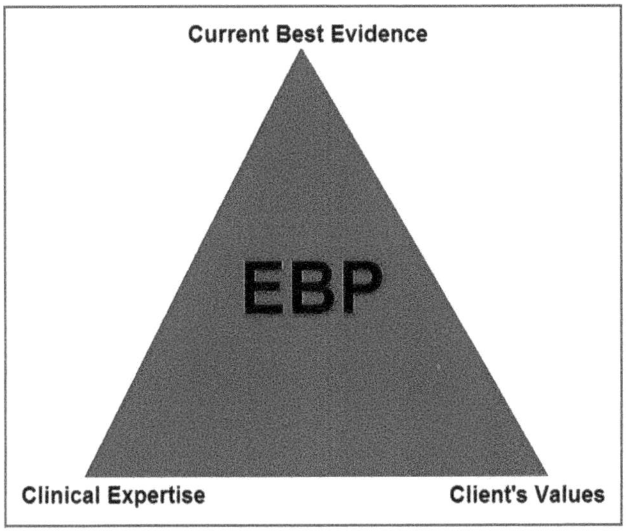

FIGURE 1–15. Triangle illustrating the processes and responsibilities of professionals who adopt evidence-based practice (EBP).

CULTURAL CONSIDERATIONS AND COMMUNICATION DISORDERS

Population centers throughout the world are becoming increasingly diverse both culturally and linguistically. To effectively meet the needs of a diverse population, audiologists and speech-language pathologists need to be **culturally competent**. This competency involves sensitivity to issues that can influence both the identification and management of communication disorders. Multilingual and culturally diverse clients are those who use languages and dialects other than that of the audiologist or speech-language pathologist, or do not share the same cultural background as the audiologist or speech-language pathologist. Clients may belong to a different culture and communicate in a language different from the audiologist or speech-language pathologist or may share the same language to some degree while belonging to a different culture. By misunderstanding or misinterpreting a client, the audiologist or speech-language pathologist may inadvertently mistake certain communication behaviors as signs of a disorder. There also are cultural differences in beliefs about health, disability, and delivery of clinical services. The differences can influence how an individual would either perceive a communication disorder or accept certain treatment for the disorder. Professionals providing services to individuals from different cultural backgrounds need to be aware of unique perspectives or communication styles common to those cultures. The complexities of communication in a multicultural environment are depicted as a series of layers in Figure 1–16. These layers apply to both the client and the professional providing services to the client. Some observations about different cultural styles that should be considered by audiologists and speech-language pathologists when communicating with individuals of differing cultural and linguistic backgrounds are listed later (Roberts, 2001).

Audiologists and speech-language pathologists should also strive to be **culturally responsive**. The difference between being culturally competent and culturally responsive is that the latter does not imply that one has attained all the skills and views needed to work with culturally diverse clients (Hyter & Salas-Provance, 2023). It assumes one just has the openness to adapt to the cultural needs of those with whom they work. Being culturally responsive requires having the ability to adapt and understand cultural differences and look beyond differences to work productively with clients whose cultural contexts are different from the clinician. Clinicians who may come from a white middle-class background and who do not reflect the diversity of their clients may inadvertently conflict with the needs of the client. To become culturally responsive, audiologists and speech-language therapists should engage in an ongoing process of

- understanding that culture has a role in their clinical practice
- actively learning about their clients' cultures and communities
- broadening their awareness and gaining insight into issues facing diverse clients, families, and communities

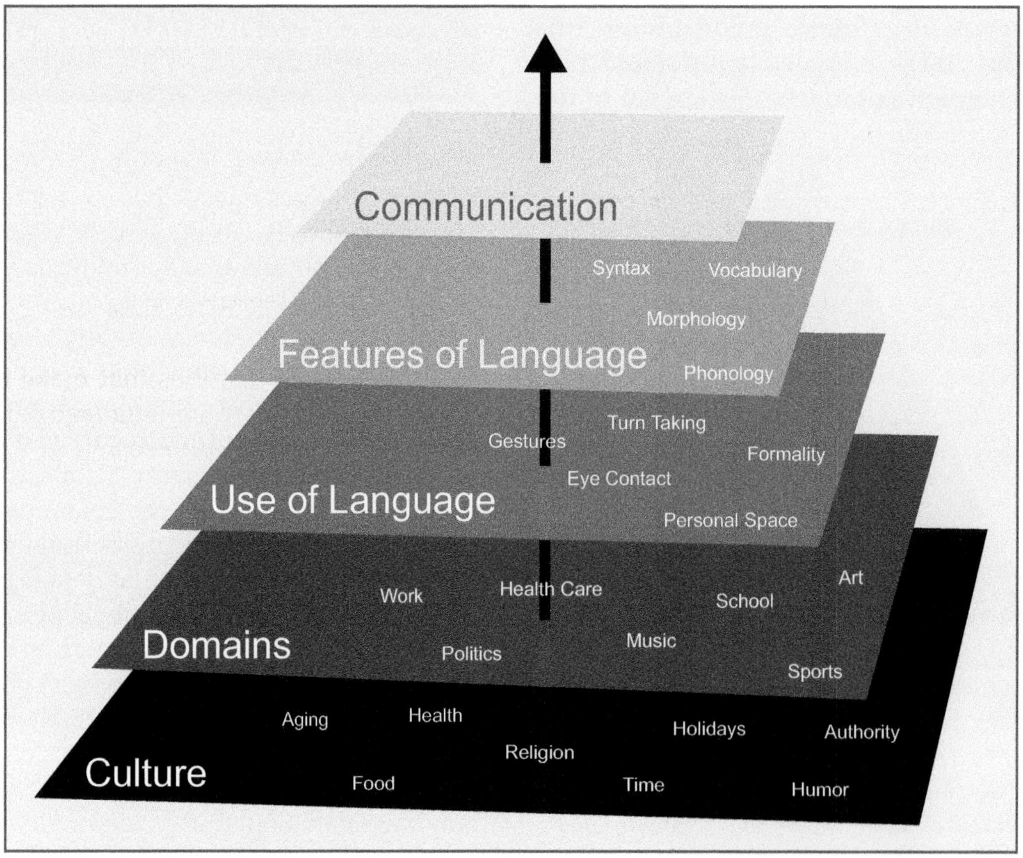

FIGURE 1–16. Depiction of the various layers of communication within a cultural context.

SUMMARY OF CHAPTER

A communication disorder is one of the most common types of disabilities found throughout the world, and they occur across the life span—from children to adults. Communication disorders can be grouped into two general categories related to the timing and cause of the disorder. A developmental or congenital communication disorder is one that occurred prior to birth. An acquired communication disorder is characterized by a medical or health condition found to occur later in life (i.e., after birth), typically because of injury or illness. An organic communication disorder refers to condition in which the cause of the disorder is known. The condition may be visible to the naked eye or more subtle, such as a result of a genetic abnormality. In contrast, a functional (or idiopathic) communication disorder is one whereby the cause is unknown. In the absence of knowing the cause of the disorder, it is still possible to successfully treat the condition.

The professionals dedicated to helping individuals with communication disorders are audiologists and speech-language pathologists. Both degrees require intensive study related to the identification and management of communication disorders. There are a variety of work settings in each profession, including hospitals, clinics, schools, and private practice. Professionals providing services to individuals from different cultural backgrounds need to be aware of unique perspectives or communication styles common to those cultures.

THE PROFESSIONS OF AUDIOLOGY AND SPEECH-LANGUAGE PATHOLOGY ON THE WORLD WIDE WEB

The following are websites that provide further information on the professions of audiology and speech-language pathology. At the time of publication, each website was freely accessible.

Exploring Nonverbal Communication Video
http://nonverbal.ucsc.edu

AT&T Archives: The Speech Chain
https://www.youtube.com/watch?v=v-IPapef3BQ

A Guide to Internet Resources in Audiology
https://www.audiology-worldnews.com/

A Guide to Internet Resources in Speech Pathology
https://www.speechpathologyaustralia.org.au

American Speech-Language-Hearing Association
http://www.asha.org/students

Audiology and Speech-Language Pathology Professions Videos
https://study.com/
https://www.youtube.com/watch?v=_OIcPbndZMo

STUDY QUESTIONS

1. Describe the speech chain.
2. List and describe the verbal and nonverbal forms of communication.
3. Describe the classifications used for the various types of communication disorders.
4. Who are some of the pioneers that contributed to the creation of the audiologist and speech-language pathologist professions?
5. Compare and contrast the two models for educating audiologists and speech-language pathologists.
6. What are the qualities that make for a good audiologist or speech-language pathologist?
7. What is cultural competency?

REFERENCES

American Speech-Language-Hearing Association. (2023). *Code of ethics* [Ethics]. http://www.asha.org/policy

Denes, P., & Pinson, E. (1973). *The speech chain: The physics and biology of spoken language*. Anchor Books.

El Amin, M., Borders, J., Long, H., Keller, M., & Kearney, E. (2023). Open science practices in communication sciences and disorders: A survey. *Journal of Speech, Language, and Hearing Research*, *66*, 1928–1947.

Hyter, I., & Salas-Provance, M. (2023). *Culturally responsive practices in speech, language and hearing sciences* (2nd ed.). Plural Publishing.

Roberts, P. (2001). Aphasia assessment and treatment for bilingual and culturally diverse patients. In R. Chapey (Ed.), *Language intervention strategies in adult aphasia* (3rd ed., pp. 208–232). Lippincott, Williams & Wilkins.

Shannon, C., & Weaver, W. (1949). *Mathematical theory of communication*. University of Illinois Press.

2

ANATOMY OF SPEECH AND HEARING

OBJECTIVES

After reading this chapter, the student should be able to:

- Identify major anatomical structures related to speech, language, and hearing.
- Describe the physiological functions of these structures.
- Name individuals who have made historical contributions to our understanding of the anatomy of speech and hearing.
- Describe the essential physiological processes involved in the production of speech.
- Describe the essential physiological processes involved in hearing.
- Understand how impairments in one or more anatomical structures can contribute to a communication disorder.

KEY TERMS

Anatomy
Dissection
Physiology
Gross Anatomy
Cellular Anatomy and Physiology
Upper Respiratory Tract
Lower Respiratory Tract
Nasal Cavity
Cilia
Mouth Breathing
Adenoids
Pharynx
Esophagus
Bronchial Tubes
Bronchitis
Bronchioles
Alveoli
Lungs
Rib Cage
Diaphragm
Respiratory Cycle
Inhalation Phase
Exhalation Phase
Active muscular process
Passive muscular process
Larynx
Thyroid Cartilage
Laryngeal Prominence
Epiglottis
Hyoid Bone
Cricoid Cartilage
Vocal Folds
Arytenoid Cartilages
Glottis
Phonation
Fundamental Frequency
Articulation
Vocal Tract
Oral Cavity
Pharyngeal Cavity
Movable Articulators
Lips
Ventriloquism
Tongue
Soft Palate
Uvula
Velopharyngeal Closure
Mandible
Pipe Speech
Fixed Articulators
Hard Palate
Alveolar Ridge
Teeth
S * T = P
Source
Transfer Function
Laryngeal System
Articulatory System
Audition
Peripheral Auditory System
Central Auditory System
Auricle
Pinna
Helix
Tragus
Lobule
Front-Back Confusion
External Auditory Meatus
Temporal Bone
Cerumen
Tympanic Membrane
Malleus
Incus
Stapes
Ossicular Chain
Tensor Tympani
Stapedius
Acoustic Reflex
Eustachian Tube
Vestibular Apparatus
Cochlea
Semicircular Canals
Basal
Apical
Scala Vestibuli
Scala Tympani
Scala Media
Helicotrema
Perilymph
Endolymph
Organ of Corti
Basilar Membrane
Hair Cells
Tonotopic Organization
Auditory Nerve
Cochlear Nucleus
Brainstem Nuclei
Auditory Cortex
Henry Gray
Henry Vandyke Carter
Bartolomeo Eustachi
Antoine Ferrein
Alfonso Corti
Albert von Kölliker
Anna Morandi Manzolini
Sir Victor Negus
Willard R. Zemlin
Anthropometry
Alphonse Bertillon

INTRODUCTION

Anatomy is the study of the structure of the body and its parts. The word **anatomy** comes from the Greek *ana* meaning "up" or "through," and *tomie* meaning "a cutting." The early science of anatomy was based on "cutting up" structures of the body because our knowledge of the body was learned through **dissection** of human cadavers. However, less invasive methods are now available to examine the living body, using such devices as endoscopic cameras and body scans (e.g., computed tomography [CT] scan, MRI scan). **Physiology** is the study of the functions of the body and its parts. This word is also Greek in origin with *physis* meaning "nature," and *logia* meaning "to speak." So, physiology involves describing the nature of things. **Gross anatomy** and physiology involve examination of the structure and function of body parts that can be seen with the naked eye. **Cellular anatomy and physiology** (or histology) entails examining those body parts best seen under the microscope. Traditionally, both gross and cellular anatomy and physiology are foundation courses that beginning medical students are required to take as part of their degree program. This is no different for students of the audiology and speech-language pathology professions. To fully appreciate the nature of normal communication and disorders of communication, knowledge about the structure and function of the speech and hearing mechanism is essential. This chapter provides some introductory exposure to speech and hearing anatomy and physiology. The material presented is referenced again in later chapters concerning communication disorders resulting from anatomical and physiological abnormalities of the speech and hearing mechanisms.

SPEECH ANATOMY

The anatomy we use to produce speech is the same anatomy used for doing nonspeech things such as breathing, swallowing, and coughing. The anatomical structures can be divided into three subsystems: (a) respiratory, (b) laryngeal, and (c) articulatory. As humans, we have learned to exploit these structures that were originally designed for basic survival and to use them to communicate with other humans. A survey and description of the structure and function of the respiratory, laryngeal, and articulatory systems are provided.

Respiratory System

The respiratory system consists of the lungs, diaphragm, rib cage, trachea, pharynx, and oral and nasal passages. The general location of each of these anatomical structures is shown in Figure 2–1. When referring to human anatomy, a tract is an area of the body that consists of a series of related structures. The respiratory system is divided into two tracts: the **upper respiratory tract** (including the oral and nasal cavities and the pharynx) and the **lower respiratory tract** (the trachea, bronchi, and lungs). Air is inhaled primarily through the nostrils into the **nasal cavity**. The nasal cavities are lined with mucous membranes that are covered with tiny hairs known as **cilia**. These features within the nasal cavity serve to warm, moisten, and filter the air of possible contaminants. For most of us, breathing is breathing, and it does not matter whether it is from the mouth or nose. **Mouth breathing** may appear to be a harmless form of breathing; however, there are many negatives associated with breathing through the mouth. Excessive mouth breathing is problematic because air is not filtered and warmed as much as when inhaled through the nose, as it bypasses the nasal cavity. The dust and dirt deposited in the membranes cannot be disposed of as they would typically be by the nasal cavity. Consequently, these contaminants remain to produce irritation and inflammation. Mouth breathing is thought to contribute to a higher-than-average occurrence of upper respiratory infections and may exacerbate the occurrence of asthma. Excessive mouth breathing may also be indicative of situations in which the nasal cavity is obstructed, thereby preventing nasal breathing from occurring naturally. In cases such as this, mouth breathing is done out of necessity. Situations like enlarged adenoids can lead to excessive mouth breathing. **Adenoids** (e.g., tonsils) consist of a paired mass of tissue in the back of the nasal cavity that serves to filter out debris that is inhaled through the nose.

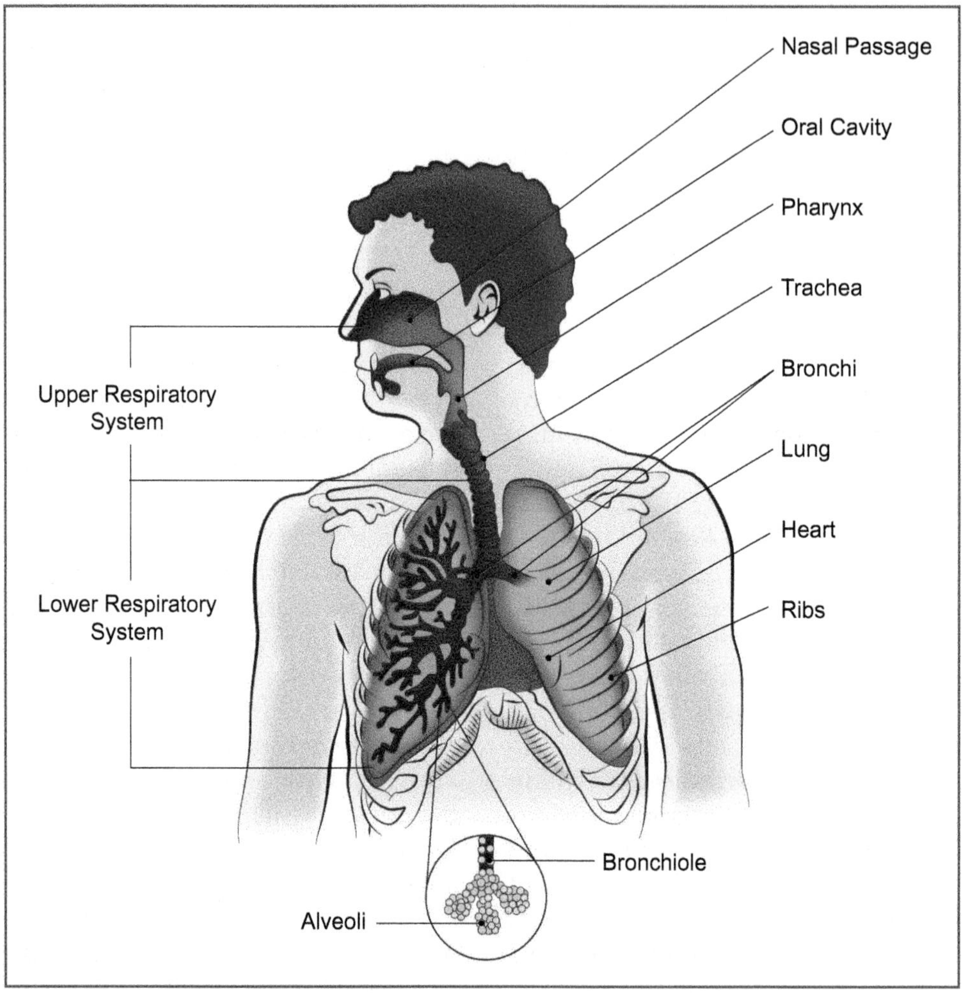

FIGURE 2–1. Anatomical features of the human respiratory system.

The **pharynx** is a hollow tube about 5 in. (12.7 cm) long that starts behind the nose and ends at the top of the trachea. The tube is made of a series of overlapping muscles that encircle the throat. At the bottom of the pharynx the tube splits, with one tube running down the front of the neck to form the trachea (i.e., windpipe) and the second tube running down the back of the neck to form the **esophagus** (i.e., food tube). The pharynx serves a twofold purpose. During the process of eating, food enters the oral cavity and is ready for swallowing. When swallowing begins, the food is directed down the pharynx. The muscles surrounding the pharynx contract and push the food toward the esophagus and onward to the stomach. During the process of breathing, air inhaled through the nose is directed toward the pharynx and down through the trachea to the lungs.

> **FYI**
>
> At rest, a healthy adult breathes about 14 to 16 times per minute. After exercise, the rate could increase to more than 60 times per minute. New babies at rest breathe between 40 and 50 times per minute. By age 5 years, the rate decreases to about 25 times per minute.

The trachea is the principal tube that carries air to and from the lungs and is made up of elastic tissues and about 20 rings of cartilage. This anatomical structure is designed to be flexible so that we can twist and turn our head and neck while, at the same time, being able to breathe normally. The trachea branches into two main tubes supplying air to the right and left lobes of the lung, respectively. These are called **bronchial tubes**. An inflammation of these airway tubes results in a serious health condition known as **bronchitis**. The tubes continue to divide again and again becoming narrower and narrower tubes, referred to as **bronchioles**. The very ends of these airway tubes look like spongy sacs termed **alveoli**. Tiny blood vessels surround each of the alveoli. At this point in the process of breathing, oxygen that is inhaled into the lungs is delivered to the bloodstream and carried to the rest of the body. Each cell in the body always needs oxygen. At the same time, these tiny sacs remove carbon dioxide from the blood, which is then exhaled from the body.

Collectively, the bronchial tubes, bronchioles, and alveoli serve to make up the lungs. The **lungs** are so large that they occupy most of the space in the chest. The lungs are cone shaped. Although the lungs come as a pair, they are not the same size, as is typical for other paired anatomical structures such as our eyes, ears, or nostrils. Instead, the lung on the left side of the body is a bit smaller than the lung on the right. This extra space on the left leaves room for the heart to occupy space within the chest. The lungs, as well as the heart and other internal organs, are protected by 12 sets of rib bones, creating the **rib cage**. Beneath the lungs is the **diaphragm** muscle, which extends across the bottom of the rib cage. The diaphragm is the principal muscle of respiration. When we inhale to take a breath, the diaphragm is drawn downward, and the rib cage is expanded and elevated. The combined actions of the rib cage and diaphragm serve to enlarge the overall chest area, and air then passes into the lungs to fill the larger space. We rely heavily on the diaphragm for our respiratory function. When the diaphragm is impaired, it can seriously compromise our breathing.

FYI

Lung cancer is the second most common cancer in both men and women. Roughly two out of three people diagnosed with lung cancer are older than 65 years. In 2023, approximately 130,000 people in the United States died of lung cancer—about 70,000 men and 60,000 women.

The primary functions of the respiratory system are to help sustain life through the exchange of gases. When a person takes a breath, the air taken in consists of several gases. The mixture is mostly composed of oxygen, nitrogen, and carbon dioxide. Oxygen is an odorless gas that makes up about 20% of air and is essential to life because it is used for chemical reactions that occur in the cells of the body. Oxygen is brought in and utilized by the body, whereas carbon dioxide and nitrogen are expelled from the body.

A single breath occurs during a **respiratory cycle**. This cycle consists of two phases: an inhalation phase and an exhalation phase. During the **inhalation phase**, the muscles are used to expand the size of the lungs so that outside air naturally flows inward toward the lungs. The process of inhalation requires us to actively engage several respiratory muscles. During the **exhalation phase**, the lungs recoil back to their original size and naturally expel air out toward the oral/nasal cavities. The process of exhalation is viewed as a passive muscular process. An example of **active** and **passive muscular processes** is seen by raising your arm to the side. The process of arm raising involves active muscular movement. Lowering of the arm simply involves passively releasing control of these same muscles.

During quiet, relaxed breathing, the amount of time dedicated to each phase of the respiratory cycle is approximately equal. During the process of speaking, the respiratory cycle is dramatically altered. The inhalation phase uses only 10% of the overall time of the cycle, whereas exhalation consumes the remaining 90% of the cycle (Figure 2–2). The reason for this is obvious: We need to prolong exhalation in order to produce strings of words and sentences on one breath. Two ways in which we can prolong the exhalation phase are to (a) inhale a larger amount of air than would normally occur during quiet breathing and (b) prolong expiratory airflow by using vocal tract resistance. The balloon analogy is useful to understand vocal tract resistance (Figure 2–3). Blowing up a large balloon is analogous to inhaling a large amount of air into the lungs. Upon releasing air from the balloon, one could either let the balloon naturally deflate or pinch the end of the balloon (i.e., create resistance) to prolong the expiratory airflow. Ways in which we prolong expiratory airflow for speech include vocal fold resistance (vibration) and oral cavity resistance (consonant articulation). These

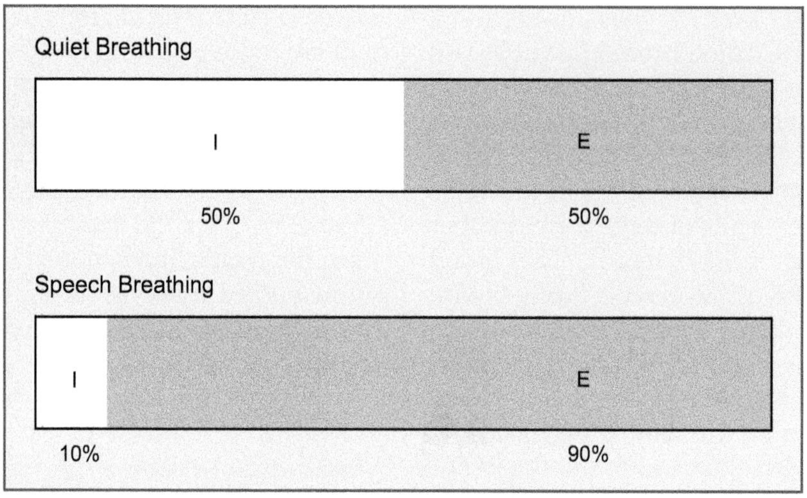

FIGURE 2–2. Comparison of the inspiratory and expiratory proportions of the respiratory cycle required for quiet breathing and speech breathing.

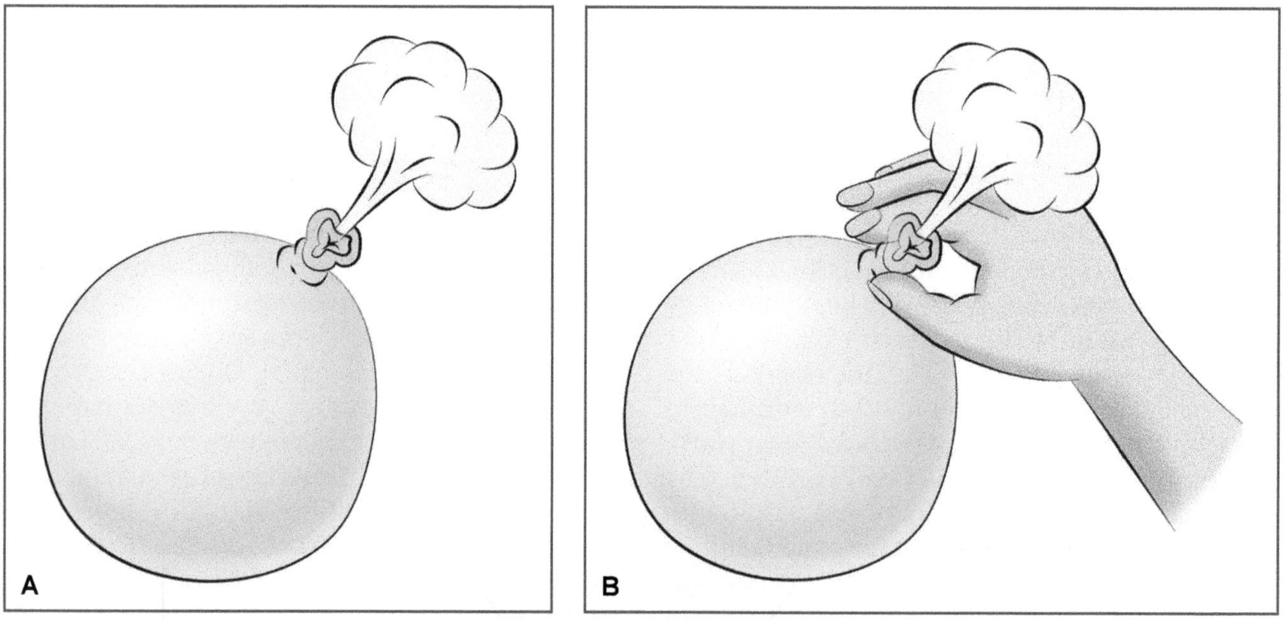

FIGURE 2–3. Balloon analogy for breathing during quiet and speech production. **A.** No resistance during expiratory airflow. **B.** Resistance to airflow resulting in longer expiratory airflow.

structures impede air flow and serve to alter the expiratory phase. In addition, the respiratory muscles relax gradually so that the air is not pushed out of the lungs in a short rush.

Laryngeal System

The anatomical structures that form the laryngeal system include cartilage, muscles, and bone. The **larynx** (pronounced "lare-rinks") is not a single structure but rather a framework of many structures. These major structures are shown in Figure 2–4. The largest of these is the thyroid cartilage, which is approximately in the middle of the larynx. The **thyroid cartilage** is formed by two large plates that are joined anteriorly (in the front) to create a slight bump in the neck. This bump is called the **laryngeal prominence** (or

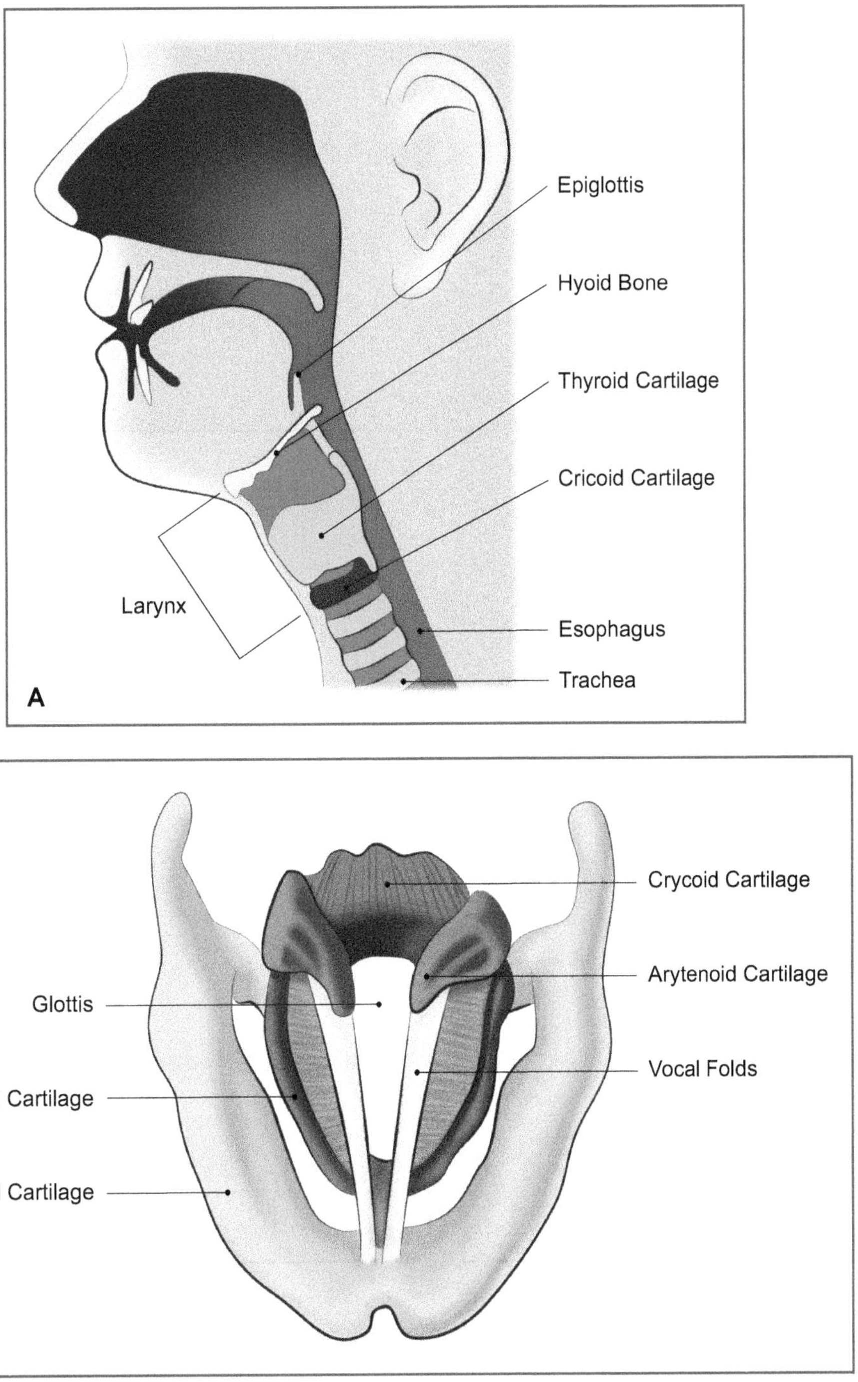

FIGURE 2–4. Anatomical features of the human laryngeal system. **A.** Side (lateral) view. **B.** View from above (superior).

Adam's apple) and is most visible in adult males. The thyroid cartilage has nothing to do with the thyroid gland, which is also located in the neck. A leaf-shaped cartilage that arises from above the laryngeal prominence is the **epiglottis**. This structure does not play an important role in producing speech, although during swallowing, the tip of the epiglottis helps to direct food away from the lungs and toward the stomach. Located above the thyroid cartilage is the **hyoid bone**, which is shaped like a horseshoe and situated very high in the neck. This bone serves as a point of attachment for muscles of the tongue (from above) and for muscles of the larynx (from below). It is sometimes called a "floating bone" because it has no direct attachments to other bones. At the base of the larynx lies the **cricoid cartilage**. The cricoid cartilage is ring shaped and rests directly on top of the trachea. Collectively, the hyoid bone, thyroid cartilage, and cricoid cartilage compose the structural framework of the larynx from top to bottom.

Inside the laryngeal framework lie the **vocal folds** (i.e., vocal cords). The technical name for the vocal folds is the thyroarytenoid muscle. The name of the muscle specifies the precise location of the vocal folds within the larynx. This is a paired muscle that makes up the right and left vocal folds. The vocal folds are attached at the front of the larynx at a point inside the thyroid cartilage (just below the Adam's apple). The vocal folds are attached at the back of the larynx to the **arytenoid cartilages**, which sit on top of the cricoid cartilage. The arytenoid cartilages swivel to allow the vocal folds to open and close as well as to shorten and lengthen. During quiet, relaxed breathing, the vocal folds remain open to allow air to flow in and out of the lungs. The space between the open vocal folds is called the **glottis**. In most cases, the vocal folds remain in an open position; otherwise, we would be unable to breathe. You can purposely close the vocal folds when you wish to hold your breath. The primary reason for closing the vocal folds is to either swallow or speak. During swallowing, the vocal folds close to prevent food and liquid from entering the trachea. These materials need to be directed into the esophagus. During the production of speech, we inhale air and then close the vocal folds. The vocal folds lie stretched across the top of the trachea. As we begin to exhale, air pressure is built up under the closed vocal folds. When enough pressure is achieved, the vocal folds are forced open and vibrate rapidly during expiratory airflow. Think of how you can make a squealing noise by blowing through two blades of grass held between your thumbs—the action of exhaling is similar.

The process of converting the air pressure from the lungs into audible vibrations is called **phonation**. The basic rate at which the vocal folds vibrate is referred to as the **fundamental frequency** (F0) of voice. It is the F0 of our voice that is perceived by others as being our voice pitch. For young children, F0 is approximately 350 cycles per second (or hertz, Hz). For women and men, the average F0 is around 240 Hz and 120 Hz, respectively. The reason for the lowest F0 being found among men is because the vocal folds are large and bulky, and they naturally vibrate at a slower rate compared with those that would be short and thin, as found in women and children (Figure 2–5). A visual depiction of vocal fold vibration is shown in Figure 2–6.

Articulatory System

The term **articulation** refers to the movement of one structure against another. Speech articulators are those structures that are in contact with another structure for the purpose of creating the sounds of speech. The major structures that form the articulatory system are shown in Figure 2–7. The system runs from the larynx to the lips and includes a combination of cavities, muscles, and boney structures. The entire articulatory system is contained within the **vocal tract**. In this case, vocal tract refers to an extended area of space within the body that is used for vocalization. The vocal tract consists of three cavities: (a) the mouth or **oral cavity**, (b) the nose or nasal cavity, and (c) the throat or **pharyngeal cavity**. Each of these cavities plays a role in the production of speech and in the process of respiration, as noted earlier. The articulators within the vocal tract can be categorized as either movable or fixed.

Movable articulators are those that make contact with either another movable structure or a permanently fixed structure. The movable articulators include the lips, tongue, soft palate, pharynx, and mandible. The **lips** are two folds of tissue that surround the mouth and play a role in eating, speaking, and, of course, kissing. The lips are required to produce consonant sounds such as /p/, /f/, and /m/. An exception to this might be found in **ventriloquism**, which is the art of speaking without moving the lips, so that an illusion of the voice coming from another source is created.

The **tongue** probably is the most important speech articulator. The tongue is not a single muscle but rather a collection of many overlapping and connected muscles. The tongue is extremely

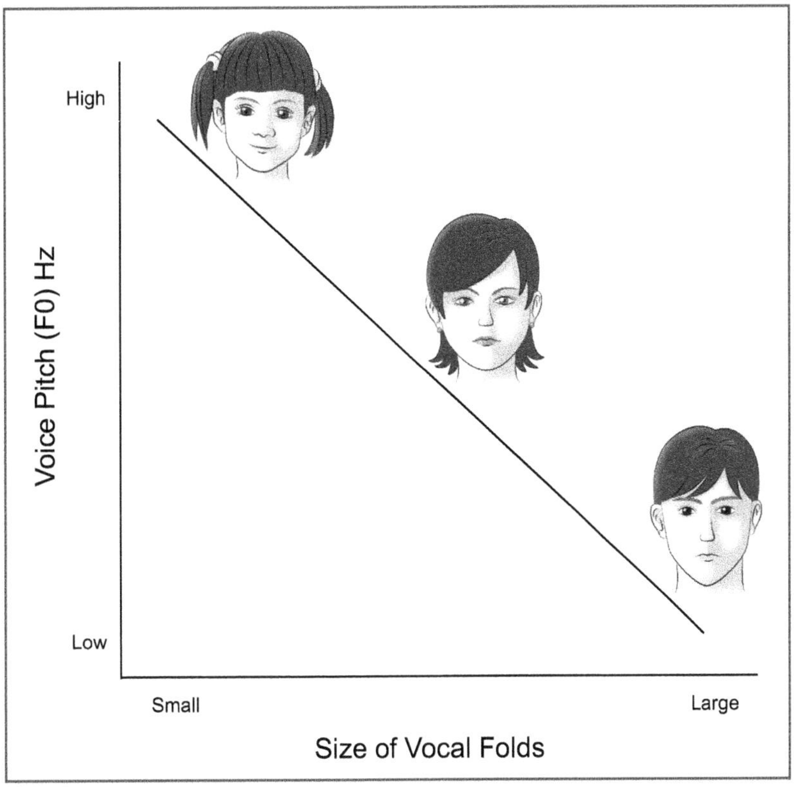

FIGURE 2–5. Relationship between vocal fold size and voice pitch (F0).

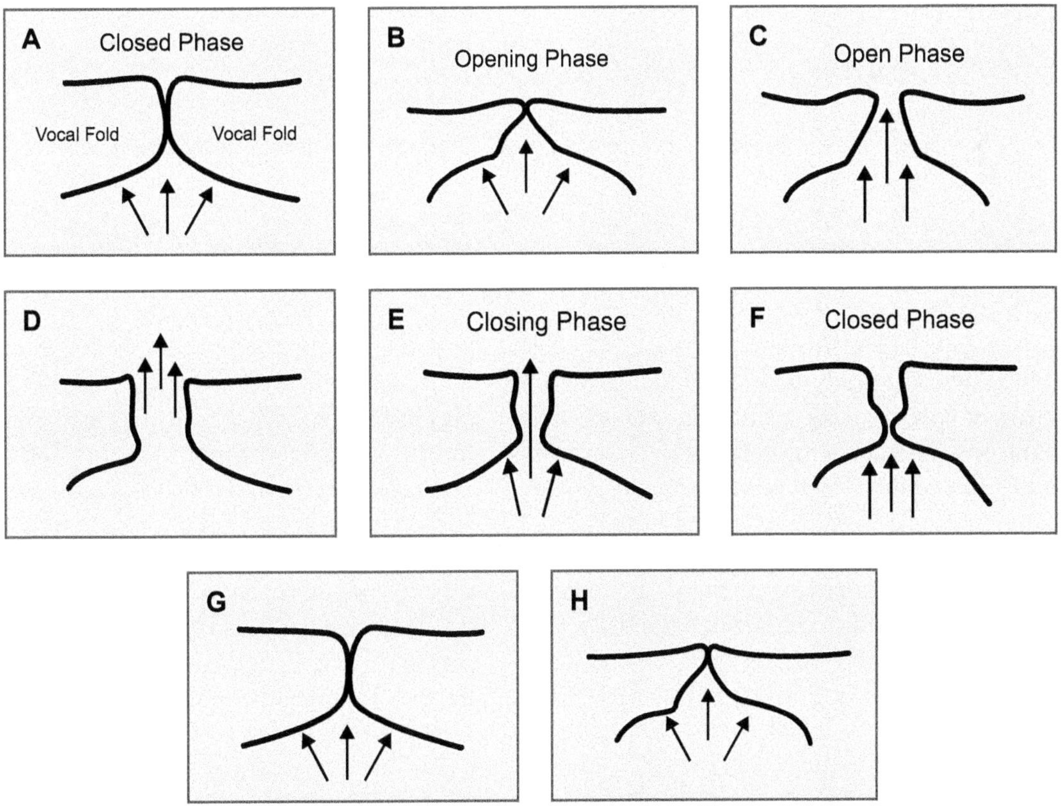

FIGURE 2–6. Frontal view of the vocal folds showing the sequential steps involved in the process of vocal fold vibration. The arrows indicate the buildup and direction of airflow from the trachea through the vocal folds.

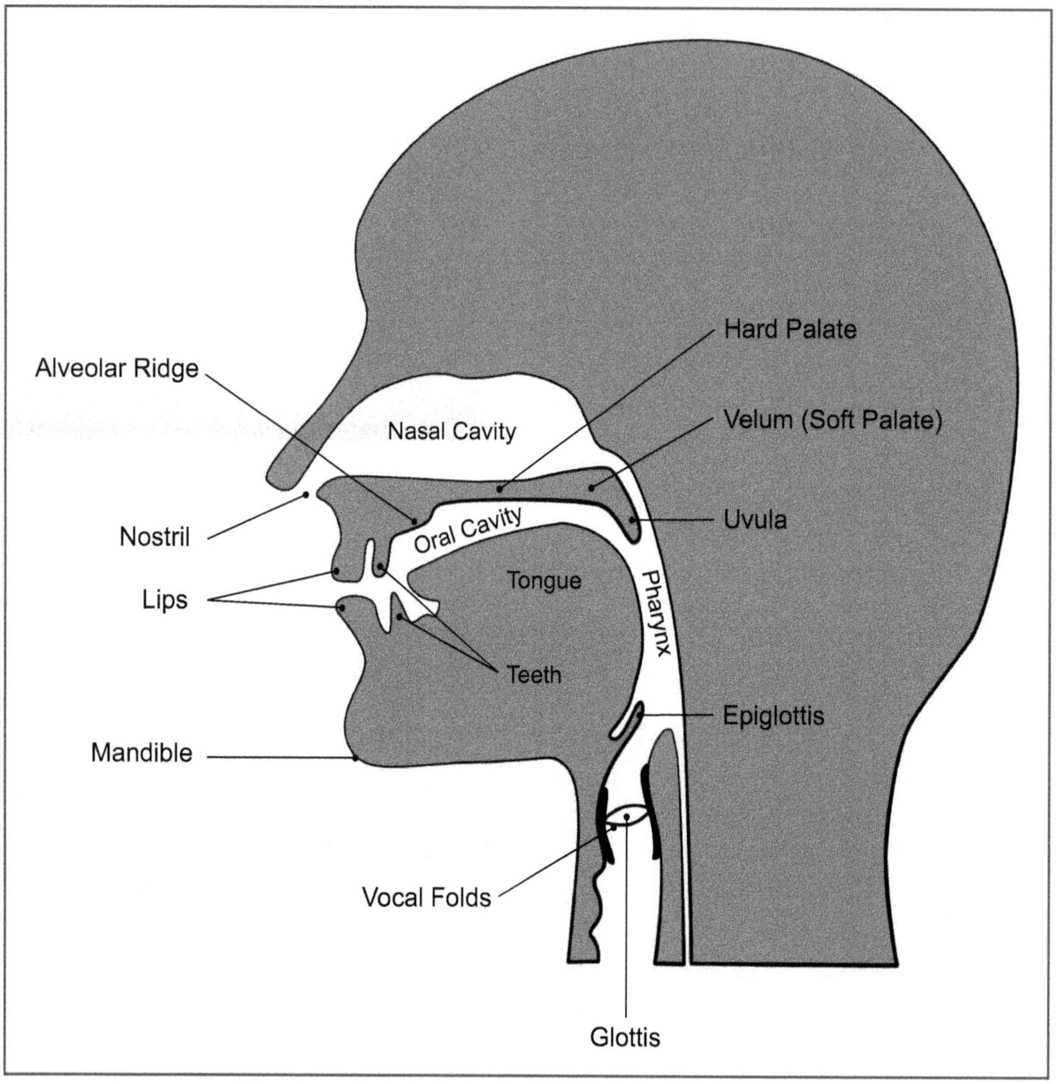

FIGURE 2–7. Anatomical features of the human speech articulatory system.

strong, as it must move food around in our mouths as we chew. The tongue is required for the production of all vowel sounds and a majority of consonants such as /s/, /l/, and /th/ (e.g., the consonants in the word "sloth"). The **soft palate** (or velum) is the soft tissue located at the back of the roof of the mouth. The soft palate, unlike the hard palate at the front of the mouth, does not contain bone. The very tip of the soft palate is called the **uvula**, which is a tiny "punching bag" of flesh. The soft palate serves to close off the oral and nasal cavities by articulating with the back of the pharynx. This process is known as **velopharyngeal closure**. All vowels and consonants, except for "m," "n," and "ng" (e.g., the consonants in the word "meaning") involve velopharyngeal closure. That is, most sounds are articulated only within the oral and pharyngeal cavities. If the soft palate was to remain lowered during the production of consonants and vowels, our speech would become highly nasalized because the flow of speech would be simultaneously directed through the oral and nasal cavities. The pharynx is not only a cavity within the vocal tract but also a movable articulator. The muscular walls of the pharynx move and squeeze the soft palate to assist with velopharyngeal closure. The **mandible**, which forms the lower jaw and holds the lower teeth in place, works as a bilateral hinge with a connection to the temporal bone on each side of the skull. It serves as a "fine-tuner" of speech articulation and moves continuously during typical speech production. Although it is not imperative for the mandible to move to produce speech, when it does, the quality of speech markedly improves. An example of this fine-tuning is demonstrated in what is known as **pipe speech**. Pipe speech (speaking with a tobacco pipe clenched between the teeth) imposes constraints on jaw movement, although speech can still be articulated. Once the pipe is removed from the mouth, speech becomes noticeably clearer.

Fixed articulators are those that cannot be moved by muscles. They include the hard palate, alveolar ridge, and teeth. The **hard palate** is the front portion of the roof of the mouth that is made of bone and serves as the base of the skull. It is used for the articulation of sounds such as "sh" (as in the word "shoe"). The **alveolar ridge** is located at the roof of the mouth between the upper teeth and hard palate. It contains the sockets of the teeth and can be felt with the tongue in the area right behind the upper teeth where there is a change in the angle of the roof of the mouth. Speech sounds such as "t," "d," and "z" (e.g., the consonants in the words "two" and "dice") are articulated with the tongue at the alveolar ridge. The **teeth** are also involved in the articulation of speech sounds. The upper and lower central incisors (i.e., front teeth) are necessary for articulation of consonants such as "v," "f," and "th" (e.g., as in the words "vie" and "faith").

FYI

The term *glossectomy* refers to surgical removal of all or part of the tongue. A glossectomy is performed to treat cancer of the tongue. Removing the tongue is recommended if the patient has a cancer that does not respond to other forms of treatment. In most cases, however, only part of the tongue is removed (partial glossectomy). Many people are still able to produce speech even when a considerable portion of the tongue is removed.

FYI

One of the strongest muscles in the human body is the masseter muscle located in the jaw. When chewing, this muscle is capable of exerting a force as great as 200 pounds.

THE PROCESS OF SPEECH PRODUCTION

As noted in Chapter 1, the process of speech production involves the encoding of a message. The starting point for speech encoding is the brain. The centers of the brain responsible for generating language organize the message to be spoken and send neural commands to the anatomical structures involved in speech production. The details of brain anatomy and the nervous system are provided in Chapter 9; however, it is important to recognize that without the brain's control of the respiratory, laryngeal, and articulatory systems, speech production would be impaired, if not impossible.

The normal process of speech production entails a transformation of aerodynamic into acoustic energy. The anatomical and physiological processes involved in the generation of speech can be depicted in the formula $S * T = P$. The *S* symbol refers to the **source**. To produce speech, there needs to be a source of energy that provides the driving force behind the act of uttering a sound. The anatomical system that provides the source for speech production is the respiratory system. The *T* symbol refers to a **transfer function**. The concept of a transfer function is like that of a filter, in which the original source is altered or transformed. In the case of speech production, the original source (i.e., the expiratory air flowing upward from the lungs) is transformed by movements from the **laryngeal system** and the **articulatory system**. The final symbol in the formula, *P*, refers to the product in the generation of speech. The end product reflects the contributions of the respiratory system, laryngeal system, and articulatory system to the acoustic generation of sound. This acoustic energy is ultimately perceived by a listener as words and sentences. An anatomical representation of $S * T = P$ is provided in Figure 2–8.

> FYI
>
> The auditory nerve is referred to by a variety of names. It is also known as the acoustic nerve, the eighth cranial nerve, and the vestibulocochlear nerve. The nerve is essential for both hearing and balance.

HEARING ANATOMY

The act of hearing is referred to as **audition**. The anatomical aspects of audition can be divided into two main components: the **peripheral auditory system** and the **central auditory system**. The peripheral auditory system consists of structures beginning with the outer ear and ending with the auditory nerve. The central auditory system begins at a point beyond the auditory nerve and terminates at the auditory centers in the brain. A basic survey and description of the structure and function of the peripheral auditory system and central auditory system are provided.

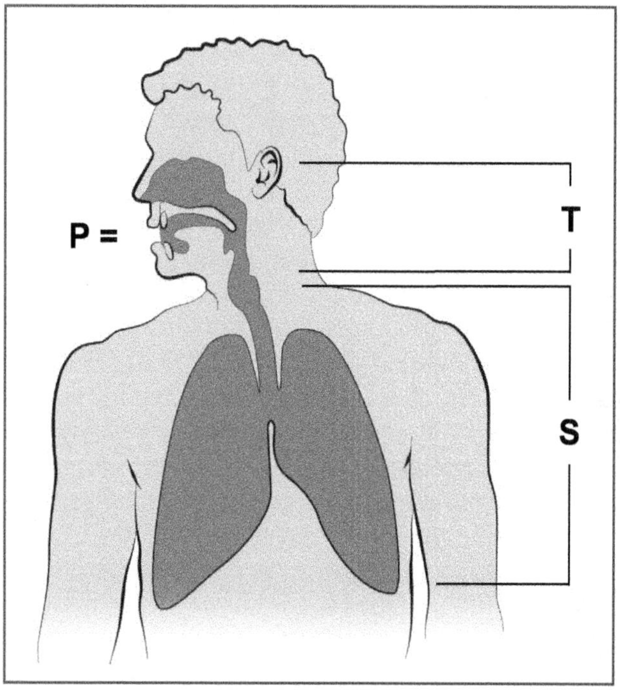

FIGURE 2– 8. The process of speech production according to the $S * T = P$ formula. *S* refers to the source of speech, namely, the respiratory system. *T* refers to the transfer function of the vocal tract involving the laryngeal and articulatory systems. *P* is the end product of the contributions from the various systems.

Peripheral Auditory System

Outer Ear

An illustration of the outer ear as well as the entire peripheral auditory system is provided in Figure 2–9. The outer ear consists of two parts: (a) auricle and (b) ear canal, or the external auditory meatus. The **auricle**, sometimes called the **pinna**, is the most visible part of the entire auditory system and is made of elastic cartilage (Figure 2–10). Some of the prominent landmarks of the auricle include the **helix**, which is the outer rim. The **tragus** is the small cartilaginous notch that is in front of the external opening of the ear. The **lobule** is the dangling fleshy part of the auricle and is the location where ears are normally pierced. The auricle serves two purposes. The first is to protect the middle ear from damage, particularly the eardrum. The auricle also serves to help eliminate **front-back confusion** by assisting in distinguishing sounds that arise from in front of the listener from those that arise from behind the listener. The movement of the auricle, particularly advanced in several types of animals, developed as a means of detecting predators. One simply needs to watch the ear movements of a dog or cat when presented with sounds coming from various directions. As humans, our auricles have evolved into fixed, immobile structures. However, it is common to find an individual who is hard of hearing cupping a hand behind the ear as an aid to improve localization of sound. The **external auditory meatus** is a 2.5-cm canal that runs from the auricle to the eardrum. The term *meatus* refers to a natural opening or canal. The outer one third of the canal, that is nearest to the auricle, is made of elastic cartilage. The inner two thirds of the canal is carved into the **temporal bone** of the skull. The entire canal is lined with skin and very fine hair.

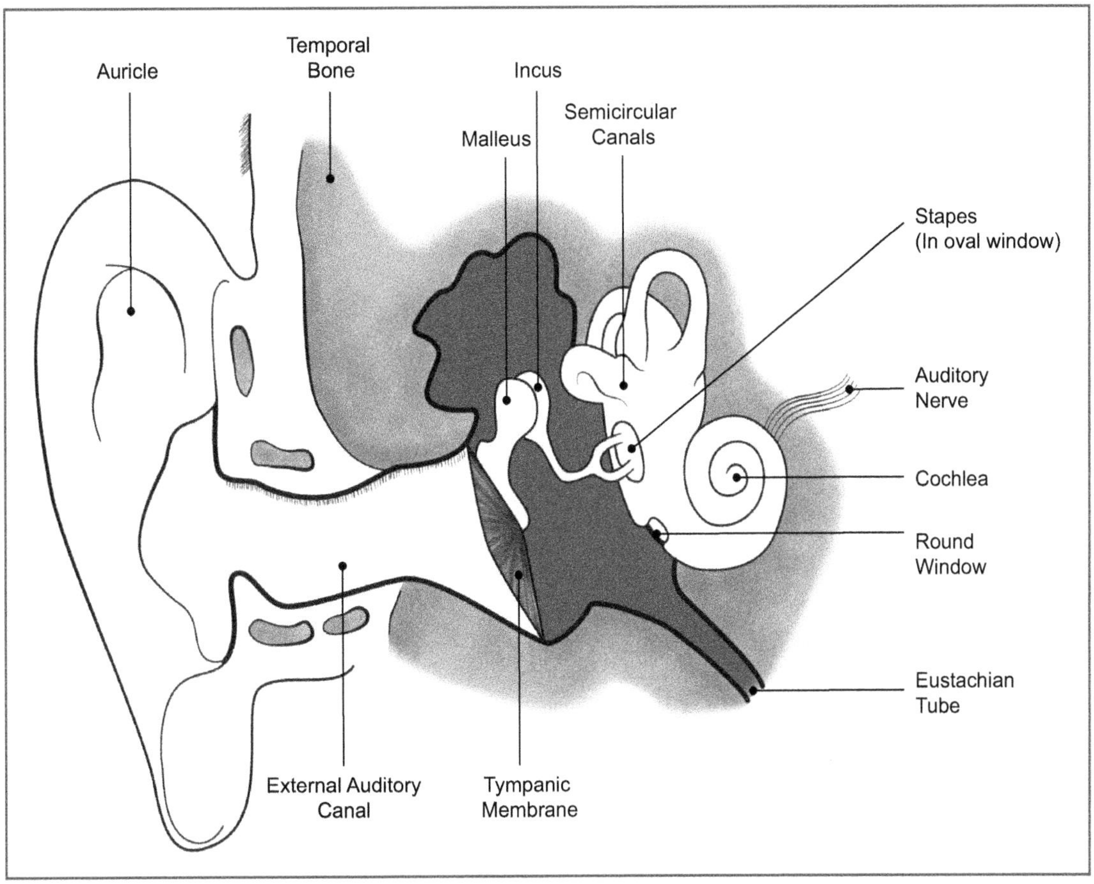

FIGURE 2–9. Cross-sectional view of the peripheral auditory system showing some anatomical detail of the outer, middle, and inner ear structures.

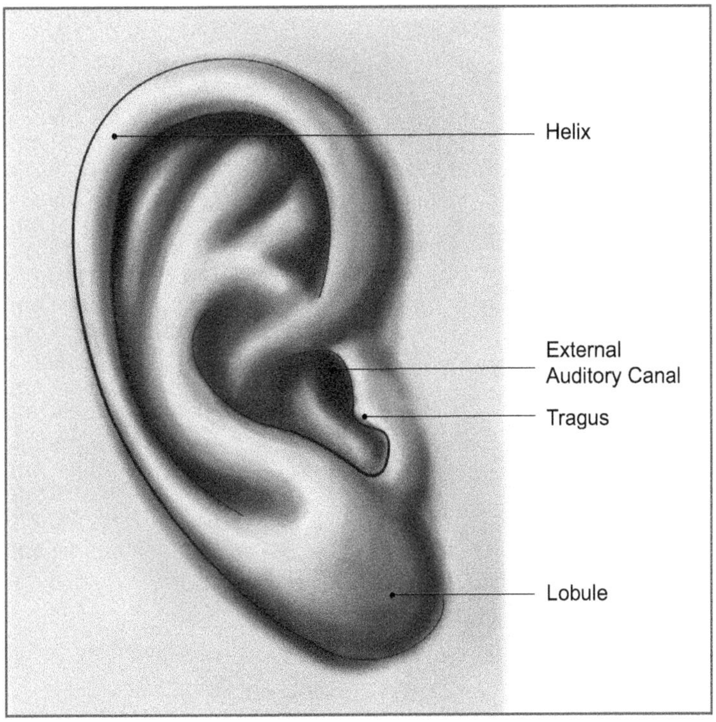

FIGURE 2–10. Landmarks of the auricle.

The ear canal also contains glands known as ceruminous glands. These glands secrete a substance called **cerumen**, commonly referred to as earwax. Cerumen plays an important role in preventing the ear canal from drying out. Cerumen also has been found to be useful in preventing intruders, such as insects, from entering the ear because they find this waxy substance to be noxious. The function of the external auditory meatus is to funnel sound toward the eardrum. In addition, the general shape of the external auditory meatus serves to provide a slight "boost" in loudness for high-frequency sounds, which are found to resonate in the canal.

Middle Ear

The middle ear is a tiny air-filled space located entirely within the temporal bone. The major structures of the middle ear include the tympanic membrane, three miniature bones, two muscles, and the eustachian tube. The **tympanic membrane** (or eardrum) is a thin, tough, fibrous membrane that spreads out across the ear canal. The tympanic membrane is a very durable and tightly stretched membrane that vibrates as incoming sound pressure waves reach it. Suspended within the middle ear space is a series of three small bones that form a bridge between the tympanic membrane and the inner ear. These three bones are the **malleus** (or hammer), **incus** (or anvil), and **stapes** (or stirrup). They are the smallest bones in the human body and make up what is known as the **ossicular chain**; each bone is an ossicle (from the Latin word *ossiculum* for "diminutive bone"). The malleus is in contact with the tympanic membrane. At the other end of the chain, the stapes is inserted into the oval window of the cochlea (inner ear). Collectively, these bones provide a mechanical link between the outer ear and the inner ear.

Two small muscles are located within the middle ear and make contact with the ossicular chain. The **tensor tympani** muscle runs from the front wall of the middle ear cavity and attaches to the malleus bone. The **stapedius** muscle runs from the back wall of the middle ear cavity and attaches to the stapes bone. These muscles provide a form of protection to the inner ear by stiffening the ossicular chain in the presence of very loud sounds, typically in excess of 90 dB.

FYI

Cotton swabs are not designed for cleaning ears. Instead, they are meant to be used for household use, as well as for applying first aid. Using cotton swabs in ears can do more damage than good. Attempts to use cotton swabs to remove cerumen can result in impacting cerumen deeper into the ear canal. This can lead to ear infections, tympanic membrane damage, as well as hearing loss.

In essence, the ossicular chain is prevented from functioning normally and causes a decrease in the loudness of sounds entering the inner ear. The contraction of these middle ear muscles is involuntary and known as the **acoustic reflex** (see also Chapter 14). The **eustachian tube** runs from the middle ear space down toward the upper region of the pharynx (Figure 2–11). The function of the eustachian tube is to protect, aerate, and drain the middle ear. It also serves to equalize middle ear air pressure with environmental air pressure. The eustachian tube is normally closed and opens only under changes in pressure. The reason your ears "pop" on an airplane is that the eustachian tube has briefly opened and equalized air pressure. In adults, the eustachian tube is approximately 35 mm (1.3 in.) long and runs from the middle ear to the pharynx along a 45° angle.

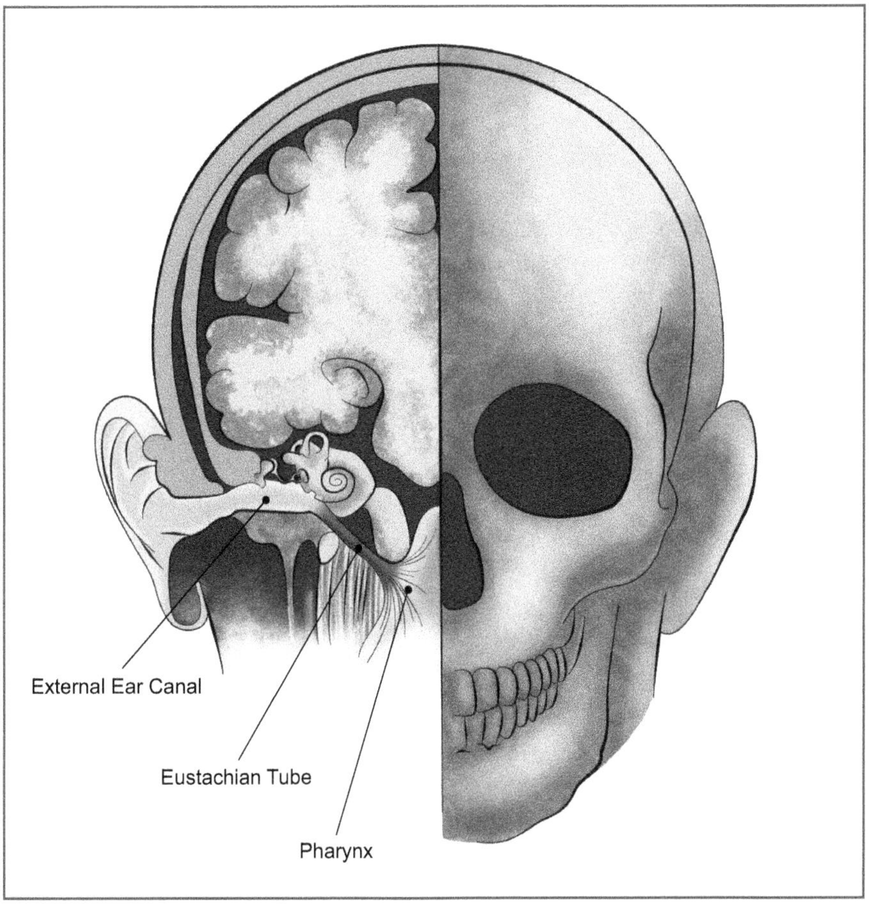

FIGURE 2–11. Depiction of the anatomical location of the eustachian tube.

In young children, the tube measures only 17 mm and is nearly horizontal in angle. This nearly flat angle in young children makes for poor drainage of fluid from the middle ear and predisposes young children to middle ear infections.

Inner Ear

Just like the middle ear, the inner ear is housed entirely within the temporal bone of the skull. Whereas the middle ear is an air-filled space, the inner ear is a fluid-filled space. The inner ear consists of two main organs. The **vestibular apparatus** serves as the body's balance organ, and the **cochlea** serves as the body's hearing organ. A key structure in the vestibular apparatus consists of **semicircular canals**, which work with the brain to sense, maintain, and regain balance and a sense of where the body and its parts are positioned in space. Most causes of dizziness are inner ear problems associated with the vestibular apparatus. Specialty occupations such as astronauts and fighter pilots require an unusually intact vestibular apparatus that allows them to function during potentially dizzying environmental situations.

> **FYI**
>
> People diagnosed with diabetes are 70% more likely to have vestibular dysfunction compared to those without diabetes. This dysfunction can lead to problems with balance and falls. An older adult with diabetes is at particularly high risk.

The cochlea has an appearance that is somewhat like that of a small snail. Indeed, the term *cochlea* is Greek for the word "snail shell." The cochlea has approximately 2.75 turns in humans. The largest turn (the one nearest the stapes) is the **basal** end of the cochlea, and the smallest turn is called the **apical** end. A helpful way to visualize the cochlea is to examine the structure from the inside. A cross-sectional view (Figure 2–12) reveals that the inside of the cochlea consists of three compartments. The upper compartment is called the **scala vestibuli**, the lower compartment is the **scala tympani**, and the middle compartment is the **scala media** (or cochlear duct). At the apical end of the cochlea is a small hole called the **helicotrema**, which connects the scala vestibuli and scala tympani compartments. Both compartments are filled with a fluid called **perilymph**, which is comparable in density with plasma or cerebrospinal fluid. The scala media is filled with a thick fluid substance called **endolymph**, which is a unique fluid unlike that found anywhere else in the body.

The **organ of Corti** lies inside the scala media of the cochlea. This organ is responsible for converting the mechanical sound energy of the ossicular chain coming from the middle ear into electrical impulses. The organ of Corti sits on the **basilar membrane**, which is the wall that separates the scala tympani from the scala media. The organ of Corti consists of four rows of **hair cells** that run the entire length of the cochlea from basal to apical ends. In total, there are approximately 20,000 hair cells. At the top of each cell, a minute fiber from the auditory nerve is attached. These hair cells sense the sounds received from the middle ear and transmit the signals to the auditory nerve that, in turn, forward the signals to the brain. A fascinating feature of the organ of Corti is its **tonotopic organization** (Figure 2–13). When sounds of varying pitch (hertz) enter the cochlea, the hair cells in the cochlea do not all respond in the same way. Different regions of the cochlea are selectively responsive to different frequencies of sound. The basal end of the cochlea vibrates most at high-frequency tones, and the apical end vibrates most at low-frequency tones. Assuming each hair cell reflects a specific frequency, the normal range of hearing extends from 20 Hz up to 20,000 Hz. Research has shown that humans are unable to

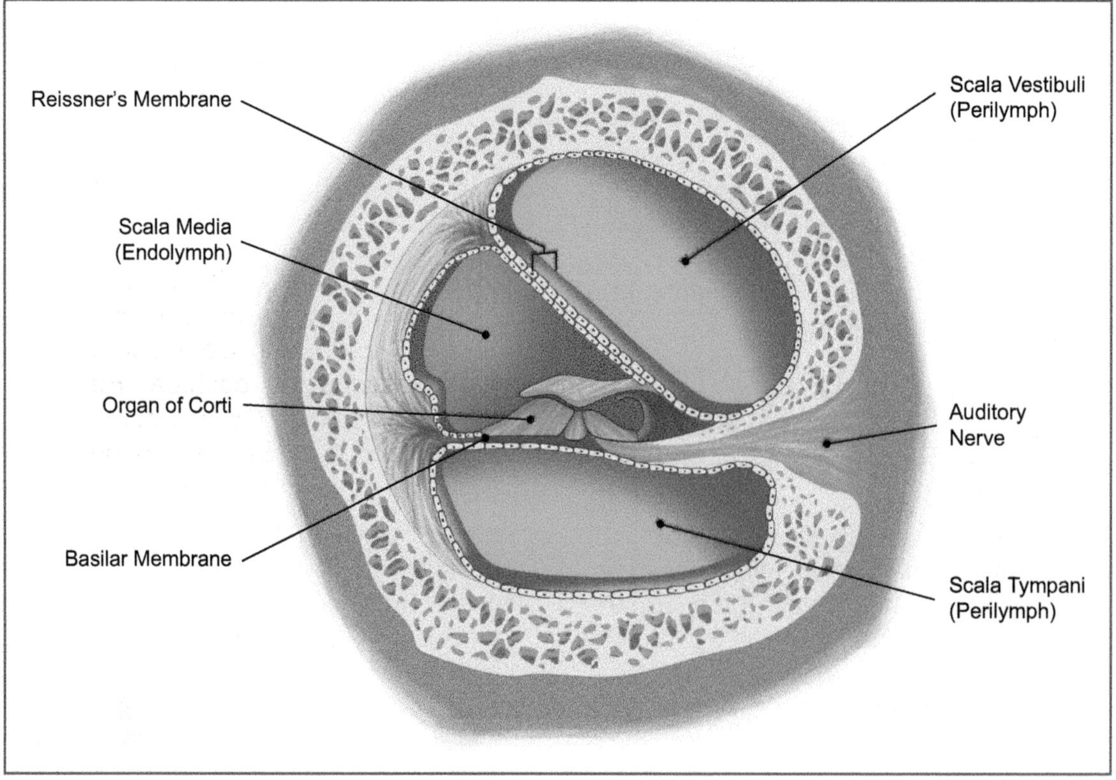

FIGURE 2–12. Cross-sectional view of the cochlea and associated landmarks.

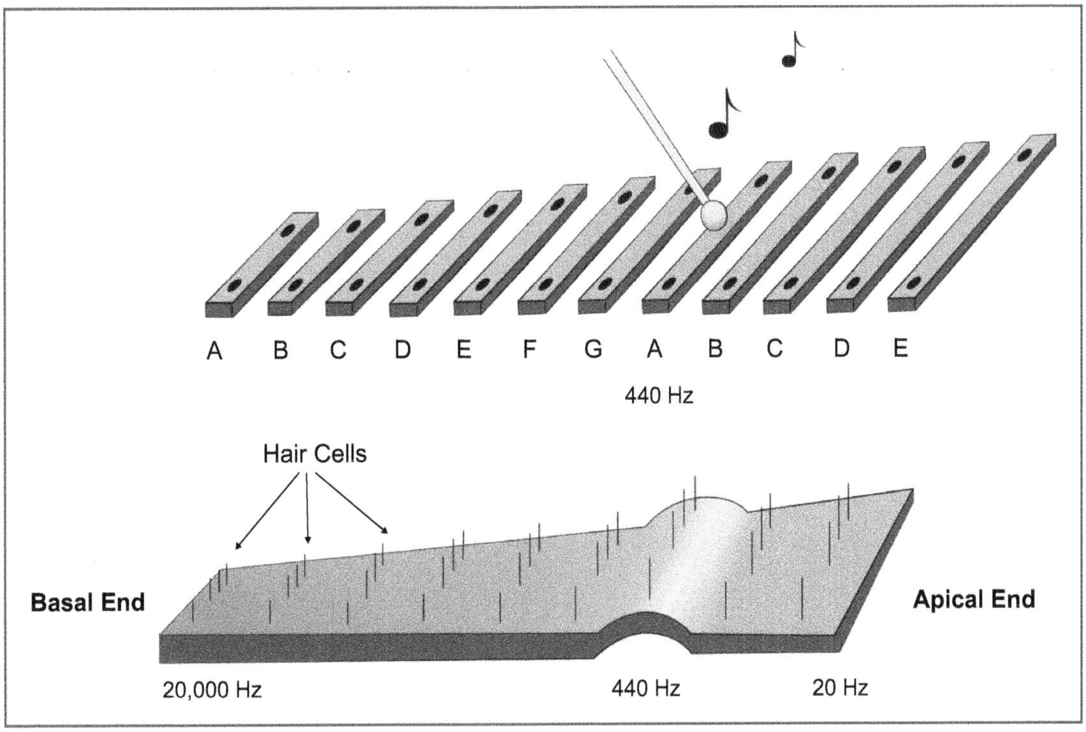

FIGURE 2–13. The tonotopic organization found within the cochlea (basilar membrane).

FYI

Empedocles, the Greek philosopher known for numbering the four basic elements (fire, air, earth, and water), was the first to describe the cochlea. He called the structure "κσΧλΟς," the name of a seashell found in the Mediterranean region. However, his discovery fascinated him more for the perfect shape of the anatomical structure than its function or relation to hearing.

perceive sounds lower than 20 Hz. The **auditory nerve** is a bundle of more than 30,000 nerve fibers that carries hearing and balance information from the inner ear to the brain. The nerve consists of the cochlear branch, carrying information about hearing to the brain, and the vestibular branch, carrying information about balance. The fibers from the auditory nerve extend into the brainstem, where they make contact with the cochlear nucleus, the next stage of the auditory system.

Central Auditory System

Once the electrical impulses generated in the cochlea are transmitted through the auditory nerve, the nerve fibers carry information about the sound to the brainstem. Figure 2–14 shows a simplified diagram of the central auditory system. All the nerve fibers from the auditory nerve terminate at the **cochlear nucleus**, which is located in the medulla region of the brainstem. The cochlear

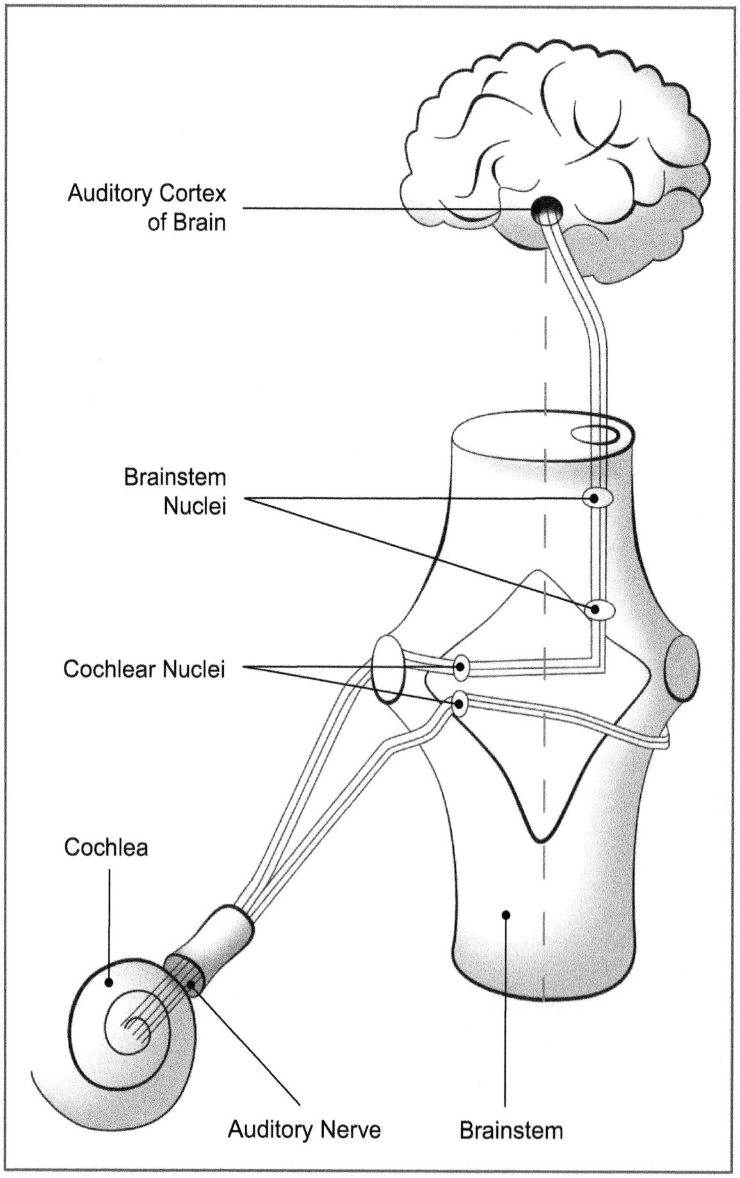

FIGURE 2–14. Simplified depiction of the anatomical structures composing the central auditory system.

nucleus is one of the most studied structures of the central auditory system in humans and animals and reflects a high concentration of neurons. Beyond the cochlear nucleus, the auditory system is characterized by a neural pathway in which most of the nerve fibers cross the midline of the brainstem. Prior to this crossing over, sound that enters one ear involves anatomical structures on the same side of the head. The auditory pathway courses upward through higher regions of the brainstem, including the pons and midbrain. At various locations along the way, the pathway terminates at clusters of **brainstem nuclei**. Eventually, the auditory pathway exits the brainstem and enters the temporal lobe of the brain. The precise location in the temporal lobe where the final process of hearing takes place is the **auditory cortex** of the brain (or Heschl's gyrus). Sound entering the left ear is ultimately processed in the auditory cortex of the right hemisphere of the brain, and vice versa.

THE PROCESS OF HEARING

Each part of the ear serves a specific purpose in the act of audition. The usual manner by which humans hear is via an airborne signal. Once sound is generated, it travels through the air in a disturbance called a sound wave. The outer ear serves to collect and channel the sound wave toward the middle ear. Thus, its function is to act as a transmission line in carrying the signal from one point to another. The sound is then transformed into mechanical energy by the tympanic membrane of the middle ear and the ossicular chain. The mechanical vibrations in the middle ear are an exact copy of the original airborne sound wave vibrations. As the vibrations reach the last bone in the ossicular chain (stapes), they enter the fluid-filled inner ear via the oval window of the cochlea. The mechanical vibrations of the stapes at the oval window are then transduced into a hydraulic wave, called a traveling wave. This wave enters the cochlea and displaces (stimulates) hair cells within the cochlea. The stimulation of specific hair cells is converted to nerve impulses that are an exact match to the frequencies composing the original airborne sound wave. The transduction of mechanical energy to nerve impulses continues all the way to the brain. The physical characteristics of the original sound are preserved at every energy change along the way until the sound becomes one the brain can recognize and process. Figure 2–15 provides a simplified breakdown of the act of hearing. Although this process is viewed as a linear (left to right) one, it is worth noting that there are various points in the hearing process where the original sound is channeled backward. However, that is beyond the scope of this introductory chapter.

> **FYI**
>
> Echolocation, also called biosonar, is the process of determining the distance and direction of objects by using sound. Animals such as bats, shrews, dolphins, and whales emit pulses of high-frequency sounds that bounce off things in their surroundings like insects, branches, or fish. The reflected sounds, or echoes, are picked up by their sensitive ears to locate food or obstacles in darkness, such as in caves and in the ocean.

HISTORIC ASPECTS OF ANATOMY AND PHYSIOLOGY

Henry Gray (1827–1861; Figure 2–16) was an English anatomist and surgeon. His most famous accomplishment was achieved in 1858, when he published *Gray's Anatomy: Descriptive and Surgical*. Intended for medical students, physicians, and surgeons, the first edition of the book contained 750 pages and 363 figures. **Henry Vandyke Carter** (1831–1897) assisted Gray by providing the illustrations for the book. In 1861, at the age of 34 years, Gray contracted smallpox from his nephew and died. *Gray's Anatomy* has lived on as the authoritative anatomy text and an indispensable teaching tool. The book has more than double the number of pages from its first appearance in 1858, including details about speech and hearing

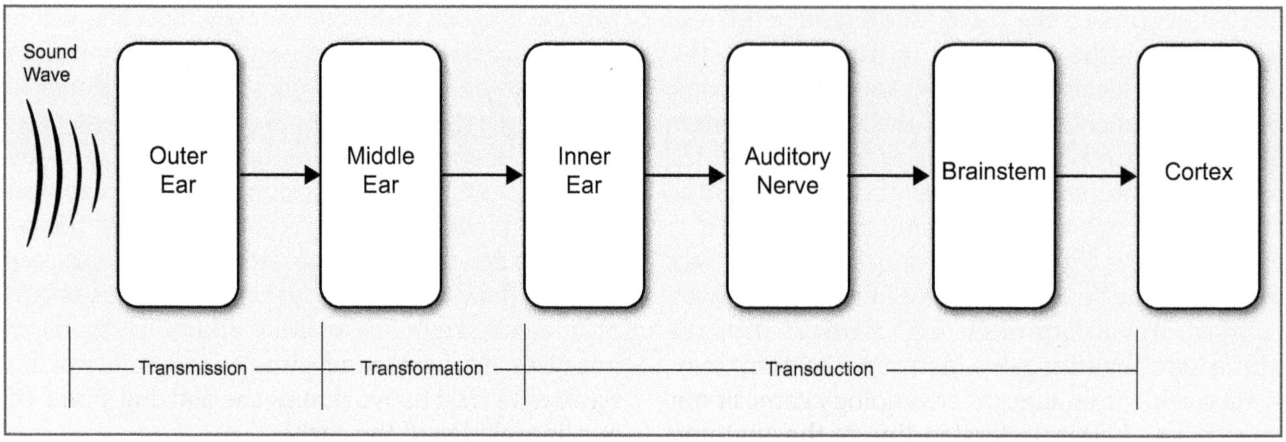

FIGURE 2–15. Process of hearing showing the flow of sound through the entire auditory system.

FIGURE 2–16. Henry Gray, an accomplished anatomist and surgeon in the early 1800s.

FIGURE 2–17. Bartolomeo Eustachi, the 16th-century Italian physician who studied anatomical features of the ear.

anatomy. Gray accomplished much as a young man; imagine what he could have accomplished had he lived a full life.

Gray's contribution to the fields of anatomy and physiology were immense and spanned the entire range of the human body. Several individuals made contributions that more directly impacted the fields of audiology and speech-language pathology. For example, **Bartolomeo Eustachi** (1510–1574; Figure 2–17) was a 16th-century Italian physician. In 1562 and 1563, he produced a remarkable series of reports (called treatises) on various parts of the body including the kidneys, teeth, and ears. In his report concerning the ear, he provided an accurate description of the tensor tympani and stapedius muscles as well as the *tuba auditiva*, which has since been referred to as the eustachian tube. The discovery by Eustachi of the connection between the middle ear and the pharynx is thought to have later inspired Shakespeare to write his play *Hamlet*, a story in which Hamlet's father is killed by poison poured into his ear.

Antoine Ferrein (1693–1769) was a French anatomist who was the first person to coin the term *vocal cords*. In 1741, while dissecting corpses, he discovered in the center of the larynx two strips of muscle that ran horizontally (front to back). He concluded that speech and song were produced entirely by the vibration of these bands of muscles caused by air being blown outward from the lungs. He compared the structures with that of a violin, in which the strings or "cords" work to produce sound. Vocal fold is now the preferred term over vocal cord. The change in terminology came about because of a better understanding of the anatomy and function of the larynx. Rather than looking and functioning like a stringed instrument, the vocal folds more closely resemble a lip of tissue.

Alfonso Corti (1822–1876; Figure 2–18) was born in Italy. As a medical student, he was enrolled first at the University of Vienna, where he became interested in the field of anatomy. Corti began his scientific career studying the cardiovascular systems of reptiles. Later he turned his attention to the mammalian auditory system. In the years 1850 and 1851, he worked in the laboratory of **Albert von Kölliker** (1817–1905) at the University of Würzburg (Germany) and examined more than 200 cochleas from cats, dogs, pigs, sheep, rabbits, and rats. It was there that he developed new coloring techniques in microscopic anatomy, which enabled him to describe individual components inside the cochlea. Prior to this time, it was notoriously difficult to preserve inner ear structures because they quickly deteriorated once removed from their fluid-filled compartments. In 1851, he published a paper describing a structure located on the basilar membrane of the cochlea containing hair cells that convert sound vibrations into nerve impulses. This structure came to be known as the *organ of Corti*. His work was the starting point of our knowledge of the cochlea.

Anna Morandi Manzolini (1714–1774; Figure 2–19) was both an anatomist and artist who was born in Bologna, Italy. She is often overlooked for her outstanding contributions to anatomical dissection and the creation of wax anatomical models. Her work involved meticulously deconstructing anatomical organs such as the eye and ear, which were then reconstructed as wax models. Her anatomical sculptures brought human anatomy to life, and she ushered in a new way of visualizing and understanding human organs.

Sir Victor Negus (1887–1974) was born in London and received his medical education in laryngology at King's College Hospital in 1912.

FIGURE 2–18. Alfonso Corti provided detailed anatomical descriptions of the inner ear.

FIGURE 2–19. Anna Morandi Manzolini was the first female anatomist and wax modeler with a special interest in the anatomy of the eye and ear.

He had a long and meritorious career in laryngology. He was a pioneer in detailing the anatomy of the human and animal larynx. In 1929, he published a monumental work titled *The Mechanism of the Larynx* that had a profound influence on laryngologists, anatomists, and many other scientists throughout the world. In this publication, he was able to demonstrate which structures of the human larynx serve to differentiate man from other species.

The work of Negus on the structure of the larynx eventually contributed to the development of theories regarding the evolution of man and speech. In particular, Phillip Lieberman and Edmund Crelin (1971) argued that man's need to produce a wide range of sounds for communication led to the development of a unique two-tube (oral and pharyngeal) vocal tract. The two tubes are reflected in a clear separation between the oral cavity and the larynx, which rests low in the neck. All other animal species have a single-tube vocal tract, reflected by the close approximation between the oral cavity and larynx (Figure 2–20). This single-tube anatomy allows for easy ingestion of food and drink with no danger of food entering the lungs. This anatomical configuration also permits breathing to occur simultaneously. Anthropologists believe a single-tube vocal tract is a form of "survival" anatomy that allows animals to smell danger while eating. The two-tube vocal tract of adult humans is less efficient for eating and actually makes humans more susceptible to choking because of the large gap between the oral cavity and the esophagus. Additionally, adult humans cannot breathe and drink simultaneously. Most interesting, human infants do not show a two-tube vocal tract at birth, but rather a single-tube vocal tract. With the larynx located high in the neck, it is not possible for liquids to enter the airway, which is what makes it possible for an infant child to suckle the nipple while still being able to breathe. As the child grows, the larynx slowly descends to form a two-tube vocal tract. Among animals, the single-tube vocal tract does not permit the production of a wide range of sounds, although the two-tube vocal tract allows for a wide range of speech sounds, prompting theorists to suggest that the lowering of the larynx in man is an anatomical specialization for human speech.

Willard R. Zemlin (1929–1998; Figure 2–21), born in Minnesota, made an enormous contribution to the field of speech and hearing science through his work in basic anatomy and physiology. Zemlin was a faculty member in the department of speech and hearing science at the University of Illinois. He was the first speech-language pathologist in the world to develop a textbook on the anatomy and physiology of the speech and hearing mechanism that was designed for students pursuing a degree in communication disorders. Based on his own dissection work, Zemlin set about detailing

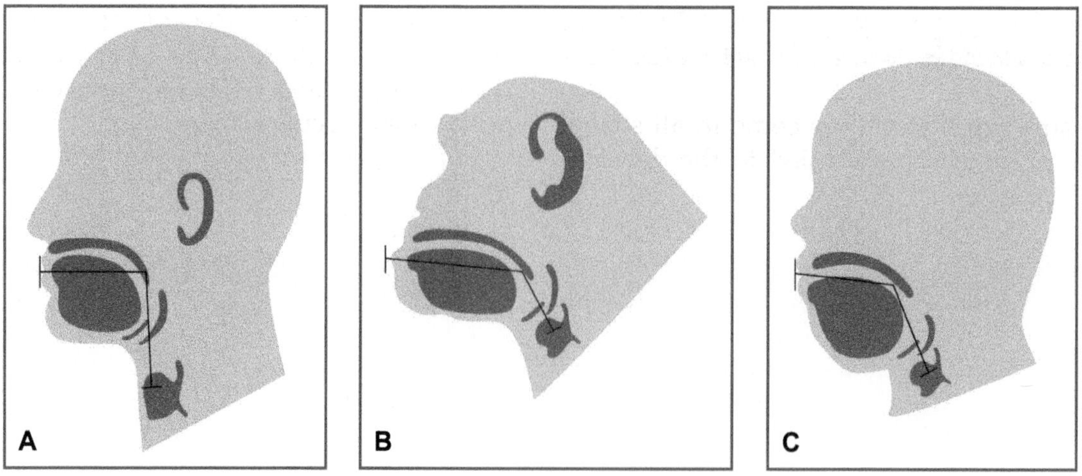

FIGURE 2–20. Comparison of the vocal tract anatomy of an adult human, nonhuman primate, and human infant. Only adult humans have a distinct two-tube vocal tract, whereas nonprimates and human infants have a sloping one-tube vocal tract.

FIGURE 2–21. Willard R. Zemlin, who was interested in the anatomy and physiology of the hearing and speech mechanisms. (From the Willard R. Zemlin Memorial website. Permission granted by Eileen Zemlin.)

essential anatomy using line drawings and photographs. The result was the publication of the classic textbook *Speech and Hearing Science, Anatomy and Physiology*, first published in 1964. The book continues to be in widespread use.

CULTURAL CONSIDERATIONS IN ANATOMY AND PHYSIOLOGY

It is no surprise that people come in all shapes and sizes. This observation led to the development of **anthropometry**, which is the scientific study of the measurements of the human body. The field was established to assist in understanding human physical variations and aid in anthropological classification. The term is derived from the Greek terms *anthropos*, meaning "man," and *metron*, meaning "measure." Anthropometry was first introduced in the late 19th century to the field of criminology as a supposedly useful means of identifying criminals based on their physical characteristics. Paris police clerk **Alphonse Bertillon** (1853–1914) devised a system that was used to identify people held in police custody; the system was based on classification of facial and bodily characteristics, and the description of scars and tattoos. Eventually, it was discovered that use of physical characteristics as a form of criminal profiling was not effective and served to perpetuate social racism. Probably the most infamous abuse of anthropometrical research occurred in the years leading up to, and surrounding, World War II. Anthropometric studies performed by German Nazis were used in the classification of Aryan and non-Aryan races and led to the decimation of countless individuals who did not fit into established categories.

Putting these extreme examples of anthropometric misuse aside, contemporary anthropometry studies continue to be conducted for various purposes (Figure 2–22). One body measurement that is currently used in criminology is fingerprinting. Academic anthropologists often investigate the evolutionary changes in human body shape and size stemming from ancestors from different environmental settings. For example, there is undisputable evidence that human populations exhibit similar climatic variation to other large-bodied mammals, such as the finding that indigenous individuals who reside in colder climates tend to be larger than individuals residing in warmer climates, and that individuals in cold climates tend to have shorter, thicker limbs than those in warm climates. Health practitioners use body measurements as an index of physiological development and nutritional status. Determining a child's weight at a given age provides information about the child's overall nutritional status. Measuring a child's weight and height can be used to detect acute malnutrition. Measuring mid-upper arm circumference provides an index of muscle wastage. Measurement of skinfold thickness is related to the amount of subcutaneous fat as an index of too much or too little nutrition.

Differences in body shape and size are also a consideration in the field of disabilities, including communication disorders. Anthropometry of people with disabilities, such as those confined to a wheelchair, is important in the design of home facilities as well as workspaces. Anthropometry has been used with increasing frequency to characterize syndromes and to establish ranges of variation within syndromes. There is research revealing

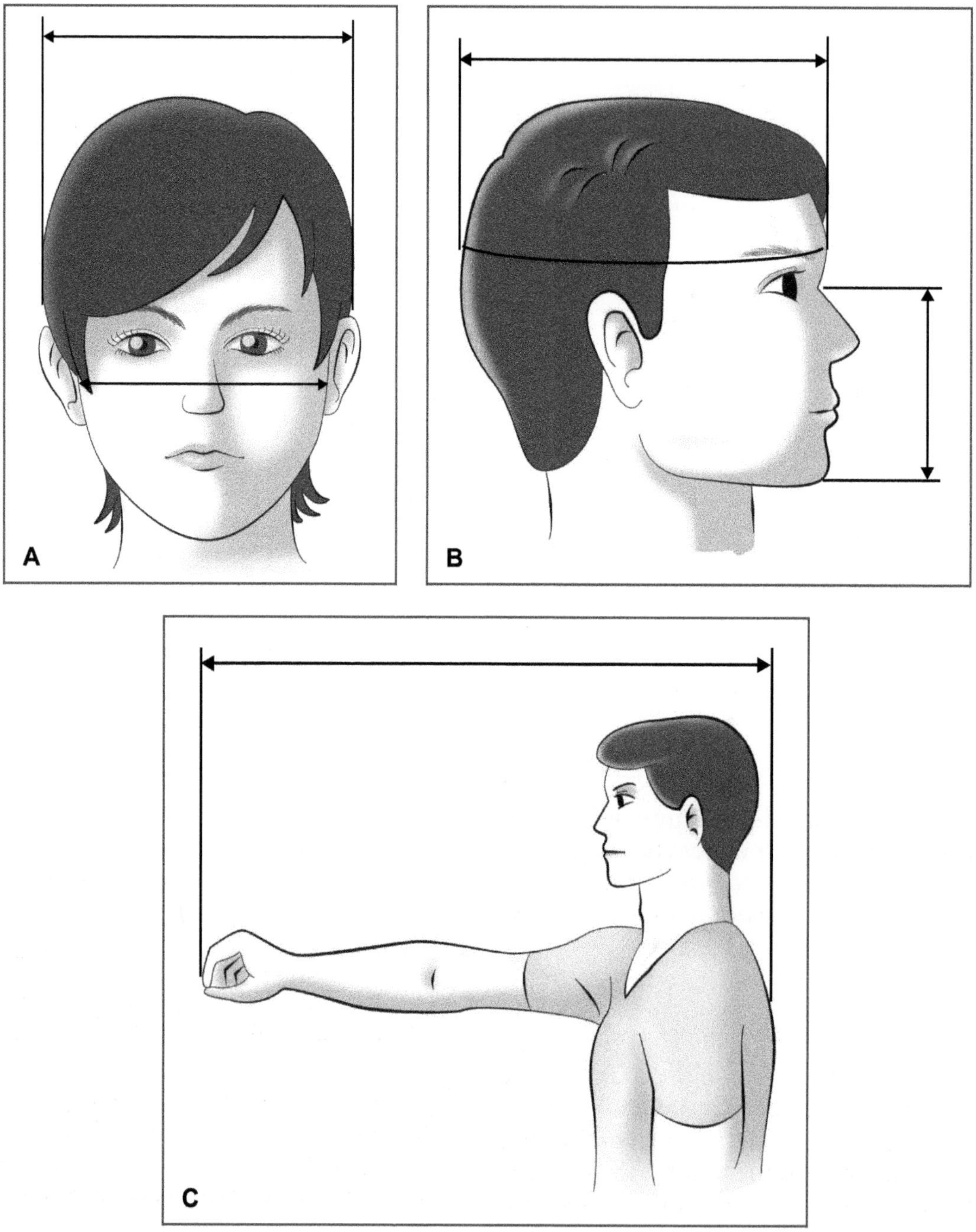

FIGURE 2–22. Examples of anthropometry for various parts of the body. *continues*

that children with autism may exhibit unusual physical characteristics such as wide-set eyes or a broad forehead (Ali et al., 2022). Noting anatomical differences in the structure and function of a person's oral-peripheral speech mechanism is a routine consideration in the speech-language pathologist's assessment of communication disorders. Audiologists too are routinely confronted with anatomical differences in ear anatomy that are a major consideration in the appropriate fitting of hearing aids. Clearly, anatomical and physical differences among people across all walks of life are the norm rather than the exception. Anthropometry has evolved to serve a useful role in the clinical evaluation and management of individuals with known and suspected disabilities.

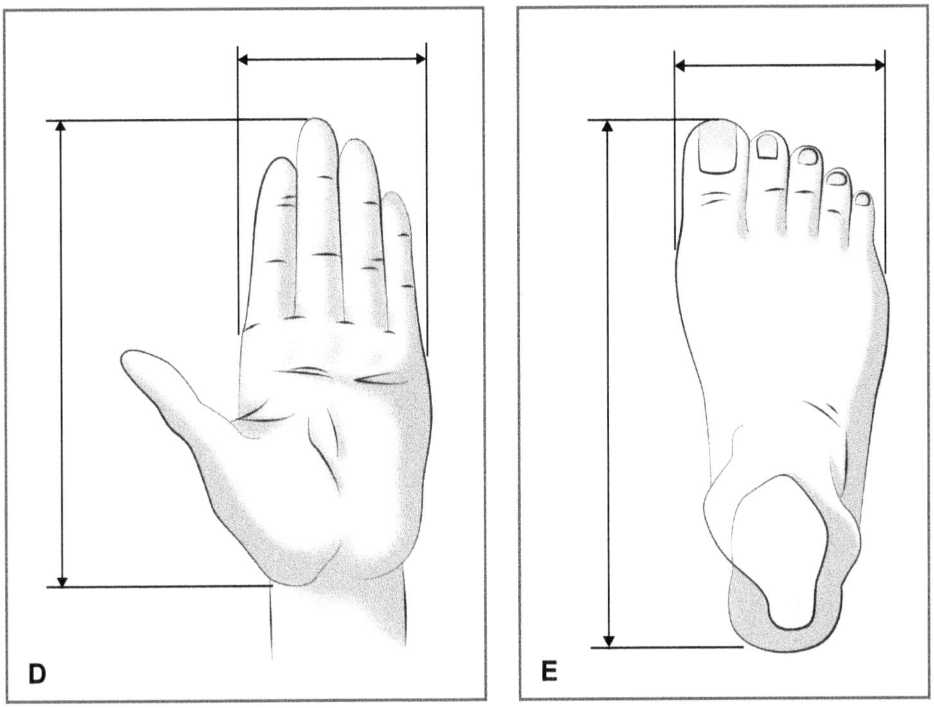

FIGURE 2–22. *continued*

SUMMARY OF CHAPTER

The anatomy we use to produce speech is the same anatomy used for doing nonspeech things such as breathing, swallowing, and coughing. The anatomical structures used for speech can be divided into three subsystems: (a) respiratory, (b) laryngeal, and (c) articulatory. As humans, we have learned to exploit these structures that were originally designed for basic survival and to use them to communicate with other humans. The anatomical structures used to produce speech consist of fixed and movable articulators. Together, they are involved in the generation of speech by transforming aerodynamic energy into audible acoustic energy, depicted in the formula $S * T = P$. The act of hearing is referred to as audition. The anatomical aspects of audition can be divided into two main components: the peripheral auditory system and the central auditory system. Together, they are involved in the process of hearing that occurs in three stages: transmission, transformation, and transduction. Anatomical and physical differences among people across all walks of life are the norm rather than the exception. Anthropometry has evolved to serve a useful role in the clinical evaluation and management of individuals with known and suspected disabilities.

ANATOMY AND PHYSIOLOGY ON THE WORLD WIDE WEB

The following are websites that provide further information on the topic of anatomy and physiology of speech and hearing. At the time of publication, each website was freely accessible.

Bartleby.com Edition of Gray's Anatomy of the Human Body
https://www.bartleby.com/107

W. R. Zemlin Memorial Website
http://zemlin.shs.uiuc.edu

How the Ear Functions Video (1940s Classic)
https://archive.org/details/HowtheEa1940

Larynx and the Voice Video (1950s Classic)
https://archive.org/details/larynx_and_the_voice

STUDY QUESTIONS

1. List and describe the three subsystems of speech anatomy.
2. Who are some of the pioneers who contributed to our understanding of hearing and speech anatomy and physiology?
3. List and describe the two main components of hearing anatomy.
4. Explain the processes of speech production.
5. Explain the process of hearing.

REFERENCES

Ali, M., El Nakieb, Y., Elnakib, A., Shalaby, A., Mahmoud, A., Ghazal, M., . . . El-Baz, A. (2022). The role of structure MRI in diagnosing autism. *Diagnostics*, *12*(1), 165.

Lieberman, P., & Crelin, E. S. (1971). On the speech of Neanderthal man. *Linguistic Inquiry*, *2*, 203–222.

SECTION 2

Developmental Communication Disorders

3

CHILD LANGUAGE DISORDERS

OBJECTIVES

After reading this chapter, the student should be able to:

- Differentiate elements of language (phonology, morphology, syntax, semantics, and pragmatics).
- Understand basic concepts of each element of language, such as morpheme or phoneme.
- Explain the course of normal spoken language development.
- Understand the distinctions between different disabilities that are characterized by a language disorder, including specific language impairment, intellectual disabilities, and autism spectrum disorders.
- Know the difference between language disabilities and cultural language differences.
- Understand the definition and implications of a language disorder.
- Understand basic principles of formal, standardized language assessment.
- Understand basic principles of informal language assessment.

KEY TERMS

Language
Linguistics
Lois Bloom
Margaret Lahey
Language Form
Language Content
Language Use
Phonology
Morphology
Free Morpheme
Bound Morphemes
Syntax
Semantics
Denotative
Connotative
Idioms
Pragmatics
Infant
Prelinguistic
Gaze Coupling
Vocalizations
Crying
Cooing
Babbling
Single Words
Verbalizations
Sound-to-Symbol Relationship
Onomatopoeia
Fast Mapping
Two-Word Combinations
Idioglossia
Metalinguistic Awareness
Written Language
Jean-Marc Gaspard Itard
Wild Boy of Aveyron
Roger Brown
Mean Length of Utterance
Specific Language Impairment
Intelligence Quotient
Behaviorist Theory
Jean Piaget
Burrhus Frederic (B. F.) Skinner
Nativist Theory
Noam Chomsky
Language Acquisition Device
Interactionist Theory
Eve Clark
Statistical Learning Theory
Case History
Standardized Testing
Language Sampling
Nonstandardized Testing
Norms
Orthographic Transcription
SALT
Language Delay
Language Deviance
Adult-Centered Therapy
Child-Centered Therapy
Self-Talk
Parallel Talk
Description
Language Expansions
Bilingualism
Simultaneous Bilingualism
Consecutive Bilingualism
Language Difference
L1
L2
Elective Therapy

INTRODUCTION

Language is a uniquely human process that involves the sharing of information. This sharing is based on a system of signs, sounds, and gestures that convey meaning. Language provides the foundation upon which communication, problem-solving, and synthesizing knowledge take place. The academic studying of language is called **linguistics**. A disorder of language can have a profound impact on a person's ability to function competently in the world. Among children, a language disorder can affect their ability to learn. A language disorder is impairment in the ability to understand and/or use words in a social communicative context. Some characteristics of language disorders include improper use of words and their meanings, inability to express ideas, inappropriate grammatical patterns, reduced vocabulary, and an inability to follow directions. Children may hear or see a word but are not able to understand its meaning. They may have trouble getting others to understand what they are trying to communicate. Concern regarding a child's language development is one of the most common reasons for parents of preschool children to seek the advice of their family doctor. Although some children initially may take longer than normal to acquire language, they may show rapid improvements. For other children, their language difficulties may be more persistent, requiring intervention by a speech-language pathologist. A long-term deficit in language can adversely affect an individual's academic progress as well as social relationships. The focus of this chapter is to provide background on normal aspects of language development and then use this information as a basis for describing child language disorders.

FIGURE 3–1. Lois Bloom developed a framework for describing the various strands of language. (Permission granted by L. Bloom.)

TERMINOLOGY AND DEFINITIONS

Language is complex and involves multiple domains, such as nonverbal language, oral language (i.e., listening and speaking), and written language (i.e., reading and writing). A classic framework for describing the various strands of language was proposed by **Lois Bloom** and **Margaret Lahey** in 1978 (Figure 3–1). They divided language domains into three areas of skill that contribute to overall communicative competence. These skills consist of (1) **language form**, (2) **language content**, and (3) **language use**. The form of language is created through the features of phonology, morphology, and syntax. **Phonology** refers to the knowledge a person has of the consonant and vowel sounds in the language. Although the number of sounds that exist in a language is limited, a nearly endless number of words can be constructed from these sounds.

Morphology refers to the smallest meaningful unit of language. Morphology involves the stringing together of sounds (phonemes) and includes such structures as prefixes and suffixes. Morphemes are of two types: free morphemes and bound morphemes. A **free morpheme** is a stand-alone word. Examples of free morphemes are *play*, *safe*, and *elephant*. Each of these words contains only one morpheme because they cannot be divided into smaller units and still retain their meaning. Examples of **bound morphemes** include prefixes and suffixes, such as those attached to the words: *playing*, *unsafe*, and *elephants*. Each of these words contains two morphemes, and each morpheme within the word contributes uniquely to the word's overall meaning. However, the morphemes "ing," "un," and "s" have no stand-alone meaning. They contribute to word meaning once they are attached, or bound, to a free morpheme. **Syntax** refers to the rules used for combining words to make a sentence. As with the sounds of language, the rules for combining words to structure a sentence in a particular language are finite. For example, the rules of English require that a noun occurs before a verb in a sentence, such as *"He is running,"* as opposed to *"Running is he."*

The content of language includes the meanings of individual words and words in combination. Another name for language content is **semantics**. The words we use symbolize concepts. If there was no meaning to what was being said, there would be no point in using language. The meaning of words constrains how words may or may not be used together. For example, the sentence *"I saw the tree swimming in the lake"* makes little sense, although it is syntactically correct. Content involves knowledge of vocabulary and the relationships between words. Words can have denotative or connotative meaning. **Denotative** is the literal (dictionary) meaning of a word. **Connotative** involves use of words for a meaning other than their literal meaning. For example, the denotative meaning of the word *mother* is female parent. The connotative meaning of mother could evoke alternative meanings such as love and security. Other nonliteral aspects of language content can be found in **idioms**, such as, *"If the shoe fits, wear it"* or *"It's raining cats and dogs."*

The final component in the Bloom and Lahey model is language use. Another term for language use is **pragmatics**. The pragmatic functions of language involve the use of language in context for a particular purpose or reason. Pragmatics entails three major communication skills:

- *using* language for different purposes, such as greeting (e.g., hello, goodbye), informing (e.g., I'm going to get a cookie), demanding (e.g., Give me a cookie), and requesting (e.g., Could I please have a cookie?);
- *changing* language according to the needs of a listener or situation, such as talking differently to a baby than to an adult, or speaking differently in a classroom than on a playground; and
- *following* rules for conversations, such as taking turns in a conversation, introducing topics of conversation, staying on topic, the physical proximity to/from a speaker, and the use of facial expressions and eye contact.

Collectively, the skills of language form, content, and use compose our language competence.

FYI

For years, scientists have argued that language is what sets humans apart from all nonhuman species. Although other animals can communicate, it seems that only humans are capable of using symbols (i.e., words) that have meaning. However, some researchers have suggested that apes are capable of learning sign language, which provides evidence of their ability to use symbols that have meaning. The most famous of these apes was a gorilla called Koko who learned more than 200 signs.

LANGUAGE DEVELOPMENT

Knowledge of the normal, developmental features of language is important for determining the existence of a language disorder. The area of expressive language development, particularly the form of language, has been studied extensively over the past 60 years. Some of the most well-established features of normal language are described next as they occur across the period of infancy to school-age development.

Infant/Toddler Language Development

The term **infant** has its origins in Latin and means *"without speech."* So, when referring to the period of infant development, we are considering a period during which the child has yet to utter a single word. That is not to say children remain silent during infancy. The wide array of sounds made by the infant is well-documented, and these sounds are thought to contribute to the child's eventual abilities to learn language. Thus, it seems that development of language begins before a child says her first word. Indeed, some may argue that language begins in the mother's womb.

FYI

It is often reported that a child's first words are either *mom* or *dad*. The reason for this is twofold. First, these are important people in a young child's daily life. Second, the /m/ and /d/ sounds are the earliest and easiest consonant sounds for young children to articulate, which helps pave the way for saying these two words.

Before children begin talking, they communicate using a combination of vocal and gestural behaviors known as **prelinguistic** communication. One form of prelinguistic communication is that which occurs between mother and child. We know that as early as 3 months of age, infants take part in a conversational turn-taking with their mothers, called **gaze coupling**. Gaze coupling occurs when an infant turns toward the speaker and gains eye contact; this act establishes a bond between mother and infant. The infant also produces a rich array of **vocalizations**. The production of vocalizations is not unique to human infants. To vocalize simply means to produce voice, and many nonhuman species also vocalize (e.g., birds, cats, chimpanzees). Among human infants, a distinct developmental pattern of vocalizations has been charted covering the first 12 months of life. The stages of vocal development are illustrated in Figure 3–2. A similar pattern of vocal development is found in infants throughout the world. This has led experts to theorize that these vocal behaviors represent necessary milestones that need to be achieved to acquire language.

The earliest vocalization produced by infants is **crying**. A baby's crying at birth is used as an indicator of health status. Within the first 2 months following birth, the infant learns to produce cries for varying reasons such as when hungry, fussy, or experiencing discomfort. The melodic pattern of these differentiated cries is believed to be an important vocal skill for the eventual production of words (Wermke & Mende, 2011). Between 2 and 4 months of age, the infant begins to use vowel-like sounds and consonant-like sounds similar to /k/ and /g/. These sounds are referred to as **cooing** (or gooing) and are produced when the infant is in a pleasurable comfort state. Around 5 months of age and continuing to 11 months of age, infants produce a wide range of **babbling** sounds. These babbles consist of strings of syllable combinations that are either reduplicated (e.g., *baba-ba-ba*) or non-reduplicated (*ma-ba-da-ba*) and that also have strong intonation patterns. Babbling represents a rich form of vocal behavior that represents improvements in the young child's maturation and coordination of the speech musculature. The infant is truly on the cusp of talking during the babbling period.

> *FYI*
>
> Professor Ray Kent (1984) theorized that the reason children produce repetitive strings of babbling is part of a larger human developmental process. During the first year of life, children demonstrate a number of rhythmic motoric behaviors such as leg, arm, and finger movements. These rhythmic behaviors are thought to reflect a necessary activity in the development of motor control (skilled performance). Thus, babbling is just one of many rhythmic behaviors related to the development of physical coordination.

By the time an infant reaches her first birthday, she is referred to as a toddler. The period of toddlerhood covers the approximate ages of 1 to 2 years of life and reflects a period of rapid development in motor, cognitive, and linguistic abilities. During this time, the toddler is now standing upright and learning to walk. This is a period of discovery for the child and corresponds with the uttering of **single words**. These single-word productions mark the moment when the child is no longer just producing vocalizations but rather **verbalizations** (i.e., language based). These verbalizations represent a distinct **sound-to-symbol relationship**. One of the earliest types of sound-to-symbol relationship is found in the production of **onomatopoeia**, whereby the toddler makes a sound to suggest a thing or action (cow says "moo," car goes "beep"). Children's

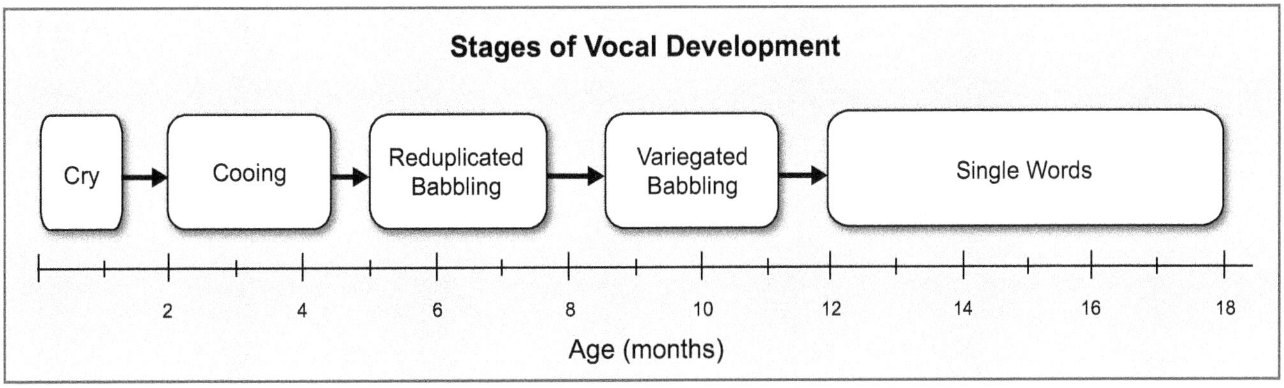

FIGURE 3–2. The stages of early vocal development from the period of birth to 18 months of age.

early vocabularies tend to include the names of important people in their environments and referents that they can interact with, manipulate, or change. For example, children are more likely to say something like *ball* rather than *tree* because a ball has movement, and the child can manipulate the object. A child's understanding (comprehension) of vocabulary normally is more advanced than the child's expressive vocabulary. Research has shown that children comprehend their first 50 words at about 13 months of age, but they cannot produce 50 different words until they reach 20 months of age. Another language behavior that begins to surface by 18 to 24 months is **fast mapping**. Fast mapping refers to the process by which children connect a word to an underlying concept after minimal physical exposure (i.e., seeing the object and quickly linking a word to the object). By the time a child reaches the age of 2 years, the production of **two-word combinations** should be apparent (e.g., *"more juice"* or *"daddy go"*). Two-word combinations occur once a child achieves a single-word vocabulary in excess of 50 different words. Many of these early two-word combinations are simply a combination of two single words that are in the child's existing vocabulary. Examples of the first 50 words produced by children are shown in Table 3–1.

Table 3–1. Example of First 50 Single Words Produced by Three American Children

Daniel: Age = 12–16 months		*Will: Age = 11–16 months*		*Sarah: Age = 12–19 months*	
1 light	26 nose	1 baby	26 apple	1 uh-oh	26 ticktock
2 uh-oh	27 fire	2 mommy	27 nose	2 alldone	27 ball
3 wha that	28 hot	3 doggie	28 bird	3 light	28 go
4 wow	29 yoghourt	4 juice	29 alldone	4 down	29 bump
5 banana	30 pee-pee	5 bye-bye	30 orange	5 shoes	30 pop-pop = fire
6 kitty	31 juice	6 daddy	31 bottle	6 baby	31 out
7 baby	32 ball	7 milk	32 coat	7 don't throw	32 hee-haw
8 moo	33 wack-wack	8 cracker	33 hot	8 moo	33 eat
9 quack	34 frog	9 done	34 bib	9 bite	34 neigh
10 cookie	35 hello	10 ball	35 hat	10 three	35 meow
11 nice	36 yuk	11 shoe	36 more	11 hi	36 sit
12 rock	37 aoole	12 teddy	37 ear	12 cheese	37 woof-woof
13 clock	38 Big Bird	13 book	38 nite-nite	13 up	38 bah
14 sock	39 walk	14 kitty	39 paper	14 quack-quack	39 hoo-hoo = owl
15 woof-woof	40 Ernie	15 hi	40 toast	15 oink-oink	40 bee
16 daddy	41 horse	16 Alex	41 O'Toole	16 coat	41 tree
17 bubble	42 more	17 no (no)	42 bath	17 beep-beep	42 mi-mi = ferry
18 hi	43 mommy	18 door	43 down	18 keys	43 ss = snake
19 shoe	44 bunny	19 dolly	44 duck	19 cycle	44 ooh-ooh = monkey
20 up	45 my	20 wha tha	45 leaf	20 mama	45 yack-yack = talk
21 bye-bye	46 nut	21 cheese	46 cookie	21 daddy	46 hohoho = Santa
22 bottle	47 orange	22 oh wow	47 lake	22 siren sound	47 bye bye
23 no	48 block	23 oh	48 car	23 grr	48 doll
24 rocky	49 nite-nite	24 button	49 rock	24 more	49 kite
25 eye	50 milk	25 eye	50 box	25 off	50 Muriel

Source: From "Patterns of Early Lexical and Phonological Development," by C. Stoel-Gammon and J. Cooper, 1984, *Journal of Child Language*, *11*, pp. 247–271. Reprinted by permission of Cambridge University Press.

Preschool Language Development

A great deal is known about the language development that occurs during the age period of 2 to 5 years. A child's development of morphology and semantics is well-charted. During this time frame, the length of the child's expressive utterances begins to increase by leaps and bounds. This increase is accompanied by the acquisition and use of grammatical morphemes (see later discussion). By 3 years of age, a child is producing short phrases of three or more words. As children gain mastery over language skills, they also become more sophisticated in their conversational abilities. Between the ages of 4 and 5 years, they can follow complex directions and enthusiastically talk about things they do. They can make up stories, listen attentively to stories, and retell stories. At this age, children usually can understand that letters and numbers are symbols of real things and ideas. By the age of 5 years, a child's expressive vocabulary is between 1,000 and 2,000 words, and a child can understand twice as many words spoken. They know the gender and names of family members. They often play with words and make up silly words and stories. Toward the end of the preschool period, a child should have clear speech pronunciation, although there may be some mild speech misarticulations. A summary of the language milestones covering the first 6 years of life is provided in Table 3–2.

Table 3–2. Normal Language Development Across the First 6 Years of Life

Age	*Language Level*
Birth	Cries
2–3 months	Cries differently in different circumstances; cooing/gooing
3–4 months	Babbles randomly
5–6 months	Babbles rhythmically
6–11 months	Babbles in imitation of real speech, with expression
12 months	Produces jargon-like utterances and a small number of single words; recognizes name; imitates familiar sounds
18 months	Single-word vocabulary of 5 to 20 words, understands simple instructions
2 years	Expressive utterances of two words; vocabulary is growing; waves goodbye; makes "sounds" of familiar animals; make wants known; understands "no"
2–3 years	Identifies body parts; combines nouns and verbs; has a 450-word vocabulary; uses short sentences; matches three to four colors, likes to hear the same story repeated; forms some plurals
3–4 years	Can tell a story; expressive utterances of four to five words in length; vocabulary of about 1,000 words; knows last name, name of street, several nursery rhymes
4–5 years	Expressive utterances of four to five words in length; uses past tense; vocabulary of about 1,500 words; identifies colors, shapes; asks many questions like "why?" and "who?"
5–6 years	Utterances of five to six words in length; vocabulary more than 2,000 words; knows spatial relations (like "on top" and "far"); knows address; understands same–different; identifies simple currency, knows right and left hand; uses all types of sentences

FYI

A popular myth is that twin children, when learning to talk, develop their own form of communication known only to them. This has been termed **idioglossia**. However, the phenomenon is actually a case of one twin copying the immature or disordered speech pattern of their co-twin in their attempts to use language.

FYI

Children with low levels of education and who also exhibit behavioral problems are known to be at risk for communication difficulties. These same features also place an individual at risk for criminal activity. Perhaps it is not surprising to find an unusually high number of inmates in the prison population who have some form of speech, language, or hearing disorder.

School-Age Language Development

As children progress through the elementary school years, their language skills continue to develop. Growth in all aspects of language occurs with obvious changes seen in the areas of semantics (vocabulary) and pragmatics (language use). It is estimated that a 6-year-old child has a vocabulary of anywhere from 8,000 to 14,000 words. Beginning with the production of single words at 12 months of age, this means the child must (on average) acquire four to eight new words every day. By school age, a child should be able to speak in complete sentences with minor grammatical errors. The school-age period also marks the development of **metalinguistic awareness**. Metalinguistic awareness is the ability to reflect consciously on the nature and properties of language. Understanding that words and sentences can have more than one meaning is a form of metalinguistic awareness. Children begin to appreciate language in terms of humor, puns, poetry, and use in different situations. The knock-knock joke told by a 6-year-old captures metalinguistic awareness in the form of word play:

Knock knock. Who's there? Cargo.

Cargo who?

Cargo BEEP BEEP!

Written Language Development

Most of what is currently known about child language development is based on examining comprehension and production of spoken (oral) language. Less attention has been given to the relationship between oral language competency and **written language**. Yet a child's written language skills begin to surface as early as 2 years of age, and these abilities provide insight into a child's overall knowledge of language (Table 3–3). Children acquire an understanding of the relationship between oral language and written language before they enter elementary school. Learning to write involves the ability to translate the sounds of a word to discrete letters (i.e., spelling). So, a child's mastery in writing represents an achievement in generalizing language across modalities of communication (Taslim et al., 2019). As covered in Chapter 15, the analysis of a written language sample among individuals with deafness is thought to provide an indication of a person's oral language abilities as well.

HISTORIC ASPECTS OF CHILD LANGUAGE DISORDERS

To speak about language is to speak about the development of the human race (Butler, 1986). There is evidence to suggest that language originated during the Ice Age, approximately 30,000 years ago. When language was created, it is likely that language disorders were soon to follow, frequently because of a physical accident or intellectual disability. One of the earliest detailed reports of a language disorder was by the French physician **Jean-Marc Gaspard Itard** (1774–1838; Figure 3–3). The report was based on the case of the **wild boy of Aveyron**. Discovered in 1799, the boy (named Victor) had been lost or abandoned

Table 3–3. Stages of Written Language Development

Stage	*Age*	*Ability*
I. Random scribbling	2 to 3 years	Children make marks on paper randomly with little muscular control.
II. Controlled scribbling	3 years	Children "write" across the paper in linear fashion, repeating patterns over and over showing increased muscular control.
III. Letter-like forms	3 to 4 years	Children make mock letters. These are written lines of letters that have letter characteristics but are misshapen and written randomly. They like to pretend they are writing and are able to separate writing from drawing. They have purpose to their letter-like forms.
IV. Letter/symbol relationship	4 years	Children write letters to create words. They can write their name. They know the word that represents their name. They can copy words. Letter reversals are frequent.
V. Invented spelling	4 to 5 years	Children make the transition from letter forms to invented spelling. They use a group of letters to form a word. Many of the letters will be consonants. They understand that letters relate to sounds. Some punctuation appears. They can copy words from their environment.
VI. Standard spelling	5 to 7 years	Most of the words the children use are written correctly. They organize their words in lines with spaces between the words; they move from left to right, and from the top of the page to the bottom.

FIGURE 3–3. Jean-Marc Gaspard Itard provided one of the earliest detailed reports of a language disorder based on the wild boy of Aveyron.

in childhood, apparently surviving on his own in the wild up to the age of approximately 11 years. The boy spoke no language, and Itard undertook to educate Victor. Itard believed that two things separated humans from animals: empathy and language. He wanted to be the first person to fully civilize a wild child and attempted to teach Victor to speak and show human emotion. Although initially successful in understanding language and reading simple words, Victor 's abilities eventually plateaued to the point where Itard abandoned the experiment. The only words that Victor ever actually learned to speak were *lait* (milk) and *oh Dieu* (oh God). Victor died at the age of 40 years. This early study supported the theory that an enriching environment is vital to the acquisition of normal language.

In the early 1960s, **Roger Brown** (1925–1997) from Harvard University performed some pioneering research in the area of normal language development in a longitudinal study of three children: Adam, Eve, and Sarah (Brown, 1973). Brown recorded the conversations of these children with their parents at home every 2 weeks for the first 5 years of life as a way of estimating the type and amount of language produced by each child. Brown calculated a measure called **mean length of utterance** (MLU). A child's MLU is calculated by taking 100 utterances produced by a child (excluding all cases where the utterance is a repetition of a statement made by an adult) and then working out the average length in morphemes. The number of morphemes in an utterance often is the same as the number of words because in children's early multiword speech, their words usually consist only of a single unbound morpheme. For example, the utterance *"Daddy go"* consists of two morphemes. However, as a child's speech becomes more complex, the child begins to modify words by the addition of bound morphemes, such as plural "s" or present progressive "ing," resulting in utterances such as *"Daddy going"* (three morphemes).

A great deal of what is currently known about the development of expressive language during the preschool period is based on the classic research of Brown. He was able to show that MLU reflected a child's increasing ability to combine words and produce complex utterances. He identified five sequential stages in language development that were organized according to the child's MLU. There was an orderly development in 14 grammatical morphemes across the first 5 years of life that corresponded to the child's MLU (Table 3–4). The order of acquisition was similar for the three children. Brown suggested that the order in which all children acquire various grammatical morphemes is identical, with the progression from simple morphemes to more complex ones. However, more recent studies have shown that by the end of the preschool period, most children have acquired a full range of grammatical morphemes in their expressive language, although the precise order in which they are acquired may not be identical.

TYPES OF CHILD LANGUAGE DISORDERS

Language disorders in children are characterized by deficiencies in the production and/or comprehension of spoken and written language (Figure 3–4). Deficiencies in language can have a profound impact on a child's academic, social, and emotional development. Roughly 7% of preschool and school-age children exhibit significant limitations in language ability. Some language disorders in children can result from physical factors, such as intellectual impairment, hearing loss, and head injury. Often, child language disorders are functional in nature, where a specific etiology for the disorder cannot be determined. Later chapters in this book address language disorders resulting from specific conditions such as genetic abnormalities (Chapter 13) and hearing impairment (Chapter 15). Some common conditions indicative of child language impairment follow.

Specific Language Impairment

Specific language impairment (SLI) is characterized by difficulty with language that is not caused by known neurological, sensory, intellectual, or emotional deficit. SLI can affect the development of vocabulary, grammar, and conversation (discourse) skills. Children with SLI may be intelligent and healthy in all regards, except for an isolated difficulty with language. They may in fact be extraordinarily bright. Children with SLI usually learn to talk late. It is not unusual to first encounter a child with SLI who has limited vocabulary and short utterances at the age of 3 or 4 years. A child with SLI may do things such as omit the plural "s" at the end of words or omit various verbs. An example would be to say, *"He drive the car"* rather than *"He drives the car."* As children with SLI mature and the problem goes undetected, they may be described by teachers as being smart but unmotivated. SLI affects approximately 8% of 5-year-old children. Although SLI is not a reading disability, 50% to 75% of children with SLI also experience problems in learning to read. If gone untreated, the impact of SLI can continue into adulthood. Studies of young adults with SLI in their 30s have shown that these individuals tend to have fewer educational qualifications and may have difficulty finding stable employment.

Intellectual Impairment

The acquisition of language is a remarkable human achievement. Within a few short years, children make the transition from cooing and babbling to becoming fully communicative individuals. Generally, children acquire the essential components of language by the age of 3 or 4 years.

Table 3–4. Brown's (1973) Stages of Grammatical Morpheme Development and the Approximate Age at Which Each Stage Should Be Attained

Stage	*MLU*	*MLU Range*	*Age in Months*	*14 Grammatical Morphemes*	*Examples*
I	1.75	1.5–2.0	15–30	Combine basic words	more juice daddy go
II	2.25	2.0–2.5	28–36	(1) Present progressive	daddy go*ing* fall*ing* down
				(2) Preposition "in"	*in* house
				(3) Preposition "on"	*on* top
				(4) -s plurals (regular)	my toy*s*
III	2.75	2.5–3.0	36–40	(5) Irregular past tense	I *fell* down She *sat* on
				(6) 's possessives	Mommy*'s* house
				(7) Uncontractible copula	*Are* they here?
IV	3.5	3.0–3.7	40–46	(8) Articles	*a* ball *the* cat
				(9) Regular past tense "ed"	He walk*ed* She danc*ed*
				(10) Third-person regular present tense	He push*es* She *walks*
V	4.0	3.7–4.5	46–52+	(11) Third-person irregular	Kathy *has* He *does*
				(12) Uncontractible auxiliary	*Is* he going? What *are* you doing?
				(13) Contractible copula	*Matt's* tall *I'm* short
				(14) Contractible auxiliary	*They're* walking *He's* running

Note. MLU = mean length of utterance.

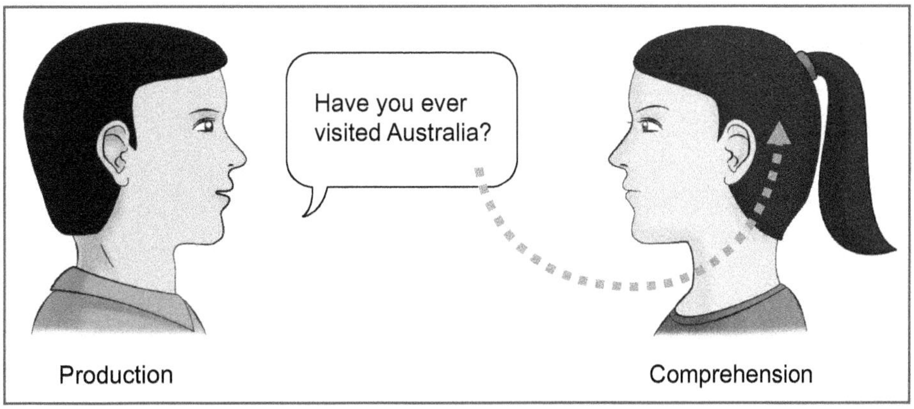

FIGURE 3–4. Conceptualization of the processes of language production and comprehension.

However, this may not be true for children with an intellectual disability. Intellectual impairment is characterized by significantly subaverage intellectual functioning, which is determined based on a mathematical ratio known as an **intelligence quotient** (IQ). A standard way of determining IQ is to note the discrepancy between an individual's true chronological age (CA) and mental age (MA), as derived from a test of intelligence. The formula for calculating IQ is *100 × MA/CA*. So, two possible IQ examples would be:

- MA = 6 years /CA = 5 years (IQ = 120, which means gifted)
- MA = 6 years /CA = 9 years (IQ = 66, which means impaired)

In the late 1800s, intellectual disability was classified using descriptive terms such as idiot (IQ = 0–19), imbecile (IQ = 20–24), moron (IQ = 25–49), simpleton (IQ = 50–69), and dullard (IQ = 70–99). Over time, these terms began to be abused by the rest of society. The terms are now obsolete, and intellectual impairment is currently defined by an IQ of approximately 70 or below. Four degrees of impairment severity can be specified: mild (IQ = 50–70), moderate (IQ = 35–49), severe (IQ = 20–34), and profound (IQ = 0–19). The prevalence of intellectual impairment in the noninstitutionalized population of the United States is 7.8 people per 1,000. If institutionalized individuals are included in the prevalence rates, the number increases to 8.7 per 1,000.

Intellectual impairment is associated with limitations in learning and can have a profound effect on a child's ability to talk. At one time, it was believed that the language acquisition of all persons with an intellectual impairment represented a slow-motion version of normal language development. That is, children with an intellectual impairment demonstrated normal language behavior; however, it was behavior expected in younger, nonimpaired children. An example of this view would be to suggest that a 10-year-old child with an intellectual impairment has the language abilities of a 5-year-old. We now know there is no consistent pattern of language behavior shown in children with an intellectual impairment due to differences in the type and severity of impairment. The overall picture of early language development in children with intellectual impairment is one of differences and similarities in comparison to nonimpaired children. Impaired children appear to follow the same set of universal principles in the acquisition of word meaning, although this is not always the case for profoundly impaired children. Intellectually impaired children are found to acquire syntactic and morphological knowledge in the same order as normally developing children. Children with intellectual impairments also can acquire basic pragmatic skills; yet more subtle aspects of conversational competence are less commonly displayed. Intellectual impairments are associated with some of the genetic-based communication disorders covered in Chapter 13.

Late Talkers

The term *late talker* is used to describe a group of children who have an impoverished expressive vocabulary, usually within the age range of 18 to 30 months of life. These children are late bloomers and are slow to acquire their first 50 words. They also take longer to begin uttering two-word combinations. By 24 months of life, most children have an expressive vocabulary of approximately 200 words, whereas late talkers may have a vocabulary of approximately 20 words. These children are developing typically in the areas of language comprehension, play, motor, and cognitive/learning skills, with the sole exception being language expression. Children who are late talkers are thought to be at risk for subsequent language problems. The challenge presented to the speech-language pathologist is determining which of these children will simply outgrow the delay and which will not. As a rule, it is advisable for these children to be involved in language enrichment activities. Research has indicated that children who are diagnosed early show more positive outcomes in their language development.

CURRENT THEORIES REGARDING CHILD LANGUAGE DEVELOPMENT AND DISORDERS

Theories regarding the cause of a child language disorder usually attribute the disorder to biological (nature) or environmental (nurture) factors. For example, a biological cause would be seen in a child born with a profound hearing loss that interfered with his ability to hear and subsequently learn language. Alternatively, an environmental cause would be seen in a child deprived of human contact (e.g., wild boy of Aveyron), thus preventing the child from experiencing the language of others. Both situations would influence a child's subsequent language development. However, it is equally possible for the combined effects of nature and nurture to contribute to a language disorder. One possible scenario would be a situation where a child born with an intellectual disability (a biological condition) receives inadequate language stimulation in the home environment. Of course, a wide range of situations can contribute to a language disorder. Four major theories concerning normal language acquisition are presented. These are the (a) behaviorist, (b) nativist, (c) interactionist, and (d) statistical learning theories. Regardless of the theory one may ascribe to, a disruption in the normal process of language acquisition more than likely will lead to a language disorder.

The **behaviorist theory** is perhaps the oldest theory about language development. This theory assumes that children learn language the same way they learn everything else, namely through imitation and reinforcement. The Swiss psychologist **Jean Piaget** (1896–1980) and American psychologist **Burrhus Frederic (B. F.) Skinner** (1904–1990) were strong proponents of a behavioral influence on language acquisition. The child's path to learning language involves a trial-and-error process. In other words, the child tries and fails to use correct language until the child succeeds. The child's success with language is based on reinforcement and shaping provided by the parent's gestures (smiles, attention, and approval), which are pleasant to the child. Parents who ignore unfamiliar sounds produced by the young child and show increased attention to the child's production of word-like utterances further shape the child's language learning. Although research has shown that children who imitate the actions of those around them during their first year of life generally are those who also learn to talk more quickly, there is also evidence that imitation alone cannot explain how children acquire language.

The **nativist theory** of language stresses the contribution of the child's biological makeup to language acquisition. This theory was advocated in the early 1960s by the American linguist **Noam Chomsky** (b. 1928; Figure 3–5). He suggested that humans are born with a special biological brain mechanism, called a **language acquisition device**. This theory supposes that the ability to learn language is inborn, that nature is more important than nurture, and that experience using language is necessary only to activate the language acquisition device.

Chomsky claimed that it would be little short of a miracle if children were to learn their language strictly through the imitation of others. This is because children are exposed to very little correctly formed language. When people speak, they constantly interrupt themselves, change their minds, and make slips of the tongue. Yet children manage to learn their language despite all of these inconsistencies. Children do not simply copy the language that they hear around them. They deduce rules from it, which they can then use to produce sentences that they have never heard before. This also accounts for the common observation of young children inventing novel words such as "*throwed*." Because it is highly unlikely such a word was previously modeled to the child, it is doubtful this reflects imitation by the child.

FIGURE 3–5. Noam Chomsky, American linguist.

An alternative to the behavioral and nativist theories of language acquisition is the **interactionist theory**. The interactionist theory recognizes that both behavioral and nativist processes are important for a child to acquire language. According to this theory, language learning is influenced by the desire of children to communicate with others in their environment, namely parents and caregivers. The role of the social environment is of major importance in learning a language. **Eve Clark** (b. 1942; Figure 3–6) is a British pioneer in the field of first language acquisition who has examined how children learn to acquire their vocabulary, particularly in the context of social interaction with adults. She has shown that these social interactions lead to an uptake of new words in the child's lexicon.

Some researchers believe that language acquisition is based primarily on general learning mechanisms, namely statistical learning (Kujala et al., 2023). Imagine that as an infant you are placed in an environment where you overhear an immense language system that contains thousands of unusual sounds. As an infant, you must discover the underlying structure of this system that consists of the individual sounds of language, and the larger pieces that are the words, which in turn combine to form sentences. Somehow you must rapidly figure out the structure of this system so that you can use it appropriately early in your childhood. The use of statistical cues may help young children discover some of the consistent patterns found in the language they overhear. This theory proposes that infants and toddlers are highly sensitive to the structure of their environment and learn statistical probabilities in spoken language, such as natural breaks between syllables, words, and sentences. The **statistical learning theory** of language asserts that, with repeated exposure to many language examples, the statistical structure of the language is deciphered, which streamlines the process of language acquisition.

FIGURE 3–6. Eve Clark has done extensive research on how children acquire language. (Permission granted by E. Clark.)

ASSESSMENT OF CHILD LANGUAGE DISORDERS

The classic diagram developed by Bloom and Lahey shows the relationship between the three components of language: form, content, and use (Figure 3–7). Communicative competence is achieved when a child can manage all these components effectively. In the event of a language disorder, the speech-language pathologist identifies whether the problem is one of form, content, or use—or some combination of these components. Once the problem is isolated, an intervention plan can be developed to target the specific domain of language that is hindering communicative competence. When a child has a suspected language disorder, the child is usually brought to the speech-language clinic for an assessment by a speech-language pathologist. The assessment is a process of observation and measurement of the child's language behaviors to determine: (a) whether a language disorder exists and (b) the nature and severity of the disorder.

Does A Language Disorder Exist?

To answer this question, the speech-language pathologist must examine and assess the child's comprehension and production of the various lan-

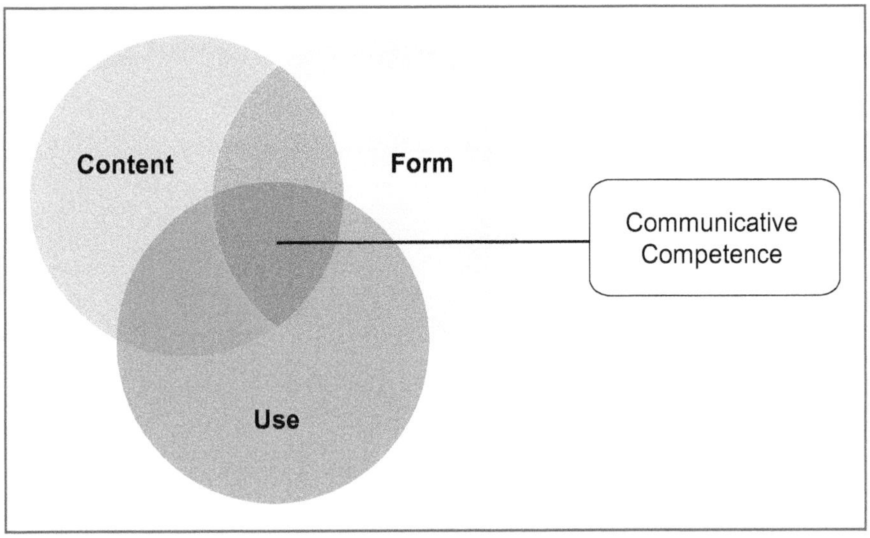

FIGURE 3–7. A Venn diagram showing the three components of language and their contribution to communicative competence.

guage components. Some features of a language assessment include (a) a **case history**, (b) **standardized testing**, and (c) **language sampling** or **nonstandardized testing**. Each of these features is briefly defined.

Case History

The collection of a case history is vital to any assessment of communication disorders. The collection of this information typically is done via a questionnaire-type format (Table 3–5) and can be completed by the parents prior to their visit to the clinic or as part of an interview with the parents at the beginning of the assessment session. The speech-language pathologist uses the case history gathering as an opportunity to become acquainted with the parents and ascertain their understanding of their child's problem and their concerns for the child. As part of the case history, the speech-language pathologist collects information about the child's general development as well as communication behavior as reported by the parents. The speech-language pathologist also learns about the possible coexistence of complicating conditions such as ear infections. One cannot overemphasize the role of parents in the assessment process. The collection of information during the case history can be crucial in situations where the child may be quite young and/or severely disabled, where more emphasis is placed on the parent interview process rather than on the child assessment process.

Standardized Testing

The use of standardized testing is a central feature of assessing a child's language abilities. There are many standardized measures of language ability. Some provide a comprehensive view of all language functioning; others measure specific features of language. Standardized tests are those that are sold by publishing companies. When using a standardized test, children are assessed in precisely the same fashion, with specific instructions provided by the tester. Every standardized test has a consistent, uniform way in which a child's language behavior is elicited and evaluated. Many standardized tests have **norms** that provide a way for the speech-language pathologist to compare the child being tested with normally developing children of the same age and socioeconomic status. Standardized tests are the basis for many decisions in our culture. They are used for determining school placement, university entrance, and intelligence level. The score a child receives on a standardized test predicts a certain level of performance. A variety of standardized tests are available to evaluate a wide range of language abilities. Two popular tests

Table 3–5. Abbreviated Example of a Case History Questionnaire

Identifying Information	
Child's Name: ______________________________	Sex: F M
Date of Birth: ______________________________	Age: ______
Statement of Problem	
Describe your child's communication problem: ______________________________	
When did you first notice the problem? ______________________________	
Has your child's communication problem changed since then? ______________________________	
Is your child aware of their communication problem? ______________________________	
Is there a history of communication problems in your family? ______________________________	
Communication Development	
At what age did your child begin to babble? ______________________________	
At what age did your child produce single words? ______________________________	
At what age did your child say two-word sentences? ______________________________	
Developmental History	
Was the pregnancy normal? ______________________________	
When did your child sit upright? ______________________________	
When did you child begin to walk? ______________	run? ______________
Medical History	
Has your child had any illnesses or accidents? ______________________________	
Has your child experienced any ear infections? __________	Frequency? __________

are the Peabody Picture Vocabulary Test (Dunn, 2018), which is designed to estimate vocabulary comprehension abilities, and the Clinical Evaluation of Language Fundamentals (Wiig et al., 2013), which involves myriad language comprehension and expression abilities (Table 3–6). Tests such as these examine a child's language abilities based on picture-pointing tasks. The tester presents the child with a specific language model, and the child is required to match a specific picture to the language model. Figures 3–8 and 3–9 provide examples of picture stimuli that might be used in standardized testing.

Language Sampling

It is important to recognize that standardized tests generally are not sensitive to the subtleties of natural, spontaneous communication. Therefore, in addition to standardized tests, a language assessment should include a collection of a naturalistic sample of the child's language. The key to language sampling is to obtain a representative sample of the child's typical expressive language behavior. Language sampling is a form of nonstandardized (or informal) testing because there is no consistent or standardized way the sample

Table 3–6. Various Subtests Comprising the Clinical Evaluation of Language Functions Standardized Test

Subtest/Scale	*Description*
Concepts and Following Directions	Measures auditory comprehension and recall of utterances of increasing length and complexity
Word Structure	Assesses morphology and pronoun use
Recalling Sentences	A sentence imitation task
Formulated Sentences	Child is given a word or words and must generate spoken sentences in reference to a picture cue
Word Classes (Receptive and Expressive)	These subtests measure the student's comprehension of relationships between words
Word Definitions	A measure of word meanings
Sentence Structure	A measure of auditory comprehension
Sentence Assembly	A measure of verbal expression
Semantic Relationships	Assesses comprehension of complex language relationships
Expressive Vocabulary	Vocabulary
Understanding Spoken Paragraphs	A measure of auditory comprehension, memory, and logic
Number Repetition—Forward	A measure of attention and memory
Number Repetition—Backward	A measure of attention and memory
Familiar Sequences (1 and 2)	Assess retrieval of well-learned information
Rapid Automatic Naming	Assesses naming speed
Word Associations	Assesses semantic knowledge
Phonological Awareness	Assesses phonological knowledge
Pragmatics Profile	Assesses comprehension of social rules
Observational Rating Scale	Assesses the impact of language functioning across situations

Source: From *Clinical Evaluation of Language Fundamentals* (5th ed.), by E. Wiig, E. Semel, and W. Secord, 2013, Pearson Education.

is collected. Language samples can be obtained through checklists or observational recording systems, or through casually conversing with the child. Language sampling is a four-step process. The first step involves eliciting and recording the language sample. Eliciting good language samples takes time, training, and practice. The sample is obtained by encouraging the child to speak while playing with toys, describing pictures, and answering open-ended questions (e.g., "How does that toy work?"). The sample is audio- and/or video-recorded for later analysis. The remaining three steps are completed using the recorded language sample. The second step is transcribing the language sample. The child's utterances are transcribed verbatim. This is also referred to as **orthographic transcription**. The third step in this process entails analyzing the language sample in a number of ways, including calculating the child's size of vocabulary and MLU, and noting the use of various syntactic structures and sentence types. The fourth step in the language sampling process requires interpretation of the analyses. The child's language abilities noted in the sample

FIGURE 3–8. Example of test pictures used for standardized testing of vocabulary comprehension. The clinician would prompt the child by stating, "Point to giraffe."

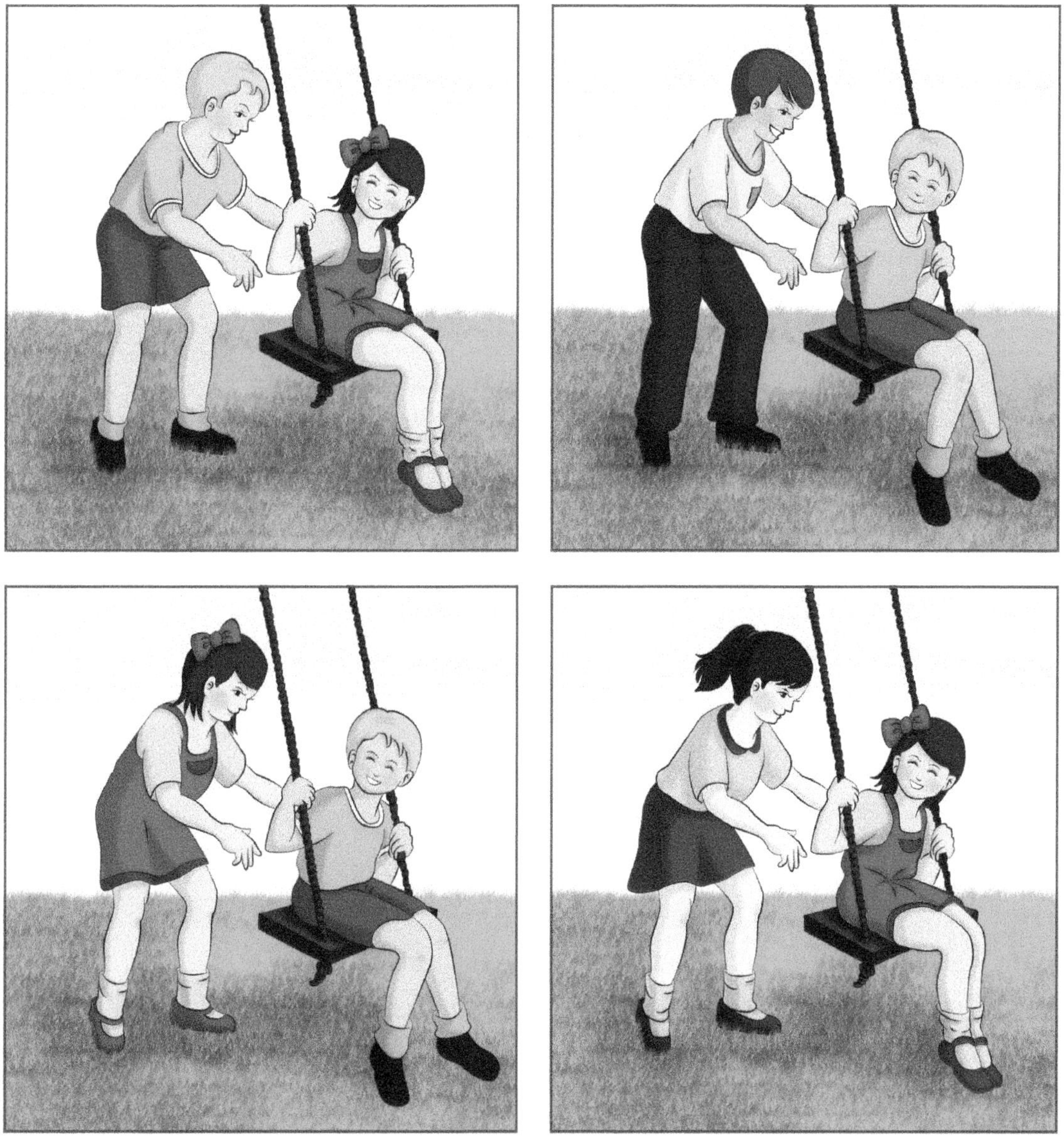

FIGURE 3–9. Example of test pictures used for standardized testing of language comprehension of sentences. The clinician would prompt the child by stating, "Point to 'The girl pushes the boy.'"

can be compared with reference databases of typical children to provide an indication of the child's expressive language and whether the child may exhibit a language disorder. Computer software known as **SALT (systematic analysis of language transcripts)** is in regular use for transcribing and analyzing language samples, as well as for comparing them with reference databases of typical children. The SALT program was developed by Dr. Jon Miller and Dr. Robin Chapman at the University of Wisconsin–Madison. An example of MLU calculation is shown in Table 3–7.

What Is the Nature and Severity of the Disorder?

Based on the information collected from the child and parents, the speech-language pathologist makes a number of decisions regarding the child's language abilities. The most immediate decision is a determination of whether the child exhibits a language disorder. The disorder could be in any area of language form, content, or use. If the child's language abilities are not equivalent to those found for same-aged normally developing peers, then the initial diagnosis of a language disorder is made. If a disorder is present, the speech-language pathologist next determines the nature of the disorder, whether the impairment is indicative of a **language delay** or **language deviance** (Figure 3–10). A language delay means that the child's language system is similar to younger, non-disordered children. The various components of the child's language system are not unusual. Rather, the child's language is trailing behind in development compared with the child's peers. Some children with a language delay may catch up without the need for treatment, such as the case with late talkers. A child demonstrating a language deviance is exhibiting a linguistic system that is unlike that of younger non-disordered children. A language deviance often is found in situations where a child may exhibit a variety of physical and or cognitive impairments. Children exhibiting a language deviance are less common than those showing a language delay. The speech-language pathologist also makes a decision concerning the severity of the language disorder; that decision is based on a determination of the extent to which the child's language abilities are impaired. Generally, a language deviance is considered more severe than a language delay. However, a language delay also can be severe if several language abilities are impaired, such as vocabulary size, utterance length, and language syntax.

Table 3–7. Example of Mean Length of Utterance Calculation

Utterance Transcription	*Number of Grammatical Morphemes*
I see daddy.	3
More juice.	2
What man doing.	4
Mommy driving.	3
Ball in cup.	3
Baby pulled the wagon.	5
The girl likes eating.	6
He's falling down.	5
The bus is yellow.	4
Where mommy go?	3
Number of utterances = 10	
Number of grammatical morphemes = 38	
MLU = 38/10 utterances = 3.8	

Note: A typical mean length of utterance (MLU) calculation is based on a sample of 100 utterances.

TREATMENT OF CHILD LANGUAGE DISORDERS

Prior to treatment of child language disorders, the speech-pathologist determines the goals and best course of action to assist the child. There is no standard agreed-upon approach to treating child language disorders. Some approaches work better for some children than others. The approach and success of an approach are dependent on factors such as the child's age, attention span, and

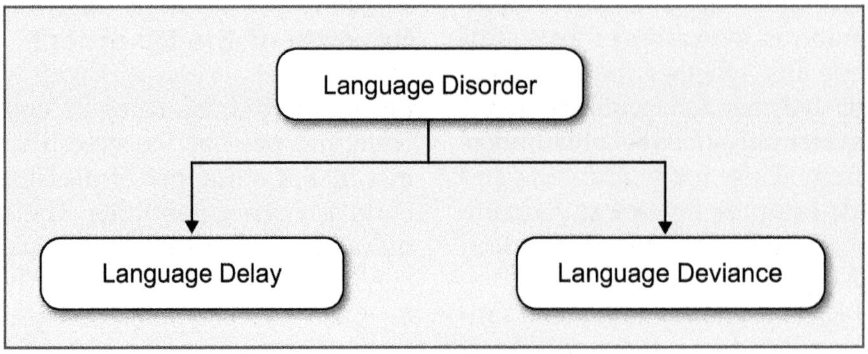

FIGURE 3–10. Classification of language disorders.

type and cause of language disorder. The set of goals and treatment strategies are unique to the child and their particular difficulties with language. An overarching theme in the treatment of child language disorders is to help the child improve communication. Parents and teachers can contribute a great deal to the child's success in therapy. The child may spend only a few short hours each week receiving formal therapy from a speech-language pathologist. The remainder of the time is spent outside the clinic in the home and school environments. So, the speech-language pathologist is likely to provide parents and teachers with activities that can be used in these settings to help facilitate improvement in the child's language abilities. Goals developed for helping children improve their language comprehension abilities might be to help the child increase receptive (listening) vocabulary, comprehension of directions, understanding of grammar, and recognition of the role of a listener in a conversation. Examples of expressive language goals would be to expand vocabulary development and the child's use of language (pragmatics) in various speaking contexts.

Once specific goals of treatment are identified, the speech-language pathologist can opt to use either an adult-centered approach or a child-centered approach in helping the child achieve these goals. Language therapy is characterized as **adult-centered therapy** if the therapist takes a direct approach to teaching specific language skills to the child. This approach has been in widespread use for many years and involves giving the child frequent prompts to produce the desired utterances. The speech-language pathologist may also use instructional materials such as charts that focus on the language skill being taught. The treatment goal of a session might be, for example, to get the child to correctly use verb forms such as "is walking," "is playing," and "is eating," or learning to follow directions. Adult-centered therapy is found to be most effective with school-age children.

In contrast, **child-centered therapy** uses a less directive path to improving the child's language abilities. This approach has been referred to as "speech on the run," whereby the speech-language pathologist provides therapy by following the child's lead and using a more conversational give-and-take, rather than an instructional format. In these therapy sessions, a speech-language pathologist interacts with a child by playing and talking. The therapist may use pictures, books, objects, or ongoing events to stimulate language learning. Four therapy techniques used in child-centered therapy are (a) self-talk, (b) parallel talk, (c) description, and (d) language expansion. **Self-talk** involves the speech-language pathologist (or parent) talking out loud about what they are doing while engaging with the child. As part of self-talk, the therapist provides a rich array of spoken language models for the child in a noninvasive, natural fashion. For example, while playing with a doll, the speech-language pathologist may say, "*Oh there's my doll; she is sitting on the chair*," as a natural language model for the child to overhear. **Parallel talk** involves the speech-language pathologist describing out loud what the child is seeing, hearing, or thinking during the play activity. For example, if the child is playing with a train set, the speech-language pathologist may comment, "*You put the train in the tunnel*" as a language model for the child to overhear. **Description** involves the use of labeling or explanations by the speech-language pathologist that call the child's attention to objects or happenings in the play setting. The speech-language pathologist may say, "*Here comes the train*." The use of **language expansions** by the speech-language pathologist requires a restatement of the child's utterances, however with a fuller and grammatically correct language model. For example, the child may say, "*train go*," and the speech-language pathologist responds with, "*Yes. The train is going*." The speech-language pathologist adds the missing parts to the utterance and elaborates on the utterance, without overtly correcting the child or interfering with the flow of communication. All four techniques are based on communicating to the child by using statements rather than questions. By avoiding posing questions to the child, there is less communicative demand placed on the child. This, in turn, results in a more natural give-and-take in language use between the speech-language pathologist and child. The use of these child-centered techniques is particularly effective in providing language remediation to preschool-age children.

These two therapy approaches are not mutually exclusive. It is quite possible that the speech-language pathologist may develop some sort of hybrid therapy approach involving both adult- and child-centered techniques. One situation when a hybrid approach may likely be used is when the speech-language pathologist wishes to implement a therapy program that involves both the home and school settings. The parents could be using speech-on-the-run techniques to model general language skills for the child at home, and the speech-language pathologist could use direct therapy techniques when the child is attending school.

CULTURAL CONSIDERATIONS AND CHILD LANGUAGE DISORDERS ASSESSMENT

As the world becomes more globally connected, the diversity of cultural and language backgrounds represented among today's children is expanding. Most speech-language pathologists working in schools are likely to be confronted with children who differ in culture and dialect, as well as in primary language compared with their own. Culturally and linguistically diverse children exhibit differences in behaviors, expectations, and belief systems. They use languages other than English and/or dialectical variations different from those used in the school setting. Special considerations must be made to address the complex issues of these populations (Hyter & Salas-Provance, 2023). The percentage of children living in the United States who are Hispanic has risen from 9% in 1980 to 26% in 2022. Approximately 4 million residents in England are of Asian/Indian and Black African/Caribbean background. More than 2 million Australians, or about 14% of those aged 5 years and older, speak a language other than English at home, including Greek, Italian, Arabic, Chinese, and German.

Bilingualism is defined as the ability to communicate in two languages (Figure 3–11) but not necessarily at the same level of proficiency. Varying levels of proficiency can be found across the domains of reading, writing, speaking, and listening. There are two forms of bilingualism: (a) simultaneous and (b) consecutive. **Simultaneous bilingualism** also is referred to as spontaneous bilingualism. In this form of bilingualism, an individual has presumably spoken (or has been spoken to) two or more languages in the home since birth. In **consecutive bilingualism**, an individual learns one language after already knowing another. This is the situation for individuals who become bilingual as older children and adults. Consecutive bilingualism is by far the most common form of bilingualism. Most linguistically diverse children speak a form of English that varies from Standard English. These variations should not automatically be considered a language disorder.

FIGURE 3–11. Bilingualism is becoming a part of our everyday world.

The challenge for the speech-language pathologist when confronted with a bilingual child is to distinguish between aspects of linguistic variation that represent regular patterns in the speaker 's language or dialect and those that represent true disorders in language. This is known as the "difference versus disorder paradox." A **language difference** is a situation in which the language features of a community differ from the majority language. The rules are normal for the smaller community. Consider the case of a child who is speaking Spanish-accented English. The child's first or dominant language (**L1**) is Spanish, and the second language (**L2**) is English. The speech-language pathologist must determine whether the child's differences with the English language are due to variation caused by normal linguistic processes resulting from the competition between two languages or by a more basic language disorder problem. If the child's L2 is found to be disordered, it is highly likely the L1 also is disordered. It is inappropriate to label a child as language disordered if the second language is in transition. It is also inappropriate to overlook a child who is speaking L2 when the L1 may be disordered.

Great care must be taken to ensure that language assessment of bilingual children is culture free and dialect sensitive. Problems may arise when the language tester (the speech-language pathologist) and the child being assessed come from different linguistic or cultural backgrounds. In addition, there are few language tests that have been adapted to the bilingual population. Most tests are developed using speakers of Standard English. So, in addition to the mismatch between the speech-language pathologist and the child regarding cultural and linguistic differences, there is also a mismatch in the tools available to evaluate the child's language abilities. According to the American Speech-Language-Hearing Association, fewer than 8% of speech-language pathologists identify themselves as being bilingual. If the speech-language pathologist is monolingual and is not fully aware of the possible factors influencing a child's L1 on the L2, the therapist should recruit the services of an interpreter or family member as part of the assessment protocols. It is crucial that speech-language pathologists exercise diligence in distinguishing between a language difference and a language disorder.

Intervention

The traditional role of the speech-language pathologist has been to provide therapy services to individuals with diagnosed communication disorders. It is also within the scope of practice for speech-language pathologists to provide what is termed **elective therapy**. Given that a standard form of English is often required to be successful in business, economic, and educational sectors, speakers of nonstandard English may be at a disadvantage. In these cases, the role of the speech-language pathologist is to help the client acquire the desired competency in speaking a standard form of English and reduce the effects of the accent resulting from the individual's L1 or primary dialect. Normally, the services of the speech-language pathologist would not be required because the language demonstrated by the client technically is not disordered. In these cases, the client chooses to receive therapy on an elective basis.

> **FYI**
>
> Children who misbehave are often labeled as manipulative or stubborn. However, we now know that language impairment is sometimes associated with behavior problems. Children with either receptive or expressive language difficulties often use inappropriate actions to get attention or escape a situation. Difficulty with using language can also restrain the child from asking a question or stating that they do not understand.

SUMMARY OF CHAPTER

Language disorders in children are characterized by deficiencies in the production and/or comprehension of spoken and written language. Deficiencies in language can have a profound impact on a child's academic, social, and emotional development. Some language disorders in children can result from physical factors, such as intellectual impairment, hearing loss, and head injury. Often, child language disorders are functional in nature, where a specific etiology for the disorder cannot be determined. SLI is characterized by difficulty with language that is not caused by known neurological, sensory, intellectual, or emotional deficit. The term *late talker* is used to describe a group of children who have an impoverished expressive vocabulary, usually within the age range of 18 to 30 months of life. To diagnose a language disorder, the speech-language pathologist must examine and assess the child's comprehension and production of the various language components. Some features of a language assessment include (a) a case history, (b) standardized testing, and (c) language sampling or nonstandardized testing. There is no agreed-upon approach to treating child language disorders. Some approaches work better for some children than others. The specific approach and success of an approach are dependent on factors such as the child's age, attention span, and type and cause of language disorder. The set of goals and treatment strategies are unique to the child and their particular difficulties with language. Culturally and linguistically diverse children exhibit differences in behaviors, expectations, and belief systems. They use languages other than English and/or dialectical variations different from those used in the school setting.

CHILD LANGUAGE DISORDERS ON THE WORLD WIDE WEB

Following are websites that provide further information on the topic of child language disorders. At the time of publication, each website was freely accessible.

Language Development
https://www.cincinnatichildrens.org/service/s/speech/patients/development

Specific Language Impairment

Autism
https://www.autismspeaks.org

Late talkers
https://latetalkers.org/index.php?p=about
https://vimeo.com/160930988

Bilingualism
https://www.youtube.com/watch?v=9Wc5qI-qqT4

https://www.youtube.com/watch?v=_CAv7S5NiNY

STUDY QUESTIONS

1. List and describe the stages of infant vocal development.
2. Who are some of the pioneers that contributed to our knowledge related to child language development?
3. List and describe three common conditions indicative of language impairment.
4. How do standardized and nonstandardized approaches to language assessment differ?
5. What is the difference between adult-centered and child-centered language therapy?

REFERENCES

Brown, R. (1973). *A first language*. Harvard University Press.

Butler, K. (1986). *Language disorders in children*. Pro-Ed.

Dunn, D. M. (2018). *Peabody Picture Vocabulary Test* (5th ed.). Pearson Education.

Hyter, Y., & Salas-Provance, M. (2023). *Culturally responsive practices in speech, language, and hearing sciences* (2nd ed.). Plural Publishing.

Kent, R. D. (1984). Psychobiology of speech development: Co-emergence of language and a movement system. *American Journal of Regulatory Integrative and Comparative Physiology, 246*, R888–R894.

Kujala, T., Partanen, E., Virtala, P., & Winkler, I. (2023). Prerequisites of language acquisition in the newborn brain. *Trends in Neurosciences, 46*(9), 726–737.

Stoel-Gammon, C., & Cooper, J. (1984). Patterns of early lexical and phonological development. *Journal Child Language, 11*, 247–272.

Taslim, T., Asrifan, A., Chen, Y., & Nurdania, N. (2019). Correlation between student's vocabulary mastery and speaking skill, *Journal of Advanced English Studies, 2*, 65–76.

Wermke, K., & Mende, W. (2011). From emotion to notion: The importance of melody. In J. Decety & J. Cacioppo (Eds.), *The Oxford handbook of social neuroscience*. Oxford University Press.

Wiig, E., Semel, E., & Secord, W. (2013). *Clinical evaluation of language fundamentals* (5th ed.). Pearson Education.

4

CHILD SPEECH SOUND DISORDERS

OBJECTIVES

After reading this chapter, the student should be able to:

- Describe consonants and vowels according to categories of articulation.
- Explain theories related to phonological development and disorders.
- Identify individuals who have made historical contributions to the area of speech sound disorders.
- Compare, contrast, and discuss typical and atypical speech sound development.
- Compare, contrast, and discuss articulation versus phonological assessment.
- Compare, contrast, and discuss articulation versus phonological treatment.
- Describe phonological awareness.
- Describe cultural considerations in speech sound disorders.

KEY TERMS

Speech Sound Disorder
Phonological Disorder
Phonemes
Virgules
International Phonetic Alphabet (IPA)
Place of Articulation
Bilabial
Labio-Dental
Lingua-Dental
Lingua-Alveolar
Lingua-Palatal
Lingua-Velar
Glottal
Glottal Stop
Manner of Articulation
Stops
Nasal
Fricatives
Affricates
Liquids
Glides
Approximates
Consonant Voicing
Voiceless Consonants
Tongue Elevation
Tongue Advancement
Misarticulations
Edward Wheeler Scripture
Lee Edward Travis
Grant Fairbanks
Charles Van Riper
Psychological Disturbance
Jane Beasley Raph
Mildred Templin
Articulation Disorders
Structural
Cleft Lip or Palate
Dentition
Occlusion
Malocclusion
Class I Malocclusion
Class II Malocclusion
Class III Malocclusion
Temporomandibular Joint
Ankyloglossia
Reverse Swallow
Lingual Frenulum
Tongue Thrust
Parkinson Disease
Amyotrophic Lateral Sclerosis
Childhood Apraxia of Speech
Speech Delay
Residual Errors
Behaviorist Theory
Natural Theory
David Stampe
Optimality Theory
Constraints
Speech Spontaneity
Structure
Picture-Naming Task
Phonetic Inventory
SODA
Substitutions
Omissions
Distortions
Additions
Phonological Processes
Age of Mastery
Age of Suppression
Qualitative
Quantitative
Percentage of Consonants Correct
Range of Motion
Strength
Rate of Movement
Articulation Approach
Traditional Approach
Maximal Contrast Approach
Phonological Approach
Cycles Approach
Minimal Pair
Phonological Awareness
Dialect
Geographic Dialects
Socioeconomic Dialects
Accent
Orlando Taylor
Bilingualism
Multilingualism
English as a Second Language (ESL)
Phonological Interference
Phonological Difference

INTRODUCTION

A landmark achievement of a child's acquisition of language is the production of single words. The earliest of these single words typically consist of only one or two syllables and are created using a small number of consonants and vowels. As the child ages, the corresponding length and complexity of spoken utterances increases. The advances in language development are accompanied by increases in the number and variety of consonants and vowels. Children progress through phases of speech sound acquisition so that, by no later than 6 to 7 years of age, they should be overheard producing the entire repertoire of speech sounds in the English language. For a variety of reasons, children may be unable to accurately produce certain consonants and vowels by the age at which they are expected. Such children are described as having a **speech sound disorder**. The severity of a speech sound disorder can range from speech that is completely incomprehensible, even to a child's immediate family members, to speech that can be understood by everyone but with a few slightly mispronounced sounds. A speech sound disorder has long been recognized as the most common type of communication disorder shown by children. In this chapter, the nature of speech sound disorders is described.

TERMINOLOGY AND DEFINITIONS

The consonant and vowel sounds that make up a language are called **phonemes**. The term *phonology* refers to the study of how sounds are organized and used in a language. Diagonal marks (/) known as **virgules** are used to signify the individual phonemes of a language (e.g., /m/, /b/, /z/). The a-b-c symbols of the English alphabetic system serve as a poor example of depicting the sound–symbol relationship of the English language. The English alphabet consists of 26 letters (5 vowels and 21 consonants), yet these individual letters or combinations of these letters can represent far more than 26 sounds. For example, the /s/ sound is depicted differently in the words ba<u>ss</u>, ba<u>se</u>, and fa<u>ce</u>. In the word *scissors*, the /s/ sound is written as "sc," whereas the remaining /s/ symbols in this same word are produced more like a /z/ sound. This rather fuzzy sound–symbol relationship is not unique to English. This situation prompted a group of French and English linguists to gather in 1886 and develop a symbol system called the **International Phonetic Alphabet** (IPA), which has become the standard notation system used worldwide by linguists and speech-language pathologists to describe the sound patterns of various languages. The basic idea behind developing the IPA was to create an alphabet in which each sound would have its own distinctive symbol. According to the IPA system, the English language consists of 42 distinct sounds (or symbols; 18 vowels and 24 consonants). A portion of the IPA symbol system is shown in Figures 4–1 and 4–2. The figures depict the various ways in which consonant and vowel sounds can be classified. This classification relates to the pattern of articulation within the vocal tract.

Consonant Classification

When a consonant is articulated, there is almost always some form of obstruction or at least a narrowing of the vocal tract that causes a disruption in the air flowing upward from the lungs. The three major ways of classifying the pattern of consonant articulation are according to (a) place of articulation, (b) manner of articulation, and (c) consonant voicing.

Place of Articulation

Place of articulation refers to the location where the constriction or obstruction of the vocal tract occurs. An illustration of the various places of consonant articulation is shown in Figure 4–3. The following sections discuss the places of consonant articulation beginning at the front of the mouth and working toward the back of the throat.

Bilabial. As the name implies, the place of articulation for a **bilabial** consonant is at the front of the mouth, by using both lips for articulation. The bilabial consonants are /p/, /b/, and /m/.

Labio-Dental. In **labio-dental** articulation, the place of articulation involves the lower lip and

Place of Articulation

Manner of Articulation

		Bilabial	Labiodental	Lingua-Dental	Lingua-Alveolar	Lingua-Palatal	Lingua-Velar	Glottal	Examples
Stops	Voiceless	/p/			/t/		/k/		pin tin kin
	Voiced	/b/			/d/		/g/		bust dust gust
Fricatives	Voiceless		/f/	/θ/	/s/	/ʃ/		/h/	fin thin sin shin hit
	Voiced		/v/	/ð/	/z/	/ʒ/			van the zoo treasure
Affricates	Voiceless					/tʃ/			cheap
	Voiced					/dʒ/			jeep
Nasals	Voiced	/m/			/n/		/ŋ/		seem scene sing
Liquids	Voiced				/l/	/r/			late rate
Glides	Voiced	/w/				/j/			well yell

FIGURE 4–1. Categorization of consonants according to place, manner, and voicing features of articulation. Where there are voiced and voiceless consonants within the same manner of articulation, the voiceless consonants are listed in the top of the box.

Tongue Advancement

Tongue Elevation	Front	Central	Back
High	i (heed) ɪ (hid)		u (hude) ʊ (hood)
Mid	e (hayed) ɛ (head)	ʌ ə (hud)	o (hoed)
Low	æ (hat)		ɔ (hawed) ɑ (hod)

FIGURE 4–2. Categorization of vowels according to tongue elevation and tongue advancement categories.

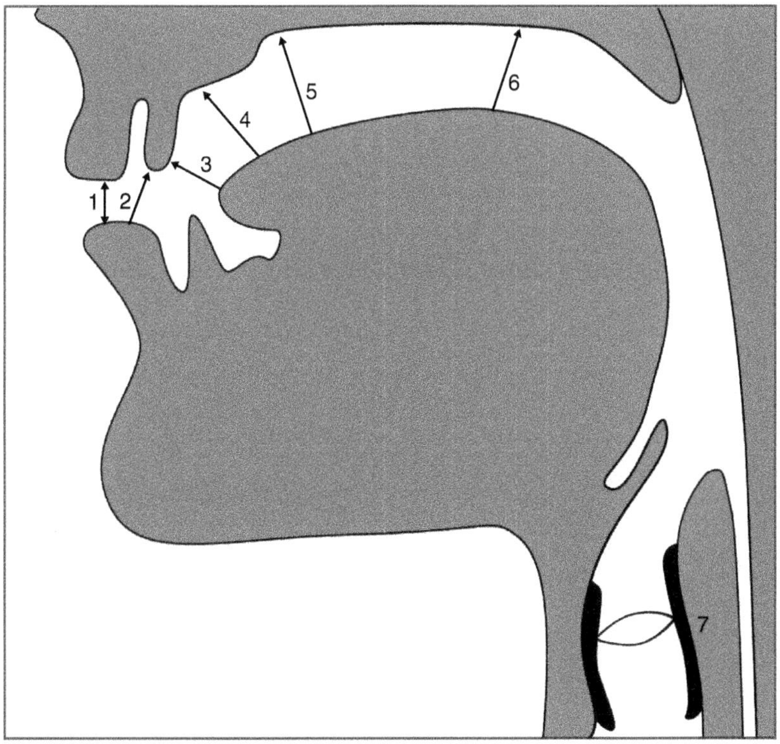

FIGURE 4–3. Cross-sectional view of the vocal tract depicting consonant places of articulation. 1 = bilabial, 2 = labio-dental, 3 = lingua-dental, 4 = lingua-alveolar, 5 = lingua-palatal, 6 = lingua-velar, and 7 = glottal.

the upper teeth, which act together to produce the consonant sound. The labio-dental consonants are /f/ and /v/.

Lingua-Dental. Articulation of the **lingua-dental** consonants involves placement of the tongue between (or just behind) the teeth. The sounds /θ/ and /ð/ are included in this category.

Lingua-Alveolar. The alveolar ridge, situated just behind the upper teeth, is a common place of **lingua-alveolar** articulation for English consonants. No less than six sounds are produced there, including /t/, /d/, /n/, /s/, /z/, and /l/.

Lingua-Palatal. Moving farther back in the vocal tract, the creation of **lingua-palatal** consonants involves the tongue making direct (or close) contact with the region of the hard palate. Similar to lingua-alveolar consonants, this is a popular place of articulation for English consonants and includes /ʃ/, /ʒ/, /tʃ/, /dʒ/, /j/, and /r/.

Lingua-Velar. As the name indicates, the place of articulation for **lingua-velar** consonants is the tongue (mid-to-back portion of the tongue) and the velum (soft palate). The lingual velar consonants are limited to the /k/, /g/, and /ŋ/ sounds.

Glottal. The **glottal** place of articulation is located at the back of the throat at the lower end of the pharynx (i.e., near the glottis). The primary glottal consonant is /h/, although there is another, less frequently produced consonant known as a **glottal stop** /ʔ/.

Manner of Articulation

The term **manner of articulation** refers to how the obstruction inside the oral cavity is made. Some of these obstructions are quite strong, while others are very subtle. In total, there are six distinct manners of articulation as discussed in the following sections.

Stops. To produce **stops**, the manner in which these consonants are articulated involves a solid obstruction within the oral cavity. The obstruction entails a complete blockage of the airstream coming up from the lungs. This blockage is then abruptly released so the air that was compressed behind the obstruction can escape with a kind of explosive movement. The stop consonants are /p/, /b/, /t/, /d/, /k/, and /g/.

Nasals. The manner in which **nasal** consonants are articulated involves a lowering of the velum. This lowering allows air to escape through the nasal cavity rather than the oral cavity. Nasal consonants in English are fairly limited in number. There are only three: /m/, /n/, and /ŋ/.

Fricatives. Where stops are produced with complete obstruction in the oral cavity, **fricatives** are produced by creating a partial obstruction of the airstream. This makes turbulence arise at or near the point of obstruction, where the airstream is forced through a greatly narrowed channel. Fricatives compose the largest class of English consonants according to manner of articulation, including /f/, /v/, /θ/, /ð/, /s/, /z/, /ʃ/, /ʒ/, and /h/.

Affricates. **Affricates** are a combination of a stop and a following fricative, where the quality of the stop remains largely the same, but the fricative part tends to be shorter than a "pure" fricative. The affricates are /tʃ/ and /dʒ/.

Liquids and Glides. The **liquids** and **glides** are consonants that differ from the other consonants by the fact that they are produced with far less obstruction in the vocal tract. Instead, there is a subtle narrowing of the vocal tract. These consonants are sometimes referred to as **approximates** because their manner of articulation seems to lie between true consonants and pure vowels. The liquid consonants are /l/ and /r/. The glide consonants are /w/ and /j/.

Consonant Voicing

Consonant voicing requires vocal fold vibration. These voiced consonants include /b/, /d/, /g/, /v/, /ð/, /z/, /ʒ/, /dʒ/, /w/, /j/, /l/, /r/, /m/, /n/, and /ŋ/. Not all consonants involve vocal fold vibration. These are referred to as **voiceless consonants** and include /p/, /t/, /k/, /f/, /θ/, /s/, /ʃ/, /tʃ/, and /h/. Collectively, all consonants can be described using the categories of voicing, place, and manner of articulation. The phoneme /b/ is an example of a voiced bilabial stop. The phoneme /ʃ/ is an example of a voiceless lingua-palatal fricative (see Figure 4–1).

> *FYI*
>
> The ability to articulate an innumerable number of speech sounds in an oral cavity that is less than 3 in. in length is considered the most sophisticated and coordinated activity performed by the human body.

Vowel Classification

As noted earlier, consonants are characterized by an obstruction of the vocal tract, which causes a disruption in airflow. The opposite is true of vowels. Here, the characteristic feature is the absence of closure of the vocal tract so that air can flow through the vocal tract in a relatively unimpeded fashion. The articulation of vowels is organized according to the positioning of the tongue body within the oral cavity. The two vowel classifications are tongue elevation and tongue advancement (Figure 4–4).

Tongue Elevation

As implied, **tongue elevation** (or tongue height) refers to the distance that the tongue is moved from the base of the mouth toward the roof of the mouth to produce vowels (see Figure 4–4). However, in no instance does the tongue physically contact any other structures in the vocal tract. There are three general locations of vowels according to tongue elevation: high /i, ɪ, u, ʊ/, mid /e, ɛ, ə, ʌ, o/, and low /æ, ɔ, ɑ/.

> **FYI**
>
> American English uses a vowel that is found in less than 1% of the world's languages. The vowel is found in words such as *fur*, *stir*, and *her*.

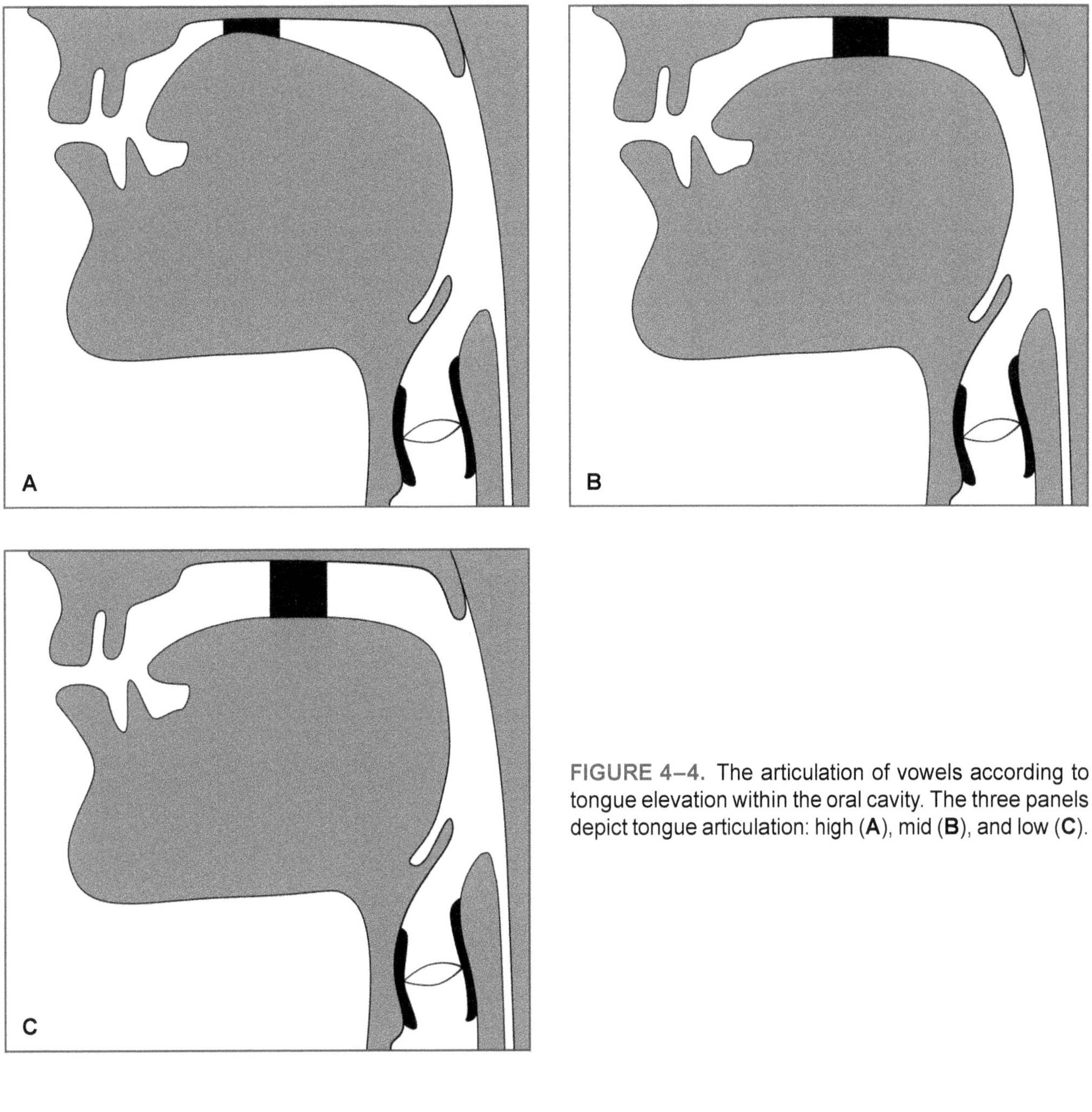

FIGURE 4–4. The articulation of vowels according to tongue elevation within the oral cavity. The three panels depict tongue articulation: high (**A**), mid (**B**), and low (**C**).

Tongue Advancement

The classification of vowels according to **tongue advancement** (or tongue carriage) refers to the movement of the tongue body from the front of the oral cavity toward the back (Figure 4–5). There are three locations of vowels according to tongue advancement: front /i, ɪ, ɛ, e, æ/, central /ə, ʌ/, and back /u, ʊ, o, ɔ, ɑ/. Collectively, all vowels can be described using the categories of tongue elevation and tongue advancement. The phoneme /u/ is an example of a high-back vowel. The phoneme /æ/ is an example of a low-front vowel (see Figure 4–2).

Phonological Development

Children do not learn to pronounce all the consonant and vowel sounds of their language at once; the process is gradual and covers the approximate age range of 1 year to around 6 years of age.

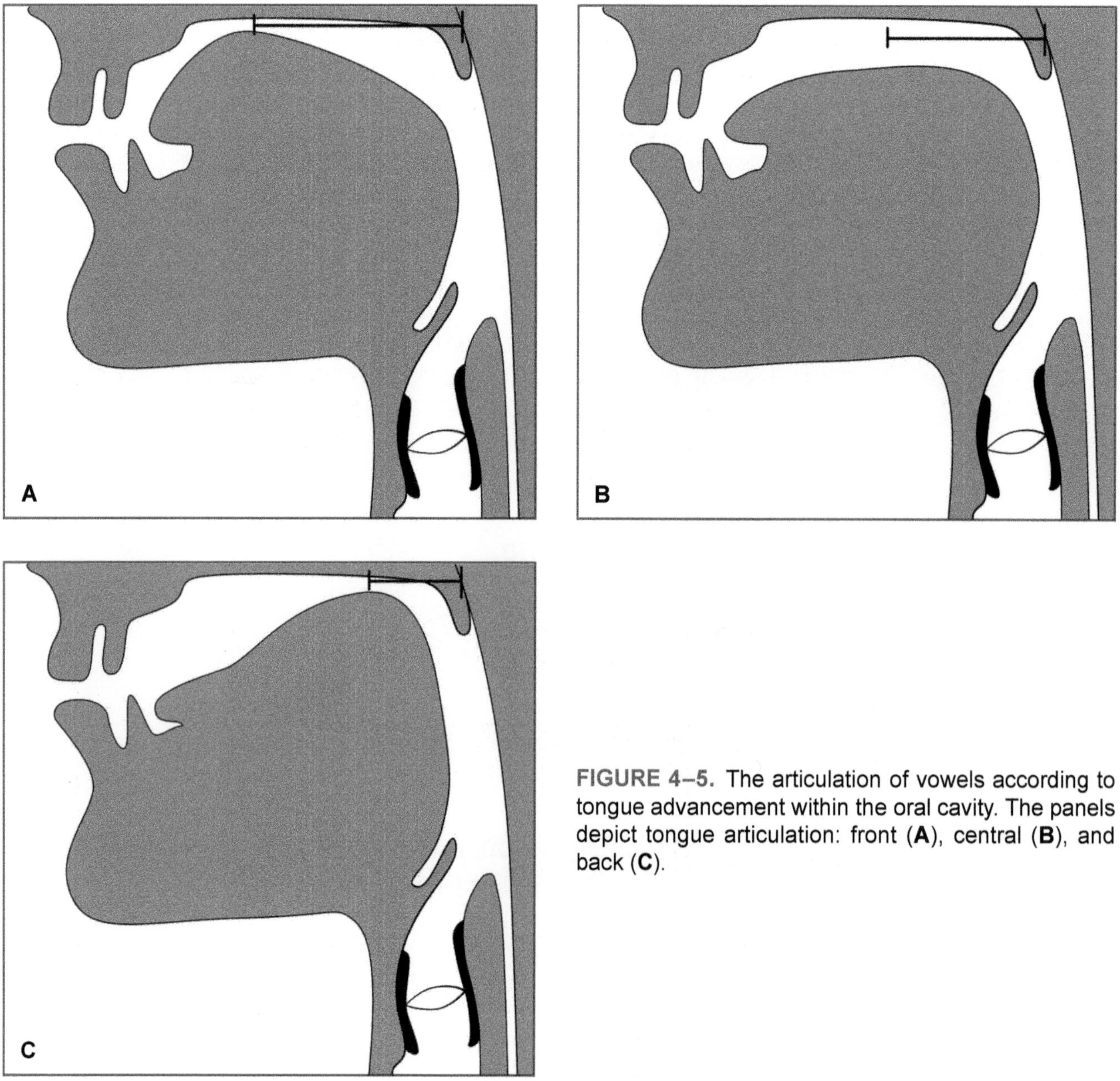

FIGURE 4–5. The articulation of vowels according to tongue advancement within the oral cavity. The panels depict tongue articulation: front (**A**), central (**B**), and back (**C**).

Although some variability is naturally expected between children, most tend to acquire the sounds of speech in an orderly fashion. As a rule, vowels of the English language are acquired by children slightly earlier than consonants. The 24 consonant phonemes of English can be loosely organized into four steps of development (Figure 4–6). The first step contains the earliest consonant sounds such as the phonemes /m/, /b/, and /w/ that emerge around 2 to 3 years of age. At 4 years of age, children learn to produce another seven consonants such as "l," "ch," "s," and "sh." Another three consonants are learned at 5 years of age and include /r/ and voiced "th" and "zh." The last sound to be learned by children emerges at around 6 years of age, which is the voiceless "th." The sounds acquired during the later phases of development generally involve more precise articulatory movements compared with early developing sounds, so it is not unusual for children to require more time to master these articulations. Some children may not acquire these consonants in precisely the same order. So, it is important to emphasize that these steps are not set in stone. Children are known to show variability in the order and pace at which they acquire speech sounds, especially those occurring between 4 and 6 years of age. If a child's speech does not consistently contain these various consonants by a particular age range, suspicion is raised about the possibility of a speech sound disorder.

Any deviation, great or small, in the articulation of phonemes can lead to **misarticulations**, or what is simply referred to as a speech sound disorder (or **phonological disorder**). Speech sound disorders affect 15% of preschool children. In a majority of cases, the type of speech sound disorder demonstrated by children results from inaccurate production of consonants. This is not always the case, especially among children with severe phonological disorders who demonstrate impaired consonant and vowel production. By the time children enter school, approximately 6% continue to exhibit a speech sound disorder ranging from mild to severe. For 80% of children with a speech sound disorder, the condition is sufficiently severe that they will require the services of a speech-language pathologist to help them improve the quality of their speech. As noted in other chapters, many medical conditions found to occur during the childhood period seem to affect boys more often than girls. Speech sound disorders are no exception. Estimates suggest that two to four times as many boys as girls exhibit the disorder.

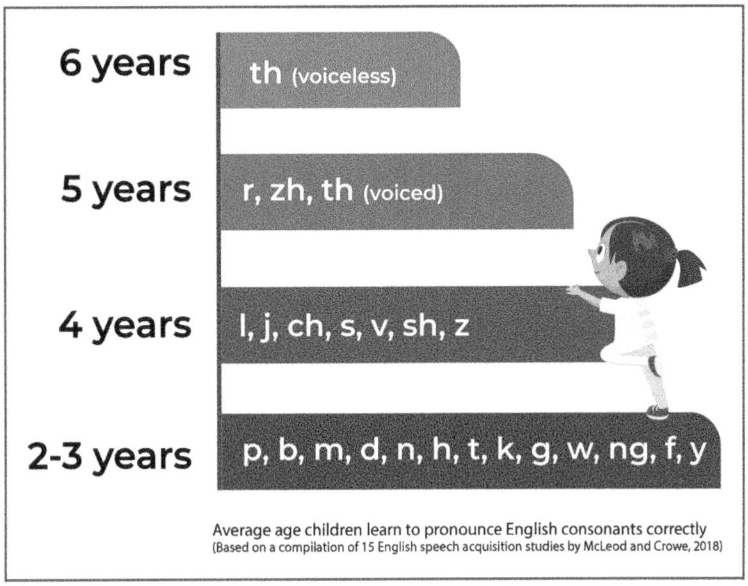

FIGURE 4–6. The average age when children learn to pronounce English consonants correctly. (Based on a compilation of 15 English speech acquisition studies by McLeod and Crowe (2018).)

As of 2023, approximately 90% of speech-language pathologists working in the United States reported that their caseloads included individuals with a speech sound disorder. There is no other speech or language disorder that receives more attention from a speech-language pathologist.

Children who have a speech sound disorder are more likely to have additional difficulties with their communication, such as language problems and academic difficulties. Children who show a speech sound disorder that persists into the entrance of school are thought to be at risk for developing literacy skills. The skills related to accurately producing speech sounds are the same skills that are required for learning to read. Most children who develop speech and language skills normally go on to develop literacy skills with no problem. There is thought to be a "critical age" in which speech difficulties (if present) can pose a significant barrier in learning to read. The relationship between literacy development and speech and language development is complex. We now know that a number of children who have poor oral language skills, as well as poor phonological awareness, experience difficulty learning to read and spell (Hayiou-Thomas et al., 2017).

HISTORIC ASPECTS OF CHILD SPEECH SOUND DISORDERS

Over the last century, a great deal of research has examined speech sound disorders. A large body of this historical research has centered on approaches to correcting the disorder. In the early 20th century, **Edward Wheeler Scripture** (1864–1945; Figure 4–7), who was a professor of psychology at Yale University, recommended specific treatment approaches for a speech condition he called *negligent lisping*. In current times, we would refer to this speech sound disorder as stopping of fricatives, where the fricative /s/ might be produced with a stop consonant /t/ ("soup" is produced as "toup"). Scripture attributed the condition to mental carelessness, and his cure for the condition consisted of teaching the individual to carefully correct his faults. To elicit correct articulation for /s/, for example, Scripture (1912) wrote,

FIGURE 4–7. Edward Wheeler Scripture, early 20th-century psychologist who recommended specific treatment approaches for speech sound disorders.

> One cure consists [of] inserting a probe, an applicator, a toothpick, or a pencil just over the middle of the tongue and pressing it down as the person begins to speak a word beginning with "s." . . . He cannot close the passage completely, and instead of saying "t," he is forced to say "s." This catches his ear, and he notices the difference in sound. Constant repetition enables him to train his tongue in the new way. (pp. 132–133)

Lee Edward Travis (1896–1987) made contributions to several areas in the field of communication disorders, including speech sound disorders (see also Chapter 1). He developed treatment programs that differed depending on whether the cause of the disorder was organic (anatomical) or functional (nonanatomical) in nature. Travis (1931) wrote,

> The articulatory case frequently shows inferior ability in controlling the lips, tongue, jaw and diaphragm in voluntary rhythmical movements not involved in speech. This would imply, as does the speech defect itself, that he possesses poor control of these structures in speech. (p. 223)

Grant Fairbanks (1910–1964) was a well-respected speech scientist at the University of Illinois who wrote a therapy manual known as the *Voice and Articulation Drillbook*, published in 1940. The book was filled with a number of word- and sentence-naming activities for correcting the speech misarticulations of children and adults. Fairbanks firmly believed that good listening skills in addition to repeated practice in producing specific misarticulated speech sounds were essential for the correction of any phonological disorder. He wrote,

> When articulating a sound in isolation it is valuable to start with prolonged examples, since you can listen carefully, make the necessary adjustments and perceive the position of your articulators. (Fairbanks, 1940, p. xxi)

Charles Van Riper (1905–1994; Figure 4–8), a contemporary of Fairbanks, was undoubtedly one of the leading researchers in child speech sound disorders and stuttering during the mid-20th century. Van Riper was a skilled speech-language pathologist who also happened to stutter. He devoted his career to developing effective treatment approaches. In his seminal publication *Speech Correction* (Van Riper, 1947), he recommended a series of procedural steps for the treatment of phonological disorders. The steps begin with helping to establish a new sound (that is misarticulated) in a person's speech and working through increasingly complicated speaking situations, with the end goal of producing the new sound in natural conversational speech. This management program has since been referred to as the **traditional approach**, and the essential components of the approach are still used today. Additional details regarding the traditional approach are provided later in this chapter.

FIGURE 4–8. Charles Van Riper established what is now known as the traditional approach to treating speech sound disorders. (Reprinted with permission from "An Early History of ASHA," by C. Van Riper, 1981, *ASHA Magazine*, *23*[11], pp. 855–858.)

There was a short period during the 1950s where a group of researchers attempted to link speech sound disorders to a larger emotionally based disorder (Rousey, 1957). Apart from obvious physical impairments of the speech anatomy, the assumption was that a nonorganic functional speech sound disorder was indicative of a **psychological disturbance**. The treatment was thus focused on techniques of psychotherapy. This view was prompted by existing research at the time, which indicated that children showed considerable variability in acquiring speech sounds. This variability was attributed to developmental differences between children in their social and emotional development. A few theories were proposed concerning the psychological underpinnings of specific consonant and vowel misarticulations. For example, substitution of the /d/ for the /ð/ ("th") sound ("the" is produced as "duh") was assumed to be related to an oral expression of aggression; that is, a pattern of speech utilized by "tough guys."

The resultant therapy focused on reducing aggression as a means of improving speech clarity. This perspective on speech sound disorders was short lived. Large-scale studies examining the acquisition of speech sounds have since confirmed there is considerable similarity across children in achieving normal milestones. Furthermore, we now have a much clearer understanding of the patterns of speech sound misarticulations that are produced by children, which attribute the problem to either motor- or language-based difficulties, as opposed to psychological difficulties.

Around this same time, **Jane Beasley Raph** (1917–2002; Figure 4–9) developed a novel approach to treating speech sound disorders. Beasley Raph was an American professor of speech-language pathology who is credited with developing a treatment approach that focused on social/conversational interaction. Beasley Raph believed that treating speech sound disorders in a social context rather than an individual (one-on-one) setting was an effective treatment approach for three reasons: (a) the approach provides a way of working on the mechanics of speech production, (b) development of such skills within a social context is a more real-world way of speaking, and (c) these social situations can improve the child's overall confidence and abilities as a speaker.

Finally, no history of speech sound disorders would be complete without mentioning the contributions of **Mildred Templin** (1913–2008; Figure 4–10). Templin earned her doctorate in child development from the University of Minnesota in 1947. She conducted a series of longitudinal and cross-sectional studies of spelling, vocabulary, and cognitive behavior of children with hearing disabilities and normally developing children. Her work led to the publication of *Certain Language Skills in Children* (1957). At the time, this was a definitive work in the field. Together with her colleague Frederick Darley in 1969, she created the Templin–Darley Tests of Articulation, which are still used today to evaluate speech sound production skills in children.

TYPES OF SPEECH SOUND DISORDERS

The types of speech sound disorders can be organized into three categories based on the presumed cause of the disorder: (a) structural, (b) neurological, and (c) functional. Structural and neurological disorders are sometimes referred to as **articulation disorders** because the cause of the disorder is related to problems in the motor movements required to produce clear speech. Functional disorders are simply referred to as speech sound disorders because there are no clearly identifiable

FIGURE 4–9. Jane Beasley Raph, American professor of speech-language pathology who developed a social interaction approach to treating speech sound disorders in children. (Permission granted by the family of Jae Beasley Raph.)

FIGURE 4–10. Mildred Templin, expert in the communication disorders of children. (Printed with permission of the Trustees for the Estate of Mildred Templin.)

motor problems. Instead, the difficulty observed in producing speech sounds appears to be related to a problem in learning to organize the sounds of the language.

Structural Cause

Structural problems involve abnormalities of the mouth, such as the teeth, tongue, or palate, that are necessary for accurate speech sound production. These abnormalities make it difficult for children or adults to produce certain sounds and in some cases make it impossible to produce the sounds at all. The structural problem causing the speech sound disorder generally needs to be surgically or medically treated before the child receives any sort of speech therapy. Correction of the structural problem is likely to greatly assist in correction of the speech sound difficulties. One such example is a **cleft lip or palate.** Chapter 6 is specifically dedicated to this condition. A cleft of the lip and palate is one of the most common and obvious speech sound disorders that has a structural cause. Another structural problem contributing to a speech sound disorder is **dentition.** It is not unusual for children to develop a temporary speech sound disorder during the time when primary teeth are being replaced by permanent teeth. This condition is found in nearly all first graders (see Chapter 1, Figure 1–4). Indeed, the child who loses her front two teeth experiences considerable difficulty producing consonants that require articulation between the tongue tip and central incisors (e.g., "s" and "t").

More permanent forms of dental-related articulation problems concern the alignment of the upper and lower teeth, which is referred to as **occlusion.** An uneven alignment between the upper and lower teeth is called a **malocclusion.** This situation occurs in approximately 90% of the population. There are three types of malocclusion patterns that help to create the overall appearance of our faces (Figure 4–11). A **Class I malocclusion** involves normal alignment of the upper and lower teeth with only one or two teeth slightly misaligned. A **Class II malocclusion** (or distocclusion) is an overbite. This pattern can result from one of two conditions, the first being an overly large maxilla (upper jaw) with a normal-sized mandible (lower jaw). The second condition is a result of a normal-sized maxilla but a small mandible. The third type is referred to as a **Class III malocclusion** resulting in an underbite (or mesiocclusion). In this condition, the maxilla may be unusually small with a normal-sized mandible, or the mandible may be unusually large with a normal-sized maxilla. In extreme instances of either a Class II or Class III malocclusion, oral surgery may be required to correct the alignment pattern. However, this situation usually is prompted by other medical conditions, aside from speech problems. Most notable is a condition in which the **temporomandibular joint** works abnormally.

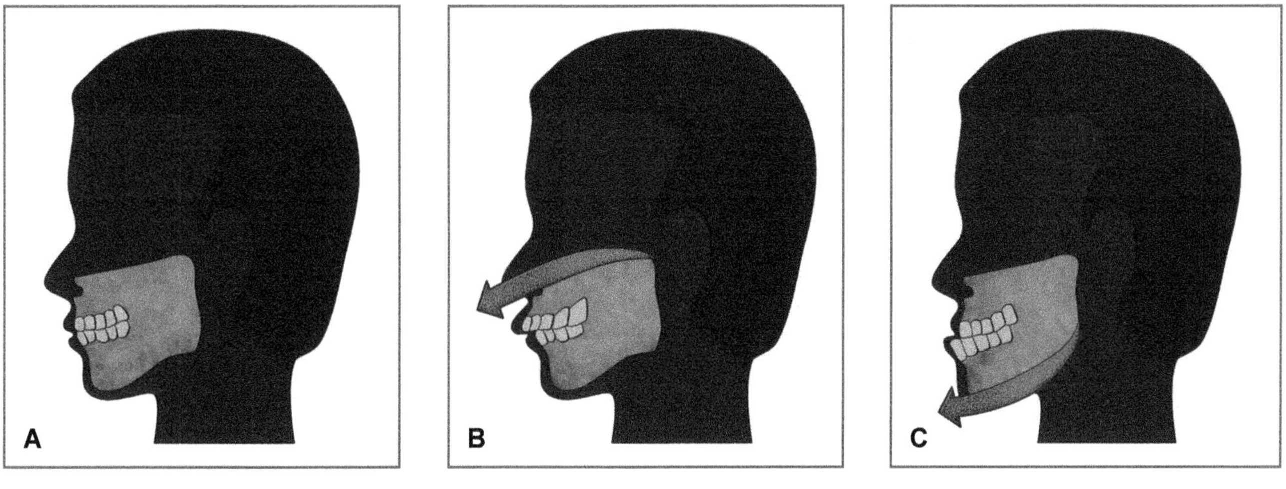

FIGURE 4–11. Dental and jaw alignment (occlusion) patterns. The patterns represent Class I (**A**), Class II (**B**), and Class III (**C**) malocclusions.

This joint serves as the socket location where the mandible fits into the side of the skull (temporal bone). When the temporomandibular joint fails to function normally, an individual may experience severe headaches. There also are extreme instances of temporomandibular joint dysfunction when the jaw may open and stay locked (i.e., lockjaw).

Two conditions concerning *tongue mobility* contribute to a structurally based speech sound disorder: **ankyloglossia** and **reverse swallow**. The first condition involves the **lingual frenulum**, which is the tendon that extends from the floor of the mouth to the underside of the tongue. A child may be born with a condition where the length of the tendon is abnormally short. The short length of the tendon restricts tongue mobility and possibly tongue-related speech sounds. In the past, there were suggestions that clipping the tendon would help to improve speech clarity. There is little evidence to indicate that undergoing this rather drastic surgical procedure serves to correct a speech sound disorder, and it should be considered only when the tendon is so short that it impairs more basic biological functions such as swallowing. Another term for ankyloglossia is "tongue tie." An illustration of a lingual frenulum is provided in Figure 4–12.

The condition of reverse swallow also is called **tongue thrust**. The condition is reflective of an orofacial muscular imbalance. A reverse swal-

FYI

Some famous people who have a Class III malocclusion (underbite) include the former U.S. First Lady Michelle Obama; musician Bruce Springsteen; former Prime Minister of Canada Brian Mulroney; and film actors Woody Harrelson, Keira Knightley, and Quentin Tarantino.

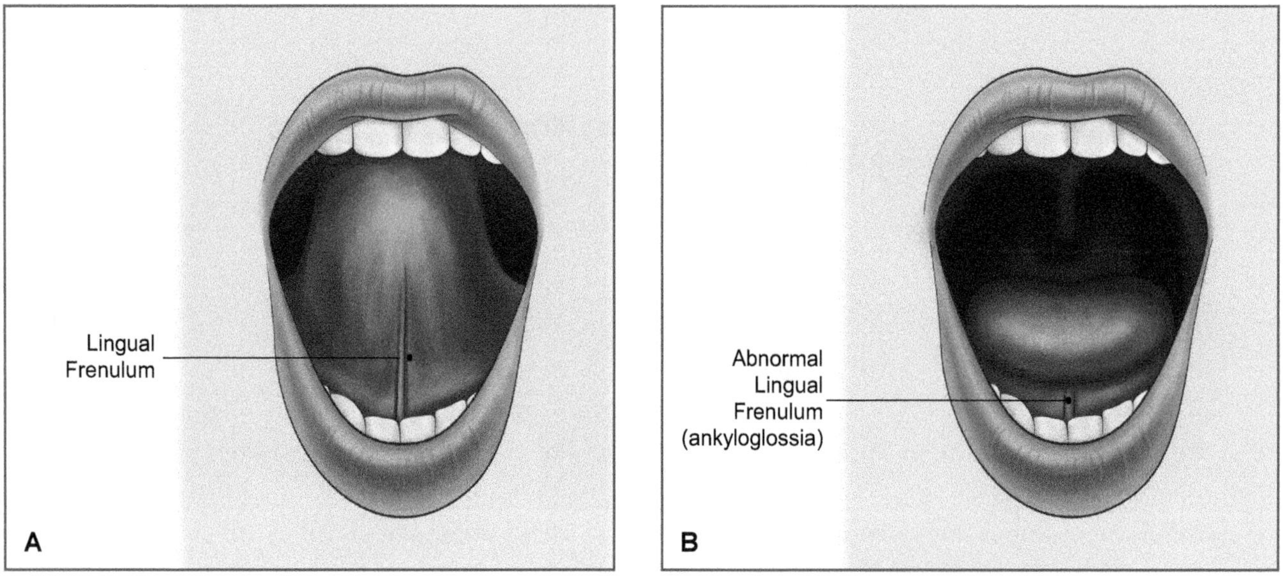

FIGURE 4–12. **A.** Normal lingual frenulum. **B.** An abnormally short frenulum (ankyloglossia).

low normally is seen during the early infancy and toddler periods of normal development. During this period, swallowing is achieved by pushing the tongue forward, rather than backward, to assist with the digestion of food and liquid (Figure 4–13). By the time children reach the age of 6 years, most have automatically changed to a normal swallowing pattern, which involves squeezing the tongue against the roof of the mouth instead of pushing it forward against the teeth. Research suggests that hereditary factors, learned behavior such as thumb sucking, and/or medical conditions may be responsible for tongue thrust. For whatever reason, a child may experience a delay or interruption in the oral maturational process and fail to progress to an adult swallowing pattern. This delay may also affect motor skills required for speech sound production.

Neurological Cause

The second category of speech sound disorders reflects neurological problems attributed to the nervous system. The nervous system is responsible for activating and controlling the various structures and muscles needed for producing speech sounds. Depending on the location of the nervous system impairment, an individual could show excessive speed or stiffness in the execution of speech. It is equally possible for nervous system impairment to result in slow or labored speech production. Some neurological conditions that are known to cause a speech sound disorder are **Parkinson disease** and **amyotrophic lateral sclerosis**. Chapter 10 is dedicated to speech sound disorders of this particular neurological origin. One type of neurologically based speech sound disorder that has been discussed for more than 30 years is **childhood apraxia of speech**. Childhood apraxia of speech is thought to be a disorder of the nervous system that affects a child's ability to organize and sequence the sounds of speech when producing words. This difficulty occurs in the absence of any muscle weakness or paralysis. The problem lies with the inability to plan movements of the speech articulators for the purpose of volitional (i.e., on command) speech. The child has difficulty making speech movements when the child is consciously aware of trying to do so or in instances when the child is requested to do so by others. The same speech movements are produced correctly when the child is producing natural, conversational speech. A key feature of childhood apraxia of speech is that the child's misarticulations are inconsistent. Childhood apraxia of speech is a relatively rare, poorly understood speech sound disorder that continues to be a topic of debate among researchers. There are varying opinions regarding the existence, cause, symptoms, and treatment of childhood apraxia of speech. There is no clearly defined set of speaking behaviors that identify the presence of childhood apraxia of speech, rather it is a spectrum of characteristics, and consequently, no two children with childhood apraxia of speech are alike.

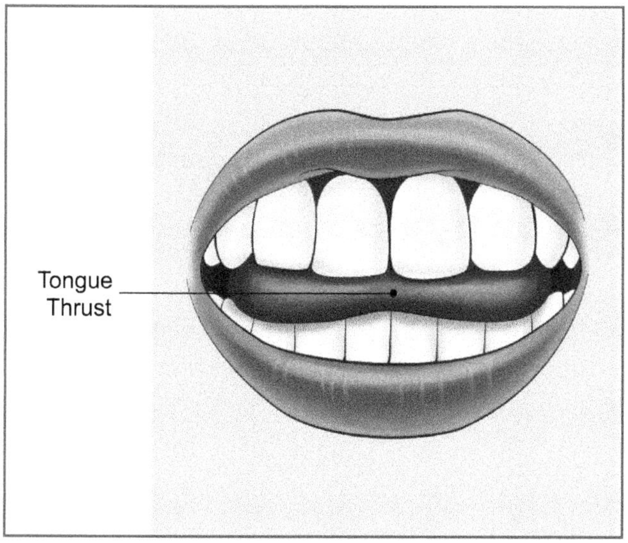

FIGURE 4–13. Tongue thrust during moments of swallowing.

Functional Cause

The third category of speech sound disorder is considered functional because the precise cause of the disorder is unknown. In this condition, the speech sound disorder results from impairments in the organization of phonemes and/or their application in speech. A child may be able to say a sound correctly but not use it appropriately in all words containing the sound. The child may also display a reduction in the total number of consonant and vowel sounds in their speech repertoire. In either case, the speech patterns displayed by the child are different from those of same-age peers. Speech sound disorders of a functional nature make up the largest percentage of child-based speech sound disorders. A functional disorder can be further divided into disorders that reflect a **speech delay** or those that reflect **residual errors**. A delay is characterized by speech pronunciations that are unclear (or unintelligible) and contain many consonant misarticulations. Children with speech delays also are found to be at an increased risk for broader communication and academic difficulties. Children with a speech delay represent the most severe form of functional disorder. Children with a speech sound disorder who show residual errors are those who may have only one or two speech sounds that are misarticulated. The speech sound in error is usually one of the later-developing consonant sounds such as a fricative (e.g., thumb is produced as *fumb*) or liquid consonant (e.g., rabbit is produced as *wabbit*). This category represents a less severe form of functional speech sound disorder.

CURRENT THEORIES REGARDING CHILD SPEECH SOUND DISORDERS

Several theories have attempted to explain the fashion in which children normally learn the consonant and vowel sounds of their language. The same theories have been used as a backdrop for the assessment and treatment of speech sound disorders. Three of these theories are (a) behaviorist theory, (b) natural phonology theory, and (c) optimality theory.

Behaviorist Theory

The **behaviorist theory**, developed by Mowrer (1960), suggests that a child's acquisition of consonants and vowels has its roots in early prelinguistic babbling behavior. The vocal interaction that takes place between the infant and caregiver during this early period of life sets the stage for establishing the child's speech development. The child's babbling is shaped and directed toward the adult pronunciation of words through selective reinforcement of sounds that approximate the target language. According to this theory, children may not acquire speech sounds in an identical fashion. Instead, their speech development is based on the environment in which they are reared. In the case of a speech disordered child, a faulty environment would be viewed as contributing to the child's speech difficulties.

Distinctive Features and Natural Phonology Theory

Chomsky and Halle (1968) proposed that the unique sound systems of all the world's languages could be described according to a specific number of phonological patterns, which they termed distinctive features. By simply noting the presence or absence of these features, the phonology of a particular language could be captured. Examples of distinctive features include nasality, consonantal, vocalic, and lip rounding. This approach to describing phonology according to patterns represented a dramatic shift in the way theorists viewed a child's acquisition of speech sounds.

The early work of Chomsky and Halle was a turning point in phonological theory and led to the development of other theories examining patterns of speech sound development. Notable among these theories was the **natural theory** proposed by **David Stampe** (1938–2020) (Donegan & Stampe, 1979). In this theory, a child's speech development is thought to be affected by naturally occurring phonological patterns (or "processes"), some of which remain active and others that are suppressed (or disappear) as the child learns their language. The child's task is to either "allow" or deliberately "suppress" various sound patterns that match those of the native language. The phonological system of a particular language is based on retaining some of these patterns while suppressing others. An example of a phonological pattern would be *final consonant deletion* (i.e., producing words that do not end with a final consonant—only vowels). A child acquiring English would learn to deliberately suppress this pattern because many of the words of English contain final consonants. On the other hand, a young child learning Mandarin would naturally accept this phonological pattern as part of the language because the words of Mandarin contain few, if any, final consonants. The notion of phonological patterns has received widespread attention over the past 30 years as a framework to evaluate and treat the speech of children with severe speech sound disorders. The theory provides an approach to treating entire classes of misarticulated speech sounds rather than individual phonemes.

Optimality Theory

Optimality theory is a general model of how grammar is structured. The theory was originally developed in the field of linguistics but has since been applied to phonological disorders. In its approach to the acquisition of phonology, optimality theory focuses on two important aspects of any phonological system: (a) the patterns that are impossible for a language and (b) the patterns that are possible. It is distinguished from other theories of phonological development in the role that is assigned to **constraints** (Geruit & Morrisette, 2005). A constraint is a limit on what constitutes a possible pronunciation of a word. The child's role in learning the sounds of the language is to learn these constraints. For example, in English some of the various phonological constraints are as follows:

- No word may end in /tp/, although /pt/ is possible.
- No word may start with /tl/ or /dl/, but /pl/, /bl/, /tr/, and /dr/ are possible.
- No word may start with /mr/ or /nr/, although /br/ and /fr/ are possible.

ASSESSMENT OF CHILD SPEECH SOUND DISORDERS

The goal of assessment is to obtain and establish an accurate profile of the child's speech sound production abilities. The diagnosis of a speech sound disorder depends greatly on the age of the child in question. Children who are 3 years old may show mispronunciation of words, but these mispronunciations may well be expected (normal) for their age. On the other hand, an 8-year-old child who makes the same mispronunciations may have a speech sound disorder. The following are some of the fundamental steps in performing an assessment. These steps include (a) conducting speech sampling, (b) collecting a phonetic inventory, (c) describing speech patterns, (d) estimating age expectancy, (e) estimating severity, and (f) performing an oral-facial examination.

Speech Sampling

The first step in determining whether a speech sound disorder exists is to collect a sample of the child's speaking behavior. There are numerous ways of collecting the sample that vary according to **speech spontaneity** and **structure**. Spontaneity refers to whether the child is asked to speak freely or whether the child is required to say specific words or sounds. Structure refers to the environment in which the speech sample is being collected. At one end of the continuum, the sample could involve collection of a spontaneous sample of speaking behavior in a typical environment such as the child's home. The advantage of this approach is that the sample is natural and reflects normal speaking behavior. A particular disadvantage to this approach is that it is time consuming and may not elicit from the child a broad sample of speech containing all possible consonants and vowels. On the other end of the continuum, the speech sample may be based on having the child name specific pictures that result in a one-word response. This type of activity usually occurs in a clinical setting. The advantage of this approach is that the child is required to deliberately produce specific consonants and vowels, although a disadvantage is that this is not a typical, natural setting of free speaking. Despite this unnaturalness, picture naming is the preferred approach to speech sampling. Several commercially available tests exist that are designed to sample a child's phonology using a **picture-naming task**. The pictures composing the test have been chosen because they contain consonants and vowels in various locations within a word (initial, medial, and final). There is no universally accepted picture-naming test used across English-speaking countries. A depiction of a picture-naming task and the associated scoring sheet is shown in Figure 4–14.

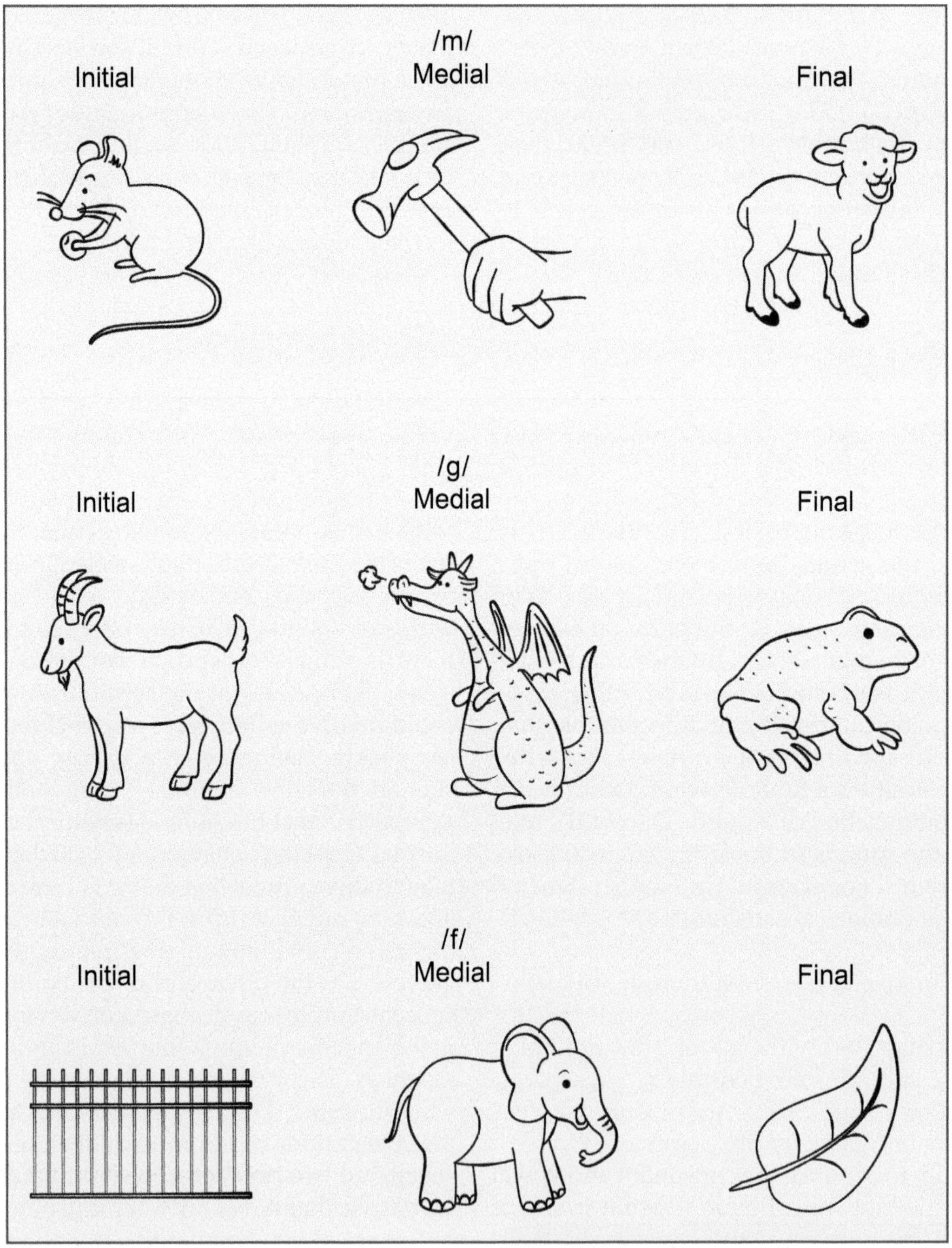

A

FIGURE 4–14. **A.** Example of a picture inventory test in which each item is named aloud.
continues

Phonetic Inventory

Once the speech sample is collected, the speech-language pathologist next transcribes the sample using symbols of the IPA. Based on the transcribed sample, a **phonetic inventory** is created. A phonetic inventory is a list of the consonants and vowels in the speech sample that were accurately pronounced. The list can be organized in several ways, such as noting those sounds that occurred at the initial, medial, or final position of a word. The inventory provides useful information regarding a

Picture-Naming Test

Word	Phoneme	Initial	Medial	Final
Mouse	/m/	x		
Hammer	/m/		x	
Lamb	/m/			x
Goat	/g/	x		
Dragon	/g/		x	
Frog	/g/			x
Fence	/f/	x		
Elephant	/f/		x	
Leaf	/f/			x

B

FIGURE 4–14. *continued* **B.** Corresponding test form.

child's ability to produce the consonant and vowel sounds of the language. Sounds absent from the inventory may be indicative of a speech sound disorder.

Description of Speech Patterns

Based on the phonetic transcription, the speech-language pathologist then compares the child's actual pronunciation of each word to the intended pronunciation of the word. This comparative analysis allows the speech-language pathologist to describe the pattern of the child's pronunciations. There are two notational systems for the description of disordered speech patterns.

The first notational system is the **SODA** system. This system considers four general types of misarticulations: (a) **substitutions**, (b) **omissions**, (c) **distortions**, and (d) **additions** (SODA). Examples of these patterns are provided in Table 4–1. The speech sound misarticulations demonstrated by children with a functional disorder that are of a residual nature are often described using the SODA system. The second notational system is used in instances when a child exhibits a severe speech sound disorder (e.g., speech delay). The system describes the speech pattern according to

Table 4–1. The SODA Patterns of Speech Misarticulations and Some of the More Commonly Occurring Phonological Processes

Error Patterns	*Examples*	
SODA Patterns		
Substitution	rabbit → wabbit	cat → tat
Omission	hat → at	blue → bue
Distortion[a]	soup → *oup	ladder → *adder
Additions	green → gareen	swim → sawim
Phonological Process		
Final consonant deletion	hat → ha	leaf → lea
Stopping of fricatives	fish → pish	zoo → doo
Cluster reduction	spoon → poon	broom → boom
Gliding of liquids	lazy → wazy	broom → bwoom

Note. [a]Distortions involve the substitution of a phoneme with an undecipherable sound. The * is used to denote an undecipherable sound.

large classes of sounds that may be misarticulated; these patterns are referred to as **phonological processes** (or patterns). Examples of common phonological patterns are shown in Table 4–1.

Age Expectancy Estimation

Once the speech patterns demonstrated by the child are determined, the speech-language pathologist decides whether these patterns are acceptable or disordered. The child's age is an important factor when determining whether a speech sound disorder exists. Normative data are available to the speech-language pathologist to guide in the decision. The normative data are presented in two ways: (a) age of mastery and (b) age of suppression. Using **age of mastery** norms involves examining each misarticulated sound produced by the child about the age at which the sound should be acquired.

If a child is unable to produce a sound after the age at which it should normally be acquired, the child is assumed to be disordered in the production of the sound. For example, the /g/ sound is normally acquired by the age of 3 years (see Figure 4–6). If a 6-year-old child demonstrated misarticulations of /g/, there would be cause for concern. **Age of suppression** norms refer to the age at which specific phonological patterns should no longer be apparent in a child's speech. If a child still demonstrates a particular phonological pattern after the age at which it should have disappeared, the child would be exhibiting a disorder. For example, the phonological pattern of final consonant deletion ("hat" is produced as "*ha*") should disappear by the age of 3 to 6 years. If a 4-year-old child is observed deleting final consonants, there would be cause for concern. Some age of disappearance (suppression) norms for phonological patterns are listed in Table 4–2.

Severity Estimation

For a child found to demonstrate a speech sound disorder, the speech-language pathologist next determines the severity of the disorder. Severity refers to the effect of the disorder on the intelligibility of speech. Intelligibility is defined as a listener's ability to understand a speaker's words. This judgment can be based on **qualitative** and **quan-**

Table 4–2. Age of Suppression for Some of the More Commonly Occurring Phonological Patterns

Phonological Pattern	*Example*	*Age of Suppression*
Velar fronting	gun → dun	3 years
Final consonant deletion	bat → ba	3;6 years
Unstressed syllable deletion	balloon → loon	4 years
Gliding of liquids	rabbit → wabbit	4 years
Vowelization	flower → flowa	4 years

titative criteria. A qualitative criterion involves an impressionistic judgment as to the impact of the disorder on the clarity of the child's communication. This may simply involve a judgment by the speech-language pathologist using a continuum of good-fair-poor. This estimation is generally influenced by the characteristics of the speech sound disorder. For example, a pattern involving a high number of consonant omissions is likely to result in a severity judgment of "poor," compared with a pattern involving a simple substitution of one sound for another such as "f" used in place of "th" (thumb is pronounced as "*fumb*," which would be a judgment of fair). Another qualitative scale of speech severity involves judgments by the child's parents or teachers regarding how well the child communicates. For example, a teacher might be asked to rate how well they understand the child on a 10-point scale, with 1 meaning all the time and 10 meaning never.

A quantitative estimate of severity is based on more objective criteria such as (a) the exact number of misarticulated phonemes, (b) the length of time the disorder has existed, and (c) the age of the child. A popular measure of severity is known as the percentage of consonants correct (Shriberg, 2003). The **percentage of consonants correct** is calculated from the phonetic inventory by tabulating the total number of consonants produced in a speech sample (both correct and incorrect) and dividing this into the total number of consonants that were produced correctly. The formula is as follows:

$$\frac{\text{Number of correct consonants}}{\text{Total number of consonants}} \times 100 =$$

$$\text{\% of consonants correct}$$

On the basis of the percentage of consonants correct calculation, the severity of the disorder is categorized as normal to mild (85%–100%), mild to moderate (65%–84%), moderate to severe (50%–64%), or severe (below 50%).

Oral-Facial Examination

The assessment continues with an examination of the child's oral-facial patterns. This aspect of the assessment is designed to rule out whether there are anatomical reasons for the child's speech sound difficulties. Assessment of the oral-facial mechanism is divided into two key areas: (a) structure and (b) function. Some individuals with a speech sound disorder may show structural and/or functional peculiarities that affect speech sound production, including dental malocclusion, cleft palate, and tongue abnormalities. Structural assessment includes examination of the lips, teeth, tongue, hard palate, and soft palate. The functional assessment involves examination of the same structures in a variety of speaking and nonspeaking tasks. These tasks are designed to evaluate the **range of motion**, **strength**, and **rate of movement**. The information derived from this examination helps to guide the speech-language pathologist in determining the nature of the speech sound disorder. The information also can shed light on the client's general oral-motor skills, which can be useful when developing a treatment program. A simple checklist of features considered in an oral-facial examination is provided in Table 4–3.

TREATMENT OF CHILD SPEECH SOUND DISORDERS

Decisions about whether to treat and how often the child should be seen are based primarily on the severity of the disorder. Treatment for a speech sound disorder is important not only for the child

Table 4–3. Example of Typical Oral-Facial Examination

Oral Facial Examination		
	Structure	***Function***
Lips	Symmetry: ________ Scarring: ________	Purse: ________ Retract: ________ Purse and retract: ________
Teeth	Alignment: ________ Gap or missing teeth: ________ Facial pattern: ________	
Tongue	Scarring: ________	Moves side to side: ________ Moves up and down: ________ Moves in and out: ________
Hard Palate	Vault height: ________ Vault width: ________ Scarring: ________	
Soft Palate	Symmetry: ________ Scarring: ________	Lifts on sustained "ah": ________ Lifts on repeated "ah": ________ Symmetry of movement: ________

to be able to accurately form speech sounds but for other reasons as well. Children who have a speech sound disorder may also have academic difficulties in subject areas such as spelling or reading. Furthermore, children whose speech articulation differs from that of their peers can find themselves frustrated and bullied and may become less willing to participate in play or classroom activities. The prognosis for children with speech sound disorders generally is good. For many children, the problem resolves spontaneously. It is reported that in 75% of children with mild or moderate forms of the disorder, and whose problems do not stem from a medical condition, the disorder is resolved by the age of 6 years. In many other cases, children who receive treatment eventually develop normal or close to normal speech. In some instances, there may be mild misarticulations that last until adulthood, but speech is completely understandable. For children with a phonological disorder due to a structural or neurological cause, the outcome generally is dependent on how well the underlying cause of the problem is treated.

The types of treatment available to resolve a speech sound disorder can be categorized into two primary approaches: (a) the articulation approach and (b) the phonological approach. Within each of these approaches, there are variations in management techniques.

Articulation Approach

The **articulation approach** focuses on motoric aspects of producing individual consonants and vowels. Techniques include the use of mirrors, tongue depressors, oral-motor exercises, and sensory motor training. Repetitive practice in correctly saying the misarticulated sounds is an integral part of treatment. Two well-known techniques that use a motor-oriented framework of speech treatment are the traditional approach and the maximal contrast approach.

> **FYI**
>
> Children with a speech sound disorder typically receive individualized treatment from a speech-language pathologist on a twice weekly basis. The duration of each therapy session lasts between 30 min and 1 hr, depending on the age of the child and the severity of the disorder.

Traditional Approach

The traditional approach was first developed by Charles Van Riper. This style of treatment emphasizes correct articulation of individual speech sounds. Through a series of graduated steps, the child is taught to consciously learn to produce the sound. The child must be successful at each step before proceeding to the next level of speaking complexity. The first step involves sensori-perceptual (ear) training, whereby the child must first be able to correctly perceive the target speech sound as spoken by others before attempting to produce the sound. The ensuing steps entail teaching the child to articulate the sound in short syllables, followed by words, then sentences, and eventually, in a conversational speaking context. The sounds targeted for treatment are those that should have been mastered earliest by the child but are not yet articulated correctly (see Figure 4–6).

Maximal Contrast Approach

There is debate over the way children with more severe forms of a speech sound disorder should be treated. A child with a severe speech sound disorder may exhibit misarticulations of early developing as well as later-developing speech sounds. Some speech-language pathologists believe sounds that are learned later in development should be addressed first in therapy, even if the child has not yet learned to produce some of the earlier developing sounds. Research has shown that earlier developing sounds are likely to improve on their own, so it may not be necessary to target them in therapy. The focus of the **maximal contrast approach** is to enact widespread change in children with a severe speech sound disorder. Rather than targeting early developing sounds, later-developing sounds are the focus of therapy. Presumably, targeting these more difficult sounds assists in filling the gap for less difficult sounds.

Phonological Approach

Whereas traditional and maximal contrast approaches focus on teaching the child to articulate specific sounds correctly, the **phonological approach** focuses on having the child change their phonological system using cognitive techniques such as semantic images. The phonological approach is used in cases where children have multiple misarticulations (e.g., speech delay) and highly unintelligible speech. Presumably, using a phonological treatment approach with severely unintelligible children shortens the length of time necessary to improve their sound systems. Two phonological treatment approaches are the cycles approach and minimal pairs approach.

Cycles Approach

This **cycles approach** was developed by Hodson and Paden (1991). The general idea behind the approach is to facilitate the emergence of speech sound patterns rather than attempt to work on mastery of individual speech sounds. For example, if a child is showing the phonological patterns of final consonant deletion (e.g., "hat" is produced as "ha"), cluster reduction (e.g., "blue" is produced as "bue"), and stopping of fricatives (e.g., "see" is produced as "tee"), the treatment program would involve working on each of these patterns in a staggered fashion. A typical treatment cycle might involve working on final consonant deletion for 2 weeks, then switching to cluster reduction for 2 weeks, followed by stopping of fricatives for 2 weeks. At the conclusion of this cycle, the speech-language pathologist probes to determine whether the child's overall pattern of speech sound production is improving. If not, another cycle of therapy would commence with possible changes to the particular sounds targeted during a treatment session.

FYI

The electropalatograph is a recording device that provides a form of biofeedback to a client with speech articulation difficulties. A specifically designed acrylic palate is created that contains touch-sensitive sensors spaced along the surface of the palate. The device is attached to the roof of a person's mouth and can detect the location and amount of contact between the tongue and palate during the articulation of speech. A visual display of the location of tongue–palate contact is provided on a computer monitor. The device is used primarily for research but is gaining popularity as an alternative approach to the treatment of some speech disorders (Lee, 2021).

Minimal Pairs Approach

A **minimal pair** refers to a situation where two words differ in pronunciation by only one sound, and the change in sound results in a change in word meaning. For instance, the words "sea" and "seat" differ only by the absence or presence of the last consonant /t/, and this difference signals a change in meaning. For a phonologically disordered child who deletes final consonants, it is likely the child would produce "seat" as "sea." A minimal pair treatment approach might involve the speech-language pathologist presenting pictures of "sea" and "seat" simultaneously to the child. In a game format, the child would be instructed to name one of the pictures, with the speech-language pathologist guessing which picture was named. Because the child is likely to produce both words as "sea," the speech-language pathologist would deliberately point to the picture of "sea" even when the child had intended the alternate "seat." Thus, to resolve this confusion, the child must learn to revise productions until the speech-language pathologist is no longer confused between the two words.

Phonological Awareness

As an adjunct to both articulation and phonological approaches to the management of speech sound disorders, it is important to consider the child's understanding of the speech sound system. Treatment programs often rely on the repeated production of speech sounds and may fail to link the child's awareness with production. **Phonological awareness** refers to the ability to think about and manipulate the sound system apart from meaning. Children with impaired phonology may have incomplete (or inaccurate) awareness of their speech sound system. Training in the types of skills that deliberately involve phonological awareness has been shown to help children change their disordered phonological system as well as help children with literacy (reading) problems (Gillon, 2018). A simple phonological awareness task involves the child's recognition of words that rhyme (e.g., asking the child, "Do the words 'cat' and 'hat' sound alike?"). A more complicated phonological awareness task involves the child's ability to segment sounds and words (e.g., asking the child, "How many words do you hear in the sentence, '*I have a blue pen*'?"). Examples of phonological awareness tasks, ranging in level of complexity, are provided in Figure 4–15.

CULTURAL CONSIDERATIONS AND CHILD SPEECH SOUND DISORDERS

English is spoken throughout the world. Although the English of England might be construed as the true mother tongue of the language, there are enormous varieties in spoken English. Each variety of English is often described in reference to the geographic region where the language is spoken, with geographically rich varieties of the language. We find English varieties such as British English, Irish English, Australian English, American English, New Zealand English, South African English, Indian English, and Singapore English, to name a few. Each variety is characterized by

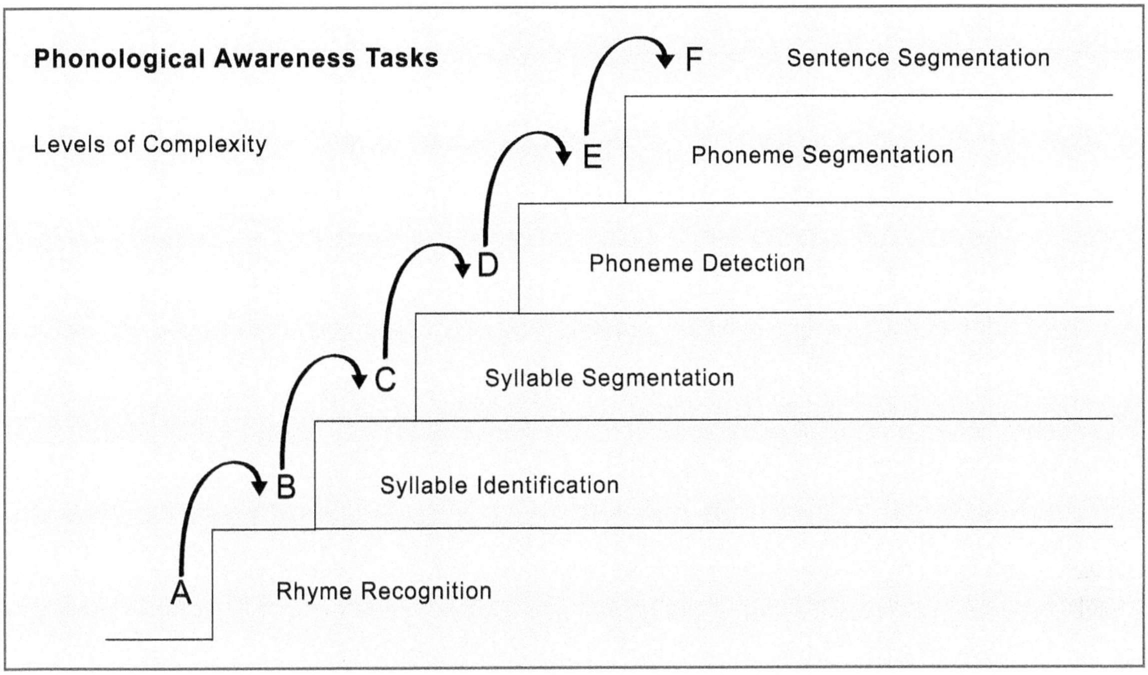

FIGURE 4–15. Examples of phonological awareness tasks according to increasing levels of complexity.

dialectical features, including unique vocabulary and specific phonological patterns. **Dialect** refers to a regional variety of a particular language. Dialects are distinguished by variations in vocabulary (word choice), grammar, and pronunciation. They are based on geography or socioeconomic level. **Geographic dialects** are the most common form of dialect. They are thought to be related to the immigration of certain ethnicities to specific regions of a country. The dialect reflects the vestiges (i.e., roots) of the original language. Examples of geographic dialects found in England and the United States are shown in Figure 4–16.

Socioeconomic dialects are less common, with word choice being one of the more obvious features. Individuals who vary in income level, educational level, and occupation may be found to speak differently than individuals residing within the same geographic region. For example, consider the term used in England to describe pieces of candy. Individuals from high economic levels often use the term "sweets," whereas someone from a lower economic class is likely to use the term "lollies."

The term **accent** refers to the manner of pronunciation of a language. Accents are found in all varieties of English. For example, a common feature of New Zealand English is the "vowelization" of postvocalic /r/ ("bear" → "bea-ah") that is produced throughout most of the country. Yet in the most southern region of the same country, the postvocalic /r/ is clearly produced. This peculiar variation in pronunciation is attributed to a large Scottish immigrant population in the southern part of New Zealand, which is known to produce a distinct /r/. A wide range of variation is also found in American English production, including New England English, Appalachian English, and African American English.

There is a popular misconception that African American English (AAE) is incorrect, lazy, defective, ungrammatical, and broken English. On the contrary, evidence from many years of linguistic investigation establishes that AAE is a legitimate, rule-governed, socially constructed variety of American English. **Orlando Taylor** (b.1936; Figure 4–17) was a speech-language pathology professor who stressed that the variety of English spoken by Black/African Americans was distinct rule-governed system rather than a "deficient" use of standard English (Taylor, 1969). Taylor and several other colleagues coined the term *ebonics*, derived from the combination of *ebony* and *phonics*, to describe the patterns of AAE. Taylor was a

FIGURE 4–16. **A.** The approximate geographic boundaries for various accents of English spoken in England. **B.** The approximate geographic boundaries for various accents of English spoken in the United States.

fierce advocate of Black children and maintained they were often objects of racial and linguistic prejudice inflicted upon them by their teachers and peers because of the way they talked. He helped raise awareness of the rich cultural history and origins of AAE. Charity (2008) and Green (2002) noted that speakers of AAE can be at different points on a continuum, ranging from mainstream English to AAE. The evaluation of children who may produce phonological features of AAE needs to consider that some speech patterns reflect an acceptable variety of English rather than a speech sound disorder. Some examples of phonological variation found in AAE are listed in Table 4–4.

FIGURE 4–17. Orlando Taylor, American professor who identified and described the rule-governed speech and language characteristics of Black/African American English.

Bilingualism refers to the ability to communicate in two languages. This ability can be found in four modalities: (a) speaking, (b) understanding, (c) reading, and (d) writing. **Multilingualism** is the ability to communicate in more than two languages. An individual who is multilingual can also be referred to as a polyglot (i.e., multiple tongues). Approximately 50% of the world's population is bilingual. Indeed, individuals who speak only one language (i.e., monolingual) are becoming the exception rather than the norm. The learning of two or more languages can occur simultaneously or consecutively. A simultaneous bilingual is one who has learned two or more languages at precisely the same time and continues to use multiple languages. Simultaneous bilinguals use both languages effortlessly and will not display any form of foreign accent when speaking various languages. A consecutive bilingual is one whose second language was learned sometime after learning a first language. In this case, the first language is referred to as L1, and the second language is L2. The majority of the world's bilinguals are consecutive and exhibit an accent in their L2 speech. When the L2 spoken is English, the term **English as a second language (ESL)** is used.

Table 4–4. Variation Found to Occur in Spoken African American English

Consonant Feature	***Examples***
ask/aks alternation	*I aks him a question*
ing/in alternation	*He's runnin' fast*
Final consonant deletion in clusters	find as *fine*; hand as *han*
Initial "th" as [d]; final "th" as [d,t,s,z,f,v]	they as *day,* with as *wif,* with as *wit*
/s/ as [d] before /n/	isn't as *idn't*; wasn't as *wadn't*
Glide [j] as consonant	computer as *compooter*, Houston as *Hooston*
Syllable stress shift from second to first syllable	POlice, UMbrella

Source: From "African American English: An Overview," by A. H. Charity, 2008, *Perspectives on Communication Disorders and Sciences in Culturally and Linguistically Diverse Populations*, *15*, pp. 33–42.

When we encounter a foreign language, our natural tendency is to hear it in terms of the sounds of our own language. We perceive it differently from the way native speakers do. Equally, when we speak a foreign language, we tend to attempt to do so using the familiar sounds and sound patterns of our mother tongue. This is the well-documented phenomenon known as **phonological interference.** Our L1 (mother tongue) interferes with our attempts to produce the L2 (target language). Phonological interference can occur in many ways. Perhaps the most common interference concerns sounds in the L2 that are not found in the L1. In these cases, the speaker of the L2 may either replace the foreign sound with one found in the L1 or completely delete the sound. Some aspects of accented speech are generally attributed to differences in the phonemic inventories of a speaker's native language and their second language. Some examples for French, Spanish, and Mandarin are provided next, all of which pertain to production of the phoneme /ð/ (the first sound in the English word "this"). In each of these languages, this particular phoneme is not found in the native L1.

- *French.* In French-accented English, the French phoneme /z/ is often produced as a substitute for the English phoneme /ð/. For example, the word "thee" is likely to be produced as "zee."
- *Spanish.* In Spanish-accented English, the Spanish phoneme /d/ is often produced as a substitute for the English phoneme /ð/. So instead of saying "this," the speaker is likely to say "dis."
- *Mandarin.* In Mandarin-accented English, the English phoneme /ð/ frequently sounds like a soft "d," produced with the tongue either immediately behind the front teeth or protruding slightly from the mouth.

An issue that confronts the speech-language pathologist when evaluating the speech of an ESL speaker is determining whether the speech pattern demonstrated is indicative of a phonological difference or a phonological disorder. A **phonological difference** is a pattern where the sound productions are within the norms for the community but different from the standard. For instance, a person who produces Mandarin-accented English is likely to pronounce English in the same way as other speakers of Mandarin-accented English (Miao et al., 2023). Speech therapy is not warranted for an ESL speaker showing a phonological difference. Rather, the speech pattern is considered normal and serves a communicative function as well as a social solidarity function. Sometimes an accent or dialect may be a problem if it interferes with a person's goals in life. For example, an ESL speaker may choose to receive therapy to help reduce their accent, such as a Japanese executive who wishes to do business with American companies. Another situation might be when an aspiring actor from a European country wishes to "lose" his foreign accent by learning the standard form of the L2. This type of therapy would be considered elective as opposed to mandatory and could be provided by the speech-language pathologist.

FYI

Click sounds serve as phonemes in some South African languages. Clicks are produced on ingressive (inward) airflow compared with all other phonemes, which are produced on egressive (outward) airflow. However, click sounds are sometimes found in languages when we least expect them, including English. For example, consider the ingressive sound sometimes used to express regret or disapproval, written as tsk-tsk.

It is possible that a bilingual speaker might show a speech sound disorder. In this condition, the sound productions of the speaker fall outside the norms of the community. Referring to a Mandarin-accented English speaker, this would be a situation in which the individual's speech productions of English differ from those of other Mandarin-accented English speakers. As is often the case, if the person's L2 speech is found to be disordered, the L1 speech is most likely disordered as well. For the speech-language pathologist to make this diagnosis, they would need to be aware of the phonological rules of the accent.

SUMMARY OF CHAPTER

Children who have a speech sound disorder are unable to accurately produce certain consonants and vowels by the age at which they are expected. The severity of a speech sound disorder can range from speech that is completely incomprehensible to speech that can be understood by everyone but with a few slightly mispronounced sounds. The types of speech sound disorders can be organized into three categories based on the presumed cause of the disorder: (a) structural, (b) neurological, and (c) functional. Structural and neurological disorders are sometimes referred to as articulation disorders because the cause of the disorder is related to problems in the motor movements required to produce clear speech. Functional disorders are simply referred to as speech sound disorders because there are no clearly identifiable motor problems. The goal of assessment is to obtain and establish an accurate profile of the child's speech sound production abilities. Some of the fundamental steps in performing a phonological assessment include (a) conducting speech sampling, (b) collecting a phonetic inventory, (c) describing speech patterns, (d) estimating age expectancy, (e) estimating severity, and (f) performing an oral-facial examination. Treatment of a speech sound disorder is important for improving the child's communication abilities and may also facilitate the child's academic skills in areas such as spelling or reading.

CHILD SPEECH SOUND DISORDERS ON THE WORLD WIDE WEB

Following are websites that provide further information on the topic of speech sound disorders. At the time of publication, each website was freely accessible.

Sounds of Speech (App)
http://soundsofspeech.uiowa.edu/index.html#english

Introduction to Phonetics
https://www.youtube.com/watch?v=Kxsw7eS270w

Speech Sound Disorders
https://www.youtube.com/watch?v=VPQ6txx3FQw

Childhood Apraxia of Speech Association of North America (CASANA)
http://www.apraxia-kids.org/

Phonological Awareness
https://www.canterbury.ac.nz/education/research/phonological-awareness-resources/

STUDY QUESTIONS

1. List and describe the consonant and vowel classification systems.
2. What are the three categories of speech sound disorders?
3. List and describe the six steps involved in performing an assessment of child speech sound disorders.
4. What are the two approaches to treating child speech sound disorders?
5. What is phonological interference, and how does this influence the diagnosis of a speech sound disorder?

REFERENCES

Charity, A. H. (2008). African American English: An overview. *Perspectives on Communication Disorders and Sciences in Culturally and Linguistically Diverse Populations, 15*, 33–42.

Chomsky, N., & Halle, M. (1968). *The sound pattern of English*. Harper & Row.

Donegan, P., & Stampe, D. (1979). The study of natural phonology. In D. A. Dinnsen (Ed.), *Current approaches to phonological theory* (pp. 126–173). University Press.

Fairbanks, G. (1940). *Voice and articulation drillbook*. Harper & Brothers.

Geruit, J., & Morrisette, M. (2005). The clinical significance of optimality theory for phonological disorders. *Topics in Language Disorders, 25*, 266–280.

Gillon, G. (2018). *Phonological awareness: From research to practice* (2nd ed.). Guilford Press.
Green, L. (2002). *African American English: A linguistic introduction*. Cambridge University Press.
Hayiou-Thomas, M., Carroll, J., Leavett, R., Hulme, C., & Snowling, M. (2017). When does speech sound disorder matter for literacy? The role of disordered speech errors, co-occurring language impairment and family risk of dyslexia. *Journal of Child Psychology and Psychiatry, 58*, 197–205.
Hodson, B. W., & Paden, E. P. (1991). *Targeting intelligible speech* (2nd ed.). College-Hill Press.
Lee, A. (2021). Electropalatography. In M. Ball (Ed.), *Manual of clinical phonetics* (pp. 339–355). Routledge.
McLeod, S., & Crowe, K. (2018). Children's consonant acquisition in 27 languages: A cross-linguistic review. *American Journal of Speech-Language Pathology, 27*, 1546–1571.
Miao, Y., Rose, H., & Hosseini, S. (2023). The interaction effect of pronunciation and lexicogrammar on comprehensibility: A case of Mandarin-accented English. *Language and Speech*. https://doi.org/10.1177/00238309231156918
Mowrer, O. H. (1960). *Learning theory and behavior*. Wiley.
Rousey, C. (1957). The psychopathology of articulation and voice deviations. In L. E. Travis (Ed.), *Handbook of speech pathology and audiology* (pp. 831–853). Prentice-Hall.
Scripture, E. W. (1912). *Stuttering and lisping*. Macmillan.
Shriberg, L. (2003). Diagnostic markers for child speech-sound disorders: Introductory comments. *Clinical Linguistics and Phonetics, 17*, 501–505.
Taylor, O. (1969). *An introduction to the historical development of Black English: Some implication for American education*. Presented at the Institute of Speech and Language of Rural and Urban Poor, Ohio University.
Templin, M. (1957). *Certain language skills in children*. University of Minnesota Press.
Travis, L. E. (1931). *Speech pathology: A dynamic neurological treatment of normal speech and speech deviations*. Appleton-Century.
Van Riper, C. (1947). *Speech correction: Principles and methods*. Prentice-Hall.

5

FLUENCY DISORDERS

OBJECTIVES

After reading this chapter, the student should be able to:

- Define and describe speech fluency and factors that interfere with fluency.
- Understand the cross-cultural and cross-linguistic differences that may impact communication.
- Understand the etiologies of various types of fluency disorders, including stuttering, neurogenic and psychogenic fluency disorders, and cluttering.
- Understand the nature, characteristics, and onset of stuttering.
- Understand past and present theoretical models concerning the etiology of stuttering.
- Describe methods for evaluating and measuring disfluent speech.
- Describe the role of family involvement in the prevention and intervention strategies for young children and adolescents.
- Describe procedures for the treatment of stuttering.
- Understand the role of age and culture in the management and treatment of stuttering.
- Understand the diagnostic and treatment principles for clients who demonstrate cluttering, neurogenic disfluency, and psychogenic disfluency.

KEY TERMS

Fluency Disorder
Fluency
Disfluency
Stuttering
Cluttering
King Louis II
Rudolf Schulthess
Phonophobia
Lalophobia
A. Thome
James Hunt
Johann Friedrich Dieffenbach
James Yearsley
Lee Edward Travis
Charles Van Riper
Wendell Johnson
Bryng Bryngelson
Sigmund Freud
Lena Rustin
Deso Weiss
National Institute on Deafness and Other Communication Disorders
Stammering
Primary Characteristics
Between-Word Disfluencies
Within-Word Disfluencies
Stuttering-Like Disfluencies
Other Disfluencies
Bodily Movements
Psychosocial Behaviors
Temperament
Neurogenic Stuttering
Psychogenic Stuttering
Demands and Capacities Theory
Covert Repair Theory
Neuropsycholinguistic Theory
Iowa Scale for Rating the Severity of Stuttering
Stuttering Severity Instrument
Severity Scale
Speaking Rate
Fluency Shaping
Continuous Phonation
Stuttering Modification
Parent-Directed Therapy
Lidcombe Program
Hypnotherapy
Drug Therapy
Electronic Devices
Altered Auditory Feedback

INTRODUCTION

Most of us have met someone with a fluency disorder or know of someone who has a **fluency disorder** (Figure 5–1). The peculiarity of the disorder is undeniable and is one of the most identifiable communication disorders by both trained and untrained listeners. When speech-language pathologists are asked to provide a general description of their occupation to a layperson, mentioning the treatment of individuals with a fluency disorder is readily recognizable. After holding a conversation with a person who has a fluency disorder, one may wonder: (a) What caused the disorder? (b) Can the disorder be cured? and (c) What can I, as a listener, do to best communicate with a person who has a fluency disorder? The answers to some of these questions are still unknown, but we do know a great deal about fluency approaches that help improve a person's ability to produce speech fluently. It is interesting to note that some of the world's leading experts in the area of fluency disorders were drawn to the field because they themselves have a fluency disorder. Who would be a better expert than someone who has first-hand experience with the disorder? There is a documented history of research on fluency disorders that has led to a wealth of information on the topic. The information presented in this chapter is an introduction to the fascinating area of fluency disorders.

FIGURE 5–1. Pictures drawn by children in response to instructions, "draw a picture of what it feels like to stutter." (Permission granted by Andriana diGrande, New England Fluency Program, United States.)

TERMINOLOGY AND DEFINITIONS

The term **fluency** refers to the effortless flow of speech. Fluency encompasses many features that contribute to this effortless flow, such as (a) the rate or quickness of a person's speech, (b) the silent periods or pauses that may occur within or between words, (c) the stress or emphasis placed on various syllables or words, and (d) the inflection or intonation used by the speaker during the production of an utterance. Collectively, we think of fluent speech as the pleasant sing-song pattern of talking. Fluency encompasses qualities that make speech sound natural and normal. This definition is specific to the spoken word; however, fluency can also apply to other areas of communication such as written language.

The term **disfluency** is the opposite condition, whereby a disruption or breakdown in the flow of speech occurs. A change in any single feature, or combination of features, that contributes to fluent speech can result in disfluent speech. For example, excessively fast speaking can interfere with the correct articulation of vowels and consonants, thereby affecting the naturalness of speech. Unusually long pauses between the syllables of words can likewise affect speech naturalness. It is important to keep in mind that speech disfluencies naturally occur. We all encounter moments of disfluent speech, although this does not necessarily mean we have a fluency disorder. The simple interjection of "um" between words or changing our choice of words in midconversation would classify as forms of disfluency. The job of the speech-language pathologist is to distinguish between what are considered normal, natural speech disfluencies and those that are unnatural speech disfluencies. When speech disfluencies fall outside the boundary of what is considered natural, they are deemed to represent a fluency disorder. The two fluency disorders profiled in this chapter are **stuttering** and **cluttering**.

There is a bit of confusion in the terminology surrounding fluency disorders. Students frequently ask whether the terms *<u>dis</u>fluency* and *<u>dys</u>fluency* are interchangeable. The answer is no, although the terms have been used interchangeably as recently as the 1990s. The prefix *dis* has its origins in Latin and is used to form words that are the opposite of the core word, such as *honor* versus *dishonor*, and *able* versus *disable*. Alternatively, the prefix *dys* has its origins in Greek and refers to something bad, harsh, or wrong, such as *function* versus *dysfunction*. We all demonstrate disruptions in fluency. To ascribe the prefix dys to this condition would be too strong a description. Rather, the disruption in fluency simply reflects the opposite state. Therefore, the term disfluency is preferred for the disruptions in speech that occur normally in most speakers.

HISTORIC ASPECTS OF FLUENCY DISORDERS

Observations regarding fluency disorders, specifically stuttering, can be traced back centuries. A list of notable individuals (past and present) known (or thought) to have a fluency disorder is provided in Table 5–1. Some of the earliest documented reports of individuals who stuttered include Moses. There is a report in the Old Testament that Moses stuttered as depicted in the passage, "*O Lord, I have never been a man of ready speech, never in my life, not even now that thou has spoken to me; I am slow and hesitant of speech*" (Exodus 4:10). The Roman Emperor Claudius (10 BC to AD 54) was assumed to produce stuttered speech and showed signs of deafness. **King Louis II** of France (843–879; Figure 5–2) was also known to produce a stutter. He was called *le Begue* or "the Stammerer." The 2010 film *The King's Speech* profiled the impact of stuttering on the life of King George VI of England (1895–1952).

Because of the unusual pattern of speaking associated with stuttering, the disorder has been of high scientific and medical curiosity. The interest has centered on determining either the cause of stuttering or how to cure the condition. During the late 1700s and early 1800s, the root cause of stuttering was thought to be related to faulty functioning of the tongue and/or larynx. Jean-Marc Gaspard Itard (1774–1838), a physician at the Institute of Deaf Mutes in Paris, was the first to view stuttering as a pathological condition. In his opinion, stuttering was caused by a spasm induced by a weakness of the motor organs of the larynx and tongue. The Swiss scientist **Rudolf Schulthess** (1802–1833) also believed stuttering was due to spasms of the larynx and suggested using the terms **phonophobia** or **lalophobia** to describe the condition.

FYI

The origins of the word "stuttering" are unclear, but there are a few possibilities as to its derivation. The word *stue* is from a Greek word that means "to strike." There is a Nordic word *stytta*, which means "to stop." There is also an old German word *stutten* that means "to make a series of repeated sounds."

Toward the middle of the 19th century, there was a shift from viewing the tongue and larynx as causal factors of stuttering toward viewing stuttering as a disturbance in the breathing patterns

Table 5–1. Famous People Known to Have Displayed Stuttering

Rowan Atkinson	British actor	Marilyn Monroe	American actor
Emily Blunt	British actor	Sam Neill	New Zealand actor
Joseph Biden	46th president of the United States	Isaac Newton	Scientist
Lewis Carroll	Author of Alice in Wonderland	Ed Sheeran	British singer
Winston Churchill	Former prime minister of England	George Springer	American baseball player
Charles Darwin	British naturalist	Megan Washington	Australian musician
King George VI	Former King of England	Bruce Willis	American actor
James Earl Jones	American actor		

FIGURE 5 –2. King Louis II of France was called "le Begue" or "the Stammerer."

for speech. For example, the German scholar **A. Thome** (1867) held the opinion that stuttering was a result of spasms of the respiratory organs that were linked to an individual's emotional state. The disturbance of stuttering was triggered by emotionally based disruptions in the nervous system. Two types of emotional conditions were assumed to contribute to moments of stuttering: (a) embarrassment or lack of confidence and (b) excessive rapidity of thought. **James Hunt** (1833–1869) was a British speech therapist who wrote an early textbook on the topic of stuttering entitled *Stammering and Stuttering: Their Nature and Treatment*. The book was first published in 1861 and was continually reprinted up to 1967. Hunt was also known to provide speech therapy to some famous individuals at the time who happened to stutter, including Lewis Carroll.

During the 1800s, approaches to the treatment of stuttering also varied widely. Believing the tongue was responsible for stuttering led Itard to develop a small forked golden plate that was placed under the tongue to provide support while speaking. More drastic treatment of the tongue was proposed by German surgeon **Johann Friedrich Dieffenbach** (1792–1847; Figure 5–3) who recommended cutting the tongue with scissors and removing a triangular wedge from the back of the tongue. **James Yearsley** (1805–1869) was a British surgeon who advocated removal of the tonsils as a form of treatment for stuttering. All these invasive procedures were ultimately abandoned for two reasons. First, performing surgery in this region of the body carries a level of danger because the speech organs receive heavy blood supply (i.e., they are highly vascular). Therefore, surgery performed in this part of the body was risky. A surgical error could lead to considerable blood loss and subsequent death. The second reason for abandoning invasive techniques was that the various surgical procedures were not found to be successful in curing stuttering.

During the first half of the 20th century, there was continued interest in isolating the cause and cure of stuttering. Although research undertaken during this period was less invasive than in earlier years, the approaches were no less unusual. **Lee Edward Travis** (1896–1987; Figure 5–4), who

FIGURE 5–3. Johann Friedrich Dieffenbach, German surgeon who recommended cutting out portions of the tongue to treat stuttering.

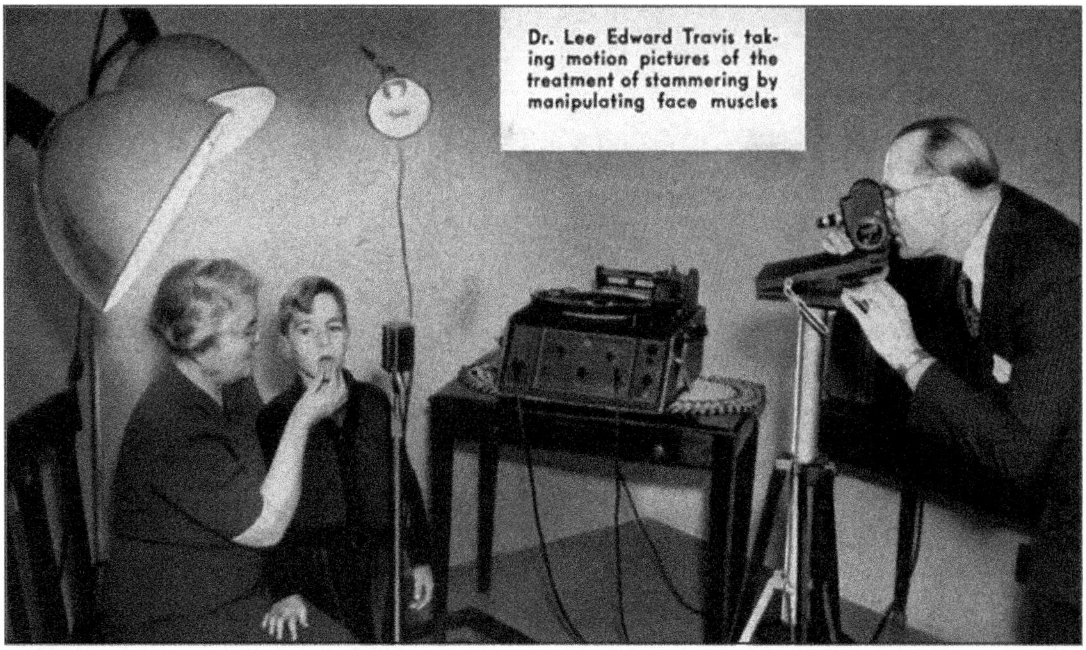

FIGURE 5–4. Lee Travis (in 1940), known as the father of speech-language pathology, had a strong research interest in stuttering.

is considered a founding father of the speech-language pathology profession in the United States, devoted a majority of his career to understanding the cause of stuttering. Travis held the view that people who stutter have speech centers in both cerebral hemispheres of their brain instead of just the left hemisphere. According to Travis, stuttering resulted from a lack of brain dominance when it came to producing speech. As a result of this condition, when an individual began to organize the act of speech in their brain, the two sides of the brain were competing for control of the speech muscles. This competition led to a breakdown in the forward flow of speech and resulted in a stutter. This theory was based on Travis's observation that people who were naturally left-handed but "forced" to be right-handers were more likely to stutter than pure right-handers. Presumably, this situation led to a lack of clear brain dominance in motor execution, which included speech execution. In the early 1930s, Travis studied a group of people who stuttered that were naturally left-handed individuals but had been forced at an early age to write and perform other tasks with their right hand. Two of these research participants later became eminent scholars in the field of stuttering: **Charles Van Riper** (1905–1994) and **Wendell Johnson** (1906–1965). Van Riper (1981) is quoted as saying that to restore their left-handedness, "Both of us [Van Riper & Johnson] wore plaster casts upon our right arms to enforce left-handedness and again I found myself doing the interminable pages of talking and writing each day." The activity did little to alleviate the production of stuttered speech.

Bryng Bryngelson (1892–1979) received his doctorate from the University of Iowa and went on to have a successful career at the University of Minnesota. Bryngelson is remembered for his research on the relationship between stuttering and left-handedness. However, after spending nearly 30 years on the topic, there was little evidence to suggest that shifting handedness would alleviate the production of stuttered speech. One of Bryngelson's important contributions to the field of stuttering therapy was his concept of voluntary stuttering. Having an individual who stutters do so deliberately in public settings helped to lower the anxiety associated with speaking situations. This reduction in anxiety led to a corresponding decrease in the frequency of stuttering. Gradually, deliberate stuttering was decreased with the aim of always producing stutter-free speech.

The area of stuttering in the early 1900s was also influenced by **Sigmund Freud's** (1856–1939) psychoanalytic theory. The cause of stuttering was felt to be a result of a deep-seated psychological disturbance, and family relationships, especially parent–child relationships, were thought to lay at the root of the problem. An adaptation of this perspective was proposed by Wendell Johnson who felt stuttering was caused by the parents' misinterpretations of their child's speech (Figure 5–5). Parents confused the child's normal disfluency for stuttering. According to Johnson (1961), "Stuttering begins not in the child's mouth but in the parent's ear." Because of this confusion, parents required from the child a level of speaking performance that the child could not attain. The subsequent reactions of both child and parents resulted in a worsening of the child's speech, leading to stuttering. In 1939, Johnson tested this theory in what is now known as the Iowa Stuttering Study. In this study, 12 nonstuttering children who were residents in an orphanage were induced to stutter. Of these 12 children, one half were told they had symptoms of stuttering, and their caregivers were instructed to correct their speech disfluencies whenever they occurred. These six children eventually developed symptoms of stuttering. The other six children were part of a control group and received no instructions to correct their speech disfluencies. These children never developed stuttering. By today's standards, the research would be considered unethical because of the lack of protection for the participants. The University of Iowa made a public apology in 2001 and subsequently agreed to pay approximately $1 million to the six children and their heirs (American Speech-Language-Hearing Association [ASHA], 2007).

FIGURE 5–5. Wendell Johnson believed the development of stuttering had a strong environmental influence. (Reprinted with permission from "An Early History of ASHA," by C. Van Riper, 1981, *ASHA Magazine*, *23*[11], pp. 855–858.)

Lena Rustin (1928–2004; Figure 5–6) was an inspirational pioneer in the treatment of stuttering. Born in England, Rustin was a dedicated clinician who spent her career helping children who stutter and their families. She founded the Association for Research into Stammering in Childhood in 1991. She also was the cofounder of the Michael Palin Centre for Stammering Children in London.

Deso Weiss (1901–1971) was a Hungarian psychiatrist and speech-language pathologist who is remembered for his research related to cluttering. He believed cluttering was caused by a central language imbalance. His description of a person who clutters was that they are mostly carefree, rapid-fire conversationalists, whose speech is studded with repetitions, hesitations, and incomplete sentences.

TYPES OF FLUENCY DISORDERS

Stuttering

The **National Institute on Deafness and Other Communication Disorders** (National Institutes of Health [NIH]) defines stuttering as, "A speech disorder characterized by repetition of sounds, syllables, or words; prolongation of sounds; and interruptions in speech known as blocks. An individual who stutters exactly knows what they would like to say but has trouble producing a normal flow of speech." Speech-language pathology associations worldwide such as ASHA, the Royal College of Speech and Language Therapists, and Speech Pathology Australia have developed their

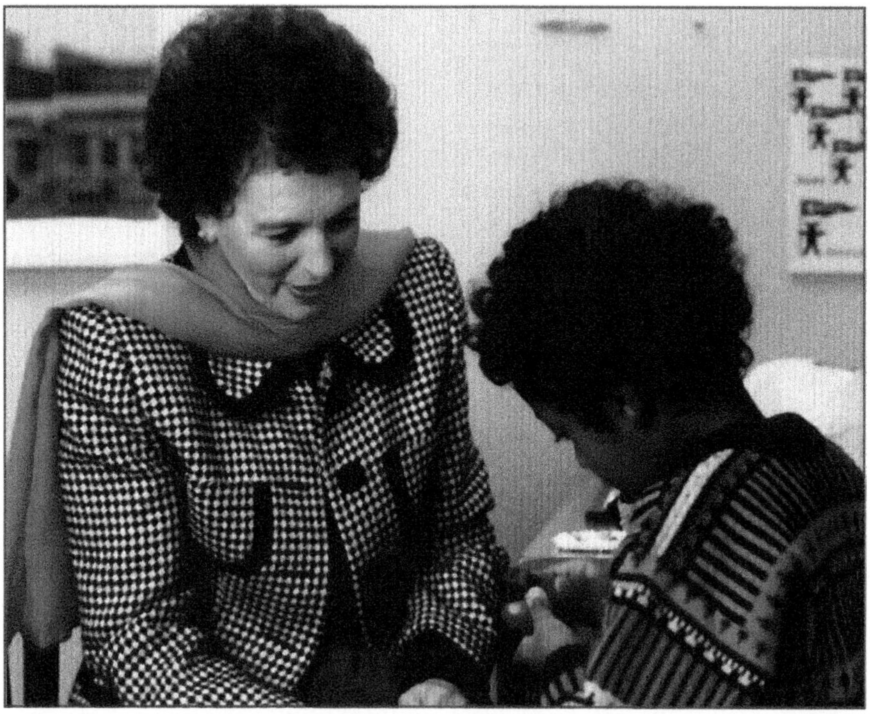

FIGURE 5–6. Lena Rustin, inspirational pioneer in the treatment of stuttering. (Photo courtesy of the British Stammering Association [http://www.stammering.org].)

own definitions of stuttering that vary slightly from the NIH definition, but the general tenets of the definition are the same. Stuttering is a disruption in the flow of speech. Stuttering is also viewed as a developmental disorder. A child who eventually develops a stutter is considered to have been born with this condition; however, the condition is not perceptually apparent until the child begins using connected speech. The term **stammering** is synonymous with stuttering and is used often in the United Kingdom. Either term is appropriate and acceptable.

Stuttering is found to occur in all languages of the world, although precise estimates of its prevalence are unknown. Evidence of its occurrence around the world is provided by noting whether a word for stuttering exists in the vocabulary of the language. Table 5–2 provides some examples of various words for stuttering in languages around the world. If a language does not have a word for stuttering, that does not necessarily mean the disorder is absent from the population. Rather, the condition may not be viewed as a disorder. As a rule, stuttering is thought to occur in 1 out of every 100 individuals, or approximately 1% of the population. The percentage of stuttering in preschool children is somewhat higher, with approximately 3% of children showing early signs of stuttering behavior. However, this number lowers to 1% once children enter school. Stuttering is three times more likely to occur in boys compared with girls (3:1 ratio). There are also reports of stuttering occurring more often among twins and for the disorder to run in families across generations, suggesting a genetic (hereditary) predisposition for the disorder among some individuals.

The development of stuttering is not sudden. The appearance of the disorder is often equated with phases of the moon, whereby the condition waxes and wanes. There will be periods in the child's daily or weekly speaking behavior when it seems like nearly every word produced is disfluent. The same child may then show long periods of time when nearly every word is produced fluently. The onset of stuttering typically occurs at 3 years of age but may vary in children anywhere

Table 5–2. Words From Around the World Used to Refer to Stuttering

Language	*Word*
Afrikaans	hakkel
Arabic	rattat
Cherokee	a-da-nv-te-hi-lo-squi
Chinese (Cantonese)	hau hick
Chinese (Mandarin)	kou chi
Dutch	stotteren
Egyptian	tuhuhtuhuh
English	stuttering
Fijian	kaka
French	begaiement
German	stottern
Hawaiian	uu uus
Hebrew	gimgum
Hindi	hakalaanaa
Hungarian	dadogo
Icelandic	stama
Italian	balbuzie
Japanese	domori; kitsuon
Korean	maldeodum
Māori	kīkiki
Nigerian	nsu
Punjabi	totalaanaa
Russian	zaikatsia; zaikanie
Spanish	tartamudez
Swedish	stamning

FYI

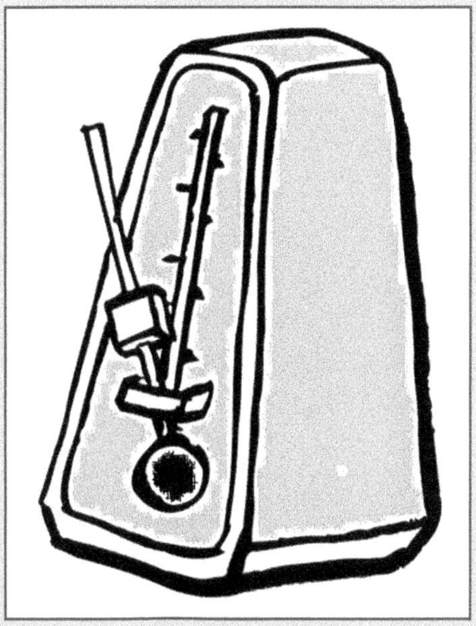

Speaking to the rhythmic beats of a metronome has been shown to help reduce stuttering. Although speaking in such a fashion may sound highly unnatural, the device has been used at the beginning of a therapy program to help gain control over severely disfluent speech.

from 2 to 5 years of age. We also know that some situations can serve to raise or lower moments of stuttering in children and adults alike. Situations that tend to require high communicative demand, such as answering questions, speaking to a stranger, or speaking on the telephone, are likely to increase moments of disfluent speech. On the other hand, speaking one-on-one with a familiar individual (or even to a pet) is likely to be a situation of low communicative demand, resulting in more fluent speech.

Stuttering involves both overt (observable) and covert (nonobservable) behaviors. The combination of these behaviors has been likened to the shape of an iceberg. The tip of the iceberg that rises from the water reflects the overt behaviors, which are the audible and visible signs of stuttering (Figure 5–7). Van Riper (1982) referred to overt behaviors as the **primary characteristics** of stuttering. Yet far greater and perhaps more detrimental is the portion of the iceberg that is submerged. This portion reflects covert behaviors, which comprise feelings of fear, shame, guilt, anxiety, hopelessness, isolation, and denial. Van Riper referred to covert behaviors as the secondary characteristics of stuttering.

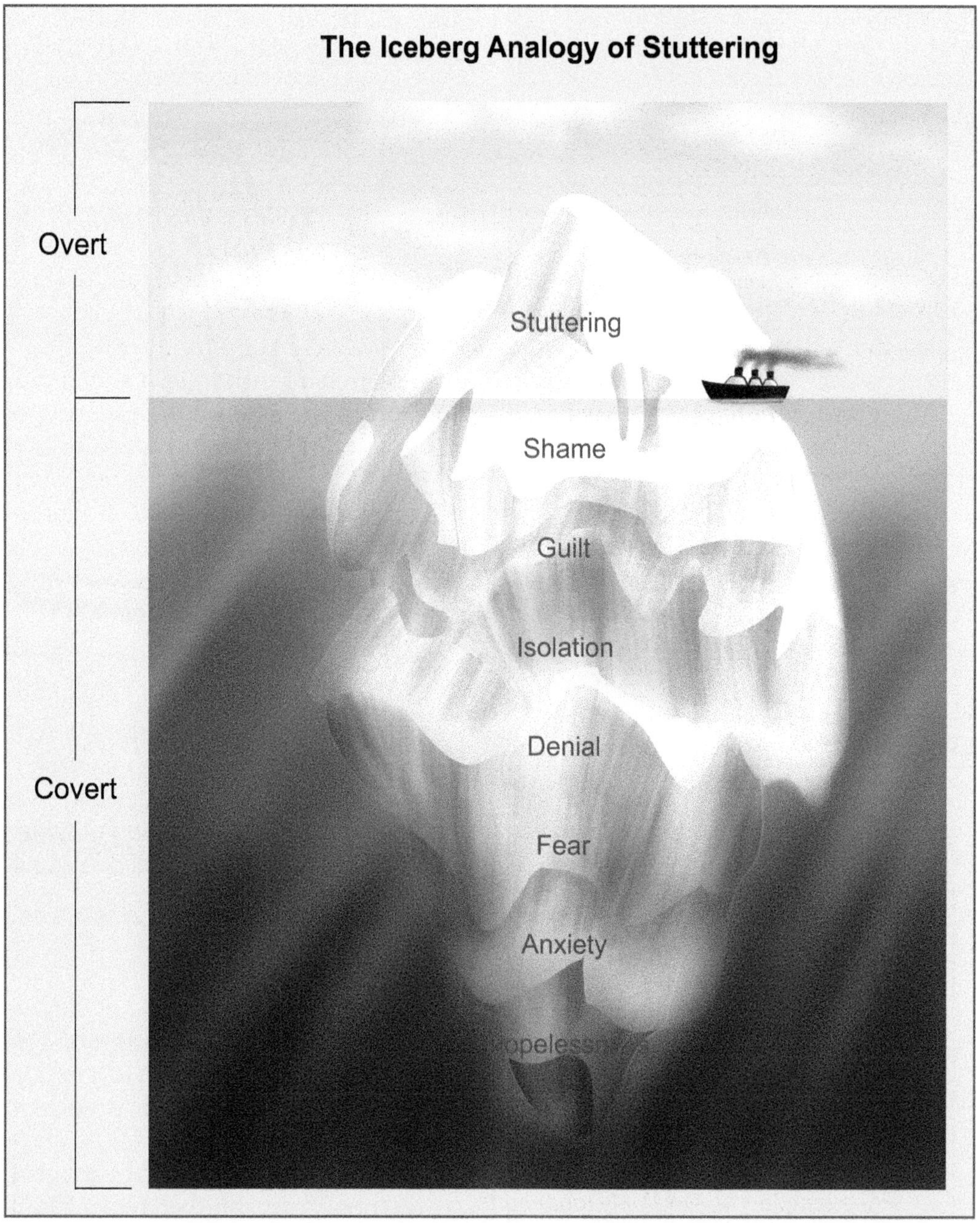

FIGURE 5–7. Classic depiction of the many facets of stuttering as analogous to the shape of an iceberg.

FYI

As the development of stuttering progresses from young children to adults, the earliest types of disfluencies tend to be repetitions of phrases and single words. Later, the types of disfluencies include blocks and prolongations, in addition to repetitions. However, adults who stutter show considerable variability, with some producing primarily repetitions rather than blocks/prolongations.

Primary Characteristics of Stuttering

A popular approach to describing overt stuttering is to differentiate and label the various types of disfluencies. The premise for identifying disfluency types is that some types of disfluencies are most often associated with chronic stuttering. Therefore, differentiating disfluency types should aid in the assessment and diagnosis of stuttering. Johnson (1961) identified eight disfluency types (Table 5–3). One thing to note with these various disfluency types is that some disfluencies occur within a specific word, whereas other disfluencies occur between (or across) words. Johnson suggested that the production of **between-word disfluencies** was a common feature in the speech of people who do not stutter. The production of **within-word disfluencies** (in addition to producing between-word disfluencies) most often was associated with stuttering behavior. The typology developed by Johnson is still used in research and clinical settings; however, it has since been simplified to two broad categories of disfluencies: **stuttering-like disfluencies** and **other disfluencies** (Yairi & Ambrose, 1992). Stuttering-like disfluencies are those disfluencies indicative of chronic stuttering (i.e., partword repetition, single-syllable word repetition, disrhythmic phonation, tense pause), and other disfluencies are reflective of normal nonfluent speech (i.e., multisyllabic word repetition, phrase repetition, interjection, and revision-incomplete phrase). The reason for reducing the types of disfluencies to only two categories was to simplify the identification process for researchers and clinicians while still being able to capture the essence of stuttering behavior. An illustration of two common types of stuttering-like disfluencies—sound repetitions and sound prolongations—is shown in Figure 5–8.

Secondary Characteristics of Stuttering

The secondary characteristics of stuttering are more difficult to classify than the primary characteristics. These features of stuttering seem to develop gradually over time. Many of these

Table 5–3. Disfluency Notation Systems

Johnson System	*Yairi and Ambrose System*
(1) Part-Word Repetition For example, *"My t-t-t-tooth hurts"* (2) Single-Syllable Word Repetition For example, *"I-I-I-I want to go home"* (3) Multisyllabic Word Repetition For example, *"The ba-ba-ba-baby is crying"* (4) Dis-Rhythmic Phonation (sound prolongation) For example, *"MMMMMMy tooth hurts"* (5) Tense Pause (silent prolongation or "block") For example, *". . . The baby is crying"*	SLD
(6) Phrase Repetition For example, *"I want- I want- I want to go home"* (7) Interjection For example, *"I um, well, um, want to go home"* (8) Revision-Incomplete Phrase For example, *"My too . . . my molar hurts"*	OD

Note, The Johnson (1961) system is based on consideration of eight disfluency types. Types 1–5 are considered within-word disfluencies. Types 6–8 are considered between-word disfluencies. The Yairi and Ambrose system (1992) is based on the original Johnson system but is simplified to consider two major types of disfluencies, stutter-like disfluencies (SLD) and other disfluencies (OD).

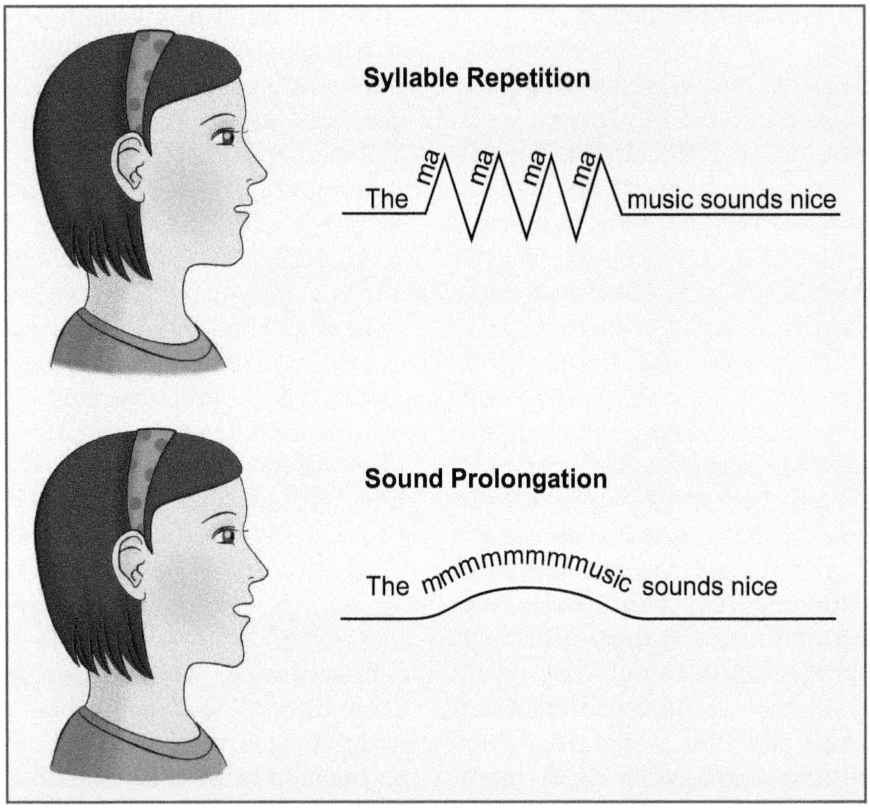

FIGURE 5–8. Sound repetition and sound prolongation during production of the sentence, "The music sounds nice."

behaviors may be absent among young children during the earlier years of stuttering and begin to develop only as the child grows older and stuttering becomes more fixated. These secondary characteristics can be organized into two categories: **bodily movements** and **psychosocial behaviors**. Bodily movements typically are related to facial activity that accompanies a moment of stuttering. These might include eye blinks, facial grimaces, head movements, and loss of eye contact. In more extreme cases, there also might be torso and limb movements. Some theorists believe these body movements reflect a coping strategy by the individual, whereby the behavior was voluntarily used successfully at some point in time to aid the individual in speaking fluently. However, over time, these behaviors were less successful in preventing moments of stuttering. Consequently, stuttering continued, and the coping strategy (i.e., bodily movements) became involuntarily linked to moments of stuttering. Psychosocial behaviors are the feelings experienced by the individual who stutters. A person's feelings can be as much a part of the disorder of stuttering as the speech behaviors. These feelings, which are usually negative, include fear, frustration, embarrassment, sadness, and anger, as well as overall **temperament**. As a person's stuttering worsens, these psychosocial behaviors can become more enhanced and may lead to complete withdrawal from speaking.

Nondevelopmental Stuttering

Stuttering does not occur as a single form of speech but rather in a variety of ways. Although childhood-onset stuttering is the most frequently occurring form of stuttering, there are forms of the disorder that arise later in life. These nondevelopmental forms of stuttering occur far less often, but this does not minimize their importance in the caseload of a speech-language pathologist. Two nondevelopmental forms of stuttering are neurogenic and psychogenic.

Neurogenic Stuttering

Conditions affecting various areas of the brain, including the cortex, cerebellum, and brainstem, can cause **neurogenic stuttering**. The disfluency pattern in neurogenic stuttering is characterized by a high number of involuntary repetitions or prolongations of speech that do not seem to be a result of poor (hesitant) language formulation difficulties or because of psychiatric problems. Secondary behaviors may not be present, and if they do exist, they are not associated with moments of disfluency. One example of neurogenic stuttering can be found among individuals with Parkinson disease. Past reports have suggested that increases in dopamine associated with taking medication designed to boost the amount of dopamine in the brain contribute to an increase in stuttering. However, this excess dopamine theory was challenged by Im et al. (2019) who found no major differences in the amount of stuttering either before or following medication, indicating that either more or less dopamine may influence speech fluency.

Psychogenic Stuttering

There are far fewer reports of **psychogenic stuttering** compared with neurogenic stuttering. Whereas neurogenic stuttering is associated with various known pathologies in the brain, psychogenic conditions are less obvious. Psychogenic stuttering is a condition describing people for whom a psychological disturbance is clearly diagnosed. Because of the psychological nature of this disorder, the diagnosis of psychopathology falls outside the expertise of the speech-language pathologist. The speech disfluencies produced by the individual are strongly linked to psychological distress. The types of disfluencies are less consistent than both developmental stuttering and neurogenic stuttering. An example would be a situation where the person's speech disfluencies may change noticeably, either for better or worse. A reduction in stuttering during a person's disclosure of emotionally sensitive information is a strong indicator of a psychogenic stutter. Further evidence of a psychogenic basis for stuttering is related to response to treatment. If a person's speech fluency returns to normal or near normal, it is likely there was a psychological basis because this level of improvement is not found in developmental stuttering.

Cluttering

A third type of nondevelopmental stuttering that is considered a separate type of fluency disorder is known as cluttering. Cluttering is a disorder of speaking rate. In a person who shows cluttering, their speaking rate can be either abnormally fast, irregular, or both. Among normally fluent adult speakers, the typical rate of speaking is approximately 240 syllables per minute (spm). Individuals with cluttering will often demonstrate a speaking rate in excess of 300 spm. In cluttered speech, the rapid rate of speaking contributes to (a) higher than normal speech disfluency, (b) types of disfluencies not like those found in stuttering, and (c) slurred speech misarticulations, such as consonant deletions and consonant substitutions during spurts of rapid speech. The general impression when listening to the speech of an individual with cluttering is that the individual is speaking so fast that their speech fluency deteriorates. A comparison of cluttered and stuttered speech is provided in Table 5–4. Treatment for individuals with cluttering tends to focus on reducing speaking rate, which results in marked improvement in the overall fluency and clarity of their speech.

> **FYI**
>
> A peculiar pattern of stuttering is the production of a disfluency cluster, which is the production of two or more disfluencies on the same word and/or adjacent words. An example of a disfluency cluster would be the production of a sound repetition followed by a prolongation such as, "The b-b-boy wwwent." Disfluency clusters seem to occur only in the speech of people with a diagnosed stuttering disorder.

Table 5–4. Comparison of the Characteristics of Cluttering and Stuttering

Characteristic	*Cluttering*	*Stuttering*
Speaking rate	Irregular: +300 syllables per minute	Regular: 240 syllables per minute
Speech articulation	Slurred and/or omissions	Normal
Speech disfluencies	Primarily other disfluencies	Primarily stuttering-like disfluencies
Self-perception/anxiety	May be unaware of disfluent speech/no anxiety	Aware of disfluent speech/anxious
Expressive language	Disorganized	Organized

CURRENT THEORIES REGARDING STUTTERING

Modern theories about stuttering have been shaped over many years of research. Although stuttering is the most researched of the various communication disorders, pinpointing the actual cause of stuttering remains controversial. There is no unified theory of stuttering. The consensus is that stuttering has a multidimensional etiology. The various theories include several factors that may contribute to the disorder, including genetics, the environment, language complexity, motor coordination, and psychological influences. In essence, modern theories suggest both nature and nurture influences on stuttering. Some of the most popular theories to date include the demands and capacities theory, covert repair theory, and neuropsycholinguistic theory.

Demands and Capacities Theory

The **demands and capacities theory** was proposed by Starkweather (1997) and views stuttering as occurring when the intrinsic and extrinsic social demands placed on a child for producing fluent speech exceed the child's cognitive, linguistic, motor, or emotional capacities for fluent speech. Children who eventually develop stuttering have a genetic predisposition for the disorder and will encounter a mismatch between their speaking capabilities and self-imposed or environmental demands.

Covert Repair Theory

The **covert repair theory** was proposed by Postma and Kolk (1993) and links together the production of language and moments of stuttering. This theory assumes that people who stutter have an internally disordered phonological system. During the internal planning for speech, we naturally form (i.e., encode) the necessary sounds for words and sentences before physically producing speech. People who stutter experience frequent planning errors in speech organization that need to be repaired before the words leave the speaker's mouth. Speech disfluencies occur when a speaker interrupts ongoing speech to repair these errors. This is why we often observe the frequent production of repetitions and pauses in people who stutter. These repairs do not occur at a conscious level.

Neuropsycholinguistic Theory

The **neuropsycholinguistic theory** proposed by Perkins et al. (1991) assumes that producing fluent speech involves sophisticated timing between the formulation of language and the actual motor execution of speech movement. Stuttering results in a situation where there is a disruption in the timing (integration) of linguistic formulation and speech movement. People who stutter will often report experiencing a loss of control in producing speech, which is enhanced when there is time pressure to produce speech.

ASSESSMENT OF FLUENCY DISORDERS

The aim of fluency assessment is to determine whether the disfluency behavior demonstrated by an individual is typical or atypical of what we might expect of most people speaking on an everyday basis. Two questions to be addressed in a fluency assessment are as follows: (a) Are speech disfluencies present in the person's speaking behavior? and (b) What is the nature of speech disfluencies? The speech-language pathologist answers these questions according to the age of the individual being assessed. The assessment differs between children and adults because parent input is vital to the diagnosis of the condition in young children.

Are Speech Disfluencies Present?

To answer the first question, a large sample of conversational speech is collected from the person. The sample needs to be large enough so that a representation of natural speaking behavior is obtained. The generally accepted minimum amount of speech is 300 words of conversation. Once this sample is collected (usually audio-recorded), the speech-language pathologist listens to the sample and identifies and tallies moments of speech disfluency occurring across the 300-word sample. This tally is then converted to a percentage of occurrence. For example, if 21 moments of disfluency were identified across the 300-word sample, the percentage of disfluency would be 7%. Conversational speech that is 3% disfluent or higher is usually a rough indication of a fluency disorder. Alternatively, 2% disfluency or lower would be considered within normal limits for people speaking on an everyday basis.

What Is the Nature of Speech Disfluencies?

The answer to the second question involves further analysis of the specific moments of disfluency. The stuttering typology systems developed by Johnson (1961) and Yairi and Ambrose (1992) can be used to assess the nature and severity of the fluency disorder. Generally, the greater the occurrence of within-word (or stuttering-like) disfluencies, the greater is the severity of the stuttering disorder. The **Iowa Scale for Rating the Severity of Stuttering** was developed by Johnson et al. (1963) more than 60 years ago and remains quite popular. To use the scale, the speech-language pathologist must first calculate the average percentage of disfluency produced by an individual. Based on the percentage of disfluency, a corresponding severity ranking is assigned ranging from 0 (no stuttering) to 7 (very severe stuttering; Table 5–5).

A commercially available test used to determine the nature of speech disfluencies is the **Stuttering Severity Instrument** for children and adults (Riley, 2009). This test considers the frequency of disfluencies, the duration of disfluencies, and the physical concomitants of speaking to formulate a diagnosis. A perceptual scale can also be used to

Table 5–5. Iowa Scale for Rating the Severity of Stuttering

Severity Ranking	*Description*
0	*No stuttering*
1	*Very Mild*—Stuttering on less than 1% of words
2	*Mild*—Stuttering on 1% to 2% of words
3	*Mild to Moderate*—Stuttering on 2% to 5% of words
4	*Moderate*—Stuttering on 5% to 8% of words
5	*Moderate to Severe*—Stuttering on 8% to 12% of words
6	*Severe*—Stuttering on 12% to 25% of words
7	*Very Severe*—Stuttering on more than 25% of words

Note. The table is a condensed version of the overall scale.

FYI

Stuttering disappears once a person begins to sing. The reason for this is twofold. First, the strings of words being sung are familiar and well-rehearsed, which helps to reduce stuttering. Second, singing involves the natural blending together of sounds and words in a melodic fashion, with the vocal folds in a constant state of vibration. This is a form of continuous phonation that likewise helps to reduce stuttering.

determine the nature of speech disfluencies. Perceptual scales bypass any formal measurement of disfluent speech. The philosophy behind using a perceptual scale is that one simply needs to hear a moment of stuttering to make a judgment as to the existence and severity of the disorder. One such scale is a 9-point **severity scale** that requires a listener to assign a value ranging from 1 (not stuttering) to 9 (extremely severe stuttering) after listening to a sample of conversational speech (Figure 5–9).

Other variables that are considered when describing the nature of disfluencies are the presence or absence of secondary behaviors, including bodily movements and psychosocial behaviors. Bodily movements can be ascertained by visually examining the person during moments of disfluency. Psychosocial behaviors can be assessed by simply asking the person about their feelings and attitude toward speaking. A more thorough assessment of psychosocial behaviors can be obtained by administering the Overall Assessment of the Speaker's Experience of Stuttering instrument (Yaruss & Quesal, 2010). This is a questionnaire-based tool that is used to evaluate the perceived impact of stuttering on a person's life.

The calculation of **speaking rate** can also aid in the diagnosis of a fluency disorder, particularly regarding cluttering. This calculation can be made using the same 300-word conversational sample that was collected for noting the frequency and type of disfluencies. It is equally important to examine a person's fluency behavior in the context of overall communication abilities. So, assessment of the person's phonology and language abilities is also performed.

Once a diagnosis of a fluency disorder is made, the next step is to enroll the individual in a treatment program. There are instances when the speech-language pathologist may recommend monitoring the client rather than direct therapy. This may be the case for young children who are on the cusp of developing a fluency disorder or when a child appears to be at low risk for persistent stuttering.

TREATMENT OF FLUENCY DISORDERS

There is no 100% cure for stuttering. Because we still do not know what causes stuttering, it is not surprising to find there is no unified approach toward its treatment. Although there is general agreement that stuttering cannot be completely remedied, a great deal can be done to help reduce the frequency of disfluent speech. Regardless of the treatment approach, there are three general goals to therapy: (a) to change the speaking behavior of the person, (b) to change the way the person feels about their speech, and (c) to change the way the person interacts with their speaking environment. Each goal is equally important to the success of treatment. Most treatment approaches fall into one of two categories: traditional and nontraditional.

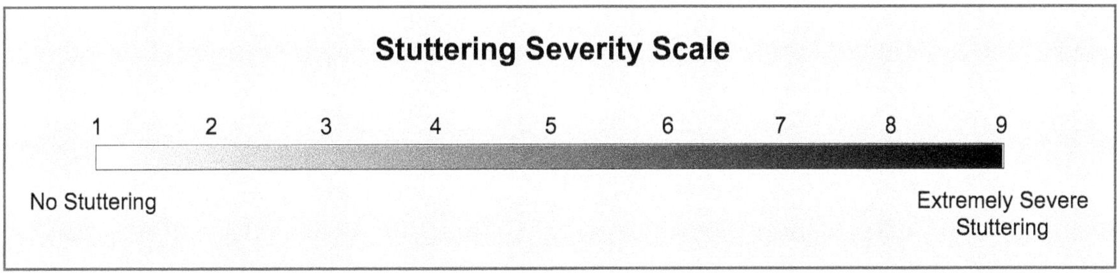

FIGURE 5–9. Example of a 9-point scale for perceptually rating the severity of stuttering.

Traditional Treatment Approaches

The traditional approaches to treating fluency disorders can be broadly organized into two types: (a) fluency shaping and (b) stuttering modification (Maruthy & Kelkar, 2023). Both approaches use principles of behavior modification to change the existing pattern of speaking. Often, the speech-language pathologist may try one or the other approach with the client to determine which seems to work best. The speech-language pathologist may also develop a hybrid approach that incorporates features of both types of therapy. Ultimately, the client's response to a particular approach serves as the best gauge to the preferred treatment approach.

The **fluency shaping** approach is designed to modify all aspects of the client's speaking behavior. That is, every syllable, word, and sentence uttered by the client are modified into an overall new pattern of speaking. This modification is made by instructing the client to (a) speak at a reduced rate, (b) prolong the vowel portions of words, and (c) use slow and smooth speech initiation. A term associated with this pattern of speaking is **continuous phonation**, where the client attempts to maintain constant vocal fold vibration during the production of entire utterances of speaking. These are the same principles of phonation that are at play when singing, which has likewise been shown to result in a reduction of disfluent speech. The aim of this treatment is for the client to become completely "stutter free." A particular criticism of this treatment approach is that the client's speech sounds somewhat unnatural because of the modification in overall speaking behavior.

> **FYI**
>
> Speech-language pathologists typically advise that when speaking with a person who stutters, it is appropriate to allow the person to complete their utterances. It is important to maintain good eye contact and refrain from interrupting or finishing a stuttered utterance for the person.

The **stuttering modification** approach is designed to address individual moments of stuttering, as opposed to changing the entire pattern of speaking behavior. People who stutter are aware of upcoming moments of stuttering during their ongoing speech. This technique addresses these upcoming instances of stuttering by teaching the client to (a) stutter with less tension, (b) use light articulatory contacts during speaking, and (c) reduce situational fears and negative attitudes of stuttering. A person applying this treatment approach will produce speech that is more natural sounding compared with speech produced with continuous phonation. A criticism of this approach is that there may still be moments of stuttering, although significantly reduced in occurrence.

One treatment approach to working with preschool children during the earliest years of stuttering is **parent-directed therapy** (Maruthy & Kelkar, 2023). As indicated, parents are taught to play a key role in the remediation of their child's stuttering behavior. Receiving treatment in a clinical setting may typically involve only one or two (1-hr) sessions per week, which accounts for only a fraction of a child's weekly speaking activity.

Therefore, by involving parents in the delivery of treatment, they are taught to reinforce goals established in the clinical setting. This form of therapy places emphasis on increasing desirable speaking behavior instead of trying to lessen undesirable behavior. Attention is directed away from the perception of what is happening to the child, toward those things the child is doing to both facilitate and interfere with talking. Emphasis is also placed on increasing the child's awareness of physical aspects of speaking that contribute to fluent speech, such as articulatory tension and breathing patterns.

A popular form of parent-directed therapy is the **Lidcombe Program** of early stuttering intervention (Onslow et al., 2003). The program was developed at the Australian Stuttering Research Centre and was designed primarily for preschool children who stutter. The essence of the treatment is for parents to provide direct feedback to their child about stuttered, as well as nonstuttered, speech during conversational settings.

Nontraditional Treatment Approaches

Nontraditional approaches are not used as often as traditional approaches to manage a person's stuttering. These approaches are also typically not applicable to most individuals who may stutter or show a related fluency disorder. Nontraditional approaches to treating stuttering include hypnotherapy, drug therapy, and electronic devices. **Hypnotherapy** is a psychologically based approach to the treatment of stuttering. Psychological techniques emphasizing anxiety reduction and building self-confidence are presented under hypnosis to help the individual speak confidently. By reducing anxiety and increasing self-confidence, the person's severity of stuttering presumably will lessen. Use of this technique remains controversial, but there is evidence to suggest the approach may be particularly effective for individuals with a mild stuttering disorder.

The use of **drug therapy** to manage stuttering focuses on an individual's anxiety, which is often greatly heightened when anticipating moments of speaking. A few antianxiety drugs have been shown to reduce moments of stuttering; however, only a small number of individuals tend to show a long-lasting reduction in stuttering once under the drug's influence. Those who do respond usually show only a modest reduction in stuttering.

Electronic devices that closely resemble hearing aids are inserted into one ear. These fluency aids serve to alter the individual's overall speaking behavior (i.e., a form of fluency shaping). Some devices use a technology called **altered auditory feedback**. When fitted with the device, an illusion is created where the client hears their own voice with either a delay or slight shift in pitch. The client needs to reduce their speaking rate and prolong vowels in order to minimize the effect of the alteration, which subsequently results in fluent speech. Some devices transmit white noise, which is acoustically similar to the sound of a waterfall. By introducing noise into the speaker's ear, the individual is unable to hear their own voice. This form of distraction has shown to decrease moments of stuttering in some, but not all, individuals.

The use of electronic devices Is often considered at two points in the continuum of therapy. Based on consultation with a speech-language pathologist, a client may use such a device when first entering treatment to assist with gaining initial control over severe stuttering. Once control is established, the device is no longer used, and the person transitions into a traditional treatment program. Alternatively, an electronic device might be used when other forms of treatment have proved unsuccessful. In this case, the device is used on an everyday basis.

CULTURAL CONSIDERATIONS AND FLUENCY DISORDERS

Careful considerations are required in the diagnosis and management of fluency disorders among individuals from diverse cultural backgrounds. The multicultural perspectives of the client can (and should) influence clinical practice. For example, in some cultures, such as Chinese, stuttering is not considered to be a prevalent communication disorder; thus, there is not a great deal of attention placed on correcting the disorder. In some African nations, the cause of this speech problem and its treatment are deeply rooted in folk ideas. Some of the reported causes of stuttering include tickling a baby too much or leaving a newborn child out in the rain. Corresponding treatments include praying or applying ointments to the throat. Therefore, a speech-language pathologist should not assume there is a universally agreed upon approach to the management of fluency disorders.

To illustrate this point, consider the two common traditional approaches to treating stuttering: stuttering modification and fluency shaping. Stuttering modification therapies utilize a counseling-based methodology with a primary aim of developing positive attitudes toward communication. Although this goal may seem to hold wide universal appeal, the structuring of this form of therapy requires cultural sensitivity. Counseling has its roots in psychology; therefore, it is important to consider features such as race, language, economic class, and differing worldviews as potential barriers to the counseling process (Üstün-Yavuz et al., 2021). The stuttering modification treatment approach has the potential to become a complex and multidimensional process, especially in a context of varying multicultural perspectives and beliefs.

There are reports that fluency shaping therapies appear to have better acceptance compared with stuttering modification therapy by clients of diverse backgrounds (Cooper & Cooper, 2001). Fluency shaping approaches, at least in the earliest phases of treatment, tend to focus exclusively on gaining control of speech fluency and have less emphasis on counseling. Fluency shaping has its roots in behavioral conditioning and programmed instruction, so this approach tends to bypass matters concerning cultural sensitivity. Regardless of the treatment approach selected, those that are currently available to the speech-language pathologist will likely need to be modified to make them applicable in a multicultural context.

Person-centered practice (PCP) is a form of health delivery that involves a partnership between the clinician and client. It is an attempt to "humanize" care by including input from the client. Each client is considered unique and contributes important knowledge to the management of their own health care. PCP is gaining popularity in the treatment of various communication disorders, including fluency disorders (Forsgren et al., 2022). Person-centered goals are those identified by the client (adult, child, family) in partnership with the clinician that allow participation in meaningful therapy activities. This active participation has the effect of optimizing client engagement and satisfaction in therapy.

Another multicultural consideration when dealing with fluency disorders is the influence of bilingualism. More than 50% of the world's population is bilingual. Thus, the trend is that most people can speak more than one language, and people who speak only one language are becoming far less the norm. Also consider that roughly 1% of the population stutters. So in the context of bilingualism, it would seem that at some point in the career of speech-language pathologists, they will be confronted with a bilingual speaker who stutters. There are mixed views concerning the characteristics of stuttering in bilingual speakers. Although it would seem obvious that a bilingual person who stutters in one language will show the same pattern in another language, the research to date does not support this view. Individuals are likely to stutter in both languages; however, the less dominant or least proficient language will show a higher percentage of stuttering (Chaudhary et al., 2021). Therefore, the bilingual person who stutters poses unique concerns about diagnosis and management of the disorder. For example, can the speech-language pathologist make an accurate diagnosis of a fluency disorder when listening to a language that is foreign? Is it possible to differentiate stuttering from cluttering? Should the treatment of fluency disorders focus on only one language or both? These are important questions that still await answers.

SUMMARY OF CHAPTER

Disfluency is a disruption in the forward flow of speech. When speech disfluencies fall outside the boundary of what is considered natural, they are deemed to represent a fluency disorder. The two fluency disorders profiled in this chapter are stuttering and cluttering. Stuttering involves both overt (observable) and covert (nonobservable) behaviors. The combination of these behaviors has been likened to the shape of an iceberg. Cluttering

FYI

There are several apps that can be used on a smartphone or tablet that are specifically designed for people who stutter. Some of these apps provide altered auditory feedback. Others are targeted to addressing speech-related anxiety.

is a disorder of speaking rate. In a person who shows cluttering, their speaking rate can be either abnormally fast, irregular, or both. The aim of fluency assessment is to determine whether the disfluency behavior demonstrated by an individual is typical or atypical of what we might expect of most people speaking on an everyday basis. The traditional approaches to treating fluency disorders can be broadly organized into two types: (a) fluency shaping and (b) stuttering modification. Both approaches use principles of behavior modification to change the existing pattern of speaking. The multicultural perspectives of the client can (and should) influence clinical practice. The job of the speech-language pathologist is to distinguish between what are considered normal, natural speech disfluencies and those that are unnatural speech disfluencies.

FLUENCY DISORDERS ON THE WORLD WIDE WEB

Following are websites that provide further information on the topic of fluency disorders. At the time of publication, each website was freely accessible.

International Stuttering Association
https://www.isastutter.org

International Fluency Association
https://www.theifa.org

Stuttering Foundation Video
https://www.stutteringhelp.org/videos

Therapy Techniques
https://www.youtube.com/@StutteringTherapyResources

https://www.speechandlanguagekids.com/stuttering-therapy-activity-ideas/

Stuttering Documentaries
https://www.youtube.com/watch?v=bNkOeIBKZNs

https://www.youtube.com/watch?v=-V_4chECIos

STUDY QUESTIONS

1. What are the similarities and differences between stuttering and cluttering?
2. What are the primary and secondary characteristics of stuttering?
3. What are some of the most popular theories related to the cause of stuttering?
4. Compare and contrast the fluency shaping and stuttering modification approaches to treating stuttering.
5. Who are some of the pioneers in stuttering, and what were their contributions?

REFERENCES

American Speech-Language-Hearing Association. (2007, November). Iowa stuttering study settlement. *ASHA Leader*, *8*.

Chaudhary, C., Maruthy, S., Guddattu, V., & Krishnan, G. (2021). A systematic review on the role of language-related factors in the manifestation of stuttering in bilinguals. *Journal of Fluency Disorders*, *68*, e105829.

Cooper, E. B., & Cooper, C. S. (2001). Fluency disorders. In D. Battle (Ed.), *Communication disorders in multicultural populations* (3rd ed., pp. 189–211). Butterworth-Heinemann Medical.

Forsgren, E., Ake, S., & Sladert, C. (2022). Person-centred care in speech-language therapy research and practice for adults: A scoping review. *International Journal of Language and Communication Disorders*, *57*, 381–402.

Im, H., Adams, S., Abeyesekera, A., Pieterman, M., Gilmore, G. & Jog, M. (2019). Effect of levodopa on speech dysfluency in Parkinson's disease. *Movement Disorders Clinical Practice*, *6*, 150–154.

Johnson, W. (1961). *Stuttering and what you can do about it*. University of Minnesota Press.

Johnson, W., Darley, F., & Spriestersbach, D. (1963). *Diagnostic methods in speech pathology*. Harper & Row.

Maruthy, S., & Kelkar, P. (2023). *Understanding and managing fluency disorders*. Routledge.

Onslow, M., Packman, A., & Harrison, E. (2003). *The Lidcombe program of early stuttering intervention: A clinician's guide*. Pro-Ed.

Perkins, W. H., Kent, R. D., & Curlee, R. R. (1991). A theory of neuropsycholinguistic function in stuttering. *Journal of Speech, Language, and Hearing Research*, *34*, 734–752.

Postma, A., & Kolk, H. (1993). The covert repair hypothesis: Prearticulatory repair processes in normal and stuttered disfluencies. *Journal of Speech and Hearing Research*, *36*, 472–487.

Riley, G. (2009). *The Stuttering Severity Instrument for adults and children* (SSI-4; 4th ed.). Pro-Ed.

Starkweather, C. W. (1997). Therapy for younger children. In R. F. Curlee & G. M. Siegel (Eds.), *Nature and treatment of stuttering* (2nd ed., pp. 257–279). Allyn & Bacon.

Üstün-Yavuz, M., Warmington, M., Gerlach, H., & St. Louis, K. (2021). Cultural difference in attitudes towards stuttering among British, Arab and Chinese students: Considering home and host cultures. *International Journal of Language & Communication Disorders*, *56*, 609–619.

Van Riper, C. (1981). An early history of ASHA. *ASHA Magazine*, *23*(11), 855–858.

Van Riper, C. (1982). *The nature of stuttering* (2nd ed.). Prentice-Hall.

World Health Organization. (1977). *Manual of the international statistical classification of diseases, injuries, and causes of death*.

Yairi, E., & Ambrose, N. (1992). A longitudinal study of stuttering in children: A preliminary report. *Journal of Speech, Language, and Hearing Research*, *35*, 755–760.

Yaruss, J. S., & Quesal, R. (2010). *Overall Assessment of the Speaker's Experience of Stuttering* (OASES). Pearson.

6

CLEFT LIP AND PALATE

OBJECTIVES

After reading this chapter, the student should be able to:

- Demonstrate knowledge of the biological aspects of embryonic development that impact the process of developing a cleft.
- Understand the differences between normal lip/palate and cleft lip/palate anatomy and physiology.
- Describe the characteristics of different types of cleft lips and palates.
- Identify the impact of cleft lip and palate on speech and language development.
- Demonstrate knowledge regarding the fundamental aspects of assessing individuals with cleft lip and palate.
- Have a basic knowledge of the surgical and nonsurgical management techniques for cleft lip and palate.
- Demonstrate basic knowledge of and be able to accurately identify the articulation, voice, and resonance characteristics that are typical of clients with cleft lip and palate.
- Demonstrate basic knowledge of the team concept in the habilitation of individuals (and families) who have cleft lip and palate.
- Identify cultural issues impacting individuals with cleft lip and palate.

KEY TERMS

Birth Defect	Karl Ferdinand von Graefe	Obturator
Schisis	Johann Friedrich Dieffenbach	Otitis Media
Craniofacial Abnormality	Bernard von Langenbeck	Eustachian Tube
Embryology	Philip Gustav Passavant	Pressure Equalization Tubes
Zygote	Carl Casper von Siebold	Orthognathic
Embryo	Matthew Wilson	Velopharyngeal Closure
Fetus	Herbert K. Cooper	Velopharyngeal Inadequacy
Columella	Edna Hill Young	Hypernasal Speech
Nares	Unilateral Cleft Lip	Nasometer
Philtrum	Bilateral Cleft Lip	Compensatory Strategy
Cupid's Bow	Complete Cleft Lip	Glottal Stop
Vermilion Border	Incomplete Cleft Lip	Pharyngeal Fricative
Fistula	Microform Cleft	Cleft Palate Team
Ambroise Pare	Complete Cleft Palate	Pharyngeal Flap
Jehan Yperman	Incomplete Cleft Palate	Pharyngoplasty
Pierre Franco	Submucous Cleft	Operation Smile
Philibert Joseph Roux	Multifactorial	Smile Train

INTRODUCTION

The birth of a child is one of the most joyous experiences in a parent's life. However, it is not uncommon for expectant parents to alternate between visions of a healthy baby and worries that the baby will be born with health problems. A **birth defect** is a problem that happens while a baby is developing in the mother's body. Birth defects are defined as abnormalities of structure, function, or body metabolism that are present at birth. Most birth defects happen during the first 3 months of pregnancy. Most babies with birth defects are born to two parents with no obvious health problems or risk factors. A woman can do everything her doctor recommends to deliver a healthy child and still have a baby with a birth defect. A cleft of the lip or palate (CL/P) is a birth defect that affects an estimated 7,000 infants annually in the United States. According to the Centers for Disease Control and Prevention, approximately 2,700 babies are born with a cleft palate, and another 4,500 babies are born with a cleft lip with or without a cleft palate. Among the various types of communication disorders covered in this text, cleft lip and palate are by far the most physically obvious types of communication disorder.

TERMINOLOGY AND DEFINITIONS

A CL/P is defined as an elongated opening resulting from failure of parts of the mouth to fuse or merge. The medical term is **schisis**, which means opening in Greek. A CL/P is an organic, developmental communication disorder. A CL/P is also a type of **craniofacial abnormality**, reflecting involvement of the bony features of the skull as well as tissue features of the face. A CL/P is the most common congenital abnormality. Because it is present at birth, the developmental disruptions that result in a CL/P occur during the prenatal period of growth.

The scientific study of prenatal growth and the developing process of an individual is called **embryology**. Human pregnancy is approximately 9 months (40 weeks) in duration. This time period starts immediately after conception, when the ovum is fertilized by sperm. The prenatal period is divided into three phases of pregnancy: the first phase is **zygote**, which is the period of conception through the first 2 weeks of pregnancy; the second phase is **embryo**, which is the period of 2 weeks through the eighth week; and the third phase of pregnancy is **fetus**, which is the period of 9 weeks through birth.

Physical formation of the face occurs during the period of embryonic development and early fetal development. A visual timeline of facial development is provided in Figure 6–1. Late in the first month of pregnancy, the baby's developing face and mouth are effectively split into two halves with the eyes and nose spread out toward the sides. The two sides gradually start growing closer together beginning around the fourth week of prenatal development. First to fuse are the

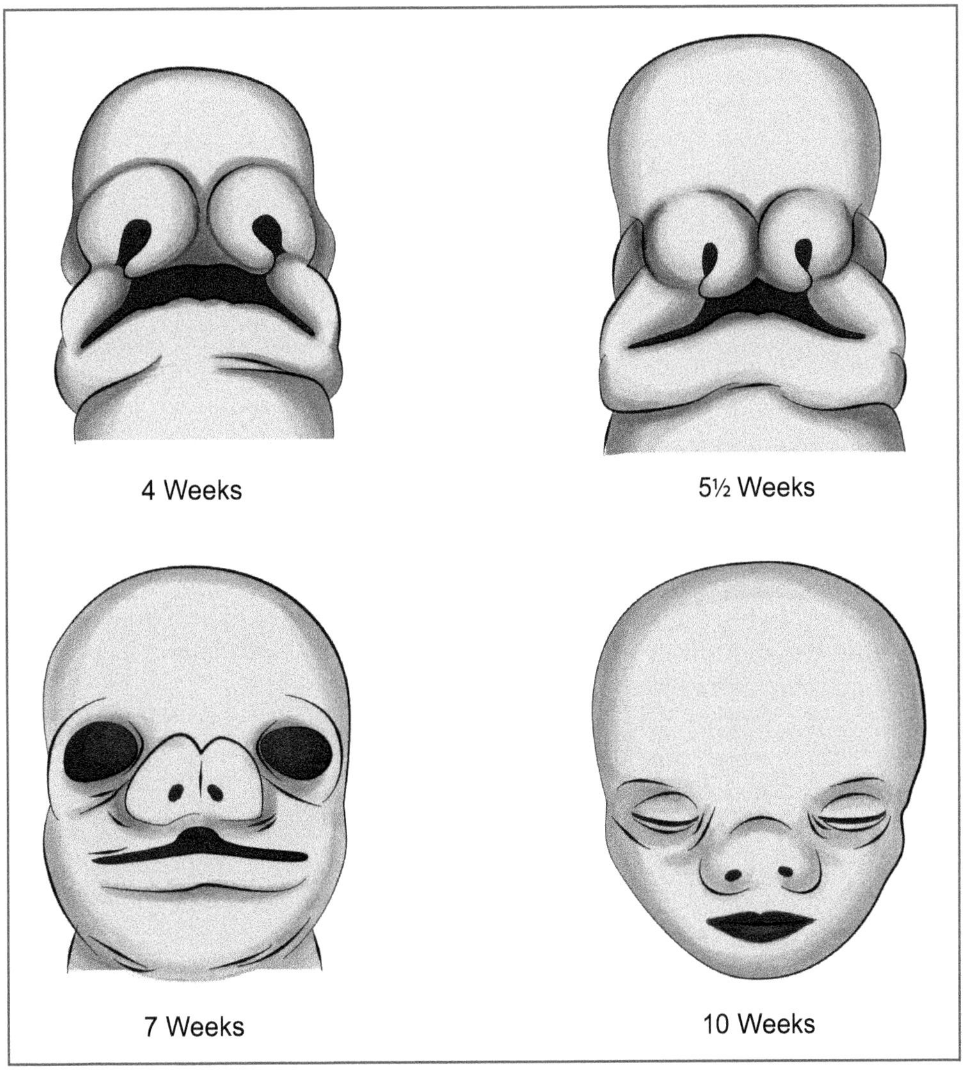

FIGURE 6–1. Prenatal development of the face.

FYI

Source: aphrodite-in-nyc from new york city, CC BY 2.0 <https://creativecommons.org/licenses/by/2.0>, via Wikimedia Common

Some well-known people who were born with a CL/P include Wendy Harmer (comedian), Jesse Jackson (politician), Stacy Keach (actor), Nikki Payne (comedian), Joaquin Phoenix (actor, pictured), Peyton Manning (professional football player), and Cheech Marin (comedian). According to diagnostic imaging of the Egyptian Pharaoh Tutankhamun (1341–1323 BC), he too may have had a CL/P.

lips. The face continues developing and changing shape considerably. The eyes move forward, the nose comes together, and the face appears much narrower. Following fusion of the lips, the alveolar ridge is formed, which is the boney gum ridge that has sockets for our upper teeth. Next, the fusing seam travels backward to form the hard palate and then the soft palate (i.e., velum). The tip of the soft palate is called the *uvula* and is recognized as the teardrop-shaped tissue that hangs at the back of the throat. By the 12th week of pregnancy, the mouth is fully formed (Nasreddine et al., 2021). An illustration of the timeline of palate development is provided in Figure 6–2.

Various landmarks on the face (Figure 6–3) that can be affected by a CL/P include the **columella**, which is the fleshy strip underneath the nose that separates the right and left nostrils (also called **nares**). The **philtrum** is the midline groove in the upper lip that runs from the top of the lip to the nose. The slight curve in the upper lip directly below the philtrum is called **Cupid's bow**, said to resemble the bow of Cupid, the Roman god of love and beauty. The **vermilion border** is the edge of red pigment around the upper and lower lips of the mouth. Normally, these facial landmarks are quite prominent in children and young adults. Because of normal aging, the philtrum and Cupid's bow regions of the upper lip tend to flatten and become less distinct.

HISTORIC ASPECTS OF CLEFT LIP AND PALATE

During the 1500s, research and interest in cleft lip and palate were lacking because the deformity was thought to occur because of syphilis transmitted to an infant by its infected mother. An effect of syphilis was severe inflammation of the hard palate that resulted in the creation of a **fistula**, or narrow opening. At the time, surgeons viewed such openings as unrepairable. Many children born with a CL/P were unable to nurse and subsequently failed to survive because of malnutrition. Others were simply left to die either because the birth defect was too hideous for society or as a result of superstition. One of the earliest reports of a CL/P was by a French surgeon **Ambroise Pare** (1510–1590; Figure 6–4) who is considered the greatest surgeon of the 16th century. When discussing a patient with a cleft, Pare first coined the phrase *le bec-de-lièvre*, with an English transition of "lip of the hare." He was merely observing that the lip was split, as is the lip of a rabbit (and several other animals). Among these animals, the split lip is used like forceps in picking up food (Figure 6–5).

FYI

The occurrence of a CL/P is not unique to humans. CL/Ps also are found in the animal world, including in dogs and cats. Purebred dogs and cats are at the highest risk for a CL/P, and they are most common in Boston terriers, Pekingese, bulldogs, beagles, cocker spaniels, dachshunds, and Siamese cats. Heredity is considered the primary cause of a CL/P in animals.

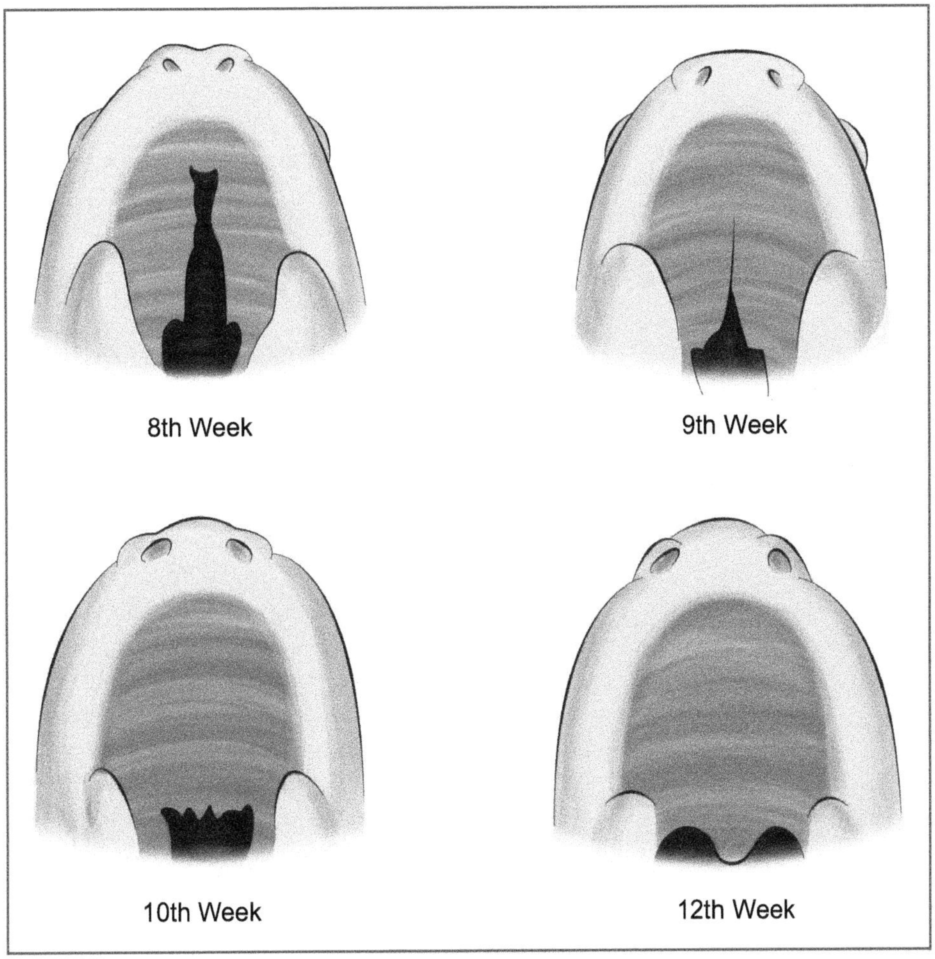

FIGURE 6–2. Major stages of hard and soft palate development during the 12 weeks of prenatal development.

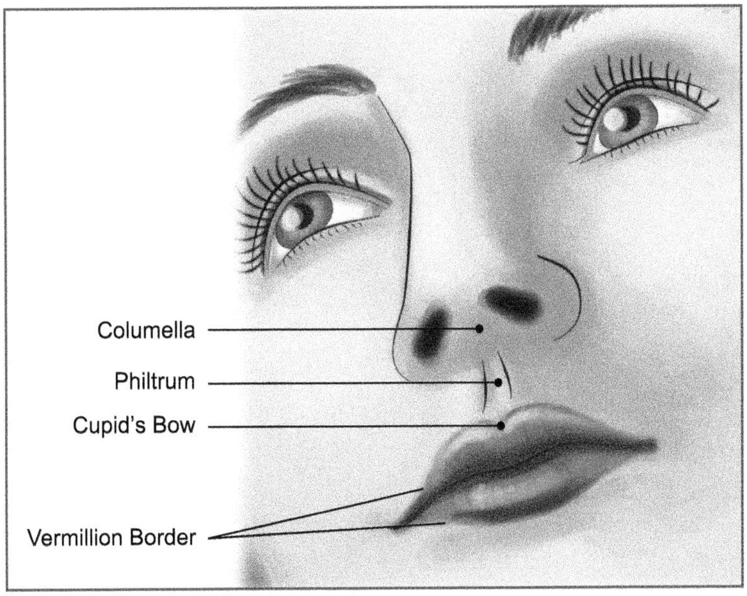

FIGURE 6–3. Some anatomical landmarks of the face.

FIGURE 6–4. Ambroise Pare, considered one of the greatest surgeons of the 16th century.

Unfortunately, this terminology led to the development of superstition as to the cause of the disorder. For example, it was once believed that children with cleft lips were born to women who, when pregnant, were frightened by the devil, who had assumed the shape of a hare. In 1887, a passage was published in the journal *Lancet* stating that one of the laws of heredity is that hideous physical impressions on the mind of a mother can produce deformity and monstrosity in the offspring. Support of this notion was based on a report at the time of a pregnant woman attending a carnival. One of the attractions she observed involved a trained horse pulling the trigger of a pistol, pretending to shoot a rabbit. Upon shooting, the rabbit was replaced with a stuffed (toy) rabbit that appeared to have had its head shot off. This greatly distressed the pregnant woman who later gave birth to a child resembling a rabbit. Fortunately, the term *harelip* is no longer in use and is considered demeaning. However, as a society, we have not yet moved beyond using names of animals to describe human conditions. For example, the phrase *pigeon-toed* is used to refer to the turning in of feet while walking, and *crow's feet* is a phrase used to refer to small wrinkles around the outer corners of the eyes.

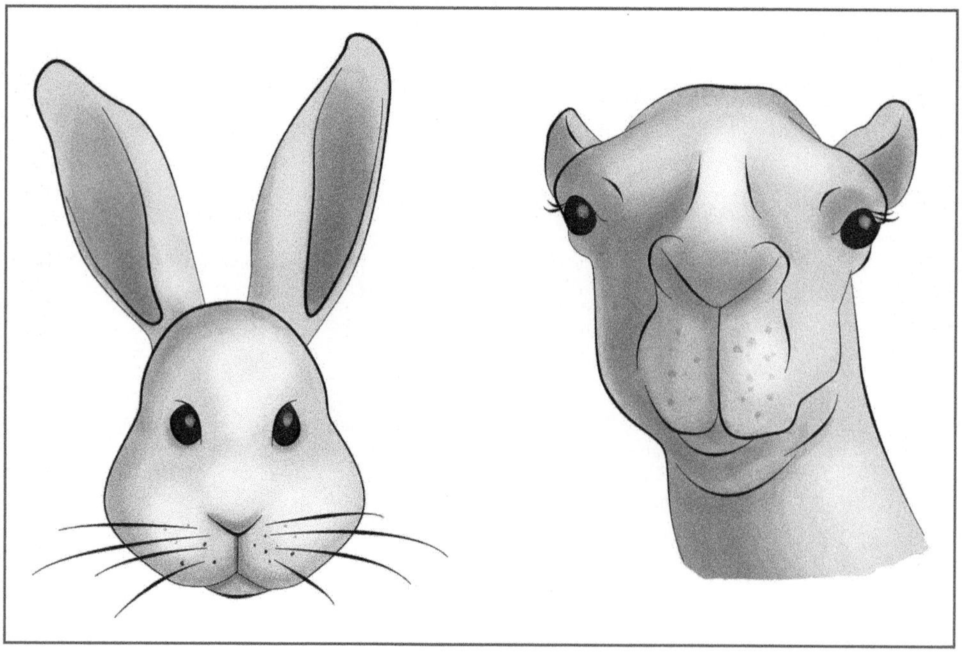

FIGURE 6–5. Example of two animals that have a split lip used for grasping food during eating.

Cosmetic surgery began in the ancient world. The Romans performed simple techniques such as repairing damaged ears. Physicians in ancient India used skin grafts for reconstructive work as early as 800 BC. The first report of surgical cleft lip repair came from China in 390 when an 18-year-old named Wei Yang Chi received the surgery. Chi subsequently became the Governor General of six Chinese Provinces (Rogers, 1971). The treatment consisted of cutting and stitching the edges of the cleft lip together, followed by 100 days of complete bed rest, when the patient could eat only thin gruel and was not allowed to smile or talk.

Jehan Yperman (1260–1331; Figure 6–6) was a medieval Belgian surgeon who is believed to have been the first person to provide a detailed description of cleft lip repair, although he made no mention of cleft palate repair. Yperman published a treatise on surgery that so meticulously described the details of needle-and-suture "pinning" surgery that some of his advice is still considered in modern surgical procedures.

The Swiss surgeon **Pierre Franco** (1506–1580) is known as the "father of cleft palate surgery." In 1556, he described in detail the principles and techniques for repairing a cleft of the palate. Because of the dangers associated with surgery in any form, especially that involving the head or face, the repair of a CL/P was almost nonexistent until the 19th century. Besides, in the absence of anesthesia, the operation was extremely painful. The first general surgery using an anesthetic known as ether was not performed until 1840, and it was not until 1860 that a cleft palate was repaired using anesthesia. It is also worth noting that the light bulb was not invented until around 1880, so many of these early surgeries were performed using lanterns. Ether is a highly flammable chemical, so its use around lanterns was extremely dangerous. Not until the 19th and 20th centuries did CL/P surgeries become commonplace.

Some of the well-known CL/P surgeons during the 1800s included the Frenchman **Philibert Joseph Roux** (1790–1854) and the Germans: **Karl Ferdinand von Graefe** (1787–1840), **Johann Friedrich Dieffenbach** (1792–1847), **Bernard von Langenbeck** (1810–1887; Figure 6–7), and **Philip Gustav Passavant** (1815–1893). Roux was best known for having performed the first surgical repair of a cleft palate in that country. Von Graefe was a pioneer of plastic and reconstructive surgery. Dieffenbach applied his surgical talents to the correction of a CL/P as well as other communicative disorders such as stuttering (see also

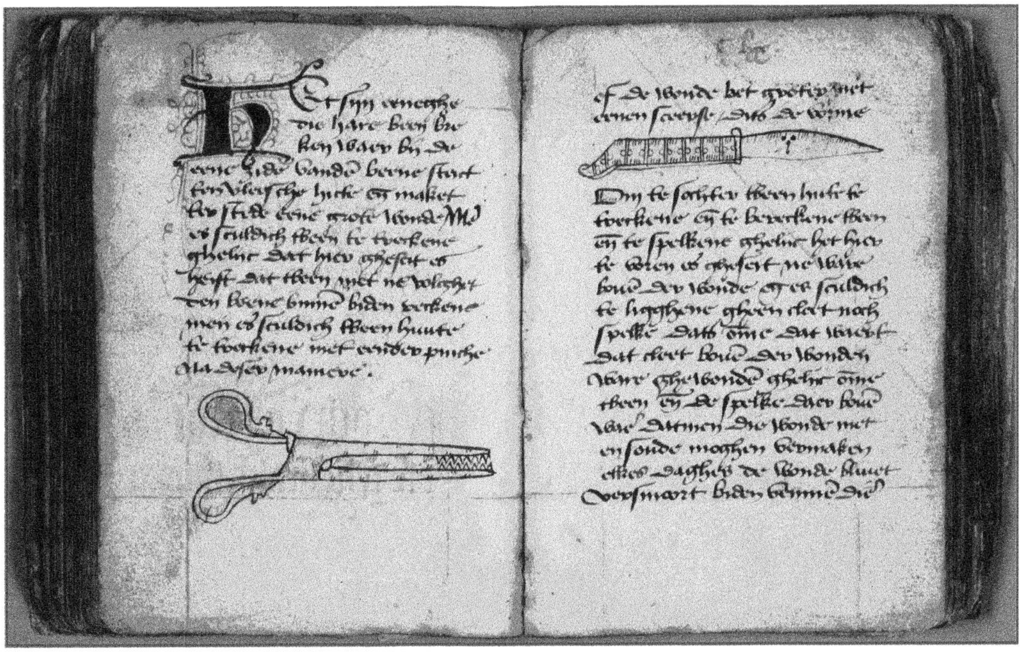

FIGURE 6–6. Example of the 13th–14th century surgical treatise written by medieval surgeon Jehan Yperman. Techniques related to cleft lip repair were included in the treatise.

FIGURE 6–7. Bernard von Langenbeck was a skilled surgeon who developed a procedure for the closure of the hard palate.

Chapter 5). Von Langenbeck was a skilled surgeon who developed a procedure for the closure of the hard palate. Passavant was a dedicated surgeon who was interested in developing surgical techniques to help improve speech production. In particular, he recommended reconstruction of the velar muscles and lengthening of the soft palate as important steps to helping individuals develop normal speech.

During the time of CL/P repairs in the mid-1800s, infants and children were rarely operated on, and most patients were mature adults with speech defects that were nearly impossible to correct. However, as improvements were introduced in surgical techniques and use of anesthesia, the age of the patients receiving surgery gradually became younger (Figure 6–8). One of the first surgeons to recognize the importance of speech therapy was **Carl Casper von Siebold** (1736–1807). He conducted detailed studies of the speech difficulties of a 3-year-old boy with a CL/P and noted that he had difficulty pronouncing the

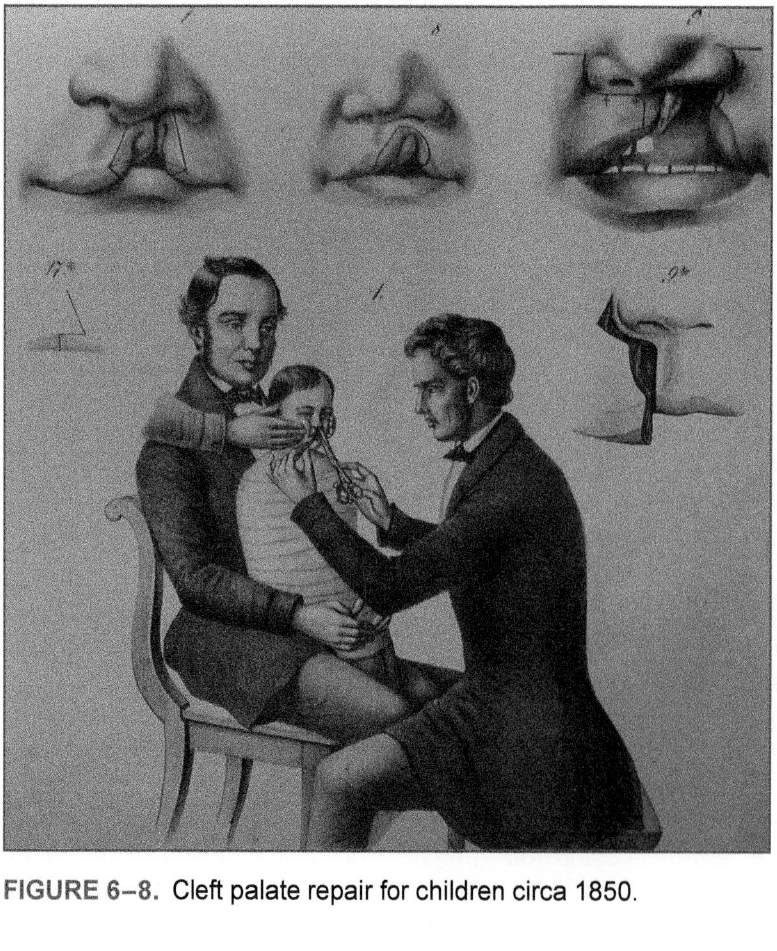

FIGURE 6–8. Cleft palate repair for children circa 1850.

letters b, s, z, and r. Siebold expressed deep regret at the impossibility of correcting the child's speech defect surgically.

The effect of a CL/P on speech was also studied in the United States by **Matthew Wilson** (1734–1802). Wilson served as both a minister and a surgeon during the American Revolutionary War. During this period in the United States, it was extremely rare for surgeons to have held a medical degree. Wilson wrote a compendium of medicine called the *Therapeutic Alphabet* that contained an alphabetical listing of diseases, symptoms, and their cures. Among the various listings was a reference to CL/P and the poor speech pronunciation that accompanied the affliction. At the time, only surgery of the lip was performed. Surgery of the palate was unheard of.

Herbert K. Cooper (1897–1978) established the first CL/P clinic in the United States when his recognition of the need for multidisciplinary involvement resulted in the formation of a unique clinic in 1938. It was the first of its kind, having all the necessary dental, surgical, and speech-language pathology specialists in one location. The team concept Cooper created is still the accepted standard of care for children with a CL/P. The clinic remains in existence in Pennsylvania and has been renamed the Lancaster Cleft Palate Clinic.

Edna Hill Young (1878–1968; Figure 6–9) was known for developing the moto-kinesthetic method of speech therapy for children. Her developments in speech therapy came from her own experiences having difficulties speaking. She had been a schoolteacher before transitioning to speech therapy. She created the Hill-Young School of Speech in Minnesota aimed to help children and adults with speech disorders and developed therapy principles for children born with a CL/P.

FIGURE 6–9. Edna Hill Young was known for developing the moto-kinesthetic method of speech therapy for children with CL/P.

DISORDERS OF CLEFT LIP AND PALATE

Clefts of the lip and palate can be categorized according to the affected structures and location of the cleft. The degree of clefting is related to the amount of embryonic damage to the lip and palate.

Cleft Lip

If the cleft does not affect the palate structure of the mouth, it is referred to as cleft lip. When the cleft occurs on only one side of the upper lip, it is called a **unilateral cleft lip**. The occurrence of a cleft on both sides of the upper lip is called a **bilateral cleft lip**. When the cleft results in a gap that goes all the way from the lip and mouth into the nostril, it is referred to as a **complete cleft lip**. If the gap does not extend from the mouth all the way into the nostril, it is referred to as an **incomplete cleft lip**. When the incomplete cleft lip is very minor (a groove or a notch), it is called a **microform cleft**. A microform cleft can appear as small as a slight indentation in the vermilion border of the lip or look like a scar from the lip up to the nostril. Examples of the various types of cleft lip are shown in Figure 6–10.

Cleft Palate

A cleft palate can be either complete or incomplete. A **complete cleft palate** involves an opening between the hard and soft palates that extends

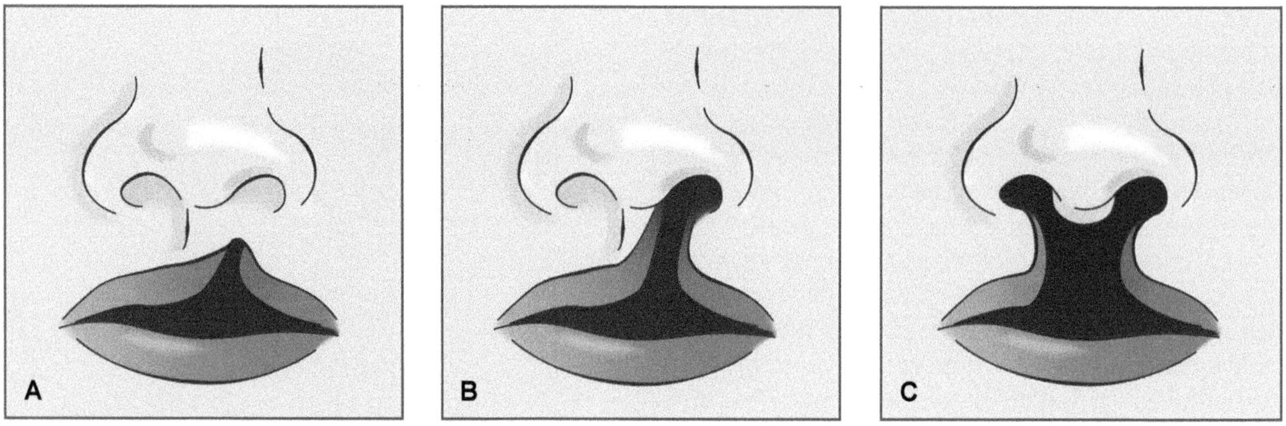

FIGURE 6–10. Types of cleft lip. **A.** Unilateral incomplete cleft lip. **B.** Unilateral complete cleft lip. **C.** Bilateral complete cleft lip.

through to the uvula. In most cases, a cleft lip is also present in conditions of a complete cleft of the hard palate. An **incomplete cleft palate** is a condition in which the hard palate may be fully developed with a cleft found only for the soft palate. In these cases, it is likely there is no cleft of the lip. Another less common and minor form of cleft palate is known as a **submucous cleft**. In this condition, there is a cleft of the muscular layer of the soft palate with an intact layer of mucosa lying over the defect. A telltale sign of a submucous cleft is a bifid (or notched) uvula. In most cases, a submucous cleft does not adversely affect swallowing and speech production. Examples of various types of clefts to the hard palate are shown in Figure 6–11.

FYI

Although most conditions of a CL/P are of a congenital nature, it is possible for a CL/P to be acquired. Oral cancer affecting either the hard or soft palate would necessitate removal of these structures, thereby creating a cleft condition. Cancer of either the hard or soft palate accounts for approximately 2% of all head and neck cancers.

Characteristics of Cleft Lip and Palate

Approximately 50% of all clefts involve a cleft of both the lip and palate. Cleft of the lip alone, or the palate alone, each account for 25% of all clefts, respectively. Instances when there are isolated clefts of the lip or palate alone are most often associated with birth defects affecting other parts of the body and/or brain. Ten percent of cleft lips are incomplete. Approximately 85% of cases of bilateral cleft lip and 70% of unilateral cleft lip also involve a cleft of the palate. Cleft lip and palate is more common on the left side, less common on the right, and least common bilaterally. There are sex differences in the occurrence of various types of clefts. Males are twice as likely to have a cleft lip and palate or an isolated cleft of the lip compared with females. Females are twice as likely to have an isolated cleft of the palate compared with males. Across the various types of clefts, males are far more likely to be born with some form of cleft compared with females.

The occurrence of a CL/P varies considerably according to race. In the United States, American Indians show the highest occurrence of clefting with 7 per 10,000 live births, followed by Latinos with a prevalence of 5 per 10,000 live births. Among the Japanese population, the occurrence of CL/P is 4.5 per 10,000. Among the Chinese population, the occurrence is 3.4 per 10,000 live births. Among the White population, the occurrence of CL/P is approximately 2 per 10,000 births. The lowest occurrence of CL/P is found among the Black population with only 0.6 per 10,000 births.

According to the International Perinatal Database of Typical Orofacial Clefts, the worldwide prevalence of CL/P is 6.64 per 10,000 individuals. However, the prevalence of CL/P differs among various countries around the world. The prevalence of children born with a CL/P in the United Kingdom is around 3 per 10,000 live births, similar to what is found in Arab countries. In Australia, Canada, and New Zealand, the prevalence is approximately 7 per 10,000 births. At the extreme ends of the continuum, Cuba and South Africa show fewer than 2 children with a cleft of the lip or palate per 10,000 births, whereas Finland and Malta have more than 14 cleft of the lip or palate births per 10,000.

CURRENT THEORIES OF CLEFT LIP AND PALATE

The exact cause of CL/P is not completely understood. Cleft lip and/or cleft palate are caused by multiple genes inherited from both parents as well as environmental factors that scientists do not yet fully understand. About 25% of occurrences of CL/P can be attributed solely to genetic inheritance. If either parent has a cleft, the relative risks become about 5% higher for having a baby with a cleft, compared with nonclefted parents. If both parents have clefts, the risks are much greater. When a combination of genes and environmental factors causes a condition, the inheritance is called **multifactorial** (i.e., many factors contribute to the cause). By far, the majority of children born with a CL/P acquire the condition as a result of combined genetic and environmental factors. There are a number of environmental conditions that interact with one or more genes to increase the risk of CL/P. These include (a) lack of a balanced diet, (b) maternal illness, (c) cigarette smoking, (d) alcohol consumption, and (e) chronic use of nonprescribed drugs or substance abuse. The risk of CL/P is found to be higher among teenage pregnancies as well as among parents (both mother and father) who are older than 35 years of age (Bille et al., 2005).

FYI

The cause of a CL/P is most often attributed to a combination of genetic and environmental factors. However, a group of scientists at the University of Bonn in Germany recently found that a genetic variant on chromosome 8 occurs with significantly higher frequency in people with CL/P than those without a cleft. Although the exact gene on chromosome 8 has yet to be identified, these results point to genes playing a far more important role in the formation of CL/P than previously thought.

ASSESSMENT OF CLEFT LIP AND PALATE

Because clefting causes obvious physical changes, diagnosis of the condition is straightforward. As ultrasound testing becomes increasingly common in routine obstetric practice and its accuracy improves, prenatal diagnosis of a CL/P is

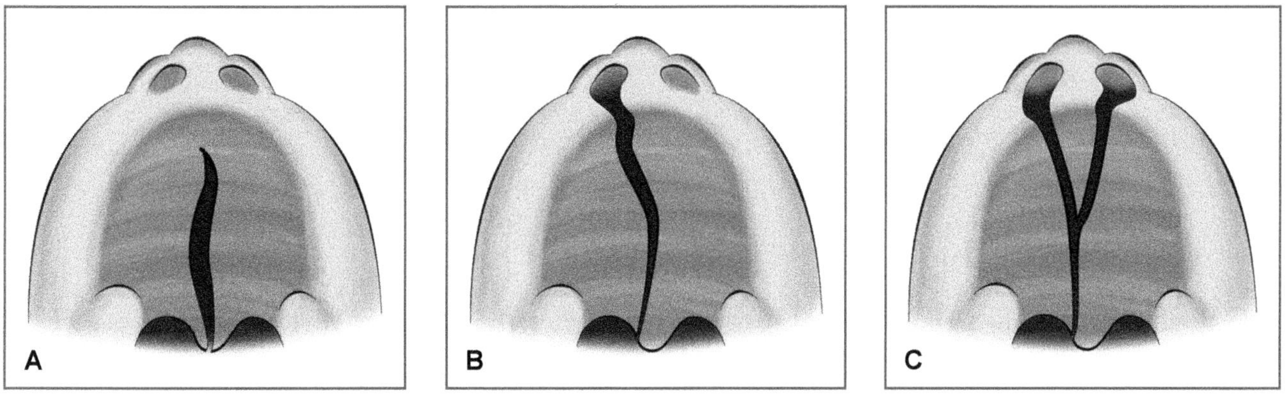

FIGURE 6–11. Types of cleft palate. **A.** Incomplete cleft of the soft palate only. **B.** Unilateral complete cleft of lip and palate. **C.** Bilateral complete cleft of lip and palate.

now a reality. Developments in ultrasound technology have enabled the identification of major facial anomalies as early as 12 weeks' gestation. If the cleft has not been detected in an ultrasound prior to the baby's birth, a physical examination at birth of the mouth, nose, and palate confirms the presence of a CL/P. Aside from the visible physical features that serve to confirm the diagnosis of a CL/P, there are related areas that are also assessed in regard to the child's health status, including (a) feeding, (b) hearing, (c) dentition, and (d) communication.

FIGURE 6–12. Feeding a baby with a cleft lip and palate. The infant is positioned in an upright position to prevent milk from entering the nasal cavity.

Feeding

Normally, in order for an infant to feed (suck), the infant needs to squeeze the nipple with the lips between the tongue and alveolar ridge at the same time, maintaining suction during the act of swallowing. The muscular motions of the jaw and soft palate at the back of the mouth allow suction to draw the milk. For an infant with a CL/P, sucking is a much more difficult task. Depending on the location and severity of the cleft, it is a challenge for the infant to maintain suction of the breast or bottle. Swallowing air is likely, so babies with clefts need thorough burping. Most babies with a CL/P are fed with a bottle, although breastfeeding is not precluded and may be attempted in some cases. It is possible that the infant may need to wear a prosthetic palate called an **obturator** to help the infant eat properly. The device helps to close off the nasal cavity from the oral cavity. The infant needs to be positioned in a nearly upright position during feeding to prevent milk from coming through the nose (Figure 6–12). Positioning the baby upright also limits choking and helps to decrease the risk of ear infections.

Hearing

Almost all babies with a CL/P are likely to acquire **otitis media** (ear infections) at some point during the first year of life. The common occurrence of otitis media is due to the fact that the muscles that move the palate also open the **eustachian tube**, which runs from the back of the throat into the middle ear space (see Chapter 14). Its primary function is to ventilate the middle ear and also to drain any accumulated secretions or debris from the middle ear space. The eustachian tube is usually closed, but among children with a CL/P, these muscles are deficient or abnormal. The tube may remain open, which results in any bacteria in the child's throat traveling into the middle ear space. Although short bouts of otitis media are common in most children, persistent otitis media may lead to permanent hearing loss. Treatment for this problem typically involves careful observation by the family physician and audiologist. In most instances, **pressure equalization tubes** (sometimes called "grommets") are surgically inserted through the eardrum to improve ventilation in the middle ear. These temporary tubes enable the child to hear better and serve to decrease the number of ear infections (see also Chapter 15).

Dentition

Children with a CL/P, particularly a cleft affecting the alveolar (gum) ridge, are likely to develop dental problems such as missing or malformed teeth. These dental problems may occur unilaterally or bilaterally (depending on the cleft). Because the young infant is not born with teeth, and the first set of teeth will eventually fall out, special planning is needed to solve the functional and cosmetic dental problems that a cleft can create. In about 25% of children with a unilateral CL/P, the upper jaw (maxilla) growth does not keep up with the lower jaw (mandible) growth, which can lead to the development of an underbite. If this occurs, the child may need **orthognathic** surgery. This type of surgery involves manipulation of various facial bones to restore the proper anatomical and functional relationship between the teeth and jaws. Fortunately, dental experts can successfully treat most problems resulting from a CL/P.

Communication

It is common for children who are born with a CL/P to have communication problems at some time in their young lives. Children with a CL/P are likely to experience problems in two domains of communication: (a) voice and (b) speech articulation. Over 50% of them will require speech therapy during early childhood. However, many children who are born with a CL/P are able to develop normal speech by the time they enter school.

Voice

The particular voice problem associated with a CL/P concerns the ability to regulate air flowing through the nasal cavity during speech production. During normal speech production, the nasal cavity is typically closed off from the oral cavity by elevating the velum against the back of the throat (pharynx). This process is referred to as **velopharyngeal closure** (Figure 6–13). You can observe velopharyngeal closure by facing a mirror, opening your mouth, and saying "ahhh," as your doctor might have you say during a routine visit. At the precise moment of turning on your voice, you should observe the uvula elevate and press against the back of the throat. This physiological movement may be impaired in an individual with a CL/P.

In cases of a CL/P, the palatal structures may be impaired, resulting in a lack of closure between the oral and nasal cavities. The inability to close off the nasal cavity from the mouth is called **velopharyngeal inadequacy**. The end result is that excessive air flows through the nasal cavity during talking, which results in **hypernasal speech**. Children who have velopharyngeal inadequacy may sound like they are "talking through their noses." Prior to surgery, it is likely all children with a cleft palate will exhibit hypernasal speech. Approximately 25% of children who undergo repair of a cleft palate may still show signs of velopharyngeal inadequacy. Assessment of velopharyngeal inadequacy can be accomplished in a number of ways. By placing a small mirror directly below the nose and having the child speak, one is able to determine whether excessive nasal airflow is occurring by simply noting whether the mirror fogs up.

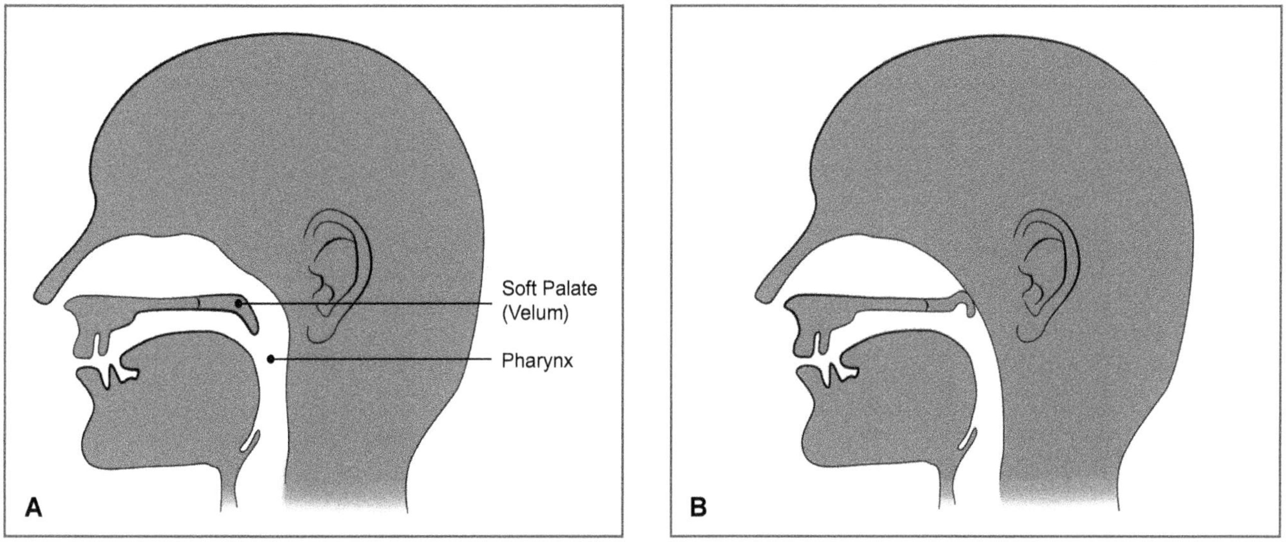

FIGURE 6–13. Depiction of velopharyngeal opening (**A**) and velopharyngeal closure (**B**).

A second approach involves either directly listening to nasal airflow or using an instrument to measure the amount of airflow exiting the nose during speech production (Figure 6–14). A commercially available instrument known as a **nasometer** has been specially created to measure nasal airflow.

Speech Sound Production

Not only are the lips and palate essential for eating, but like the teeth, tongue, and other throat and mouth structures, they are also used to produce speech. When we speak, the stream of air from the lungs passes through the vocal tract and is shaped to produce the many different consonant and vowel sounds used to create strings of words. Nearly all the sounds of English involve closure of the nasal cavity, and the sounds are directed through the mouth. The only exceptions are the nasal consonants /m/ (e.g., me), /n/ (e.g., no), and /ŋ/ (e.g., sing), which all have a natural nasal quality to their production. In the case of velopharyngeal inadequacy, the consonants and vowels that normally are produced through the mouth are now produced through the mouth *and* nose.

Because of advances in surgical techniques, speech articulation is seldom a problem. However, if problems with speech sound production do exist, they are related to two particular classes of

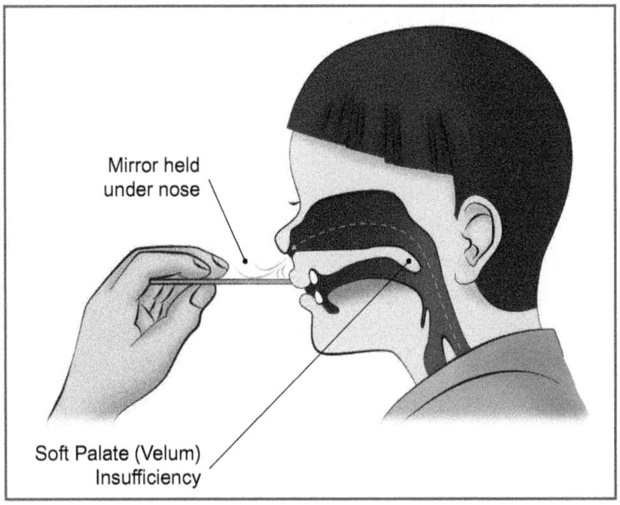

A

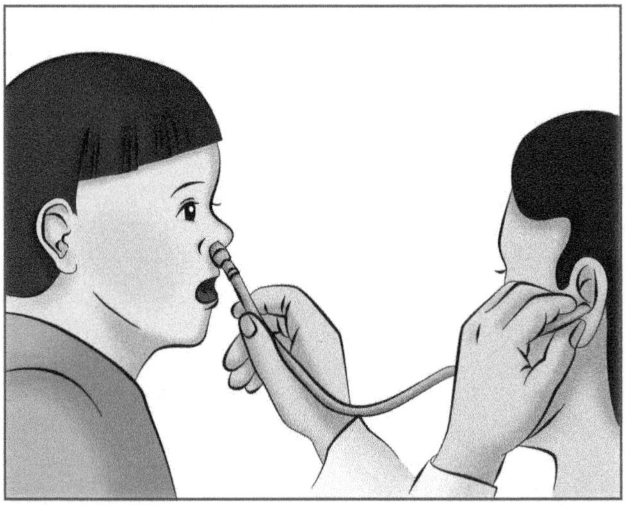

B

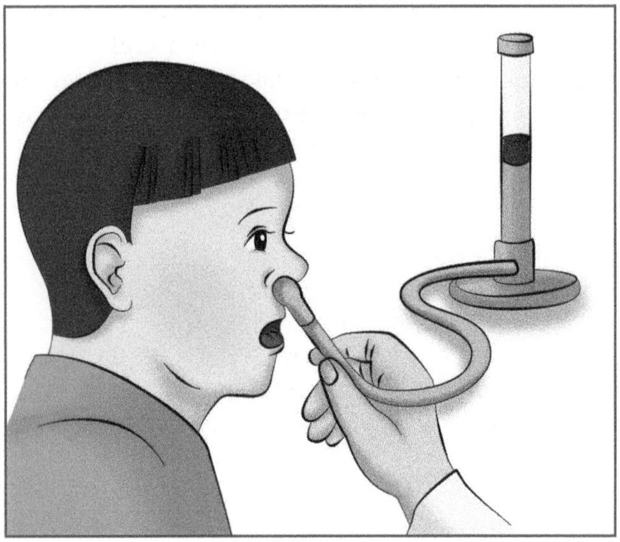

C

FIGURE 6–14. Devices for detecting velopharyngeal insufficiency (hypernasal airflow). **A.** Mirror. **B.** Listening device. **C.** Airflow detecting instrument.

speech sounds. These are stop consonants (i.e., p, t, k, b, d, g) and fricative consonants (e.g., s, z, f, v, th, sh). To be produced correctly, these consonants require the buildup of a large amount of air pressure inside the oral cavity. For stop consonants, air pressure is created behind a point of constriction (such as the closed lips for /p/) and then suddenly released. If the child is unable to maintain a sufficient amount of pressure at this point of constriction because of air escaping through the nose, the subsequent production of this consonant is likely to be weak. The child may acquire a **compensatory strategy** to this situation by producing a **glottal stop** (ʔ). A glottal stop is articulated deep in the vocal tract and thus bypasses any possible nasal emission that would occur in the forward flow of speech. Acoustically, it sounds like the break separating the syllables of the interjection *uh-oh*. To produce fricatives, high oral air pressure is required to maintain a forward flow of air friction (such as in the production of /v/). If the child is unable to maintain enough air pressure for fricatives, the sound will be substituted by a fricative-like sound made in the pharynx. This sound is called a **pharyngeal fricative** (ʕ) and is produced by vibrations set up between the back of the tongue and the pharyngeal wall. Acoustically, the sound resembles the /h/, but it is made with increased friction in the back of the throat.

TREATMENT OF CLEFT LIP AND PALATE

A child with a CL/P will need to see a variety of specialists who work together as a team to treat the condition and improve the quality of life. Treatment usually begins in the first few months of an infant's life, depending on the health of the infant and the extent of the cleft. Various forms of treatment can extend until the patient reaches early adulthood (Table 6–1). The need for assembling a team of health professionals is related to the notion of the *whole child* and the many facets related to human growth and cognitive development that are found across various health disciplines. The use of a team also is an ideal way of managing complex medical problems and avoids rigid compartmentalization of various specialties in medical practice. The idea that many brains are better than one prevails in working with children who have complex needs. The concept of a **cleft palate team** was first developed by Herbert Cooper in 1938 and has continued to serve as the preferred model of health care for children with a CL/P. The principal role of the multidisciplinary team is to provide integrated case management for the child and to ensure the quality and continuity of care and long-term follow-up. A typical cleft palate team consists of the following:

- audiologist, who manages ongoing hearing status
- geneticist, who screens child for possible syndromes and counsels parents for future pregnancies
- orthodontist, who straightens the teeth and aligns the jaw
- otolaryngologist, who monitors middle ear problems
- pediatrician, who monitors the child's overall health and development
- pediatric dentist, who makes prosthetic devices for the mouth
- psychologist or social worker, who supports the family and assesses any adjustment problems
- speech-language pathologist, who treats communication and feeding problems
- surgeon, who manages the cleft repair

All of the specialties contributing to the cleft palate team are important and provide a valuable contribution to the well-being of a child with a CL/P. Specific forms of treatment offered by the surgeon, speech-language pathologist, and psychologist are detailed later.

> FYI
>
> Young children who have dental problems resulting from a CL/P are treated by a pedodontist. A pedodontist is a dentist who manages the treatment plan for these children. Generally, treating a child may take two or three times longer than treating an adult with the same procedure.

Table 6–1. Typical Timeline of Treatment for a Child Born With Cleft Lip and Palate

Age	*Treatment*
1 month	Evaluation of feeding Hearing evaluation Dental evaluation Emotional support for families Planning for upcoming surgery
3 months	Repair of cleft lip
3–12 months	Continued dental evaluations Hearing evaluation Speech evaluation
1 year	Repair of cleft palate Insertion of pressure equalization tubes if required
1–5 years	Annual hearing and speech evaluation Dental evaluation Evaluation of child's emotional development Occasional lip and palate revision surgery to minimize deformity
5–9 years	Orthodontic preparation before permanent teeth erupt Continued speech evaluations
9–20 years	Orthodontic treatment Minor lip and nose surgical revisions

Surgery

Cleft palates must be surgically repaired before the baby is ready to speak. There is no worldwide consensus on the surgical techniques for repair of a CL/P. The decision as to when and how to repair a cleft lip or palate is based on a variety of factors such as facial growth, speech development, and psychological impact on the child and family. As a general rule, a child born with a cleft of the lip (with or without a cleft of the palate) usually has the lip repaired at approximately 3 months of age. By waiting a few months following birth, the size of the lips increases and makes the repair more precise. The primary reason for repairing the lip earlier than the palate is to permit as near normal feeding as possible. Another reason is to improve the appearance of the child in regard to social acceptance. Repair of the palate, usually between 9 and 15 months of age, is performed primarily for speech purposes. Without an intact hard and soft palate, it would be nearly impossible for the child to produce intelligible speech.

Other surgical treatments for cleft deformities occur during the teenage years and may include nasal reconstruction and possibly jaw alignment. However, this latter surgery is typically delayed until growth of the facial skeleton is complete. In addition to the surgical procedures that are designed to repair the palatal and facial structures, there are other procedures performed to assist with speech production. Some children may continue to demonstrate velopharyngeal inadequacy following initial palate repair. Sometimes the palate is still not able to close off the nose from the mouth. This may be because it is too short, does not stretch far enough backward and upward, or does not move quickly enough. A widely performed surgical procedure to eliminate velopharyngeal inadequacy is the creation of a **pharyngeal flap**, which is usually performed between 6 and 12 years of age (Figure 6–15). Another surgical procedure is the sphincter **pharyngoplasty**. In this procedure, the surgeon moves tissue from the back of the throat closer to the back of the palate. This surgery is recommended when the surgeon decides that the palate is working as well as it can, but the back of the throat (pharynx) is not moving correctly (see Figure 6–15).

> **FYI**
>
> The type of doctor who usually performs a CL/P operation is a craniofacial surgeon, which is a subspecialty of plastic surgery. Craniofacial surgery deals with congenital and acquired deformities of the skull, face, and jaw.

Another option for improving velopharyngeal function for some patients is a prosthetic device (i.e., obturator). These speech aids are placed in the mouth, much like an orthodontic retainer. One common type of obturator is a speech bulb (Figure 6–16), which is designed to partially close off the space between the soft palate and the throat. An acrylic ball is attached to an acrylic (dental) retainer held by the teeth. The bulb is tailored to the vocal tract anatomy and physiology of the patient. Many professionals feel that prosthetic appliances work best in children who are at least 5 years of age.

Cleft of the Lip or Palate Fetal Surgery

While the surgical correction of cleft lip and palate has improved dramatically over the past decades, patients still show residual effects of the surgery, such as a visible scar or speech disorder. The advent of fetal surgery has been suggested as a way of alleviating these residual effects. The procedure involves partially removing the fetus from inside a pregnant woman's uterus, performing the surgery, and then resealing the fetus into the mother's womb. A major risk in this type of open surgery is that premature labor can be induced, thereby further threatening the life of the baby. The development of feto-endoscopic surgery is far less invasive and may ultimately serve as an approach to the treatment of a CL/P. In addition to scarless fetal wound healing, an advantage of this fetal surgery would contribute to better skeletal development of the midface. Presently, fetal surgery is considered as a last-resort option, primarily for such medical conditions that will prove fatal if the repair is delayed until delivery. At the moment, this type of surgery does not apply (nor is it warranted) for children who have been

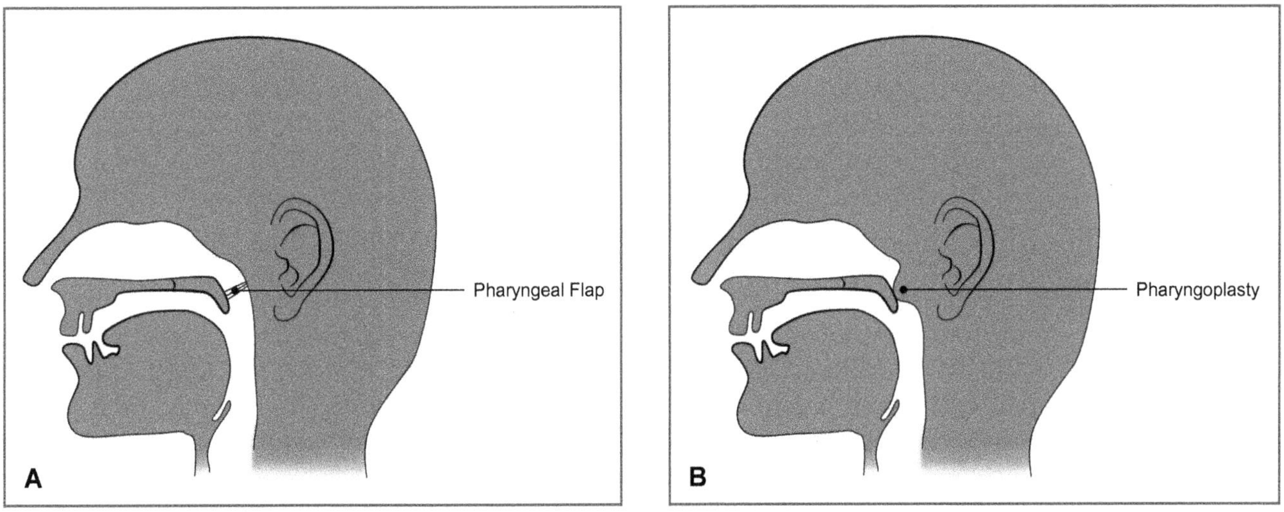

FIGURE 6–15. **A.** Pharyngeal flap. **B.** Pharyngoplasty.

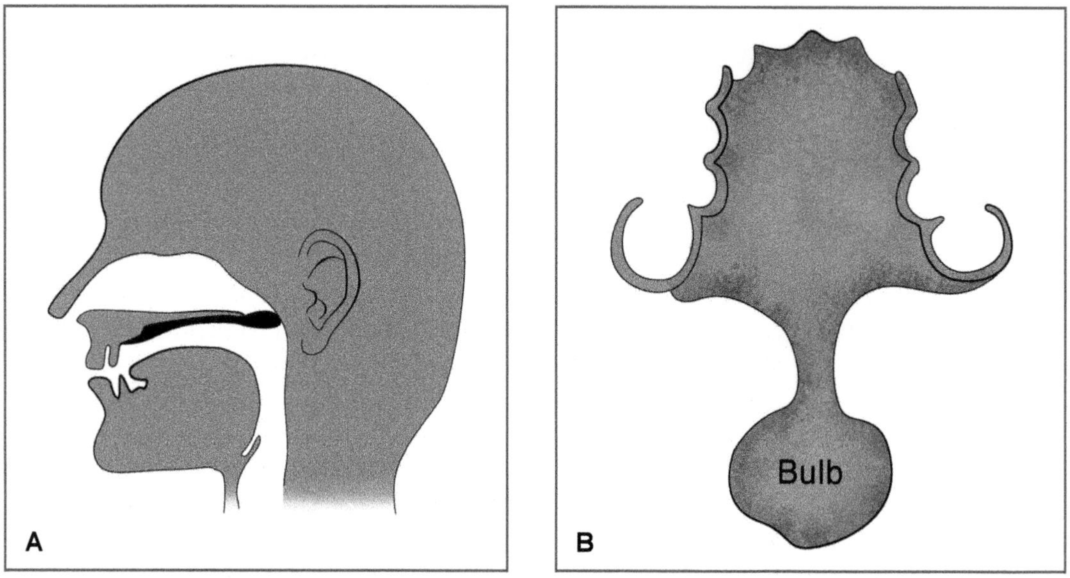

FIGURE 6–16. Example of a prosthetic device called a bulb obturator that is fit to the hard palate similar to a dental retainer. The bulb assists with maintaining velopharyngeal closure for speech production.

prenatally diagnosed with a CL/P. Surgeons are not clinically ready to repair a fetal CL/P, and potential issues for the fetus and mother from the surgery are far too high. Theoretically, fetal surgery for a CL/P would significantly advance treatment of the condition; however, the current risks associated with the surgery outweigh the benefits (Vardhan & Verma, 2023).

Speech-Language Therapy

Since the early development of the speech-language pathology profession, there has been heightened interest in the communication characteristics exhibited by individuals with a CL/P. From 1940 to 1960, many speech-language pathologists believed that children with a CL/P showed oral-motor problems that prevented them from producing clear speech. As a means of addressing this assumed problem, children with a CL/P were asked to undergo a number of activities designed to strengthen the speech musculature. Some of these strengthening exercises involved swallowing, sucking, blowing, and whistling. Tasks such as these were later discredited during the 1960s and 1970s because research failed to substantiate an improvement in speech articulation. That is, the children may have shown improvements in their abilities to blow and whistle, but these nonspeech activities did not transfer to speaking ability. We now know that a typical child with a CL/P does not have oral-motor problems.

Although current medical technology is not advanced enough to prevent the occurrence of a CL/P, most of the speech problems associated with a CL/P can be improved or even corrected. There is no doubt that a child with an unrepaired CL/P will experience severe speech difficulties. However, this is becoming the exception rather than the norm. Following surgery, only 10% of children are likely to experience a communication disorder. For those whom speech articulation difficulties may persist, the use of conventional articulation/phonology therapy approaches is preferred. Aside from speech problems, another area of concern is in regard to the child's voice, specifically the production of hypernasal speech. This condition may be corrected surgically (see previous section). However, if the child still demonstrates velopharyngeal inadequacy, some form of therapy may be required. The use of devices that provide the child with visual or auditory feedback regarding the amount of speech nasality has proven to be successful. The feedback guides the child in learning alternative strategies for maintaining appropriate closure between the oral and nasal cavities during speaking activities.

Psychology

Psychosocial issues are a critical part of the assessment and management of the child with a CL/P and must be addressed from the onset of care. The birth of a child is always a time of great family adjustment, and it is especially stressful when the child is born with a birth defect such as a CL/P. Parents often experience feelings of sadness, guilt, anger, and fear for their child's future social acceptance. Our society often focuses on people's appearance, which can make childhood, especially the teenage years, an emotionally challenging time for someone with a physical difference. Depending on the severity of the cleft, quality of the surgery, and the effect on speech clarity, a child with a CL/P may experience painful teasing or seclusion, which can damage self-esteem. Chung et al. (2019) summarized the research examining the psychosocial influences on a cleft of the lip or palate and found that 70% of children with a CL/P and their parents reported having to deal with teasing and ostracism because of their cleft. Teachers have been found to misjudge the intelligence of students with a CL/P and noticeable facial disfigurement, and this may lead to reduced teacher expectations and poor school performance. Teachers also have rated school-aged children with a CL/P as more withdrawn and inhibited compared with children without a CL/P, and this tendency has been associated with academic underachievement of children with a CL/P. Upon entering the workforce, people with a CL/P have been viewed negatively by prospective employers. Although the majority of children and adults may not experience major psychosocial consequences as a result of a CL/P, research has indicated that behavioral problems, depression, and anxiety are associated with the disorder for some individuals (Guillén et al., 2020). One role of the cleft palate team is to provide psychological and emotional support personnel who can help address emotional and social issues. A major goal for parents is to nurture their children so that they have a positive sense of self and ultimately make a contribution to their community.

CULTURAL CONSIDERATIONS AND CLEFT LIP AND PALATE

The management of children with a CL/P may require special multicultural considerations. The cultural variations that are likely to exist should be recognized in order to encourage the family's participation in the team approach. Traditional religious, as well as philosophical, beliefs are known to affect the attitudes of various cultural groups toward birth defects such as a CL/P. For example, Loh and Ascoli (2011) examined the cultural attitudes and perceived causes of a CL/P in Chinese, African, and Indian communities. Among the perceived causes were (a) the will of God and (b) punishment for past wrongdoings. Bebout and Arthur (1997) surveyed a group of Cantonese-speaking Americans and found that some individuals considered the speech produced by individuals with a CL/P as indicative of an emotional disturbance and felt that persons with a CL/P could try harder to speak in a less disordered manner. Meyerson (1990) noted that Latinos from many geographic subgroups (e.g., Mexico, Central America) have attributed the cause of a CL/P to a number of folk theories including (a) an eclipse of the moon, (b) God's punishment of sins, (c) paternal alcoholism, (d) venereal disease, and (e) emotional stress during pregnancy. Mednick et al. (2013) surveyed Russian parents of children with a CL/P and found the majority attributed the cause of the cleft to external environmental factors. Several of the parents reported living near nuclear plants when pregnant with their child. Even if folk explanations or folk treatments are rejected by members of the cleft palate team, these should not be viewed as negatively influencing the goals for the patient. Unless these alternative treatments are suspected of causing physical or mental harm to the patient, they should be viewed as an adjunct to the treatment plan.

An important cultural consideration when assessing individuals with CL/P is the use of language-specific norms for the occurrence of nasality. Some languages, such as Hindi, have a high occurrence of nasalance compared to others, such as Icelandic, with minimal nasalance. Keeping this in mind, the assessment of nasality in a person with CL/P should use nasalance norms if possible. Nasality norms are available for a variety of languages, including English, French, Spanish, Portuguese, Flemish, Greek, Malay. Mandarin, Hungarian, Estonian, Turkish, Swedish, Japanese, and Vietnamese.

In many countries, there is limited medical and rehabilitation support for people with a CL/P. Individuals may go through their entire lives with an unrepaired CL/P. In 1982, an American plastic surgeon, William Magee, and his wife Kathleen, a nurse and clinical social worker, traveled to the Philippines and volunteered their time to help repair facial clefts for those who did not have access to medical care. The country's demand for repair of clefts far exceeded what the couple was able to accomplish during their visit. In response to this initial visit to the Philippines, various volunteer agencies have since been established that are designed to provide assistance to some of the world's poorest countries in the management of cleft lips and cleft palates. Two of the better-known agencies are **Operation Smile** and **Smile Train**. Trained surgeons and other members of a cleft palate team donate their time and services to travel to various countries and quickly treat a high number of cases in a 1- to 2-week period. The stated mission of these organizations is to provide free CL/P surgery for millions of poor children in developing countries—until there are no more children who need help, and the problems contributing to a CL/P have been completely eradicated.

SUMMARY OF CHAPTER

A CL/P is defined as an elongated opening resulting from embryonic failure of parts of the mouth to fuse or merge. A CL/P is also a type of craniofacial abnormality, reflecting involvement of the bony features of the skull as well as tissue features of the face. A CL/P is the most common congenital abnormality and one of the most physically obvious types of communication disorder. If the cleft does not affect the palate structure of the mouth, it is referred to as cleft lip. When the cleft occurs on only one side of the upper lip, it is called a unilateral cleft lip. The occurrence of a cleft on both sides of the upper lip is called a bilateral cleft lip. When the cleft results in a gap that goes all the way from the lip and mouth into the nostril, it is referred to as a complete cleft lip. If the gap does not extend from the mouth all the way into the nostril, it is referred to as an incomplete cleft lip. Children with a CL/P are likely to experience problems in two domains of communication: (a) voice and (b) speech articulation. The inability to close off the nasal cavity from the mouth is called velopharyngeal inadequacy that results in hypernasal speech. If the child is unable to maintain enough oral pressure because of air escaping through the nose, the articulation of some consonants may be impaired. A child with a CL/P will need to see a variety of specialists who work together as a team to treat the condition and improve the quality of life. Treatment usually begins in the first few months of an infant's life and can extend until the patient reaches early adulthood. The management of children with a CL/P may require special multicultural considerations.

CLEFT LIP AND PALATE ON THE WORLD WIDE WEB

Following are websites that provide further information on the topic of cleft lip and palate. At the time of publication, each website was freely accessible.

American Cleft Palate Craniofacial Association
https://acpacares.org

Lancaster Cleft Palate Clinic
https://www.cleftclinic.org/about/history-legacy/

Smile Train
https://www.smiletrain.org

Operation Smile
https://www.operationsmile.org

WebMD
https://www.webmd.com/oral-health/guide/cleft-lip-cleft-palate

Cleft Lip and Palate Description
https://www.hopkinsmedicine.org/health/conditions-and-diseases/cleft-lip-and-palate

STUDY QUESTIONS

1. What are the milestones in face and lip/palate development?
2. What are the types of cleft lip and palate?
3. How has the historical treatment of cleft of the lip or palate changed over time?
4. List and describe the various areas that are assessed in a cleft of the lip or palate.
5. How is cleft of the lip or palate surgically treated?

REFERENCES

Bebout, L., & Arthur, B. (1997). Attitudes toward speech disorders: Sampling the views of Cantonese-speaking Americans. *Journal of Communication Disorders*, *30*, 205–229.

Bille, C., Skytthe, A., Vach, W., Knudsen, L., Andersen, A., Murray, J., & Christensen, K. (2005). Parent's age and the risk of oral clefts. *Epidemiology*, *16*(3), 311–316.

Chung, K., Sorouri, K., Wang, L., Suryavanshi, T., & Fisher, D. (2019). The impact of social stigma for children with cleft lip and/or palate in low-resource areas: A systematic review. *Plastic Reconstructive Surgery Global Open*, *7*(10), e2487.

Guillén, A., Peñacoba, C., & Romero, M. (2020). Psychological variables in children and adolescents with cleft lip and/or palate. *Journal of Clinical Pediatric Dentistry*, *44*, 116–122.

Loh, J., & Ascoli, M. (2011). Cross-cultural attitudes and perceptions towards cleft lip and palate deformities. *World Cultural Psychiatry Research Review*, *6*, 127–134.

Mednick, L., Snyder, J., Schook, C., Blood, E., Brown, S., & Weatherley-White, R. (2013). Causal attributions of cleft lip and palate across cultures. *Cleft Palate-Craniofacial Journal*, *50*(6), 655–661.

Meyerson, M. (1990). Cultural considerations in the treatment of Latinos with craniofacial malformations. *Cleft Palate Journal*, *27*, 279–288.

Nasreddine, G., Hajj, J., & Ghassibe-Sabbagh, M. (2021). Orofacial clefts embryology, classification, epidemiology, and genetics. *Mutation Research/Reviews in Mutation Research*, *787*, 108373.

Rogers, B. (1971). History of cleft lip and palate treatment. In W. Grabb, S. Rosenstein, & K. Bzoch (Eds.), *Cleft lip and palate: Surgical, dental, and speech aspects* (pp. 371–390). Little, Brown.

Vardhan, H., & Verma, M. (2023). Prenatal management in clefts. *Journal of Cleft Lip Palate and Craniofacial Anomalies*, *10*(1), 26–30.

7

AUTISM SPECTRUM DISORDER

OBJECTIVES

After reading this chapter, the student should be able to:

- Understand the diagnostic features of autism spectrum disorder.
- Understand some of the historical contributions in the area of autism spectrum disorder.
- Describe current theories related to the cause of autism spectrum disorder.
- Describe the communication features of a person with autism spectrum disorder.
- Understand the basic principles of communication assessment in autism spectrum disorder.
- Understand the basic principles of treatment in autism spectrum disorder.
- Describe cultural features and considerations in autism spectrum disorder.

KEY TERMS

Autism	Leo Kanner	Developmental Screening
Autism Spectrum Disorder	Hans Asperger	Developmental Diagnosis
Neurotypical	Victor Lotter	Family-Centered Practice
Pervasive Developmental Disorder	Bernard Rimland	Applied Behavior Analysis
Asperger Syndrome	Lorna Wing	Discrete Trial Training
Savant	Triad of Impairments	Early Intensive Behavioral Intervention
Pica	Greta Thunberg	Naturalistic Developmental Behavioral Intervention
Down Syndrome	Echolalia	Pivotal Response Training
Fragile X Syndrome	Theory of Mind	
Williams Syndrome	Executive Functioning Disorder	
Hyperlexia	Weak Central Cohesion Theory	
Henry Maudsley	Developmental History	
Eugen Bleuler	Developmental Monitoring	
Grunya Sukhareva		

INTRODUCTION

Autism is a term that refers to impairment in social interaction and communication and restricted repetitive and stereotypic patterns of behavior. The term **autism spectrum disorder** (ASD) is now preferred to capture the wide range of symptoms and behaviors that a child may exhibit. Some individuals diagnosed with ASD may consider their autism to be central to their self-identity and refer to themselves as an "autistic person" rather than a person who has ASD. Some autistic people prefer to use the term *autism* as they dislike the negative meaning implied by the word *disorder* in ASD. The presence of ASD is not a result of illness or disease but rather a neurodevelopmental condition that affects how a person perceives and interacts in the world. ASD is considered an invisible disability since there are no visible physical markers compared to **neurotypical** individuals. Being a developmental condition, the signs of ASD are exhibited differently as the person grows from early childhood to later childhood to adulthood (Lord et al., 2006). Being a spectrum disorder, no two people with autism are the same. Some people with ASD are affected more than others, and they vary in their challenges and abilities. Some may require daily support in their lives, while others may require minimal support and live independently.

The precise cause remains unknown, but most researchers agree that it is a difference in brain function that makes people with ASD hear, see, and feel the world differently than other people. Public awareness of ASD has grown over the past 50 years from once being a condition that was rarely discussed in public. Today, we find information about ASD across all forms of public and social media, including the views of celebrities sharing their experiences. There are many well-known people with ASD (Table 7–1).

Autism is a lifelong condition that cannot be "cured." However, depending on the individual there are approaches that may help the individual learn key life skills. Over time, and with the right kind of support, strategies may be learned to overcome some of the challenges associated with

Table 7–1. Famous People Known or Thought to Have Autism Spectrum Disorder

Susan Boyle	Scottish singer
Henry Cavendish	British philosopher
Emily Dickinson	American poet
Albert Einstein	German physicist
Temple Grandin	Professor of animal science
Daryl Hannah	American actor
Heather Kuzmich	American fashion model
Tom Malone Jr.	British TV personality
Clay Marzo	Professional surfer
Elon Musk	South African entrepreneur
Dawn Prince-Hughes	American anthropologist
Satoshi Tajiri	Japanese video game designer
Nikola Tesla	Austrian electrical engineer
Greta Thunberg	Swedish activist
Stephen Wiltshire	British architectural artist

FYI

Source: Jonathunder, GFDL 1.2 <http://www.gnu.org/licenses/old-licenses/fdl-1.2.html>, via Wikimedia Commons

Dr. Temple Grandin is certainly one of the most well-known individuals with autism in the world. She is a professor of animal science with a focus on the humane treatment of livestock animals. Dr. Grandin went on to become a well-respected scientist and a public figure for the ASD community as one of the first individuals to openly disclose that she was autistic.

autism. The information presented in this chapter is an introduction to the fascinating topic of ASD and the areas of communication affected by the condition. A speech-language pathologist can play a pivotal role by assisting people with ASD to improve their communication and ability to interact with others.

TERMINOLOGY AND DEFINITIONS

The word *autism* is derived from the Greek word *autos* meaning self. The literal meaning of autism is "alone." When this condition was first formally documented in the 1940s (see Historic Aspects later in this chapter), it was thought to be a psychiatric condition with intellectual disability as the characteristic feature of the disorder accompanied by social awkwardness (Mody & Belliveau, 2013). We now have more detailed descriptions of the behavioral features of ASD that have led to a more accurate diagnosis. A medical diagnosis of ASD is made by a psychologist, pediatrician, or other specialized doctor based on an assessment of tests and symptoms. The diagnosis is most frequently made according to the *Diagnostic and Statistical Manual of Mental Disorders, Fifth Edition* (*DSM-5*) (APA, 2013). The manual lists five criteria for the diagnosis of ASD. These criteria are (a) social communication deficit, (b) fixed interests and repetitive behaviors, (c) present since early childhood but may not be evident until later in life, (d) the behaviors impair daily functioning, and (e) the impairment is not better explained by intellectual disability. There are three levels of ASD that are differentiated by the amount of support needed by the individual. Level 1 means *requiring support*, Level 2 requires *substantial support*, and Level 3 requires *very substantial support*. ASD is also known as a type of **pervasive developmental disorder** because it can cause a severe impairment in thinking, feeling, language, and the ability to relate to others.

Prior to publication of *DSM-5*, **Asperger syndrome** was considered a separate form of autism. The person met the criteria for diagnosis of autism apart from having no language delay in childhood. Under the current *DSM-5* criteria, people who were previously diagnosed with Asperger syndrome are now diagnosed with ASD at Level 1 (*requiring support*).

The number of people known to have ASD has increased dramatically since the 1980s, partly due to changes in diagnostic practice. ASD is more prevalent than childhood diabetes, AIDS, and cancer combined. As of 2023, the rate of occurrence is approximately 1 in 40 children. The condition is about 4.5 times more common among boys than girls. Parents who have a child with ASD have a 2% to 18% chance of having a second child with the same disorder. Current estimates suggest that roughly 500,000 individuals in England and the United States and more than 12,000 people in Australia have ASD. ASD affects approximately 95,000 New Zealanders. Autism occurs in individuals of all levels of intelligence. Approximately 50% are of low intelligence, whereas around 10% show **savant** skills such as extraordinary abilities in specific areas like music and mathematics.

A variety of physical and mental health conditions frequently co-occur with ASD that are found to affect anywhere from 10% to 70% of individuals. These conditions include epilepsy (seizure disorder), gastrointestinal problems (e.g., diarrhea), restricted food habits (e.g., overeating, food aversions, **pica** [the eating of nonfood items]), disrupted sleep, attention deficit hyperactivity disorder, and social anxiety. Some of the early signs and symptoms of ASD are listed in Table 7–2. Research has shown that many people who display autistic behaviors have related but distinct disorders.

Table 7–2. Early Signs and Symptoms of Autism Spectrum Disorder

Communication Patterns
• Delays in development of spoken language • Idiosyncratic repetitive language • Lack of pragmatic aspect of language • Uses a robotic or singsong speaking voice • Inability to initiate or maintain language • Responds to a question by repeating it, rather than answering it • Has difficulty communicating needs or desires
Social Patterns
• Lack of appropriateness in verbal and nonverbal behavior • Lack of ability to develop peer relationships • Lack of apparent social and emotion reciprocity • Prefers not to be touched, held, or cuddled • Has trouble understanding feelings or talking about them • Does not share interests or achievements with others (drawings, toys)
Behavior Patterns
• Restricted, repetitive, and stereotyped patterns of behavior • Difficulty in motor control • Peculiar attachment to inanimate objects • Distressed by a change in routine • Lining up toys • Head banging • Rocking back and forth • Upset by certain sounds, smells, or textures

Note. Adapted from the American Autism Association.

These include **Down syndrome**, **Fragile X syndrome**, and **Williams syndrome**, to name a few.

While most of the information covered earlier focuses on the various challenges that characterize ASD, individuals with ASD can also display strengths and abilities that are related to their diagnosis, such as logical thinking and problem-solving skills, and academic excellence in areas like engineering, mathematics, and music. A summary of some of the common ASD traits is provided in Figure 7–1.

FYI

Hyperlexia is when a child starts reading early and far beyond the level expected for their age. *Hyper* means "better than," while *lexia* means "vocabulary" or "language." Hyperlexia is often accompanied by obsessive interest in letters and numbers. This particular strength and ability can be a feature related to the eventual diagnosis of autism.

HISTORIC ASPECTS OF AUTISM SPECTRUM DISORDER

Numerous people have made contributions to our current understanding of autism that dates back to the late 1800s. A sampling of some of the earliest documented reports as well as pioneers in the field are profiled next.

In 1867, the British psychiatrist **Henry Maudsley** (1835–1918) made early observations of children who showed a marked deviation in development that appeared to be indicative of autism. The children were found to have severe cognitive and behavioral difficulties. The term *autism* was first used by the Swiss psychiatrist **Eugen Bleuler** (1857–1939) in 1908 to describe an adult schizophrenic patient who was withdrawn and self-absorbed.

The pioneering work of **Grunya Sukhareva** (1891–1981; Figure 7–2) is often overlooked when documenting the timeline of historic contributions. Sukhareva was a Russian child psychiatrist who is believed to have provided the earliest detailed descriptions of autistic behavior in six boys in 1925. Although she did not specifically use the term *autism*, she described the children as being pathologically avoidant, which is a hallmark feature of autism.

In 1943, American child psychiatrist **Leo Kanner** (1894–1981; Figure 7–3) studied 11 children with a disturbance of affect contact. The children exhibited difficulties in social interactions, sensitivity to stimuli (especially sound), good intellectual potential, linguistic problems such as a propensity to repeat the words of the speaker, and difficulties in spontaneous activity. Kanner made

Source: MissLunaRose12, CC BY-SA 4.0 <https://creativecommons.org/licenses/by-sa/4.0>, via Wikimedia Commons.

FIGURE 7–1. Some of the more common features found among individuals with autism spectrum disorder.

FIGURE 7–2. Grunya Sukhareva, a clinical psychiatrist, was credited with identifying some of the primary characteristics of autism.

FIGURE 7–3. Leo Kanner was an American psychiatrist known for his contributions to defining autism spectrum disorder.

no estimate of the possible occurrence of autism but felt the condition was rare.

During the same time that Kanner was describing observable features of autism, the Austrian psychiatrist **Hans Asperger** (1906–1980; Figure 7–4) was studying a group of children who were also having problems in social interactions with their peers. They showed behavioral problems similar to those reported by Kanner, but the children did not have deficits in speech and language and were able to function independently in the community. Unlike the group that Kanner observed, most of these children were very bright and had specific areas of interest in which they could excel. Asperger referred to their condition as "autistic personality disorder."

Important work in the 1960s occurred in estimating the occurrence of autism in the general population. The South African psychologist **Victor Lotter** (d. 1988) was the first to estimate the prevalence of autism. He screened the entire 8- to 10-year-old population of children residing in Middlesex County, located in the southeastern region of the United Kingdom. He identified 35 children on the autism spectrum, and based on the population in the area, estimated the prevalence rate to be 4.5 out of 10,000 children or nearly 1 in 2,000.

FIGURE 7–4. Hans Asperger was an Austrian psychiatrist who identified a form of autism termed *autistic personality disorder.* The condition was later named Asperger syndrome.

Bernard Rimland (1928–2006) was an American psychologist who published a groundbreaking book in 1964 titled *Infantile Autism* that served to shift the focus of autism research. Prior to this publication, there was a long-held view that autism was primarily due to emotional neglect. Rimland hypothesized that autism resulted from a complex interaction of genetics, neurology, and the environment.

The British psychiatrist and autism researcher **Lorna Wing** (1928–2014; Figure 7–5) was among the first to realize that autism could be considered along a spectrum, having many different causes and affecting all age groups of people at all levels of intellectual ability. She first used the term *Asperger syndrome* to describe Hans Asperger's autistic personality disorder and speculated about the cause. Wing suggested that autism was a **triad of impairments** that involved difficulties with social interaction, communication, and imagination. She was the founder of the National Autistic Society in the United Kingdom in 1962.

FYI

Source: European Parliament, CC BY 2.0 <https://creativecommons.org/licenses/by/2.0>, via Wikimedia Commons.

Greta Thunberg (b. 2003) is a Swedish environmental activist. She has been open about her ASD diagnosis. Thunberg noted that autistic people get involved in environmental activism due to an inability to look away from the growing climate crisis.

AUTISM SPECTRUM DISORDER AND COMMUNICATION

The communication problems of ASD vary, depending on the intellectual and social development of the individual. Some may have rich vocabularies and be able to converse in great detail. Others may have very limited speaking skills and may require some form of augmentative or alternative communication (AAC). (See Chapter 12 for the topic of AAC.) For most, communication development is uneven with difficulty in language skills and social communication. Some of the more commonly affected areas of language, social and nonverbal communication, are highlighted in the following sections.

FIGURE 7–5. Lorna Wing was a British psychiatrist who recognized that autism could be considered along a spectrum, having many different causes. (*Source:* Photo courtesy of Steve Silberman.)

Language

Individuals with ASD can have difficulty effectively using language. Some children have a good vocabulary and are able to deliver an in-depth monologue about a topic that holds their interest, even though they may not be able to carry on a two-way conversation about the same topic.

A strong preference for routine and order is a common feature of ASD, which can lead to restricted or repetitive behaviors and interests. Rigid or repetitive behavior can also be found in the individual's communication. A child with ASD might say things that have no meaning or do not relate to the topic of conversation. For example, a child may count from one to five repeatedly amid a conversation that is not related to numbers. Or a child might continuously repeat words they have heard, which is a condition referred to as **echolalia**. One form, *immediate echolalia*, may occur when the individual repeats the question, "Do you want something to drink?" instead of replying with a "yes" or "no." In another form called *delayed echolalia*, an individual might say, "Do you want something to drink?" whenever the individual is asking for a drink.

Individuals with ASD are sometimes unresponsive to the language of others, such as not responding to their own name. This difficulty understanding others is sometimes mistakenly thought to indicate a possible hearing loss. Some other features of language impairment may be as follows:

- have difficulty maintaining the topic of conversation
- have difficulty with figurative language such as idioms and metaphors
- respond to questions and suggestions or directions in a literal manner
- appear to have difficulty understanding and responding to "Wh-" questions (what, where, who, why, when)
- have a pattern of speech that may have an unusual tone, pitch, or accent

Social Communication

A social communication deficit is one of the main *DSM-5* criteria for diagnosis of ASD.

The simple act of communication involves two individuals, a talker and a listener. People with ASD can fail to interact with others, related to a difficulty with perception of social cues or information and related challenges with communication (Williams, 2018).

Examples of reduced social interaction found in ASD that can affect communication include the following:

- appear disinterested in other children or people
- have a tendency to prefer to play or be alone
- may not respond to other people's greetings or smiles
- have difficulty with social situations and understanding social rules
- children may not show pretend play or "make-believe" play

FYI

Savant syndrome is a juxtaposition of severe intellectual disability and prodigious (narrow) mental ability. Individuals have an IQ generally below 70. The syndrome occurs more often in males. The most common savant skills are music (playing piano by ear), art (painting or drawing), lightning-quick mathematical calculating, calendar calculating, and mechanical/spatial skills. Savant skills were highlighted in the classic 1988 film *Rain Man*. The condition was first identified in 1887 by **John Langdon Down** (1828–1896), who used the term "idiot savant." The condition known as Down syndrome was also first identified by Down.

Nonverbal Communication

Difficulty with nonverbal conversation skills is common among people with ASD. These skills allow a person to connect and communicate with others. Problems using and being able to understand nonverbal communication cause children and adults with ASD to become frustrated in their attempts to make their feelings, thoughts, and needs known. The following are examples of nonverbal communication difficulties:

- may not understand facial expressions, body language, gestures
- avoid or do not maintain eye contact
- are unable to understand the meanings of a talker's different vocal tones
- could appear to be clumsy and have poor motor skills

CURRENT THEORIES REGARDING AUTISM SPECTRUM DISORDER

A common question after an autism diagnosis is what is the cause of autism? Earlier it was thought that autism was caused by the child's upbringing, the parents' attitude, lack of love, or being afraid of establishing and maintaining social relationships. Although we would like to think that parents are no longer blamed, all-too-frequent examples demonstrate how autism is still widely misunderstood. We now know that autism is a neurodevelopmental disorder, which is most likely caused by a combination of genetic and environmental factors. No one knows exactly what lies at the root of autism, but that has not deterred researchers from speculating. No single theory can explain all the behaviors exhibited by a person with ASD. A brief description of three popular theories is provided in the following sections.

Theory of Mind

One of the most common theories of autism is the **theory of mind** that was proposed by Baron-Cohen (1999). An individual with a theory of mind should be able to identify mental states within themselves and others and use this information to make predications regarding others' behavior. It is the capacity of a person to think or reason about mental states within themselves and recognize that their own mental state is distinct from others. This ability is vital for the development of social communication. Researchers suggest the inability to anticipate the mental state of others, especially when it is different than the child's own, may contribute to the social communication difficulties experienced by most individuals on the spectrum. "Mind reading" is something most neurotypical individuals do effortlessly, a necessary skill to predict and participate successfully in social interactions. Utilizing years of research as a foundation, Baron-Cohen concluded that children with autism suffer from "mind-blindness"—an impairment in mind reading. There is an abundance of literature and research showing theory of mind is impaired in those with ASD (Rosello et al., 2020).

Executive Functioning Disorder

The **executive functioning disorder** theory was proposed by Pennington and Ozonoff (1996). These researchers observed that individuals with ASD struggled in complex tasks involving abstract concepts such as reasoning and planning. Individuals with ASD are often observed to struggle more than their peers when their brain needs to process more information at once. As the complexity of tasks increases, individuals with autism are more impaired than those without autism. A deficit in executive functioning means that children with ASD may struggle in planning ahead, keeping things organized, following multistep directions, and combining information from several sources to problem-solve.

Weak Central Cohesion

The **weak central cohesion theory** was proposed by Happé and Frith (2006) as an inability to *see the big picture*. According to these researchers, individuals with autism tend to focus on and remember details, instead of the global form or meaning (i.e., "big picture"). This theory has been used to describe both assets and deficits in individuals with ASD. For example, this would explain why individuals with autism quite frequently develop very strong skills in math or science but have difficulty grasping the gist of a story. Individuals with ASD usually score high on tasks favoring part or detail processing. On the other hand, they may struggle in areas such as reading comprehension, literal thinking (i.e., "black-and-white" thinking), and generalizing information learned to different domains.

> **FYI**
>
> A common misconception is that vaccines cause ASD. The widespread fear that vaccines increase risk of autism originated with a 1997 study published by Andrew Wakefield, suggesting that the measles, mumps, rubella vaccine was increasing autism in British children. The paper has since been completely discredited due to serious procedural errors. Wakefield lost his medical license, and the paper was retracted.

ASSESSMENT OF AUTISM SPECTRUM DISORDER

Parents are typically the first individuals to observe autistic-like behaviors in their child. The young child may be unresponsive at an early age or show intense focus on an item/action for lengthy periods of time. Alternatively, the initial signs of autism might surface after a period of normal development. The child may begin to withdraw from social interactions and become silent. A formal diagnosis of ASD can be made as early as 18 months, and by 2 or 3 years of age, the signs of ASD are usually apparent. There are instances when individuals are not diagnosed until they are adolescents or adults. The delay in diagnosing ASD can negatively impact receiving services and support. An early diagnosis leads to early intervention.

Assessing and diagnosing ASD can be challenging because there is no specific medical test to detect the disorder. Instead, a team of professionals from various health and educational disciplines provide input. The team can include a pediatrician, neurologist, psychologist, audiologist, and speech-language pathologist, as well as family members. Observation of the child's **developmental history** is an important consideration in the diagnosis. By observing how the child's behavior changes over time, predictions can be made as to whether the child is developing normally. The speech-language pathologist is primarily interested in assessing the child's language development, nonverbal communication, speech prosody, and social skills. The Centers for Disease Control and Prevention (CDC) recommend a three-step process of developmental observation to assess and diagnose ASD: (a) monitoring, (b) screening, and (c) diagnosis.

Developmental Monitoring

Developmental monitoring is an ongoing process of observing how the child is growing and whether the child is meeting the developmental milestones in playing, learning, speaking, and behaving that most children reach by a certain age. Maintaining good communication between parents and providers about a child's skills and abilities is vital to successful monitoring.

Developmental Screening

Developmental screening involves a more formal examination of the child's development compared to developmental monitoring. The screening uses checklists that compare the child's behavior to that of same-aged children. The checklists contain items related to social-emotional behavior, language use, and motor development. Screenings are often a feature of regularly scheduled "well-child" visits. The American Academy of Pediatrics recommends that all children be screened specifically for ASD at 18 and 24 months of age.

Developmental Diagnosis

A **developmental diagnosis** is the final step in the assessment process. If the results of the developmental screening identify an area of concern, a more in-depth assessment of the child's development is undertaken, usually by a developmental pediatrician, child psychologist, or speech-language pathologist. The assessment includes administration of structured tests, parent questionnaires, and behavioral observation, designed to determine whether the child meets the *DSM-5* criteria for diagnosis of ASD. The results also determine whether there is a need for early intervention services.

> **FYI**
>
> The unemployment rate for those with autism is high. Recent research suggests that approximately 20% of autistic adults are absent from the workforce. There is encouraging news that companies are recognizing the value of fostering a diverse workforce and including those with ASD for the unique perspective they contribute.

TREATMENT OF AUTISM SPECTRUM DISORDER

Supporting individuals with ASD to improve their communication skills is essential for helping them reach their full potential. The treatment of communication difficulties related to ASD is specific to the individual due to the heterogeneity of the disorder. Every person with ASD is unique, with a range of skills and deficits. As the saying goes, "*If you've met one person with ASD, you've met one person with ASD!*" There is no cure for ASD; however, there are several therapeutic approaches that can improve how a person with ASD communicates. The speech-language pathologist has an important role in the development of an appropriate treatment program. In addition, the speech-language pathologist might make a referral to an audiologist for a hearing test to make sure the child's hearing is normal.

Treatment Programs

The focus of treatment for individuals with ASD is to address social behavior and communication skills (Hsieh et al., 2018). There are many different approaches. Ideally treatment should commence as soon as a concern is identified. So, if a diagnosis of ASD is made at 18 months of age, intervention should take place shortly thereafter. For young children, focus is placed on the child's primary interests. For older children with ASD, communication training is more guided and teaches basic language skills, such as production of single words and phrases. Advanced treatment focuses on language spontaneity and use, such as learning to hold a conversation with another person and maintaining the topic of conversation. **Family-centered practice** is an important consideration in treatment of ASD. Parents or primary caregivers, as well as other family members, have intimate knowledge of the child's strengths and needs. The collaboration between family members and the speech-language therapist has been found to lead to better outcomes for children with ASD.

Depending on the age of the child, the speech-language pathologist might work with the client individually or in small groups. Most children with ASD respond well to highly structured, specialized programs. There are many types of treatments available, including educational, social-relational, psychological, behavioral, and naturalistic. The behavioral and naturalistic approaches are especially popular because there is a large body of evidence that supports these approaches for treating symptoms of ASD. Behavioral approaches focus on changing behaviors by understanding what happens before and after the behavior. A behavioral intervention for people with ASD is known as **applied behavior analysis** (ABA). ABA works mainly on reducing problem behaviors and encourages desired behaviors. This method uses rewards or reinforcement to help the child learn and maintain desired behaviors and skills. The child's progress is closely monitored by the therapist. Two ABA therapy approaches are briefly described—Discrete Trial Training and Early Intensive Behavioral Intervention (Shinall & LaRue, 2019):

- **Discrete Trial Training:** The desired behavior or communication skill is broken down into a series of steps. These discrete steps are repeated until they are mastered to obtain the desired behavior/skill. Positive reinforcement and incentives are used to reward correct answers and behaviors. Undesired answers and behaviors are ignored.

- **Early Intensive Behavioral Intervention:** A type of ABA that is aimed at reducing atypical behaviors (e.g., poor eye contact) in young children with ASD. Children receive treatment prior to 5 years of age (usually between 2 and 3 years of age). As the title suggests, the intervention is intense and consists of 20 to 40 hours per week of individualized instruction.

The provision of treatment for ASD within the context of more naturally occurring social activities within natural environments is known as **Naturalistic Developmental Behavioral Intervention (NDBI)** (Schreibman et al., 2015). Some of the core elements of NDBI include (a) be face-to-face on the child's level, (b) follow the child's lead, (c) use positive affect and animation, (d) model appropriate language, (e) respond to communicative attempts, and (f) provide frequent direct teaching episodes (Frost et al., 2020). One type of NDBI treatment is Pivotal Response Training (Hyman et al., 2020):

- **Pivotal Response Training:** This form of training focuses on four "pivotal" areas of the child's overall development: motivation, self-management, initiation of social interaction, and responsiveness to multiple cues. The therapy is play-based within a natural environment and initiated by the child because the therapist often uses an activity or an item that interests the child to teach and help the child reach a goal. PRT takes place in a natural setting rather than a clinic setting. The goal of PRT is to improve a few pivotal skills that will help the person learn many other skills. For example, if a child makes a meaningful attempt to request a stuffed animal, the reward is the stuffed animal, not an unrelated reward. Children are rewarded for making a good attempt, even if it is not perfect (Vismara & Bogin, 2009).

Treatment Areas

The American Speech-Language-Hearing Association (https://www.asha.org/public/speech/disorders/autism/) has identified some of the primary areas of treatment for children with ASD. Depending on the needs of the person, the speech-language pathologist may work on skills such as

- getting along with others in different settings
- using a variety of communication supports
- taking turns in conversation
- moving from one task or setting to another
- accepting change and expanding interests, including trying new foods and activities
- reading and writing skills

Parents or primary caregivers, as well as other family members, should be involved in the treatment program so that it becomes part of the child's daily life. The speech-language therapist can teach families how to facilitate their child's communication during play activities by

- talking about what you are saying/doing
- talking about what a child is saying/doing
- adding extra words for what a child has said
- providing enough help to complete a task while still letting the child do it themselves
- providing sensory supports during play

Some further examples of strategies a parent or therapist could implement when communicating with an autistic person are provided in Table 7–3.

Augmentative and Alternative Communication and Autism

Approximately one third of children with ASD who fail to develop functional speech and language could benefit from AAC (see Chapter 12). Yet, historically, children with ASD were not considered ideal candidates for an AAC system because many demonstrated some expressive language ability. Educators and caregivers were hesitant about using AAC and viewed it as a last resort for children who failed to show functional expressive language. A review of research by Iacono et al. (2016) found that there is growing evidence that the use of AAC is indeed beneficial to either replacing or augmenting a person's existing communication skills. The approaches used with these children involve unaided AAC such as manual signs and/or aided AAC such as communication boards or books.

Table 7–3. Strategies for Communicating With an Autistic Person

Get and Maintain Attention
• Use the person's name so they know you are talking to them. • Use the person's hobbies or interests in an activity to engage them.
Process Important Information
• Use specific key words and pause between words and phrases to provide time to process. • Avoid using nonverbal communication (facial expressions, gestures, body language).
Avoid Open-Ended Questions
• Keep questions short and ask only the most necessary questions. • Be specific and structure the questions (e.g., offer options or choices).
Enforce Reactions of "No"
• "No" is often used when someone is putting themselves or others in danger. If it is a safety issue, look at ways of explaining danger and safety. • Set clear boundaries and explain why and where it is acceptable and not acceptable to behave in certain ways.

Note. Adapted from the National Autistic Society.

FYI

Source: Photwik Photographer for Kiddle.co, CC BY-SA 4.0 <https://creativecommons.org/licenses/by-sa/4.0>, via Wikimedia Commons

Research suggests that owning a pet dog can significantly improve the quality of life in autistic children, helping to reduce stress and aggressive behavior, and positively impact functioning in families who have a child with ASD.

CULTURAL CONSIDERATIONS AND AUTISM SPECTRUM DISORDER

Individuals of all races, ethnicity, and socioeconomic backgrounds show signs of ASD. A 2020 report produced by the *Autism and Developmental Disabilities Monitoring Network* examined the occurrence of ASD in 4-year-old and 8-year-old children living in the United States. Across both age groups, the percentage of children with ASD was higher among Black/African American, Hispanic, and Asian/Pacific Islander children compared with White children. More Black/African American children with ASD also had an intellectual disability than White and Hispanic children. In the United States, racial and ethnic differences are apparent in the age at which the diagnosis occurs. A study of Medicaid-eligible children with ASD in Philadelphia County found that on average, White children receive a diagnosis about 1.5 years earlier than Black/African American children and 2.5 years earlier than Hispanic children. Further, Black/African

American children spend more time in treatment before receiving the diagnosis of ASD (Kogan et al., 2009).

An example of how cultural beliefs can impact the accurate diagnosis of ASD can be found by considering impaired social interaction. One of the core problems with ASD is absent or poor social interaction. In some Asian cultures (e.g., Japanese), maintaining eye contact with others is considered disrespectful, while indirect eye contact is a sign of politeness. However, reduced eye contact is a part of the impaired nonverbal behavior criteria for diagnosis of ASD. Children raised in an Asian culture may avoid eye contact not because of ASD but because of the social norms of their culture (Bernier et al., 2010).

Upon receiving the news of a diagnosis of ASD, parents need to modify their original expectations of raising a neurotypical child. Whereas changes can occur associated with development and response to intervention, ASD cannot be cured. Having a child with ASD can significantly alter the family system. Cultural factors affect the family's ability to accept the child and provide the resources necessary to promote the child's adaptation and development (Bernier et al., 2010). It is essential for health/education professionals to consider the stigma associated with ASD in many cultures and how it influences their work with families and the family's perception of the child with ASD. To consider stigma at the societal and cultural levels, speech-language pathologists must be aware of their own cultural biases on how ASD is characterized and treated (c.f., Hyter & Salas-Provance, 2023).

FYI

There are over 200 movie theaters in the United Kingdom that offer Autism Friendly Screenings, where the volume is lower and the lighting is darker. These conditions reduce the sensitivity to sound and light that many people with ASD experience. These conditions make the moviegoing experience more comfortable for autistic people and their families.

SUMMARY OF CHAPTER

ASD refers to impairment in social interaction and communication and restricted repetitive and stereotypic patterns of behavior. Individuals with ASD may have difficulty effectively using language. Poor nonverbal conversation skills are common, resulting in a potentially severe communication disorder. ASD is a lifelong condition that cannot be cured; however, there are approaches that may help the individual learn key life skills. A speech-language pathologist can play a pivotal role by assisting people with ASD in improving their communication skills and ability to interact with others. Two popular forms of intervention for people with ASD are applied behavior analysis and NDBI that focus on reducing problem behaviors and encourage desired behaviors. Treatment for ASD should strive to be family centered, which provides a collaboration between the family and therapist to achieve maximal benefits. Health/education professionals need to consider the stigma associated with ASD in many cultures and how it influences their work with families and the family's perception of the child with ASD.

AUTISM SPECTRUM DISORDER ON THE WORLD WIDE WEB

Following are websites that provide further information on the topic of ASD. At the time of publication, each website was freely accessible.

American Academy of Pediatrics Council on Children with Disabilities
https://www.aap.org/en/community/aap-councils/council-on-children-with-disabilities

Autism Society
https://www.autismsociety.org

Autism Speaks
https://www.autismspeaks.org

Interagency Autism Coordinating Committee
https://iacc.hhs.gov/publications/publications-analysis/2012/treatments.shtmlexternal icon

National Institute on Child Health and Human Development
https://www.nichd.nih.gov/health/topics/autism

STUDY QUESTIONS

1. List and describe the primary features of ASD.
2. Who are some of the pioneers who contributed to our knowledge related to ASD?
3. List and describe the types of communication difficulties exhibited by people with ASD.
4. Describe some of the common theories about the underlying cause of ASD.
5. List and describe some of the behavioral and naturalistic approaches to treating ASD.

REFERENCES

American Psychiatric Association. (2013). *Diagnostic and Statistical Manual of Mental Disorders* (5th ed.). American Psychiatric Publishing.

Baron-Cohen, S. (1999). The evolution of a theory of mind. In M. C. Corballis & S. E. G. Lea (Eds.), *The descent of mind: Psychological perspectives on hominid evolution* (pp. 261–277). Oxford University Press.

Bernier, R., Mao, A., & Yen, J. (2010). Psychopathology, families, and culture: Autism. *Child and Adolescent Psychiatric Clinics of North America, 19*, 855–867.

Frost, K. M., Brian, J., Gengoux, G. W., Hardan, A., Rieth, S. R., Stahmer, A., & Ingersoll, B. (2020). Identifying and measuring the common elements of naturalistic developmental behavioral interventions for autism spectrum disorder: Development of the NDBI-Fi. *Autism, 24*(8), 2285–2297.

Happé, F., & Frith, U. (2006) The weak coherence account: Detail-focused cognitive style in autism spectrum disorders. *Journal of Autism and Developmental Disorders, 36*(1), 5–25.

Hsieh, M., Lynch, G., & Madison, C. (2018). Intervention techniques used with autism spectrum disorder by speech-language pathologist in the United States and Taiwan: A descriptive analysis of practice in clinical settings. *American Journal of Speech-Language Pathology, 27*, 1091–1104.

Hyman, S. L., Levy, S. E., Myers, S. M., & AAP Council on Children with Disabilities, Section on developmental and behavioral pediatrics. (2020). Identification, evaluation, and management of children with autism spectrum disorder. *Pediatrics, 145*(1), e20193447

Hyter, Y., & Salas-Provance, M. (2023). *Culturally responsive practices in speech, language, and hearing sciences* (2nd ed.). Plural Publishing.

Iacono, T., Trembath, D., & Erickson, S. (2016). The role of augmentative and alternative communication for children with autism: Current status and future trends. *Neuropsychiatric Disease and Treatment, 12*, 2349–2361.

Kogan, M. D., Blumberg, S. J., Schieve, L. A., Boyle, C. A., Perrin, J. M., Ghandour, R. M., . . . van Dyck, P. C. (2009). Prevalence of parent-reported diagnosis of autism spectrum disorder among children in the US. *Pediatrics, 124*(5), 1395–1403.

Lord, C., Risi, S., DiLavore, P. S., Shulman, C., Thurm, A., & Pickles, A. (2006). Autism from 2 to 9 years of age. *Archives of General Psychiatry, 63*(6), 694–701.

Mody, M., & Belliveau, J. (2013). Speech and language impairments in autism: Insights from behavior and neuroimaging. *North American Journal of Medical Sciences, 5*, 157–161.

Pennington, B. F., & Ozonoff, S. (1996). Executive functions and developmental psychopathology. *Journal of Child Psychology and Psychiatry, 37*(1), 51–87.

Rosello, B., Berenguer, C., Baixauli, I., García, R., & Miranda, A. (2020). Theory of mind profiles in children with autism spectrum disorder: Adaptive/social skills and pragmatic competence. *Frontiers in Psychology, 17*(11), 567401.

Schreibman, L., Dawson, G., Stahmer, A., Landa, R., Rogers, S., McGee, G. G., . . . Halladay, A. (2015). Naturalistic developmental behavioral interventions: Empirically validated treatments for autism spectrum disorder. *Journal of Autism and Developmental Disorders, 45*(8), 2411–2428.

Shinall, J., & LaRue, R. H. (2019). Research synopsis: Community implementation of early behavioral intervention—Higher intensity gives better outcome. *Science in Autism Treatment, 16*(12), 92–109.

Vismara, L. A., & Bogin, J. (2009). *Steps for implementation: Pivotal response training*. The National Professional Development Center on Autism Spectrum Disorders, The M.I.N.D. Institute, University of California at Davis School of Medicine.

Williams, D. (2018). Executive function and complex processing models. In J. Johnson, G. Goodman, & P. Mundy (Eds.), *The Wiley handbook of memory, autism spectrum disorder, and the law*. John Wiley & Sons.

SECTION 3

Acquired and Genetic Communication Disorders

8

VOICE DISORDERS

OBJECTIVES

After reading this chapter, the student should be able to:

- Demonstrate an understanding of anatomical, neurological bases of vocal behavior, and physiological processes of normal voice production.
- Demonstrate an understanding of the historical aspects of normal voice production and advances in the profession of otolaryngology.
- Demonstrate an understanding of current theories in voice production.
- Demonstrate knowledge of the occurrence, classification, and symptoms of voice disorders.
- Describe appropriate counseling strategies and features of vocal hygiene.
- Demonstrate knowledge of laryngectomy including physiological changes, and the various options for alaryngeal speech.
- Describe sociocultural influences in voice disorders.

KEY TERMS

Voice Disorders
Larynx
Trachea
Thyroarytenoid Muscle
Vocal Folds
Abducted
Glottis
Adducted
Phonation
Pitch
Voice Quality
Breathy Voice
Hoarse Voice
Hyper-/Hyponasal Voice
Register of Voice
Pulse Register
Modal Register
Falsetto
Loudness
Dysphonation
Aphonia
Phonatory Disorder
Edema
Hyperfunctional Voice
Hypofunctional Voice
Otolaryngologist
Ingo Titze
Vocology
Hippocrates
Aristotle
Claudius Galen
Julio Casserius
Antoine Ferrein
Henri Dutrochet
Manuel García
Indirect Laryngoscopy
Elizabeth Blackwell
Margaret F. Butler
Minoru Hirano
Friedrich Brodnitz
Phoniatrics
Phonotrauma
Vocal Misuse
Vocal Abuse
Laryngitis
Acid Reflux
Vocal Nodules
Vocal Polyp
Puberphonia
Psychogenic Disorder
Parkinson Disease
Amyotrophic Lateral Sclerosis
Monotonic Voice
Spasmodic Dysphonia
Adductor-Type Spasmodic Dysphonia
Abductor-Type Spasmodic Dysphonia
Papillomas
Raoul Husson
Neurochronaxic Theory
Myoelastic Aerodynamic Theory of Phonation
Janwillem van den Berg
Personality and Emotional Adjustment Theory
Subjective Assessment
Objective Assessments
Direct Laryngoscopy
Voice Rest
Lee Silverman Voice Treatment (LSVT)
Vocal Function Exercise
Respiratory Training
Confidential Voice
Phonosurgery
Hans von Leden
Phonomicrosurgery
Laryngectomy
Stoma
Alaryngeal Speech
Electrolarynx
Esophageal Speech
Tracheoesophageal Speech
Vocal Hygiene
Voice Feminization
Voice Masculinization

INTRODUCTION

The use of voice is an integral part of communication. Dogs bark, growl, and howl. Cats purr and mew. Birds use different calls to warn other birds about threats or food. Each animal has a distinct voice, and all animal species have some form of vocal patterns they use to communicate. The use of voice allows animals to recognize one another and convey messages like "get away," "danger," and "that feels good." Humans also use voice to communicate basic needs and wants. Because humans have also developed the capacity to use language, our use of voice has become more specialized. When we open our mouths to speak, the voice we use is uniquely special to us. Our voice shares a lot of information about us and is one of the defining features of our individuality. Infants can recognize their caregivers based on voice. Our voice tells others whether we are happy or sad, healthy or unwell, young or old. Our voice can also reveal to others our background, such as the region of the world where we live, and even our social economic status. Although some people are experts at voice impersonations, our voice is what helps to define who we are. Indeed, many past and present celebrities are readily identifiable by their voices. A list of some well-known voices is provided in Table 8–1. A "normal voice" is one that is pleasing to the ear, has a balance of sound through the mouth and nose, and matches a person's size, age, and sex. When a voice is produced that is perceived by others as unusual or strange and draws attention to the person who is speaking, it is quite likely the person is demonstrating a voice disorder.

Voice disorders occur in people of all ages. Voice disorders are also likely to be found among individuals whose occupation is dependent on having a healthy voice. These vocal performers work in a variety of settings, such as the music industry, theater, clergy, the courtroom, or the classroom. Voice disorders reflect a special form of communication disorder that involves a close working relationship between the patient, speech-language pathologist, and medical personnel. Amazingly, most instances of voice disorders are preventable by simply taking the proper precautionary steps. The fact that many voice disorders could be prevented also makes this form of communication disorder unique.

FYI

Our mood can be reflected by our body language, as well as by the characteristics of our voice. Whether we are happy, sad, angry, or afraid, there are telltale signs in our voice that signal these various moods. Research has uncovered a strong connection between our voice and corresponding mood.

Table 8–1. Unmistakable Voices of Well-Known and Some Not-So-Well-Known Celebrities

Humphrey Bogart	Actor
Bette Davis	Actor
Morgan Freeman	Actor
Janeane Garofalo	Actor
Cary Grant	Actor
Arnold Schwarzenegger	Actor
Sylvester Stallone	Actor
Alan Rickman	Actor
Luciano Pavarotti	Singer
Elvis Presley	Singer
Justin Timberlake	Singer
Madonna	Singer
Kanye West	Singer
Bing Crosby	Singer
Amy Winehouse	Singer
Christopher Martin	Singer
Nat King Cole	Singer
Dan Castellaneta	Voice of Homer Simpson
James Earl Jones	Voice of Darth Vader
Andy Serkis	Voice of Gollum — *Lord of the Rings*
Frank Oz	Voice of Yoda — *Star Wars*
Mel Blanc	Voice of Looney Tunes cartoon characters
Jim Henson	Voice of Kermit the Frog

TERMINOLOGY AND DEFINITIONS

The key anatomical structures required to produce voice can be found within the framework of the larynx. The **larynx** consists of several muscles and cartilage that work cooperatively to produce voice. To appreciate the nature of various voice disorders, it is necessary to reacquaint ourselves with the basic anatomy and physiology of the larynx (see Chapter 2). The larynx is positioned between the base of the tongue and the top of the **trachea** (windpipe), the passageway to the lungs. The larynx is not designed for the daily wear and tear we place on it to produce voice. The key function of the larynx is to protect the breathing airway from foreign matter (i.e., food, liquid) that may be heading toward the lungs. The primary muscle involved in the generation of voice is the **thyroarytenoid muscle**, which is the formal term for the **vocal folds**. The thyroarytenoid muscle is composed of two bands of smooth muscle tissue that lie opposite each other and sit prominently over the trachea. One end of the muscle is attached to the inside of the thyroid cartilage. The other end is attached to the arytenoid cartilages. When the vocal folds are **abducted** (open), a space forms between the two folds known as the **glottis**. During breathing, air flows in and out of the lungs and passes through the glottis. When the vocal folds are **adducted** (closed), the space (or glottis) disappears. During strenuous physical activities such as lifting or pulling, as well as during moments of swallowing, the vocal folds are adducted. A depiction of the vocal folds in abducted and adducted positions is shown in Figure 8–1.

FYI

A bird's larynx, called a syrinx, is anatomically simpler than that found in humans. Instead of being located at the top of the windpipe (trachea), it is located at the bottom, much closer to the lungs. This proximity to the lungs is what allows very small birds to sing so loudly.

To produce voice, we exploit the structures of the larynx by adducting the vocal folds and causing them to vibrate. The technical term for the physiological process of generating voice is **phonation**. To produce voice, the brain precisely coordinates a series of events involving the three subsystems of voice: (a) respiration, (b) phonation, and (c) resonance. The respiratory system serves as the driving force of voice production. Without the forward (exhaled) flow of air from the lungs, we would not be able to produce voice smoothly. Upon exhalation of inspired air, the phonatory system is then responsible for closing the vocal folds in a deliberate but relaxed fashion. Once the vocal folds close, air from the lungs builds up underneath them until they are blown open, causing them to vibrate and produce sound. This sound then travels outward through the oral and

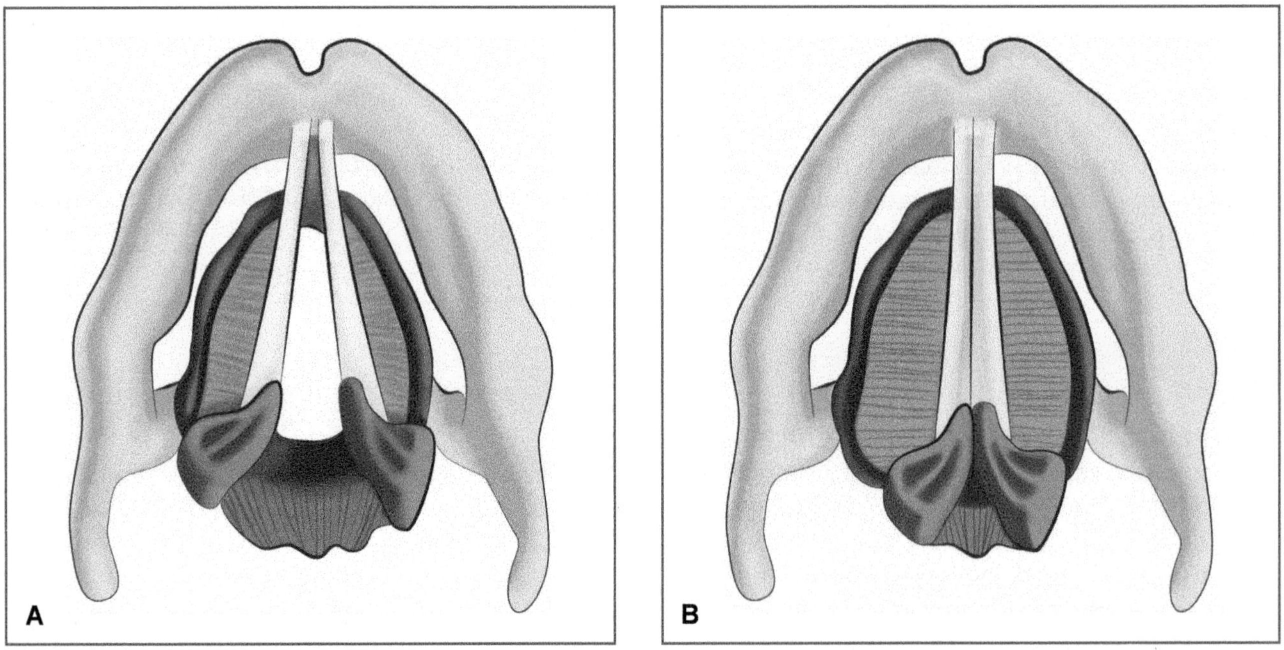

FIGURE 8–1. Superior (top-down) view of the larynx. **A.** Abducted (open) vocal folds. **B.** Adducted (closed) vocal folds.

nasal cavities, which serve to shape or resonate the sound quality as it leaves our mouth. The number of vocal fold vibrations per second determines the fundamental frequency (F0; or **pitch**) of our voice. A person's voice pitch can be high or low, variable (singsong) or flat (monotonic). An individual might also demonstrate natural pitch breaks, such as the case when young males undergo puberty. These hormonal changes can affect voice production as a young male's voice pitch begins to lower with age.

Voice quality refers to the subjective aspect of voice that is perceived by listeners. The size and shape of the vocal folds, as well as the size and shape of the oral and nasal cavities, help to determine the quality of voice. Terms such as a **breathy voice** (i.e., excessive and audible air leakage), **hoarse voice** (i.e., a grating voice with pitch breaks), or **hyper-/hyponasal voice** (e.g., too much or too little voice through the nasal cavity) are examples of qualitative descriptions of voice. Another aspect of voice quality is the dynamic range or **register of voice.** The term *register* was originally used to describe church pipe organs, where different regions of pipes combined to produce specific tones. A typical speaking voice has three registers that cover the low, middle, and high ranges of voice. The lowest register is called the **pulse register** and refers to the pulse-like quality that is produced with a low pitch. The middle register is called the **modal register** and is the region of our voice that is used during normal speaking behavior. The top range is called the **falsetto** and is rarely used in daily speaking. This voice quality may come into play when laughing loudly or when singing a high note. Voice **loudness** is somewhat self-explanatory. A voice can be produced excessively soft or loud. The term **voiced sounds** encompasses all vowels, as well as approximately one half of all consonants.

> **FYI**
>
> The whistle register is the highest register of the human voice. The sound in this register resembles a flute. The ability to produce a voice in this register is believed to be rare. Minnie Riperton (1947–1979) was a famous vocalist of the 20th century who popularized the whistle register. This style of singing is also used by the pop artist Mariah Carey.

> **FYI**
>
> A castrato is a male singer with an artificially created falsetto (high-pitched) voice, the result of castration in childhood that stunts the growth of the larynx. The combination of the larynx of a boy and the chest and lungs of a man produces a powerful voice of great range and unique sound. Castrati were especially popular in churches and opera in Europe during the 17th and 18th centuries.

A voice disorder is a condition whereby a person's voice pitch, quality, or loudness differs from that of people of the same sex, age, geographic region, or cultural background. **Dysphonation** refers to any type of impaired voice and includes a condition called **aphonia**, which is the inability to produce any sort of voice. The term **phonatory disorder** is synonymous with a voice disorder. **Edema** is a buildup of fluid in tissue that is a natural, protective reaction to trauma or misuse. The vocal folds make up a delicate muscle that is prone to edema, even under the slightest instances of misuse. Edema may also develop in tissue as a side effect to certain drugs. **Hyperfunctional voice** refers to speaking with excessive muscular effort and force resulting in a tense, high-pitched voice. In contrast, **hypofunctional voice** reflects inadequate muscle tone of the laryngeal mechanism during the production of voice, often resulting in a weak, low-pitched voice that may also sound breathy. An **otolaryngologist** is a surgeon who specializes in disorders of the **e**ar, **n**ose, and **t**hroat (i.e., ENT surgeon or otolaryngology, head, and neck surgeon). These professionals provide the initial diagnosis of a voice disorder. Most recently, the physicist **Ingo Titze** (Figure 8–2), who is one of the world leaders in the scientific study of the human voice, coined the term **vocology** to reflect the clinical practice of voice rehabilitation.

HISTORIC ASPECTS OF VOICE DISORDERS

People have sung through the ages, and so it is not surprising to find accounts of normal or unusual voice production dating back many centuries.

FIGURE 8–2. Ingo Titze, one of the world leaders in the scientific study of human voice. (Permission granted by I. Titze.)

Hippocrates described the importance of the lungs, trachea, lips, and tongue in phonation in the early fifth century BC. In 350 BC, **Aristotle** was the first to mention the larynx in his book *Historia Animalium*, in which he described the neck as the part between the face and the chest. He noted that the larynx was located at the front of the neck, and it was through this structure that speech and breathing occurred.

Claudius Galen (129–200) of the ancient Greek city of Pergamum was a physiologist considered the most important contributor to medicine following Hippocrates and the founder of laryngology and voice science. Because dissections of human corpses were against Roman law in the second century, Galen uncovered information about laryngeal physiology and anatomy based on dissections of apes and pigs. Galen was the first to recognize the larynx as the primary organ of voice and the regulation of breathing and called it "an instrument of pneuma." Galen theorized that the larynx functioned similar to a flute, where the vocal folds were the beak (mouthpiece), and the trachea was the body of the flute. Even though Galen learned much about the larynx, he had no ability to observe how it worked in a living person; therefore, knowledge regarding the specific aspects of voice production would not come about for many centuries.

Julio Casserius (1552–1616) was an Italian anatomist who made a major contribution to the study of voice with his 1600 publication of *The Anatomy of Voice and Hearing*. The book contained remarkably accurate artistic renderings of the anatomy of the larynx in humans and mammals.

In 1741, French anatomist **Antoine Ferrein** (1693–1769; Figure 8–3) concluded that the larynx functioned like that of a stringed instrument, in which the loudness and variety of tones produced by the voice were a result of different degrees of tension and length. The concept of a vibrating string led Ferrein to develop the term *vocal cords*.

Henri Dutrochet (1776–1847) was a French botanist who was primarily interested in plant physiology. His research involved investigations of the mechanisms responsible for physical movement in plants that led to his discovery of cell biology. His interest in the natural biological movement of organisms also carried over to the examination of certain excitability responses in animals, namely, the production of voice. In 1806, he published *A New Theory of Voice* and theorized about the way the vocal folds vibrated. His view was different from that of Ferrein; Dutrochet recommended dropping the term *vocal cords* in favor of the term *vocal folds* because of the observation that the vocal ligaments of the larynx did not act as cords but rather like a reed of a clarinet.

In ancient Greece, the larynx was often singled out as the root cause of various diseases.

FIGURE 8–3. Antoine Ferrein, 18th-century French anatomist who coined the term *vocal cords*.

The primary symptom of many diseases, such as diphtheria, typhus, and tuberculosis, was a marked change in voice or coughing. Because the voice failed to function normally, considerable interest grew in examining the larynx from both a physiological and a clinical viewpoint. By the early part of the 19th century, there was an overwhelming curiosity to visualize the interior of the larynx through the development of various types of viewing instruments. However, it was not until the Spaniard **Manuel García** (1805–1906) created the laryngeal mirror in 1855 that clear examinations of the larynx were possible. García was an opera singer who had a personal interest in the physiology of voice production. Using a dentist's mirror placed in the back of his own throat and positioning it at a proper angle, he was able to see the reflection of his vocal folds in an opposing mirror (Figure 8–4). The procedure was originally referred to as auto-laryngoscopy but today is referred to as **indirect laryngoscopy**. García was hardly the first to investigate the physiology of voice, but what made his work different was that he experimented on himself, seeking the cause of his own voice ailment.

Elizabeth Blackwell (1821–1910; Figure 8–5) was the first woman to obtain a medical degree in the United States by graduating at the top of her class from the Geneva Medical College of New York in 1849. Blackwell enabled many more women to follow in her footsteps, including one of the first female otolaryngologists, **Margaret F. Butler** (1861–1931; Figure 8–6). Butler initially decided to specialize in gynecology but recognized the need for her skills in otolaryngology.

FIGURE 8–5. Elizabeth Blackwell. The first female physician in the United States.

FIGURE 8–4. Manuel García performing an indirect laryngoscopy. Note that the light source is an oil lamp.

FIGURE 8–6. Margaret Butler, one of the first female otolaryngologists.

FIGURE 8–7. Minoru Hirano, known for his contributions to vocal fold anatomy.

A clinical professor of laryngology and chief of the nose and throat department at the Woman's Medical College of Pennsylvania in 1906, she was the sole representative from the United States at the First International Congress of Rhinolaryngology held in Vienna in 1908. She invented several ENT surgical instruments, including a device to remove tonsils, called the *Butler tonsil snare*.

Minoru Hirano (1932–2017; Figure 8–7) of Kurume, Japan, was a laryngologist and pioneer in the use of video stroboscopy to visualize the vibration of the vocal folds. In 1974 he proposed his theory of voice production that is now known as the cover-body theory. He demonstrated that the vocal folds were not a single-body structure but actually a multilayered muscle. His publication, *Histological Color Atlas of the Human Larynx*, is widely used in clinical practice.

> FYI
>
> As late as 1947, there were 77 approved medical colleges in the United States with four still closed to women, including the world-renowned Harvard Medical College. Of the colleges that accepted both women and men during that time, most limited their enrollment of women to 5%. Today, the enrollment of men and women in medical schools is equal.

The assessment and management of voice disorders remained exclusively within the domain of otolaryngologists or singing teachers throughout the 19th century and the early 20th century. **Friedrich Brodnitz** (1899–1995; Figure 8–8) was a German physician who introduced the concept of **phoniatrics** (i.e., voice science) in the late 1930s. When he arrived in the United States in 1937, he was something of a novelty among ENT surgeons, having been trained in both otolaryngology and speech therapy. Prior to this time, there was little interest in the field of voice disorders among otolaryngologists. He established one of the first clinics in the United States for voice disorders and devoted his life to problems of the voice, especially when they interfered with the livelihoods

FIGURE 8–8. Friedrich Brodnitz, German physician who introduced the concept of phoniatrics.

of opera singers, actors, or others who used their voice professionally. Brodnitz was a pioneer in the so-called chewing method, which consisted of exercises designed to strengthen and realign the throat muscles to produce less strain and better control of the vocal folds.

The development of the speech-language pathology profession served to greatly advance assessment and treatment approaches to voice disorders. Two textbooks, designed specifically for use by speech-language pathologists in their clinical practice, were published in the 1930s and contained material concerning voice disorders. The first of these books was *The Rehabilitation of Speech* (West, Kennedy, & Carr, 1937), followed by *Speech Correction: Principles and Methods* (Van Riper, 1939).

TYPES OF VOICE DISORDERS

Voice problems rarely occur instantaneously. Such problems do not occur overnight. Rather, it is likely voice disorders result from daily lifestyle behaviors, including occupational or social demands on the voice, as well as issues related to overall health. Voice disorders are classified according to the causal basis of the disorder. Colton, Casper, and Leonard (2011) organized voice disorders into three categories, those resulting from (a) vocal misuse, (b) nervous system involvement, or (c) organic disease and trauma. Some of the more frequently encountered voice disorders found in each of these categories are highlighted next. A comprehensive list of the wide range of voice disorders can be found in Table 8–2.

Vocal Misuse

The first types of voice disorders are those related to vocal misuse. In these instances, the basic anatomy of the larynx is normal, but the manner in which the larynx is being used contributes to a voice disorder. Vocal misuse (also called **phonotrauma**) is any improper or inefficient speaking behavior that can damage the vocal folds and cause temporary or permanent changes in vocal function, voice quality, and possible loss of voice. Examples of vocal misuse include excessive talking, throat clearing, coughing, inhaling of irritants, smoking, screaming, or yelling. The term **vocal misuse** is preferred over **vocal abuse** because "abuse" places blame for the disorder on

FYI

Source: Indiapuppet, CC BY-SA 3.0 <https://creativecommons.org/licenses/by-sa/3.0>, via Wikimedia Commons

The term *ventriloquism* comes from the Latin venter (belly) and loqui (to speak), which translates to "belly-speaking." It is not actually possible to throw your voice across the room. Rather, the effect used by ventriloquists is to disguise their voice to make it appear that it is coming from another voice (i.e., a dummy). This unusual manner of speaking can place strain on the voice.

Table 8–2. Types of Voice Disorders and the Vocal Quality Associated With Each Disorder

Classification	*Type and Vocal Quality*
Vocal misuse/ phonotrauma	*Nodules*—breathiness and lowered pitch *Polyps*—breathiness and lowered pitch *Edema*—lowered pitch *Laryngitis*—breathiness and lowered pitch *Aphonia*—total loss of voice in spite of apparent normal vocal anatomy *Puberphonia*—unusually high pitch in spite of normal vocal anatomy
Nervous system involvement	*Parkinson disease*—monopitch and reduced loudness *Myasthenia gravis*—breathiness *Spasmodic dysphonia*—vocal strain/struggle *Lesions of peripheral nerves*—breathiness *Huntington chorea*—hoarseness *Motor neuron disease*—hoarseness or strain/struggle *Multiple sclerosis*—impaired loudness control and hoarseness
Organic disease and trauma	*Laryngeal granuloma*—hoarseness *Contact ulcer*—hoarseness *Papilloma*—hoarseness *Vocal fold hemorrhage*—hoarseness and intermittent aphonia *Laryngeal web*—hoarseness *Inhalation trauma*—hoarseness *Carcinoma*—hoarseness

Source: From Colton et al., 2011.

the patient for purposeful damaging actions. In reality, there are instances when the patient is simply using their voice incorrectly with little knowledge as to any vocal wrongdoing. Disorders of vocal misuse are the most prevalent and preventable types of voice disorders. People of all ages who use their voice excessively may experience phonotrauma. Young children, teachers, lawyers, cheerleaders, and others who use their voice professionally, such as singers and actors, are prone to voice disorders of this nature. Some disorders resulting from vocal misuse are laryngitis, vocal nodules, and vocal polyps. Each of these various disorders of vocal misuse represents a form of hyperfunctional voice disorder.

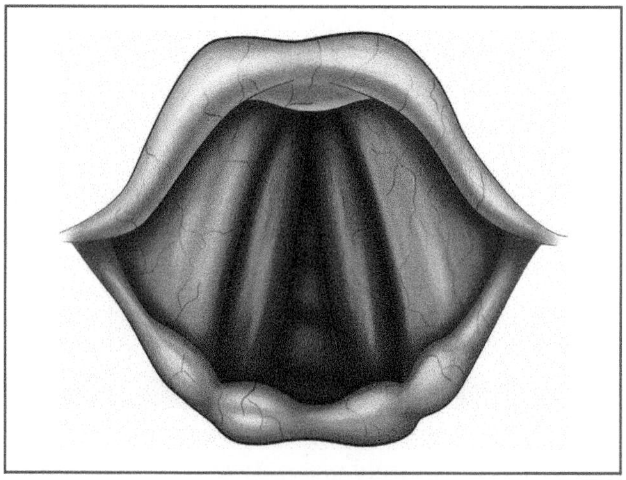

FIGURE 8–9. Example of laryngitis.

Laryngitis

Inflammation or swelling of the vocal folds results in **laryngitis** (Figure 8–9). Some symptoms associated with laryngitis are a sore throat and swallowing difficulty. The condition may be caused by excessive use of the voice, bacterial or viral infections, or irritants such as inhaled chemicals or the backup of stomach acid into the throat (i.e.,

acid reflux). The voice of someone with laryngitis will often sound breathy and hoarse. Laryngitis occurs in two forms: (a) acute, which lasts only a few days; and (b) chronic, which persists over a period of weeks or months. Chronic laryngitis can result in the development of a more severe and long-lasting voice disorder. In addition, children who experience severe forms of laryngitis can run the risk of breathing difficulty because inflamed vocal folds can serve to narrow the air passage leading to the lungs.

Vocal Nodules

Small, benign (noncancerous), callus-like bumps that form on the vocal folds are called **vocal nodules** (Figure 8–10). They can form on one or both folds, are located on the front one third of the vocal folds, and range in size from a pinhead to a split pea. Nodules develop from irritation caused by repeated pressure on the same area of the vocal folds, much like how a callus forms on areas of a person's hands or feet following repeated physical activity. During normal voice production, the vocal folds should naturally meet together at a midline position. However, when a vocal nodule is present, the vocal folds are unable to close completely, resulting in excessive air escaping during the production of voice. Not surprisingly, the voice of a person who has vocal nodules usually sounds hoarse and slightly breathy. Voice pitch is also abnormally low as a result of the additional mass of the nodule on the vocal folds during vibration. Vocal nodules are a prevalent type of voice disorder resulting from vocal misuse. This condition is also referred to as "singer's nodes" because it is a frequent problem among professional singers. The inability to sing high notes is a hallmark feature of nodules. When the individual tries to sing in a high voice, there is a delay in the onset of the sound with an audible escape of air.

Vocal Polyp

A small, noncancerous growth on one or both vocal folds results in a **vocal polyp** (also termed *polypoid degeneration*). While a vocal nodule is much like a hard callus, a vocal polyp is much like a soft blister (Figure 8–11). Symptoms of vocal polyps include abnormal voice quality, vocal fatigue, and the sensation of a lump in the throat that involves constant throat clearing. A polyp typically forms on only one vocal fold. Although polyps occur most often because of sudden vocal trauma, a specific type of polyp (known as *Reinke edema*) results from long-term cigarette smoking, creating the well-known smoker 's voice. People who develop a vocal polyp usually have a low-pitched, hoarse, breathy voice, similar to the voices of people who have vocal nodules.

Puberphonia

A fourth type of vocal misuse is **puberphonia**, also called *mutational falsetto*. Puberphonia refers to a condition in which an adult (usually an adolescent male) continues to speak with a high-pitched voice well after the age when a natural

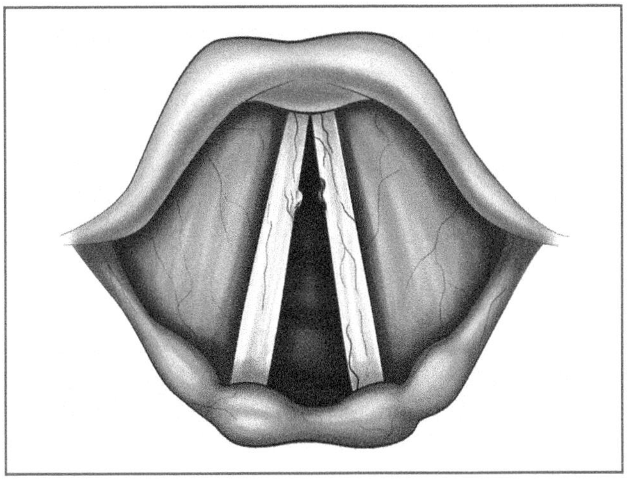

FIGURE 8–10. Example of vocal nodules.

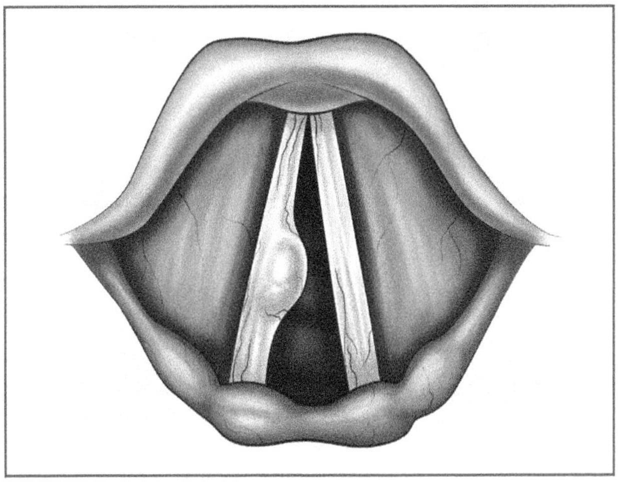

FIGURE 8–11. Example of vocal polyp.

lowering in voice pitch should have occurred. The condition is rare and is believed to reflect a form of **psychogenic disorder**. A psychogenic voice disorder is thought to result from an underlying psychological disturbance. In the case of puberphonia, there is no structural reason for the voice disorder. However, because the voice is not being used normally, a condition such as puberphonia is classified as a disorder of vocal misuse.

Nervous System Involvement

The nervous system consists of the brain, spinal cord, and an enormous network of sensory and motor nerves throughout the body. Malfunctions of the nervous system may result from disease, abnormal growths, or trauma. Nervous system damage can also impair normal voice production. Two conditions that reflect voice disorders having a nervous system origin are (a) neurogenic disorders and (b) spasmodic dysphonia. These disorders are not related to trauma, which forms the basis of organic voice disorders (see later section).

Neurogenic Voice Disorders

Two nervous system disorders that have an associated voice disorder are **Parkinson disease** and **amyotrophic lateral sclerosis**. The condition of Parkinson disease is a progressive neurological disorder affecting movements such as walking, talking, and writing. The disease generally affects people beyond the age of 40 years. The three main symptoms of Parkinson disease are tremor, stiffness, and bradykinesia (i.e., slowness of movement). These conditions can carry over into the production of voice, with approximately 50% to 80% of all patients with Parkinson disease demonstrating a voice disorder. The voice features found in Parkinson disease are **monotonic voice** and a low-pitched voice, as well as considerable variation in the loudness of voice. Amyotrophic lateral sclerosis, also known as *motor neuron disease*, is a progressive chronic disease of the nerves that are responsible for supplying electrical stimulation to the muscles used for all movement. The disease causes gradual muscle weakness and wasting. The disease generally affects people over the age of 40 years, with a typical life span of less than 3 years from the date of diagnosis. The muscles responsible for producing voice are not spared among individuals with amyotrophic lateral sclerosis. Early symptoms include a hoarse voice accompanied by vocal spasm. As the disease progresses, the voice becomes weaker and is characterized by breathiness and hypernasality. The increase in nasality results from weakness in the muscles responsible for closing off the nasal cavity from the oral cavity during normal voice production.

Spasmodic Dysphonia

A spasm is an involuntary and abnormal contraction of a muscle. In the case of **spasmodic dysphonia**, the specific voice disorder appears to be one of involuntary and abnormal functioning of the muscles responsible for voice production. Spasmodic dysphonia is perhaps the most mysterious of all voice disorders because we still do not know what causes it and how best to treat it. The disorder was originally thought to be a type of psychogenic condition, and because there was no identifiable physical cause to the problem, researchers believed it must result from some level of mental distress. This way of thinking is evident in the use of the term *hysterical dysphonia*, which has since been dropped in favor of the term *spasmodic dysphonia*. Research over the past 30 years now indicates that the disorder probably reflects a motor disturbance deep in the brain.

There are two types of spasmodic dysphonia, based on whether the spasm affects the closing or opening phases of vocal fold vibration. **Adductor-type spasmodic dysphonia** results in a severe hyperfunctional voice. The patient demonstrates obvious struggle in attempting to produce a clear voice. The vocal folds show intermittent spasms causing them to close and stiffen. Patients find it difficult, if not impossible, to shout, but surprisingly the spasms are usually absent while laughing, singing, or speaking on inhalation. **Abductor-type spasmodic dysphonia** is rarer and essentially the opposite to that of the adductory type. In abductor spasmodic dysphonia, sudden involuntary muscle movements or spasms cause the vocal folds to open. The vocal folds are unable to vibrate when fully abducted causing periods of aphonia. The open position of the vocal folds also allows air to escape from the lungs during speech. As a result, the voices of these individuals sound weak and breathy. As with adductor spasmodic dysphonia, the spasms are often absent during activities such as laughing or singing. The prevalence of either type of spasmodic dysphonia in the general population is unknown. There is no difference regarding its occurrence in men and women. The disorder is rarely found in children and young adults, with most cases occurring in middle-aged adults.

Organic Disease and Trauma

The third type of voice disorders are those that affect the structure of the vocal mechanism as a result of an organic disease or some form of physical trauma. Two examples of voice disorders resulting from these conditions are (a) papilloma and (b) cancer of the larynx.

Papilloma

Papillomas are benign epithelial (surface-level) tumors caused by infection with the human papillomavirus. The tumors can develop in various parts of the body, including the larynx. Laryngeal papillomas appear as numerous warty growths on the surface of the vocal folds (Figure 8–12). Laryngeal papillomas are most often found among children, and between 60% and 80% of cases occur in children, usually before the age of 3 years. Although papillomas are benign, their rapid growth on the vocal folds can cause obstruction of the airway that could potentially lead to asphyxiation if not promptly treated. Like warts, papillomas are very stubborn lesions that tend to grow back even if they have been completely removed. This is particularly the case among children. In adults, laryngeal papillomas tend to be less aggressive. Papillomas generally cause no physical pain, with the most obvious symptom of the disorder being a hoarse-sounding voice.

Carcinoma

Cancer can develop in any part of the body, and the larynx is no exception (Figure 8–13). Laryngeal cancer composes approximately 5% of all forms of cancer. If allowed to develop without treatment, the condition can be life threatening. The primary cause of laryngeal cancer is smoking. In addition to laryngeal cancer, smoking is the major cause of cancers of the lungs, oral cavity, and esophagus. The ratio of men to women who develop laryngeal cancer is 3 to 1, with approximately 60% of individuals surviving longer than 5 years once diagnosed. Smoking serves as an irritant to the vocal folds, causing edema. It also decreases lung function, and without good lung power, more stress is placed on the larynx when speaking or singing. This is why heavy, long-term smokers' voices are often hoarse and low in pitch. These voice features are also the prime symptoms or warning signs of laryngeal cancer.

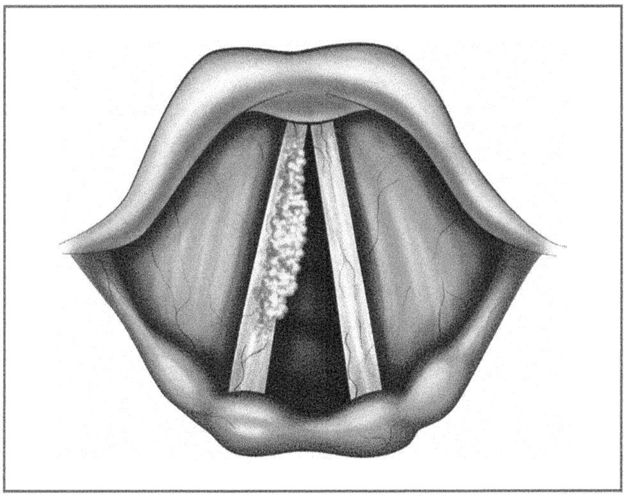

FIGURE 8–12. Example of vocal papilloma.

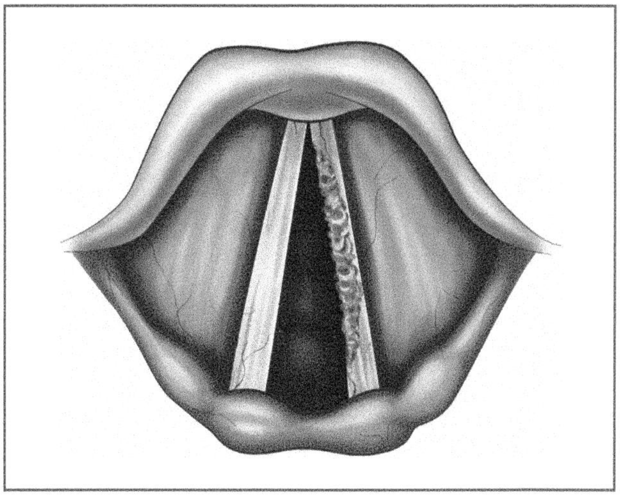

FIGURE 8–13. Example of vocal carcinoma.

CURRENT THEORIES OF VOICE DISORDERS

One of the earliest modern theories of normal voice production was proposed by the French scientist **Raoul Husson** in 1950, who sparked considerable debate concerning the physiology of the vibration of the vocal folds. In his **neurochronaxic theory**, he suggested that the frequency of vocal fold vibration is dependent on excitation of nerve cells from the laryngeal nerve (part of cranial nerve X). For example, if the vocal folds were to vibrate at a rate of 200 Hz, this theory suggests that 200 nerve impulses per second are sent to the thyroarytenoid (vocal fold) muscle. Husson's theory was eventually found to be invalid because we now know that nerves are unable to discharge at such high rates. This theory was eventually replaced by the **myoelastic aerodynamic theory of phonation** in 1959 by the Dutch scientist **Janwillem van den Berg** (1920–1985; Figure 8–14). The title of the theory is self-explanatory regarding the process of producing voice. The theory is that normal vocal fold vibration involves coordination of muscle tension and breath pressure. To produce voice, there needs to be air pressure and flow. Elastic muscular movement of the structures composing the vocal mechanism is also necessary, and the entire process is dynamic, involving movement and change. Over the past 60 years, the various intricate steps in vocal fold vibration have been more critically examined; however, the general concept of producing voice is still captured within the myoelastic aerodynamic theory of phonation.

FIGURE 8–14. Janwillem van den Berg proposed the myoelastic aerodynamic theory of phonation.

Roy and Bless (2000) proposed a **personality and emotional adjustment theory** of voice disorders. The premise of the theory is that an individual's personality and behavioral patterns may contribute to the eventual development of a voice disorder such as nodules. In turn, the subsequent voice disorder that develops creates further emotional problems and personality effects for the individual with the disorder. For example, a person with an impulsive, preservative personality who is misusing their voice may be unable to normally cease in misusing it, thereby contributing to a more long-lasting voice disorder. The role of personality and issues such as impulsivity have not been considered in previous theories concerning voice disorders. If personality issues are found to show a direct link to some voice disorders, advancements in the diagnosis and treatment of these disorders will likely occur.

ASSESSMENT OF VOICE DISORDERS

At any given time, approximately 6% of the general population experience a voice disorder, and most of these individuals tend to be female (Stemple et al., 2020). Approximately 30% of the entire population will experience a form of voice disorder, either fleeting or long term, at some point in their lives. Most instances of voice disorders occur in people between the ages of 40 and 60 years, although voice disorders are also found in children. Among children, there is a greater likelihood of voice disorders in boys compared with girls, with boys more often implicated in vocally abusive behaviors such as shouting and screaming. Anyone who experiences vocal discomfort for more than 2 weeks should consider seeking an assessment of their voice. In some cases, the speech-language pathologist may be the first individual to encounter a patient complaining of a voice problem. The speech-language pathologist may perform an initial evaluation of the patient's voice; however, appropriate ethical practice requires the speech-language pathologist to immediately refer the patient to an otolaryngologist because of the possibility of an underlying medical condition. The otolaryngologist examines the individual's laryngeal mechanism and determines whether a medical condition is indeed the root cause of the voice problem.

The assessment of voice disorders involves subjective and objective procedures. Both approaches are essential to obtaining the detail necessary to accurately diagnose the cause, type, and severity of a voice disorder. A **subjective assessment** of voice entails listening and observing the patient while speaking and collecting a case history. When listening to the patient's voice, the speech-language pathologist completes a rating of the patient's voice quality, which is based on having the patient prolong isolated vowels, read aloud, and speak in a conversational setting. This is where the speech-language pathologist may use terms such as "breathy" or "hoarse" to describe the patient's voice. The speech-language pathologist also observes the patient's general body movements during speaking, in particular examining for excessive neck tension and irregular breathing patterns. Obtaining a patient's case history provides background information that may hold relevance to diagnosing the voice disorder. The speech-language pathologist collects information about the patient's occupation, daily use of voice, onset and duration of the voice problem, and expectations for improving the individual's voice. An example of a voice case history form is provided in Table 8–3.

Objective assessments involve use of instruments to examine the dynamic process of voice production. Two frequently employed instrumental approaches in voice diagnosis are indirect and direct laryngoscopy (Collins, 2014). Both approaches are illustrated in Figure 8–15. The steps to performing an indirect laryngoscopy have changed little since the original method established by García in 1855. The patient is seated upright, and the otolaryngologist inserts a small hand mirror to the back of the throat. Prior to inserting the mirror, an anesthetic is sprayed in the back of the throat to prevent gagging. A light is projected into the throat and deflected off the mirror toward the vocal folds to illuminate the area. The same mirror is also used to visualize the vocal folds. The patient is asked to prolong individual vowels ("say eee") during the examination. A **direct laryngoscopy** is most often performed after the indirect method to allow for viewing of a greater area of the larynx. Direct laryngoscopy is easily accomplished using a flexible endoscope, which consists of hundreds of fiberoptic strands that serve as both a light source for illumination as well as a camera for examination. The scope is inserted through one of the nostrils and guided toward the back of the throat to rest slightly above the vocal folds. This view is valuable for direct examination of the surface of the vocal folds and any existing vocal pathology.

TREATMENT OF VOICE DISORDERS

The wide range of possible voice disorders and their occurrence in children and adults results in individualized treatment programs varying from one patient to the next. The general goal of voice therapy is to restore the best voice possible. An acceptable voice is one that is functional for purposes of general communication. Ideally, the best form of treatment is one aimed at eliminating the vocal behavior that created the voice disorder in the first place. In the case of voice therapy with singers, therapy involves working on both the speaking and singing voice to achieve an easy natural voice without strain. When the healthiest possible voice is achieved, the speech-language pathologist may refer the patient to a singing teacher, whose role is to provide advice on singing style and technique. Four approaches to the management of voice disorders are (a) indirect therapy, (b) direct therapy, (c) phonosurgery, and (d) prevention. These approaches seek to eliminate potentially harmful vocal behaviors, enhance vocal fold tissue healing following injury, and/or alter the manner of voice production.

Table 8–3. Example of a Case History Form Used in the Assessment of Voice Disorders

Voice History Form

Name: ______________________ Age: ________ Sex: ☐ Female ☐ Male

Did concern over your voice begin with: ☐ Illness ☐ Trauma (injury) ☐ Surgery?

Voice History

Please list previous voice problems: ______________________

Please list previous voice treatments: ______________________

Current Status of Voice

Is your voice today typical of how it sounds since the voice problem began? ☐ Yes ☐ No

Does your voice vary with: ☐ Seasons/Weather? ☐ Time of day?

Do you ever experience voice loss where you are only able to whisper? ☐ Yes ☐ No

Medical History

Do you currently have or have you ever had any of the following conditions?

☐ Pain, tightness in throat ☐ Sinus ☐ Allergies ☐ Breathing difficulties

Please list current medications: ______________________

How much caffeine (coffee, tea, soft drinks, etc.) do you drink per day? Cups: ________

How much alcohol do you drink? ______________________

Do you smoke? ☐ Yes ☐ No How much? ______________________

Are you frequently in a situation where you are breathing noxious fumes? ☐ Yes ☐ No

Voice Use

How many hours do you spend?

- In conversation (friends, family, work, etc.): ________
- Talking in noise (work, machines, restaurants, taverns, crowds, etc.): ________
- Yelling (sporting events, coaching, etc.): ________
- Teaching, giving instructions, or training: ________
- Singing: ________

Are you using your voice less than usual because of the problem? ☐ Yes ☐ No

Self-Perception of Voice Concern

Please rate the importance of the following:

Use of voice for work: ☐ Unimportant ☐ Somewhat Important ☐ Very Important

Use of voice for socializing: ☐ Unimportant ☐ Somewhat Important ☐ Very Important

Please rate each of the following potential problems that most closely apply to you.
(1 = No problem, 2 = Slight problem, 3 = Moderate problem, 4 = Severe problem)

- My voice is not loud enough for people to hear me in some situations. ______
- My voice is too loud for some situations. ______
- My pitch is too high. ______
- My pitch is too low. ______
- My voice quality is not good. I sound harsh or hoarse. ______
- I'm bothered by the way people react to my voice. ______
- My voice gets tired and fatigued with talking. ______

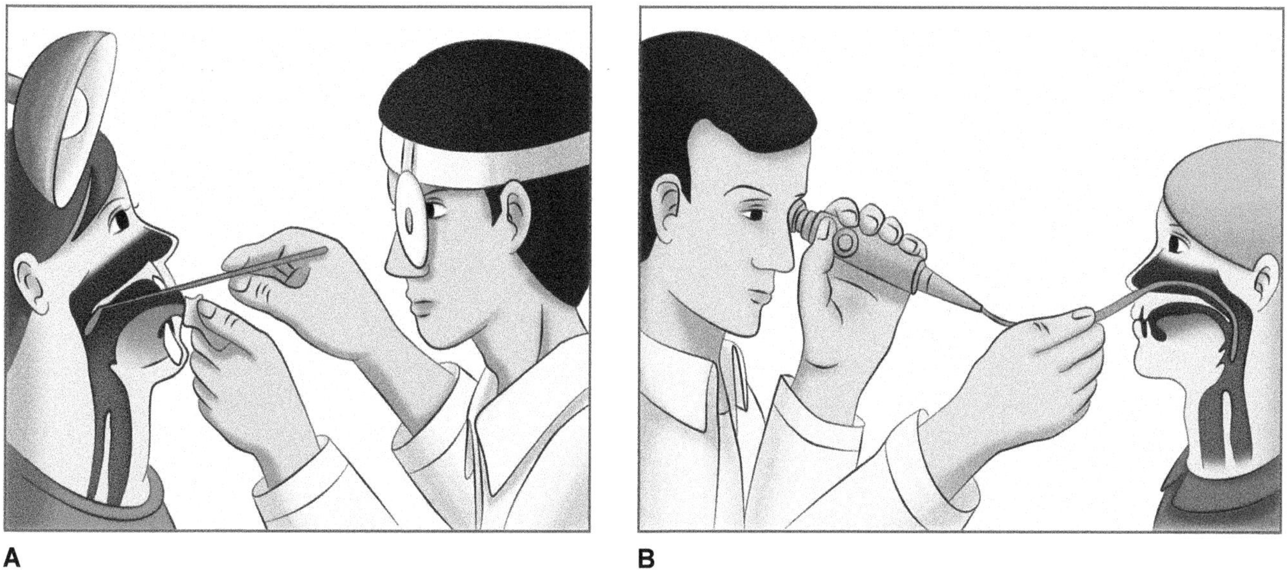

FIGURE 8–15. Examples of indirect and direct approaches to examining the larynx. **A.** Indirect examination of the larynx using a lamp and head mirror. **B.** Direct examination of the larynx using a flexible fiberoptic endoscope.

Indirect Therapy

Techniques associated with indirect therapy include voice rest and patient education. **Voice rest** is the process of easing the strain placed on the vocal folds by not allowing any form of speaking, singing, or whispering for several days. Voice rest is not a cure for most disorders. The purpose of voice rest is to hasten recovery time in conditions where the vocal folds have been traumatized. It is generally believed that if a person must absolutely speak during a prescribed period of vocal rest, regular phonation is preferred over whispering. The use of whispering does not allow the voice to rest. During whispering, the vocal muscles are still active. This action, combined with air passing between the vocal folds, actually has an irritating effect on the vocal folds. Patient education consists of informing the patient about laryngeal anatomy and the way voice is produced. This might include a simplified interpretation of the myoelastic aerodynamic theory of phonation. As well, the patient is educated about the subsequent long-term vocal damage that may result from not producing voice normally.

Direct Therapy

The use of direct therapy involves alteration of a patient's existing speaking behavior in an attempt to increase vocal efficiency and improve voice quality. Four examples of direct therapy are (a) vocal function exercises, (b) respiratory training, (c) use of confidential voice, and (d) the **Lee Silverman Voice Treatment (LSVT). Vocal function exercises** are a form of calisthenics designed to strengthen and improve coordination of laryngeal musculature. Examples of vocal function exercises include maximum vowel prolongations and smoothly raising and lowering pitch along a musical scale. **Respiratory training** is one of the major methods for enhancing vocal function. Respiratory training focuses on coordinating muscles used for breathing and vocalizing. Professional singers are aware of the importance of respiration in maintaining a normal healthy voice. **Confidential voice** therapy involves using a soft, breathy voice. The term is based on the concept of speaking softly with another individual so as to not be too obvious. This is not the same as using a whispered voice. From a physiological standpoint, speaking with a soft voice reduces laryngeal muscle tension. Somewhat opposite to confidential voice therapy is LSVT. The LSVT is a structured, programmatic approach to voice therapy. The premise of the approach is to encourage a full, loud speaking voice to improve overall voice quality as well as to improve aspects of speech clarity. The treatment has gained widespread acceptance for working with individuals with Parkinson disease (see also Chapter 10).

Phonosurgery

In some instances, indirect or direct therapy is not sufficient to improve one's voice. In these cases, an operation may be necessary to repair or remove growths from the vocal folds. The term **phonosurgery** denotes restoration of voice by using various surgical techniques. The term was originally used by the otolaryngologist **Hans von Leden** (1918–2014) in the 1950s to describe any surgery performed specifically to improve voice. In most cases, some form of indirect or direct voice therapy is required following surgery. Two routine types of phonosurgeries performed by an otolaryngologist are (a) phonomicrosurgery and (b) injection laryngoplasty. Both surgeries take place in an operating room with the patient under sedation. **Phonomicrosurgery** involves use of a microscope to view the area of surgery, and the operation is carried out using special microinstruments and lasers (Figure 8–16). Phonomicrosurgery is performed to remove vocal nodules and polyps. A guiding principle of this surgery is to maintain normal vocal function by removing only the growth found on the superficial tissue of the vocal folds. This surgery is seldom performed on children's voices because nodules and polyps often reappear in developing children, so repeated phonosurgery would likely cause long-lasting damage to the vocal folds. Injection laryngoplasty entails use of a syringe to insert material (such as collagen) into one or both vocal folds to "plump up" the overall size and shape of the muscle. Injection laryngoplasty has been successfully used to treat vocal fold paralysis. An effective treatment for reducing the symptoms of spasmodic dysphonia is the injection of very small amounts of botulinum toxin (Botox) directly into the affected muscles of the larynx. The toxin weakens muscles by blocking the nerve impulses to the muscle. Botox has gained widespread attention for its use as a form of cosmetic facial surgery. For treating spasmodic dysphonia, the toxin blocks nerve activity to the vocal folds, thereby freeing up

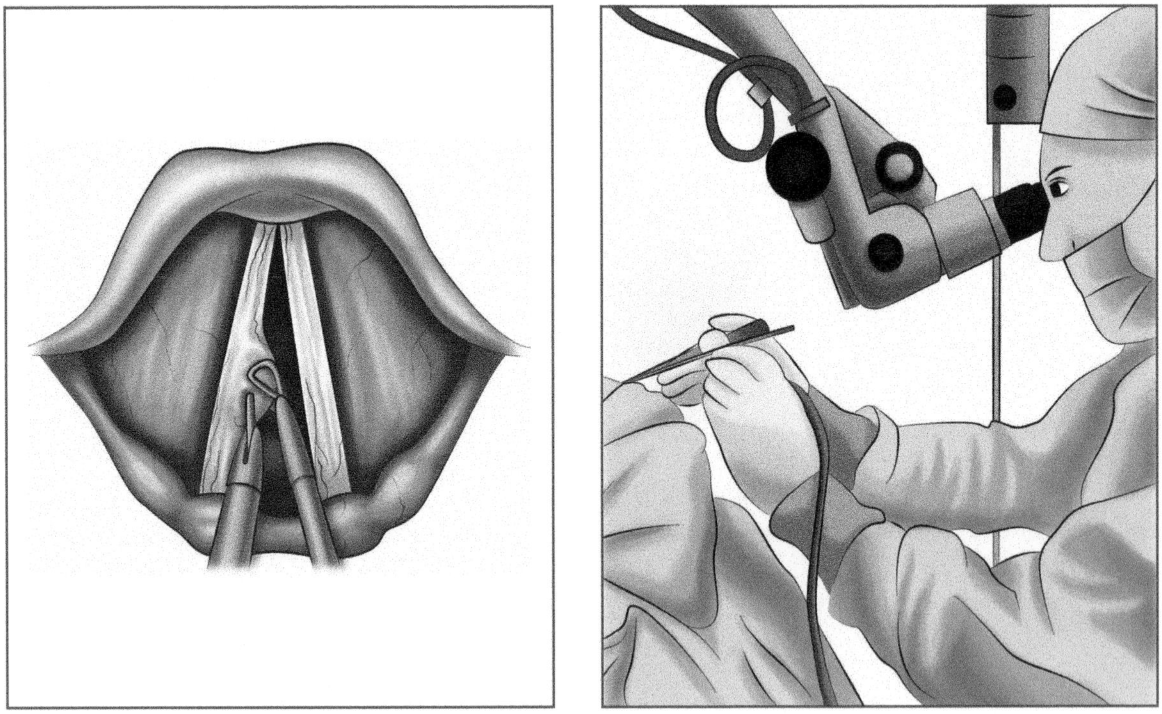

A B

FIGURE 8–16. The process of phonosurgery. The surgeon uses delicate instruments to remove a growth from the vocal folds.

the muscle to vibrate in a more normal fashion. Botox injections improve the voice for a period of 4 months after which voice symptoms gradually return. This treatment requires continual injections to maintain a good speaking voice.

A **laryngectomy** is the complete surgical removal of the larynx, most likely because of cancer of the larynx. In nearly all cases of laryngectomy, the individual was a cigarette (or cigar) smoker. A person who has undergone a laryngectomy no longer breathes through the nose or mouth but through an opening in the neck called a **stoma**. The individual is incapable of producing a normal voice because the primary laryngeal structures needed to generate voice have been removed (Figure 8–17). Several alternative methods exist for producing **alaryngeal speech**. One of these methods involves use of a small handheld device known as an **electrolarynx** (see Figure 8–18). The device produces a buzzing sound that is transferred into the vocal tract by holding it firmly against the neck. The patient learns to modulate this sound by shaping the lips, tongue, and jaw as they normally would if the individual still had a larynx. The quality of the sound is unnatural, but many patients use the device for basic communication needs. Another method for producing speech is referred to as esophageal speech. **Esophageal speech** is a type of speaking in which air is purposely injected into the back of the esophagus in a manner similar to burping to create speech. This form of speaking is difficult to master. Although most of us are probably able to utter one or two words in a single burp, a skilled esophageal speaker is able to produce short phrases. A very popular method of speech used following laryngectomy is **tracheoesophageal speech**, which is like esophageal speech but uses a device to redirect air from the trachea into the esophagus. This is done through a small shunt placed through an opening made between the trachea and esophagus, called a tracheoesophageal puncture. A small one-way valve placed into this opening allows the patient to force air from the lungs into the mouth to create speech (Figure 8–18).

Prevention

Most voice disorders are preventable. Strategies that raise a person's awareness of inappropriate voice use and vocal health are essential to

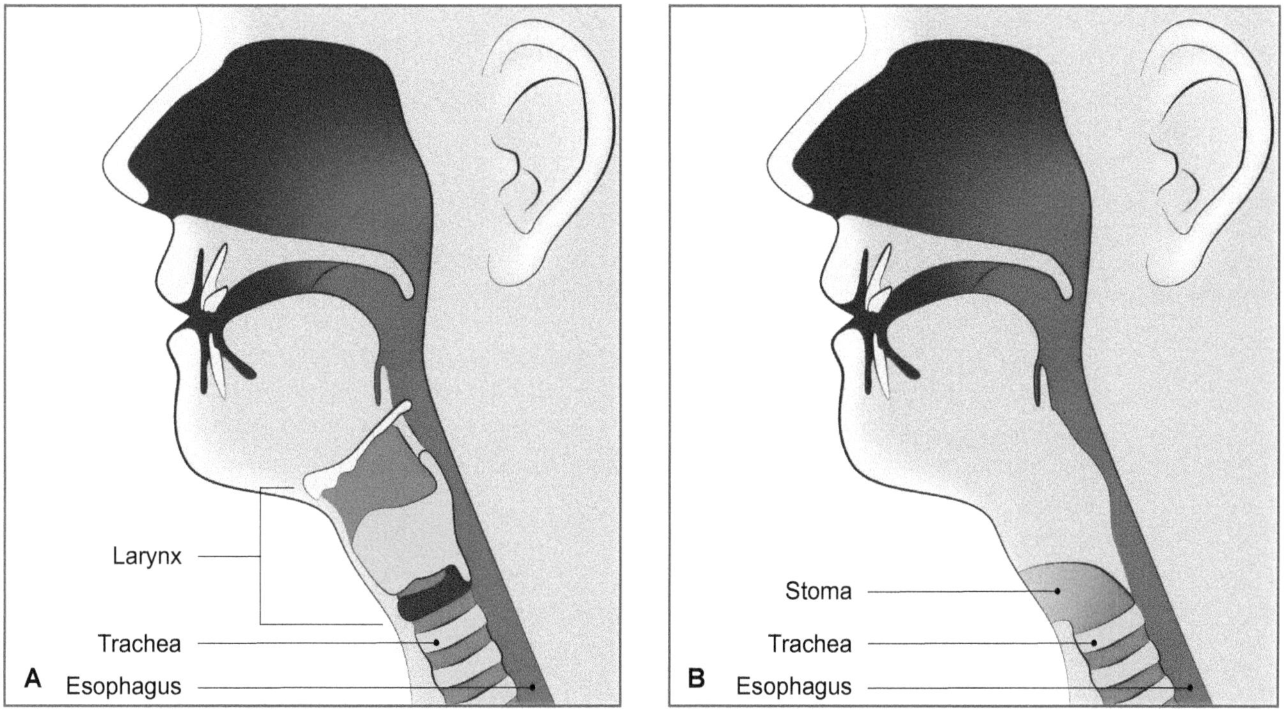

FIGURE 8–17. Vocal anatomy before (**A**) and after (**B**) a laryngectomy.

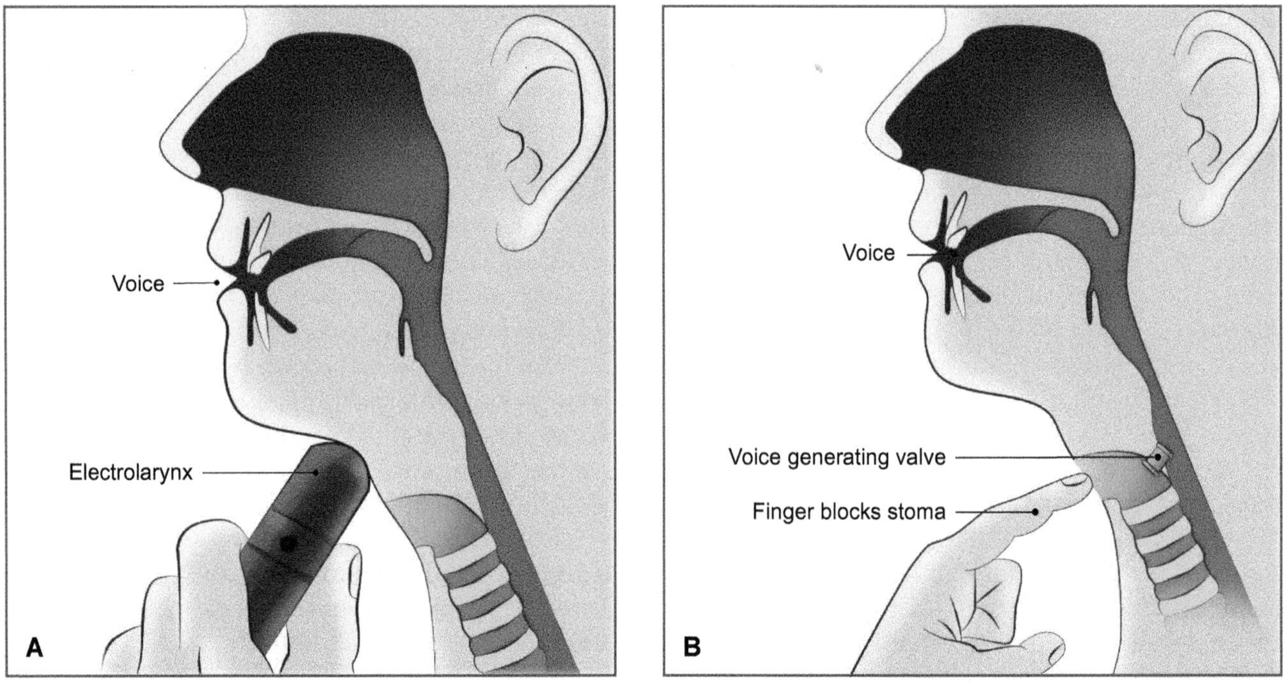

FIGURE 8–18. **A.** Use of an electrolarynx following a laryngectomy. **B.** Use of tracheoesophageal speech.

the prevention of voice disorders. **Vocal hygiene** refers to the healthy habits that patients should follow to take care of their voices. This includes being aware of how various speaking behaviors, as well as food and drinks, can affect one's voice and overall health. Vocal hygiene is analogous to taking care of your automobile. When you drive your car, you expect it to always work perfectly. For this to happen, you need to be aware of how the car works and the steps needed to keep the car mechanically sound. The same logic applies to using and taking care of your voice. Examples of good vocal hygiene are listed in Table 8–4. The various examples can be summarized using the acronym developed by those hosting The Voice Problem Website (see https://voicefoundation.org/health-science/voice-disorders/introduction [see information about Voiceproblem.org]), VOICE:

V = Value your voice through healthy diet and lifestyle.

O = Optimize your voice with vocal warm-ups before use.

I = Invest in your voice with training in proper voice technique.

C = Cherish your voice by avoiding voice misuse, overuse, and abuse.

E = Exercise your voice to increase endurance and power.

Over the years, several recommendations concerning vocal hygiene have been presented. Some of these recommendations are related to general health voice practice, while others are related to recovery of voice following surgery. Many of these suggestions have never been critically evaluated as to their effectiveness. DiRenzo et al. (2016) identified some of the more common suggestions (hypotheses) that represent the current view among voice experts:

Hypothesis 1: E-cigarettes are not as harmful to the vocal folds as traditional cigarettes.

Current View: E-cigarettes may not be as harmful as traditional cigarettes; however, they may still act as a gateway to nicotine addiction, especially among adolescents.

Hypothesis 2: Drinking water improves vocal hygiene.

Table 8–4. Examples of Good Vocal Hygiene

- Control the amount of shouting or yelling.
- Minimize or avoid using a whispered voice.
- Control the amount of caffeine and alcohol consumption.
- Reduce and avoid excessive coughing and throat clearing.
- Minimize grunting or vocalization during exercise.
- Limit the amount of talking in loud and noisy environments.
- Do not smoke and limit your exposure to secondhand smoke.
- Conserve your voice during periods of excessive fatigue and stress.
- Keep hydrated by drinking water every day.
- Maintain a healthy diet, and minimize laryngopharyngeal reflux.
- Be aware of potentially traumatic vocal behaviors.

Current View: Experts do not agree on whether changes in hydration serve to improve vocal function.

Hypothesis 3: Seven days of voice rest following vocal surgery improves outcomes.

Current View: Experts generally agree that there may be some early benefit of voice rest to stabilize the surgical "wound," but complete rest for 7 days may not be warranted.

Hypothesis 4: Excessive voice use at habitually high levels can contribute to vocal fold lesions.

Current View: Abnormally high vocal intensity and pitch can indeed lead to the development of vocal fold lesions.

CULTURAL CONSIDERATIONS AND VOICE DISORDERS

The occurrence of various types of voice disorders does not appear to differ significantly across racial and ethnic groups. However, a combination of social and cultural factors seems to influence voice and the subsequent development of voice disorders. For example, Japanese women tend to speak with a higher pitch (F0) level than their Western female counterparts. The high-pitch voice is assumed to project a vocal image associated with femininity. In contrast, Japanese men tend to use a lower-pitch (F0) level compared with Western males. The lower-pitch voice is used to emphasize masculinity. In both situations, the differences in F0 are not due to anatomical differences in size of the larynx. Rather, the use of F0 is altered due to sociocultural reasons. Presumably, this somewhat unnatural use of F0 may place Japanese speakers at a higher risk for voice disorders due to possible misuse of the voice.

Socioeconomic status (SES) may be a contributing factor to voice disorders. Individuals from low SES backgrounds have less access and are less informed about appropriate health care. An example can be found by considering the occurrence of smoking, which is significantly higher among low SES groups. The roll-on effect of smoking is the risk of developing laryngeal cancers. Impoverished countries such as Pakistan and Cuba lead the world in the occurrence of laryngeal cancer. In the United States, there is a racial disparity in laryngeal cancer with Black men more likely than White men to develop and die from laryngeal cancer.

Society and culture also impact individuals who are biologically born as male or female but whose gender does not correspond with their

FYI

Each of us has a habitual pitch, or level at which we speak most frequently, and an optimum pitch, or level at which we can produce our strongest voice with minimal effort. One way to determine an individual's optimum pitch is through the yawn–sigh technique. Have the individual do just what the technique describes: yawn (or take a deep breath) and then sigh (usually we sigh, "ahh"). The pitch of the sigh is the person's optimum pitch.

FYI

LOUD Americans

Surveys consistently show that Americans are viewed as loud talkers, which is especially apparent when traveling abroad. One reason suggested for this finding is that Americans are accustomed to a larger "personal space" compared to other countries. With this increased personal space is a natural tendency to talk loudly in social situations.

sex at birth. Gender typically is demonstrated in several physical and behavioral ways, one of which is speaking voice. Transgender individuals frequently undertake voice therapy as part of a female/male gender transition to make their voices sound appropriate and, therefore, facilitate their entrance (and acceptance) as females/males in society. **Voice feminization** is the desired goal of changing a perceived male-sounding voice to a perceived female-sounding voice. **Voice masculinization** is the opposite of voice feminization —the change of a voice from feminine to masculine. There is a greater likelihood of vocal misuse occurring in the process of voice feminization compared with masculinization due to the need to consistently maintain hyperadducted vocal fold behavior when speaking.

FYI

Adult men have a lower speaking voice (F0) than adult women; however, among some older adult individuals, the reverse can be found. The raising of pitch among older adult men is attributed to a stiffening (calcification) of the vocal folds. The lowering in pitch among older adult women is attributed to a thinning and loss of elasticity (tension) of the vocal folds.

Other examples of society and culture influencing voice production can be found from the music industry and sporting events. A common anthem shared by today's youth is: *If it's too loud—you're too old.* Examples of this perspective can be found in musical groups whose song lyrics delivery tends to verge on shouting and yelling. Although this form of music may be accepted culturally and socially, there are clear risks of entertainers developing phonotrauma. Most sporting events consist of teams of athletes competing against each other, with the added sideline attraction of cheerleaders (both male and female). There is a cultural and social expectation that cheerleaders shout and yell as a means of supporting their team. Not surprisingly, cheerleaders are at high risk of developing voice disorders due to vocal misuse.

Children at a young age understand that the volume of their voice has an impact on others in social situations. Williams et al. (2015) showed that children as young as 2 years of age are aware of situations that require a quiet voice (e.g., bedtime) or a loud voice (e.g., calling for a parent). Clearly the perception and use of voice are an important feature of early child development.

SUMMARY OF CHAPTER

Voice disorders occur in people of all ages and are likely to be found among individuals whose occupation is dependent on having a healthy voice. Voice disorders reflect a special form of communication disorder that involves a close working relationship between the patient, speech-language pathologist, and medical personnel. Most instances of voice disorders are preventable by simply taking precautionary steps. Voice disorders are classified according to the causal basis of the disorder, resulting from (a) vocal misuse, (b) nervous system involvement, or (c) organic disease and trauma. The assessment of voice disorders uses subjective and objective procedures. A subjective assessment of voice entails listening and observing the patient while speaking and collecting a case history. Objective assessments use instruments to examine the dynamic process of voice production. Four approaches to the management of voice disorders are (a) indirect therapy, (b) direct therapy, (c) phonosurgery, and (d) prevention. These approaches seek to eliminate potentially harmful vocal behaviors, enhance vocal fold tissue healing following injury, and/or alter the manner of voice production. The occurrence of various types of voice disorders does not appear to differ significantly across racial and ethnic groups. However, a combination of social and cultural factors seems to influence voice and the subsequent development of voice disorders.

VOICE DISORDERS ON THE WORLD WIDE WEB

Following are websites that provide further information on the topic of voice disorders. At the time of publication, each website was freely accessible.

Examples of Voice Disorders
http://www.fauquierent.net/voice.htm
https://www.voicedoctor.net/media/videos

The Voice Foundation
http://www.voicefoundation.org

Treatment of Voice Problems
https://dysphonia.org/about-sd/treatment-for-sd/voice-therapy

STUDY QUESTIONS

1. What are the major structures of the larynx, and how is voice produced?
2. What are the classifications and types of voice disorders?
3. What are the similarities and differences in indirect and direct laryngoscopy?
4. List and describe four examples of direct voice therapy.
5. What are the various types of phonosurgery?

REFERENCES

Collins, S. (2014). Direct and indirect laryngoscopy: Equipment and techniques. *Respiratory Care, 59*, 850–864.

Colton, R. H., Casper, J., & Leonard, R. (2011). *Understanding voice problems: A physiological perspective for diagnosis and treatment* (4th ed.). Lippincott Williams & Wilkins.

DiRenzo, E., Tanner, K., & Thibeault, S. (2016). Voice health conventional wisdom: Unknown, plausible or confirmed? *ASHA Leader, 21*.

Roy, N., & Bless, D. M. (2000). Personality traits and psychological factors in voice pathology: A foundation for future research. *Journal of Speech, Language, and Hearing Research, 43*, 737–748.

Stemple, J., Roby, N., & Klaben, B. (2020). *Clinical voice pathology: Theory and management* (6th ed.). Plural Publishing.

Van Riper, C. (1939). *Speech correction: Principles and methods.* Prentice-Hall.

West, R., Kennedy, L., & Carr, A. (1937). *The rehabilitation of speech: A textbook of diagnostic and corrective procedures.* Harper and Bros.

Williams, R., Brooks, R., & Meltzoff, A. (2015). The sound of social cognition: Toddlers' understanding of how sound influences others. *Journal of Cognition and Development, 16*, 252–260.

9

NEUROGENIC LANGUAGE DISORDERS

OBJECTIVES

After reading this chapter, the student should be able to:

- Demonstrate knowledge concerning neuroanatomy and neurophysiology and their relationship to language.
- Identify individuals who have made historical contributions to the fields of neurology and neurogenic language disorders.
- Demonstrate theoretical and clinical knowledge of neurogenic language disorders in the adult population.
- Describe etiologies and characteristics of neurogenic language disorders, including site of lesion.
- Describe current approaches to the assessment of adults with neurogenic language disorders.
- Identify current professional issues relevant to treatment and intervention of neurogenic language disorders.
- Demonstrate knowledge concerning the multicultural aspects of neurogenic language disorders.

KEY TERMS

Neurogenic	Apoplexy	Hemiparesis
Central Nervous System	Alzheimer Disease	Laceration
Peripheral Nervous System	Dementia	Concussion
Cerebrum	Traumatic Brain Injury	Contrecoup
Cortex	Localism Theory	Phineas Gage
Gryri	Holism Theory	Hemispatial (Left) Neglect
Sulcus	Franz Joseph Gall	Spontaneous Recovery
Fissure	Paul Broca	Neuroplasticity
Hemispheres	Cortical Localization	Right Hemisphere Theory of Recovery
Computed Tomography	Karl Wernicke	Initial Assessment
Electroencephalography	Korbinian Brodmann	Primary Assessment
Magnetic Resonance Imaging	Brodmann Areas	Premorbid State
Near-Infrared Spectroscopy	Alois Alzheimer	Person-Centered Approach
Frontal Lobes	Karl Lashley	International Classification of Functioning, Disability, and Health (ICF)
Broca's Area	Hildred Schuell	Stimulation
Parietal Lobes	Wilder Penfield	Memory
Temporal Lobes	Connectionism	Inhibiting
Primary Auditory Center	Martha Taylor Sarno	Validation Therapy
Occipital Lobes	Aphasia	Graphic Cuing
Limbic System	Cognitive Communication Disorder	Montessori-Based Interventions
Spinal Nerves	Right Hemisphere Syndrome	Race
Cranial Nerves	Fluent Aphasia	Ethnicity
Cerebrovascular Accident	Anomic Aphasia	Geographic Region
Stroke	Nonfluent Aphasia	Socioeconomic Status
Thrombosis	Broca Aphasia	
Embolism	Global Aphasia	
Hemorrhage	Circumlocutions	

INTRODUCTION

The term **neurogenic** refers to having its origin or starting with the nervous system. Therefore, a neurogenic communication disorder is usually a brain-based disorder. Individuals who have a neurogenic communication disorder are frequent clients of speech-language pathologists who work in a health care setting, ranging from acute care hospitals to long-term (nursing home) settings. Although the brain is likely to be involved in nearly all types of communication disorders, neurogenic disorders represent a special set of communication difficulties that are attributed to disease or damage of the nervous system, of which the brain is a major component. These disorders can affect speech sound articulation as well as language formulation and production. Neurogenic communication disorders typically are acquired disorders. That is, they reflect a disorder that occurred later in life, following a period of normal communication behavior. Although neurogenic communication disorders can be found in children, they tend to be more prevalent in adults. The focus of this chapter is the neurogenic communication disorders that impact language comprehension and production. Chapter 10 is dedicated to neurogenic communication disorders that affect speech sound production, commonly referred to as motor speech disorders.

TERMINOLOGY AND DEFINITIONS

When the nervous system is compromised due to developmental abnormalities, acquired damage, or illness, communication can be compromised as well. To fully appreciate the nature of neurogenic communication disorders, understanding the anatomy and physiology of the nervous system is essential. The detail of the human nervous system is immense and cannot be adequately covered in an introductory textbook on communication disorders; therefore, the terminology covered in this section is somewhat abbreviated and simplified.

The human nervous system can be generally divided into two parts: the **central nervous system** and the **peripheral nervous system**. An illustration of the basic division of the nervous system is shown in Figure 9–1. The central nervous system is made up of the cerebrum, brainstem, cerebellum, and spinal cord. The **cerebrum**, which is commonly referred to as the brain, is a major landmark of the central nervous system. The brain allows humans to engage in high-level functions such as thinking, learning, and speaking. The brain has specialized areas that are designed for purposes of receiving, organizing, and producing language. The surface of the cerebrum is called the **cortex**, which has a variety of ridges and grooves. The ridges are called **gyri**, and the grooves are referred

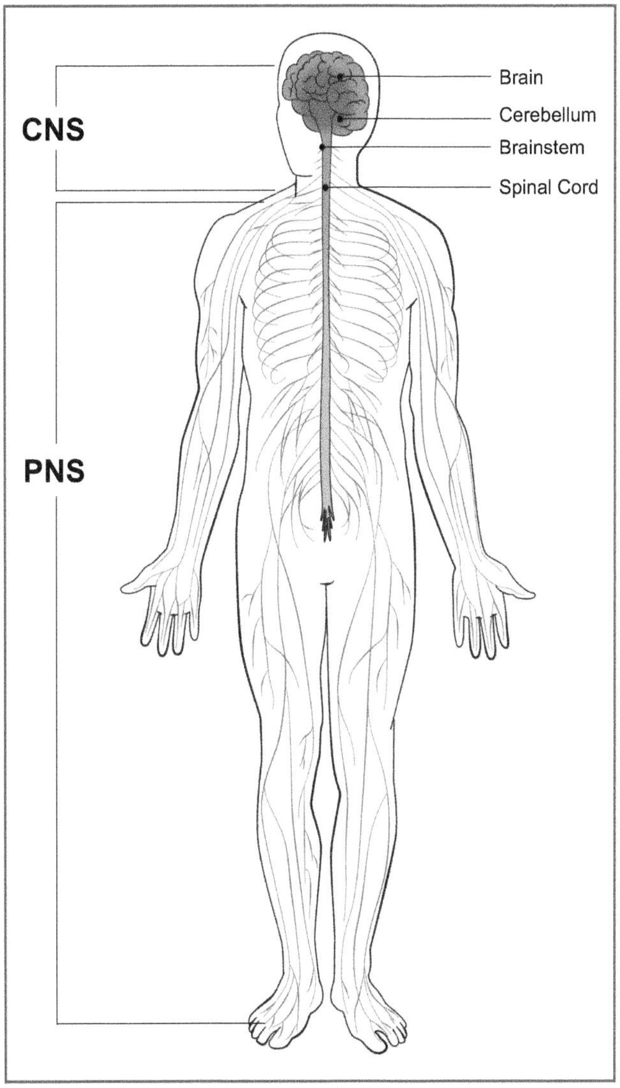

FIGURE 9–1. Nervous system consisting of the central nervous system and the peripheral nervous system.

to as either a **sulcus** (i.e., a shallow groove) or a **fissure** (i.e., a deep groove), depending on the depth of the groove. Based on the grooves along the surface of the cortex, the cerebrum can be divided into two halves, known as the left and right **hemispheres**. The grooves in each hemisphere serve to further subdivide the cerebrum into four parts, or lobes. Each of these lobes is found in both the left and right hemispheres of the cerebrum.

The **frontal lobes**, as aptly named, are found in the front of the cerebrum and play a major role in the planning of physical (i.e., motor) movement for all parts of the body. An important language feature of the frontal lobe is **Broca's area**, which is located in the left hemisphere only. As

FYI

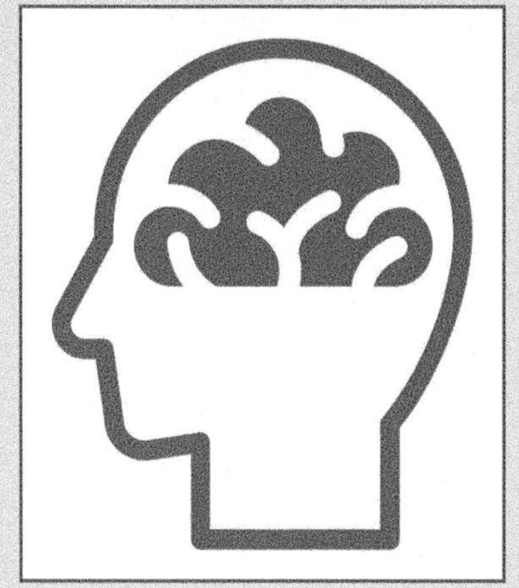

Source: AomAm, CC BY 3.0 <https://creativecommons.org/licenses/by/3.0>, via Wikimedia Commons

Brain imaging has the potential to identify as well as predict various types of communication disorders. A variety of techniques are available for brain scanning. Some of the more common techniques are computed tomography (CT), electroencephalography (EEG), positron emission tomography (PET), magnetic resonance imaging (MRI), and near-infrared spectroscopy (NIRS). Each technique provides a specialized view of the brain. The use of MRI has become perhaps the most important tool for evaluating regions of the brain affected by injury.

detailed later, Broca area plays a pivotal role in the expression of speech and language. The left and right **parietal lobes** are located at the top of the cerebrum, behind the frontal lobes. The role of the parietal lobes is to process incoming sensory information (e.g., the mental sensation of touching something hot or cold). The **temporal lobes** are located along the side of the cerebrum. There are two important landmarks in the temporal lobes that are relevant to communication. The first of these is the **primary auditory center** (also called Heschl's gyrus), found in both left and right temporal lobes. This is the endpoint location in the brain responsible for hearing. Sound, initially entering the ears, travels along a specific nervous system pathway and terminates in the primary auditory center. Further information regarding the anatomy and physiology of hearing can be found in Chapter 2. The second landmark of the temporal lobe is **Wernicke's area**. As noted later, Wernicke area is found only in the left temporal lobe and is responsible for the understanding (or comprehension) of language. The fourth lobes are the **occipital lobes** and are found at the back of the cerebrum. A major function of the occipital lobes is the processing of incoming visual information. Deep within the cerebrum is an area known as the **limbic system** (or lobe) that includes part of most of the other lobes (i.e., frontal, parietal, and temporal). The limbic system is involved in affective behaviors such as emotion and motivation. An illustration of the lobes of the cerebrum is provided in Figure 9–2.

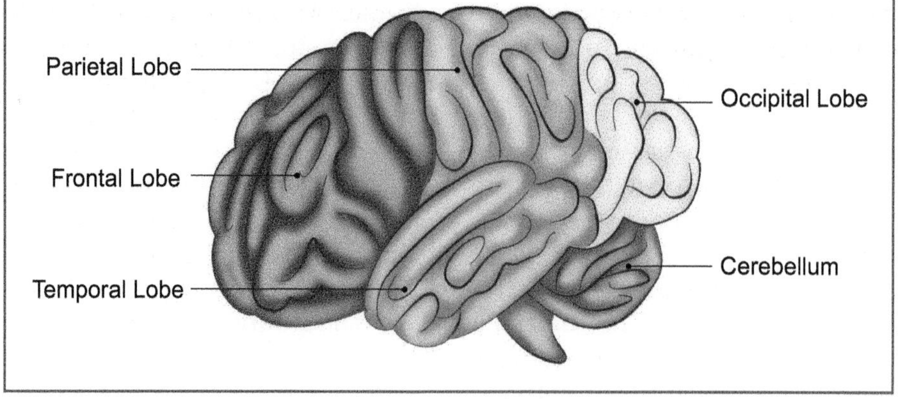

FIGURE 9–2. The four lobes of the left hemisphere of the cortex. The location of the cerebellum is also shown.

The remaining parts of the central nervous system include the brainstem, spinal cord, and cerebellum. These structures contain bundles (or pathways) of nerve fibers that transmit sensory and motor information. Sensory pathways are those that carry information from the periphery toward the cerebrum. For example, the sensory pathway associated with stubbing your toe would begin at the toe and end in the cerebrum. Motor pathways carry information away from the cerebrum toward the peripheral regions of the body. So, the motor pathway associated with wiggling your toes would begin in the cerebrum and end at the toes. Damage to the sensory and motor pathways can have an adverse impact on speech and language because these pathways either originate or terminate in the brain.

The peripheral nervous system consists of all the remaining nerves that lie outside the cerebrum, brainstem, and spinal cord. The peripheral nervous system connects the brain to the outside world. Foremost among these nerves are a collection of **spinal nerves** and **cranial nerves**. There are 31 pairs of spinal nerves that are connected to the spinal cord and pass into the central nervous system where neural signals are processed. There are 12 pairs of cranial nerves (CNs) that emerge from the base of the brain and are commonly identified by the Roman numerals I through XII. Several cranial nerves are involved in various aspects of speech, hearing, and swallowing, particularly CNV, CNVII, CNVIII, CNIX, CNX, CNXI, and CNXII (Table 9–1). Damage to any of these cranial nerves could have a negative effect on communication and swallowing.

Table 9–1. The 12 Cranial Nerves Comprising the Peripheral Nervous System and Their Associated Primary Functions

Cranial Nerve	*Function*
Olfactory (I)	Smell
Optic (II)	Vision
Oculomotor (III)	Eye movement (opening)
Trochlear (IV)	Eye movement (closing)
Trigeminal (V)	Facial sensation and chewing
Abducent (VI)	Eye movement
Facial (VII)	Facial expression and taste
Auditory (VIII)	Balance and hearing
Glossopharyngeal (IX)	Taste and salivation
Vagus (X)	Swallowing and talking Taste and respiration
Accessory (XI)	Pharynx/larynx muscles Neck and shoulder movement
Hypoglossal (XII)	Tongue movement

There are a wide range of conditions that can contribute to neurogenic language disorders. These conditions result from damage to either the central nervous system or the peripheral nervous system, and sometimes both. Foremost among these damaging conditions is a **cerebrovascular accident**, or what used to be called *apoplexy*. The term *apoplexy* is a Greek word meaning "struck down," because this was believed to be a condition that would strike an otherwise healthy person at random. Physicians now commonly refer to this condition as a **stroke**. A stroke is an injury to blood vessels in the brain (not the heart), usually in the form of a clot or hemorrhage (i.e., bleeding). Because blood is the means by which oxygen is transferred to the brain, injury to blood vessels results in a lack of oxygen to brain cells that can lead to brain cell death within only a few minutes. There are two types of blood clots: (a) **thrombosis**, which is a stationary blood clot, and (b) **embolism**, which is a blood clot that is carried to a brain artery where it lodges permanently. Approximately 80% of strokes result from a blood clot. A **hemorrhage** is a condition where a blood vessel bursts, resulting in internal bleeding in the brain. This condition makes up 20% of all strokes. The occurrence rates for stroke show that men are at a slightly higher risk than women. The occurrence of stroke increases with age—approximately 75% of all strokes occur in people over the age of 65 years. Stroke is the second, single most common cause of mortality worldwide. Strokes are typically unilateral, affecting only one side of the brain. There is no difference in the frequency of occurrence of left-hemisphere and right-hemisphere strokes. When a stroke is not fatal, it can leave people physically impaired (Figure 9–3). The American Stroke Association has identified warning signs that might signal the impending occurrence of stroke. These signs include **B**alance problems, **E**ye/vision problems, **F**ace drooping, **A**rm weakness, **S**peech difficulty, and **T**ime to call 9-1-1. The acronym of these signs spells out the phrase "*be fast*" and indicates the need to quickly seek medical attention in the event of their occurrence (Hallowell, 2023; Figure 9–4).

Aside from strokes, there are various diseases affecting the nervous system that contribute to communication disorders. **Alzheimer disease** is a frequent form of dementia among older people. **Dementia** is a brain disorder that seriously affects a person's ability to carry out daily activities. The

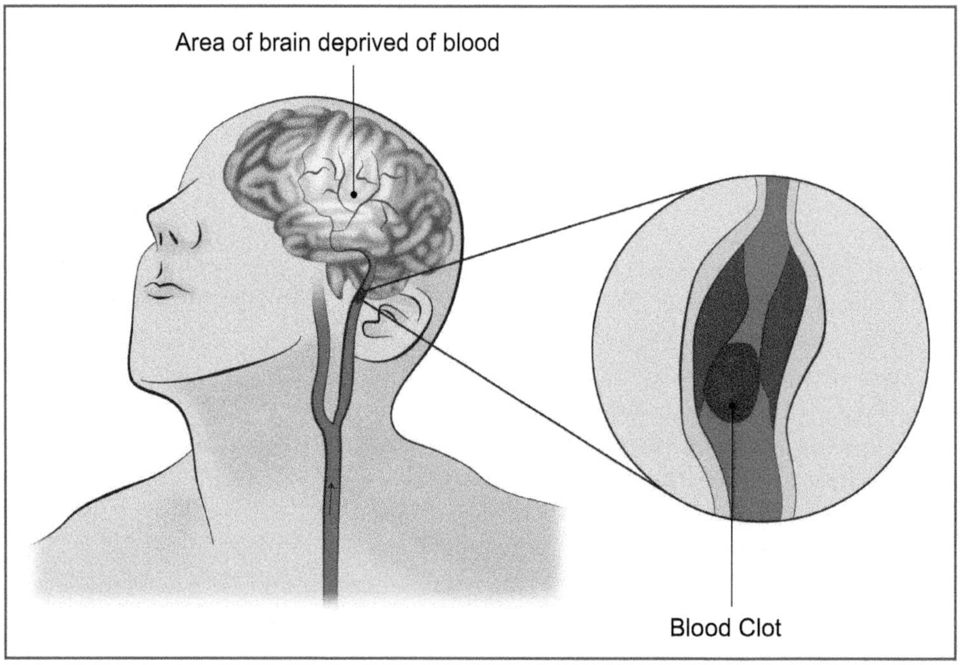

FIGURE 9–3. A cerebrovascular accident (i.e., stroke). A blood clot prevents the flow of blood and oxygen to the brain.

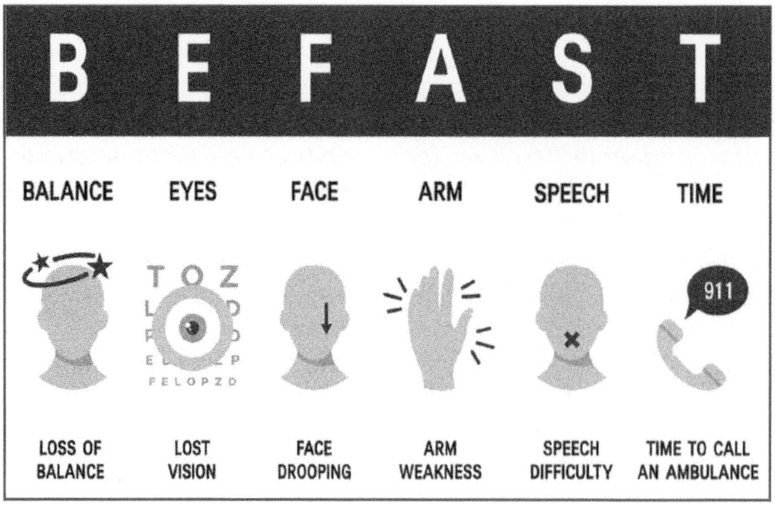

FIGURE 9–4. Warning signs for the occurrence of a stroke (taken from Hallowell, 2023, Figure 6.2).

FYI

Apoplexy is bleeding into an organ or loss of blood flow to an organ. When bleeding occurs within the brain or due to a blood clot, the term *stroke* is used most often. However, apoplexy can also occur in other regions of the body such as adrenal or pituitary glands.

disease begins slowly and initially involves the parts of the brain that control thought, memory, attention, and language. Over time, symptoms get worse, and people may not recognize family members or have trouble speaking, reading, or writing. An estimated 5 million Americans have Alzheimer disease, most of whom are older than 65 years of age. The disease is the sixth leading cause of death in the United States.

Traumatic brain injury (TBI), also called a head injury, occurs when a sudden blow to the head causes damage to the brain. A TBI can result when the head suddenly and violently hits an object, or when an object pierces the skull and enters brain tissue. Most instances of TBI are caused by motor vehicle accidents. Other cases occur from sporting activities (football, rugby) or military combat. The remaining cases are a result of falls and physical assaults. Symptoms of a TBI can be mild, moderate, or severe, depending on the extent of the damage to the brain. If various centers of the brain that affect speech, language, or hearing are affected by trauma, it is likely that a communication disorder will occur. TBI has been referred to as a silent epidemic because the condition does not receive much public attention, and the results are not visible to the naked eye. Yet TBI is a major public health problem and is a leading cause of disability among children and young adults. Males between the ages of 14 and 25 years are the most affected group because they tend to be higher risk takers than females, leading to sometimes devastating consequences. Many face lasting impairments that affect their independence and daily lives. Each year the number of new cases of TBI is approximately 1.7 million in the United States and 60,000 in the United Kingdom.

FYI

Many famous people have died from a stroke, including Bill Paxton (actor), Winston Churchill (politician), Charles Dickens (writer), Catherine the Great (Empress of Russia), Luke Perry (actor), Isaac Hayes (singer), Curly Howard (one of the Three Stooges), Judy Mazel (author), Jawaharlal Nehru (politician), Kirby Puckett (baseball star), Franklin Roosevelt (politician), Joseph Stalin (politician), and Luther Vandross (singer).

HISTORIC ASPECTS OF NEUROGENIC LANGUAGE DISORDERS

The history of neurogenic language disorders has its origins in the discipline of neuroscience. A key issue in the historical developments of neuroscience was the debate over the functioning of the brain, particularly whether areas of the brain had specific functions (**localism theory**) or whether the brain functioned as a single organ (**holism theory**). **Franz Joseph Gall** (1758–1828) was a German anatomist and an early advocate of localism. He developed a theory in 1800 known as phrenology, in which he claimed that character and personality traits, as well as criminal intentions, could be determined based on the shape of the head. That is, a person's mental characteristics were physically engraved in the brain and were signified by bumps on the surface of the head. Reportedly, Gall was jealous of a friend who showed outstanding memory skills and language proficiency. Because this friend had big bulging eyes, Gall thought the brain was particularly large at this location in the head and thus concluded that the brain functions for language and memory must be located behind the eyes. Gall's theory was very popular in the 19th century. A phrenology example is provided in Figure 9–5.

Paul Broca (1824–1880; Figure 9–6) was a French neurologist and surgeon who also believed that the brain functioned in a localized matter; however, he rejected phrenology and instead was part of a group of scholars who thought there were

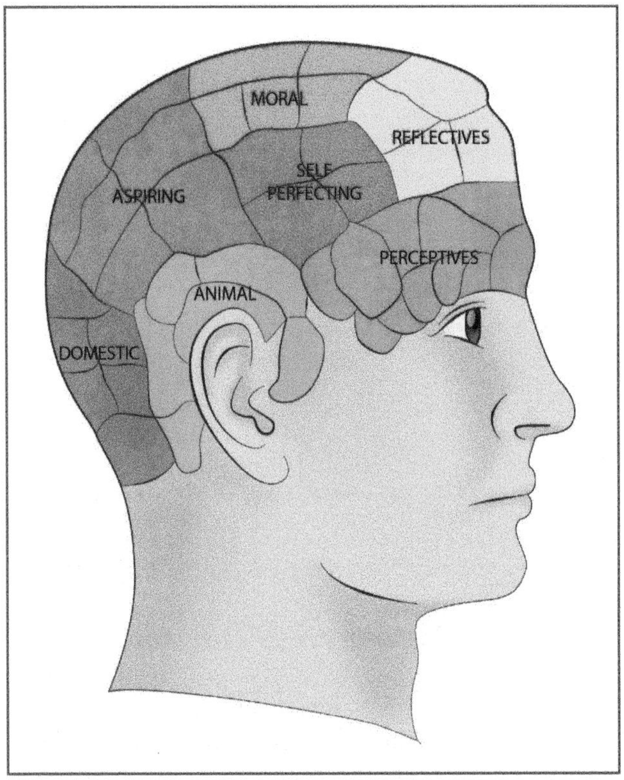

FIGURE 9–5. Franz Joseph Gall's model of phrenology.

unique centers within the brain responsible for specific motoric functions. This perspective was referred to as **cortical localization**. Broca became convinced of localization based on observations of two of his patients. The first was a 30-year-old who had progressive neurological problems. Near the time of his death, at the age of 51 years, the man was able to utter only the word "tan." The second patient was an 84-year-old who lost his speech after falling down a flight of stairs (most likely due to the sudden occurrence of a stroke). After the accident, the individual could utter only four words: "yes," "no," "always," and "three." Upon each person's death, Broca performed an autopsy of the brain and found specific damage to a region of the frontal lobe on the left hemisphere. Broca deduced that this region of the brain, which was later termed Broca's area, must be responsible for the production of speech.

Karl Wernicke (1848–1905; Figure 9–7) was a German neurologist. In 1873, Wernicke examined a patient who had suffered a stroke. Although the man was able to speak, he showed considerable difficulty understanding what was said to him.

FIGURE 9–6. Paul Broca identified a region in the frontal lobe of the left hemisphere responsible for language formulation and production.

FIGURE 9–7. Karl Wernicke identified a region in the temporal lobe of the left hemisphere responsible for language comprehension.

He also showed difficulty understanding written language. When the man died, Wernicke performed an autopsy of his brain and found a lesion in the temporal lobe of the left hemisphere. Wernicke deduced that this region in the brain must be localized for understanding language. This unique and highly specialized area of the brain was later termed Wernicke's area.

Korbinian Brodmann (1868–1918) was a German neurologist who supported the theory of localism. By staining tissues in various parts of the brain, he was able to show that different cell types (i.e., the histology) of various brain regions differed. In total, he was able to categorize the brain into 52 distinct areas (now referred to as **Brodmann areas**) based on the cellular organization of the cortex. The notation system developed by Brodmann is still in use today. A map of Brodmann areas is shown in Figure 9–8. Brodmann's research career was influenced by his close working relationship with another German neurologist, **Alois Alzheimer** (1864–1915) who is credited with publishing the first case of senile dementia (later known as Alzheimer disease.

Karl Lashley (1890–1958) was an American psychologist who believed that certain parts of the brain were indeed holistic based on his search for the location in the brain responsible for memory. From work with rats, he reasoned that memory is not found in a specific location within the brain but rather the sum of many locations throughout the brain.

> **FYI**
>
> A coma is a deep state of unconsciousness during which an individual is not able to react to their environment and which often can occur following a brain injury. The Glasgow Coma Scale is the most widely used scoring system for quantifying the level of consciousness following TBI. The scale is based on evaluating the complexity of the patient's eye movements, verbal behaviors, and motor responses.

Hildred Schuell (1906–1970; Figure 9–9) received her doctorate from the University of Iowa in 1946. Shortly after she graduated, she joined the Minneapolis veteran's hospital where she worked for most of her professional life. She was interested in both the evaluation and treatment of aphasia, and over her career, became known worldwide for her research in the area of aphasia. She published *Differential Diagnosis of Aphasia with the Minnesota Test*, portions of which are still used today. Schuell

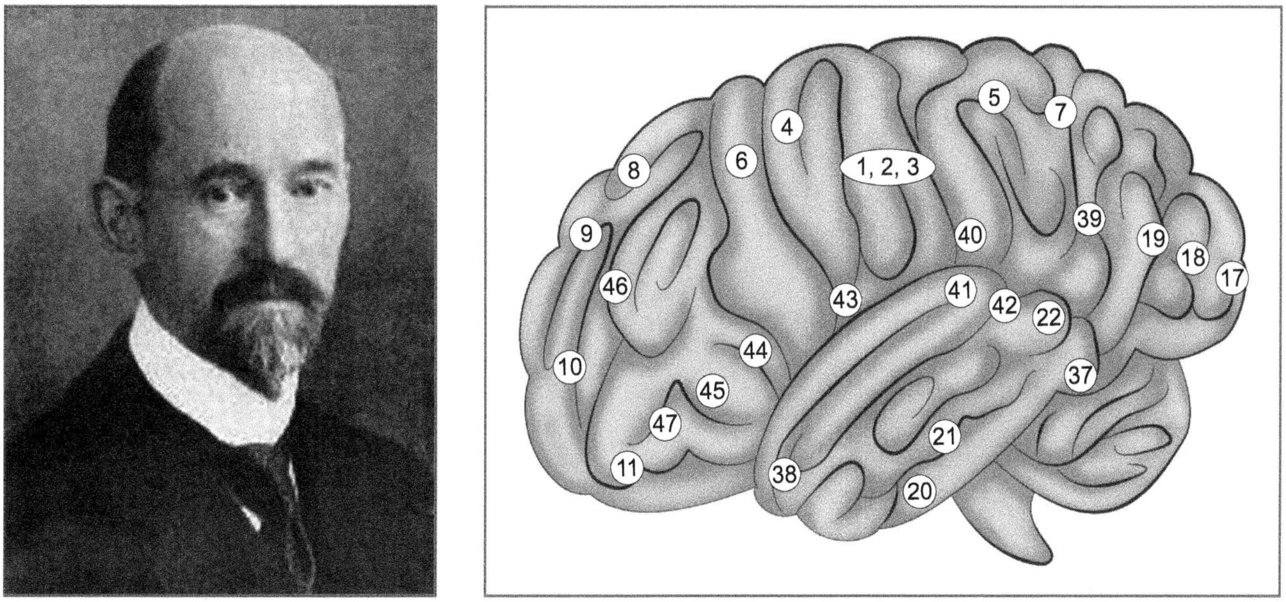

A **B**

FIGURE 9–8. **A.** Korbinian Brodmann. **B.** The Brodmann numbering system for various brain functions.

was reputed to be a skilled clinician, working with many war veterans who had experienced aphasia. Her philosophy was that most individuals with aphasia could improve their communication abilities under the right conditions.

Wilder Penfield (1891–1976) was an American neurosurgeon who was an expert in the area of epilepsy, a brain disorder involving recurrent seizures. While performing brain surgery in several patients in a wide-awake state, Penfield would stimulate different sections of their cerebrum. He found that by stimulating specific regions of the brain, the patients would provide a specific response. Based on this direct brain stimulation, he provided compelling support for the view of brain localism.

The debate over brain localism versus holism has long since subsided. With advances in technology, we are now able to identify and visualize many aspects of brain functioning. The results have shown that it is incorrect to assume a one-to-one mapping between brain structure and function. The preferred term regarding the functions of the brain is now **connectionism**. This view essentially supports a mix of both localized and holistic functions in the brain. Lower-level or primary sensory and motoric functions seem to be strongly localized, but higher-level functions, such as memory and language, are the result of interconnections among brain areas.

Martha Taylor Sarno (b. 1927; Figure 9–10) has been an innovator in the field of clinical aphasiology and neurogenic communication disorders ever since she entered the field of speech-language pathology, over 60 years ago. As the first speech-language pathologist to work in a medical rehabilitation setting, Sarno designed the framework and developed rehabilitation assessment and therapy methods that have had a lasting impact in the field of speech-language pathology. Sarno is perhaps best known in the field of speech-language pathology for the creation of a functional approach to assessment and intervention. She was also among the first to have recognized the importance of examining quality of life changes associated with speech and language therapy.

FIGURE 9–9. Hildred Schuell made major contributions to the clinical evaluation and treatment of aphasia.

FIGURE 9–10. Martha Taylor Sarno recognized the importance of considering quality of life changes associated with aphasia.

TYPES OF NEUROGENIC LANGUAGE DISORDERS

Neurogenic language disorders are **aphasia** and **cognitive communication disorder**. There are also communication difficulties associated with damage to the right hemisphere referred to as **right hemisphere syndrome**.

Aphasia

Aphasia is a language disorder associated with brain injury, usually a stroke. Aphasia refers to a collection of clinically diverse disorders that affect the production and comprehension of language and the ability to read, write, or calculate. This disorder accounts for roughly one quarter of all neurogenic communication impairments. Hallowell (2023) defines aphasia according to four primary elements: (a) it is acquired; (b) it has a neurological cause; (c) it affects reception and expression of language across modalities; and (d) it is not a sensory, psychiatric, or intellectual disorder.

There are four primary types of aphasia, each of which involves damage to the left hemisphere of the cerebrum; they are categorized according to the fluency of language expression (Table 9–2). People with **fluent aphasia** have major problems understanding spoken and written language, although their language expression seemingly appears to be within normal limits. **Wernicke's aphasia** and **anomic aphasia** are examples of fluent aphasia. People with **nonfluent aphasia** have difficulty expressing themselves when speaking or writing, although their ability to understand language seems to remain relatively intact. **Broca's aphasia** and **mixed (or global) aphasia** are examples of nonfluent aphasia.

Wernicke's aphasia is so named because of the location in the brain where damage has occurred. Wernicke's area is found in the temporal lobe of the left hemisphere at Brodmann area 22 (Figure 9–11; also see Figure 9–8). The lesion does not damage the frontal region of the brain, which is responsible

Table 9–2. Various Types of Aphasia

Type of Aphasia	*Language Examples*
Fluent aphasia: Wernicke	• May say words that make little sense. • May use made-up words such as "frangle" and are not aware of doing so. • May produce a full-length sentence that has no meaning. It sounds like a sentence, but there is no content to what is being spoken.
Fluent aphasia: Anomia	• May have difficulties naming certain words. • Patients tend to produce grammatically correct, yet empty, speech. • Language comprehension tends to be preserved.
Nonfluent aphasia: Broca	• May struggle to say words and form a sentence. • Affected people often omit small words such as "is," "and," and "the." • Often aware of their difficulties and can become easily frustrated by their speaking.
Nonfluent aphasia: Mixed (or global)	• May be totally nonverbal and/or only use facial expressions and gestures to communicate. • May understand some words.

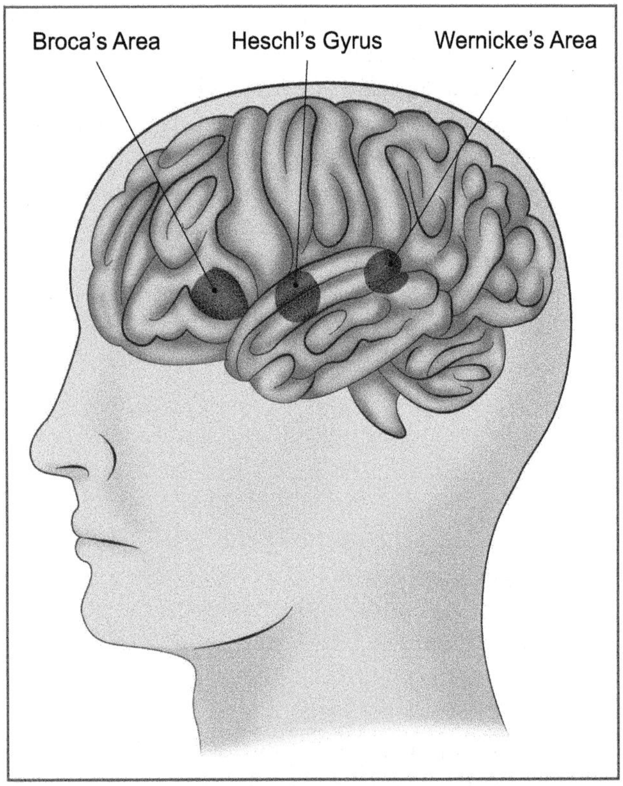

FIGURE 9–11. Location of Broca's area, Heschl's gyrus, and Wernicke's area. Broca's and Wernicke's areas are found only in the left hemisphere of the brain.

for all motor behavior. Therefore, one obvious feature of Wernicke's aphasia is that there are no signs of body paralysis. The condition is characterized by fluent language expression but impaired language comprehension. To a naive listener, the individual with Wernicke's aphasia may seem to have no expressive language difficulty because their production of speech is effortless. However, when listening closely, it becomes evident that the content of what is being spoken about may be missing. Anomic aphasia generally results from damage to an isolated region in the Wernicke's area of the brain. Similar to Wernicke's aphasia, there are no obvious signs of body paralysis. This communication disorder is characterized by difficulty with word retrieval. The patient's speech is essentially fluent; however, there are high number of instances of **circumlocutions** (i.e., roundabout talking) due to word-finding problems.

Broca's aphasia results from a lesion to Broca's area, which is in the left frontal lobe at Brodmann area 44 (see Figures 9–8 and 9–11). The lesion is accompanied by one-sided (right-side) body weakness or paralysis (i.e., **hemiparesis**). This type of aphasia is characterized primarily by fairly intact language comprehension skills but nonfluent expressive language. The nature of the expressive language is confined to short utterances of approximately four words or less, and speech articulation is likely to be slow and labored because of dysarthria cooccurring. Mixed aphasia and global aphasia are nonfluent forms of aphasia that relate more to the severity of the brain lesion rather than to the distinctive communication disorder. The brain lesion is usually deep and covers portions of both Wernicke's and Broca's areas. In mixed aphasia, the problems with expressive and receptive language are generally no more than moderate in severity. Global aphasia reflects a severe to profound communication disorder due to a massive widespread brain lesion. In mixed and global aphasias, speech dysarthria is likely to be present as well.

Cognitive Communication Disorders

The term cognitive communication disorder is used to describe a broad range of communication problems that are caused by damage to the frontal lobe regions of the brain. The damage can be a result of a stroke, TBI, brain infection, brain tumor, or degenerative disease such as multiple sclerosis, Parkinson disease, or Alzheimer disease. Individuals with a history of drug and/or alcohol abuse can also develop a cognitive communication disorder. Along with controlling motor movement, these regions of the brain also manage our thinking (i.e., cognition), memory, and problem-solving abilities. Damage to these areas of the brain result in an impairment of the verbal ability to transform thoughts into meaningful expressive language, resulting in a state of language confusion. The impairment is also found in a person's nonverbal ability to use gestures, write, and use appropriate social skills. This language disorder should not be confused with aphasia. The American Speech-Language-Hearing Association has defined cognitive communication disorders as difficulty with any aspect of communication that is affected by disruption of cognition. A cognitive communication disorder can result from damage to the right hemisphere as well as to the left hemisphere. These disorders compose approximately 15% of all neurogenic communication disorders.

Symptoms of cognitive communication disorders vary widely depending on the type and cause of brain damage, and the communication problems can range from minor to severe. Individuals who have experienced a TBI are at a high risk for developing a cognitive communication disorder. Injury to the frontal lobes can occur in several ways, including (a) laceration, (b) concussion, and (c) contrecoup. A **laceration** is a wound or cut to the brain that involves direct tearing of brain tissue. A **concussion** is a direct blow to the head that may result from violent shaking of the head or a whiplash type of injury. A **contrecoup** injury involves a secondary injury that is opposite to the primary injury, whereby the brain essentially rocks back and forth. Examples of the types of TBI are illustrated in Figure 9–12.

FYI

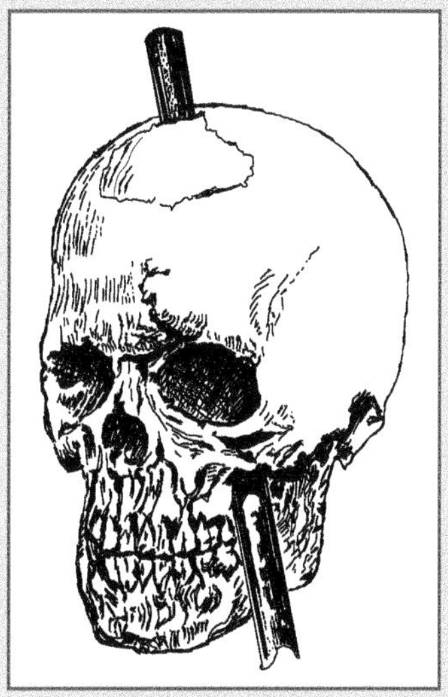

Source: John M. Harlow, M.D., Public domain, via Wikimedia Commons.

Phineas Gage (1823–1860) is by far the most famous case demonstrating the alteration of personality resulting from a brain injury. Gage was a railway worker in Vermont. On September 13, 1848, an accidental explosion of a charge he had set blew a 3-ft iron rod upward through his palate, exiting out of his left frontal skull region. Amazingly, he recovered from this massive open head wound, but something had changed. Over a course of time, Phineas' personality changed from his old friendly self to an impulsive, crude-mouthed individual. This case further solidified the belief that regions of the brain are dedicated to specific human functions and attributes.

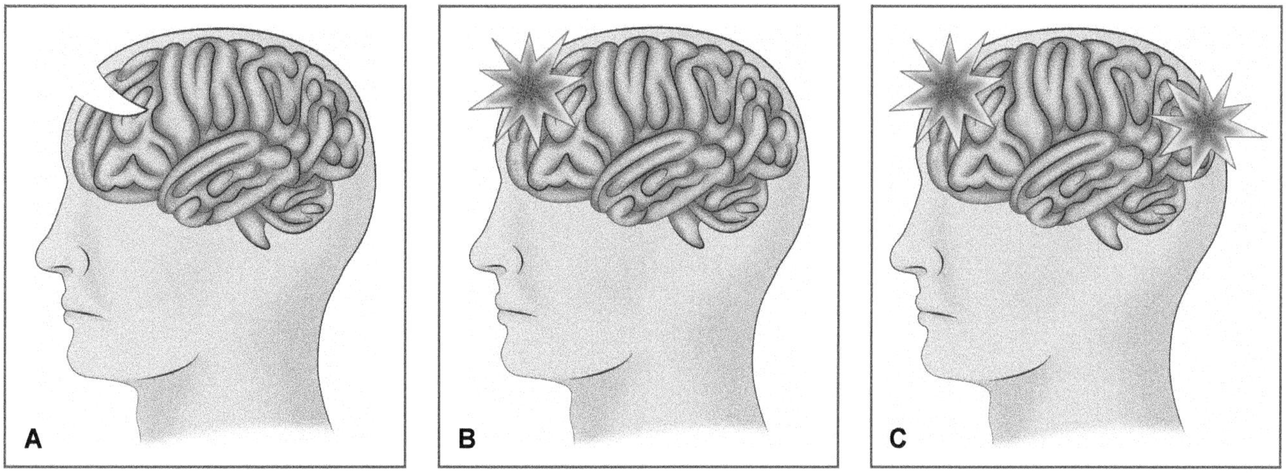

FIGURE 9–12. Types of traumatic brain injury including laceration (**A**), concussion (**B**), and contrecoup (**C**).

Right Hemisphere Syndrome

As the label indicates, right hemisphere syndrome refers to a condition in which atypical behaviors occur as a result of damage to the right side of the cerebrum. Possible causes of the damage include stroke, TBI, and brain disease, all of which affect the right hemisphere. Because damage can occur in any region of the hemisphere, there are no universal characteristics that are found among individuals with this syndrome. Further, the characteristics vary as a function of the severity of the damage. Not everyone with right hemisphere damage will exhibit communication difficulties, but some of the more common problems are listed in Table 9–3. It is important to note that the language problems exhibited by people with right hemisphere damage are not commonly found in people with aphasia (i.e., left hemisphere damage), although there may be some common symptoms between people of either group (Hallowell, 2023).

An individual who experiences a stroke in the right hemisphere can acquire a condition known as **hemispatial (left) neglect**. This is a type of attention disorder where the individual no longer acknowledges the left side of the body or any environmental space that is in the person's left visual field. The person may not shave the left side of their face or may avoid eating food on the left side of the plate. The neglect is also found in the individual's reading, writing, and drawing behavior (Figure 9–13).

Table 9–3. Possible Communication Difficulties in a Person With Right Hemisphere Syndrome

- Word retrieval difficulty, sometimes using the incorrect word
- Poor topic maintenance during a conversation, including turn-taking
- Difficulty understanding and appreciating word-based humor
- Misinterpretation of sarcasm
- Flat affect or inappropriate emotional expression
- Poor nonverbal communication, such as facial expression or body language
- Problems recognizing faces (prosopagnosia), leading to awkward communication exchanges
- Visuospatial difficulties affecting reading and writing
- Problem-solving difficulties
- Decreased awareness or insight of their communication difficulties

CURRENT THEORIES REGARDING NEUROGENIC LANGUAGE DISORDERS

One unique aspect of brain injury relates to a concept known as **spontaneous recovery**. This concept concerns a patient's natural reestablishment of skills that initially were lost immediately following the brain injury. Spontaneous recovery is not specific to communication but can refer to motor and sensory abilities as well. All patients are expected to show some level of spontaneous recovery because of brain healing (e.g., reduction in swelling). Yet no two patients are alike regarding the extent of their spontaneous recovery.

FIGURE 9–13. Example of *left neglect*. An individual with right hemisphere syndrome was asked to draw a clock illustrating the time of 6 o'clock.

Patients may fully recover their communication abilities, recover only a portion of their abilities, or show minimal recovery. In addition, the time span of spontaneous recovery varies, ranging from a few days to several years post injury. The investigation of spontaneous recovery is linked to a fascinating area of neurobiological research known as neuroplasticity (Cappa & Vignolo, 2020). **Neuroplasticity** refers to the changes that occur in the organization of the brain because of trauma. A dedicated area in the brain associated with a given function can transfer to a different location in the brain as a consequence of brain damage or recovery. Regarding aphasia, researchers are intrigued as to why and how recovery from aphasia takes place. One of the earliest hypotheses about neuroplasticity was that due to damage to the left hemisphere (e.g., stroke), the right hemisphere simply takes over all linguistic functions that normally would have occurred in the left hemisphere. The **right hemisphere theory of recovery** is still a popular theory, and with advances in functional imaging of the brain, the specific role of the right hemisphere as part of spontaneous recovery can be examined more directly.

ASSESSMENT OF NEUROGENIC LANGUAGE DISORDERS

Aphasia

Assessment of aphasia is a problem-solving activity. The speech-language pathologist must first determine whether the patient actually demonstrates aphasic symptoms. If so, the speech-language pathologist will try to determine the nature or type of aphasia (e.g., fluent, nonfluent). Next, the speech-language pathologist should appraise the patient's existing functional communication abilities. The assessment occurs in two stages. The first stage is the **initial assessment**, which happens at the patient's bedside while the patient is still a hospital inpatient. During this initial assessment, the speech-language pathologist obtains a sample of the patient's spoken language and also assesses general language comprehension abilities. Within approximately 1 week following the initial assessment, the patient should have regained enough strength to sit at a table and tolerate the demands of a more sustained interaction. The **primary assessment** occurs at this time, and the patient's language expression and comprehension are fully evaluated, as well as reading and writing abilities.

A dilemma when performing a language assessment in a person with aphasia is that often there is no baseline record of the person's language abilities prior to the brain injury (i.e., the **premorbid state**). It is vital for the speech-language pathologist to take a **person-centered approach** when assessing the client. That is, the client's needs are of foremost importance. Information regarding the person's prior vocabulary and reading abilities, as well as general loquaciousness would be useful to the speech-language pathologist in determining the severity of aphasia. The most logical source of this information would be to consider the person's prior vocation and educational background, or to simply ask the patient's family members. Those individuals closest to the patient may be at a loss as to how best to communicate with their loved one following a brain injury. Some common approaches to communication with people who have aphasia have been developed by the National Aphasia Association and are shown in Table 9–4.

Cognitive Communication Disorders

A cognitive communication disorder encompasses difficulty with any aspect of communication that is affected by an impairment of cognition. Therefore, an assessment of this disorder should involve examination of all aspects of communication, particularly listening, speaking, gesturing, reading, and writing. The assessment also needs to include close inspection of the individual's cognitive abilities, including behaviors like attention, memory, organization, and social skills. An important consideration in the evaluation of individuals who may have a cognitive communication disorder is the impact of the disorder on overall functioning. Therefore, the assessment incorporates observations of the individual in their home or daily environment and includes interviews with caregivers and other frequent communication partners.

Table 9–4. Suggestions to Help Communicate With a Person Who Has Aphasia
Make sure you have the person's attention before you start talking.
Minimize or eliminate background noise (TV, radio, other people).
Keep your own voice at a normal level.
Keep communication simple, but adult. Simplify your own sentence structure and reduce your rate of speech. Emphasize key words. Do not "talk down" to the person with aphasia.
Give them time to speak. Resist the urge to finish sentences or offer words.
Communicate with drawings, gestures, writing, and facial expressions in addition to speech.
Confirm that you are communicating successfully with "yes" and "no" questions.
Praise all attempts to speak and downplay any errors. Avoid insisting that each word be produced perfectly.
Engage in normal activities whenever possible. Do not shield people with aphasia from family or ignore them in a group conversation. Rather, try to involve them in family decision-making as much as possible. Keep them informed of events but avoid burdening them with day-to-day details.
Encourage independence and avoid being overprotective.

Note. From National Aphasia Association.

FYI

Long-term alcohol consumption could possibly lead to the development of a cognitive communication disorder. Brain damage is a common and potentially severe consequence of regular alcohol consumption. Even mild to moderate drinking can adversely affect cognitive functioning, including memory loss and various language processes. Traces from a single standard drink of alcohol can remain in the body for up to 4 days.

Right Hemisphere Syndrome

A person with right hemisphere syndrome would be assessed similarly to someone with a known cognitive communication disorder. Difficulties are likely to be discovered in areas of communication, attention, and cognition. The diverse nature of symptoms noted for the syndrome requires a broad range of standardized testing and clinical observation. Individuals with right hemisphere syndrome may range from exhibiting subtle problems such as poor eye contact or social inappropriateness to more obvious difficulties with language understanding and expression. The challenge for the speech-language pathologist when performing an assessment is to determine *"What is normal?"* (Hallowell, 2023).

International Classification of Functioning, Disability, and Health Framework

When considering assessment of neurogenic communication disorders, it is important to recognize that a brain injury can have a devastating, life-changing impact on a patient's everyday existence. Therefore, it is imperative to consider the patient's overall lifestyle and take steps to reduce any barriers to everyday functioning. The **International Classification of Functioning, Disability, and Health (ICF)** framework was developed by the World Health Organization (2001) as a model of practice for rehabilitation clinicians. The WHO ICF model shifts the concept of disability from one that focuses on impairments to one that focuses on the individual. From an ICF perspective, a patient's disability can be assessed according to two factors: (a) functioning and disability and (b) contextual factors. Functioning and disability includes (a) body functions and structures, which describe the actual anatomy/physiology and psychology of the human body; and (b) activity and participation, which describes the person's functional status, including communication, mobility, interpersonal interactions, self-care, learning, and application of knowledge. Contextual factors include (a) environmental factors, which are those factors that are not within the person's control, such as family, work, government agencies, laws, and cultural beliefs; and (b) personal factors, which include race, gender, age, educational level, and coping styles. The characteristics of the ICF make it attractive to speech-language pathologists for the holistic treatment of patients with a communication disorder. Although the ICF is not a formal assessment tool, it provides a framework to identify the key issues that may impact a patient's overall rehabilitation. Research using the ICF is providing encouraging results for addressing various cognitive communication disorders. In particular, Travis Threats (Figure 9–14) has been influential in demonstrating use of the ICF for clinical practice in speech-language pathology.

TREATMENT OF NEUROGENIC LANGUAGE DISORDERS

The communication disorder resulting from nervous system damage or disease is treatable. The clinical management of individuals with a neurogenic language disorder is focused on providing these individuals with the skills and strategies to be effective communicators. Hallowell (2023) recommends that the focus of treatment should:

- facilitate brain-based recovery of abilities that have been lost or reduced

FIGURE 9–14. Travis Threats has been a leader in demonstrating use of the International Classification of Functioning, Disability, and Health framework for clinical practice in speech-language pathology.

- help compensate for language impairments and empower use of intact abilities to maximize effective communication
- support people psychologically and socially in coping with lost or reduced abilities
- encourage the fullest life participation possible for people with neurogenic communication challenges

Aphasia

Patients who experience a brain injury resulting in aphasia may spontaneously recover their original communication abilities. Although some level of natural recovery might be expected in most patients with aphasia, speech-language therapy is still an important facet in the patient's recovery. The goals of therapy for patients with aphasia are to (a) maximize recovery of impaired function, (b) assist in the development of communication strategies, and (c) help the patient adjust to the residual deficits of the brain injury. It is unlikely that any two patients with aphasia will experience an identical stroke, and patients do not come from identical backgrounds. So, the treatment program for each patient is unique.

Approaches to treating aphasia include (a) stimulation, (b) memorization, and (c) inhibition. **Stimulation** involves encouraging the patient to use all modalities of communication to foster the return of language abilities that are impaired but appear to have the potential to be regained. For example, the patient may be asked to verbally "echo" language models provided by the speech-language pathologist. The patient could be encouraged to read lips, to attempt to write symbols and shapes, and to read single words. In essence, the patient is asked to try every aspect of the expression of language.

Working on a patient's **memory** skills is thought to assist with the development of new neural pathways in the brain, which can lead to learning how to speak again. Memory tasks can include imitating/recalling motor sequences or repetition of phrases and sentences. Some individuals who have experienced a brain injury could show difficulty with **inhibiting** their emotion, especially those emotions that are generally suppressed. Patients might demonstrate uncontrollable laughing or crying or may become sexually aroused. This aspect of therapy attempts to assist the patient to recognize when these emotions are evident and to help extinguish them. For example, the speech-language pathologist could give the patient a visual or verbal prompt to purposely pretend to laugh uncontrollably and then to halt doing so. This contrived activity can serve to heighten the patient's awareness and subsequent ability to control their emotions.

Cognitive Communication Disorders

Patients with this disorder typically have some level of intellectual impairment (e.g., dementia) that affects language, attention, memory, and personality. The goal of therapy is to assist patients in increasing their reliance on more intact cognitive abilities to compensate for those abilities that have become impaired. Manasco (2021) recommended a variety of treatment approaches to working with a patient with a cognitive communication disorder. These approaches include (a) validation therapy, (b) graphic cues, (c) Montessori techniques, and (d) caregiver training. **Validation therapy** is a technique used to confirm (through words and gestures) what the person with dementia says, regardless of accuracy or basis in fact, rather than correcting or reorienting the person. **Graphic cuing** involves providing written information and/or familiar photographs to facilitate communication. This approach capitalizes on the patient's recognition memory and the ability to read aloud. **Montessori-based interventions** involve the development of structured activities that are appropriate to an individual's cognitive abilities and that take place in the context of social interaction. Finally, when working with a patient with a cognitive communication disorder, it is important to incorporate the patient's caregivers in the treatment program. Each letter in the acronym FOCUSED stands for a particular communication technique to be used by caregivers (Ripich & Ziol, 1998). The goal of the caregiver is to teach the patient a functional piece of information or behavior that can be used in everyday situations. A summary of the FOCUSED program is found in Table 9–5.

Table 9–5. Summary of the FOCUSED Approach to Caregiver Training for Patients With Cognitive-Communicative Impairments

F = Face	Face the person directly. Call the person's name. Touch the person. Maintain eye contact.
O = Orient	Orient the person to the topic by repeating key words. Repeat phrases. Use nouns and specific names.
C = Continue	Continue the same topic of conversation as long as possible. Restate the topic throughout the conversation.
U = Unstick	Help the person become "unstuck" when the person uses a word incorrectly by suggesting the intended word.
S = Structured	Structure your questions so that the person can recognize and repeat a response. Provide two simple choices at a time. Use yes/no questions.
E = Exchange	Keep up the normal exchange of ideas used in everyday conversation. Give the person clues as to how to answer questions.
D = Direct	Keep sentences short, simple, and direct. Put the subject of the sentences first. Use hand signals, pictures, and facial expressions.

CULTURAL CONSIDERATIONS AND NEUROGENIC LANGUAGE DISORDERS

A range of multicultural factors interact with neurogenic communication disorders. For example, **race** and **ethnicity** are predisposing factors for several neurological conditions that can lead to a communication disorder. In the United States, African Americans and Hispanics are at greater risk for dementia than other cultural groups (Qualls & Muñoz, 2005). Black people, Hispanic people, Native American people, and Pacific Islanders are at a particularly high risk for type 2 (adult-onset) diabetes, thus making these groups at greater risk for heart disease and stroke. The Centers for Disease Control and Prevention reported an unusually high occurrence of TBI among (a) individuals living in rural geographic areas, (b) military service members and veterans, and (c) the prison population.

The occurrence of various nervous system diseases, such as multiple sclerosis, differs according to **geographic region**. People living beyond the 40° latitude mark north or south of the equator are far more likely to develop multiple sclerosis than those living in warmer climates near the equator. This is especially true for people in North America, Europe, and New Zealand, whereas Asia continues to have a low incidence of multiple sclerosis. Caucasians are far more likely to develop multiple sclerosis than those of African heritage.

A person's **socioeconomic status** is also a consideration in neurogenic communication disorders. Individuals coming from a low socioeconomic status background are less likely to have access to appropriate health care than individuals from middle and high socioeconomic status backgrounds. Lack of access to health care places these individuals at greater risk for later appearing conditions (e.g., hypertension, diabetes) that are precursors to some neurological conditions (e.g., stroke, dementia). Also, the diet of individuals of low socioeconomic status can lead to nutritional deficiencies that affect neurological growth and development, as well as the risk of and response to neurological impairment.

The bilingual speaker who has experienced a brain injury resulting in language impairment presents a unique challenge for the speech-language pathologist, not only from a multicultural perspective, but also from a neurological perspective (Blumenfeld & Kaushanskaya, 2012). The languages of a bilingual speaker are stored in the left hemispheres, like monolingual speakers; however, the languages may not completely overlap in cortical and subcortical regions in the brain (Lahiri et al., 2021). This can result in quite different abilities in the two languages following the injury. It is important for the speech-language pathologist to recognize the likelihood of an uneven language profile in these patients. Hyter and Salas-Provance (2023) recommend using a series of 10 questions to delve into the cultural and linguistic background of a patient who is a non-native English speaker (Table 9–6). These questions serve to provide a baseline for the speech-language therapist to provide culturally and linguistically determined clinical support.

FYI

Advances in research are likely to lead to new ideas about the neurogenic bases of a variety of communication disorders, particularly those that currently have no identifiable cause, such as stuttering and specific language impairment.

SUMMARY OF CHAPTER

Neurogenic language disorders are usually a brain-based disorder. The brain damage can be a result of a stroke, brain trauma, brain infection, brain tumor, or degenerative disease such as multiple sclerosis, Parkinson disease, or Alzheimer disease. These disorders can affect language formulation, comprehension, and cognitive processing in a person who had previously acquired normal language. Aphasia and cognitive communication disorder are the most common forms of neurogenic language disorder. Aphasia refers to a collection of clinically diverse disorders that affect the production and comprehension of language and the ability to read, write, or calculate. Cognitive communication disorder is used to describe a broad range of communication problems that are caused by damage to the frontal lobe regions of the brain. Assessment of aphasia evaluates the patient's language expression and comprehension, as well as reading and writing abilities. Assessment of a cognitive communication disorder entails examination of all aspects of communication, particu-

Table 9–6. Questions on Cultural and Linguistic Background for English as a Second Language Speaker

1. How long has the family been in the country?
2. How long has the patient been in the United States?
3. What is/are the language(s) spoken at home?
4. What is the patient's level of exposure to English?
5. What is the language skill of other family members?
6. What is the patient's language development history in each language?
7. What is the education level of the family?
8. What has been the acculturation pattern of the family?
9. What is the economic level of the family?
10. What is the family's cultural dynamic?

Source: From *Culturally Responsive Practices in Speech, Language, and Hearing Sciences* (2nd ed.), by Y. Hyter and M. Salas-Provance, 2023, Plural Publishing.

larly listening, speaking, gesturing, reading, and writing. The goals of therapy for patients with aphasia are to (a) maximize recovery of impaired function, (b) assist in the development of communication strategies, and (c) help the patient adjust to the residual deficits of the brain injury. The goal of therapy for patients with a cognitive communication disorder is to assist patients in increasing their reliance on more intact cognitive abilities to compensate for those abilities that have become impaired.

NEUROGENIC LANGUAGE DISORDERS ON THE WORLD WIDE WEB

Following are websites that provide further information on the topic of neurogenic language disorders. At the time of publication, each website was freely accessible.

Aphasia Videos
https://www.aphasia.ca/

https://www.aphasia.org/stories/different-types-aphasia/

Interactive Guide to a Neurological Examination
https://neurologicexam.med.utah.edu/adult/html/home_exam.html

Cognitive Communication Disorder
http://www.traumaticbraininjury.com

https://www.rcslt.org/speech-and-language-therapy/clinical-information/brain-injury/

Right Hemisphere Syndrome
https://mrri.org/right-hemisphere-stroke-center/

STUDY QUESTIONS

1. What are the essential anatomical features of the nervous system and their role in communication disorders?
2. What are the various types of aphasia?
3. How are neurogenic language disorders assessed?
4. How are neurogenic language disorders treated?

REFERENCES

Blumenfeld, H. K., & Kaushanskaya, M. (2012). Bilingual aphasia. In J. Kreutzer, J. DeLuca, & B. Caplan (Eds.), *Encyclopedia of clinical neuropsychology* (pp. 207–208). Springer.

Cappa, S., & Vignolo, L. (2020). The neurological foundations of language. In G. Denes & L. Pizzamiglio (Eds.), *Handbook of clinical and experimental neuropsychology*. London.

Hallowell, B. (2023). *Aphasia and other acquired neurogenic language disorders* (3rd ed.). Plural Publishing.

Hyter, Y., & Salas-Provance, M. (2023). *Culturally responsive practices in speech, language, and hearing sciences* (2nd ed.). Plural Publishing.

Lahiri, D., Ardila, A., Dubey, S., Mukherjee, A., Chatterjee, K., & Ray, B. (2021). Effect of bilingualism on aphasia recovery. *Aphasiology*, *35*, 1103–1124.

Manasco, M. H. (2021). *Introduction to neurogenic communication disorders*. Jones & Bartlett Learning.

Qualls, C. D., & Muñoz, M. L. (2005). Race ethnicity, socioeconomic status, and cognitive-communicative functioning in individuals with neurogenic communication disorders: Clinical implications and research directions. *ECHO: E-Journal for Black and Other Ethnic Group Research and Practices in Communication Sciences and Disorders*, *1*(1), 30–39.

Ripich, D., & Ziol, E. (1998). Dementia: A review for the speech-language pathologist. In A. Johnson & B. Jacobson (Eds.), *Medical speech-language pathology: A practitioner's guide* (pp. 467–496). Thieme.

World Health Organization. (2001). *International classification of functioning, disability, and health*.

10

MOTOR SPEECH DISORDERS

OBJECTIVES

After reading this chapter, the student should be able to:

- Identify individuals who have made historical contributions to the fields of neurology and motor speech disorders.
- Describe current theories in motor speech disorders.
- Describe etiologies and characteristics of motor speech disorders.
- Describe current approaches to the assessment of adults with motor speech disorders.
- Identify current professional issues relevant to treatment and intervention of motor speech disorders.
- Demonstrate knowledge concerning the multicultural aspects of motor speech disorders.

KEY TERMS

Parkinson Disease	Hugo Liepmann	Phonetic-Motoric Disorder
Bradykinesia	John Hughlings Jackson	Speech Intelligibility
Multiple Sclerosis	Arnold Aronson	Electromyography
Myelin Sheath	Joseph Duffy	Vocal Function Exercises
Amyotrophic Lateral Sclerosis	Autonomic Nerves	Lee Silverman Voice Treatment
Cerebral Palsy	Sensory Nerves	Motor Learning
James Parkinson	Motor Nerves	Deep Brain Stimulation
Augusta Déjerine-Klumpke	Dysarthria	Sound Sequencing
Klumpke Palsy	Apraxia	Geographic Region
Heymann Steinthal	Mixed Dysarthria	Socioeconomic Status
	Directions Into Velocities of Articulators (DIVA)	

INTRODUCTION

Use of the term *motor* when referring to speech implies the execution of movement or action of the speech articulators. An impairment of movement can have a significant impact on speech sound production and the perceived clarity of speech. Motor refers to the production of movement or action. Motor speech disorders are a group of speech problems due to neurological abnormalities that were acquired at some point in life. The neurogenic problem can be present at birth or surface later because of a brain-based injury or disease. A motor speech disorder is not a disorder of language or cognition (which were the disorders covered in Chapter 9). However, it is possible for an individual to acquire a neurogenic abnormality that affects both speech and language. The focus of this chapter is to introduce two primary types of motor speech disorders: dysarthria and apraxia of speech.

TERMINOLOGY AND DEFINITIONS

Aside from strokes, there are various diseases affecting the nervous system that contribute to motor speech disorders. **Parkinson disease** causes a progressive loss of nerve cell function in the part of the brain that controls muscle movement. The disease is the most common later-life degenerative disease that affects approximately 1% to 2% of people aged 60 years and beyond. Degenerative means that the effects of this disease worsen over time. The four primary symptoms of Parkinson disease are (a) limb and facial tremor; (b) stiffness of the limbs and trunk; (c) **bradykinesia** (i.e., slowness of movement); and (d) postural instability, or impaired balance and coordination. As these symptoms become more pronounced, patients may have difficulty walking and talking.

Multiple sclerosis is a nervous system disease of the brain and spinal cord that is a result of damage to the **myelin sheath**, the material that surrounds and protects nerve cells. This damage slows down or blocks electrical impulses between the brain and body. The condition is characterized by sporadic episodes of symptoms that may last for weeks or months, and then periods where symptoms diminish or disappear (i.e., remissions). Approximately 2.5 million people worldwide have multiple sclerosis. The disease occurs most often among women between the ages of 20 and 40 years. There are a variety of symptoms of multiple sclerosis due to the different ways it can affect the central nervous system, including lack of energy, fatigue, clumsiness,

FYI

Source: Chuck Kennedy (Pete for America), Public domain, via Wikimedia Commons.

Michael J. Fox has a form of Parkinson disease referred to as early-onset parkinsonism. He first started displaying symptoms of the disease in 1991. He established the Michael J. Fox Foundation for Parkinson disease research, which is dedicated to finding a cure for the disease.

vision problems, and speech difficulties such as slurred speech.

Amyotrophic lateral sclerosis, also referred to as *motor neuron disease* or *Lou Gehrig disease* (because it affected this well-known American baseball player), is a nervous system disease that attacks nerve cells that transmit messages from the brain and spinal cord to voluntary muscles such as the arms and legs. The disease generally appears between the ages of 40 and 60 years and affects males more often than females. The disease occurs in 4 to 6 individuals per 100,000, as seen across the United States, United Kingdom, Australia, Canada, and New Zealand. The disease leads to severe impairments in all motor activities, including walking, writing, and speaking. The disease is fatal and, on average, runs its full course between 3 and 5 years following diagnosis. The disease eventually affects breathing ability, leading to respiratory failure. It is estimated that approximately 30,000 Americans have the disease at any given time.

Cerebral palsy is a form of permanent brain damage that occurs either during pregnancy or shortly after birth. The brain damage is a "one-time" event and does not progress further. Cerebral palsy is not a disease, but it is a disorder. The damage affects the ability to perform voluntary motor movements and maintain balance. This condition is often accompanied by involuntary spasms. Cerebral palsy is an umbrella term that refers to a group of disorders that vary depending on the parts of the body that are affected and the way the palsy affects movement. Cerebral palsy is the most common motor disability in childhood, occurring in roughly 2.5 out of every 1,000 births. There are no known cures for cerebral palsy, and the rate of occurrence has remained unchanged. Due to impaired motor movement, individuals with cerebral palsy can have problems with swallowing as well as speech. Dysarthria is a common feature of cerebral palsy. The severity of the speech disorder is dependent on the degree of motor damage.

HISTORIC ASPECTS OF MOTOR SPEECH DISORDERS

There are a variety of neurological abnormalities that exhibit motor speech disorders as both a symptom and outcome of the disorder. Following, some of the historic work that led to the discovery and management of these conditions is profiled.

Parkinson disease was first medically described as a neurological syndrome by the English surgeon **James Parkinson** (1755–1824; Figure 10–1). Parkinson found similarity across a group of six patients who demonstrated involuntary tremors, lessened muscular power, and a propensity to bend the trunk forward. He published a pamphlet in 1817 titled, *An Essay on the Shaking Palsy*. He never attached his name to the disease but was eventually given this recognition in the late 1800s.

Augusta Déjerine-Klumpke (1859–1927; Figure 10–2) was a renowned American neurologist and neuroanatomist, and an eminent physician of her time. She was a pioneer of rehabilitation therapy resulting from spinal cord injuries and contributed much to our current knowledge of spinal cord diseases. She distinguished herself as being the first woman allowed to practice in the

FIGURE 10–1. James Parkinson was the first to medically describe a neurological syndrome later referred to as Parkinson disease.

FIGURE 10–2. Augusta Déjerine-Klumpke, eminent neurologist who was a pioneer of rehabilitation therapy resulting from spinal cord injury.

hospitals of Paris. **Klumpke palsy** (or paralysis) is a condition found in childbirth where there is damage to the brachial plexus, which is the network of nerves that sends signals from the spine to the shoulder, arm, and hand.

Heymann Steinthal (1823–1899) was a German linguist who first introduced the word *apraxia* (from the Greek word αηραεια, meaning "inaction") to denote the loss of motor skills for use of everyday objects, such as a fork and knife by patients who experienced a stroke. Steinthal thought that apraxia was a brain defect in understanding the relationship between movements and the objects with which the movements were concerned. **Hugo Liepmann** (1863–1925), a German neurologist, later described apraxia as an inability to correctly perform skilled movements with the arms and hands in the absence of primary sensory or motor impairments. He identified three forms of apraxia: limb-kinetic, ideomotor, and ideational. Since then, the definition of apraxia has extended beyond the arms and hands to include the oral-motor (speech) system. **John Hughlings Jackson** (1835–1911) was an English neurologist best known for his work in the diagnosis of epilepsy. He was likely the first to observe speech apraxia. He mentioned that a patient seemed to have lost much of his power to do anything, yet the speech musculature was not impaired.

Arnold Aronson (1928–2018) was an American speech-language pathologist at the Mayo Clinic who was recognized throughout the world as an authority and master diagnostician of motor speech disorders. His pioneering work in motor speech disorders defined the field and influenced the diagnosis and care of patients for a half century and beyond. The Mayo Clinic was also the location where **Joseph Duffy** (Figure 10–3) worked as a clinician and clinical researcher. The focus of his research has been on defining the distinguishing clinical characteristics of motor speech disorders. His clinical practice has greatly improved the accuracy of clinical diagnoses of acquired communication disorders. His textbook, *Motor Speech Disorders* (Duffy, 2019), is the go-to resource for speech-language therapists.

TYPES OF MOTOR SPEECH DISORDERS

As previewed in Chapter 9, the central and peripheral nervous systems are composed of **autonomic**, **sensory**, and **motor** nerves. Autonomic nerves

FIGURE 10–3. Joseph Duffy, American speech-language pathologist who helped define the distinguishing clinical characteristics of dysarthria. (Reproduced by permission granted by J. Duffy.)

FYI

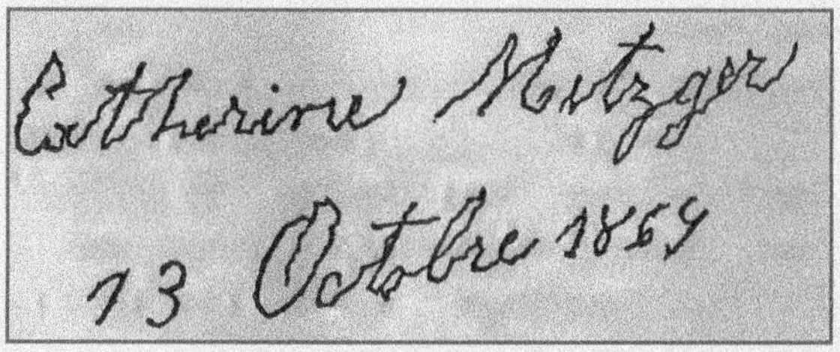

Source: Jean-Martin Charcot, Public domain, via Wikimedia Commons.

An early feature of Parkinson disease is tremor, which is caused by a problem in the deep parts of the brain that control movements. It is a rhythmic pattern resulting from unintentional (involuntary) muscle contractions. The tremor is most noticeable when the hands are at rest, giving the appearance of trying to roll a pill between the thumb and a finger. Parkinson tremor may also affect the face and legs. The tremor is not life threatening. The figure is an example of writing by an individual with Parkinson disease.

control involuntary or semivoluntary functions, such as blood pressure, digestion, heart rate, and sexual arousal. Sensory nerves send impulses from the muscles back to the spinal cord and the brain. Motor nerves send messages in the other direction—from the brain and spinal cord to all the muscles in the body. Damage to motor nerves can lead to imprecise motor movements as well as muscle weakness. A speech production deficit can occur from damage to motor nerves, resulting in a motor speech disorder. These neurologically based problems are most often acquired due to some form of damage to single or multiple areas of the nervous system (e.g., stroke, trauma, disease). They can worsen over time or remain unchanged. They can occur in children and adults of any age. The two primary types of motor speech disorder are **dysarthria** and **apraxia**.

Dysarthria

The term *dysarthria* is a combination of the Greek prefix *dys*, meaning something bad, harsh, or wrong, and the Latin term *arthr*, meaning "joint or articulation," such as the term *arthritis* (disease of the joints). The combination of these terms refers to a condition of impaired speech articulation. The disorder of dysarthria is an impairment of the motor control for speech caused by weakness, paralysis, slowness, or incoordination of the muscles responsible for producing speech sounds. The motor impairment can affect each of the three steps in the process of speech production (refer to Chapter 2, Figure 2–8), namely, the respiratory system, laryngeal system, and articulatory system. Dysarthria is not a language disorder but a disorder of speech sound production. However, a language disorder can often coexist. Individuals with dysarthria are able to comprehend language and know what they want to say but may have trouble moving the muscles necessary to clearly produce vowels and consonants. Dysarthria can also co-occur with a swallowing disorder.

Dysarthria is a collective grouping of at least six different types of impairment in speech articulation.. Each type of dysarthria reflects an impairment of a specific location in the nervous system. A detailed description of the various types of dysarthria is shown in Table 10–1. The most frequently seen form of dysarthria is **mixed dysarthria**, resulting from more diffuse damage of the nervous system compared with other forms of dysarthria. Common speech problems found

Table 10–1. The Six Types of Dysarthria

Type of Dysarthria	*Cause and Features*
Hyperkinetic	• Results from damage to the basal ganglia (deep in the brain) • Problems with involuntary movement
Hypokinetic	• Results from damage to the substantia nigra (a small region in the brainstem) • Condition most often associated with Parkinson disease
Spastic	• Results from damage to the pyramidal (motor) tract of the nervous system • Problems with executing fine motor movements
Flaccid	• Results from damage to the cranial nerves involved in speech • Problems with vocal fold movement (paralysis)
Ataxic	• Results from damage to the cerebellum • Problems regulating the force, timing, rhythm, speed, and overall coordination of movement
Mixed	• Results from simultaneous damage to two or more motor components of the nervous system • Condition most often associated with motor degenerative diseases such as Lou Gehrig disease

FYI

In some instances, dysarthria can be a temporary condition. Some medicines such as muscle relaxants may adversely affect speech articulation resulting in slurred speech. Once the medicine is discontinued, the negative effects on articulation gradually return to normal. You may have experienced this after a visit to the dentist, when a local anesthesia was used.

in dysarthria are slow and sluggish speech that is often slurred and may be accompanied by drooling. There is also reduced vocal loudness and a lack of intonation (i.e., monotone). The clarity (intelligibility) of a person's speech is adversely impacted as a result of impaired speech articulation. The precise occurrence of dysarthria is difficult to estimate because the condition varies according to the underlying cause of the motor impairment. Estimates of the cause and prevalence of dysarthria are listed in Table 10–2.

Apraxia

The Greek word *praxis* means to work or perform. The condition of apraxia, therefore, refers to an inability to voluntarily perform skilled motor movements that are not a result of muscle weakness. The term *dyspraxia* is probably a more accurate description of the condition because there is not a complete loss of volitional movement, as might be expected in true apraxia. Conditions of apraxia are found for a variety of movement behaviors such as hand and leg movements. Apraxia of speech is a motor speech disorder resulting from impairment in the ability to mentally organize the speech muscles and articulators for volitional production of speech sounds. There are two types of speech apraxia: developmental and acquired. Developmental apraxia of speech occurs in children and is present from birth for most affected individuals. Further details concerning developmental (childhood) apraxia of speech can be found in Chapter 4.

Acquired apraxia is typically found in adults and results from an identifiable neurological impairment. Acquired apraxia of speech occurs less frequently than dysarthria and accounts for approximately 5% of all neurogenic communication disorders. Precise estimates are unknown because apraxia is typically not a stand-alone condition. Instead, it usually occurs with other communication disorders such as aphasia. The condition is also apparent in degenerative diseases of the central nervous system, such as amyotrophic lateral sclerosis or Creutzfeldt-Jakob ("mad cow") disease. Individuals with speech apraxia will report that they know the words they want to say, but they will not come out the right way. A primary feature of speech apraxia is inconsistent and variable speech sound misarticulations. In some instances, a person may clearly articulate words, whereas in other instances, there is a breakdown in speech articulation. The articulatory breakdowns show up as substituting one consonant for another or completely deleting consonants. Correct articulation of multisyllabic words is more troublesome than single syllable words. People with apraxia "grope" for the correct word. They may make several attempts at a word before they are able to accurately articulate the word. Individuals may also show oral (i.e., nonverbal) apraxia. This condition is characterized by an inability to imitate or follow commands to perform volitional movements of the speech structures. For example, a patient may have difficulty whistling, coughing, or blowing out a match when requested to do so. Minutes later, when not consciously thinking of the task, a patient may naturally cough to clear their throat.

A comparison of the primary features of speech impairment evident in dysarthria and apraxia is provided in Table 10–3. In general, a person with speech apraxia demonstrates difficulty putting the sounds of words together in the correct order while speaking. A person with dysarthria has difficulty using their muscles in a coordinated fashion to produce speech. A weakness of motor movements prevents the person with dysarthria from speaking clearly.

Table 10–2. Cause and Occurrence of Dysarthria According to Some Neurological Conditions

Category	*Condition*	*Prevalence of Dysarthria*
Degenerative diseases	Parkinson disease	70%–100%
	Amyotrophic lateral sclerosis	30%–100%
Demyelinating diseases	Multiple sclerosis	25%–50%
Trauma	Traumatic brain injury	10%–65%
	Stroke	8%–60%

Source: From Duffy (2019).

Table 10–3. Some Primary Characteristics of Dysarthria and Apraxia of Speech

Dysarthria	*Apraxia of Speech*
• Impairment in muscle strength, tone, range, and steadiness.	• Primarily speech articulation and prosody impairment.
• All speech systems are affected—respiration, laryngeal, and articulatory.	• Speech misarticulations are primarily sound substitutions rather than sound distortions.
• Speech articulation errors are consistent and do not vary across word length.	• Speech articulation errors are inconsistent and vary depending on word length.
• Speech intelligibility can be severely impaired.	• Speech intelligibility is typically not severely affected.

CURRENT THEORIES REGARDING MOTOR SPEECH DISORDERS

Theories of motor control allow us to understand the complexities of speech production to develop interventions for various types of motor speech disorders. Numerous theories of speech motor control can be found in the literature. A common feature of these theories is that the mechanisms of speech motor control are complex. A popular theory of speech production is the **Directions Into Velocities of Articulators (DIVA)** model (Guenther, 2016). A key feature of the theory is that for the accurate production of speech, the articulatory movements must be planned and sequenced by the brain and then put into almost instantaneous motion. These movements need to be correctly timed with the force of muscular movements that create running speech. The DIVA model was developed with the goal of providing an interpretation of the articulatory movements that may underly neurological disorders of speech production.

There are numerous theories about the cause of acquired apraxia of speech. Because of the inconsistency in speech sound misarticulations, and the tendency for these misarticulations to occur on words containing multiple syllables, the disorder is assumed to be related to difficulty sequencing the speech articulators (e.g., lips, tongue, jaw). The prevailing theory is that acquired apraxia is a **phonetic-motoric disorder**. The manner in which speech sounds/words are organized in the brain prior to saying them is intact. The disorder occurs because of the actual execution of speech. The motor system governing our speech articulators is thought to have its own "cognitive architecture" that is activated and monitored in part by the language system (Allison et al., 2020). In the case of apraxia of speech, this cognitive architecture is faulty.

> FYI
>
> The condition of apraxia is not confined to the production of speech. The inability to perform skilled motor movements can also be found for the arms and legs, referred to as limb apraxia, or for the face, mouth, or tongue, referred to as orofacial apraxia. An example of orofacial apraxia would be demonstrating difficulty how to blow a kiss on command

ASSESSMENT OF MOTOR SPEECH DISORDERS

Dysarthria

Evaluation of the patient's speech sound articulation is a major component in the assessment of dysarthria. The examination includes evaluation of **speech intelligibility** at a variety of levels, including (a) individual speech sounds, (b) single-word production, (c) reading aloud, and (d) conversational speech. Because of the obvious physical and motoric impairments associated with this condition, a number of neuromuscular features that may influence speech sound production are examined. These include assessments of oral-motor strength, speed of articulator movement, and accuracy and steadiness of voice pitch. If possible, speech-language pathologists may use various forms of equipment to assist in the assessment of dysarthria. For example, aerodynamic testing can be performed to examine the patient's respiratory abilities, in particular breath support for producing speech. Measurement of muscle activity through the use of **electromyographic** recording also can inform the speech-language pathologist as to the role of various muscles in the production of speech. One of the most popular commercially available tests of dysarthria is the *Frenchay Dysarthria Assessment* (Enderby & Palmer, 2008), which is designed for individuals ranging from 12 years to adulthood.

Apraxia

There is no single factor that can be used to diagnose apraxia of speech. In addition, speech-language pathologists do not fully agree about which specific symptoms must exist to confirm the diagnosis of an apraxia condition. The speech-language pathologist looks for the presence of a group of symptoms, including those described earlier. Ruling out other contributing factors, such as muscle weakness or language-comprehension problems, also can help with the diagnosis. To diagnose acquired apraxia, the speech-language pathologist may ask the person to perform speech tasks such as repeating a particular word several times or repeating a list of words of increasing syllable length (e.g., wreck, reckless, recklessly). In the event of a motor sequencing problem (apraxia), it is likely that breakdowns in speech articulation would occur in the words of longer length. The patient also may be asked to engage in conversation, during which time the speech-language pathologist would note any inconsistent speech misarticulations. Aspects of nonspeech oral apraxia are also tested by having the patient perform volitional movements of the speech structures, such as whistling, coughing, or blowing. If available, the use of instruments to directly image the brain is especially helpful in distinguishing acquired apraxia of speech from other communication disorders in people who have experienced brain damage. A research-based assessment instrument known as the *Apraxia of Speech Rating Scale* (Duffy et al., 2023) has shown promise as a possible clinical tool for speech-language pathologists. A condensed version of the scale is shown in Table 10–4.

FYI

Childhood-onset stuttering (see Chapter 5) can be considered a motor speech disorder because moments of disfluency are characterized by intermittent/involuntary repetitions, prolongations, or blocks of speech sounds, syllables, and words. However, this form of stuttering is not indicative of motor weakness (dysarthria) or variable speech sound articulation (apraxia) and is typically viewed as distinct from these conditions.

TREATMENT OF MOTOR SPEECH DISORDERS

Dysarthria

The treatment of dysarthria focuses on improvement of speech clarity and speech naturalness. Specific goals for therapy are targeted toward altering speaking rate and increasing breath support, as well as strengthening muscles through exercises designed to increase mouth, tongue, and lip movement. The speech-language pathologist can help the person's caregivers or family learn to adapt to the environment so they can understand the person better. The use of **vocal function exercises** can be particularly useful in the treatment of dysarthria to strengthen and coordinate the three subsystems of voice: respiratory, laryngeal, and supralaryngeal (Stemple et al., 2020). The exercises consist of a sequence of four steps: (a) warm-up, (b) stretch, (c) contract, and (d) power exercise. The warm-up exercise involves prolonging the vowel /i/ for several seconds, followed by "gliding" the vowel /o/ from low to high pitch. Contraction entails gliding the vowel /o/ in the opposite direction—from the highest pitch to the lowest pitch. The power exercise involves sustaining voice at a range of musical notes (C-D-E-F-G) for as long as possible.

Among individuals with mild to moderate dysarthria, particularly those with Parkinson disease, a popular treatment approach known as the **Lee Silverman Voice Treatment** (LSVT LOUD) is in widespread use. The Lee Silverman Voice Treatment technique emphasizes high-effort loud phonation to improve respiratory, laryngeal, and articulatory functions during speech (Ramig & Fox, 2019; see also Chapter 8). Clients are provided instruction to produce a loud voice and (at the same time) monitor the loudness of their voices while speaking. The importance of self-monitoring of one's voice is stressed. The use of maximal effort in producing a loud voice has been shown to improve speech articulation affected by dysarthria. An illustration of the therapy technique is provided in Figure 10–4.

Motor learning is a concept related to the process by which performance of movement is improved (or acquired) based on practice. An individual repeatedly performs specific movements to the point where *practice makes perfect*. Recent neuroplasticity research has shown that synapses are constantly being re-created or removed according to how they are used. A range of principles have been developed that have proven to facilitate motor learning, whether it is for learning a golf swing, balancing on a tightrope, or improving

Table 10–4. Apraxia of Speech Rating Scale

1	**Apraxia of speech primary distinguishing features (no overlap with dysarthria or aphasia). One or more must be present for diagnosis of apraxia of speech.**	**Score (0–4)**
1.1	Distorted sound substitutions	
1.2	Distorted sound additions (not including intrusive "schwa")	
1.3	Increased sound distortions or distorted sound substitutions with increased utterance length or increased syllable/word articulatory complexity	
1.4	Increased sound distortions or distorted sound substitutions with increased speech rate	
1.5	Inaccurate (off-target in place or manner) speech alternating motion rates, as in rapid repetition of "puh-puh-puh")	
1.6	Reduced words per breath group relative to maximum vowel duration	
2	**Distinguishing features unless dysarthria present**	**Score (0–4)**
2.1	Syllable segmentation within words more than one syllable	
2.2	Syllable segmentation across words in phrases/sentences	
2.3	Sound distortions	
2.4	Slow overall speech rate	
2.5	Lengthened vowel and/or consonant segments	
2.6	Lengthened intersegment durations (between sounds, syllables, words, or phrases; possibly filled, including intrusive "schwa")	
3	**Distinguishing features unless aphasia present**	**Score (0–4)**
3.1	Deliberate, slowly sequenced, segmented, and/or distorted (including distorted substitutions) speech sequential motion rates in comparison to speech alternating motion rates	
3.2	Audible or visible articulatory groping; speech initiation difficulty; false starts/restarts	
4	**Distinguishing features unless dysarthria and/or aphasia present**	**Score (0–4)**
4.1	Sound or syllable repetitions	
4.2	Sound prolongations (beyond lengthened segments)	

Note. Scoring of each item is on a scale from 0 to 4, where 0 = not present, 1 = detectable but infrequent, 2 = frequent but not pervasive, 3 = nearly always evident but not marked in severity, 4 = nearly always evident and marked in severity.

Source: From Strand, Duffy, Clark, and Josephs (2014).

speech. These principles of motor learning can be broadly classified into two types: (a) principles pertaining to the structure of practice and (b) principles pertaining to the type of feedback provided to the individual. Because speech production is a motor skill, applying principles of motor learning for individuals with a motor speech disorder can be beneficial. Kaipa et al. (2016) explored how

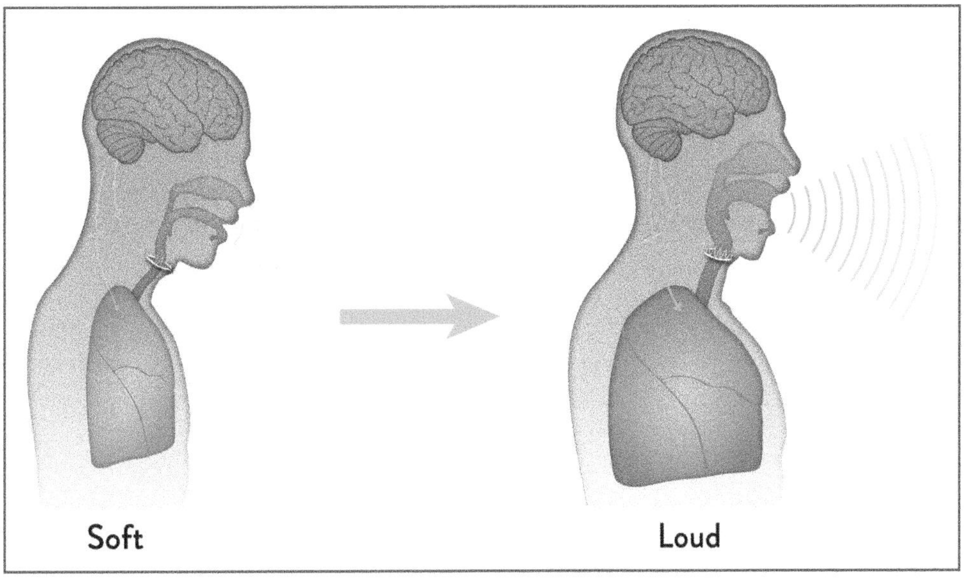

FIGURE 10–4. Modifications in breath support, posture, and voice production using the LSVT LOUD technique. (Reprinted with permission from LSVT Global.)

these principles can help to improve the motor movements required for clear speech among people with Parkinson disease. Their results indicate that repeated practice can be beneficial in assisting these individuals with speech motor learning.

Deep brain stimulation has become an established technique to treat neurologically based movement disorders. Individuals with Parkinson disease are often prescribed medications to help alleviate muscle stiffness and restricted range of movement. These drugs eventually prove to become ineffective as the severity of the disease progresses. As an alternative to drug therapy, deep brain stimulation has been attempted by directly stimulating parts of the brain to help reduce disordered movement patterns. The procedure involves inserting electrodes via a hair-thin wire through the skull into the area of the brain that controls movement (Figure 10–5). The patient is able to control the device with a neurotransmitter that sends electrical impulses down the wire into the brain. The person can turn the deep brain stimulation on when needed and turn it off during sleep (when the motor disturbance is minimal). Over the past decade, there have been technological improvements in the delivery of electrical impulses to the brain that have resulted in improved motor function, including speech production (Krauss et al., 2021).

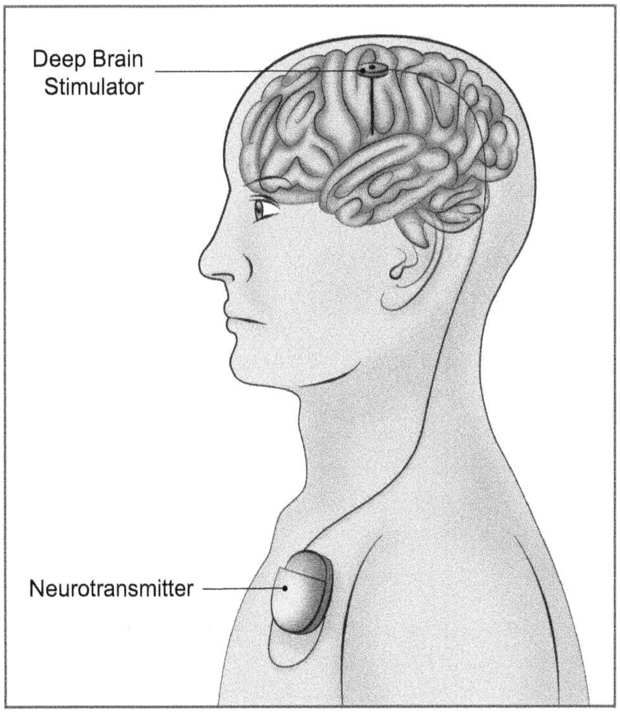

FIGURE 10–5. Deep brain stimulation.

Apraxia

A common approach used in physiotherapy for limb-based apraxia is to break down the movement task (such as reaching or walking) into isolated movements in order to stimulate pathways in the brain. These movements are rehearsed repeatedly and eventually coordinated. Treatment approaches for apraxia of speech have adopted a similar approach, dependent on the severity of the impairment. In some cases, people with acquired apraxia of speech recover some or all their speech abilities on their own. In the most severe cases of apraxia, the ability to produce clearly articulated speech may not be an option. In these cases, an alternative or augmentative form of communication should be pursued (see Chapter 12). Individuals with mild apraxia might be taught strategies to help them correctly articulate multisyllabic words that tend to give them trouble. People with moderate to severe apraxia usually need frequent and intensive therapy sessions with a speech-language pathologist. One approach to therapy is to work on **sound-sequencing** skills. In this approach, a word to be spoken is dissected into individual consonants and vowels. The patient is asked to say the individual sounds in a controlled, deliberate fashion, while also thinking about how the lips and tongue should be positioned for speaking. A gradual increase in the length of a word to be spoken is introduced by varying the number of sounds and syllables. Sometimes tapping or clapping out the rhythm of speech helps patients to speak more clearly. An alternative approach to having the patient produce individual speech sounds is to work on more complex forms of articulation first, such as two- and three-element consonant clusters (e.g., stop, street). The logic behind this approach is to help the patient gain control over more challenging forms of speech sound sequencing first, which will have a trickledown effect of naturally stabilizing the articulation of less complex (individual) speech sounds (Munasinghe et al., 2023).

CULTURAL CONSIDERATIONS AND MOTOR SPEECH DISORDERS

The occurrence of various nervous system diseases, such as multiple sclerosis, differs according to **geographic region**. People living beyond the 40° latitude mark north or south of the equator are far more likely to develop multiple sclerosis than those living in warmer climates near the equator. This is especially true for people in North America, Europe, and New Zealand, whereas Asia continues to have a low incidence of multiple sclerosis. White people are far more likely to develop multiple sclerosis than Black people.

A person's **socioeconomic status** is also a consideration in motor speech disorders. Individuals coming from a low socioeconomic status background are less likely to have access to appropriate health care than individuals of middle and high socioeconomic status. Lack of access to health care places these individuals at greater risk for later appearing conditions (e.g., hypertension, diabetes) that are precursors to some neurological conditions (e.g., stroke). A motor speech disorder is sometimes the primary evidence of some form of neurological disease. Recognizing that a change in a person's speech may be due to a neurological problem can help to diagnose a neurological disease. A late diagnosis significantly reduces the likelihood of a full recovery. Also, the diet of individuals of low socioeconomic status can lead to nutritional deficiencies that affect neurological growth and development as well as the risk of and response to neurological impairment (Qualls & Muñoz, 2005).

Motor speech disorders such as dysarthria and apraxia can cause individuals to lose confidence in their talking ability. Therefore, these individuals may avoid social interactions, leading to isolation. It is important for the speech-language pathologist to promote social interaction to help counter the potentially harmful health effects, such as depression and anxiety, from isolation.

SUMMARY OF CHAPTER

Motor speech disorders are a group of speech problems due to neurological abnormalities. The abnormalities can be present at birth or become evident when a child begins to speak, but in many cases, they emerge later in life in association with acquired neurological injury or disease. Apraxia of speech and dysarthria are two types of motor speech disorders. Apraxia of speech reflects an impaired ability to plan or program movements for speech. In contrast, dysarthria is a broad category of speech difficulties that reflect abnormalities that can include weakness, incoordination, spasticity, involuntary movements, or reduced movements.

There is no single factor that can be used to diagnose apraxia of speech. The speech-language pathologist looks for the presence of a group of symptoms that reflect variability in the production and planning of speech sound production. Evaluation of the patient's speech articulation is a major component in the assessment of dysarthria. Because of the physical and motoric impairments associated with dysarthria, a number of neuromuscular features that may influence speech sound production are examined. These include assessments of oral-motor strength, speed of articulator movement, and accuracy and steadiness of voice pitch. Treatment approaches for apraxia of speech depend on the severity of the impairment. In some cases, people recover some or all of their speech abilities on their own. People with moderate to severe apraxia usually need frequent and intensive therapy sessions with a speech-language pathologist. The treatment of dysarthria focuses on improvement of speech clarity and speech naturalness. Multicultural factors interact with motor speech disorders. For example, race and ethnicity are predisposing factors for several neurological conditions that can lead to a communication disorder.

MOTOR SPEECH DISORDERS ON THE WORLD WIDE WEB

Following are websites that provide further information on the topic of neurogenic communication disorders. At the time of publication, each website was freely accessible.

Dysarthria Videos

http://www.stroke4carers.org/?p=5409

http://library.med.utah.edu/neurologicexam/

https://neurologicexam.med.utah.edu/adult/html/mentalstatus_resources.html

https://www.youtube-nocookie.com/embed/O9mwW5r7wBQ

Apraxia Videos

https://youtu.be/8RzEeQdtc9g?t=13

https://youtu.be/bZ7pnmd9UHI

STUDY QUESTIONS

1. How is a motor speech disorder different from a neurogenic language disorder?
2. What are the various types of dysarthria?
3. How is apraxia different from dysarthria?

REFERENCES

Allison, K., Cordella, C., Iuzzini-Seigel, J., & Green, J. (2020). Differential diagnosis of apraxia of speech in children and adults: A scoping review. *Journal of Speech, Language, and Hearing Research*, *63*, 2952–2994.

Duffy, J. (2019). *Motor speech disorders: Substrates, differential diagnosis, and management* (4th ed.). Elsevier.

Duffy, J., Martin, P., Clark, H., Utianski, R., Strand. E., Whitwell, J., & Josephs, K. (2023). The apraxia of speech rating scale: Reliability, validity, and utility. *American Journal of Speech-Language Pathology*, *32*, 469–491.

Enderby, P., & Palmer, R. (2008). *Frenchay Dysarthria Assessment* (2nd ed.). Pro-Ed.

Guenther, F. H. (2016). *Neural control of speech*. MIT Press.

Kaipa, R., Jones, R., & Robb, M. (2016). Are individuals with Parkinson's disease capable of speech-motor learning? A preliminary evaluation. *Parkinsonism and Related Disorders*, *28*, 141–145.

Krauss, J. K., Lipsman, N., Aziz, T., Boutet, A., Brown, P., Chang, J. W., . . . Lozano, A. M. (2021). Technology of deep brain stimulation: Current status and future directions. *Nature Reviews Neurology*, *17*(2), 75–87.

Munasinghe, T. U., Ariyasena, A. D. K., & Siriwardhana, D. D. (2023). Speech therapy interventions for acquired apraxia of speech: An updated systematic review. *American Journal of Speech-Language Pathology*, *32*(3), 1336–1359.

Qualls, C. D., & Muñoz, M. L. (2005). Race ethnicity, socioeconomic status, and cognitive-communicative functioning in individuals with neurogenic communication disorders: Clinical implications and research directions. *ECHO: E-Journal for Black and Other Ethnic Group Research and Practices in Communication Sciences and Disorders*, *1*(1), 30–39.

Ramig, L., & Fox, C. (2019). Use of LSVT LOUD (Lee Silverman Voice Treatment) in the care of a patient with Parkinson disease. In J. Stemple & E. Hapnter (Eds), *Voice therapy: Clinical case studies* (pp.281–291). Plural Publishing.

Stemple, J., Roby, N., & Klaben, B. (2020). *Clinical voice pathology: Theory and management* (6th ed.). Plural Publishing.

Strand, E., Duffy, J., Clark, H., & Josephs, K. (2014). The Apraxia of Speech Rating Scale: A tool for diagnosis and description of apraxia of speech. *Journal of Communication Disorders, 51*, 43-50.

11

DYSPHAGIA

OBJECTIVES

After reading this chapter, the student should be able to:

- Describe anatomical and neuromuscular systems involved in swallowing.
- Demonstrate understanding of bedside methods of dysphagia assessment.
- Demonstrate understanding of instrumentation for the assessment and treatment of swallowing functions.
- Demonstrate knowledge of swallowing disorders including their etiologies.
- Describe current surgical techniques related to communicative and swallowing functions, and prosthetics.
- Describe various nonsurgical techniques related to the management of dysphagia.
- Describe multicultural considerations in the assessment and management of dysphagia.

KEY TERMS

Dysphagia	Oropharyngeal Dysphagia	Cervical Auscultation
Deglutition	Esophageal Dysphagia	Videofluoroscopic Swallowing Study
Maintenance	Functional Dysphagia	Videofluoroscopy
Ingestion	Globus	Barium
Per Oral	Cerebrovascular Accident	Fiberoptic Endoscopic Evaluation of Swallowing
Mastication	Swallowing Center	Ultrasound
Bolus	Esophagitis	Electromyography
Peristalsis	Gastroesophageal Reflux Disease	Effortful Swallow
Aspiration	Human Papillomavirus	Masako Maneuver
Reflux	Odynophagia	Feeding Tube
Aspiration Pneumonia	Pediatric Dysphagia	Enteral Tube
Oral Stage	Pediatric Feeding Disorder	Nasogastric Tube
Pharyngeal Stage	Clinical Assessment	Parenteral Tube
Esophageal Stage		Gastronomy Tube
George L. Larsen		
Jeri A. Logemann		
Andre Jean		

INTRODUCTION

We tend to think of swallowing as the activity related to drinking and eating food; however, we swallow throughout the day. In fact, people swallow a thousand times or more each day. Swallowing begins at the lips and ends at the stomach. Swallowing is an activity that we take for granted and perform easily. Yet the process of normal swallowing is actually a highly complex activity. Approximately 30 to 40 pairs of muscles, and at least six pairs of nerves, are involved in moving food from the lips to the stomach. To add to this complexity, these structures must perform in sequence with our breathing patterns to ensure the material being swallowed is directed toward the stomach rather than to the lungs.

Among some disabled children and adults, there is a breakdown in coordination of swallowing. This breakdown may be due to the person's (a) wakefulness or awareness, (b) brain functioning, and/or (c) muscular strength. The medical term for swallowing difficulty is called **dysphagia** ("dis fay ja" or "dis fah ja"). Dysphagia is a rather unique area of specialty in the speech-language pathologist profession because the condition is not a communication disorder. Speech-language pathologists are called upon tens of thousands of times every day to evaluate swallowing in the estimated 15 million adults suffering from dysphagia in the United States and many millions more internationally. Dysphagia can severely affect an individual's quality of life and can also require a person to be dependent on others to be fed. Aside from these social issues, disordered swallowing may be life threatening. A person can run the risk of choking or having the airway blocked. Malnutrition, weight loss, and increased chances of dehydration are possible outcomes of prolonged periods of swallowing difficulties. Dysphagia also could pose a threat for respiratory infections resulting from food entering the lungs rather than the stomach. What is generally considered an automatic and even pleasurable experience can be one of discomfort and worry.

FYI

Most people believe they chew their food thoroughly before swallowing, but this may not be the case. It is recommended that, on average, we should chew food between 20 and 30 times before swallowing. The more we chew, the more saliva we generate that helps break down food and facilitate the digestion process.

FYI

We swallow during our sleep, however much less compared to when we are awake. On average, we swallow approximately once per hour when sleeping.

TERMINOLOGY AND DEFINITIONS

There are a variety of terms associated with normal and disordered swallowing. The formal term used to describe the act of normal swallowing is **deglutition**. We swallow for two reasons. The first reason is maintenance. This type of swallowing is used to remove the natural buildup of saliva in the oral cavity. Maintenance swallowing tends to occur subconsciously and happens even when we sleep. **Maintenance** swallowing has also been observed in infants prior to birth. Although in most cases this type of swallowing occurs automatically, we also can swallow deliberately whenever we feel like clearing our throats. The second reason we swallow is for **ingestion**. This type of swallowing is for the consumption of liquids and foods. Ingestive swallowing of **per oral** (p.o.) nutrition (i.e., food taken by mouth) requires that we are awake and cognizant of the presence of food or fluid in the mouth. Typically, the process of swallowing food involves chewing. The technical term for chewing is **mastication**. When we chew, the food inside the mouth is turned into a soft mass referred to as a **bolus**. During deglutition, the bolus moves through the tubes of the digestive system in waves of alternating contraction and relaxation (i.e., snakelike movement) known as **peristalsis**.

The term *dysphagia* is a combination of the prefix *dys* ("disordered") and the Greek word *phagein* ("eat"). Dysphagia can occur at locations anywhere from the lips to the stomach and is found in approximately 7% of the general population. Among people aged 50 years or older, the occurrence of dysphagia ranges anywhere from 15% to 30% and may be as high as 60% in acute hospital wards and nursing homes. Between 50% and 75% of individuals who experience a stroke will develop a swallowing problem. The frequency of occurrence of dysphagia does not differ between females and males. A primary indicator of dysphagia is coughing moments after swallowing. This can lead to **aspiration**, which refers to the situation where food or liquid inadvertently enters the breathing airway (trachea) before, during, or after the swallow (Figure 11–1). Among individuals who experience a stroke, it is not uncommon for them to be susceptible to aspiration during the earliest days of recovery. A condition known as **reflux** is also indicative of dysphagia. Each year, around 60,000 Americans die from complications associated with swallowing dysfunctions because of **aspiration pneumonia**. Reflux is a backward flow of food or liquid. Esophageal reflux is a condition in which the stomach contents flow backward into the esophagus.

Because of the obvious anatomical and physiological processes underpinning swallowing behavior, it is important to be familiar with some of the primary physical structures involved in swallowing. Most of the key structures were covered in Chapter 2. A summary of these structures and their function regarding swallowing is provided in Table 11–1. A corresponding illustration of the major structures used for swallowing and their anatomical location is provided in Figure 11–2.

From start to finish, normal swallowing is an almost instantaneous activity, taking around 2 minutes to accomplish. Although the action of swallowing is relatively quick and automatic, the process of moving liquid or food toward the stomach is extremely complicated. To conceptualize swallowing, it is useful to think of the process as occurring in a series of three sequential stages: (a) oral, (b) pharyngeal, and (c) esophageal. Each

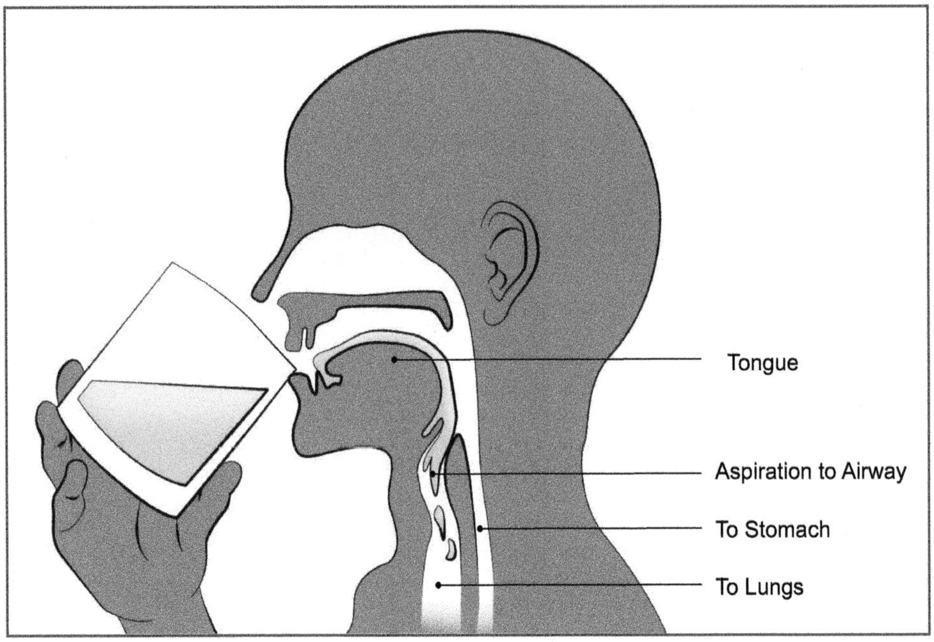

FIGURE 11–1. Aspiration.

Table 11–1. Primary Anatomical Structures Involved in Swallowing

Oral Cavity	
Lips	Responsible for sealing the oral cavity for preparation of swallow.
Tongue	Responsible for pushing food toward the hard palate and back toward the pharynx.
Teeth	Required for mastication (chewing).
Saliva	A special digestive enzyme for softening and moistening food. Glands are located in cheeks, underside of tongue, and underside of mandible.
Nasal Cavity	
Velum	The soft palate muscles that raise during swallowing to close off the nasal cavity from the oral cavity.
Pharynx	
Muscles	A series of overlapping muscles in the throat cavity. The cavity extends from the back of the nasal cavity to the top of the larynx.
Epiglottis	A leaf-shaped cartilage that protects the vocal folds from collecting foreign matter and diverts the bolus around the airway.
Valleculae	The space between the base of the tongue and the epiglottis. The collection of residue in this space indicates a problem with tongue movement during swallowing.
Upper esophageal sphincter	A specialized muscle that separates the pharyngeal and esophageal cavities.
Trachea	
Cartilage	A series of cartilaginous rings that form the windpipe. The trachea branches off from the base of the pharynx and leads to a series of smaller tubes comprising the lungs.
Esophagus	
Muscle	A long muscular tube that branches off from the pharynx and sits behind the trachea. This is the "food tube" that serves as the conduit to the stomach. The esophagus normally is collapsed and only opens during swallowing.

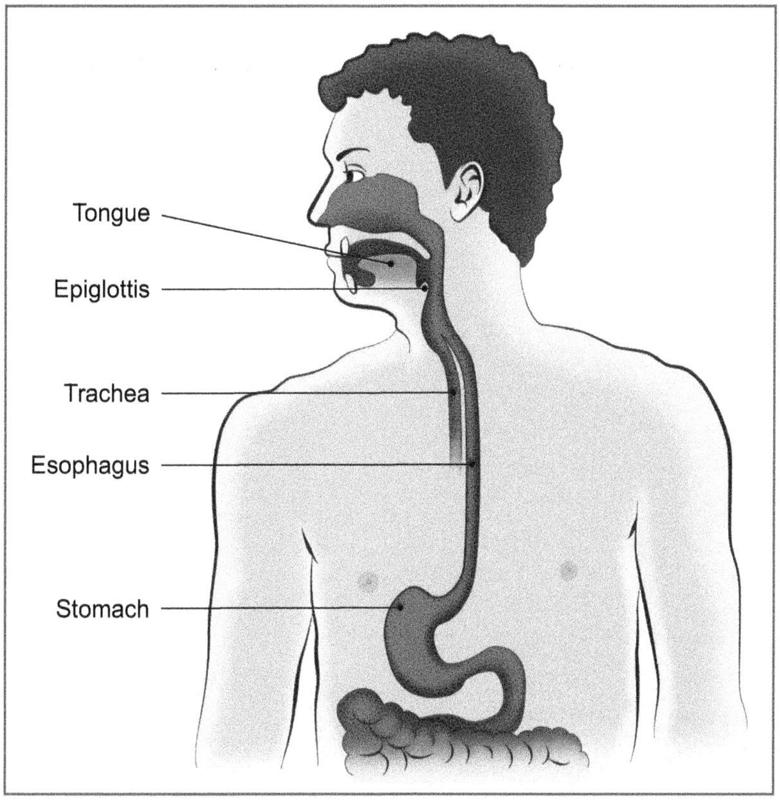

FIGURE 11–2. Anatomy of swallowing.

stage represents specific physiological activity in the progression of moving material from the mouth to the stomach. These three stages are illustrated in Figure 11–3.

Stage 1 of Swallowing: The Oral (Transfer) Stage

The **oral stage** begins when we first take food or drink into our mouths. Once material is placed in the mouth, the lips are sealed. The tongue then moves the material around the mouth for mastication. Saliva helps to soften and moisten food to create a bolus that is easy to swallow. This stage is one of preparation for swallowing by transferring the food or drink to the back of the mouth. We maintain normal nasal breathing during this stage.

Stage 2 of Swallowing: The Pharyngeal (Transport) Stage

The **pharyngeal stage** begins once the tongue transfers the food or liquid bolus to the back of

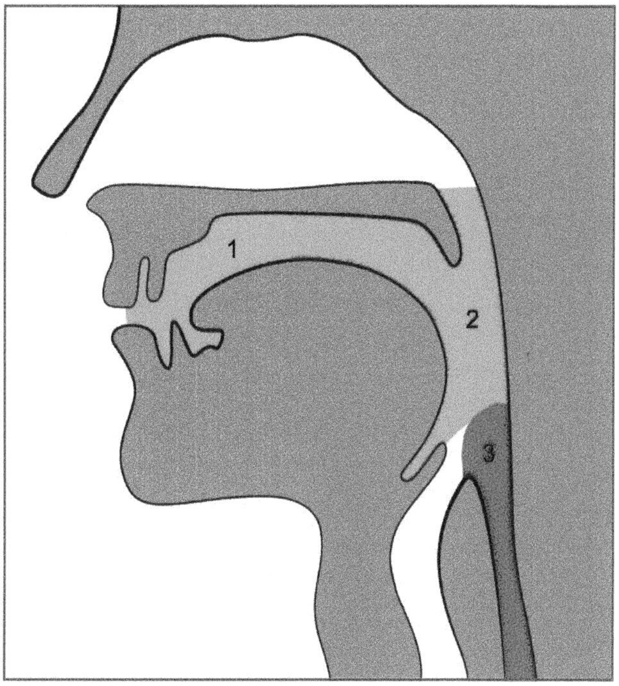

FIGURE 11–3. The three stages of swallowing: oral (transfer), pharyngeal (transport), and esophageal (entrance).

the mouth. Once the bolus reaches the back of the throat, a reflex automatically occurs that transports the bolus downward through the pharynx. During this stage of the swallow, the nasal cavity is closed off from the oral cavity to prevent food from going through the nose. Muscles of the throat serve to shorten the pharynx and push the food toward the esophagus. The vocal folds close tightly, and breathing stops to prevent food or liquid from entering the trachea.

Stage 3 of Swallowing: The Esophageal (Entrance) Stage

The **esophageal stage** begins when the bolus is directed away from the trachea and enters the esophagus (or gullet), which is the canal that carries food and liquid to the stomach. The esophagus is separated from the pharynx by a sphincter muscle that relaxes and is pulled open by muscles of the throat. After the bolus exits the pharynx, the normally collapsed esophagus is pushed open by the propelling bolus. During this process of swallowing, peristalsis occurs to move the bolus through the esophagus into the stomach. Once the bolus is fully in the esophagus and the sphincter is again closed, the airway is reopened, and normal breathing resumes.

FYI

Source: Evolution and evolvability, CC BY-SA 4.0 <https://creativecommons.org/licenses/by-sa/4.0>, via Wikimedia Commons

Grant Fairbanks (1910–1964), one of the pioneers of speech-language pathology, died by asphyxiation from choking on a piece of food that had lodged in his throat. Fairbanks died tragically while onboard an airplane in 1964 traveling from San Francisco to Chicago (see also Chapter 4).

HISTORIC ASPECTS OF DYSPHAGIA

To an outsider, a speech-language pathologist may not seem to be the most qualified individual to deal with swallowing difficulties. By the nature of their professional title, a speech-language pathologist is presumed to work exclusively with speech and language problems. Yet some speech-language pathologists have been indirectly treating aspects of dysphagia since the early 1930s. This early work was focused primarily on young children with oral-motor disorders such as cerebral palsy, as well as head and neck surgery patients. One of the core features in the educational curriculum of a speech-language pathologist student has always been knowledge of the anatomy and physiology of the head, neck, and respiratory system. This coursework, along with extensive clinical education with clients who have disordered function of the oral, pharyngeal, and laryngeal systems, made speech-language pathologists the prime candidates for assessing and treating dysphagia. Prior to the involvement by the speech-language pathologist profession, no other health professions specifically included dysphagia as part of their scope of practice.

Two individuals from the United States are often given credit for advancing the profession regarding helping people with swallowing problems. The first is **George L. Larsen**, who in the early 1960s developed the speech-language pathologist clinical services program at the Seattle Veterans Administration Hospital. Because of Larsen's employment in a hospital setting, he was aware of many people who experienced difficulties with both speech and swallowing. To his dismay, he found that most speech-language pathologists tended to address only speech difficulties, leaving the swallowing difficulties to either go unaddressed or be dealt with by some other health profession (e.g., neurologist, otolaryngologist, nurse, physiotherapist, occupational therapist). Larsen believed that when a patient showed both speech and swallowing problems, the cause was a nervous system disturbance. Therefore, by working on swallowing, it would be expected that improvements in speech production would follow. Although this was not found to be the case, Larsen is credited with establishing a range of therapeutic techniques to help individuals regain the ability to swallow. His approach to the evaluation, management, and treatment of swallowing difficulties was considered artistic and intuitive (Miller & Groher, 1993).

The next major advancement in dysphagia was made by **Jeri A. Logemann** (1942–2014; Figure 11–4) who completed a doctorate from the Department of Communication Disorders at Northwestern University, Illinois, in the early 1970s with particular emphasis in dysphagia. Logemann applied a more rigorous scientific methodology to assessing and treating dysphagia compared with Larsen by undertaking controlled examinations of swallowing physiology and treatment efficacy. Logemann also made major contributions about outlining the essential educational and clinical training required of speech-language pathologists dealing with dysphagia. She published the textbook *Evaluation and Treatment of Swallowing Disorders* in 1983, in which she described the role of the speech-language pathologist in the diagnosis and management of the condition. Education in dysphagia is now an essential component among all speech-language pathology university programs worldwide.

It is important for speech-language pathologists to recognize that due to the complex medical issues involved in management of the patient with dysphagia, this area of clinical practice is by necessity and design an interdisciplinary clinical field. Appropriate management includes input from a variety of health professionals, including but not limited to neurology, otolaryngology, radiology, and dietetics. Indeed, substantial research that guides our understanding of swallowing comes from outside of speech-language pathology. One such example involves the research of the French physiologist **Andre Jean** (Figure 11–5). Over the past 25 years, Jean has been instrumental in defining the role of the brainstem in normal and disordered swallowing.

There has been dramatic growth in the involvement by speech-language pathologists in the field of dysphagia regarding both service delivery and research. More than one third of speech-language

FIGURE 11–4. Jerilyn A. Logemann has made important clinical contributions to the field of dysphagia. (Permission granted by J. Logemann.)

FIGURE 11–5. Andre Jean has examined the role of the brainstem in normal and disordered swallowing. (Permission granted by A. Jean.)

pathologists deal with dysphagia as part of their annual caseload. For speech setting, dysphagia can often exceed 80% of the total caseload. In 1986, a research journal titled *Dysphagia* was created. This is a multidisciplinary journal dedicated exclusively to normal and disordered swallowing.

TYPES OF DYSPHAGIA

There are three generally agreed-on types of dysphagia: (a) oropharyngeal dysphagia, (b) esophageal dysphagia, and (c) functional dysphagia. The first two types are related to known anatomical or physiological difficulties with swallowing. The third type is a form of dysphagia with no known causal factors.

Oropharyngeal Dysphagia

Oropharyngeal dysphagia is the most common type of dysphagia. The anatomical description of this form of dysphagia indicates that the condition affects the transfer of liquid or food from the mouth and pharynx into the esophagus. This type of dysphagia results from abnormalities of muscles, nerves, or structures of the oral cavity and pharynx. Attempts to swallow food may be misdirected upward toward the nasal cavity. Many patients choke or cough when swallowing and may have food or fluids enter the trachea instead of the esophagus. This can allow harmful bacteria to grow in the lungs or bronchial tubes, resulting in an infectious condition known as aspiration pneumonia (Figure 11–6). Patients often complain of difficulty chewing and swallowing both liquids and foods. They appear to have a hoarse or wet-sounding voice that may be accompanied by bad breath.

Esophageal Dysphagia

Esophageal dysphagia is less common than oropharyngeal dysphagia and arises during the latter stages of the swallowing sequence. Patients with esophageal dysphagia have difficulty passing a

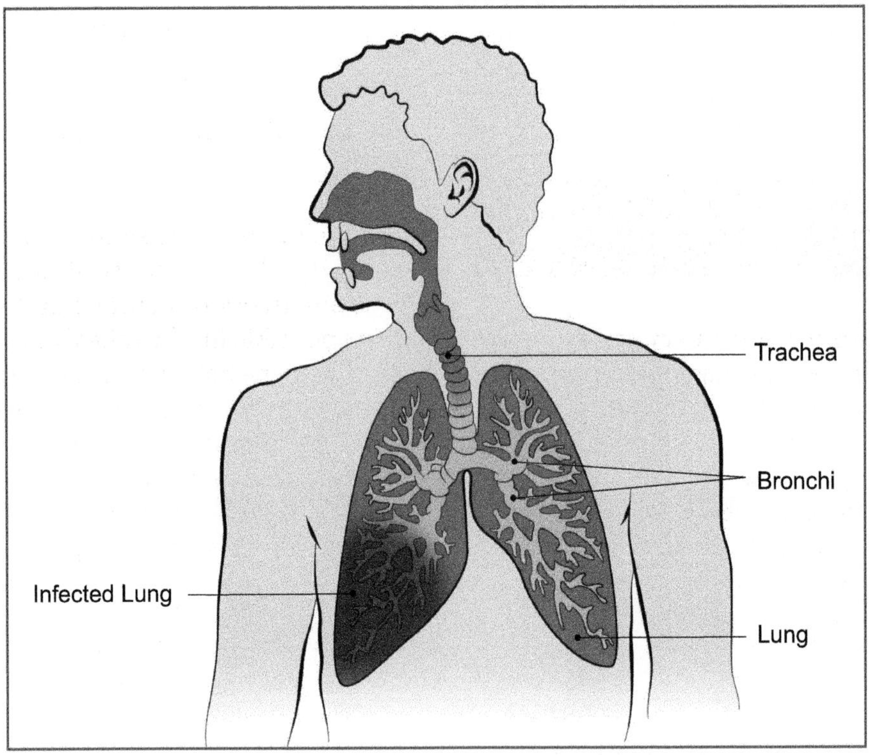

FIGURE 11–6. Lung infection that can result from aspiration.

bolus of food from the esophagus to the stomach. Patients usually complain of swallowing only solid foods, as opposed to both solid foods and liquids. Their swallowing difficulty is due to either an obstruction or stricture (i.e., narrowing) of the esophagus or problems with peristalsis (i.e., a motility problem). Patients report that it feels like food is stuck in the base of their throat or in the chest. Patients generally point to their neck as the primary region of the problem, indicating that the site is at or below this region.

Functional Dysphagia

The least frequently occurring type of dysphagia is known as **functional dysphagia**. This form of dysphagia is poorly understood, primarily because there is no identifiable anatomical cause. Examples of functional dysphagia include difficulty in swallowing pills and a condition known as **globus**, which is the sensation of having a lump in one's throat. The International Foundation for Gastrointestinal Disorders defined functional dysphagia as the sensation of solid and/or liquid foods sticking, lodging, or passing abnormally through the esophagus. Functional dysphagia is diagnosed based on symptoms present for at least 3 months and not associated with anatomical abnormalities such as reflux (Triggs & Pandolfino, 2019).

Table 11–2. Some Likely Causes of Various Types of Dysphagia

Type	*Cause*
Oropharyngeal dysphagia	Stroke
	Parkinson disease
	Muscular dystrophy
	Multiple sclerosis
	Cleft palate
	Tumors of mouth or pharynx
	Drug/radiation-induced dry mouth (xerostomia)
Esophageal dysphagia	Esophageal spasms
	Tumors of the esophagus
	Age-related changes of motor function of the esophagus
	Lack of involuntary esophageal peristalsis (achalasia)
	Pill-induced inflammation of the esophagus
	Esophagitis due to gastroesophageal reflux disease (GERD)
	Narrowing of the lower esophageal ring (Schatzki's ring)
Functional dysphagia	Stress

CAUSES OF DYSPHAGIA

Although there are three primary types of dysphagia, the causes of dysphagia are numerous. Swallowing requires healthy functioning of many different oral structures, muscles, and nerves, so a wide range of medical and even dental conditions can contribute to the cause. Dysphagia is a symptom of an underlying condition. A list of likely causes associated with the three types of dysphagia is provided in Table 11–2. A common cause of oropharyngeal dysphagia is a **cerebrovascular accident** (i.e., stroke). Dysphagia can result from strokes that affect the area of the brain that controls motor actions, particularly the frontal lobes of the cerebrum. Strokes that affect the area of the brain that houses the **swallowing center** also can lead to dysphagia. The swallowing center is made up of a network of neurons in the brainstem that are responsible for the reflexive act of swallowing. More than one half of all stroke victims experience some degree of dysphagia during the earliest days following the stroke. In most cases, normal or near-normal swallowing function returns within 1 week poststroke, although dysphagia and aspiration will persist in some patients. Additionally, people with disorders of the nervous system, such as cerebral palsy or Parkinson disease, could experience oropharyngeal dysphagia. Traumatic brain injury and progressive neurological diseases like multiple sclerosis and amyotrophic lateral sclerosis (motor neuron disease) may cause oropharyngeal dysphagia. Any number of cancers affecting the head and neck also can lead to oropharyngeal dysphagia. These various conditions may affect the coordination of the swallowing muscles or limit sensation in the mouth and throat. To compound matters, sometimes the preferred treatment for various types of cancers (e.g., radiation or drugs) has side effects that can cause dysphagia.

A frequent cause of esophageal dysphagia is a structural problem that creates a blockage within the esophagus. The blockage prevents food and liquid from moving toward the stomach. The most common structural problems are esophageal cancer, strictures, and narrowing of the lower region of the esophagus (called Schatzki rings). An infection or irritation can also cause narrowing of the esophagus, resulting in a condition known as **esophagitis.** One type of irritation is **gastroesophageal reflux disease.** Gastroesophageal reflux disease (or acid reflux) is a condition in which acid, bile, and partially digested food in the stomach back up into the esophagus. Partially digested food contains a strong acid that can inflame and damage the lining of the esophagus. Many people think that heartburn (or acid indigestion) is a separate disease. It actually is one symptom of gastroesophageal reflux disease. Heartburn is an unpleasant burning sensation behind the breastbone that usually occurs after a meal.

Cancer of the oropharynx is a form of carcinoma that occurs at the back of the throat and can include the base of the tongue and tonsils (Figure 11–7). Cancer in these regions can lead to swallowing and voice difficulties. Most oropharyngeal cancers result from **human papillomavirus** (HPV), which is the most common sexually transmitted infection in the United States. Roughly 10% of men and 4% of women have oral HPV, and oral HPV infection is more common with older age. The occurrence of HPV has become a serious public health issue that has impacted the work of speech-language pathologists in medical settings.

FYI

The term **odynophagia** refers to the feeling of pain or a burning sensation upon swallowing. Such pain may be a symptom of a serious medical condition.

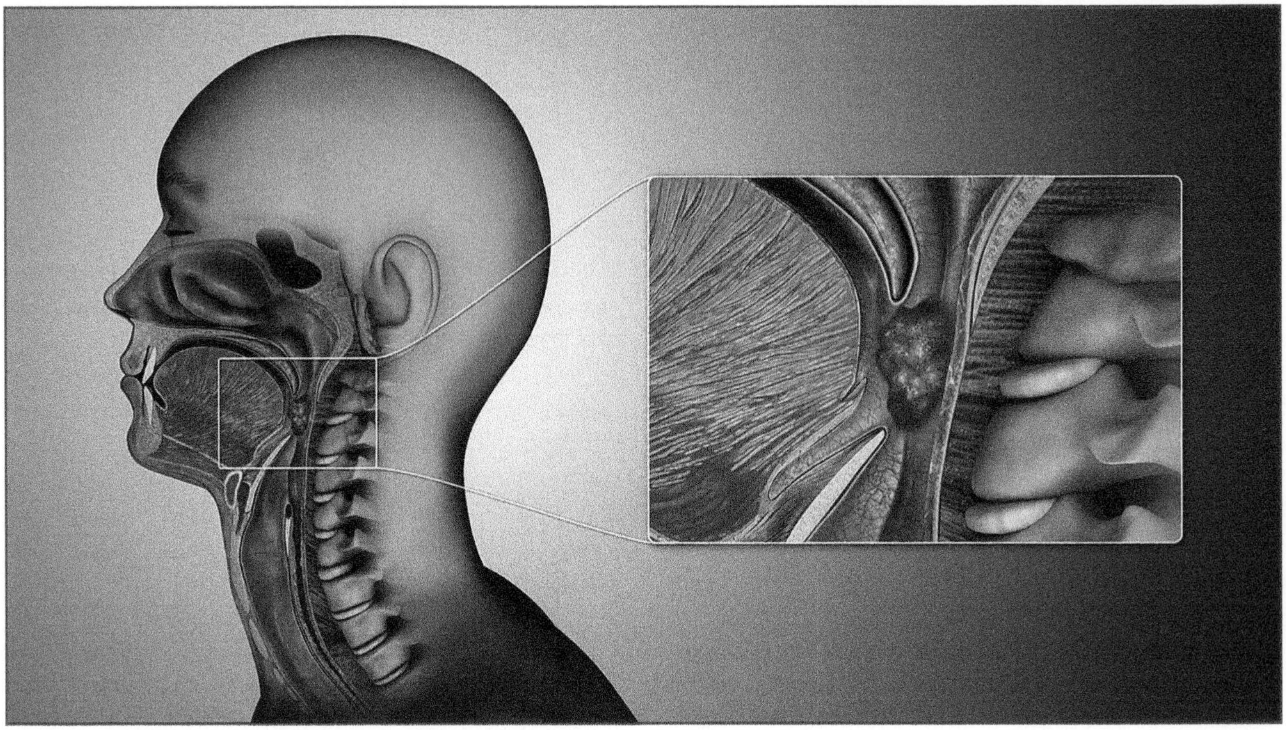

Source: http://www.scientificanimations.com, CC BY-SA 4.0 <https://creativecommons.org/licenses/by-sa/4.0>, via Wikimedia Commons.

FIGURE 11–7. Oropharyngeal cancer.

The absence of a clear anatomical reason for the occurrence of functional dysphagia leads most experts to speculate that the cause of this condition is a combination of physiological and psychosocial problems (Triggs & Pandolfino, 2019). Anecdotal information has been reported that individuals who show functional dysphagia may show significantly higher instances of anxiety and depression compared with those who do not have this form of dysphagia. An associated symptom seems to be fear of swallowing (Bülow, 2019).

Pediatric Feeding Disorder

Dysphagia is not limited to adults. Young children can experience difficulties with swallowing. **Pediatric dysphagia** is not simply an adult problem on a smaller scale. As pointed out in Chapter 2, the anatomical configuration of a young child's vocal tract is quite different from a fully grown adult vocal tract. These developmental differences in pharyngeal and laryngeal anatomy also can influence the manner of swallowing in children compared with adults. Normal adult swallowing is a complicated process, but because the underlying swallowing anatomy is fully mature, the process of swallowing is quite stable. In children, ongoing physical growth and development of motor coordination create a situation whereby swallowing behavior changes "in step" with anatomical changes (Dodrill & Gosa, 2015). **Pediatric feeding disorder** (PFD) refers to impaired oral intake that is not appropriate, lasting at least 2 weeks and associated with dysfunction in one or more of the following domains: medical, nutritional, feeding skill, and psychosocial behavior, given the age of the child (Goday et al., 2019; Table 11–3). Research has suggested that approximately 1% of children in the general population will experience swallowing difficulties. The occurrence is higher in some clinical populations such as in babies who are born prematurely or who have genetic syndromes (e.g., Down syndrome) or maxillofacial deformities. Infants who are born with a cleft lip and palate are unable to suck properly, which complicates nursing and drinking from a regular baby bottle.

FYI

The developing fetus begins to swallow as early as 10 weeks' gestation. During the last trimester, the fetus swallows up to a liter of amniotic fluid per day.

Table 11–3. Criteria for Determination of a Pediatric Feeding Disorder

Criteria	*Description*
Medical	Cardiorespiratory compromise during oral feeding Aspiration or recurrent aspiration pneumonia
Nutritional	Malnutrition Specific nutrient deficiency Significantly restricted intake of one or more nutrients Reliance on enteral feeding or oral supplements
Feeding skill	Use of modified feeding strategies Use of modified feeding positions or equipment Need for texture modification of liquid or food
Psychosocial	Active or passive avoidance behavior by child when being fed Inappropriate caregiver management of child's feeding behavior Disruption of social functioning within a feeding context

ASSESSMENT OF DYSPHAGIA

All of us at times have had trouble swallowing. Perhaps it was that time when you were taking a drink, and someone made you laugh so hard that fluid went through your nose. Or perhaps you once choked on a piece of food. For most of us, these events are fleeting; however, for some individuals, swallowing difficulties occur more often. There are several symptoms that require evaluation for a possible swallowing problem. A list of some of the warning signs for dysphagia is provided in Table 11–4.

The procedures used for assessing the presence of dysphagia fall into two general categories: (a) clinical assessment and (b) instrumental assessment. **Clinical assessment** is an approach commonly used for the initial screening of swallowing dysfunction and, as the term suggests, typically occurs while a patient is in a clinic setting. Sometimes this may involve assessing a patient sitting upright in a hospital bed. The approach is designed to determine a patient's cognitive abilities, language abilities, and readiness to eat or swallow (Immovilli et al., 2021). Clinical assessments have been criticized for being too general and lacking in necessary precision to detect pharyngeal pathophysiology or moments of aspiration. Yet most speech-language pathologists would agree there is a need for a simple bedside assessment that would at least identify patients who are "at risk" for aspiration. Detection of dysphagia at a patient's bedside requires the speech-language pathologist to be highly suspicious of swallowing difficulties and have a clear understanding of the physiological process of swallowing. An important feature of a bedside assessment requires the patient to ingest fluids and foods of different textures when seated in an upright position. While the patient is swallowing, the speech-language pathologist observes whether (a) swallowing occurred in a natural, automatic fashion; (b) there was drooling during the swallow; (c) the patient coughed during swallowing; and (d) the patient's voice sounded hoarse. Based on the bedside swallowing assessment, a patient would be diagnosed by the speech-language pathologist to have *possible* dysphagia if any one of these four observations were present.

Table 11–4. Some Warning Signs of Dysphagia

- Coughing
- Drooling
- Choking
- Food or fluid coming out of the nose
- Gurgly voice quality
- Wet-sounding breathing
- Spillage of food or liquid from the mouth
- Frequent throat clearing
- Low-grade fever
- Progressively slower rate of food intake
- Difficulty initiating a swallow
- Pain upon swallowing
- Food or liquid left in the mouth after a swallow
- Difficulty manipulating food or liquid in the mouth
- Weight loss

Another rather novel bedside approach to evaluating normal swallowing involves a procedure known as **cervical** (neck) **auscultation**. The process of auscultation is the diagnostic listening to sounds. Physicians perform this diagnostic test frequently by using a stethoscope to listen to heart and lung sounds. In the case of cervical auscultation, a stethoscope is placed in the region of the neck, and the patient is asked to swallow. By listening to the swallow, the speech-language pathologist makes a perceptual judgment of the patient's swallowing function based on the perceived "crispness" of the signal. Some experts believe there is a distinct acoustic pattern of normal swallowing that can be used as a backdrop to evaluate disordered swallowing (Enz et al., 2022); however, application of cervical auscultation as a standard clinical measure has not received widespread support.

Use of instrumentation to determine the existence of dysphagia provides a more in-depth form of assessment compared with the bedside approach. In most cases, the instruments employed by the speech-language pathologist are used to visualize the different stages of swallowing. Although this may seem the logical choice for determining the existence of swallowing difficulties, there are drawbacks associated with the various instrumental techniques. Some of the most common instrumental assessment techniques are (a) videofluoroscopic swallowing study, (b) fiberoptic endoscopic evaluation of swallowing, (c) ultrasound, and (d) electromyography.

Videofluoroscopic Swallowing Study

The **videofluoroscopic swallowing study** approach to determining the existence of dysphagia involves an imaging technique known as **videofluoroscopy**. Fluoroscopy is a procedure that allows for a dynamic x-ray to be taken of a person's bodily organs as they are moving. Because swallowing is a form of bodily movement, fluoroscopy is amenable to the visualization of swallowing. The most common anatomical view is a cross section (side view) of the entire vocal tract to allow for examination of swallowing from start to finish. A typical fluoroscopic image of the vocal tract is shown in Figure 11–8. The videofluoroscopic swallowing study procedure is usually completed under the direction of a speech-language pathologist, while working with a radiologist. The radiologist operates the videofluoroscopy equipment and, along with the speech-language pathologist, provides an interpretation of the radiographic images. So that the swallowing behavior can be visualized, the patient is required to swallow a radiopaque substance known as **barium**, which can easily be detected using an x-ray. As the patient swallows the barium substance, the movements of the swallow are videorecorded for later analysis. This x-ray helps the speech-language pathologist

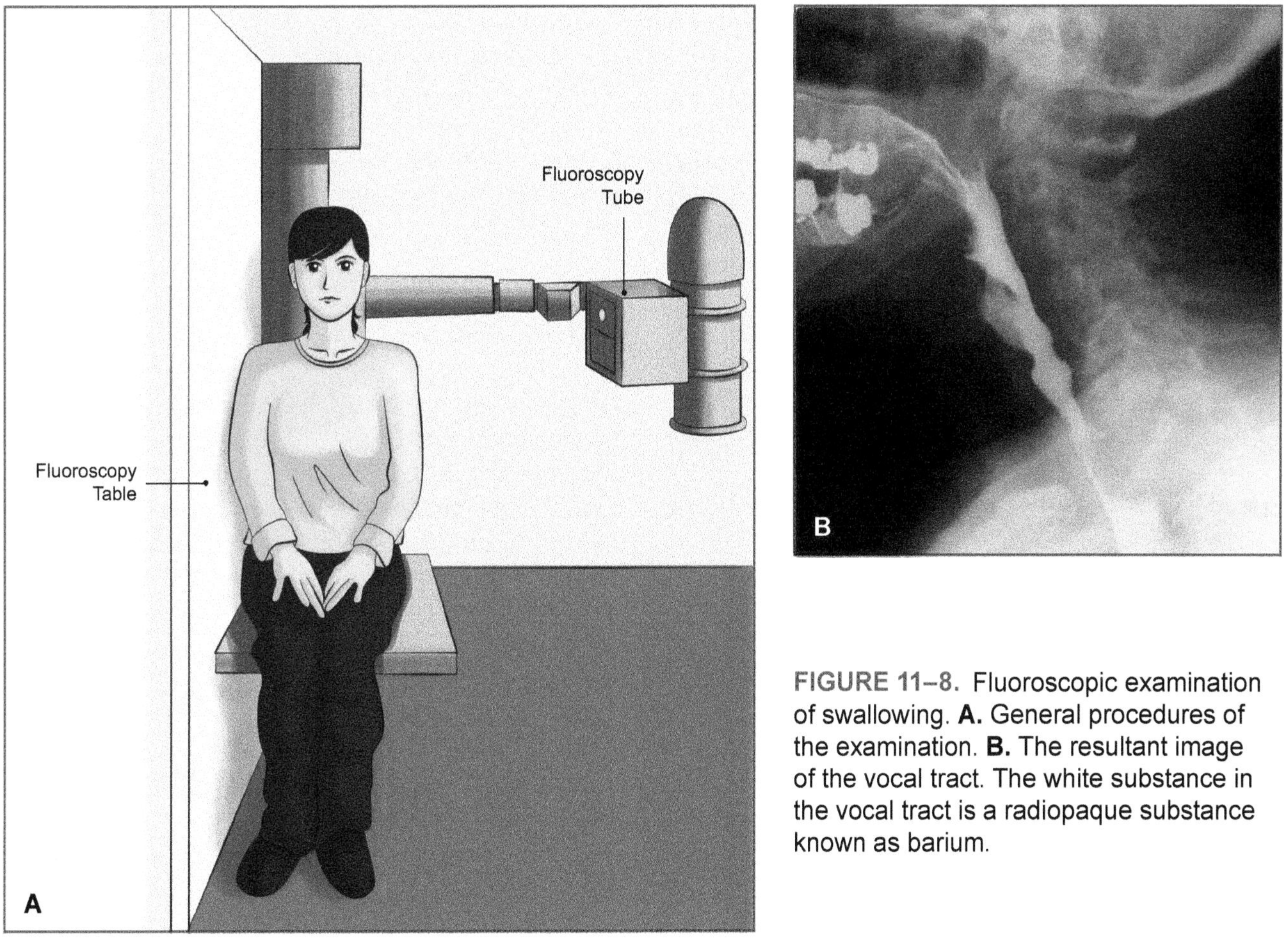

FIGURE 11–8. Fluoroscopic examination of swallowing. **A.** General procedures of the examination. **B.** The resultant image of the vocal tract. The white substance in the vocal tract is a radiopaque substance known as barium.

determine what types of food and drink are safe to swallow and what type of dysphagia therapy might be appropriate. A primary drawback with the videofluoroscopic swallowing study approach is that the x-ray beams directed into the body for visualization expose the patient to mild levels of radiation. Such radiation is cumulative on the body and is not dissipated. Therefore, it is advisable to perform this procedure as infrequently as possible. The use of the videofluoroscopic swallowing study has proven to be an effective instrumental approach to evaluating the swallowing function and will likely continue to be performed regularly for years to come.

Fiberoptic Endoscopic Evaluation of Swallowing

Although use of the videofluoroscopic swallowing study is widely considered the "gold standard" examination for oral and pharyngeal dysphagia, another instrumental approach known as **fiberoptic endoscopic evaluation of swallowing** is gaining widespread appeal. The fiberoptic endoscopic evaluation of swallowing procedure involves use of a flexible endoscope to visualize the pharyngeal and laryngeal structures involved in swallowing. An endoscope is a thin, flexible tube that contains both a light source and a camera lens that provides an image on a computer monitor. This tube can be inserted into bodily orifices that are typically difficult to visually examine (e.g., stomach, larynx, ear canal), thus providing an opportunity to assess both structure and function. Langmore et al. (1988) were the first group of researchers to describe the fiberoptic endoscopic evaluation of swallowing technique for evaluating oropharyngeal dysphagia. Fiberoptic endoscopic evaluation of swallowing originally was conceived to be used as a backup, or secondary procedure, performed only when the videofluoroscopic swallowing study was not available or convenient. For example, use of the videofluoroscopy is not feasible for patients in an intensive care unit or in a nursing home, or for patients who are extremely obese. The fiberoptic endoscopic evaluation of swallowing procedure involves the insertion of a flexible endoscope into the nose to visualize the pharynx and larynx immediately before and after eating foods and drinking liquids of different consistencies (Figure 11–9). Depending on the laws established for various countries (and states), the approach can be done exclusively by the speech-language pathologist or may require additional medical personnel. During the actual swallow, the video image on the computer monitor becomes momentarily obliterated (i.e., a whiteout). The image is restored upon completion of the swallow. A telltale sign of dysphagia is the observation of any residue of fluid that accumulates in the valleculae or piriform sinuses in the pharynx either before or after the swallow. Although the view provided by fiberoptic endoscopic evaluation of swallowing is not as dynamic as videofluoroscopy, the patient does not need to ingest barium but rather food (e.g., milk, pudding) that is dyed either blue or green to enhance the visualization. Fiberoptic endoscopic evaluation of swallowing has the advantage of being free from radiation, so patients undergoing this test can be examined for longer time intervals or at repeated intervals. A disadvantage of the fiberoptic endoscopic evaluation of swallowing is that aspiration may not be noted as reliably as the videofluoroscopic swallowing study because the whiteout phenomenon at the height of swallowing is often when aspiration occurs.

Ultrasound

Ultrasound has been used to image the human body for at least 50 years. It is one of the most widely used diagnostic tools in modern medicine. Health care professionals use ultrasound to view the heart, blood vessels, kidneys, liver, and other organs. Ultrasound is commonly used during pregnancy to examine the developing fetus (see also Chapter 13). During an ultrasound test, a special technician or doctor moves a device called a transducer over a specific body part. The transducer sends out high-frequency sound waves (inaudible to human ears), which bounce off the tissues inside the body, and the same transducer captures the sound waves that bounce back. These sound waves are then translated and assembled into a visual image on a computer monitor. This same

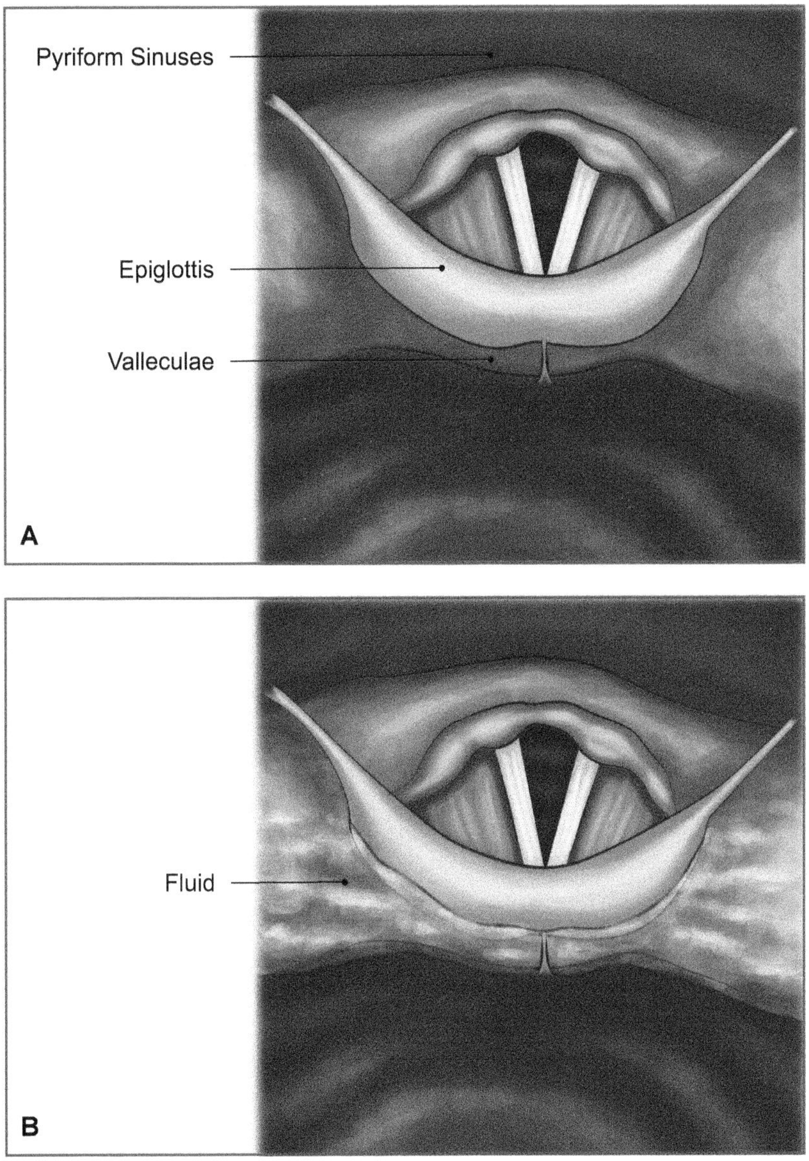

FIGURE 11–9. View of the pharyngeal area during a fiberoptic endoscopic evaluation of swallowing procedure. **A.** A normal swallow. **B.** A disordered swallow as indicated by residual fluid in the valleculae.

technology can be used to track tongue movement during a swallow. The procedure works by holding a transducer under the patient's chin; high-frequency sound waves travel through the tissues in the neck and are reflected off the tongue to create an image. Because the approach is exclusive to the tongue's role in swallowing, only the oral stage of swallowing can be evaluated; however, the approach is far less invasive than the videofluoroscopic swallowing study and the fiberoptic endoscopic evaluation of swallowing approach. An example of the ultrasound approach to evaluating swallowing is shown in Figure 11–10. The use of ultrasound to assess dysphagia has been confined to research settings, although it may ultimately serve as a clinically useful tool used in combination with other assessment procedures (Allen & Clunie, 2021).

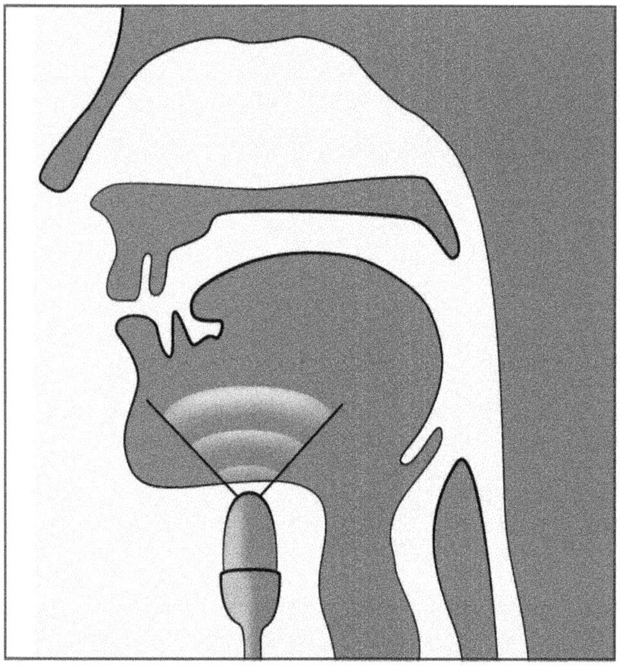

FIGURE 11–10. An ultrasound examination of the tongue during the oral stage of swallowing.

Electromyography

When a muscle is used (i.e., contracts), it generates a very small electrical signal, which can be detected with an antenna (i.e., an electrode). This instrumental procedure is known as **electromyography**. When a very thin wire electrode is inserted directly into a muscle, the activity of the muscle can be viewed and recorded. There also are less invasive disc electrodes that can simply be taped to the surface of the skin. While the patient is swallowing, a variety of muscles in the region of the mouth, larynx, and pharynx can be examined using the electromyography approach. A muscle that is not working correctly will emit an electrical signal that is different from a normal functioning muscle. In an extreme case where a muscle is paralyzed, it is possible that no electrical activity would be emitted. Examples of electromyography signals found in normal and disordered swallowing are presented in Figure 11–11. A drawback with this approach is that the procedure can be highly invasive, requiring insertion of an electrode directly into the muscle. The use of a surface electrode may also be problematic because these electrodes are attached to the surface of the skin, and the electromyography signal can be obscured due to multiple muscles overlapping or excessive adipose (body fat) tissue. The electromyography form of instrumental swallowing assessment is not routinely used in a clinical setting. Rather, it is used more often in research settings (Koyama et al., 2021).

TREATMENT OF DYSPHAGIA

There are two primary goals for the treatment of dysphagia in older children and adults. The first goal is to maintain a "safe" swallow or reduce the risk for aspiration. The second goal is to increase p.o. (per oral) intake of liquid and food. Successful management of dysphagia requires a team of various health specialists such as speech-language pathologists, occupational and physical therapists, otolaryngologists, neurologists, gastroenterologists, and dieticians. Once the cause of dysphagia is found, there are a few treatment approaches to consider, including (a) swallowing therapy, (b) lifestyle changes, (c) drugs, and (d) surgery.

Swallowing Therapy

The speech-language pathologist could be called on to test the person's ability to eat and drink and may teach the person new ways to swallow. The therapy program established for the patient is tailored to suit the individual's medical condition. Treatment may involve rehabilitation exercises to strengthen weak oral and pharyngeal muscles or to improve coordination of the overall swallowing musculature. One approach is referred to as **effortful swallow**, where the patient is required to swallow normally but squeeze forcefully with the tongue and throat muscles throughout the swallow. Another approach is known as the **Masako Maneuver**. This is an exercise designed to strengthen the pharyngeal muscles involved in swallowing. The exercise is performed by protruding the tongue between the front teeth and holding it in place by gently biting down on the anterior portion of the tongue. The patient is then

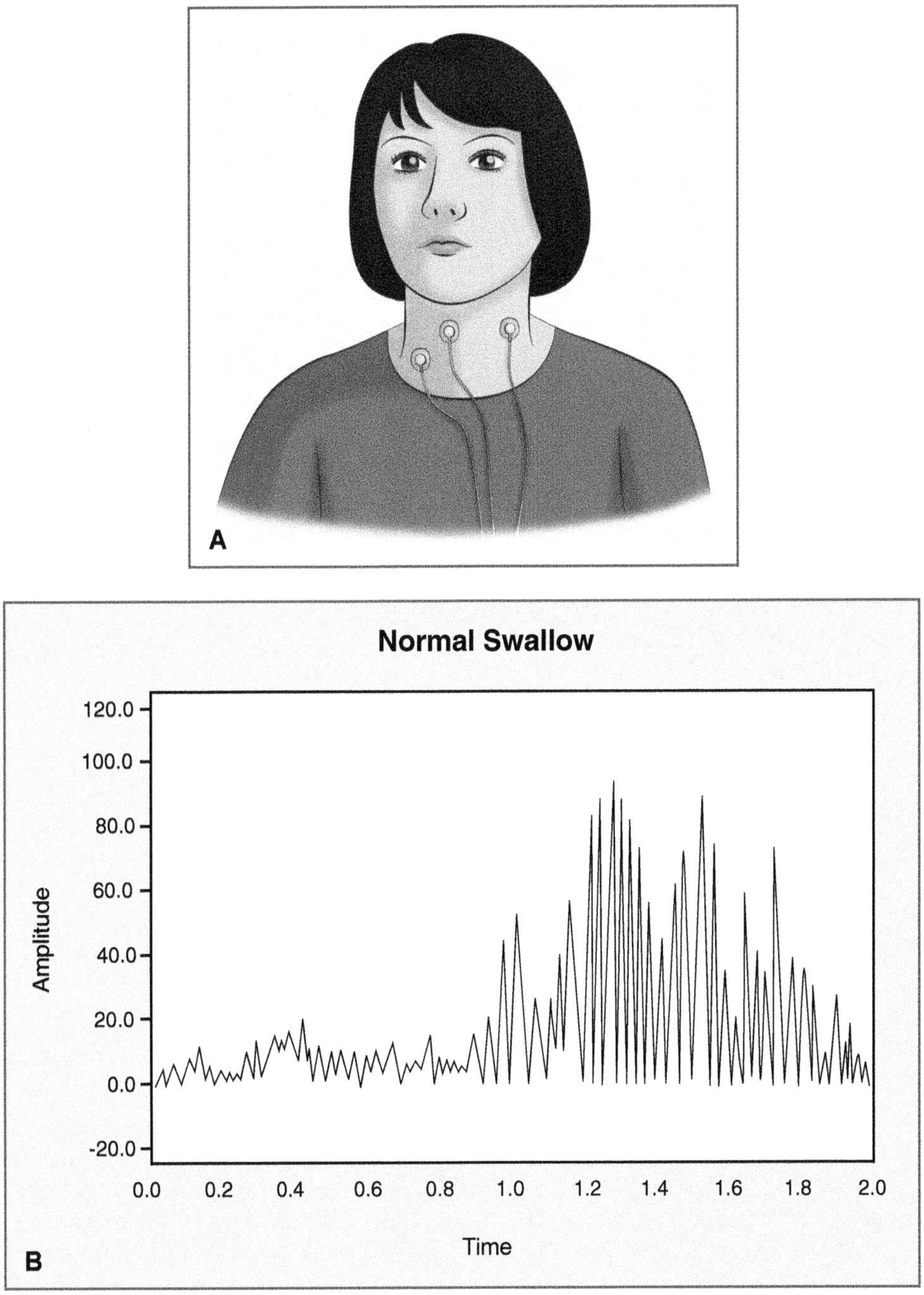

FIGURE 11–11. **A.** Surface electrode placement for electromyographic recording of swallowing. **B.** An idealized electromyographic recording reflecting normal muscle functioning during a swallow. *continues*

asked to maintain this posture while swallowing saliva. Treatment may also involve learning compensatory swallowing strategies. For example, some people might have to eat and drink with their head turned to one side or looking straight ahead. Preparing food in a certain way or avoiding certain foods can help other people. Some fluids that might normally be easily aspirated can be altered by adding a thickening agent. The patient may be discouraged from swallowing hot or cold items if the individual is particularly sensitive to reflux.

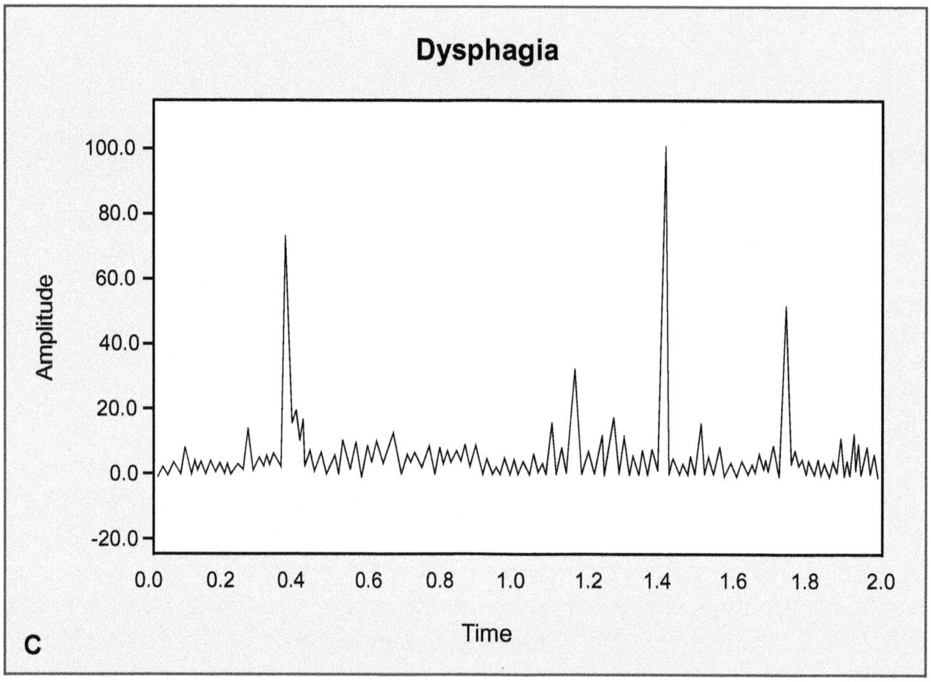

FIGURE 11–11. *continued* **C.** An impaired muscle functioning during a swallow.

FYI

Acid reflux is a warning sign of dysphagia. In addition, acid reflux can serve to impair one's speaking voice. In extreme cases of reflux, acidic juices may back up from the stomach and irritate the laryngeal mechanism, including the vocal folds.

Lifestyle Changes

As noted earlier, acid reflux is a dysphagic condition that can have serious consequences on health and quality of life. There are several steps people can take to greatly reduce the likelihood of reflux disease. These steps involve changes in lifestyle such as increased exercise and diet modification. Some common recommendations include the following:

- Eat smaller, more frequent meals.
- Eat a bland diet.
- Avoid alcohol and caffeine.
- Lose weight.
- Reduce stress.
- Avoid eating 3 hours before bedtime.
- Slightly elevate your head while sleeping.

Drugs

Prescribing drugs to treat dysphagia typically has been dictated based on the particular medical condition contributing to the disorder. Because of the wide range of causes that could contribute to dysphagia, there presently is no "magic pill" that can cure it. In many cases, drugs serve to relieve some of the symptoms of dysphagia, primarily those associated with esophageal dysphagia. The types of medications found to be useful include over-the-counter antacids that are taken before or after eating. There also are prescription medications known as proton-pump inhibitors, which substantially reduce acid production in the stomach.

Surgery

A typical surgical treatment of dysphagia involves muscle incisions to release muscle tension or to stretch/dilate an unusually narrow stricture. For some, however, consuming foods and liquids by mouth may not be possible in the immediate future. These individuals must use other methods to nourish their bodies. Usually this involves surgical intervention to create a new feeding system, such as a **feeding tube** that bypasses the part of the swallowing mechanism that is not working normally. It is common to have a feeding tube inserted during the early stages of severe dysphagia to reduce the risk of aspiration pneumonia. The tube also helps ensure that the person's nutrition and hydration are adequate. These tubes can be easily removed if and/or when the dysphagia diminishes. Two main types of feeding tubes are used: (a) enteral tubes and (b) parenteral tubes.

An **enteral tube** provides liquid nutrition directly into the stomach or small intestine. There are two general types of enteral tubes: (a) nasogastric and (b) gastrostomy. A **nasogastric tube** (or NG tube) is used on a short-term basis and entails passing a tube through the nose, pharynx, and esophagus directly into the stomach. Once the tube is correctly positioned, it is taped to the patient's nose or cheek to keep it in place. Food passes through the tube into the stomach.

A **parenteral tube** (or IV tube) involves providing liquid nutrition through the veins (Figure 11–12). The tube is essentially a catheter that provides micronutrients directly into the bloodstream. This approach is appropriate only for individuals whose stomach and intestines are not working properly. The tube allows for the digestive tract to heal after surgery to the stomach or bowel and is kept in place with a stitch. Parenteral feeding is considered riskier than enteral feeding but results in improved energy and health.

A **gastronomy tube** (or percutaneous endoscopic gastrostomy [PEG] tube) is used on a longer-term basis or for indefinite time periods. Like an NG tube, food passes through it into the stomach; but unlike an NG tube, an external opening is made in the abdomen and the tube is placed directly into the stomach. The feeding tube is held in place with either a stitch, a small inflated balloon around the tube just under the skin, or a flange around the tube just under the skin. This

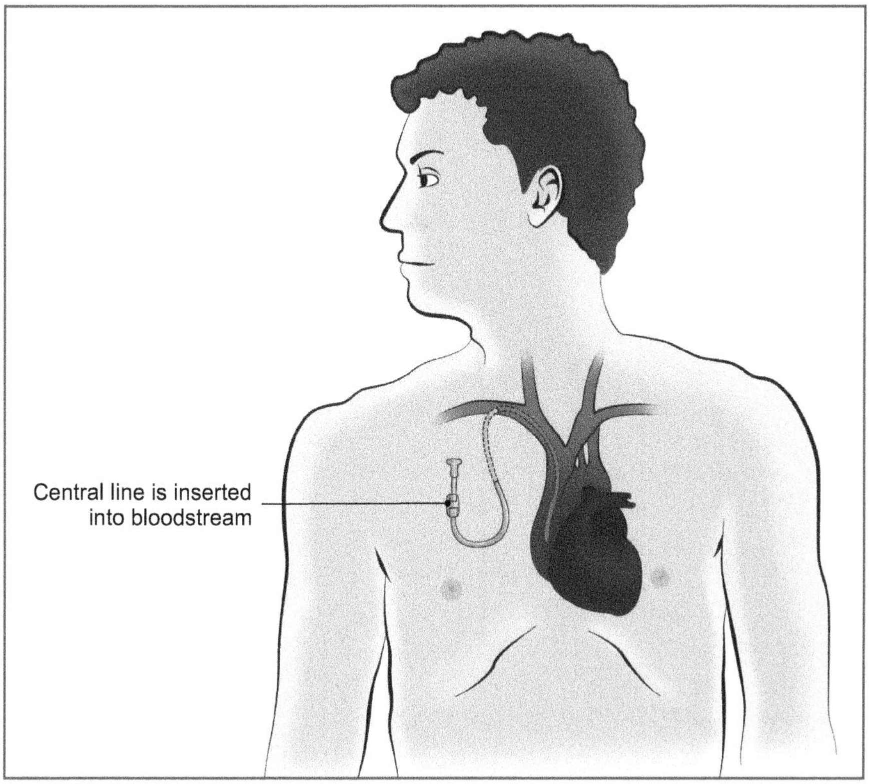

FIGURE 11–12. Parenteral tube through which nutrients are delivered directly into the bloodstream for patients who are unable to swallow.

FYI

The *abdominal thrust* procedure is a technique used in emergency situations to prevent suffocation resulting from blocked food or foreign matter. The approach involves placing one's arms around the choking individual (from behind) and delivering a series of five thrusts into the abdomen to dislodge the blockage. Back blows (with the victim leaning forward) have also been added as part of this rescue strategy for choking. The maneuver was developed by Henry Heimlich in 1974.

form of enteral feeding is more invasive than an NG tube. Examples of the two types of enteral feeding tubes are shown in Figure 11–13.

Treating Pediatric Feeding Disorders

The management of pediatric feeding disorders (PFD) involves caregivers and health professionals using a coordinated model of care. The four primary domains (medical, nutritional, feeding skill, and psychosocial) that are essential to proper feeding (see Table 11–3) serve as the framework for assessing and treating a young child with PFD. An example of how these domains can be addressed by a speech-language pathologist is provided by LaManna and Miluk (2023) for an 18-month-old child who avoids solid foods, has limited oral intake, and frequently regurgitates food after meals (Table 11–5). For children with PFD, the intake of food can be painful, scary, and potentially life threatening. However, the comprehensive plan organized across these four domains offers an affirming approach to improving a child's overall nutritional development and well-being.

CULTURAL CONSIDERATIONS AND DYSPHAGIA

The speech-language pathologist that works with patients who have dysphagia may encounter a unique set of social and cultural issues that need to be considered as part of the overall treatment plan. Riquelme (2007) identified four factors that, if not considered, may hinder speech-language pathologists' effectiveness in treating dysphagia. These factors include (a) language barriers, (b) physical space, (c) ageism, and (d) food and nutrition.

Language Barriers

Based on the introductory material presented in this chapter, it is evident that a large and unique vocabulary is used when dealing with the disorder of dysphagia. These terms are, in many cases, quite foreign even for someone who may speak the same language as the speech-language pathologist; speaking the same language may not ensure there is a cultural understanding between the clinician and client. In cases where the client speaks English as a second language, the speech-language pathologist may need to use an interpreter to communicate with the patient, and if so, great care should be taken in monitoring how the translated information is presented. Sensitivity to a patient's knowledge of medical terminology is important. Not everyone understands terms such as *no foods per oral/mouth*, *aspiration*, and *reflux*.

Physical Space

One aspect of assessing and treating dysphagia that is not found in most areas of speech-language pathology is the literal hands-on approach to assisting the patient. Any sort of touching used

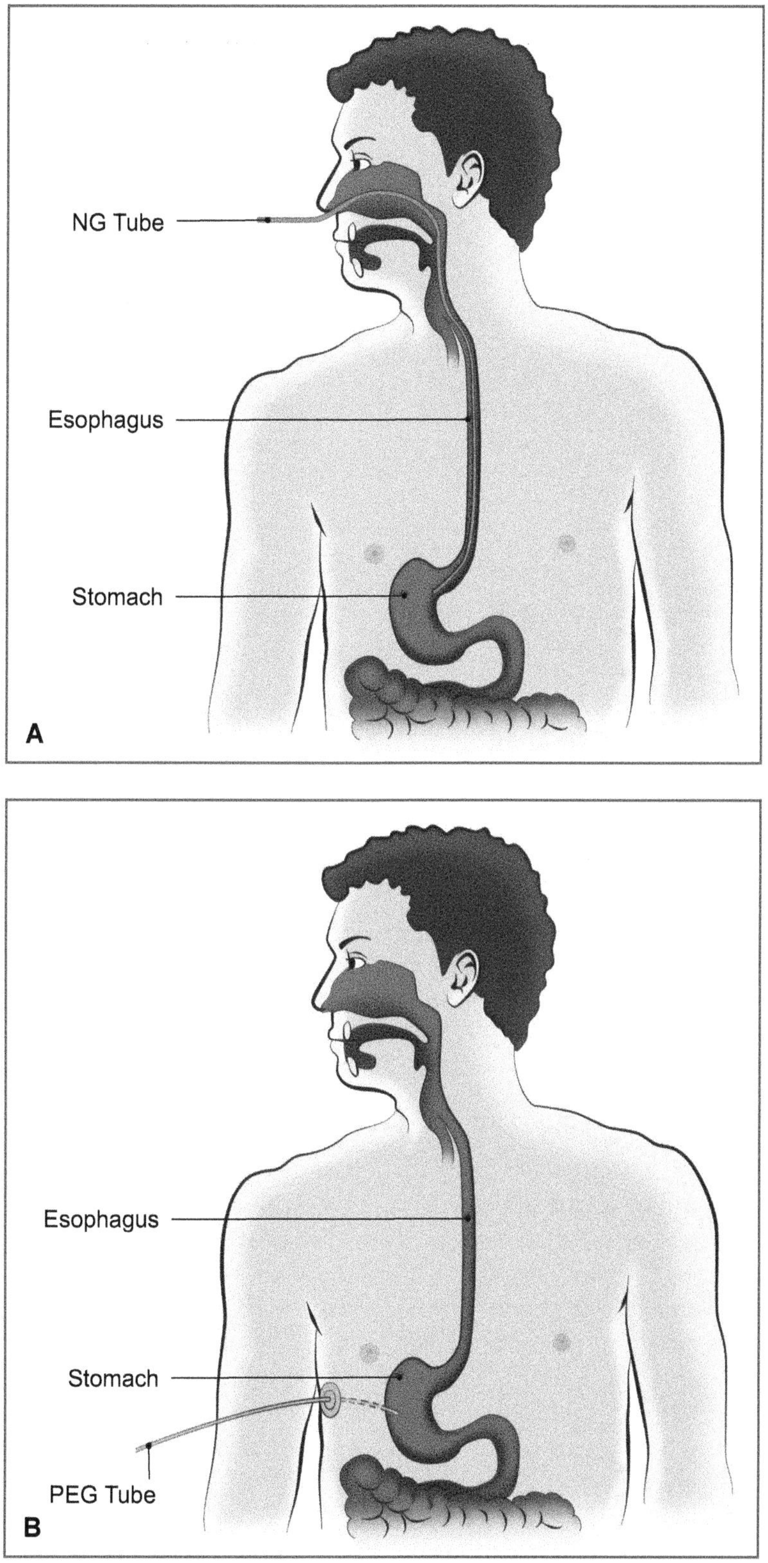

FIGURE 11–13. Examples of enteral tubes for patients to consume food and liquid if unable to swallow. **A.** A nasogastric (NG) tube or a gastronomy tube. **B.** A percutaneous endoscopic gastrostomy.

Table 11–5. Clinical Application of the Four Domains of Pediatric Feeding Disorders for an 18-Month-Old Child

Domain Problem Area	*Clinical Focus*
Medical: Gastroesophageal reflux	The clinician may work closely with the family pediatrician to manage symptoms and ensure the child is receiving appropriate medical management.
Nutritional: Lack of weight gain	The clinician and pediatrician recommend the family consult with a dietician who assists with creating a meal schedule and finds ways to increase caloric intake.
Feeding Skill: Impaired oral/pharyngeal solid structures	The child may require thickened liquids due to lack of experience with chewable foods.
Psychosocial: Parent frustration/anxiety	The clinician works with the family to create a positive feeding environment and to address emotional and behavioral issues and possibly refer to a psychologist or counselor.

Source: From "Using the Four Domains of Pediatric Feeding Disorders to Guide Assessment and Treatment," by S. LaManna and B. Miluk, 2023, *The ASHA Leader*, May 24.

by the speech-language pathologist needs to be clarified with the patient beforehand. There may be times when adjusting the patient's posture or palpating the patient's throat during swallowing could be inappropriate. The speech-language pathologist should not assume the patient understands all the procedures involved in an examination and subsequent treatment. In addition to matters concerning physical proximity, the clinical setting may also need to be considered when dealing with dysphagia. An important part of dysphagia therapy is to work with patients in the home environment. This is the most natural setting for the patient. Both the patient and the caregivers should be guided in creating a structured and safe home environment. By doing so, there is a greater likelihood of patient compliance and carryover of treatment recommendations.

Ageism

In most cases, the dysphagic patient is an older adult, and the speech-language pathologist is not. The age difference between client and clinician can impact overall interactions and patient compliance, both of which are critical to effective treatment outcomes (Riquelme, 2007). For many ethnic groups, older adults are treated with great overt respect, and these individuals hold high social status within the immediate and extended family. This needs to be acknowledged during clinical interactions. The speech-language pathologist–patient relationship needs to be equalized or at least balanced to effectively provide culturally competent care.

Food and Nutrition

Issues concerning food and nutrition for the dysphagic patient can be particularly challenging in a multicultural population. Eating a meal with others is an enjoyable and highly social activity, and in some cultures, eating implies a sense of community. The U.S. holiday of Thanksgiving is just one example of how food can be linked to culture. If the patient with dysphagia has difficulty partaking in food consumption, yet their culture places high importance on food, steps need to be taken to ensure that a balance between food and culture is maintained. When selecting types of foods, the speech-language pathologist may encounter difficulty with patients due to their prior history and culture of eating. Therefore, seeking input from a nutritionist is advisable. For example, when establishing a diet that avoids solid foods (because of increased risk of aspiration), some patients may report they "are not able to do without fish." So, when selecting specific foods, it is important to provide a patient with choices that reflect cultural preferences. For instance, the choice of pureed plantains versus potatoes may be quite important to a Latino patient who normally does not have potatoes in their diet (Riquelme, 2007).

SUMMARY OF CHAPTER

The process of swallowing occurs in a series of three sequential stages: (a) oral, (b) pharyngeal, and (c) esophageal. Each stage represents specific physiological activity in the progression of moving material from the mouth to the stomach. Dysphagia is a breakdown in coordination of swallowing. This breakdown may be due to the person's (a) wakefulness or awareness, (b) brain functioning, and/or (c) muscular strength. Dysphagia is a rather unique area of specialty in the speech-language pathologist profession because the condition is not a communication disorder. The procedures used for assessing the presence of dysphagia fall into two general categories: (a) clinical assessment and (b) instrumental assessment. Clinical assessment is used for the initial screening of swallowing dysfunction and, as the term suggests, typically occurs while a patient is in a clinic setting. Instrumentation is used to determine the existence of dysphagia and provides a more in-depth form of assessment compared to a clinical assessment. The therapy program is tailored to suit the individual's medical condition. Treatment may involve exercises to strengthen weak oral and pharyngeal muscles or to improve coordination of the overall swallowing musculature. The speech-language pathologist may encounter a unique set of social and cultural issues that need to be considered as part of the patient's overall treatment plan.

DYSPHAGIA ON THE WORLD WIDE WEB

Following are websites that provide further information on the topic of dysphagia. At the time of publication, each website was freely accessible.

Swallowing Videos
https://swallowingdisorderfoundation.com/swallow-a-documentary/

https://www.nationalmssociety.org/Programs-and-Services/Resources/Swallowing-Difficulties-in-MS-(video)

Dysphagia Resource Center
https://www.dysphagiagame.com/

Swallowing Assessment Video
https://www.youtube.com/watch?v=OufjV4UE2Oc

https://www.stroke4carers.org/?p=2413

STUDY QUESTIONS

1. What are the primary anatomical structures involved in swallowing, and how are they involved in the three stages of swallowing?
2. List and describe the three types of dysphagia.
3. What are some of the likely causes of dysphagia?
4. What are the four approaches to assessing dysphagia?
5. What are the four approaches to treating dysphagia?

REFERENCES

Allen, J., & Clunie, G. (2021). Ultrasound: An emerging modality for the dysphagia assessment toolkit? *Current Opinions in Otolaryngology, Head, and Neck Surgery*, *29*(3), 213–218.

Bülow, M. (2019). Psychiatric aspects of dysphagia. *Dysphagia: Diagnosis and treatment* (pp. 275–281). Springer.

Dodrill, P., & Gosa, M. (2015). Pediatric dysphagia: Physiology, assessment, and management. *Annals of Nutrition and Metabolism*, *66*(Suppl. 5), 24–31.

Enz, V. C. Q., Vaz, A. R. C., Nunes, M. C. D. A., Rosa, M. D. O., Nunes, J. D. A., Marques, J. M., & Santos, R. S. (2022). Accuracy of acoustic evaluation of swallowing as a diagnostic method of dysphagia in individuals affected by stroke: Preliminary analysis. *Dysphagia*, *37*(4), 724–735.

Goday, P. S., Huh, S. Y., Silverman, A., Lukens, C. T., Dodrill, P., Cohen, S. S., . . . Phalen, J. A. (2019). Pediatric feeding disorder: Consensus definition and conceptual framework. *Journal of Pediatric Gastroenterology and Nutrition*, *68*(1), 124–129.

Immovilli, P., Rota, E., Morelli, N., Marchesi, E., Terracciano, C., Zaino, D., . . . Guidetti, D. (2021). Diagnostic accuracy of a bedside screening tool for Dysphagia (BSTD) in acute stroke patients. *Journal of Stroke and Cerebrovascular Diseases, 30*(2), 105470.

Koyama, Y., Ohmori, N., Momose, H., Kondo, E., Yamada, S. I., & Kurita, H. (2021). Detection of swallowing disorders using a multiple channel surface electromyography sheet: A preliminary study. *Journal of Dental Sciences, 16*(1), 160–167.

LaManna, S., & Miluk, B. (2023). Using the four domains of pediatric feeding disorders to guide assessment and treatment. *ASHA Leader*, May 24.

Langmore, S. E., Schatz, K., & Olsen, N. (1988). Fiberoptic endoscopic examination of swallowing safety: A new procedure. *Dysphagia, 2*, 216–219.

Miller, R., & Groher, M. (1993). Speech-language pathology and dysphagia: A brief historical perspective. *Dysphagia, 8*, 180–184.

Riquelme, L. (2007). The role of cultural competence in providing services to persons with dysphagia. *Topics in Geriatric Rehabilitation, 23*, 228–239.

Triggs, J., & Pandolfino, J. (2019). Recent advances in dysphagia management. *F1000Research, 8*.

12

AUGMENTATIVE AND ALTERNATIVE COMMUNICATION

OBJECTIVES

After reading this chapter, the student should be able to:

- Explain augmentative and alternative communication (AAC) and why it is important in the field of communication sciences and disorders.
- Explain the key considerations in the development of an AAC system.
- Demonstrate an understanding of the historical aspects in the AAC field.
- Demonstrate an understanding of current theories of AAC assessment.
- Describe sociocultural influences on the selection and use of AAC systems.

KEY TERMS

Augmentative and Alternative Communication (AAC)	Beverly Vicker	Low Technology
Augmentative Communication	Shirley McNaughton	High Technology
Assistive Technology	Charles K. Bliss	Speech-Generating Device
Symbols	John Eulenberg	Digitized Speech
Direct Selection	David Yoder	Voice Banking
Indirect Selection	Gregg Vanderheiden	Synthesized Speech
Scanning	Janice Light	Dedicated System
Switch	Unaided	Open System
Hieroglyphics	Aided	Communication Needs Model
Alphabet	Multimodal Communication	Participation Model
F. Hall Roe	Intelligibility	Communicative Competency
Reginald Maling	Comprehensive Efficiency	

INTRODUCTION

Communication is not just a simple transfer of information. Among humans, communication involves an exchange of information that includes ideas, thoughts, and emotions. Our identity is reflected in our ability to communicate. It is what makes us human. We tend to take communication for granted. Everyone uses multiple forms of communication that will vary based on the partner and the context of communication. Effective communication occurs when the intent and meaning expressed by one individual are understood by another. As profiled in previous chapters, breakdowns in communication can occur as a consequence of developmental or acquired conditions. The conditions affecting normal communication can range from severe physical impairments resulting in no verbal language to more idiosyncratic conditions. Communication impairments are found for people of all ages. In cases of significant neurological impairment, some individuals have no physical capacity to produce speech that is understandable. These individuals may also have impairments in the ability to move other parts of their body that prevent them from using another form of communication such as sign language. Severe communication impairment can stem from conditions like cerebral palsy or some types of neurodegenerative disorders (e.g., amyotrophic lateral sclerosis). Cancer of the larynx or tongue can also significantly impact expression of speech and language. A disorder such as autism, where there is no obvious physical impairment, may result in some spoken language, but the effectiveness of communication is lacking. Across these various cases, it is unlikely the individual's communication will improve with traditional treatment approaches. The speech-language pathologist may recommend using another approach to facilitate communication, known as **augmentative and alternative communication** (AAC). The AAC approach is an area of clinical and educational practice that provides communication interventions for people who have little or no functional speech or who have complex communication needs.

Examples of conditions that would likely involve AAC are shown in Table 12–1. The term AAC refers to any mode of communication other than speech. There are many types of AAC, includ-

Table 12–1. Examples of Augmentative and Alternative Communication Users According to Developmental and Acquired Disability
Developmental Disabilities
• Genetic disorders • Cerebral palsy • Autism spectrum disorder • Speech apraxia • Intellectual disability
Acquired Disabilities
• Laryngectomy • Glossectomy • Amyotrophic lateral sclerosis • Multiple sclerosis • Traumatic brain injury • Cerebrovascular accident • Intubation

ing sign language, pictures, symbols, gestures, and speech-generating devices. The aim of AAC is to achieve the most effective communication possible for the individual using myriad strategies to meet the challenges of everyday communication. The goal of AAC is to provide individuals who are unable to produce speech naturally with a form of independent communication. By doing so, we can maximize their ability and opportunity to engage and participate in everyday environments. Quality of life and feelings of well-being improve when AAC is used successfully by people with complex communication needs (Antonino et al., 2019). This chapter introduces this unique and sometimes challenging area of clinical practice.

> **FYI**
>
> An unfounded myth is that the use of AAC prevents a child from ever using functional speech. Research has proven this false. AAC does not have a negative impact on speech production and may actually help to improve natural speech production.

TERMINOLOGY AND DEFINITIONS

The term **augmentative communication** refers to the use of an additional mode of communication to improve the delivery of a message—a form of communication other than natural speech. We all use various forms of AAC, such as waving and saying hello simultaneously (augmentative communication) or simply blowing a kiss (alternative communication). When a person's existing natural speech is not completely meeting communication needs or the individual has little natural existing speech, the use of AAC becomes the primary means of communication. A related term is **assistive technology**, which is technology used by individuals with disabilities to perform functions that might otherwise be difficult or impossible. Examples of assistive technology include mobility devices such as wheelchairs as well as computer hardware and software that aid people with disabilities in accessing information technologies.

The number of individuals in the United States who are unable to effectively communicate using natural speech totals 4 million. Approximately one half of 1% of the population in the United Kingdom use AAC systems (Enderby et al., 2013). As individuals age and the complexity of their disability gets greater, their need for AAC increases. The growing prevalence of autism has led to an increase in AAC users. Improved health care for individuals with severe medical conditions means a longer life span; a consequence of living longer has sometimes been accompanied by severe expressive communication deficits and prescription of AAC (Light & McNaughton, 2012).

An important feature of AAC relates to the **symbols** that are used for communication. Symbols are visual displays that represent objects, actions, events, and concepts. The user selects a single symbol or a series of symbols to create a message. There are many types of communication symbols available to AAC users. Symbols can include items such as physical objects, colored or black-and-white photographs, line drawings, and written words. A variety of commercially available symbol-based communication systems have been developed for AAC users. Some of these symbols are basic and transparent so that the symbol represents the actual word. An example of a transparent symbol system is the Widget (Rebus) system. An example of a less transparent system is Blissymbolics (discussed later). A website link to a more complete list of symbol systems is provided at the end of the chapter.

Another feature of AAC relates to the manner in which the user accesses communication symbols. The two primary means of symbol access are direct and indirect selection. **Direct selection** involves accessing the desired symbol using a finger or some sort of pointing device. The most common form of direct selection is finger pointing. Direct selection may also occur using another body part or accessing the symbols without physical contact (e.g., head/mouth stick, eye gaze, laser pointer) (Figure 12–1). **Indirect selection** (also known as **scanning**) is an alternative method of accessing symbols. This approach is recommended for individuals who are unable to choose items directly, most likely due to a physical impairment that affects motor control. Scanning involves presenting symbols on a display and progressively moving through the symbols in a predetermined pattern. For example, each item may be sequentially illuminated on a screen display in a left-to-right pattern. Scanning requires that the user wait

Source: Fezcat, CC BY-SA 4.0 <https://creativecommons.org/licenses/by-sa/4.0>, via Wikimedia Commons.

FIGURE 12–1. **A.** Example of an augmentative and alternative communication user accessing symbols with a head-mounted laser pointer. **B.** Example of a push switch.

while the system sequentially presents each symbol until reaching the item of choice. The direct or indirect access method used by an individual could change over time if the medical condition is a disease that progressively leads to weakening of different areas of the body. This means that a person who was originally using their fingers to access symbols might lose this ability and eventually must use another access method.

An electronic **switch** is a key element of some AAC systems. The user is taught to use a switch to activate symbol scanning movement and select the item or message. There are a number of switching mechanisms available to the AAC user (see Figure 12–1). The electronic switch is designed around the person's motor abilities that best allow for turning a switch on and off. Switches have been designed for a host of physical movements such as thumb flexion, jaw closing, tongue extension, eyebrow elevation, knee extension, and shoulder rotation. Various types of electronic switches are shown in Table 12–2.

FYI

There is no age limitation for using AAC. An individual is never too young or too old to be considered a candidate for AAC. Communication is a basic human right, and we should not delay providing access to that right.

HISTORIC ASPECTS OF AUGMENTATIVE AND ALTERNATIVE COMMUNICATION

The earliest forms of augmentative and alternative communication can be traced back to the creation of gestural communication and written language. As early as 25,000 BC, early humans painted pictures on cave walls that depicted events from daily life, such as hunting or planting. The earliest of these pictures were found in caves of southern France and Spain (Figure 12–2). It took primitive man thousands of years to create a written form of communication. Those civilizations that had written communication were the ones that developed most rapidly. Around 2000 BC, the Egyptians developed a writing system that used **hieroglyphics**, which means "the words of God," and was a form of writing in which the various symbols stood for certain sounds and words. It was used primarily by scribes, doctors, and priests to decorate the walls of temples and tombs. An abbreviated form of hieroglyphics, called **hieratic**, was used for more informal communication. This was a type of handwriting in which the symbols were abbreviated to the point of abstraction (see Figure 12–2).

Somewhere between 1700 and 1500 BC, the **alphabet** was established as a form of written communication. The word is derived from the Latin origin, *alfabetum*, which combines the first

Table 12–2. Examples of Electronic Switch Mechanisms Available to Users of Augmentative and Alternative Communication

Type of Switch	*Description*
Push switch	Physical pressure is applied to the switch directly by a body part (e.g., finger) or indirectly by an implement (e.g., headstick).
Position switch	A change of position in space of the switch mechanism causes activation.
Pneumatic switch	Blowing or sucking on the end of a tube changes air pressure and activates a pressure-sensitive switch.
Touch switch	Activation of switch based on touch (e.g., finger, head, foot) on a specially designed surface causes activation.
Sound-controlled switch	Switch is activated based on vocal sound energy.
Light-controlled switch	Activation of switch by directing a beam of light or by interrupting a beam of light that is directed at a device.

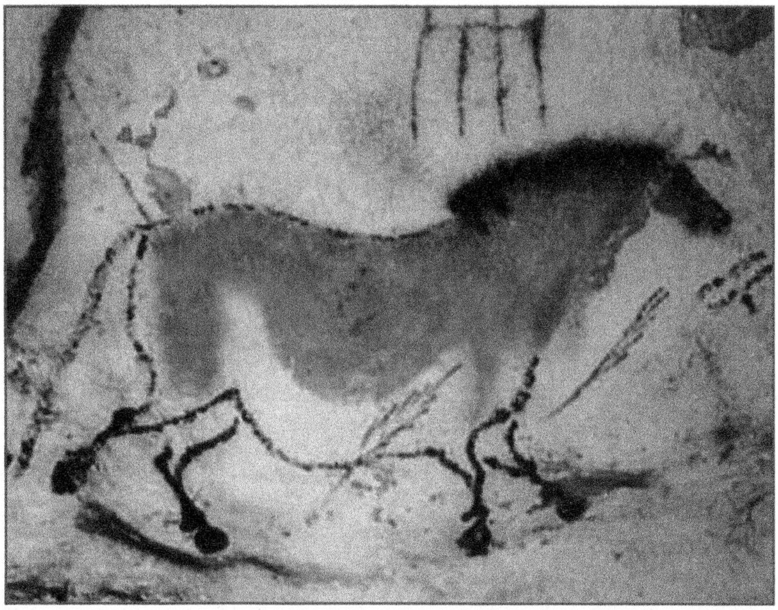

A

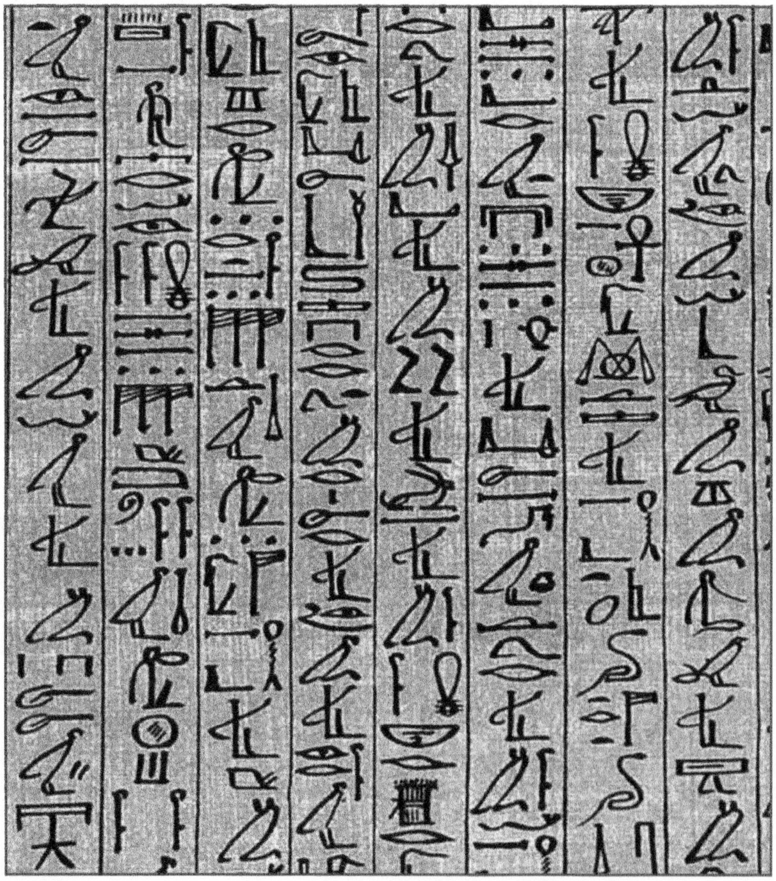

B

FIGURE 12–2. Two forms of early written communication. **A.** A cave painting discovered in Lascaux, France, ca. 1500–1000 BC. **B.** An example of abbreviated hieroglyphic writing known as hieratic, ca. 2000 BC.

two symbols of the Greek alphabet, "alpha" and "beta." Alphabetic symbols were easier and faster to draw than pictures and were more universally recognized for their meaning. The use of an alphabet allowed for the creation of words and sentences. The Greek and Hebrew alphabets were established around 100 BC. The Greek alphabet became the source for the Latin alphabet created in 7 BC, which in turn became the source of the present-day English alphabet. The version of the Hebrew alphabet that is used today dates back to 600 BC. The Greek and Latin alphabets were designed to be written from left to right. These early alphabetic systems used only uppercase letters, with lowercase letters introduced during the first century (Figure 12–3).

Manual languages were in common use during the 10th century among monks. In keeping with a vow of silence, a hand gestural system was developed as an alternative to spoken communication. During the late 1500s, manual communication was first introduced as an alternative form of communication for children and adults who were deaf (see Chapter 15). These early developments of symbolic, written, and manual communication as well as the later development of computers provided the foundation for the modern development of AAC.

The use of AAC specifically designed for individuals with severe disabilities began in the 1950s. Professionals in various disciplines, such as education, occupational therapy, speech-language pathology, and psychology, developed communication boards to assist individuals with severe disabilities such as aphasia, cerebral palsy, glossectomy, and laryngectomy. The communication boards provided a basic form of communication for children and adults to communicate with others. One of the first communication boards that was marketed broadly was the F. Hall Roe communication board (Figure 12–4). The board was originally created for **F. Hall Roe**, who had a severe expressive language disorder resulting from cerebral palsy. The boards were printed on sturdy cardboard (masonite) and could easily be mounted on wheelchairs. The boards contained letters of the alphabet, numbers, and frequently used words to allow communication between the user and those in the user's immediate environment.

One of the earliest electronic AAC devices included the patient-operated selector mechanism (POSM) (Figure 12–5). The system involved activation of a typewriter based on a sip-and-puff switch created by **Reginald Maling** (1927–2007) in 1960. The idea behind creating the device came to Maling when he observed that paralyzed people

FIGURE 12–3. The Hebrew, Greek, and Latin alphabets and the two forms of writing each alphabet.

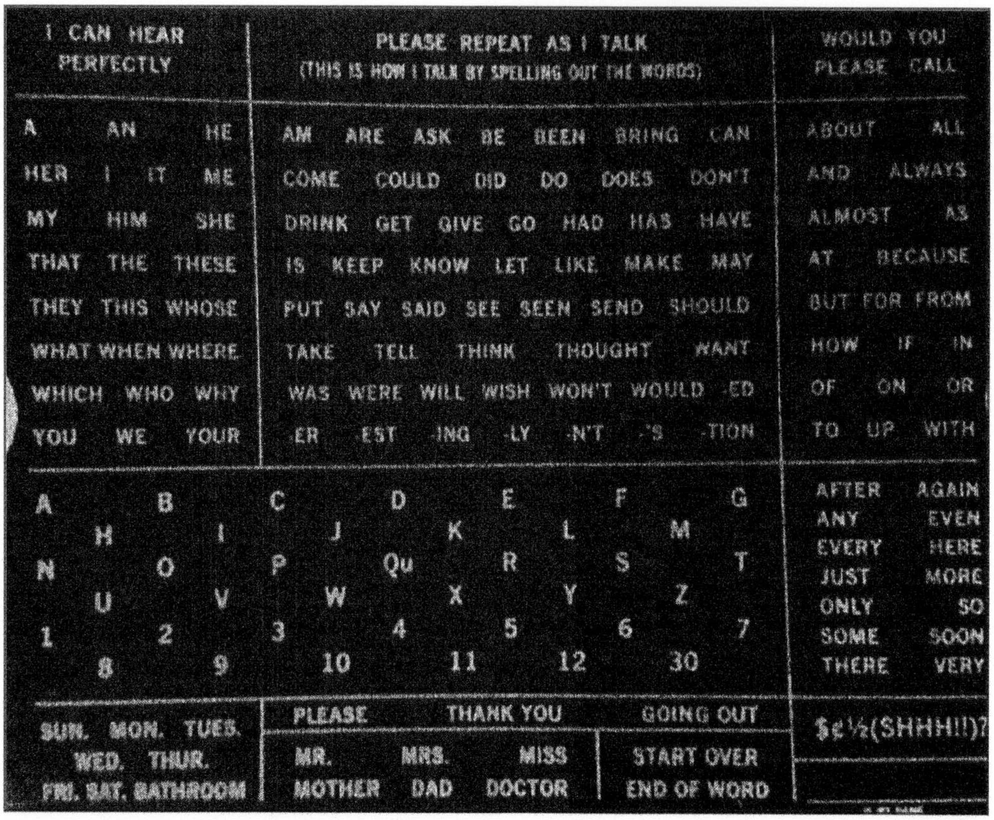

FIGURE 12–4. Early communication board created for F. Hall Roe, who had a severe expressive language disorder resulting from cerebral palsy. (Reprinted from "A Journey Through Early Augmentative Communication and Computer Access," by G. C. Vanderheiden, 2002, *Journal of Rehabilitation Research and Development*, *39*[6], pp. 39–53.)

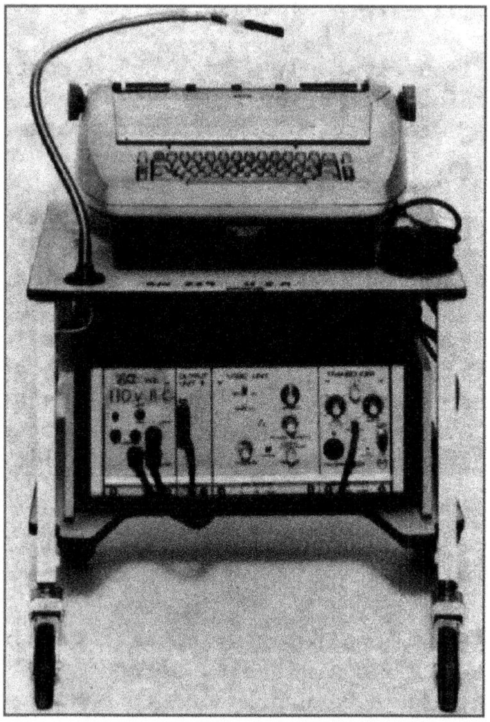

A

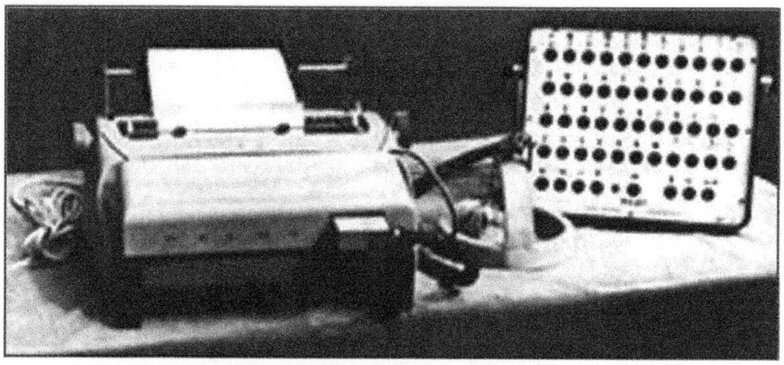

B

FIGURE 12–5. Two early electronic augmentative and alternative communication devices. **A.** The patient-operated selector mechanism (POSM). **B.** The patient-initiated lightspot-operated typewriter (PILOT). (Reprinted from "A Journey Through Early Augmentative Communication and Computer Access," by G. C. Vanderheiden, 2002, *Journal of Rehabilitation Research and Development*, *39*[6], 39–53.)

in hospitals used only a bell or whistle for communication. Maling assumed that if patients were able to control the air in their mouth to blow a whistle, then the same physical movement could be used to operate a switch. The ability to operate a switch opened a new world to activating a range of electrical devices, including a specialized typewriter. Another AAC device developed in the 1960s was the patient-initiated lightspot-operated typewriter (PILOT). This device involved pointing a beam of light at a display of letters and numbers, which was interfaced with a typewriter (see Figure 12–5).

During the 1970s, many speech-language pathologists were hesitant to provide AAC to people who were believed to have the potential to develop verbal speech (Beukelman & Light, 2020). Speech-language pathologists tended to wait until they were certain the individual would never acquire natural speech. In the mid-1960s and early 1970s, a speech-language pathologist from the University of Iowa named **Beverly Vicker** undertook a series of clinical activities using communication boards for severely disabled individuals. She published her findings in the book *Nonoral Communication System Project 1964–1973* (Vicker, 1974). The communication boards ranged from very simple pictures with a few words to elaborate boards with up to 800 words. The participants in her clinical studies accessed the symbols with pointers and head sticks. A major advance in the field of AAC occurred in the early 1970s when **Shirley McNaughton** (b. 1931; Figure 12–6) of the Ontario Crippled Children's Centre started working with Blissymbolics. She assembled a multidisciplinary team of professionals and instructed them on how to use the Bliss symbol system to facilitate the communication of physically disabled children. The symbols were used to communicate general concepts and were combined to form phrases. Bliss symbols were created in 1949 and later revised in 1965 by **Charles K. Bliss** (1897–1985). Bliss was originally interested in developing a simple picture language that would be universal. The system has a specific grammar for organizing and combining symbols (see Figure 12–6).

In the early 1980s, professional associations such as the American Speech-Language-Hearing Association (ASHA) recognized the importance of AAC to the field of speech-language pathology. The association published a position statement in 1981 detailing the justification for AAC as well as its inclusion in the scope of practice for speech-

A

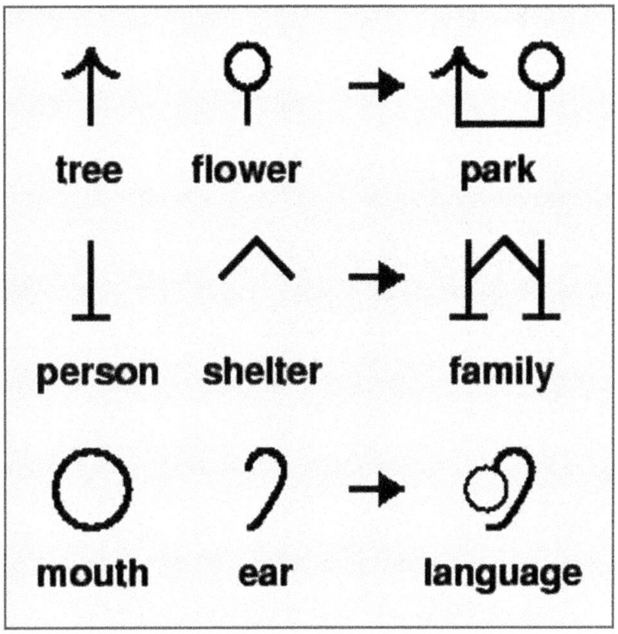

B

Source: Arno Hollosi, CC BY-SA 4.0 <https://creativecommons.org/licenses/by-sa/4.0>, via Wikimedia Commons.

FIGURE 12–6. **A.** Shirley McNaughton applied the Bliss symbol system to the communication of children with physical disabilities. (Permission granted by S. McNaughton.) **B.** Example of Bliss symbols.

language pathologists. During this time, university speech-language pathology programs began offering coursework in AAC as part of students' educational preparation. The field of AAC became organized with the formation of the International Society for Augmentative and Alternative Communication (ISAAC) in 1983. Shirley McNaughton, along with **John Eulenberg**, a computer scientist and linguist, helped to establish ISAAC as an interdisciplinary organization that included engineers, therapists, teachers, researchers, and users. In 1984, ISAAC began publishing the journal *Augmentative and Alternative Communication*, which has since become a primary journal for research concerning assessment, treatment, rehabilitation, and education of people who use or have the potential to use AAC systems.

Clinical, research, and technological advances in AAC continued throughout the 1980s and 1990s. **David Yoder** (1932–2023; Figure 12–7) was a speech-language pathologist who authored numerous articles and book chapters in the area of AAC and supervised several doctoral students. One of his students was **Gregg Vanderheiden** who was interested in the use of technology in the development of AAC systems. He is credited

FYI

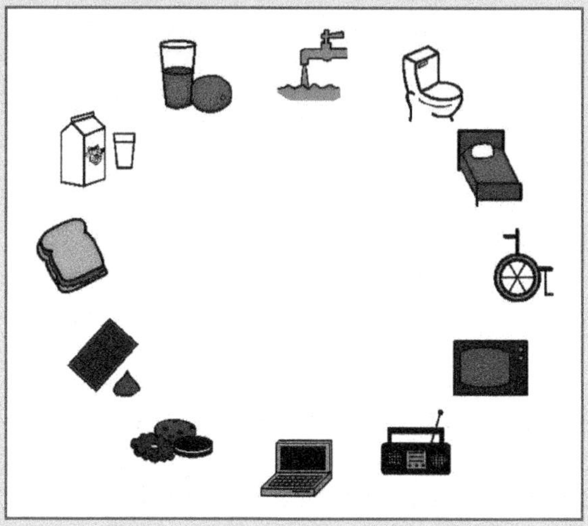

There are many shorthand terms for AAC devices including speech device, speech-generating device, communication device, aug-com device, low-tech device, high-tech device, and communication board. Regardless of the name, AAC enables people to communicate.

FIGURE 12–7. David E. Yoder made important research and clinical contributions to the field of augmentative and alternative communication. (Permission granted by D. Yoder.)

with coining the term *augmentative communication*. Advances in fast computing and cost-effective personal computers led to marked improvement in AAC technology. A variety of commercially available communication devices, including those with automated speech output, led to an era of dedicated AAC devices.

There have been exceptional advances in the past 20 years in the areas of AAC. As a result, the provision of clinical service and the communication outcomes for users of AAC have improved. During this period, one individual who has devoted her career as a researcher and clinician to improving communication outcome for individuals with complex needs is **Janice Light**. Over the course of her career, she has advanced the notion of communicative competence for individuals who require AAC (discussed later in this chapter).

TYPES OF AUGMENTATIVE AND ALTERNATIVE COMMUNICATION

The types or forms of AAC can be broadly organized into two categories: (a) **unaided** and (b) **aided**. The choice of AAC is determined by the person's needs, abilities, and communication environment. These two categories are also defined by the level of technological support required for communication. Most AAC users access a combination of unaided and aided approaches to achieve optimal communication—referred to as **multimodal communication**. It is important to remember that communication is a two-way process (encoding and decoding). So, any exchange involving AAC requires a mutual understanding of the type of communication system between the AAC user and their partner.

Developing and using an effective AAC system can be a time-consuming and complex process for the user and the likely communication partners. Training and practice are needed. An effective AAC system (a) has a high degree of intelligibility, (b) is comprehensible to others, and (c) is efficient. **Intelligibility** is defined as the degree to which a person's natural speech or artificial speech is understood by a communication partner. **Comprehensive** communication refers to the degree to which the user's expressive communication is understood when combined with available relevant information such as the linguistic context, physical environment, gestures, and conversational topic (Beukelman & Light, 2020). The **efficiency** of an AAC system is measured by the time/rate at which the communication is expressed and subsequently comprehended. The efficiency of communication can vary considerably based on the person's physical disability and how slowly or quickly that person interacts with the AAC system.

Unaided Augmentative and Alternative Communication

Unaided forms of AAC consist of nonverbal means of natural communication without the need for an external device. Unaided communication is sometimes referred to as "no-tech" AAC because there is no technological support required. The person uses whatever means is available with their own body. This may include sign language, gestures, eye gaze, facial expressions, and tone of voice. An advantage of unaided AAC is that the technique can be used in any location to supplement the person's existing communication ability. The individual may use a vocalization that is paired with gestures and body movements. A prerequisite for unaided communication is sufficient physical and motor ability to perform the necessary nonverbal movements. This communication also requires the partner to be familiar with the gestures. For example, the user may use eye blinks or subtle head movements to respond "yes" or "no." A limitation of unaided communication is that it requires good motor control to perform the nonverbal gestures, and these gestures must be recognizable to the people with whom the user is engaged.

Aided Augmentative and Alternative Communication

The use of aided AAC involves some form of external device to support communication. Aided AAC devices can be classified according to the general categories of (a) **low technology** and (b) **high technology**. In both forms of aided AAC, the user accesses the device either directly or indirectly (as described earlier).

Low-Technology Augmentative and Alternative Communication

The low-technology form of AAC does not require a power source. Most low-tech AAC systems include boards and books with letters, words, pictures, or specific symbol systems (Blissymbolics). Some examples of low-tech AAC are listed in Table 12–3. The choice of items is based on those things considered most relevant and meaningful. An example of a low-tech AAC aid in the form of a 12-symbol communication board is illustrated in Figure 12–8. Low-tech systems are simple to operate and not prone to technical difficulties. They can also be used as a backup to a person's high-tech AAC system. A limitation of low-tech AAC is that it places emphasis on requesting rather than communicating for a variety of functions.

Table 12–3. Examples of Low-Tech Aided Augmentative and Alternative Communication

• Alphabet displays	• Daily planners
• Picture or word boards	• Small objects
• Photo albums	• Memory books
• Calendars	• Schedules
• Shopping lists	• Timetables
• Labels and signs	

High-Technology Augmentative and Alternative Communication

A wide selection of high-tech AAC devices is available, as well as computer-based communication systems and AAC software. Typically, the user is required to activate a computer-like device that generates speech output to convey the message. These **speech-generating devices** (SGDs) have a voice output that can be either digitized speech or synthesized speech. **Digitized speech** refers to a human voice that has been stored on a computer. The playback of the words and phrases is natural sounding. Some individuals with a degenerative disease who may eventually lose the ability to speak are able to save and digitize samples of their own speech for future use. This procedure is known as **voice banking**. **Synthesized speech** is computer generated according to a set of rules in a mathematical algorithm known as text-to-speech synthesis. Letters and words are combined to form a near-natural-sounding artificial voice. However, not all people who use high-tech AAC want their device to talk and may prefer systems that involve built-in symbol sets for communication.

The design of a high-tech system is either dedicated or open. A **dedicated system** is one that has been created exclusively for communication—the only thing it does is speak. An **open system** is one that is multifunctional (e.g., tablet or handheld device). Not only does the system

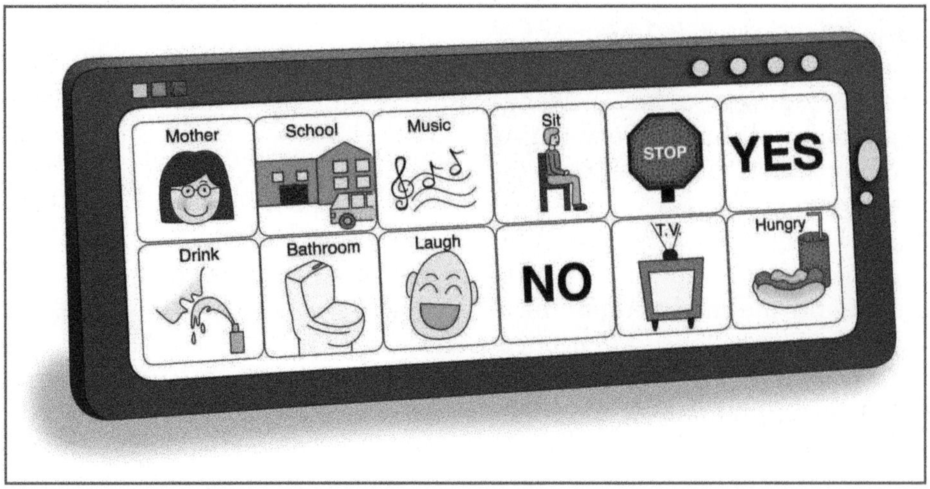

FIGURE 12–8. Simplified example of a low-technology augmentative and alternative communication device for individuals who are unable to use speech as a sole means of communication.

speak, but it also has all the functions of a regular computer (e.g., e-mail, word processing, web surfing). An example of a dedicated high-tech AAC device is provided in Figure 12–9. An advantage of high-tech AAC devices is that they are customizable and have the potential for large vocabulary and more dynamic communication. A disadvantage is that they can be quite expensive compared to low-tech AAC devices.

> **FYI**
>
> Users of AAC have been the subject of several films. Christy Brown, who could use only his left foot and toes to communicate, was featured in the movie *My Left Foot* (1989). Jean-Dominique Bauby, who communicated by blinking his left eyelid, was profiled in the movie *The Diving Bell and the Butterfly* (2008). The biography of Stephen Hawking, who communicated using his facial muscles, was the focus of the movie *The Theory of Everything* (2014).

Visual Display and Tracking

Users of an AAC system are reliant on their visual skills to access symbols for communication. The design of communication boards can vary greatly. The number, size, color, and spacing between symbols all require visual processing skills. Until recently, the visual processing skills of AAC users have either been overlooked or taken for granted. One aspect of visual processing currently being examined concerns the user's visual tracking abilities. Thistle and Wilkinson (2017) examined visual tracking speed and accuracy of a group of non-AAC users for varying symbol arrangements and colors. The researchers found that factors related to symbol size and color greatly affect visual processing, which has implications for the design of AAC systems. Research of this nature is important for assisting individuals with severe disabilities who need an opportunity to express themselves and be a part of mainstream society.

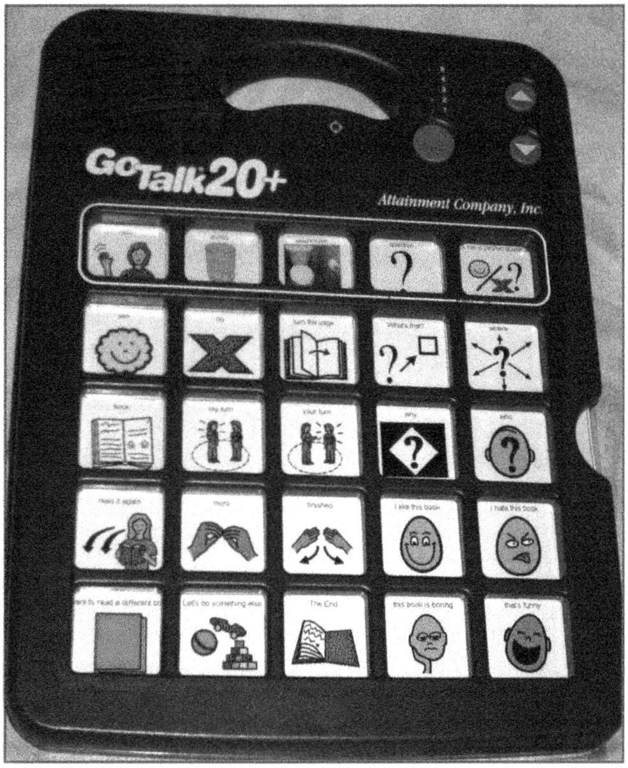

Source: Poule at English Wikipedia, CC BY-SA 3.0 <https://creativecommons.org/licenses/by-sa/3.0>, via Wikimedia Commons.

FIGURE 12–9. Example of lightweight and portable high-technology augmentative and alternative communication device.

ASSESSMENT OF AUGMENTATIVE AND ALTERNATIVE COMMUNICATION

The process of assessing an individual potential use of an AAC can be time consuming. The outcome of an assessment is to recommend an AAC system and design treatment that will assist the individual in achieving the most effective interactive communication possible (ASHA, 2023). The AAC assessment is not a single "one-off" session but is likely to occur over an extended period of time, during which several unaided and aided approaches might be tried. The assessment should address the following questions: (a) What is the cause of the person's communication disorder? (b) How does the person communicate at present? (c) Is the person able to communicate effectively using natural speech? If not, what is the best way for a person to communicate? (d) What are the person's communication needs? (e) What kind of AAC system is most appropriate to match the person's cognitive, physical, and linguistic strengths? and (f) Can the AAC system be modified in the future to keep up with the client's needs?

Seeking input from a range of disciplines is helpful when performing an AAC assessment. The team of individuals assembled varies depending on the communicative, physical (motor, hearing, vision), and cognitive characteristics of the client. In most cases, the team includes the caregiver/partner, the family physician, and a speech-language pathologist. It is not unusual for a physiotherapist, occupational therapist, and teacher to provide input as well. The speech-language pathologist is usually the team leader for the assessment because this professional most likely will continue to work with the AAC user once the appropriate system has been identified. Lloyd (2004) reported the following reasons an AAC assessment is different from a typical speech and language pathology assessment:

- Assessment instruments (tests) may need to be adapted, and the individual may require being given extra support.
- Assessments take a long time to complete and are ongoing.
- Assessments involve a whole team working together.
- Assessments place greater emphasis on communicative competence than on specific language skills.
- Assessments place heightened emphasis on environments and communication partners.
- Assessments include physical and sensory abilities.

Selection of an AAC approach is based on the needs of the individual. Beukelman and Light (2020) referred to this as the **Communication Needs Model**, where the AAC assessment seeks to identify an individual's relevant unmet needs for communication. Some of the more specific points of an assessment to consider are listed in Table 12–4. Recommendation of an AAC system needs to be based on objective and subjective evidence gathered during the evaluation. Because communication devices come in many different shapes and sizes and offer so many functions, receiving a proper evaluation is essential prior to selecting a device. A successful assessment is one that results in matching an AAC approach to the person's wants, needs, and capabilities.

> **FYI**
>
> It would be a mistake to equate using an AAC device with low intelligence. If someone is using an AAC device, it does not mean the individual is unintelligent or cannot understand what somewhat is saying. In many cases, it is just the opposite.

TREATMENT OF AUGMENTATIVE AND ALTERNATIVE COMMUNICATION

Once a decision is made regarding the ideal type of AAC approach to be used for an individual, the next step is to help the individual obtain communication success. Time should be spent training the individual in the unaided or aided AAC approach/device. This training should also involve the family, caregivers, and other professionals in the immediate environment. The treatment plan focuses on communication effectiveness. As noted earlier, effective AAC communication encompasses intelligibility, comprehensibility, and efficiency. Whenever possible, treatment should take place in a naturalistic environment in order to promote generalization. ASHA (2023) has recommended that once initial training on the approach/device has been established for functional communication, intervention should move toward incorporating use of the AAC system into a naturalistic environment and using the system to address broader communication goals such as language and literacy development and social interaction.

Effective AAC use should allow an individual to be an independent communicator. This does not mean the person no longer relies on unaided or aided AAC. Rather, independent communication permits the AAC user to interact with familiar and

Table 12–4. Example Areas to Consider in an Augmentative and Alternative Communication Assessment

Physical and social skills of AAC user • Senses (vision, hearing, touch, smell, taste) • Physical (mobility, dexterity, vocalization) • Intellectual ability (memory, language comprehension/expression, attention span) • Literacy skills (reading, writing, mathematics) • Personality (likes, dislikes) • Self-advocacy skills (self-esteem, assertiveness) • Social networks • Personal history, plans, aspirations • Previous intervention
Questions to ask AAC user • Ability to say "yes" and "no" • Communicate in everyday settings • Effectively signal a protest or rejection of something or someone • Request an object, action, or assistance • Express emotion in response to various situations • Comment or express an opinion
Skills of communication partner • Opportunities for shared interaction with AAC user • Opportunities to support choice making of AAC user • Able to acknowledge and respond to AAC user's attempts to communicate • Talking about activities and routines with the AAC user • Able to modify communication style to match the AAC user's skills

Note. AAC = augmentative and alternative communication.
Source: Adapted from Beukelman & Light (2020).

unfamiliar people. There are several models regarding approaches and techniques to guiding the AAC user to become an independent communicator. Two models—(a) the Participation Model and (b) the Communicative Competence Model—are presented next. Both models share the same goal of developing independent communication.

Participation Model

The **Participation Model**, proposed by Beukelman and Light (2020), is a functional intervention based on the person's participation requirements, particularly in relation to their same-age peers who do not require AAC. The goal of treatment is for the user of AAC to communicate easily with their peers. Treatment stresses communication opportunity and communication access, both of which must be addressed for individuals to participate fully in their lives. An important feature of the Participation Model is the creation of a participation inventory that identifies the person's communication patterns and needs. This is likely to include a list of regularly occurring activities that the individual participates in at school, at home, or in other environments. As part of the inventory, the current and desired level of independence is identified as well as any barriers that may interfere with communication.

Communicative Competency Model

Over 30 years ago, Janice Light (1989) used the term **communicative competency** to refer to the treatment goal for users of AAC. The phrase was defined as "the state of being functionally adequate in daily communication and of having sufficient knowledge, judgment, and skills to communicate effectively in daily life" (p. 138). To achieve communicative competency in the use of AAC, the individual needs to develop knowledge, judgment, and skills in four domains: operational, strategic, linguistic, and social. An example of treatment goals addressing these domains for an AAC user is shown in Table 12–5.

Operational Competence

To be a successful AAC user, the individual should attain competency in operating the device/system. Operational competency encompasses the cognitive and motor skills required to access the features of the device/system. Operational competency includes learning to use signs and gestures, accurately accessing (e.g., pointing, scanning) low-tech and high-tech devices, as well as being able to care for and maintain devices and materials.

Strategic Competence

The domain of strategic competence refers to mastering strategies to overcome limitations and barriers encountered during communicating. These limitations and barriers may occur due to the particular environment or communication partner, such as a partner who may not be familiar with the AAC system. There may also be limitations in the vocabulary available on the device that get in the way of effective communication. In cases like this, the AAC user needs to have the flexibility to adapt their communicative style to suit the environment or communication partner.

Linguistic Competence

The user of an AAC system/approach must possess adequate expressive and receptive language skills to communicate in various environments and with various partners. This includes both written and spoken language. Additionally, the individual should have sufficient skills to access language using more than one AAC system/approach.

Social Competence

The person who uses an AAC system needs to learn how to use the system/approach to engage in effective social interactions. This encompasses the skills used in typical day-to-day speaking, such as conversational turn-taking, topic maintenance, and expression of various emotions and opinions. Inter-

Table 12–5. Example of Augmentative and Alternative Communication Treatment Goals According to a Communicative Competency Framework

Competency	*Goal*
Linguistic	Use grammatically correct sentences with high-tech AAC system
Operational	Learn how to digitally pre-store frequently used requests on AAC system
Social	Express an idea or an opinion when presented with options
Strategic	Learn when to be "fast" versus "careful" when using AAC system

Note. AAC = augmentative and alternative communication.

personal communication is an important feature of social competence that carries over to the creation and maintenance of relationships with others.

CULTURAL CONSIDERATIONS AND AUGMENTATIVE AND ALTERNATIVE COMMUNICATION

Individuals with severe expressive communication disorders are found in every culture. Accordingly, individuals of all cultural groups may be among those who use AAC. Therefore, it is necessary to obtain information about culturally appropriate service delivery to AAC users needing speech-language services. Speech-language pathologists have their own set of values and belief systems, and these may dominate decision-making processes related to AAC devices. Not all individuals who use AAC will share the same attitudes, knowledge, and beliefs as the speech-language pathologist. The first step for the speech-language pathologist is to be aware of their own cultural practices and then to take the clients' social and cultural factors into consideration when conducting AAC assessments. The views of the individual and family members of an AAC user are an important factor in the development of a suitable communication system. The speech-language pathologist must recognize the clients' social and cultural factors and how the client's impairment has affected these domains. This assessment process includes observing the client in multiple contexts and with various communication partners.

The selection of unaided and aided forms of AAC, as well as the choice of symbols and manner of interaction, need to be considered from the cultural perspective of the client. For example, individuals may be culturally sensitive to the ways emotions are expressed in AAC. Therefore, it is important to consider culturally appropriate graphic symbol selection. The software and language representation of an AAC-aided system should also support diversity and divergent thinking among AAC users. This accommodation could require programming AAC devices to have a voice output that matches the dialect of the user's environment. Unfortunately, for some individuals from diverse cultural backgrounds, there is a mismatch between the device and the user, which creates a barrier rather than an aid to communication. Having a clear understanding of family members' values, beliefs, child-rearing practices, parent–child interaction styles, interpersonal styles, attitudes, and behaviors can help professionals remove barriers to culturally sensitive practice. If culturally diverse families and their family members who use AAC are not getting their needs met, the result may be abandonment of the AAC device (Kulkarni & Parmar, 2017).

There are also important considerations when working with clients who are bilingual and AAC users. Identifying a client's true communicative abilities and needs in two languages is a challenge. One of the primary barriers to using an AAC device as a functional tool is the language chosen for the device. Ward et al. (2023) recommended that when considering the language system of the device, it is important that it is programmed with culturally relevant and functional vocabulary across settings (i.e., school/academic setting versus home environment).

SUMMARY OF CHAPTER

In cases of significant neurological impairment, some individuals have minimal or no physical capacity to produce intelligible speech. These individuals may also have impairments in the ability to move other parts of their body that prevent them from using another form of communication. AAC may be recommended by the speech-language pathologist. Examples of AAC include sign language, pictures, symbols, gestures, and SGDs. The aim of AAC is to achieve the most effective communication possible for the individual to meet the challenges of everyday communication. The outcome of an assessment is to recommend an AAC system and design a treatment that will assist the individual in achieving effective and interactive communication. Selection of an AAC approach is based on the needs of the individual. Time should be spent training the individual in the unaided or aided AAC approach/device. This training should also involve the family members and other professionals in the immediate environment. Individuals of all cultural groups may be among those who use AAC, so it is important for the speech-language pathologist to ensure culturally appropriate service delivery.

AUGMENTATIVE AND ALTERNATIVE COMMUNICATION ON THE WORLD WIDE WEB

Following are websites that provide further information on the topic of AAC disorders. At the time of publication, each website was freely accessible.

Basics of AAC
https://www.youtube.com/watch?v=hWefkLfeGv4

AAC Devices
https://www.hopebridge.com/blog/what-is-an-aac-device-for-communication/

https://www.speechandlanguagekids.com/teach-your-child-to-use-an-aac-device/

Picture and Symbol Systems
http://www.everyonecommunicates.org/methods/symbols.html

https://www.isaac-online.org/english/home

AAC Evaluation Genie
https://apps.apple.com/us/app/aac-evaluation-genie/id541418407

STUDY QUESTIONS

1. What is AAC, and how is it used to assist individuals with a communication disorder?
2. What are important considerations in the development of an AAC system?
3. What are the major types of AAC systems?
4. What is communicative competency, and how does this concept apply to an AAC user?
5. Who are some of the pioneers in the area of AAC, and what were their contributions?

REFERENCES

American Speech-Language-Hearing Association. (2023). *Augmentative and alternative communication.* https://www.asha.org/public/speech/disorders/aac

Antonino Naro, M. D., Bramanti, P., Simona Portaro, M. D., & Calabrò, R. S. (2019). Augmentative and alternative communication improves quality of life in the early stages of amyotrophic lateral sclerosis. *Functional Neurology, 34*(1), 35–43.

Beukelman, D., & Light, J. (2020). *Augmentative and alternative communication: Supporting children and adults with complex communication needs* (5th ed.). Paul H. Brookes.

Enderby, P., Pickstone, C., John, A., Fryer, K., Cantrell, A., & Papaioannou, D. (2013). *Resource manual for commissioning and planning services for SLCN.* https://www.rcslt.org/about/docs/slcn_resource_manual

Kulkarni, A., & Parmar, J. (2017). Culturally and linguistically diverse student and family perspectives of AAC. *Augmentative and Alternative Communication, 33,* 170–180.

Light, J. (1989). Toward a definition of communicative competence for individuals using augmentative and alternative communication systems. *Augmentative and Alternative Communication, 5,* 137–144.

Light, J., & McNaughton, D. (2012). The changing face of augmentative and alternative communication: Past, present, and future challenges. *Augmentative and Alternative Communication, 28,* 197–204.

Lloyd, L. L. (2004, November). *What students should know about AAC.* Presentation at the ASHA Convention, Philadelphia, PA.

Thistle, J., & Wilkinson, K. (2017). Effects of background color and symbol arrangement cues on construction of multisymbol messages by young children without disabilities: Implications for aided AAC design. *Augmentative and Alternative Communication, 33,* 160–169.

Vicker, B. (1974). *University Hospital School nonoral communication system project 1964–1973.* University of Iowa.

Ward, H., King, M., & Soto, G. (2023). Augmentative and alternative communication services for emergent bilinguals: Perspectives, practices, and confidence of speech-language pathologists. *American Journal of Speech-Language Pathology, 32*(3), 1212–1235.

13

GENETICS AND SYNDROMES

OBJECTIVES

After reading this chapter, the student should be able to:

- Demonstrate a fundamental knowledge of the biological aspects of genetics that impact the process of normal human development.
- Demonstrate a fundamental knowledge of the terminology pertaining to genetics.
- Understand the historical aspects of genetics.
- Describe various genetic and chromosomal syndromes, and the respective impacts on various aspects of hearing and speech-language development.
- Demonstrate knowledge related to genetic counseling and genetic testing.
- Describe various forms of treatment for genetic conditions.
- Understand the relationship between ethnicity and genetic disorders.

KEY TERMS

Genetics	Zaccharias Janssen	Hypertelorism
Syndrome	Robert Hooke	Gene Mutation
Cell	Cytology	Teratogenic
Nucleus	Charles Darwin	Craniosynostosis
Chromosomes	Alfred Wallace	Louis Octave Crouzon
Wilhelm Waldeyer	Gregor Mendel	Craniectomy
Deoxyribonucleic Acid (DNA)	Thomas Hunt Morgan	Fetal Alcohol Spectrum Disorder (FASD)
Genes	Nettie Maria Stevens	Fetal Alcohol Syndrome (FAS)
Proteomics	James Watson	Alcohol-Related Neurodevelopmental Disorder
Centromere	Francis Crick	Genetic Counseling
Metacentric Chromosome	Congenital Anomaly	Whole Genome Sequencing
Submetacentric Chromosome	Gene Splicing	Prenatal Diagnosis
Acrocentric Chromosome	Chromosomal Syndromes	Ultrasound
Genome	Genetic Syndromes	Neural Tube Defects
Human Genome Project	Mosaicism	Spina Bifida
Heredity	Down Syndrome	Anencephaly
Genotype	John Langdon Down	Amniocentesis
Phenotype	Jerome Lejeune	Chorionic Villus Sampling
Karyotype	Hypotonia	Ethnicity
Particulate Theories	Cri du Chat syndrome	
	Microcephaly	
	Micrognathia	

INTRODUCTION

The term **genetics** refers to "life" or the "beginning." The field of human genetics is concerned with inheritance of traits. We often see family traits in various generations of family, such as facial features or body shape and size. By closely studying these traits, particularly those that may impact normal healthy functioning, we are able to answer questions about human nature, understand various diseases, and develop effective treatments for diseases. Aside from disorders resulting from physical injury, most communication disorders are genetically based. Many functional (or idiopathic) communication disorders are thought to have some form of genetic basis. For years, communication disorders have been viewed as complex disorders that are caused by the interaction of many genes. Recently, the trend in genetics has been to study families with a history of specific communication disorders. This approach is designed to identify a gene sequence or regions on a chromosome that may be unique to the disorder. Language impairment, stuttering, speech sound disorders, hearing impairment, and dyslexia are all primary communication disorders that have a genetic component. Although not all instances of these disorders are a direct cause of genetic inheritance, the search is on for identifying the primary causal genes for primary communication disorders (Den Hoed & Fisher, 2020). This is quite possibly the most popular area of research currently taking place in the fields of audiology and speech-language pathology. It is important for audiologists and speech-language pathologists to understand the rules of inheritance and the means of preventing genetic disorders (Gerber, 2011; Shprintzen, 1997).

A **syndrome** refers to a distinct group of symptoms that together are characteristic of a specific disorder or disease. For example, the common cold is a familiar syndrome, having symptoms such as a runny nose, cough, and fever (Gerber, 2011). A wide range of syndromes have communication disorders as a prevailing symptom. These syndromes are linked to a genetic abnormality. Although speech-language pathologists and audiologists are not qualified to render a genetic diagnosis, they are required to diagnose the type of speech problem or exact nature of hearing loss. Therefore, these professionals need to be aware of the way various genetic conditions can affect features of speech and hearing. The purpose of this chapter is to introduce the field of genetics and the influence of genetic-based syndromes on communication disorders. There is a long list of syndromes showing speech, language, hearing, and cognitive impairments, some of which are quite rare. The focus of this chapter is on selective syndromes that an audiologist or speech-language pathologist may encounter during their professional careers.

TERMINOLOGY AND DEFINITIONS

Prior to presenting features of various syndromes, it is necessary to provide a refresher on the terms and concepts related to human genetics. Life begins with a **cell**, which is the smallest unit of living matter. The human body comprises 100 trillion cells in many shapes and sizes. Inside the body of the cell sits the **nucleus**, which is a vast storehouse of biochemical information. Within the nucleus reside **chromosomes**. The term *chromosome* means "colored body" from *chroma* (meaning "color") and *soma* (meaning "body"). The term originated from the observation by the German anatomist **Wilhelm Waldeyer** (1836–1921; Figure 13–1), who in 1888 found that the material composing chromosomes could be observed in clear detail following staining for microscopic examination. Chromosomes are found in every cell of the body except for red blood cells, which do not contain a nucleus. Red blood cells are specially adapted to carry oxygen around the body. Each chromosome contains two very long coiled strings of **deoxyribonucleic acid (DNA)**. **Genes** are located on these DNA strings. They are the functional units of heredity that occupy a very specific place on a chromosome and have two functions: (a) they contain the basic set of instructions for putting together an organism; and (b) they regulate the function, growth, and development of an organism after birth. Genes carry information for making all the proteins required by all organisms. These proteins determine, among other things, how the organism looks, how well its body metabolizes food or fights infection, and sometimes even how it behaves. There are approximately 20,000 genes distributed among the chromosomes of the human body. Amazingly, only 2% of the DNA string contains genes. The remaining 98% of the material composing the string was once referred to as "junk DNA" because it appeared to consist of meaningless sequences. However, research is

FIGURE 13–1. Wilhelm Waldeyer, German anatomist who discovered chromosomes.

slowly unraveling the function of this remaining DNA. A future area of genetics research lies in further understanding the nature of junk DNA proteins and how they work to create an individual person. This new and burgeoning scientific field is known as **proteomics**. The basic genetic template of a cell is shown in Figure 13–2. The entire DNA of an organism, including its genes, is called the **genome**. Knowledge about the effects of DNA variations among individuals can lead to new ways to diagnose, treat, and even prevent thousands of genetic disorders.

Normal human cells contain 46 chromosomes that exist in 23 pairs. Not all species have the same number of chromosomes. For example, cats have 38 chromosomes, and fish have 78 chromosomes. Among the 46 chromosomes found in humans, 23 chromosomes are received from each parent. The number assigned to the first 22 pairs is related to chromosome length. Chromosome pair 1 is longest and contains the most genetic material. Chromosome pair 22 is the shortest. Chromosome 23 designates sex. Among females, the 23rd chromosome pairing is known as XX. The male body contains two types of sex chromosomes known as XY. The Y chromosome of the 23rd chromosome, although designating the male sex, is also found to contain the least amount of genetic material across the entire set of 46 chromosomes. Males produce both X- and Y-bearing sperm. Sex is determined by the male, depending on whether an X-bearing sperm or Y-bearing sperm joins with the female X chromosome. When the egg and sperm join at the time of conception, they form a single-cell embryo called a zygote.

Each chromosome consists of two strands that resemble an "X" in structural appearance. The point at which the two strands cross is called the **centromere**. An individual chromosome can be further described regarding the location of the centromere. A **metacentric chromosome** has a centromere in the approximate center, a **submetacentric chromosome** has a centromere that is slightly off center, and an **acrocentric chromosome** has a centromere that is near the tip of the chromosome. The top two arms of each chromosome are called the short arms or the p-arms. The letter "p" is in reference to the word *petite*, which is the French word for "small." The lower two

FYI

The number of chromosomes varies considerably across living organisms. Among animals, the mosquito is low on the list with 6 in total, cats have 38, and the hermit crab tops in at 254. Among plants, hawkweed has 8 chromosomes per cell, and ferns have 1,200 chromosomes.

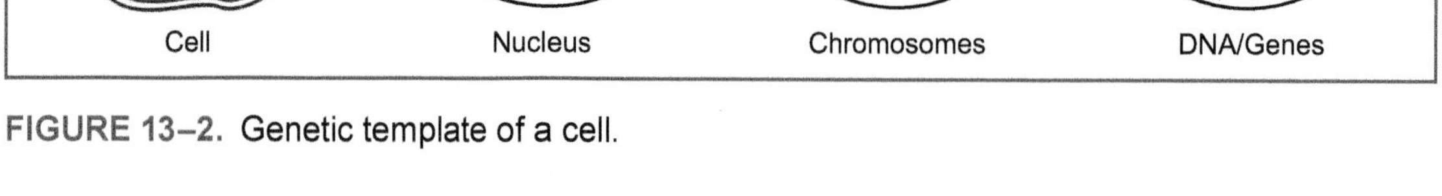

FIGURE 13–2. Genetic template of a cell.

arms are called the long arms or q-arms. The letter "q" is in reference to the word *queue*, which is the word meaning "a long line of people." Examples of various chromosome shapes are displayed in Figure 13–3.

Heredity is the genetic transmission of characteristics from parent to offspring. The term **genotype** refers to the genetic variation that separates one individual from another. No two individuals have the same genotype. But you might ask, do identical twins have the same genotype? The answer is yes and no. The answer is yes, if we consider that identical twins have the same DNA because they come from a fertilized egg cell (zygote) that gets split in half. But the answer is also no, because even though identical twins may have the same DNA, their genes are in different bodies. Alone, DNA does nothing—it is like a book sitting on a shelf. It sits there until someone (or something, like a protein) comes along to read it and assemble the information (i.e., to create a person). The way a protein interprets the gene can vary, which is why identical twins may have different fingerprints and even look different. This is because their bodies are taking the same DNA and using it in different ways. The physical expression of genetic variation (i.e., traits) is referred to as **phenotype**. The complete set of chromosomes for an individual is referred to as the **karyotype**. An example of the karyotype for a female and male is provided in Figure 13–4. Note that the most obvious difference in karyotype is related to chromosome 23, which is the sex chromosome.

HISTORIC ASPECTS OF GENETICS

A timeline of major events that shaped the field of genetics is displayed in Table 13–1. Some of the more profound events are detailed in this section. From the earliest recorded history, ancient civilizations observed patterns in reproduction. Animals bore offspring of the same species, children resembled their parents, and plants gave rise to similar plants. Some of the earliest ideas about reproduction, heredity, and the transmission of information from parent to child were the **particulate theories** developed in ancient Greece during the fourth century BC. These theories posited that information from each part of the parent had to be somehow transmitted to create the corresponding body part in the offspring. For example, the particulate theories held that information from the parent's heart, lungs, and limbs was transmitted directly from these body parts to create the offspring's heart, lungs, and limbs.

One reason particulate theories were inaccurate was that they relied on observations unaided by the microscope. The microscope was invented around 1600 by a Dutch spectacle maker, **Zacharias Janssen** (1580–1638). The English naturalist **Robert Hooke** (1635–1703) was the first to use this device to identify plant cells, specifically the cell walls in cork tissue. Hooke coined the term *cells*. The boxlike shape of cells in cork reminded him of the cells of a monastery. Over the next century,

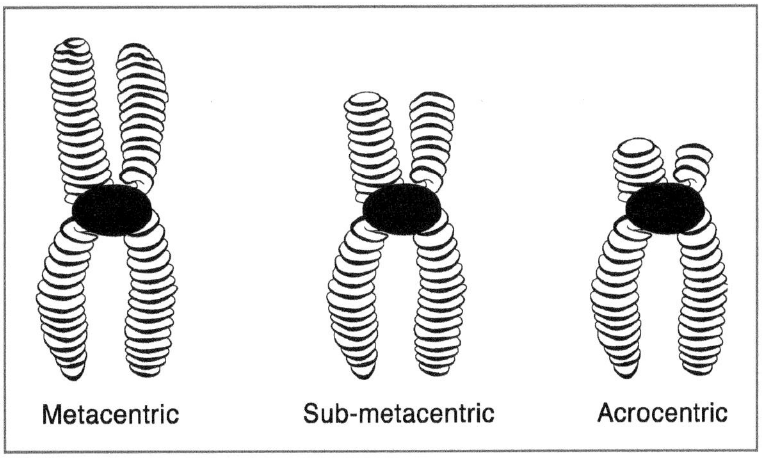

FIGURE 13–3. The various shapes of chromosomes.

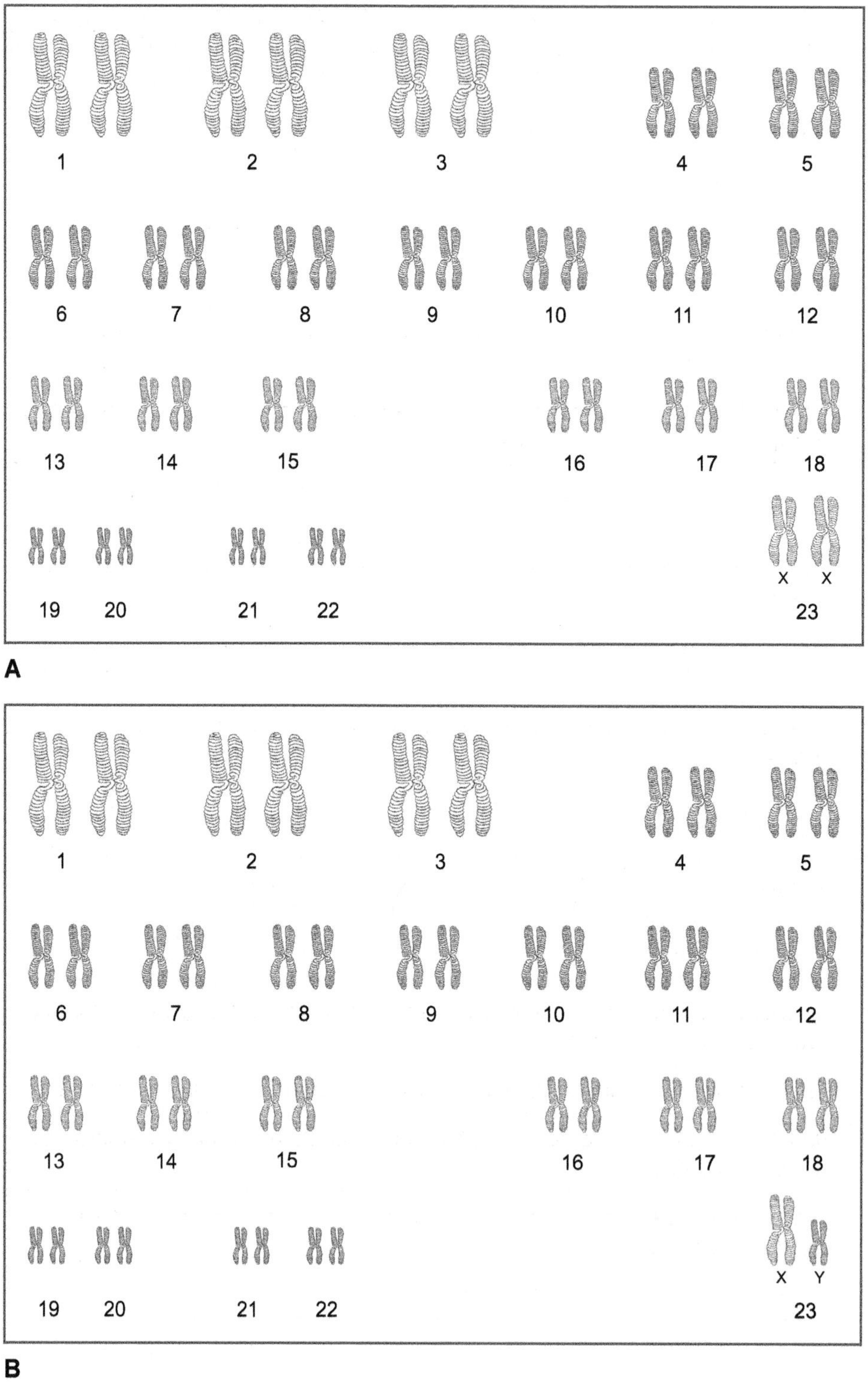

FIGURE 13–4. **A.** Female karyotype. **B.** Male karyotype. Note the obvious difference in pairing of the 23rd (sex) chromosomes.

improvements in microscopy and the increasing study of **cytology** (i.e., the formation, structure, and function of cells) enabled scientists to identify parts of the cell.

One of the most important developments in the study of hereditary processes came in 1858, when **Charles Darwin** (1809–1882) and **Alfred Wallace** (1823–1913) announced the theory of nat-

Table 13–1. Some Milestones in the Field of Genetics

Year	*Event*
1590	The microscope is invented by Zacharias Janssen.
1858	Charles Darwin announces the theory of natural selection.
1863	Studying peas, Gregor Mendel discovers that traits are transmitted from parents by discrete units, later known as genes. His observations laid the groundwork for the field of genetics.
1869	Johann Friedrich Miescher discovers DNA in human white blood cells and in the sperm of trout.
1879	Walther Fleming discovers chromatin, the rod-like structures inside the cell nucleus that are later named chromosomes.
1905	Nettie Stevens and Edmund Wilson independently describe the behavior of sex chromosomes.
1907	Thomas Hunt Morgan's work on *Drosophila* (i.e., the fruit fly) leads to further understanding of genetics.
1953	James Watson and Francis Crick publish their findings describing the double-helical structure of DNA, marking the beginning of the modern era of genetics.
1972	The DNA composition of humans is found to be 99% similar to that of chimpanzees and gorillas.
1983	James Gusella uses blood samples to demonstrate that the Huntington disease gene is on chromosome 4.
1984	The DNA fingerprinting technique is developed.
1990	The first federally approved gene therapy treatment is performed on a 4-year-old girl with an immune disorder.
1996	Discovery of a gene associated with Parkinson disease provides insight as to its cause and potential treatment.
1997	Scottish scientists report cloning a sheep, named Dolly, using DNA from adult sheep cells.
2003	*Human Genome Project* is completed and confirms humans have approximately 20,000–25,000 genes.
2007	Timothy Ray Brown becomes the first person cured from HIV/AIDS through a stem cell transplantation.
2019	England introduces a rapid DNA test to scan for rare diseases in babies and children.

ural selection. The premise of this theory was that members of a population who are better adapted to their environment will be most likely to survive and pass their traits on to the next generation. Darwin published this theory in 1859 in the classic text *On the Origin of Species by Means of Natural Selection*. At the time of publication, Darwin's work was not viewed favorably. Religious leaders believed the theory refuted the biblical interpretation of how life on Earth began. To this day, debate continues regarding evolution and creationism.

During the period of 1856 to 1863, the Austrian **Gregor Mendel** (1822–1884; Figure 13–5) conducted carefully designed genetic experiments with nearly 30,000 pea plants. Mendel was an Augustinian monk who taught natural science to

FIGURE 13–5. Gregor Mendel's genetic experiments with pea plants were designed to test the inheritance of specific traits.

FIGURE 13–6. Nettie Maria Stevens, American biologist who helped prove that chromosomes determine the sex of an organism.

high school students. He chose to study pea pods because they had distinct, identifiable characteristics that could not be confused. He cultivated pea plants in the monastery garden. His experiments were designed to test the inheritance of a specific trait from one generation to the next. For example, to test the inheritance of the characteristic of plant height, Mendel self-pollinated by hand several short pea plants, and the seeds they produced grew into short plants.

In 1907, the American **Thomas Hunt Morgan** (1866–1945) studied *Drosophila* (i.e., the fruit fly) as a means of understanding genetic traits. This research revolutionized the study of genetics because the fly's rapid life cycle and minute size enabled Morgan to undertake many experiments over a short period of time. Contrast the whole year required between generations of peas with the 2 weeks needed for the life span of a fruit fly. Morgan was able to study hundreds of fruit fly characteristics. In addition, he identified gene mutations, such as discovery of some fruit flies having a white-eyed mutation.

Nettie Maria Stevens (1861–1912; Figure 13–6) was an American biologist and geneticist who studied under the guidance of Thomas Hunt Morgan. Based on research with beetles, she helped prove that chromosomes determine the sex of an organism. Prior to this discovery, researchers assumed that the sex of an organism was influenced by food and temperature conditions during the early stages of an organism's development.

The discovery in 1953 of the double-helical structure of DNA marked the beginning of the modern era of genetics. The American anthropologist **James Watson** (b. 1928) and British physicist **Francis Crick** (1916–2004) worked together at the University of Cambridge (Figure 13–7). Many of their findings were based on examination of x-ray diffraction photographs. In 1988, Watson was appointed as head of the **Human Genome Project** at the National Institutes of Health.

TYPES OF SYNDROMES

The term *birth defect* is used as a generalized description of any genetic or nongenetic condition that occurs at birth. The term is not entirely accurate because (a) some abnormalities may not be present at birth and are evident only after the child begins to mature (such as dentition) and (b) the term does not take into account abnormalities of behavior. An example in which both physical and

FIGURE 13–7. James Watson and Francis Crick, discoverers of the double-helical structure of DNA.

behavioral anomalies may not surface until later in a child's development is fetal alcohol syndrome (FAS). The characteristics of FAS are described later in this chapter. A more accurate description of these conditions is **congenital anomaly**.

> FYI
>
> **Gene splicing** is a technique used to join segments of DNA (often from different individuals or species) to form a new genetic combination called recombinant DNA. This is one of the techniques used in genetic engineering.

Syndromes can be broadly classified into two types: (a) chromosomal syndromes and (b) genetic syndromes. **Chromosomal syndromes** involve visible changes in the chromosomal structure (i.e., karyotype) of the individual. These types of syndromes typically result in rather severe anomalies such as physical abnormalities, cognitive impairments, and communication disorders. The reason for severe anomalies is that impairment of chromosomal structure tends to affect many genes. On the other hand, **genetic syndromes** often involve a single affected gene. The outward appearance of chromosomes may seem fine. It is a specific gene that is abnormal. The problems arising from a genetic syndrome can range from mild to severe, depending on the specific gene that is affected.

Chromosomal Syndromes

Approximately 7 out of every 1,000 births is affected by a chromosomal disorder. These disorders account for approximately one half of all spontaneous abortions (i.e., miscarriages) that occur during the first trimester of pregnancy (Gerber, 2011). There are five basic abnormalities that can occur in chromosomal structure: (a) deletion of whole chromosomes, (b) deletion of parts of a chromosome, (c) addition of whole chromosomes, (d) addition of parts of chromosomes, and (e) restructuring (or rearranging) of chromosomes. Most people who have a chromosomal syndrome exhibit the chromosomal abnormality in every cell in the body. However, there are rare cases in which only a portion of the body's cells are affected. This condition is referred to as **mosaicism**. Individuals with mosaicism generally show less severe abnormalities than when all cells are affected. Two examples of chromosomal syndromes that may be accompanied by a communication disorder are Down syndrome and Cri du Chat syndrome.

Down Syndrome

Down syndrome is the most frequently occurring human chromosomal disorder. In this condition, the karyotype is characterized by a chromosomal addition to the 21st chromosome. The condition is referred to as trisomy 21, indicating the karyotype (Figure 13–8). The syndrome was named after **John Langdon Down** (1828–1896), an English physician who published *Observations of an Ethnic*

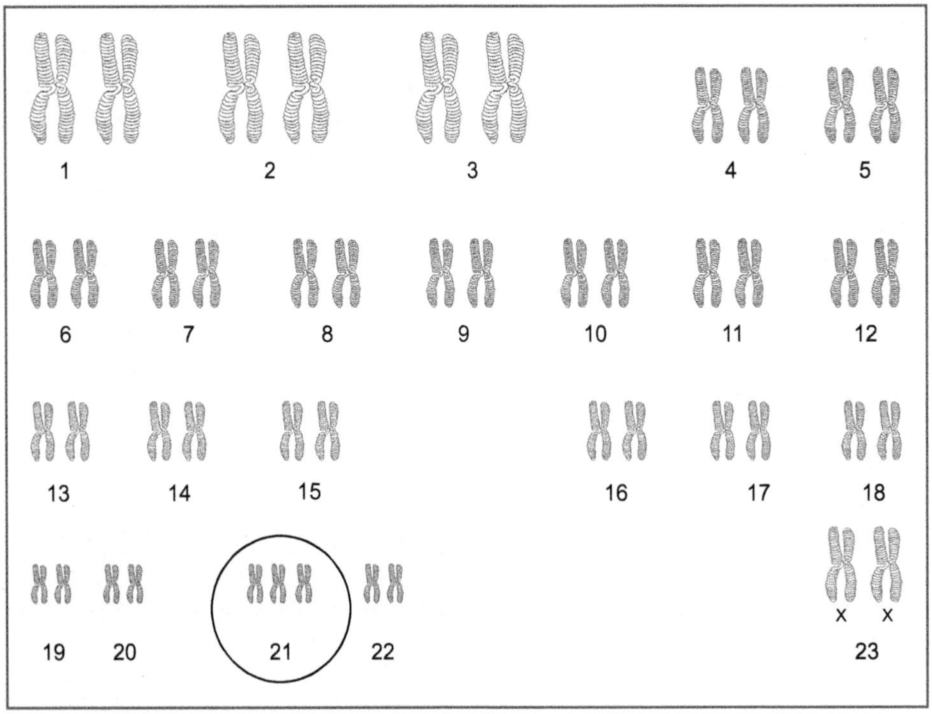

A

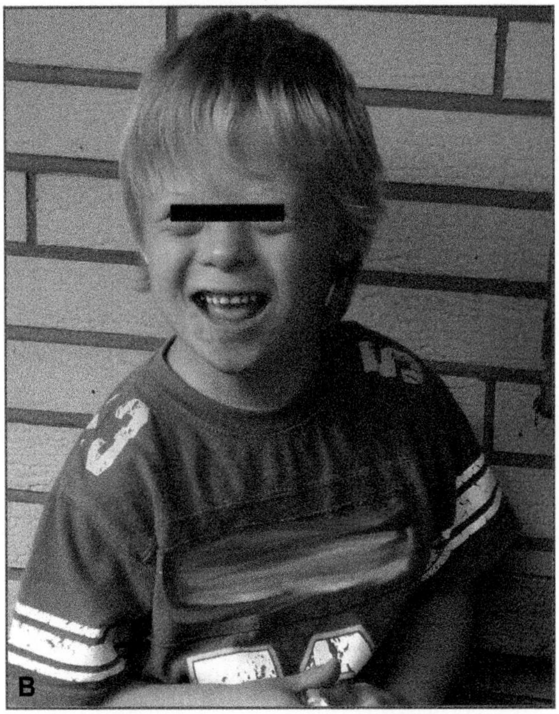

Source: Vanellus Foto, CC BY-SA 3.0 <https://creativecommons.org/licenses/by-sa/3.0>, via Wikimedia Commons.)

FIGURE 13–8. **A.** Down syndrome karyotype. **B.** A boy with Down syndrome.

Classification of Idiots in 1866. He identified a group of patients with similar features and called them mongoloid idiots. The term *idiot* was in common use at the time to describe intellectual impairment; *mongoloid* was in reference to the supposed similarity in appearance to people of East Asia. These days, neither term is socially acceptable. Although Down is credited with identifying the syndrome, the precise chromosomal structure of trisomy 21 was not identified until nearly 100 years later by **Jerome Lejeune** (1926–1994). Down syndrome is found to occur in approximately 1 out of every 800 births. Down syndrome is a chromosomal disorder caused by an error in cell division, and the likelihood of such an error increases with both parents' age (Bull, 2020), meaning that an older parent is more prone to give birth to a child with Down syndrome. The occurrence dramatically increases to 1 out of every 25 births among birthing parents over the age of 45 years (Table 13–2). However, it is important to stress that the combined effect of both parents' ages is a contributing factor. The average life expectancy of an individual with Down syndrome is 55 years of age.

The phenotype of Down syndrome is provided in Table 13–3. Included among these characteristics are heart anomalies, dry skin, fine soft hair, **hypotonia** (i.e., reduced muscle tone), brachycephaly (i.e., a widening of the skull with a flat back of head), Class III malocclusion, protruding tongue, and intellectual disability that is very rarely severe. Males with Down syndrome may also have hypogonadism—a defect of the reproductive system that results in lack of function of the gonads (i.e., sterility) in males. The communication disorder often found in Down syndrome is delayed onset of language. Although these children eventually develop communication skills, the length of utterance and size of vocabulary are reduced and dependent primarily on the severity of intellectual disability. Children with Down syndrome also may show speech articulation difficulties resulting from reduced muscle tone in the oral cavity, combined with dentition irregularities. The hearing abilities of individuals with Down syndrome usually are normal, although children can experience higher than average bouts of otitis media.

Table 13–2. Approximate Occurrence of Down Syndrome Births According to the Birthing Parent's Age

Age of Birthing Parent (years)	*Frequency of Down Syndrome (per births)*
15–19	1/1250
20–24	1/1400
25–29	1/1100
30–32	1/875
33–35	1/500
36–38	1/225
39–41	1/100
42–44	1/50
45+	1/25

Table 13–3. Phenotype of Down Syndrome and Cri du Chat Syndrome

Chromosomal Syndrome	*Phenotype*
Down syndrome	Hypotonia Protruding tongue Brachycephaly Heart anomaly Dry skin Fine soft hair Hypogonadism Obesity Short fifth finger Class III malocclusion Cognitive impairment
Cri du Chat syndrome	High-pitched voice Hypotonia Microcephaly Orbital hypertelorisim Down-slanting eyes Ear tags Small stature Occasional cleft palate Severe cognitive impairment

Cri du Chat Syndrome

Jerome Lejeune (1926–1994) first described Cri du Chat syndrome in 1963. Lejeune was a French pediatrician and geneticist who was also the first to identify the precise chromosomal structure of Down syndrome. Cri du Chat (meaning "cat's cry" in French) syndrome is named for the cat-like cry made by infants with this chromosomal disorder, which is caused by an abnormally small larynx. Cri du Chat syndrome is also called 5p minus (5p–) syndrome because it is caused by a partial deletion (p–) of the short arm of chromosome 5 (Figure 13–9). The syndrome has been estimated

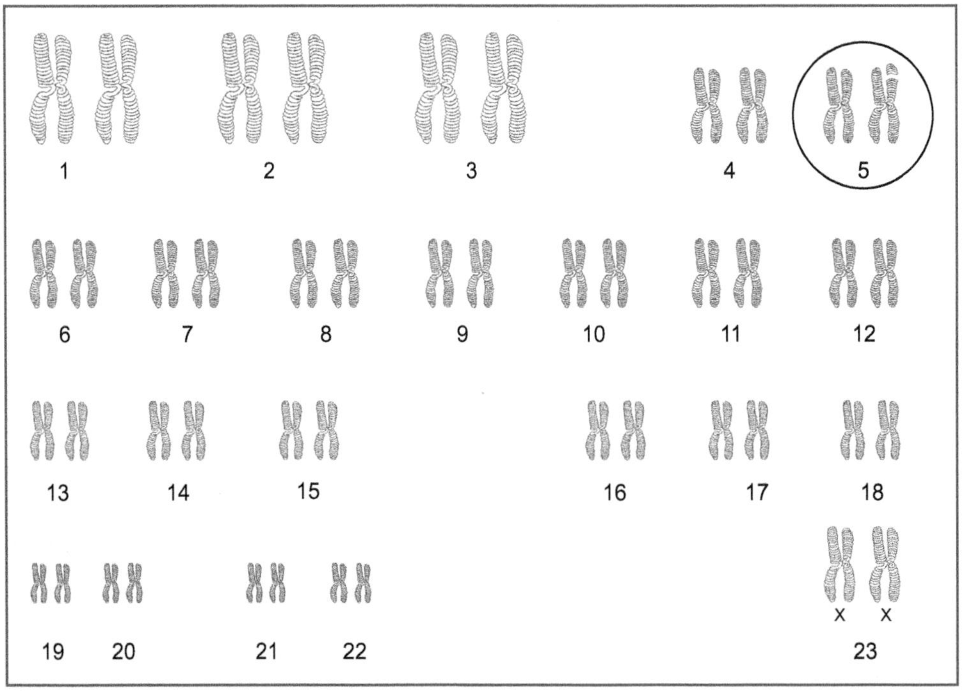

A

B

FIGURE 13–9. **A.** Karyotype of Cri du Chat syndrome. **B.** Ariella at age 6 years. (Photograph used with permission of the Cri du Chat Support Group of Australia.)

to occur in 1 of every 50,000 live births. It accounts for 1 in every 500 cases of intellectual disability. Approximately 50 to 60 children are born with Cri du Chat syndrome in the United States each year.

The syndrome is found to occur in all races and in both sexes. There is a slight female predominance with the ratio of occurrence estimated to be three girls to two boys. At birth, these children may show a failure to thrive because of feeding difficulties; however, those who do survive have a normal life expectancy. Individuals with Cri du Chat syndrome tend to be loving and highly social.

The phenotype of Cri du Chat syndrome is provided in Table 13–3. Individuals with this syndrome have unusual facial features such as downslanting eyes, ear tags (i.e., small flap of skin on front of ear), small head size (i.e., **microcephaly**), small jaw size (i.e., **micrognathia**), and a large distance between the eyes (i.e., **hypertelorism**). The children also demonstrate hypotonia and may be born with a cleft palate. A severe intellectual impairment occurs because of the large deletion of genetic material from the chromosome. In addition to the classic feature of a cat-like cry or high-pitched voice, the voice also may have a nasal quality if the child was born with a cleft palate. As a result of the severe intellectual impairments, development of oral language can be a challenge. A small number of children never learn to speak; however, most can speak and make themselves understood to some degree, which they supplement with both formal and informal gestures. A conductive hearing loss may be present, resulting from persistent otitis media.

Genetic Syndromes

Although genetic syndromes are chromosome based, they are categorized separately. These are conditions that do not have a visible cellular abnormality. Most of these syndromes involve a problem with a single gene known as a **gene mutation**. There are three possible gene mutations: (a) deletion of a gene, (b) addition of a gene, and (c) rearrangement of genes. The human body consists of approximately 20,000 genes, so there are countless possibilities for gene mutations resulting in syndromes. There are over 6,000 genetic diseases, and the list continues to grow (Genetic Disease Foundation, 2023). The problems resulting from genetic syndromes range from mild to severe, depending on the specific gene and type of gene mutation. Some genetic syndromes are inherited and may have been present in past generations of the same family. Inherited genetic syndromes often involve mutation of a single gene. There are also genetic syndromes that fall under the class of **teratogenic** disorders. The term *teratogen* translates literally from its Greek roots meaning "monster maker" (*teratos* = "monster"; *gen* = "life"). Teratogenic disorders are polygenic, meaning more than one gene is likely to be mutated. Four genetic syndromes are covered next. Two genetic-based syndromes that may be accompanied by a communication disorder are Crouzon syndrome and FAS.

Crouzon Syndrome

Crouzon syndrome is a genetic disorder characterized by the premature fusion of certain skull bones (known as **craniosynostosis**). This early fusion prevents the skull from growing normally and affects the shape of the head and face. It is a type of craniofacial syndrome (i.e., one that affects the developmental formation of the skull and face). Crouzon syndrome is caused by mutations in the *FGFR2* gene, which is found on the long arm of chromosome 10 at the location of 10q25-10q26 (Figure 13–10). The gene is associated with growth factors of the face and skull. The condition was first identified in 1912 by **Louis Octave Crouzon** (1874–1938), a French neurosurgeon, through the case of a mother and child, both with Crouzon symptoms. People with Crouzon syndrome are of normal intelligence. The syndrome occurs in 1 out of every 60,000 live births and is the most prevalent form of craniosynostosis syndrome. The condition is readily identifiable at birth because of the observable craniofacial abnormality. There is no difference in occurrence between females and males. Individuals with Crouzon syndrome have a normal life expectancy.

The phenotype of Crouzon syndrome is reflective of the premature fusion of the skull bones (Table 13–4). Abnormal growth of these bones leads to wide-set, bulging eyes and vision problems caused by shallow eye sockets, a beaked nose, and an underdeveloped upper jaw. In addition, people with Crouzon syndrome may have

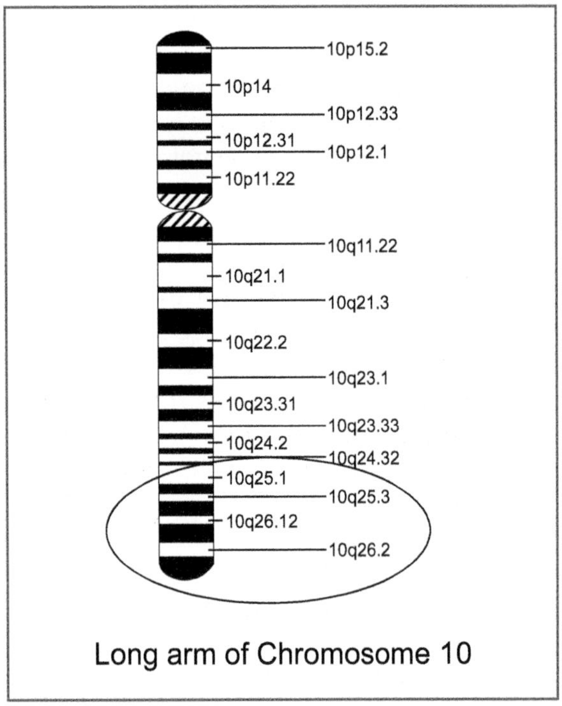

A

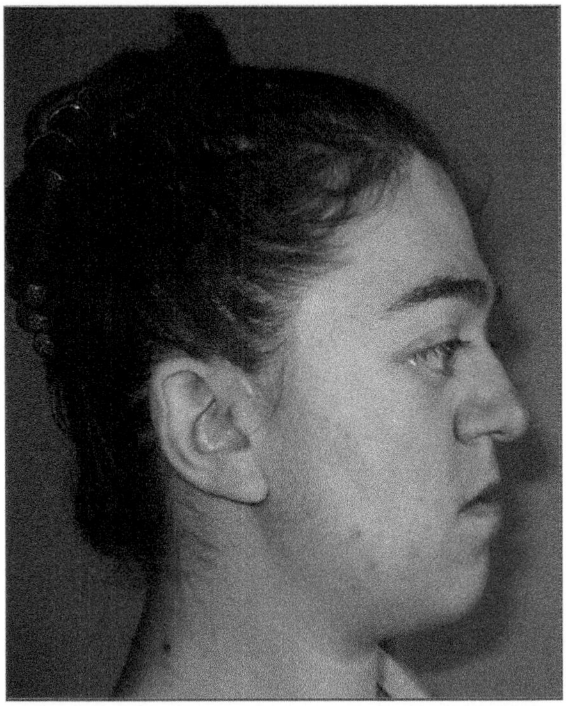

B

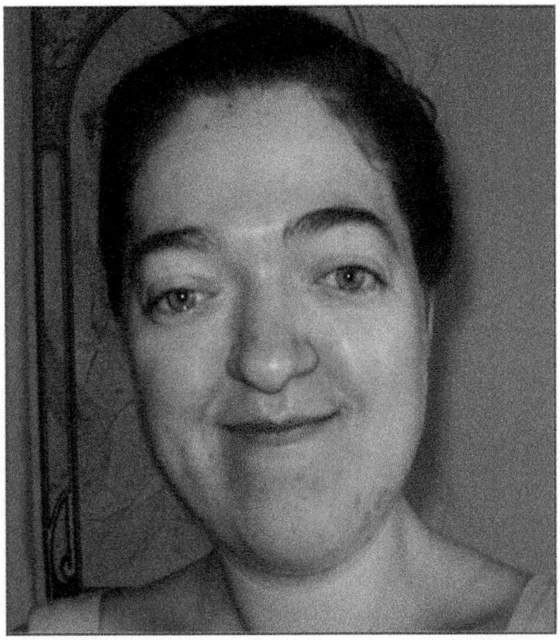

C

FIGURE 13–10. **A.** Crouzon syndrome karyotype. **B** and **C.** Candar at age 24 years. (Photographs used with permission.)

dental problems. Surgery often is necessary to correct some of the craniofacial abnormalities. The skull abnormalities are corrected using a procedure known as a **craniectomy**, which involves surgical opening of the cranium to allow for more natural growth of the brain and skull. Facial reconstruction is performed to correct midface abnormalities. Individuals with Crouzon syndrome develop speech and language normally. If any communication disorders are apparent, they are a result of physical problems related to the skull and face. For example, it is not unusual to observe speech articulation dif-

Table 13–4. Phenotype of Crouzon Syndrome

Genetic Syndrome	*Phenotype*
Crouzon syndrome	Premature fusion of cranial sutures Mid-face hypoplasia (underdeveloped) Beak-shaped nose Exorbitism (bulging eyes) Low-set ears Class III malocclusion Conductive hearing loss Possible otitis media Cognitive impairment is rare

ficulties resulting from a Class III malocclusion. There may be a hyponasal voice quality due to a small nasal port at the back of the throat. Children with this condition are also prone to chronic otitis media as a result of narrow ear canals.

Fetal Alcohol Syndrome

An infant born to a mother who drinks alcohol during her pregnancy, even in modest amounts, may give birth to a baby with **fetal alcohol spectrum disorder**, sometimes known as FASD. The term FASD is an umbrella term for a range of disorders. The most severe form of FASD is **fetal alcohol syndrome** (FAS). The condition of FAS results in growth retardation, unusual physical and facial features, and intellectual impairment. Children have suffered the consequences of their birthing parents' alcohol consumption since people began to drink alcohol. In 1973, the term FAS was coined by Kenneth Jones and David Smith, two pediatric dysmorphologists who described the signs of alcohol exposure in infants at birth and early childhood. FAS is a teratogenic disorder that causes gene mutation. On average, three out of five women drink alcohol. A woman's body metabolizes alcohol more quickly than a man's, and thus women become intoxicated more easily. When pregnant women drink, the developing fetus receives a strong dose of alcohol. The internationally recognized rate of occurrence of FAS is 1 to 3 out of every 1,000 births. In 9 out of every 1,000 births, infants show some (but not all) signs of alcohol exposure. This condition is referred to as **alcohol-related neurodevelopmental disorder** or fetal alcohol effects. It is estimated that 25% to 45% of women with chronic alcoholism give birth to children with FAS if they drink heavily during pregnancy (Table 13–5).

It is difficult to pinpoint the exact gene (or genes) that are affected because the mutation is linked to (a) the amount of alcohol consumed by the birthing parent, (b) the time of pregnancy during which alcohol is consumed, and (c) the likely interaction of alcohol consumption with other drugs. The early months of fetal growth involve development of the face, limbs, heart, and brain. Therefore, pregnant people who drink during the first trimester of pregnancy give birth to children with the most severe problems because their abuse of alcohol occurs during the period when many physical features of the child are developing. This is also a time when many pregnant people may not even realize they are pregnant. Pregnant people who abstain from alcohol in early pregnancy may feel comfortable drinking during the final months of the pregnancy. Yet it is during the last trimester of pregnancy that some of the most complex features of brain development take place. Even moderate alcohol intake, and especially periodic binge drinking, can seriously damage the developing nervous system of the fetus.

Table 13–5. Some Facts About Alcohol Consumption

- A "drink" is defined as a 12 oz. beer, 1.5 oz. shot of 80-proof liquor, or 4 oz. glass of table wine.
- In Canada, New Zealand, the United Kingdom, and the the United States, legally intoxicated is defined as a BAL of 0.08%.
- Permanent brain cell damage begins at a BAL of 0.07%.
- A 100-lb (45-kg) female consuming five standard drinks will reach a BAL of 0.25%, which is three times the legal BAL limit.
- BAL reduces 0.01% per hour.

Note. BAL = blood alcohol level.

FYI

In early 2001, a discovery was made claiming that a specific gene, *FOXP2* (located on chromosome 7), was the primary gene for learning to acquire language. This conclusion was based on genetic examination of a family with a long history of communication disorders. Members of the family showed a mutation of this gene. We now know that this gene, although contributing a major role to communication, is likely one of many genes necessary for regulating speech and language.

FYI

Genetic evidence suggests that some people are "born to smoke." Approximately 20 years ago, researchers found that people who carry the gene *SLC6A3-9*, located on chromosome 5, are less likely to become addicted to cigarette smoking than those without the gene. This specific gene is found to be important for the transfer of the neurotransmitter dopamine, which is a natural stimulant created in the brain. Those without the gene may be more vulnerable to the addictive (i.e., stimulating) effects of tobacco.

An illustration of the phenotype of FAS is provided in Figure 13–11. The phenotype found in 50% (or more) of the cases of FAS include (a) below average height and weight, (b) microcephaly, (c) micrognathia, (d) thin upper lip, (e) hyperactivity, and (f) intellectual impairment. Problems associated with FAS tend to intensify as children move into adulthood. These can include mental health problems, trouble with the law, and the inability to live independently. The communication problems found in FAS include a general overall delay in speech and language development. The child with FAS also may show speech articulation problems and swallowing problems due to poor motor coordination. If a child with FAS has an intellectual impairment, there is likely to be an associated language impairment, the severity of which is dependent on the severity of the intellectual disability. The condition of FAS, and all damage caused by prenatal alcohol exposure, is 100% preventable by

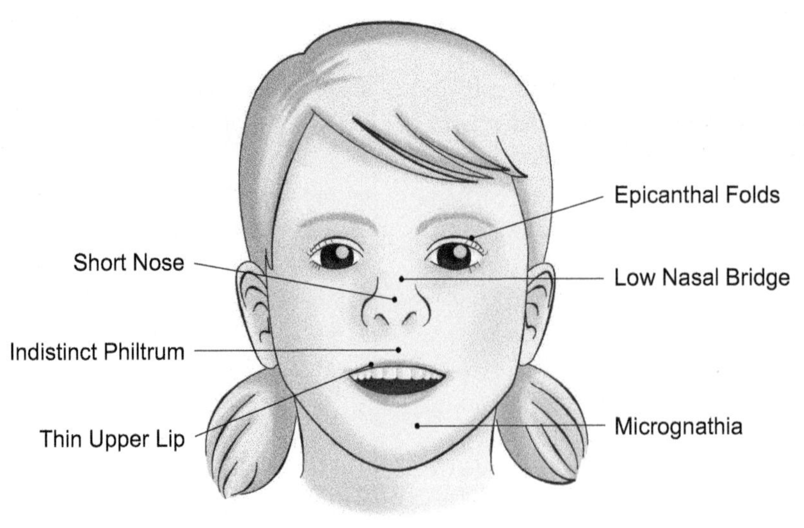

FIGURE 13–11. Phenotype of fetal alcohol syndrome.

simply choosing not to drink alcohol while pregnant. FAS cannot be cured, but the effects of the disabilities can be managed.

ASSESSMENT OF GENETIC CONDITIONS

We are continually learning more about the genetics of various diseases and syndromes, and how these conditions run in families. Two forms of assessment are (a) genetic counseling and (b) prenatal diagnosis. **Genetic counseling** is designed to help a person or family understand the risk for genetic conditions (e.g., Down syndrome), to educate the person or family about the condition, and to assess the risk of passing the condition on to children. Traditionally, a genetic counselor has a master's degree in genetic counseling and has studied genetic diseases and how they run in families. Table 13–6 provides a list of situations whereby a person may wish to seek genetic counseling. A recent trend in genetic counseling is for individuals to undergo **whole genome sequencing**. This is referred to as a form of "personalized" medicine, where a blood or saliva sample is collected and sent to a laboratory for analysis. The analysis provides the genome of the individual, and this information is used to determine whether there are any specific genes (or mutations) that place the person being tested at risk for various diseases. It is important to emphasize that being a carrier of a specific gene does not guarantee that the disease will occur.

Table 13–6. Situations Where It Is Advisable to Seek Genetic Counseling

- Individuals who are concerned they might have an inherited disorder.
- Pregnant people or those planning to be pregnant after the age of 35 years.
- Couples who already have a child with an inherited disorder.
- People who have had three or more miscarriages.
- People who are concerned that their jobs, lifestyles, or medical history may pose a risk to the outcome of pregnancy. Common causes of concern include exposure to radiation, medications, illegal drugs, chemicals, or infections.
- Couples who would like testing or more information about genetic conditions that occur frequently in their ethnic group.
- Couples who are first cousins or other close blood relatives.
- Pregnant people whose ultrasound examinations or blood testing indicate that their pregnancy may be at increased risk for certain complications.

As the term suggests, **prenatal diagnosis** involves assessing the fetus prior to birth. Two forms of prenatal testing used routinely for pregnant individuals are (a) maternal blood sampling and (b) ultrasound scanning. Between 15 and 19 weeks of pregnancy, pregnant patients are offered a blood test. A pregnancy blood test measures the exact amount of the pregnancy hormone called human chorionic gonadotropin in the bloodstream. This measurement can help give a rough estimate of the age of the fetus. It also can help determine whether the pregnancy is progressing normally.

Ultrasound scans are performed on most pregnant patients between 16 and 19 weeks of pregnancy. The process of fetal **ultrasound** testing was developed in the late 1960s and involves applying a clear, water-based conduction gel to the surface of the pregnant patient's abdomen that helps with the transmission of sound waves. A handheld probe called a transducer is then moved over the area and delivers a series of sound waves that bounce off the curves and variations inside the body, including the fetus (Figure 13–12).

FYI

In the late 1920s, it was discovered that injecting a suspected pregnant individual's urine into a rabbit served as a form of pregnancy testing. The human chorionic gonadotropin pregnancy hormone found in the urine caused spontaneous ovulation among rabbits. Unfortunately, to determine whether ovulation occurred in the rabbit, it needed to be dissected. Thus, the euphemism *the rabbit died* became associated with a positive test for pregnancy.

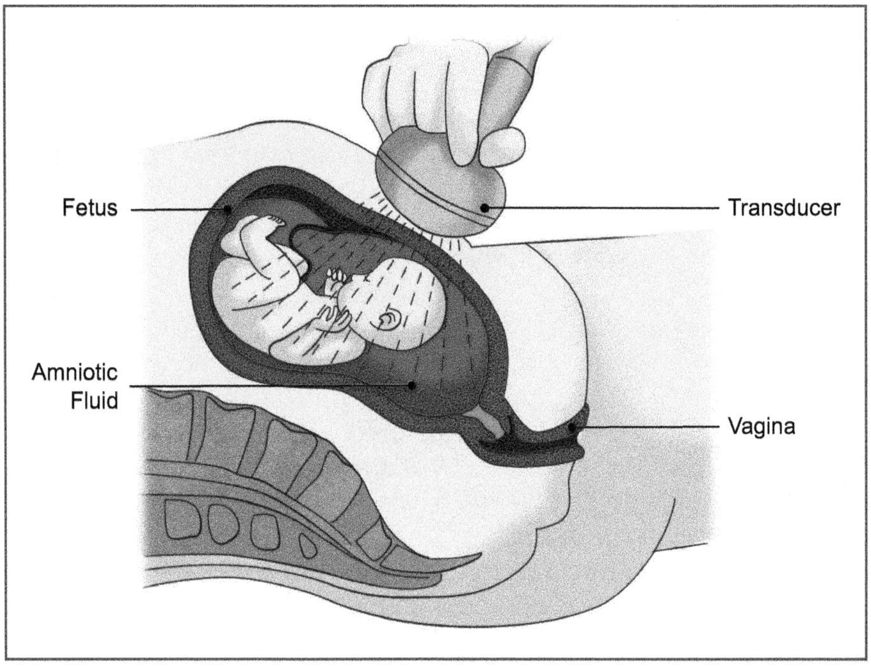

FIGURE 13–12. Ultrasound testing.

These sound waves are translated into a pattern of light and dark areas that create an image of the fetus on a monitor. The procedure is noninvasive, safe, and painless for the pregnant patient and fetus. Generally, an obstetrician performs an ultrasound test to determine whether a patient is pregnant and whether there is more than one fetus. An ultrasound test can be used to detect abnormalities in the development of the fetus, such as growth retardation, heart and kidney defects, Down syndrome, and cleft palate. The test is also useful in identifying **neural tube defects** (i.e., abnormalities) of the brain and spinal cord. Two neural tube defects are spina bifida and anencephaly. In **spina bifida**, the fetal spinal column fails to close completely during the first month of pregnancy. There is usually nerve damage that causes at least some paralysis of the legs. In **anencephaly**, much of the brain does not develop. Babies with anencephaly are either stillborn or die shortly after birth.

For pregnancies where there is a risk of the fetus having a genetic abnormality, tissue for genetic testing can be obtained either by (a) amniocentesis or (b) chorionic villus sampling. The **amniocentesis** procedure was developed in the early 1960s. The procedure involves withdrawing fluid from the amnion (the fluid-filled sack that contains the fetus). The fluid is taken from the pregnant patient's abdomen using a needle cannula (Figure 13–13). The cellular structure of the fluid is then analyzed to determine the karyotype of the fetus. Amniocentesis is performed during the 16th week of pregnancy, carries a low level of risk, and can be accomplished in an obstetrician's office.

Chorionic villus sampling was developed in 1975 by Chinese gynecologists as an aid to the early diagnosis of genetic disorders. In this approach, a catheter is inserted through the pregnant patient's cervix into the placenta. An abdominal ultrasound is also performed to determine the position of the uterus, the size of the gestational sac, and the position of the placenta within the uterus (Figure 13–14). A small piece of placental tissue (i.e., chorionic villi) is removed from the uterus and examined microscopically for the existence of chromosomal abnormalities as well as several hundred genetic disorders such as cystic fibrosis and sickle cell disease. The main advantage of chorionic villus sampling over amniocentesis is that the test can be performed earlier, generally between 11 and 12 weeks of pregnancy.

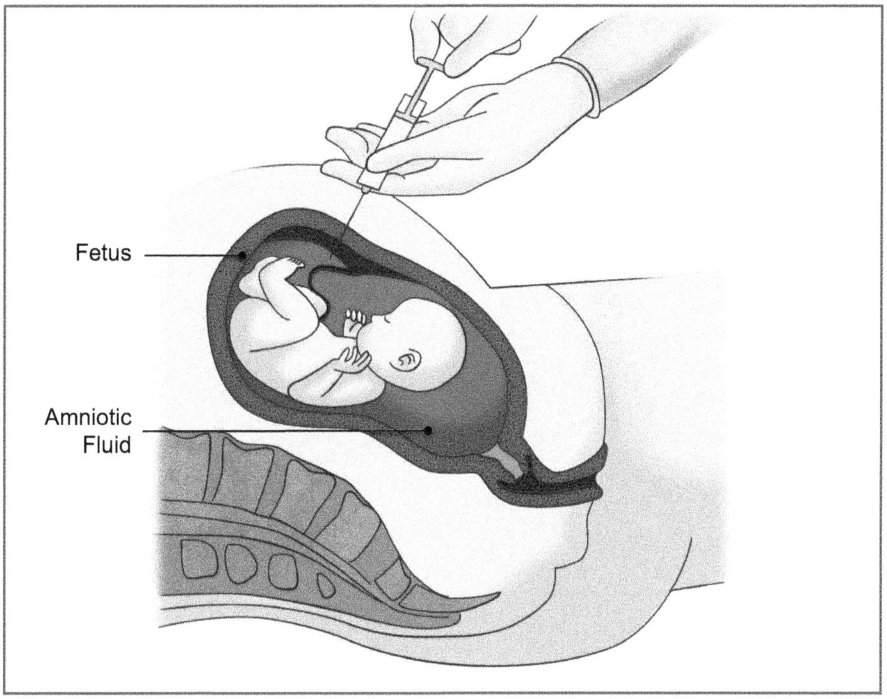

FIGURE 13–13. Amniocentesis in which amniotic fluid is withdrawn and later analyzed.

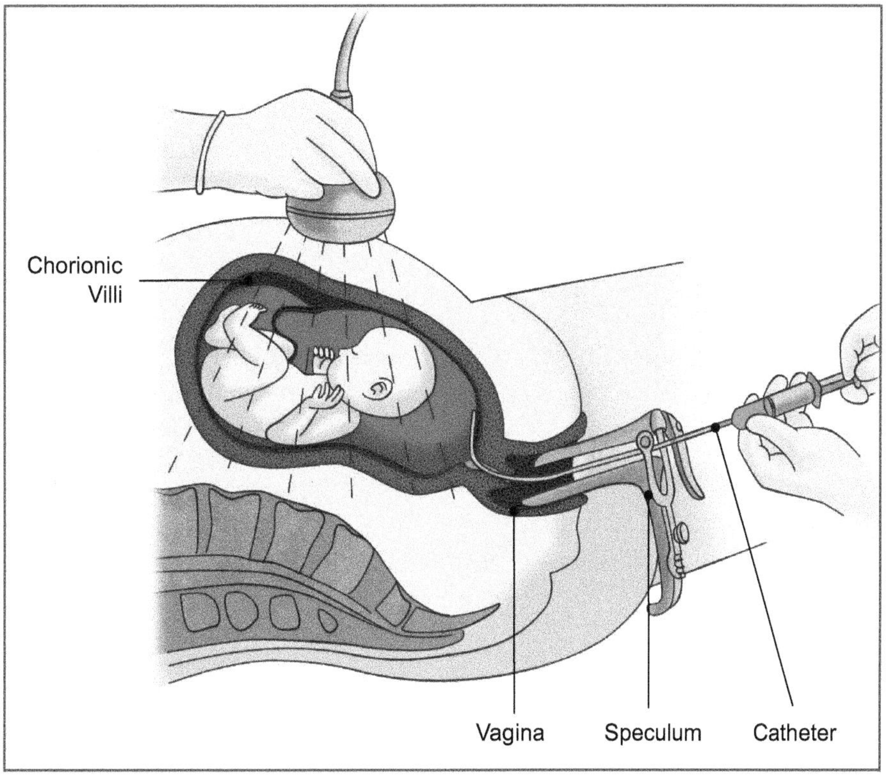

FIGURE 13–14. Chorionic villi sampling involving removal of a small piece of placental tissue (chorionic villi) from the uterus.

TREATMENT OF GENETIC CONDITIONS

Prophylactic Therapy

Prophylactic therapy involves the prevention of symptoms before they occur. One form of prophylactic therapy is the administration of vaccines to immunize against many diseases such as mumps, measles, and chicken pox. An example of prophylactic therapy involves treatment for a genetic condition known as phenylketonuria. Phenylketonuria is caused by mutations in the gene for phenylalanine hydroxylase, which is responsible for normal brain functioning. An infant's blood can be tested shortly after birth to determine whether phenylketonuria is present. If detected early, the baby's diet can be modified to ensure normal development and a normal life span.

Gene Therapy

The concept of gene therapy is that by inserting genes into a patient's cells (rather than undergoing surgery or prescribing drugs), various diseases can be either treated or prevented. The therapy involves either (a) replacing a mutated gene (i.e., protein) with a healthy copy of the same gene or (b) introducing an entirely new gene to combat the disease. For many years, such therapy has been available to individuals with conditions such as diabetes (where insulin is replaced) or growth hormone deficiency (where growth hormone is replaced). These disorders have been relatively easy to treat because the normal gene products are transported around the body in the bloodstream, and it is possible to inject the synthetic gene product intravenously. However, even for these disorders, the treatment has the disadvantage of having to be continually repeated. Groundbreaking research has shown that gene therapy is useful to repair inner ear problems (both hearing and balance) in mice (Isgrig et al., 2017). Granted, this type of gene therapy has not yet been trialed on humans, but research results are promising.

Treatment of Symptoms

For most genetic disorders, the symptoms of the disorder are treated rather than the actual affected gene/chromosome. Such treatments include surgery, the administration of drugs, and control of a patient's environment. For example, it is not unusual for people with Down syndrome to be born with heart defects, which can be corrected surgically. Treatment of communication disorders among individuals with genetic abnormalities is directed toward underlying causes such as hearing loss or impaired speech motor control. In addition, young children may be placed in early intervention programs to provide optimal input for speech and language acquisition.

CULTURAL CONSIDERATIONS AND GENETICS

It is often assumed that diseases found to occur within a family tree must be purely genetic. However, this family trend may reflect a common environment and lifestyle rather than a genetic influence. The term **ethnicity** is a complex construct that includes biology, history, cultural orientation and practice, language, religion, and lifestyle—all factors that affect an individual's health (Pearce et al., 2004). For example, the Pellagra Commission was established in 1900 to investigate the problem of pellagra (a vitamin deficiency disease) in the southern United States. The commission concluded that pellagra was purely genetic because it occurred within the same families. Unfortunately, members of the commission failed to recognize that poverty and malnutrition also were major issues in the same families, and these were the contributing factors to the disease.

Even for classic genetic diseases, environmental factors usually have an important role. In fact, genetic studies can show the importance of environmental factors. A New Zealand study of alcoholism provides one example of a health-related genetic difference. Marshall et al. (1994) found that the *ADH2-2* gene, which is believed to protect against alcoholism, was relatively common in the indigenous Maori people of New Zealand. This same gene is not found in New Zealand Europeans. Yet national statistics have revealed that alcohol-related health problems are more common in Maori, suggesting that the protective genetic factors are being outweighed by social, economic, cultural, and political factors. In summary, although various diseases are found to occur in some groups of people at a higher rate than others, the constant interaction between genes and the environment indicates that few diseases are purely hereditary.

FYI

Cloning is the creation of an organism that is an exact genetic copy of another. This means that every piece of DNA is the same between the two organisms. Cloning is an asexual process because only one parent is required. Certain plants, such as types of grapes to make fine wines, have undergone cloning for hundreds of years. Only recently has the technology become available to clone animals, and the advent of this technology has sparked ethical debate.

SUMMARY OF CHAPTER

There is a range of genetic abnormalities that have a communication disorder as a key symptom. Audiologists and speech-language pathologists are not qualified to render a genetic diagnosis, but they need to be aware of the way genetic conditions can affect features of speech, language, and hearing. This chapter provides an introduction to the field of genetics and illustrates how genetic-based syndromes can adversely affect communication. Syndromes can be broadly classified into two types: (a) chromosomal syndromes and (b) genetic syndromes. Examples of chromosomal syndromes that are accompanied by a communication disorder are Down syndrome and Cri du Chat syndrome. Two genetic-based syndromes accompanied by a communication disorder are Crouzon syndrome and FAS. Assessment of genetic conditions can be performed using prenatal diagnosis procedures or genetic counseling. For most genetic disorders, the symptoms of the disorder are treated rather than the actual affected gene/chromosome. The provision of audiological and speech-language therapy can positively impact the communication abilities of individuals with a genetic abnormality.

GENETICS AND SYNDROMES ON THE WORLD WIDE WEB

Following are websites that provide further information on the topics of genetics and syndromes. At the time of publication, each website was freely accessible.

Human Genetics Disorders Video
http://video.pbs.org/video/2328386346

Inheritance of Genetic Disorders Video
https://www.physio-pedia.com/Genetic_Conditions_and_Inheritance

Down Syndrome
https://healthify.nz/health-a-z/d/down-syndrome/

https://www.downsyndrome.org.au/about-down-syndrome/what-is-down-syndrome/

Cri du Chat Syndrome Videos
http://www.abnova.com/abvideo/Cri-du-Chat-Syndrome.html

https://www.itv.com/news/calendar/2018-07-18/yorkshire-family-raising-awareness-of-cri-du-chat-syndrome

Crouzon Syndrome Video
https://video.vice.com/en_us/topic/crouzon-syndrome

https://pulse.seattlechildrens.org/boy-with-rare-craniofacial-condition-inspires-others-with-a-simple-message/

https://www.chop.edu/video/what-craniosynostosis

Fetal Alcohol Disorders Society
http://www.faslink.org

https://www.kidshealth.org.nz/fetal-alcohol-spectrum-disorder-prevention

STUDY QUESTIONS

1. List and define the basic terms related to genetics.
2. List and describe three chromosomal syndromes. What are the communication characteristics of each syndrome?

3. List and describe three genetic syndromes. What are the communication characteristics of each syndrome?
4. What are the various types of prenatal diagnosis?
5. What are the forms of treatment for genetic conditions?

REFERENCES

Bull, M. J. (2020). Down syndrome. *New England Journal of Medicine, 382*(24), 2344–2352.

Den Hoed, J., & Fisher, S. E. (2020). Genetic pathways involved in human speech disorders. *Current Opinion in Genetics & Development, 65,* 103–111.

Genetic Disease Foundation. (2023). Retrieved from http://www.geneticdiseasefoundation.org/

Gerber, A. (2011). *Handbook of genetic communicative disorders.* Academic Press.

Isgrig, K., Shteamer, J., Belvantseva, I., Drummond, M., Fitzgerald, T., Vijayakumar, S., . . . Chien, W. (2017). Gene therapy restores balance and auditory functions in a mouse model of usher syndrome. *Molecular Therapy, 25*(3), 780–791.

Marshall, S. J., O'Brien, D., Wheeler, K., Hermans, I. F., Chambers, G. K., Robinson, G. M., & Stace, N. (1994). Genes and alcoholism: A preliminary report. *New Zealand Medical Journal, 107,* 106–107.

Pearce, N., Foliaki, S., Sporle, A., & Cunningham, C. (2004). Genetics, race, ethnicity and health. *British Medical Journal, 328,* 1070–1107.

Shprintzen, R. (1997). *Genetics, syndromes and communication disorders.* Singular Publishing.

SECTION 4

Audition

14

HEARING DISORDERS

OBJECTIVES

After reading this chapter, the student should be able to:

- Understand the concepts and terminology of the nature of sound.
- Understand basic audiology terminology.
- Describe various attributes of hearing loss, including type, degree, and configuration of loss.
- Identify the primary types, causes, and characteristics of hearing disorders in children and adults.
- Describe common disorders of hearing associated with each part of the auditory system.
- Understand theory and practice of various audiological diagnostic tests.
- Describe the primary assessment of hearing disorders in children and adults.

KEY TERMS

Sound
Sound Wave
Cycle
Frequency
Hertz Scale
Pure Tone
Complex Sound
Noise
Waveform
Amplitude
Intensity
Decibel Scale
Alexander Graham Bell
Loudness
Deafness
Congenital Deafness
Adventitious Deafness
Prelingual Deafness
Postlingual Deafness
Hard of Hearing
Hearing Aid
Prosper Ménière
Hermann von Helmholtz
Tonotopic Organization
Heinrich Hertz
Hendrik Zwaardemaker
Presbycusis
Pauline Davis
Hallowell Davis
Georg von Békésy
Rita Levi-Montalcini
Marion Downs
Conductive Hearing Loss
Sensorineural Hearing Loss
Mixed Hearing Loss
Atresia
Obstruction
Cerumen
Otitis Externa
Perforated Eardrum
Otitis Media
Otitis Media With Effusion
Otoscope
Otosclerosis
Stapedectomy
Prenatal Causes
Cytomegalovirus
Meningitis
Viral Meningitis
Bacterial Meningitis
Ototoxic Hearing Loss
Ménière Disease
Endolymphatic Hydrops
Presbycusis
Noise-Induced Hearing Loss
Retrocochlear Pathology
Acoustic Neuroma
High-Frequency Hearing Loss
Unilateral Hearing Loss
Bilateral Hearing Loss
Symmetrical Hearing Loss
Asymmetrical Hearing Loss
Progressive Hearing Loss
Fluctuating Hearing Loss
Tinnitus
Cognitive Behavioral Therapy
Neuromonics
Auditory Processing Disorder
Pure-Tone Audiometry
Audiometer
Threshold
Audiogram
Air Conduction Testing
Bone Conduction Testing
Immittance Testing
Nonbehavioral Tests
Tympanometry
Tympanometer
Tympanogram
Acoustic Reflex
Otoacoustic Emissions
Auditory Brainstem Response
Electroencephalography
Universal Newborn Screening

INTRODUCTION

Successful communication, as described in Chapter 1, involves the processes of encoding and decoding. The act of human communication can be the exchange of a message between someone producing speech and someone listening to speech. A major portion of this book thus far has been dedicated to an array of communication disorders that result from a breakdown in the process of speech production (i.e., encoding). We now turn our attention to those communication disorders that stem from a disruption in hearing (i.e., decoding). A hearing disorder can have a profound effect on one's quality of life. Loss of hearing makes even routine communication difficult, which may result in frustration, withdrawal from social activities, depression, and even marital discord. People lose the ability to appreciate sounds of everyday living such as birds singing, children's voices, and even police sirens.

Hearing loss in adults is usually a condition that tends to develop gradually over the years, and most people are not aware of the extent of their hearing loss until family or friends bring it to their attention. Even then, most adults will not seek help for their hearing until approximately 7 years from the initial diagnosis of a hearing problem. A hearing loss that occurs early in childhood can have devastating consequences to a child's ability to learn. Such impairment also interferes with a child's psychological, emotional, and speech development. Even mild forms of hearing loss can cause great difficulties for people young and old. Though loss of the ability to hear can be a serious problem, in many cases there is help available through medical or surgical treatment or with hearing aids. This chapter introduces the wide range of hearing disorders found in children and adults. Some disorders are more common than others, and there are unique ways of testing for various hearing disorders. Audiologists are professionals educated in the diagnosis and management of hearing disorders. For those interested in pursuing audiology as a career, this chapter should provide some insight into the complexities of the auditory system and the truly remarkable process of hearing.

TERMINOLOGY AND DEFINITIONS

The ear is one of the most amazing features of the human body as well as the body of many living creatures. It is one of the smallest and most complex organs in the body and is capable of transforming airborne sound waves into a form the brain can understand. **Sound** results from a disturbance in air particles (i.e., molecules). Such disturbances are typically caused by the vibration of an elastic body such as a stereo speaker, bass drum, guitar string, or vocal folds. Vibrations cause a disturbance of air particles. These particles bump into the particles close to them, which causes them to vibrate as well. When particles are disturbed, they move in a back-and-forth motion, creating a **sound wave**. One complete back-and-forth motion of a particle is called a **cycle** of vibration. The **frequency** of a sound wave refers to how fast the particles vibrate and is measured by the number of complete vibrations that occur per unit of time. If a particle of air undergoes 1,000 vibrations in 1 sec, then the frequency of the wave would be 1,000 cycles per second. The notation used to designate frequency is the **hertz** (Hz) scale (e.g., 1000 Hz). The hertz notation is used in honor of Heinrich Hertz (discussed later). Low-frequency sounds are those that have a small number of vibrations per second. These vibrations are perceived as having a low-pitched sound. Alternatively, high-frequency sounds involve many vibrations per second that we perceive as having a high-pitched quality. When a sound consists of only one frequency, it is referred to as a **pure tone**. A **complex sound** is one that contains more than one frequency. Sounds that have no consistent vibratory pattern are referred to as **noise**.

The back-and-forth motion of a pure tone can be represented graphically as a **waveform** (Figure 14–1). On such a graph, the height of the sound wave is the point at which the particle is at its maximum point of disturbance. The terms used to describe the maximum disturbance of a sound wave are **amplitude** and **intensity**. The scale for measuring intensity is the **decibel scale** (dB). One decibel (1 dB) is considered the smallest difference in sound intensity that the human ear can discern. The decibel was named in honor of **Alexander Graham Bell** (1847–1922) We perceive the intensity of a sound wave as its **loudness**. All sound waves can be described by their frequency and intensity. For example, a sound wave may be produced with a single frequency of 2500 Hz and an intensity of 40 dB, or frequency components of 50 Hz and 70 Hz with an intensity of 100 dB. The variations in frequency and intensity for types of sound waves are endless. Illustrations of sound waves of varying frequency and intensity are shown in Figure 14–1.

Some facts and figures about hearing loss are provided in Table 14–1. It is estimated that approx-

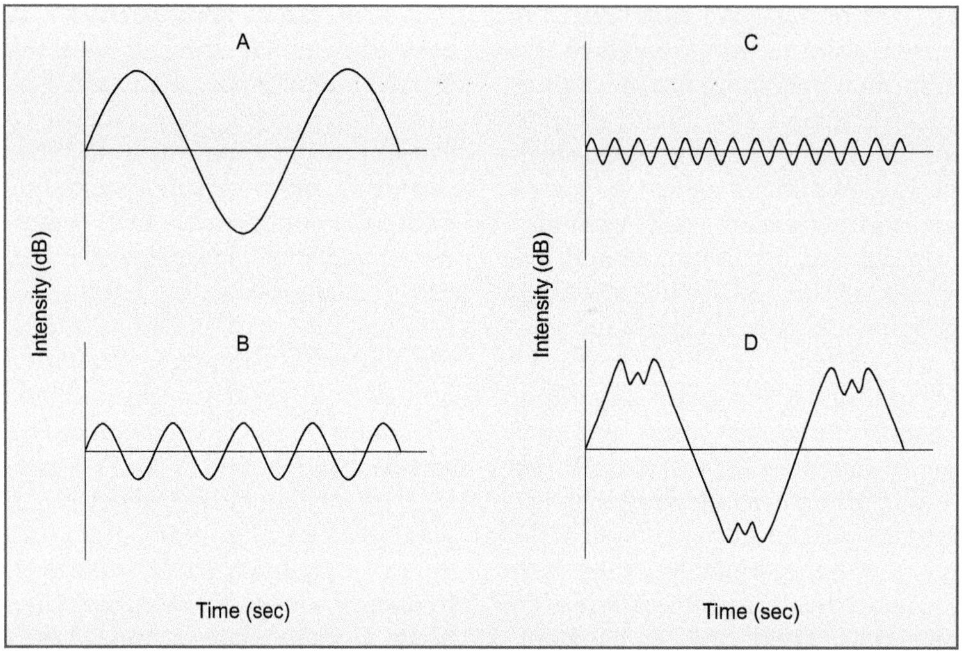

FIGURE 14–1. Examples of sound waves of varying frequency and intensity. **A.** The highest amplitude and lowest frequency, followed by **B** and **C**, respectively. **D.** A complex sound consisting of these same three sounds combined.

Table 14–1. Some Facts About Hearing Loss

- 22 million people in the United States have hearing loss.
- 9 million people in the United Kingdom have a hearing loss.
- 3.5 million people in Australia have a hearing loss.
- 4 million people in South Africa have a hearing loss.
- 400,000 New Zealanders have a hearing loss.
- Hearing loss is highly associated with aging.
- Approximately 60% of the hearing impaired are over the age of 65 years.
- Men are more likely than women to have hearing loss. Some 60% of people with hearing loss are men.
- Hearing loss is the third leading chronic disability, following arthritis and high blood pressure.
- The prevalence of hearing loss decreases as family income and education increase.
- People with hearing loss are generally less healthy than those with no hearing loss.
- Four out of five Americans with hearing loss do not use hearing aids.
- About 15% of university graduates have a level of hearing loss equal to or greater than their parents; a significant cause is listening to loud music.
- Minor decreases in hearing, especially of higher frequencies, are normal after the age of 18 years.

imately one in seven individuals has impaired hearing. This occurrence is found for countries throughout the world, including Europe, North America, and those in the southern hemisphere. Hearing impairment encompasses individuals who are deaf and hard of hearing. **Deafness** is defined as minimal hearing or complete loss of hearing. Deafness at birth is known as **congenital deafness**, whereas deafness that occurs after birth is called **adventitious deafness**. Some diseases that are known to cause adventitious deafness are meningitis, mumps, and chicken pox. Deafness that occurs prior to an individual learning to speak is called **prelingual deafness**, and **postlingual deafness** is complete hearing loss that happens after a period of language learning. **Hard of hearing** is defined as a hearing loss ranging from mild to severe for which a person usually receives some benefit from a **hearing aid**. Common causes of hearing loss are excessive noise exposure and aging. Not surprisingly, the occurrence of hearing loss is highest among older adults. By the age of 65 years, one in every four individuals has a significant hearing loss. Hearing loss is the third most self-reported health problem of individuals 65 years of age or older, listed after arthritis and hypertension. It is estimated that untreated hearing impairments cost the U.S. economy $56 billion in lost productivity, special education, and medical care. The cost exceeds 200 billion euros across the European Union.

HISTORIC ASPECTS OF HEARING DISORDERS

Paleontologists who uncovered ancient skeletal remains have shown that hearing disorders such as middle ear infections (i.e., otitis media) occurred among early human populations. Skulls dating back to the Bronze Age (2000 BC) have shown evidence of temporal bone decay. Investigations of Egyptian mummies have suggested that otitis media was present in Egyptian populations as far back as the 13th dynasty (1700 BC). Skulls uncovered from prehistoric Iran revealed evidence of otitis media among individuals from 1300 to 300 BC. Specific individuals who have either directly or indirectly contributed to our knowledge concerning hearing loss can be traced back approximately 200 years. Some of the more noteworthy contributors are mentioned here.

Prosper Ménière (1799–1862) was a French laryngologist who at the age of 39 years was appointed chief physician at the Institute for Deaf-Mutes in Paris, succeeding the renowned Gaspard Itard (noted for his work with the wild boy of Aveyron). Ménière was the first to describe the unusual ear disease that was later named in his honor. In 1861, he published a report entitled *Lesions of the Inner Ear Giving Rise to Symptoms of Cerebral Congestion of Apoplectic Type*. In this report, Ménière identified a condition in the inner ear that affected both hearing and balance. He concluded in this article that the auditory apparatus of the inner ear may be affected suddenly, causing ringing in the ear and loss of hearing. In addition, the balance structures of the inner ear could also be affected suddenly, resulting in attacks of dizziness and unsteady gait, which may be accompanied by nausea and vomiting. Ménière died in Paris of influenza pneumonia at the age of 63 years, the year after publication of his most famous work. Although Ménière's name is now known around the world, he did not receive recognition while he was alive.

Hermann von Helmholtz (1821–1894; Figure 14–2) was a German physicist who made outstanding contributions to the areas of human

FIGURE 14–2. Hermann von Helmholtz, German physicist who made outstanding contributions to the areas of human physiology, particularly eyes and ears.

physiology, particularly the eye and ear. He invented the ophthalmoscope that was used for inspecting the interior of the eye and the ophthalmometer, a device used for measuring the eye's curvature. Helmholtz was also an authority on acoustics and hearing. In 1863, he published *On the Sensations of Tone as a Physiological Basis of the Theory of Music*. In this book, he described the placement of the higher frequency fibers at the basal end of the cochlea and the lower frequency fibers near the apex, which is now referred to as **tonotopic organization.**

Heinrich Hertz (1857–1894) was a German physicist who happened to be one of von Helmholtz's students. Hertz was the first to send and receive radio waves. He proved that electricity could be transmitted in electromagnetic waves, which travel at the speed of light. His experiments with electromagnetic waves eventually led to the development of the wireless telegraph and the radio. His name also became the term used for referring to the measure of frequency per unit of time, or the number of cycles per second (Hz). The hertz designation has been an official part of the international metric system since 1933. When we use the "Hz" notation to refer to a low-frequency or high-frequency hearing loss, we are acknowledging the pioneering work of Heinrich Hertz.

FYI

Gallaudet University, located in Washington, DC, was the first university in the world specifically designed to accommodate deaf and hard-of-hearing students. The university was established in 1864 during the presidency of Abraham Lincoln. The university is named after Thomas Hopkins Gallaudet (1787–1851) who was the founder of the first school for deaf students in the United States. Hearing students are admitted to the graduate school, and degrees in audiology and speech-language pathology are offered.

Hendrik Zwaardemaker (1857–1920) was both an otolaryngologist and a physiologist who was a professor at Utrecht University in the Netherlands. He was the first individual to describe the relationship between advanced aging and a high-frequency hearing loss, for which he coined the term **presbycusis.** Zwaardemaker studied various ways of assessing hearing, including the use of whispered voice as a hearing test. He also worked on the physiology of speech production and examined acoustic properties of hearing aids. Since Zwaardemaker's initial description of presbycusis, extensive research has attempted to determine the precise physiological causes of presbycusis, which remain unknown.

Pauline Davis (1896–1942; Figure 14–3) was a physiologist who, along with her husband **Hallowell Davis** (1896–1992) was instrumental in the development of the electroencephalograph (EEG). Their work focused on using EEG to test the physiology of the inner ear. In 1939, she published the first paper demonstrating an auditory-evoked response from a human using EEG.

Georg von Békésy (1899–1972; Figure 14–4) was a biophysicist born in Budapest, Hungary. His early research interest was focused on telecommunications and finding ways of improving the acoustic quality of long-distance telephone calls. However, he later turned his attention to the physics of sound and the physical processes involved in hearing. Békésy found that sound traveling through the cochlea flows as a series of waves. He demonstrated that these waves provide maximum stimulation of hair cells (i.e., auditory nerve receptors) at different places along the cochlea: low fre-

FIGURE 14–3. Pauline Davis, American researcher who performed the first auditory-evoked test on a human using electroencephalography.

FIGURE 14–4. Georg von Békésy, Nobel Prize winner for his research on the functioning of the inner ear. (From the University of Hawaii. Reprinted with permission.)

FIGURE 14–5. Rita Levi-Montalcini, Nobel Prize winning neurologist from Italy who discovered the protein called nerve growth factor.

quencies toward the apical end of the cochlea and high frequencies near its base. He discovered that the location of this maximum nerve receptor stimulation is the most important factor in determining the pitch and loudness of sounds. His work led to advances in ear surgery and the design of better hearing aids. In 1961, Békésy was awarded the Nobel Prize in Physiology and Medicine for his research on the function of the cochlea.

Rita Levi-Montalcini (1909–2012; Figure 14–5) was a Nobel Prize–winning neurologist from Italy who discovered a protein that causes developing cells to grow by stimulating surrounding nerve tissue. She named this protein nerve growth factor. Since her initial discovery, nerve growth factor has been shown to play an important role in the growth of nerve fibers throughout the peripheral nervous system. The role of nerve growth factor in regenerating nerve fibers damaged in the cochlea of humans has yet to be proven; however, her initial discovery of this protein has opened an area of research that may someday lead to a cure for cochlea-based hearing loss.

Marion Downs (1914–2014; Figure 14–6) is widely recognized as the mother of pediatric audiology and pioneered the implementation of newborn hearing screening in the 1960s. She recognized the early detection of hearing loss coupled with early intervention led to significantly improved speech and language outcomes. Her work contributed to the development of newborn screening programs around the world.

FIGURE 14–6. Marion Downs was an American audiologist who pioneered universal newborn hearing screening.

TYPES OF HEARING DISORDERS

Hearing disorders can be described and categorized in several ways. For purposes of this introduction, they are presented according to the categories of (a) type of hearing loss, (b) degree of hearing loss, (c) location of hearing loss, and (d) configuration of hearing loss.

Type of Hearing Loss

There are three types of hearing loss: (a) conductive, (b) sensorineural, and (c) mixed.

Conductive hearing loss is due to problems affecting sound transmission through the outer or middle ear. These problems disrupt the normal flow of sound entering the inner ear. People affected by conductive hearing loss experience an overall reduction in the loudness of sounds and find it difficult to hear faint sounds. Most conductive losses are not permanent and can be treated medically or surgically. However, if left untreated, conductive hearing losses can result in permanent impairment.

Sensorineural hearing loss occurs when there is damage to the inner ear or to the nerve pathways from the inner ear leading toward the brain. In addition to affecting loudness of hearing, a sensorineural loss can affect the clarity of hearing. For example, normally we can hear sounds between the frequency range of 20 and 20,000 Hz. In the case of a sensorineural hearing loss, a person may be unable to hear sounds higher than 2000 Hz, which can have a major impact on clearly understanding what is being said. Sensorineural hearing loss results in a permanent hearing disorder that cannot be corrected, although an individual's hearing can be improved by using some sort of hearing aid. A sensorineural hearing loss accounts for 90% of all types of hearing loss.

> FYI
>
> There is research indicating that the type of filling used to repair dental cavities might contribute to hearing loss. Use of amalgam fillings (an alloy of mercury) can have ototoxic effects and might be mistaken for presbycusis, especially among middle-age and older adults who have had these fillings in their mouth over several years. Fortunately, use of amalgam fillings has become rare.

A **mixed hearing loss** is a combined conductive hearing loss and sensorineural hearing loss. The condition may result from a single pathology affecting both the middle ear and inner ear, or two independent pathologies. An example of mixed hearing would be a situation where a person may initially have a conductive hearing loss due to an ear infection and later develops a sensorineural hearing loss. Sometimes a mixed hearing loss is a temporary condition because the conductive component of the hearing loss can be successfully treated, leaving only a sensorineural hearing loss.

Degree of Hearing Loss

Degree of hearing loss refers to the severity of the loss. All types of hearing loss are defined by degrees. The severity of hearing loss can range from mild to profound, describing the lowest or softest intensity level at which sound can be heard. A classification system for degree of hearing loss is listed in Table 14–2. Depending on the degree of hearing loss, various treatment options are suggested, such as hearing aids, speech therapy, and counseling. The treatment approaches for working with hearing-impaired individuals are addressed in Chapter 15.

Location of Hearing Loss

A portion of Chapter 2 was dedicated to the anatomy of the auditory system. From that chapter, we learned that the entire auditory pathway can be neatly divided into two systems—the peripheral and central auditory systems. Each of these systems provides an important contribution to the process of audition. Damage to any of the components composing the auditory system can result in different types and varying degrees of hearing loss. Disorders of hearing that occur at various locations throughout the auditory system are described next.

Disorders of the Outer Ear

When conditions occur that interfere or block the normal transmission of sound through the outer ear, a conductive hearing loss will occur. In most cases, this condition does not result in severe hearing loss. Examples of outer ear disorders are (a) atresia, (b) obstruction of the ear canal, and (c) otitis externa. The term **atresia** refers to an absence of a normal opening. Atresia can affect many structures in the body, and one of these structures is the ear canal. The absence of the external auditory canal is a congenital condition and almost always involves abnormalities of the middle ear bones. A moderate conductive hearing loss typically is present in an atretic ear (Figure 14–7).

A common disorder of the outer ear involves an **obstruction** in the ear canal that prevents sound from normally entering the middle ear. The ear canal's natural secretion of earwax, known as **cerumen**, can become impacted to the point where

Table 14–2. Classification of Hearing Loss

Amount of Hearing Loss	*Degree of Hearing Loss*	*Ability to Hear Speech*
0–25 dB	None	No significant difficulty in hearing.
26–40 dB	Mild	Difficulty hearing soft speech and conversations but can manage in quiet environments.
41–55 dB	Moderate	Difficulty understanding conversational speech, especially when there is background noise. Higher volume levels are required for listening to the TV.
56–70 dB	Moderate-to-Severe	Speech clarity is significantly affected. Speech must be loud, and the person may have difficulty hearing in group conversations.
71–90 dB	Severe	Normal conversational speech cannot be heard. The person may also have difficulty with loud speech or only be able to understand shouted or amplified speech.
91+ dB	Profound	Unable to clearly understand even amplified speech.

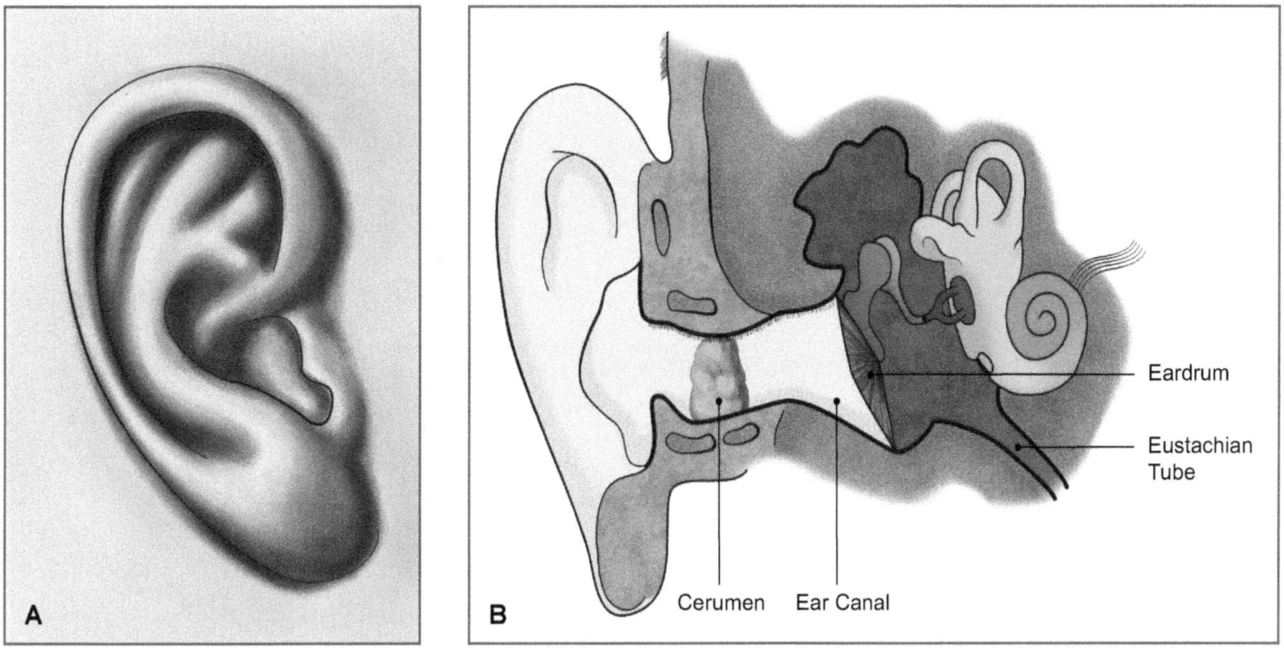

FIGURE 14–7. **A.** Atresia, where the ear canal fails to develop. **B.** An example of cerumen (earwax) impaction.

normal hearing is affected (see Figure 14–7). Impacted cerumen is not unusual, with approximately 2% to 6% of the general population having this condition. A likely cause of impaction is the misuse of cotton swabs, where the swab serves to push cerumen toward the tympanic membrane. As mentioned in Chapter 2, cerumen provides a beneficial function to the ear canal and normally does not need to be removed. Cerumen impaction is also prevalent among hearing aid users. Problematic cerumen can be removed with dissolving drops, water jets ("irrigation"), or special instruments available to a qualified specialist.

Another disorder of the outer ear is **otitis externa**. The term *otitis* is Latin with *oto* referring to the "ear" and *itis* meaning "inflammation." So, this particular condition is an infection of the outer (external) ear. The common term for otitis externa is swimmer's ear. In most cases, bacteria cause this infection in the thin layer of skin lining the canal. Our ear canals work best when they are dry, so if they are exposed to excess moisture, such as from frequent swimming, they are more likely to become infected. Swimmer's ear can be easily treated with antibiotic eardrops.

Disorders of the Middle Ear

Abnormalities of the middle ear will result in a conductive hearing loss. Examples of middle ear disorders are (a) a perforated eardrum, (b) otitis media, and (c) otosclerosis. A hole or rupture in the tympanic membrane is called a **perforated eardrum**. This condition is accompanied by decreased hearing because the tympanic membrane ceases to work normally in the transmission of sound waves along the ossicular chain. The causes of a perforated eardrum are usually due to trauma or infection. Instances of trauma include a skull fracture, or a foreign object pushed too far into the ear canal (Figure 14–8). A perforation can also result from a severe middle ear infection that causes the eardrum to rupture or tear. Most eardrum perforations heal on their own within weeks of the rupture, although some may take several months to heal. During the healing process, the ear must be protected from water to prevent further damage to the middle ear.

Otitis media refers to an inflammation of the middle ear cavity. Otitis media affects about two thirds of children at least once before they

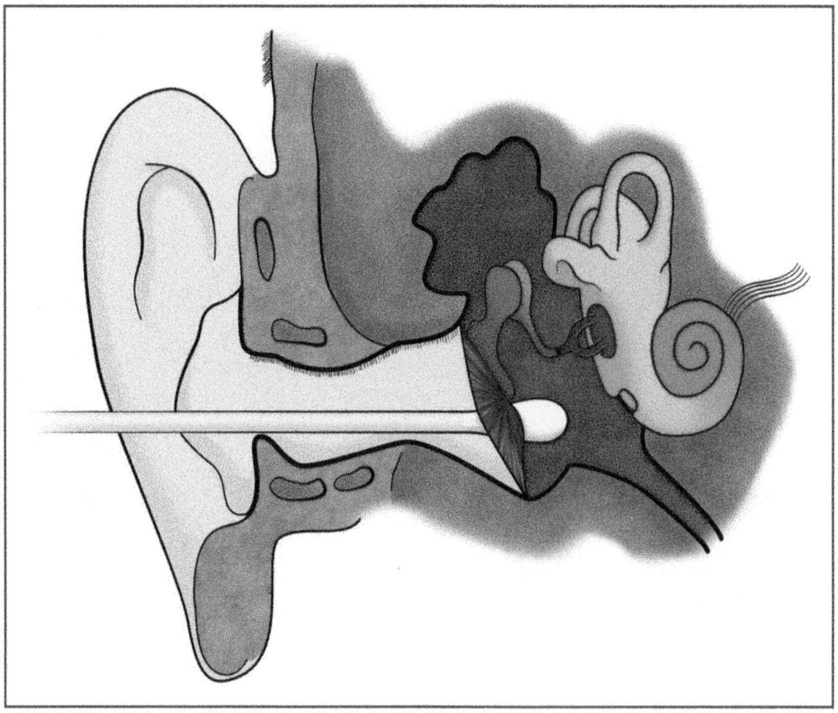

FIGURE 14–8. Example of a perforated tympanic membrane resulting from damage by a foreign object.

reach their second birthday. The only childhood illness that occurs more often than otitis media is the common cold. An earache in children is often an indication of otitis media. The frequent occurrence of otitis media in young children is usually attributed to the small size, horizontal position, and immature functioning of their eustachian tube compared with adults, making it easier for infectious organisms in the mouth and nose to gain access to the middle ear (Figure 14–9). Otitis media can be further classified according to longevity and type of condition. Acute otitis media is an infection lasting less than 3 weeks. Subacute otitis media lasts between three weeks and three months, and chronic otitis media lasts longer than three months. **Otitis media with effusion** is a condition where a watery or mucus-like fluid fills the middle ear cavity. In some countries, the shorthand term used for otitis media with effusion is glue ear. Many times, the condition of otitis media can be diagnosed by examining the coloring of the tympanic membrane using an **otoscope** (Figure 14–10). An otoscope is a standard piece of equipment found in most doctors' offices. Use of an otoscope allows for visualization of the outer

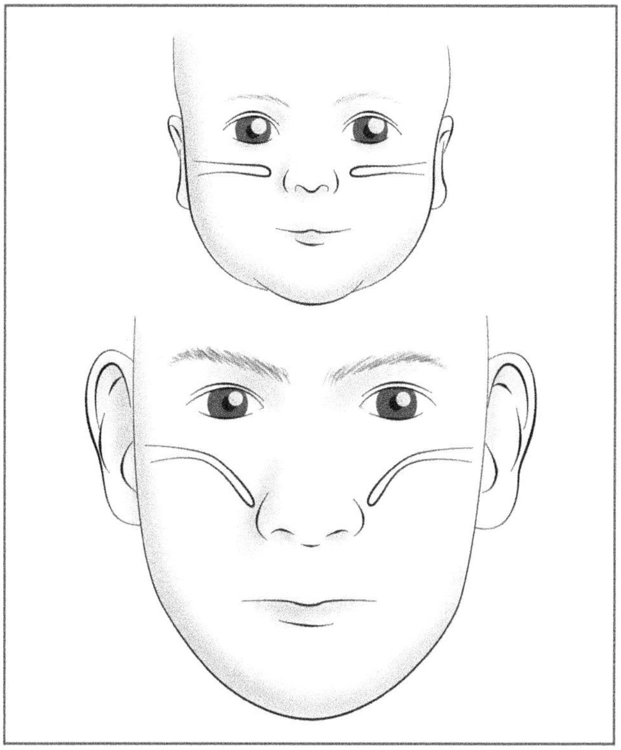

FIGURE 14–9. Depiction of infant and adult eustachian tubes. The horizontal angle of the tubes in infants makes them susceptible to ear infections.

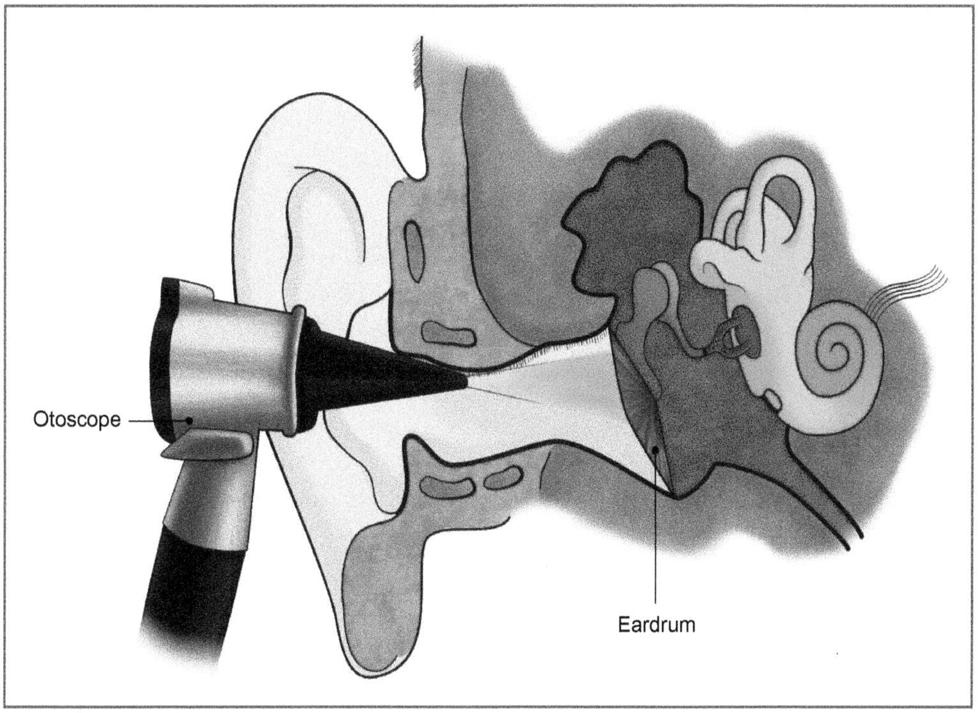

FIGURE 14–10. Example of an otoscope. The device shines a beam of light to help visualize and examine the condition of the ear canal and eardrum.

ear as well as a portion of the middle ear. Examination of the ear provides doctors with helpful information regarding a patient's overall health status.

> FYI
>
> A *malingerer* is a person who deliberately lies about a physical or psychological condition for some special gain. The term has found its way into hearing disorders, where an individual may fake a hearing loss as a means of seeking special gain, such as additional financial compensation.

Otosclerosis is the abnormal growth of spongy bone in the middle ear. This bone prevents the ossicular chain of the middle ear from working properly and causes hearing loss. The etiology of otosclerosis is not fully understood, although research has shown that otosclerosis tends to run in families, so there may be a genetic component. On average, a person who has one parent with otosclerosis has a 25% chance of developing the disorder. Women are three times more likely to acquire the disease compared with men. There are also differences in regard to ethnicity, with White people more susceptible to the disease than Asian or Black people. One way of treating otosclerosis is to surgically repair the ossicular chain. Many times, this involves **stapedectomy**, which is removal of all or a portion of the stapes and substitution of an artificial stapes.

> FYI
>
> The development of earpods is likely to significantly increase the occurrence of noise-induced hearing loss and tinnitus for future generations. Audiologists recommend what is called the 60-60 rule, which translates to a listening level of 60% (of the maximum volume) for no more than 60 min.

Disorders of the Inner Ear

Damage to the inner ear will result in a sensorineural hearing loss. Problems of the inner ear represent the largest group of hearing disorders. These disorders can affect balance as well as hearing. Examples of inner ear disorders are (a) prenatal causes, (b) meningitis, (c) ototoxic drugs, (d) Ménière disease, and (e) presbycusis. **Prenatal causes** are those that affect the mother and her developing fetus. The mother may acquire a virus during her pregnancy that has an adverse effect on the normal growth and development of the unborn child's cochlea. **Cytomegalovirus** is the most prevalent prenatal disease known to cause hearing loss. Cytomegalovirus is a common viral illness. It belongs to the herpesvirus family, which also includes viruses that are responsible for chicken pox, glandular fever, and cold sores. Between 50% and 85% of people in Australia, the United Kingdom, and the United States have had a cytomegalovirus infection by the time they are 40 years old. Cytomegalovirus infections are rarely serious in otherwise healthy children and adults. When symptoms do appear, they are similar to those seen in mononucleosis ("mono") and last a few weeks. Cytomegalovirus is a risk only when the mother develops a cytomegalovirus infection during pregnancy and passes this virus to the unborn baby before birth. The results can be severe, with as many as 20% of these children failing to survive. The children who do survive may show intellectual disabilities, visual defects, and hearing loss. The severity of hearing loss can range from mild to profound.

Meningitis is an inflammation of the thin protective tissue that surrounds the brain and spinal cord, called the meninges. **Viral meningitis** usually does not cause serious illness, although in severe cases, it can cause prolonged fever and seizures. **Bacterial meningitis** is much rarer than viral meningitis but is far more serious. Bacterial meningitis usually starts with bacteria that cause a cold-like infection. The infection can block blood vessels in the brain and lead to stroke and brain damage as well as damage to other organs such as the cochlea. Bacterial meningitis may lead to total deafness; however, early treatment with steroids can assist in reducing the severity of hearing loss.

An **ototoxic hearing loss** happens when someone takes or is given a drug that causes hearing loss as one of its side effects. There are roughly 200 prescription and over-the-counter drugs recognized as ototoxic. Sometimes the drugs are needed to save lives, and hearing loss is the price

FYI

The Dutch artist Vincent Van Gogh (1853–1890) created some of the world's most expensive and popular paintings. Was it his madness that prompted him to cut off his ear or was it his reaction to Ménière disease? Prior to his death, Van Gogh was severely depressed. He suffered from vicious, recurring attacks of dizziness, nausea, and an intense ringing in the ear, all symptoms of Ménière disease.

paid for being able to live. Common medications that are known to be ototoxic include various antibiotics, chemotherapy medications, anesthetics, cardiac medications, steroids, mood-altering drugs, and some vapors and solvents. Often an ototoxic hearing loss is reversible simply by discontinuation of the drug. People with an existing hearing loss need to be especially aware of the potential for ototoxic effects, as an ototoxic drug can worsen hearing loss.

Ménière disease is an inner ear disorder caused by increased fluid pressure in the chambers of the inner ear. The disease affects both the balance and hearing systems of the inner ear, and usually just one ear is involved. There are various symptoms that are indicative of a person having Ménière disease. These symptoms include episodes of severe dizziness (i.e., vertigo), nausea, unilateral hearing loss, ringing in the ear (i.e., tinnitus), and a feeling of ear pressure or pain in the affected ear. The disease may be extremely debilitating. Episodes of dizziness can occur without warning and may last from minutes to several hours or even days. The cause of Ménière disease is unknown, although some feel it is a result of **endolymphatic hydrops**, which is the oversecretion of endolymph (i.e., the fluid contained within the cochlea). Surgery to drain excessive endolymph is found to help reduce the debilitating aspects of the disease. Some doctors inject a corticosteroid into the middle ear space, which seems to help reduce dizziness. In extreme cases, the inner ear may be surgically destroyed to help alleviate vertigo and tinnitus, which results in permanent deafness of the affected ear.

Presbycusis is the gradual deterioration in hearing that happens as we grow older. The hearing mechanism likely begins to deteriorate shortly after birth, although most experts agree that by the age of 18 years, a natural reduction in the performance of our auditory system begins to occur. As we age, the hair cells within the cochlea become damaged through the normal wear and tear of use, particularly those that are found at the entrance (basal end) of the cochlea. This deterioration is synonymous with the entryway into a carpeted room. As years go by, the carpet fibers at the entryway of the room become flattened and damaged, whereas those at the back of the room retain their shape. As for the cochlea, this form of damage results in a high-frequency hearing loss that can start as early as middle age. The condition is to be expected in men by their early 60s and women by their late 60s. Presbycusis most often occurs in both ears. Because the process of loss is gradual, people who have presbycusis may not realize their hearing is diminishing. Between the ages of 65 and 75 years, about 35% of adults have a hearing loss. After the age of 75 years, hearing loss is found in nearly 50% of all individuals.

Whereas presbycusis reflects a natural aging of the auditory system, **noise-induced hearing loss** is a form of impairment that somewhat mirrors that of presbycusis but can be found in people at a much younger age. This hearing loss is not a result of natural aging but rather damage due to exposure to excessive noise, whether at work or play. The National Foundation for the Deaf reported that one in four teenagers is likely to experience a hearing loss as a direct result of MP3 player listening habits. Among older adults, it may be difficult to differentiate between presbycusis and noise-induced hearing loss simply because both pathologies affect hearing of high-frequency sounds. Noise-induced hearing loss is a preventable disorder that can be avoided by taking necessary precautions such as wearing noise-reduction headphones or earplugs.

Disorders of the Central Auditory System

Any damage to the auditory system running from the auditory nerve to the brain is called a **retrocochlear pathology** because the damage occurs beyond (or behind) the cochlea. One type of retrocochlear pathology is a tumor called **acoustic neuroma** (Figure 14–11). An acoustic neuroma is a noncancerous (i.e., benign) brain tumor. All types of brain tumors are rare, and acoustic neuromas account for 8 out of 100 primary brain tumors. An acoustic neuroma tends to grow very slowly and normally is not a life-threatening condition.

In rare cases, the tumor can grow large enough to press on the brain. However, most acoustic neuromas can be treated before they get to this stage. Typically, the tumor is found only on one side of the central auditory system. Approximately 50% of acoustic neuromas are treated by surgery to remove the tumor. About 25% of neuromas are treated with radiation, and the remaining 25% are monitored (i.e., left untreated). Regardless of the treatment approach, an acoustic neuroma almost always results in total hearing loss in the affected ear. Each year in the United Kingdom and the United States, approximately 13 people out of 1 million are diagnosed with an acoustic neuroma. Acoustic neuromas occur more often in women compared with men, although the reasons for this are not yet understood. People who are 30 to 60 years of age are usually affected.

Configuration of Hearing Loss

The configuration of a hearing loss refers to the extent of loss at various frequencies of hearing, ranging from low to high. The configuration of hearing loss gives an overall picture of a person's

FIGURE 14–11. An acoustic neuroma (tumor) resulting in a retrocochlear hearing loss.

hearing acuity. For example, an individual who is unable to hear frequencies within the range of 2000 to 8000 Hz at a soft loudness level would show a **high-frequency hearing loss.** Some hearing loss configurations are flat, indicating the same amount of hearing loss for low-, middle-, and high-frequency sounds. Another aspect of hearing loss configuration is whether two ears are affected: a **unilateral hearing loss** means that only one ear is affected by the loss, and a **bilateral hearing loss** means both ears are affected. In addition, hearing loss can be symmetrical or asymmetrical. A **symmetrical hearing loss** means the severity of loss and the frequencies affected are the same for both ears. **Asymmetrical hearing loss** means there is loss of hearing in both ears, but the severity of loss and frequencies affected are not identical. A final way of describing hearing loss configuration relates to the change in hearing over time. A **progressive hearing loss** is one that becomes increasingly worse. This is found in conditions such as presbycusis. A **fluctuating hearing loss** is one whereby a person's hearing may improve or worsen from one day to the next. This is often the case in conditions such as otitis media and Ménière disease.

Other Types of Hearing Disorders

There remain other types of hearing disorders that are less easily classified according to a specific location along the auditory pathway. Two such types of disorders are tinnitus and auditory processing disorder. **Tinnitus** is the medical name used to describe a continuous or intermittent noise in the ears. The term comes from the Latin word for "ringing." Some people experience a mild ringing noise, whereas others are troubled by loud, high-pitched noises. Tinnitus can occur in one or both ears. Tinnitus is divided into two types: (a) objective and (b) subjective. Objective tinnitus is rare. In this condition, the faint noise generated in the ear can be heard (using special equipment) by someone examining the patient. In such cases, the talents of an ear, nose, and throat surgeon are required to seek a surgical cure. Subjective tinnitus is by far the most frequently occurring form of the disorder. In this condition, the noise can be heard only by the patient. Subjective tinnitus is not a disease but a problem in the auditory pathway or in the central nervous system of the brain. There are many factors that have been associated with tinnitus including headaches, elevated blood pressure, emotional tension, exposure to loud noises, medications, allergies, and fatigue. Estimates from the United Kingdom, United States, Australia, and New Zealand indicate that tinnitus affects anywhere from 10% to 20% of the general population. Of these, about 1% experience the condition to a disturbing degree.

Some of the current treatment approaches for tinnitus include devices that look like hearing aids and produce sound that will mask or cover up tinnitus. **Cognitive behavioral therapy** is a treatment administered by a psychotherapist that seeks to change people's attitudes and behavior. When used to treat tinnitus, the therapy seems to improve patients' quality of life, even when the volume of noise from the tinnitus remains the same. Another new therapy is **neuromonics,** which was developed in Australia. This therapy involves the combined use of acoustic stimulation (namely music) with a structured program of counseling and support. The therapy approach needs independent assessment to demonstrate its benefits. In addition, research is underway exploring the use of a biomedical implant that stimulates the vagus nerve. The vagus nerve extends throughout the body with nerve connections to the ear. Stimulation of the vagus nerve serves to overexcite the auditory cortex, which may lead to a reduction in tinnitus symptoms (Gupta & Gupta, 2023).

FYI

Prolonged exposure to loud noise has resulted in many well-known musicians acquiring the condition of tinnitus. The list includes Belinda Butcher, Cher, Eric Clapton, Phil Collins, Mick Fleetwood, Dame Evelynn Glennie, Grimes, Dave Grohl, Chris Martin, Moby, Ozzy Osbourne, The Edge, Sting, Pete Townsend, Lars Ulrich, Neil Young, and Will.i.am.

Auditory processing refers to the way the brain makes sense out of the incoming signals from the auditory pathway. Auditory processing helps us to discriminate between different sounds, pick out sounds or speech from a noisy background, and understand speech when the sound quality is poor. The disorder known as an **auditory processing disorder** is a condition in which an individual demonstrates normal hearing and normal intelligence but may show a hearing problem in the sense that the individual is unable to process information normally. An individual can hear perfectly well but has trouble interpreting or understanding what is being said. Examples of the types of processing difficulties demonstrated by individuals with auditory processing disorder are shown in Table 14–3. The prevalence of auditory processing disorder in the general population has not been firmly established. Estimates indicate that auditory processing disorder occurs in approximately 3% of people, with a two-to-one ratio between males and females. Neurological disorders account for most instances of auditory processing disorder in adults. Among children, a definitive neurological cause for auditory processing disorder is found in only 5% of diagnosed cases. The remaining occurrences have an unknown etiology. In these cases, auditory processing disorder has been called an *invisible disability* because nothing appears to be physically wrong with the individual. The difficulty these individuals experience is often incorrectly assumed to be the result of an attention deficit or a lack of motivation. A general recommendation when treating this condition is to modify the environment by either minimizing background noise or increasing sound amplification (such as in a classroom setting) to facilitate improved auditory processing.

Table 14–3. Types of Difficulties Shown by Individuals With an Auditory Processing Disorder

- Asks for things to be repeated
- Poor listening skills
- Mishears words
- Needs more time to process information
- Difficulty following multistep instructions given orally
- Difficulty hearing in background noise
- Distracted
- Low academic performance
- Language comprehension difficulty

ASSESSMENT OF HEARING DISORDERS

Audiometry is the quantitative measurement of hearing. Measurement of auditory function enables the audiologist to determine the type, degree, location, and configuration of hearing loss. Some of the tests performed to evaluate auditory function are (a) pure-tone audiometry, (b) immittance testing, and (c) electrophysiological testing.

Pure-Tone Audiometry

In **pure-tone audiometry**, a person's hearing acuity for each ear is measured for tones as low as 250 Hz and as high as 8000 Hz. Although our entire range of hearing extends from 20 to 20,000 Hz, the 250 to 8000 Hz range is tested because this is the frequency range we use in order to clearly hear conversational speech. The device used to generate pure tones is called an **audiometer**. Pure-tone audiometry is usually completed while an individual is seated in a sound-isolated booth. During the test, the individual is asked to respond each time they hear the tone. Adult patients usually push a button when the tone is heard, and children raise their hand (Figure 14–12). As part of the test, the audiologist determines the person's threshold for each of the tones. The **threshold** represents the loudness (dB) level at which tones are barely audible. Once determined, the threshold for each frequency is recorded on a graph known as an **audiogram**. The test frequencies (pure tones) are plotted on the horizontal axis of the audiogram, and the intensity (loudness) threshold for each tone is indicated on the vertical axis. The symbols "o" and "x" are used to indicate the thresholds of the right and left ear, respectively. A threshold value of 0 to 20 dB is considered normal hearing acuity. It is possible to have scores less than 0, which indicate better than average hearing. A wide range of audiogram configurations are presented in Figure 14–13.

FIGURE 14–12. Example of pure-tone audiometry. A hand is raised in response to any sound that is heard.

Two types of pure tone testing are (a) air conduction and (b) bone conduction. During **air conduction testing**, headphones are placed over the outer ear. Small foam insert earphones are sometimes used in place of headphones. Insert earphones are placed directly in the entrance to the ear canals. Air conduction testing is designed to examine a person's hearing of sounds as they travel through the air. The sound (pure tone) leaves the earphone and travels down the ear canal as an airborne acoustic signal. Air conduction testing allows the audiologist to examine a person's hearing as sound travels through the entire peripheral auditory system (Figure 14–14). It is not possible to determine the precise location of the impairment by air conduction testing alone. If the person's hearing thresholds for air conduction fall outside the normal range of hearing, it is necessary to perform a follow-up test known as **bone conduction testing**. In bone conduction testing, the pure tones are not presented as an airborne (acoustic) signal but rather via a bone vibrator that is placed on the surface of the skull behind the ear (i.e., mastoid process of temporal bone). These tones are transmitted directly to the cochlea by vibrations in the skull and toward the central auditory system (see Figure 14–14). Bone conduction testing bypasses the outer and middle ear systems because these parts of the auditory system are located outside of the skull. If a person shows a hearing loss from air conduction testing but normal hearing from bone conduction testing, the hearing loss is likely to be an impairment of the outer or middle ear. This is called a conductive hearing loss (see Figure 14–13). A sensorineural hearing loss would be indicated if both air conduction and bone conduction hearing thresholds are higher than normal (see Figure 14–13). When both air and bone conduction thresholds are higher than normal, but bone conduction is the higher of the two, a mixed hearing loss would be indicated.

> **FYI**
>
> Sound can travel through any medium, such as air, water, rock, and steel. Sound cannot travel through a vacuum because it is devoid of matter (i.e., particles). There is no sound in outer space.

Immittance Testing

The term *immittance* refers to ease or compliance of movement. In audiological testing, **immittance testing** is the ease with which sound travels from one medium to another, as from air to bone.

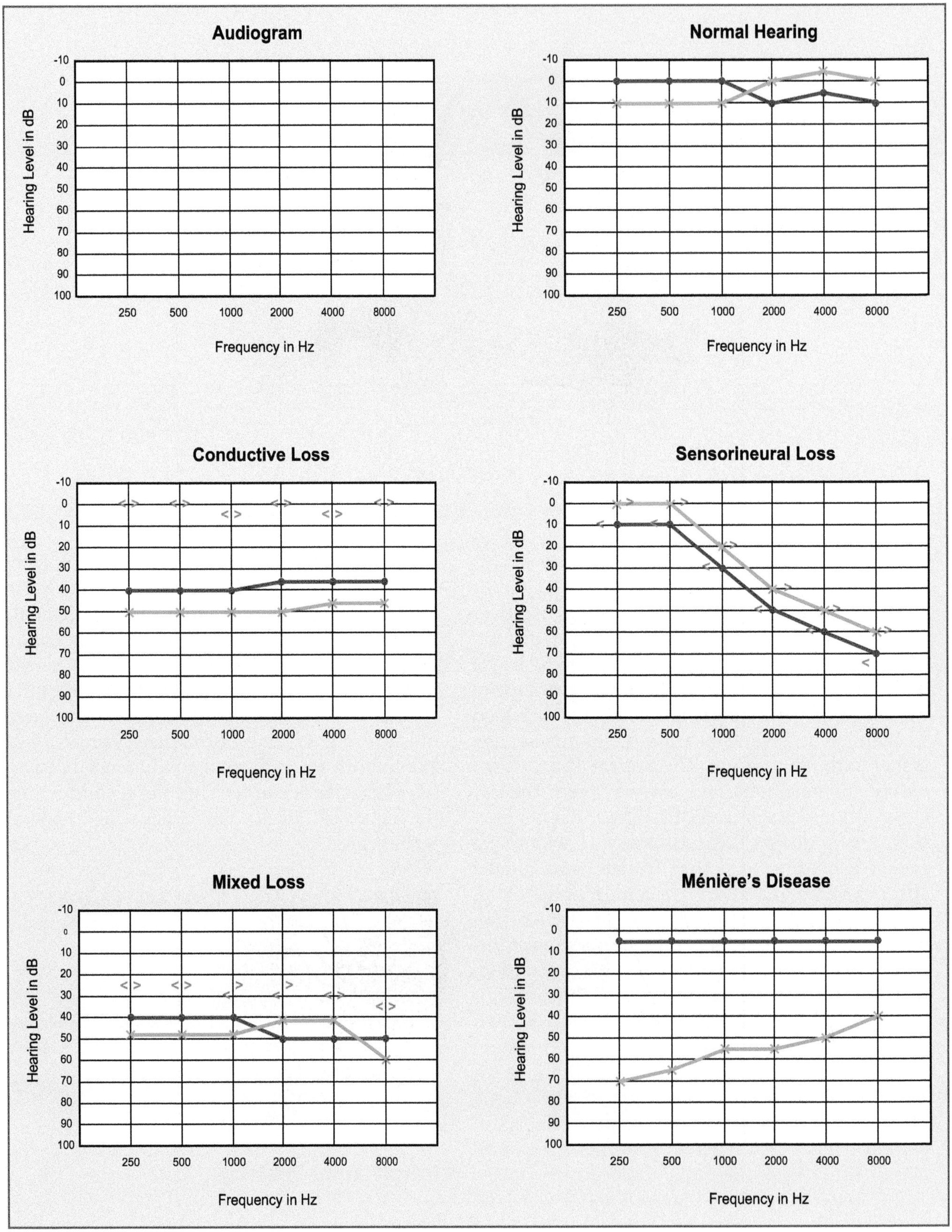

FIGURE 14–13. Audiograms depicting normal hearing and various types of hearing loss. The "x" symbol represents the left ear threshold, and the "o" symbol is the right ear. The "<" and ">" symbols represent bone conduction thresholds for the left and right ear, respectively.

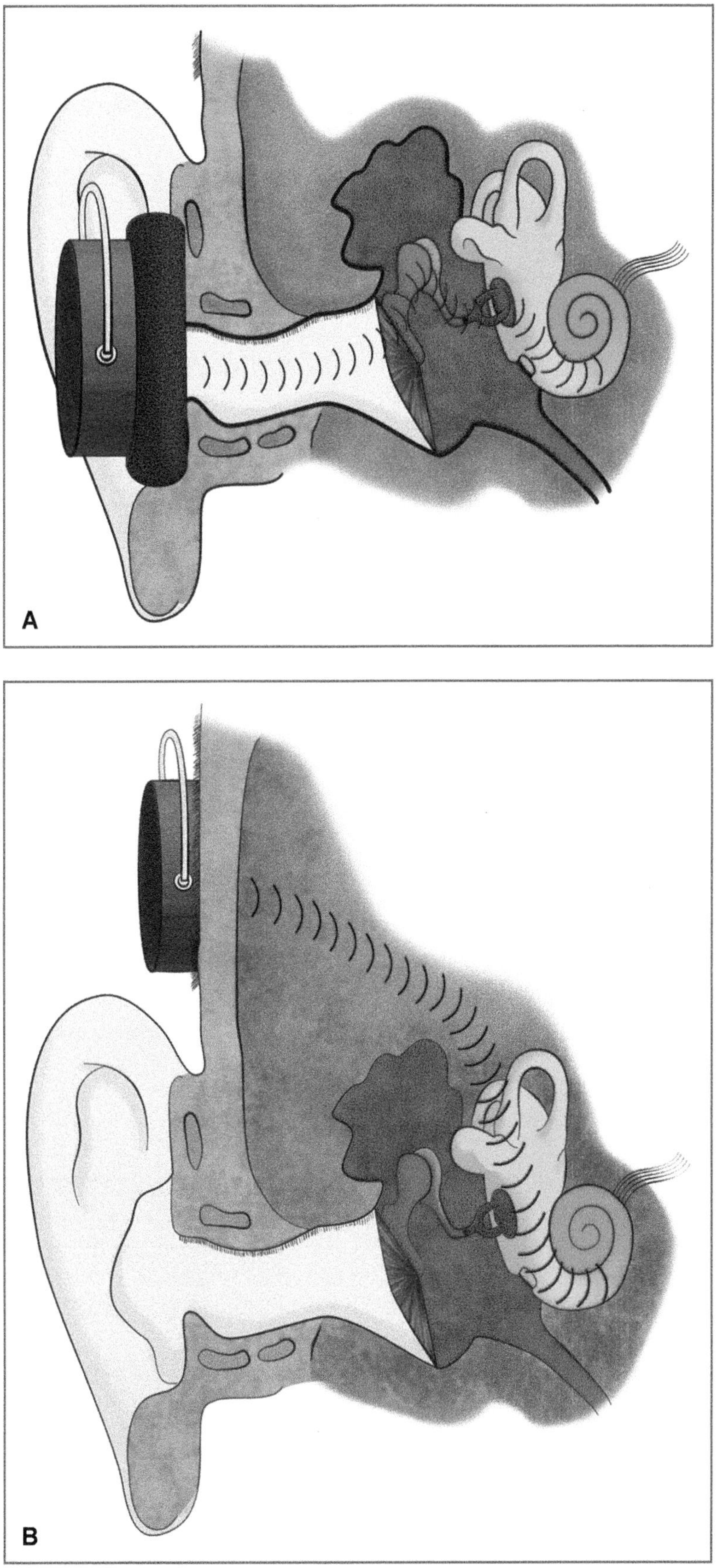

FIGURE 14–14. **A.** Example of air conduction. **B.** Bone conduction pure-tone audiometric testing.

These tests do not provide a direct measure of hearing loss but rather yield information about the mobility of the tympanic membrane and functioning of the middle ear. Immittance tests are considered **nonbehavioral tests** because the individual is not required to push a button or raise a hand for various tones. The response occurs naturally. Two types of immittance tests are (a) tympanometry and (b) acoustic reflex.

Tympanometry is a testing methodology that gives useful information about the presence of fluid in the middle ear, mobility of the middle ear system, and ear canal volume. It provides a graphic representation of the relationship between air pressure in the external ear canal compared with the movement of the tympanic membrane and middle ear ossicular chain. A **tympanometer** instrument is used to perform the test, which is noninvasive. The instrument consists of a probe that is fitted snuggly into the outer ear; the pressure within the ear canal slowly changes, and a tone is transmitted into the canal at the same time. The tone strikes the tympanic membrane, causing vibration of the middle ear. Some of this sound is reflected back and picked up by the tympanometer (Figure 14–15). The amount of sound that is reflected from the eardrum as the pressure in the ear canal varies is quantified and plotted on a graph. These **tympanogram** plots are classified as type A (normal middle ear functioning), type B (flat, indicative of middle ear fluid or punctured eardrum), and type C (off-center, indicative of eustachian tube malfunction). Examples of tympanogram plots are shown in Figure 14–15.

The **acoustic reflex** is an involuntary contraction of the stapedius muscle located in the middle ear. The reflex response is obtained by presenting high-intensity sounds (e.g., 90 dB) via a probe inserted into the ear canal. The probe detects the decibel level at which the stapedius muscle contracts. Following tympanometry, the same equipment used for tympanometry is used in each ear for acoustic reflex testing. Everyone should show an acoustic reflex to loud sounds. The reflex is a protective response of the middle ear to prevent extremely loud sounds from entering (and subsequently damaging) the cochlea. If an acoustic reflex is not present, a middle ear or brainstem disorder would be suspected, as well as a significant hearing loss.

FYI

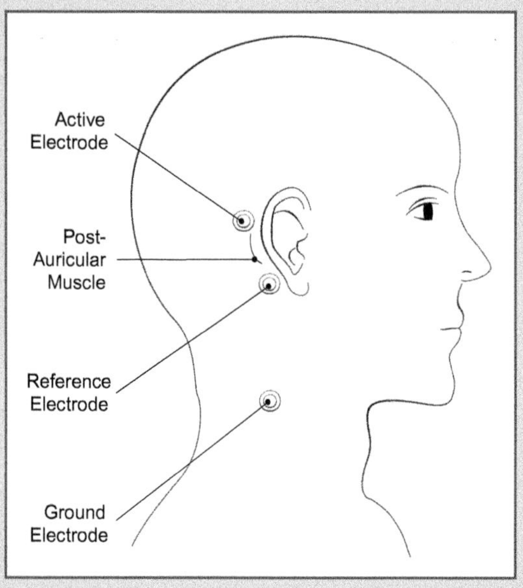

Researchers discovered that muscles located behind the ear could be deliberately activated (and measured) when sound is presented to the ears. The phenomenon has been referred to as the postauricular muscle response. This naturally occurring response has prompted researchers to consider using the postauricular muscle response as a method of screening for hearing impairment.

Electrophysiological Testing

Electrophysiological tests are nonbehavioral tests that are administered to difficult-to-assess individuals or to determine the specific site of an auditory lesion. **Otoacoustic emissions** and the **auditory brainstem response** are the most frequently performed electrophysiological tests. They are fast and easy to administer and do not require the individual to give a behavioral response (such as raising a hand). Otoacoustic emissions are faint acoustic sounds that are generated in the cochlea in response to sounds presented to the inner ear. They are considered to be epiphenomena (i.e., a secondary activity) and a by-product of a normally functioning cochlea. A healthy cochlea creates internal vibrations whenever it processes sound.

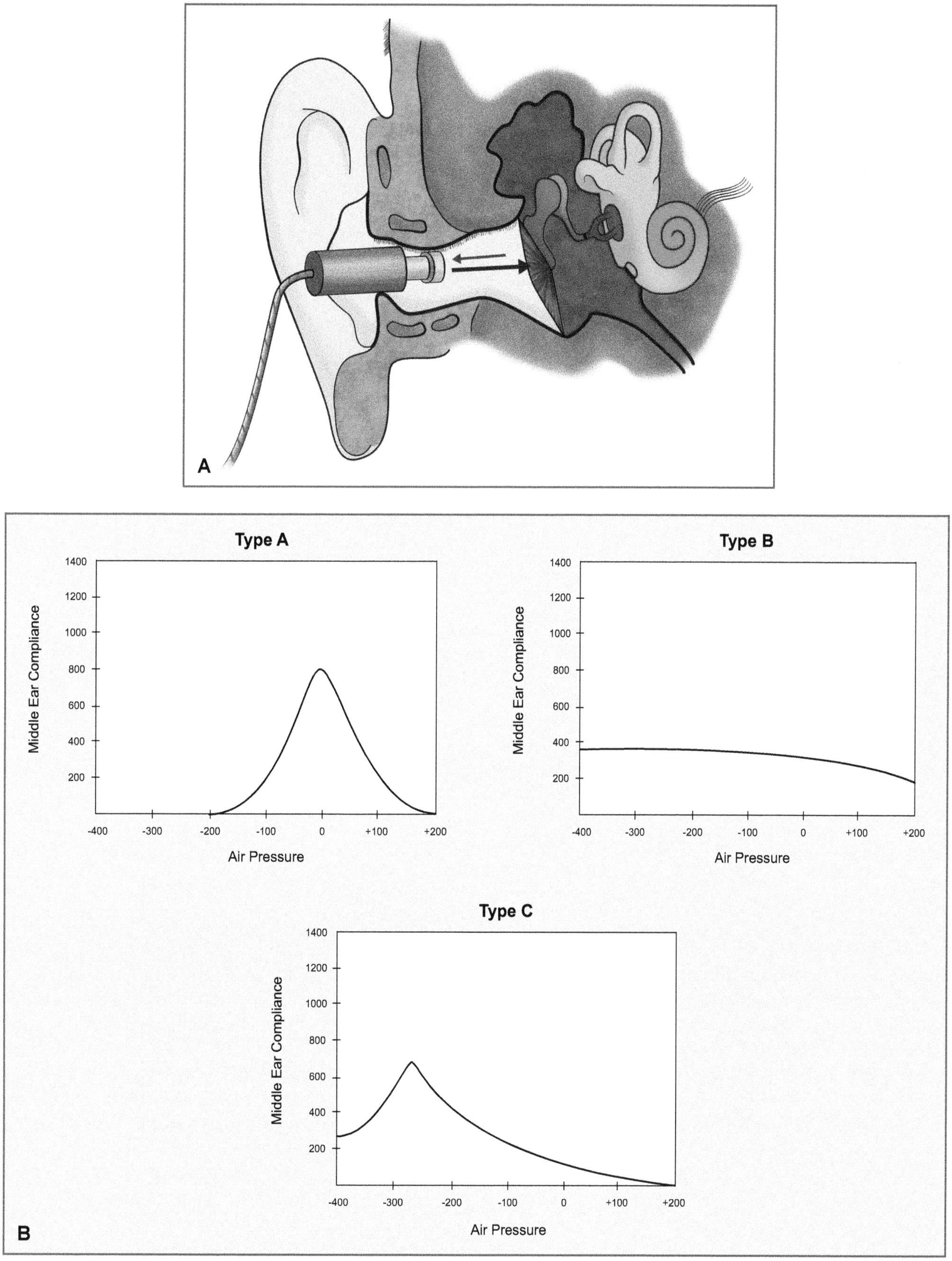

FIGURE 14–15. **A.** Tympanometry testing. A probe is inserted into the ear canal and delivers a tone to measure compliance of the tympanic membrane. Part of the probe tone is reflected backward, and some is admitted into the middle ear. **B.** Examples of three types of tympanograms.

Impaired ears usually do not. These faint sound emissions travel back through the middle ear and into the ear canal where they can be measured with a tiny microphone. Emissions are thought to be generated by the hair cells within the cochlea. Because most forms of hearing involve the loss (i.e., death) of hair cells, the lack of otoacoustic emissions is a good predictor of cochlear hearing loss. Otoacoustic emissions are measured by a probe placed at the opening of the ear canal. An illustration of the otoacoustic emissions setup is shown in Figure 14–16.

In the **auditory brainstem response** technique, **electroencephalography** is used to measure brain wave activity associated with the reception of sound. Prior to the test, three electrodes are attached, one to the forehead and one on each ear. A series of acoustic clicks is then presented to one ear via an earphone. The electrodes pick up the brain's response to those clicks, which appears as a characteristic waveform with five peaks or waves that occur within the first 10 msec of response. The waveform reflects the speed of electrical impulses traveling along the hearing pathway from the inner ear through the brainstem. The person being tested must remain very still during the test and may even be sleeping. An illustration of the auditory brainstem response setup is shown in Figure 14–17. If the auditory brainstem response waveform is missing one or more of the five peaks, or there is a time delay in the appearance of these peaks, the result is indicative of a significant hearing loss or neurological dysfunction.

Evaluating the hearing abilities of a newborn is a difficult task. Infants cannot respond with words or raise a hand to indicate what they hear and when. However, early detection of hearing problems is important. We have increasing evidence that difficulties in hearing during the infancy period may cause irreparable delays in a child's cognitive and communication development. There is a worldwide emphasis on **universal newborn screening** of hearing. Many countries (e.g., Canada, United Kingdom, United States, and New Zealand) have enacted mandatory screening of newborns shortly after birth. The otoacoustic emissions and auditory brainstem response tests are the primary instruments for evaluating a newborn's hearing.

ONLINE HEARING MEASUREMENT

It is now possible to complete a hearing test online. Several hearing aid companies, as well as universities, provide these tests to individuals at no charge. This convenience allows individuals who may be unsure of their hearing abilities the opportunity to seek information in the privacy and comfort of their home. This option is also particularly attractive to individuals who may not have health insurance, cannot afford a visit to the doctor unless it is absolutely necessary, or live in a rural community (Bhutta, 2019). These tests provide only a rough indication of a person's hearing ability. Online tests are not designed to replace a hearing evaluation performed by an audiologist but serve as a first step in the process of seeking help for hearing loss.

CULTURAL CONSIDERATIONS AND HEARING DISORDERS

A wide range of cultural and ethnic variables should be considered when evaluating hearing loss and specific types of hearing disorders. For example, the occurrence of otitis media among indigenous populations such as Hawaiians, New Zealand Maori, Australian Aboriginals, and Native Americans is unusually high. The high occurrence is attributed to the general social and physical environment, limited medical attention, allergies, and possibly also anatomical predispositions. For many nonindigenous children, especially those with good access to medical treatment, middle ear problems and associated hearing loss have been resolved by the time they arrive at school. For most indigenous children, the ramifications of chronic otitis media may disadvantage them throughout the school years and into adulthood.

Epidemiological studies have consistently demonstrated that age-related hearing loss is most common in White men, followed by White women, Black men, and Black women, suggesting that White people are more vulnerable to the

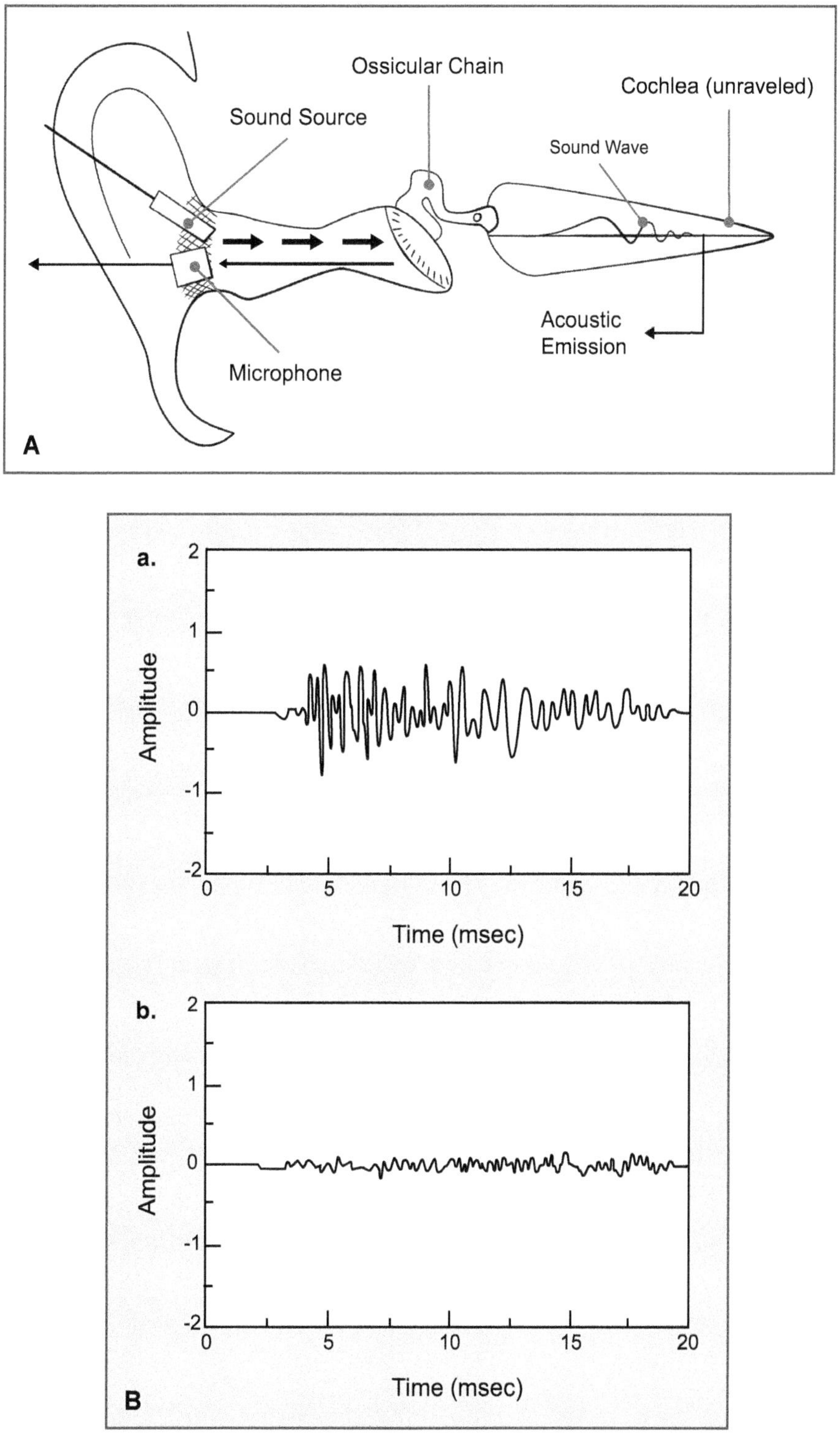

FIGURE 14–16. **A.** Equipment setup for evoking and recording an otoacoustic emission. **B.** An example of normal otoacoustic emissions (*top panel*) and a low emission level (*bottom panel*), which may indicate cochlear dysfunction.

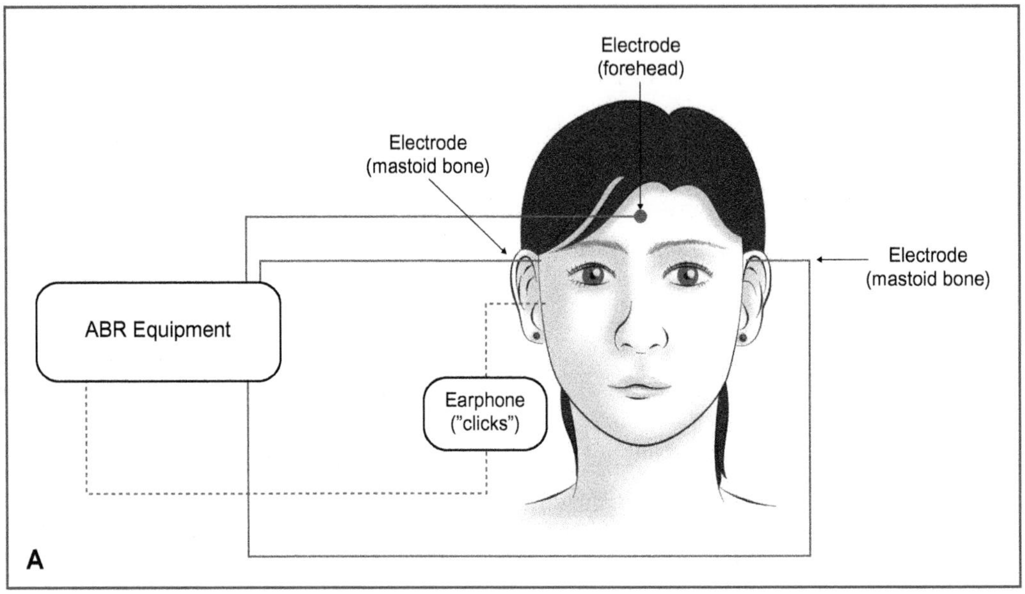

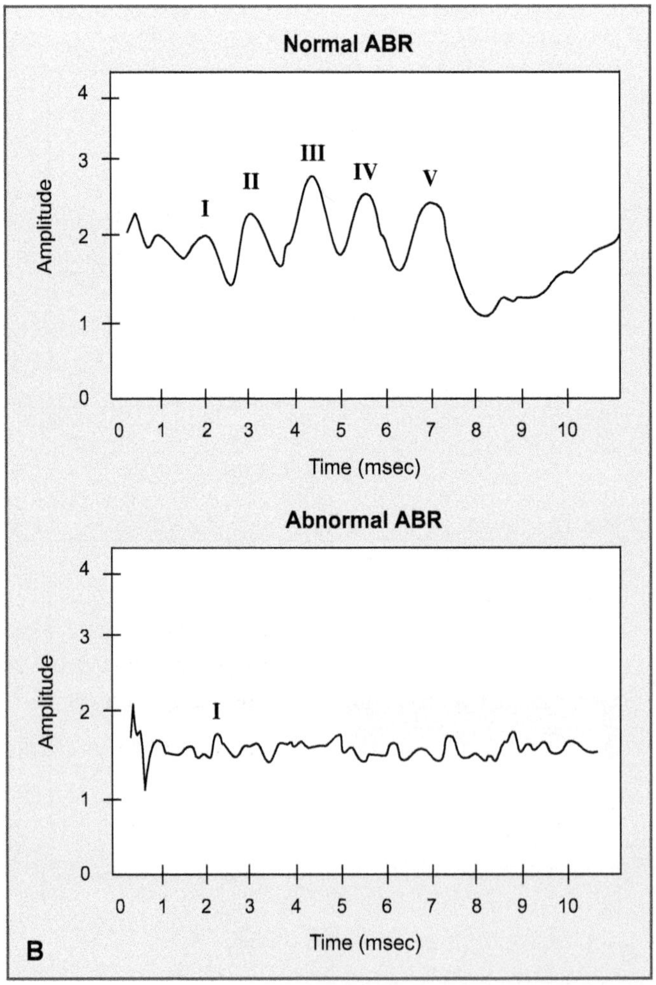

FIGURE 14–17. **A.** Depiction of the equipment setup for evoking and recording an auditory brainstem response. **B.** An example of normal auditory brainstem response with five distinct waveform peaks (*top panel*) and an abnormal auditory brainstem response indicative of a brainstem tumor (*lower panel*).

harmful effects of noise exposure than non-White people (Davis & Hoffman, 2019). It is interesting to note that tribal people in rural Africa do not seem to experience as much age-related hearing loss compared with adults with European backgrounds. One proposed explanation is that melanin-A pigment is found in higher levels among Black people compared with White people (Helzner et al., 2005). Research has shown that high concentrations of melanin-A within the cochlear hair cells may serve to protect hair cells from damage. In addition to race, gender has also been found to affect one's chances of developing an age-related hearing loss. Men are five times more likely than women to acquire a hearing loss at some point in their lifetime. This sex imbalance is attributed to likely biological differences between men and women, as well as the tendency for men to work in occupations that may increase the chance of acquiring a noise-induced hearing loss.

Hearing loss can affect one's desire to participate in cultural and social events. People with hearing loss are less likely to participate in social activities than people without hearing loss. For example, among people over the age of 65 years, those with a hearing loss are less likely to engage in community volunteer work compared with those without a hearing loss. Hearing loss can also affect an individual's emotional well-being. Among people age 70 years and older, those with a hearing loss are more likely to experience bouts of depression compared with those without a hearing loss (Lawrence et al., 2020).

FYI

Aging is inevitable, but the act of performing music seems to provide a type of exercise for the brain that can induce a youthful state. The integration of visual, auditory, motor, and cognitive (as well as emotional) activities in the creation of rhythm appears to provide a boost to the maintenance of neurons. Musical training may provide a unique approach to maintaining our auditory function.

SUMMARY OF CHAPTER

Loss of hearing can have a profound impact on a person's quality of life. Hearing loss in children is typically a condition identified shortly after birth. Among adults, hearing loss is usually a condition that tends to develop gradually over the years. Audiologists are professionals educated in the diagnosis and management of hearing disorders. Audiometry is the quantitative measurement of hearing that enables the audiologist to determine the type, degree, location, and configuration of hearing loss. Some of the tests performed to evaluate auditory function are (a) pure-tone audiometry, (b) immittance testing, and (c) electrophysiological testing. Hearing loss can affect one's desire to participate in cultural and social events.

HEARING DISORDERS ON THE WORLD WIDE WEB

Following are websites that provide further information on the topic of hearing disorders. At the time of publication, each website was freely accessible.

Types of Hearing Loss
http://www.earsite.com

https://www.soundly.com/blog/types-of-hearing-loss

Child and Adult Hearing Test Video
https://www.youtube.com/@UCSpeechAndHearing/videos

How We Hear Video
https://yais.nhs.uk/how-we-hear-bchd/

"Listen to Your Buds" Video
https://youtu.be/ieyoG-WAfy0

Pediatric Hearing Loss Videos
http://www.infanthearing.org/videos/index.html

Sound Advice for Farmers
https://nasdonline.org/4159/V000001/sound-advice-for-farming.html

Tinnitus Video
https://www.pbs.org/video/tinnitus-xomdvn/

STUDY QUESTIONS

1. List and describe the various categories of deafness.
2. How do conductive and sensorineural hearing losses differ?
3. What are the major disorders of the outer, middle, and inner ear?
4. List and describe the tests used to evaluate auditory function.
5. What are some of the cultural and ethnic variables related to hearing loss?

REFERENCES

Bhutta, M. F. (2019). Models of service delivery for ear and hearing care in remote or resource-constrained environments. *Journal of Laryngology & Otology*, *133*(1), 39–48.

Davis, A. C., & Hoffman, H. J. (2019). Hearing loss: Rising prevalence and impact. *Bulletin of the World Health Organization*, *97*(10), 646.

Gupta, J., & Gupta, R. (2023). A scoping new revolution for tinnitus management: A neuromonics narrative review. *Current Drug Targets*, *24*, 274–286.

Helzner, E. P., Cauley, J. A., Pratt, S. R., Wisniewski, S. R., Zmuda, J. M., Talbott, E. O., . . . Newman, A. B. (2005). Race and sex differences in age-related hearing loss: The health, aging and body composition study. *Journal of the American Geriatric Society*, *53*, 2119–2127.

Lawrence, B. J., Jayakody, D. M., Bennett, R. J., Eikelboom, R. H., Gasson, N., & Friedland, P. L. (2020). Hearing loss and depression in older adults: A systematic review and meta-analysis. *The Gerontologist*, *60*(3), e137–e154.

15

AUDITORY REHABILITATION

OBJECTIVES

After reading this chapter, the student should be able to:

- Define aural rehabilitation and understand why the service is necessary for those who have hearing loss.
- Describe the components of a hearing aid.
- Understand the different types and styles of amplification or assistive listening devices plus the related advantages and disadvantages of each device.
- Explain the nature and features of various auditory implants.
- Describe the speech and language features that accompany a severe hearing loss.
- Describe the types of aural rehabilitation programs available to children and adults.
- Discuss, compare, and contrast the different types of communication options, methods, training approaches, and philosophies (e.g., oral/aural, total communication, sign only, American Sign Language/British Sign Language).
- Discuss issues pertaining to Deaf culture.

KEY TERMS

Aural Rehabilitation
Aural Habilitation
Hard of Hearing
Deafness
Microphone
Amplifier
Speaker
Miller Reese Hutchison
Pedro Ponce de León
Pär Aron Borg
Laurent Clerc
Thomas Hopkins Gallaudet
Laura Bridgman
Helen Keller
Anne Sullivan
Christine Yoshinaga-Itano
Myringotomy
Ventilation Tube
Pressure Equalization Tube
Grommet
Tympanoplasty
Behind-the-Ear (BTE) Aid
In-the-Ear (ITE) Aid
In-the-Canal (ITC) Aid
Completely-in-the-Canal (CIC) Aid
Invisible-in-the-Canal (IIC) Aid
Body Aids
Assistive Listening Devices
Signal-to-Noise Ratio
Soundfield Amplification
Captioning (Closed)
Emerson Romero
Bone-Anchored Hearing Aid (BAHA)
Percutaneously
Graeme Clark
Auditory Brainstem Implant (ABI)
Middle Ear Implant
Sound Visibility
Acoustic Characteristics
Hypernasal Speech
Syntax
Speech Reading
Cued Speech
Oral
Aural
Nasometer
Visi-Pitch
Manual Communication
Sign Language
Finger Spelling
Simultaneous Communication (SimCom)
Informational Counseling
Personal Adjustment Counseling
Deaf-blindness
Print-in-Palm
Braille
Louis Braille
Tadoma Method
Medical Model
Cultural Model

INTRODUCTION

Hearing loss is referred to as an invisible condition, yet its impact is anything but invisible (Tye-Murray, 2020). Whether the severity of hearing loss is mild or profound, it can have serious consequences on an individual's overall well-being. Several devices to improve hearing and various forms of treatment have been developed to assist individuals with a diagnosed hearing loss. Decisions regarding the best approach are guided by factors such as the age of the person and the type of hearing loss that they demonstrate, with the goal of improving an individual's communication and overall quality of life. The purpose of this chapter is to provide background on the tools and approaches used to help improve hearing and minimize the consequences of a hearing loss.

TERMINOLOGY AND DEFINITIONS

Aural rehabilitation involves techniques used with people who are **hard-of-hearing** to improve their ability to communicate, and this includes both listening and speaking. Presumably, these individuals once demonstrated normal hearing earlier in life. Since then, a hearing loss has occurred, requiring assistance in improving their communication abilities in order to compensate for sounds of speech and daily living they no longer hear clearly. People who have a hearing loss at birth also require assistance in compensating for their loss. For these individuals, the more appropriate term is **aural habilitation**. Aural rehabilitation (including habilitation) is all about learning how to take advantage of what a person hears and sees in the environment. The features of a rehabilitation program are unique to everyone. A person's age, severity of hearing loss, and daily living environment are taken into consideration. For example, an individual who is hard-of-hearing shows a partial hearing impairment that may range from mild to severe. The individual's needs could be quite different from those of an individual with **deafness**, who has minimal or no hearing. Aural rehabilitation typically is provided by an audiologist, although speech-language pathologists and teachers of the deaf or hard of hearing may also make important contributions. There are various locations where aural rehabilitation occurs, including hospitals, nursing homes, and community centers, as well as the classroom.

HISTORIC ASPECTS OF AURAL REHABILITATION

Origins of Aural Rehabilitation

The concept of aural rehabilitation was developed in the 1940s as a response to World War II. Prior to this time, there was no specific program for improving the quality of life for adults with postlingual hearing loss, despite schools for the deaf having been in existence since the late 1800s. Many individuals who served in the war developed severe cases of noise-induced hearing loss. These losses could not be treated using medical or surgical techniques. Military hospitals began to develop aural rehabilitation programs to assist these injured soldiers. Specialists in fields such as speech pathology, psychology, medicine, and deaf education were brought together to design aural rehabilitation programs. Lip reading was stressed as one of the major rehabilitation approaches. During the 1940s, wearable hearing aids were also available and, along with lip reading, became a significant component of rehabilitation.

The need for a specially qualified individual to assist with the needs of people with hearing loss eventually led to creation of the profession of audiology. The establishment of audiology contributed to new techniques for diagnosing and managing hearing loss for children and adults. However, the major focus of the audiology profession during the period of 1950 to 1980 was on the diagnosis of hearing loss, with far less attention placed on the rehabilitation of hearing loss. The lack of attention to rehabilitation was driven by the view that it was unethical for an audiologist to sell a hearing aid. Such an activity was left to salespeople who had little or no training in audiological care. Ironically, this created a situation in which the actual rehabilitation of individuals with hearing loss was performed by individuals far less qualified than audiologists. All of this changed in 1978 when the American Speech and Hearing Association permitted audiologists to dispense hearing aids. Today, audiologists are able to provide comprehensive diagnostic and rehabilitative services to individuals with hearing loss. Combining these services has led to enormous improvements in the provision of audiological care.

History of Hearing Devices

Dating back to the earliest hearing devices (or aids), their function has remained essentially unchanged: to increase the loudness of sound. Prior to the 20th century, the only way to provide amplification was to reduce the amount of outside, distracting noise. The primary way to accomplish this noise reduction was to filter out other noise by directing the desired sound straight into the ear with some kind of tube or trumpet (Figure 15–1). These trumpets were large and awkward, although some models could be worn on the head and attached to a harness. Cupping your hand behind your ear gives a similar (but smaller) amplification effect.

Hearing aid technology has certainly come a long way in the past 100 years. Changes in hearing aids were linked to two important milestones in technology: (a) the advent of electricity and (b) Alexander Graham Bell's work on the telephone. Early electric hearing aids used the concept of a **microphone** that picks up sound, an **amplifier** that makes the sound louder, and a **speaker** that delivers the amplified sound to the ear. **Miller Reese Hutchison** (1876–1944) was an American electrical engineer who developed the first electoral hearing aid in 1898 that was called the "akouphone." These early electric hearing aids were so large that they sat on a table. The cost of these devices was far beyond the means of most people. In the early 1920s, hearing aid technology incorporated the use of vacuum tubes, which allowed a much more efficient method for amplifying sound. However, the early electric hearing aids were still unwieldy and could not be carried around easily. The miniaturization of batteries in the 1930s led to a significant decrease in the size of hearing aids. Hearing aids were made portable by allowing the user to wear a battery pack. By the early 1950s, vacuum tubes were replaced by transistors, and this resulted in a technological revolution in the design of hearing aids. Early transistor hearing aids were designed to fit within the frames of eyeglasses. Later, they were adapted to fit behind the ear. The 1990s saw a major shift in hearing aid technology from analog to digital circuitry, which led to major improvements in sound quality. Despite the many changes in hearing aid design and technology over the past century, they still rely on the concept of a microphone, amplifier, and speaker.

FIGURE 15–1. Early hearing aid, known as an ear trumpet. The instrument was designed to reduce the amount of distracting noise.

Deaf Education

Pedro Ponce de León (1520–1584; Figure 15–2), a Benedictine monk living in Spain, was the first teacher of the deaf in the modern era. His students were mostly children of aristocrats who had the financial means to provide their children with private tutoring. His work with deaf children focused

FIGURE 15–2. Monument of Pedro Ponce de León in Madrid, Spain. He was the first teacher of the deaf circa 1550.

on helping them learn how to speak intelligibly. He also instructed the children in sign language. The monks observed daily periods of silence and had developed a series of hand gestures to help communicate during those times. Thus, it was natural for de León to apply this form of communication with his deaf students. The prevailing opinion among most Europeans in the 1500s was that people with deafness were incapable of being educated. Many even believed that the deaf were too intellectually disabled to be eligible for salvation under Christian doctrine. So, de León's work with the deaf was considered quite bold and courageous. He was able to demonstrate that these children could learn not only to speak but also to read and write.

Pär Aron Borg (1776–1839) was from Sweden and an early educator of children with deafness. He is credited with developing the first manual sign language alphabet, and he also established a vocational school in Stockholm. Some of the current symbols used in manual alphabets around the world were originally created by Borg. **Laurent Clerc** (1785–1869) was born in a small village near Lyons, France. Although he was French, Clerc is considered by many to be the "father of deaf education" in the United States. He was born hearing but as an infant fell from his highchair, which resulted in a complete loss of hearing in both ears. He entered the Royal Institution for the Deaf in Paris where he excelled in his studies. His outstanding academic abilities, despite a profound hearing loss, caught the attention of a visiting American, **Thomas Hopkins Gallaudet** (1787–1851; Figure 15–3). Gallaudet invited Clerc to visit the United States, and the two eventually established the first school for the deaf in Hartford, Connecticut, now known as the American School for the Deaf. Clerc never returned to France and dedicated his life to educating deaf children. The American School for the Deaf remains the oldest existing school in the United States for the education of deaf and hard-of-hearing students. Gallaudet University in Washington, DC, is named in honor of Thomas Gallaudet (see also Chapter 14).

FIGURE 15–3. Thomas Hopkins Gallaudet established the first school for the deaf in the United States.

FIGURE 15–4. Laura Bridgman, the first person with deaf-blindness to be formally educated in the United States.

Laura Bridgman (1829–1889; Figure 15–4) was born in Hanover, New Hampshire. At 2 years of age, she developed scarlet fever. The illness killed two of her older sisters and one of her brothers. She survived, although she lost her vision and hearing. A courageous individual, she was the first person who was deaf-blind to be successfully educated in the modern era. She attended the Perkins School for the Blind in Massachusetts, where she learned to read, write, and sew. She eventually became a sewing teacher at the school and remained there until her death. Bridgman was famous for her accomplishments, which were described in newspapers and magazines worldwide. Her fame was later eclipsed by that of Helen Keller.

Helen Keller (1880–1968; Figure 15–5) was born in Tuscumbia, Alabama. Her birth history was quite similar to Laura Bridgman's. Helen had a normal birth, but at the age of 19 months developed scarlet fever, which left her deaf and blind. Her only companion until the age of 6 years was the family housekeeper, Martha Washington. As Keller grew older, the family became increasingly frustrated in their attempts to communicate with their daughter. Helen's mother eventually read about the success of Laura Bridgman and later visited a local expert on the problems of deaf children. This expert was Alexander Graham Bell, and he recommended that the family take Helen to the Perkins School for the Blind. It was there that Helen met her teacher **Anne Sullivan** (1866–1936), who would become Helen's companion for the next 50 years. In 1904, Helen graduated from Radcliffe College, becoming the first deaf-blind person to earn a Bachelor of Arts degree. She and Anne went on a series of lecture tours around the world, speaking of her experiences. She became a major advocate for ensuring the rights of the deaf and blind. During her lifetime, she was introduced to every U.S. president from Grover Cleveland to Lyndon B. Johnson and met many celebritiesas well.

FIGURE 15–5. The student Helen Keller and her teacher Anne Sullivan.

FYI

The life of German composer Ludwig van Beethoven (1770–1827) was affected by hearing problems. Beethoven did not become suddenly deaf; his loss of hearing was a slow process, spanning approximately 20 years. He was known to use a hearing trumpet. By the age of 50 years, he was totally deaf and could not hear music. In his years of total deafness, he completed his Ninth Symphony. It is said that after his first public performance of the symphony, he cried when he was turned around to see the audience's response to the music.

Christine Yoshinaga-Itano (Figure 15–6) was both a teacher of the deaf and hard of hearing and an audiologist. Her career focused on the impact of early identification and early intervention on the developmental outcomes of children with significant hearing loss. She was the first to demonstrate that early identification of hearing loss coupled with appropriate interventions services led to young children maintaining age-appropriate language development and intelligible speech in the first 5 years of life. As a result of this research, universal newborn hearing screening programs were implemented throughout the United States.

FIGURE 15–6. Christine Yoshinaga-Itano emphasized the importance of early identification of hearing loss and the importance of early intervention on the developmental outcomes of children with significant hearing loss. (Reproduced with permission granted by C. Yoshinaga-Itano.)

TREATMENT APPROACHES: HEARING REHABILITATION

One component of aural rehabilitation is the direct treatment of hearing loss. Three approaches to treat hearing loss are (a) surgery, (b) hearing aid fitting, and (c) auditory implants.

Surgical Treatment

Two surgical procedures that address pathology of the tympanic membrane and middle ear are myringotomy and tympanoplasty. **Myringotomy** involves making a small incision in the eardrum to drain fluid that has accumulated in the middle ear space and serves to relieve pressure within the middle ear. The surgery is often performed on children who are prone to otitis media with effusion, although adults occasionally acquire similar problems requiring the myringotomy procedure. The buildup of fluid implies that the eustachian tube is not functioning and is unable to perform its normal role of keeping the middle ear dry and ventilated. The fluid buildup creates a conductive hearing loss, and once the fluid is drained, the individual's hearing is essentially restored. As part of the surgery, a small **ventilation tube** (also called a **pressure equalization tube** or **grommet**) is placed around the incision. The tube serves to ventilate the middle ear and prevent fluid from accumulating (Figure 15–7). Most tubes are made of a synthetic plastic material, such as silicone or Teflon. They typically stay in place for approximately 9 months before they are pushed out by the rapidly healing eardrum. A small scar usually

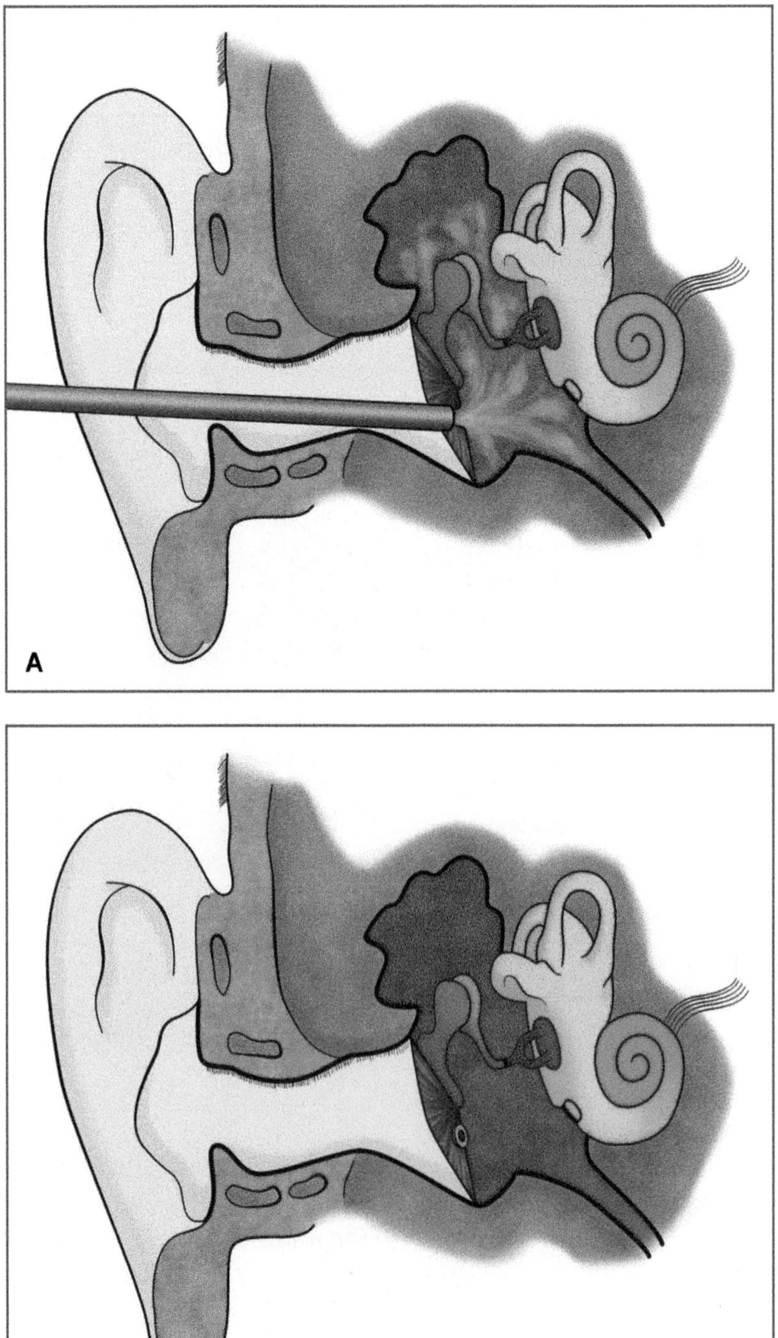

FIGURE 15–7. **A.** Myringotomy procedure. **B.** Insertion of a ventilation tube (i.e., grommet) in the tympanic membrane.

forms in the eardrum, although the scarring does not impair hearing. The surgery is an outpatient procedure, meaning the patient returns home on the same day the surgery takes place.

Tympanoplasty is a microsurgical procedure to repair a perforated tympanic membrane or reconstruct the small bones of the middle ear. The procedure can also help treat certain types of hearing loss and prevent infection of the middle ear. Three types of tympanoplasty are (a) myringoplasty, which is a repair of a tear in the eardrum; (b) tympanoplasty with ossiculoplasty, which is a repair of a tear in the eardrum and correction of a defect in middle ear ossicles; and (c) tympanoplasty with mastoidectomy, which is a repair of an eardrum tear and removal of a bony infection in the area behind the ear. An illustration of tympanoplasty is shown in Figure 15–8.

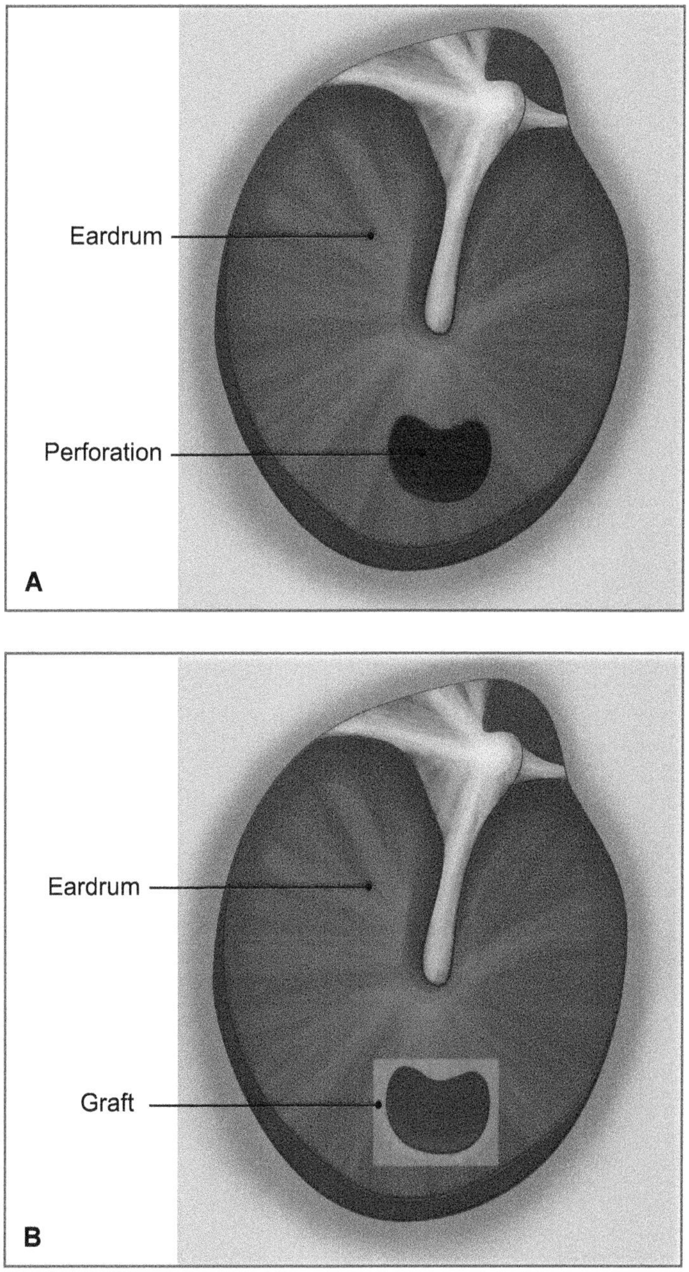

FIGURE 15–8. **A.** Example of a perforated (punctured) tympanic membrane. **B.** Tympanoplasty involving repair of the puncture.

FYI

Americans wait an average of 7 years after diagnosis of a hearing loss before deciding to purchase a hearing aid. Roughly 80% of people who would benefit from a hearing aid choose to go without. The stigma associated with wearing a hearing aid as well as the cost of an aid seem to be the reasons why.

Hearing Devices

The use of hearing aids to treat hearing loss typically is considered when no medical or surgical option is available to correct the loss. As mentioned earlier, a hearing aid consists of three major components: (a) microphone, (b) amplifier, and (c) speaker. All components are housed in a plastic case that protects them and allows the hearing aid to be fitted on the ear (Figure 15–9). The microphone serves to transform the incoming acoustic sound into an electrical signal. The amplifier then increases the intensity of the electrical signal. A programmable filter is an additional feature of the amplifier. Filters can selectively modify sound so that only the sounds needed by the person with a hearing loss are amplified. The speaker converts the electrical signal that has been amplified back into an acoustic sound, which is transmitted down the ear canal. Hearing aids function as miniature computers that are designed to deliver a "clean" signal to the cochlea.

Hearing aids tend to be expensive, and the high cost is due to the manufacturing of miniaturized components. They are built to be durable, but like any electronic device, they can be broken if dropped on a hard surface. Exposure to water also can lead to damage, so they must not be worn in the shower or when swimming. Hearing aids come in various sizes, generally corresponding to the amount of power (or amplification) that can be provided. Large hearing aids usually provide the most amplification and are prescribed for individuals with more severe hearing loss. A listing of the various types of hearing aids follows.

Behind-the-Ear Aids

A **behind-the-ear (BTE) aid** consists of two parts (Figure 15–10). One part is the actual hearing aid, and this is situated behind the ear; the other part is an acrylic/silicon earmold that fits in the outermost portion of the ear canal. The mold is connected to the hearing aid with a transparent tube that transmits the amplified sound from the hearing aid into the ear canal. People with a wide range of hearing losses, from mild to profound, can be fitted with BTE hearing aids. Because the components are housed outside of the ear, these aids tend to be the most durable. This durability makes them ideal for children, and the size of the hearing aid also provides a high level of amplification, if needed. A popular modification to BTE aids is to fit the aid without a mold but with a small plastic tip on the end of the tubing (called an open-ear fitting). The soft silicone tip has holes so that the ear canal is not sealed off. The advantage of an open-fit BTE aid is the cosmetic appeal, as well as the open feeling in the ear canal. Another variation of the BTE aid involves placing the speaker directly at the end of the tubing, called a receiver-in-the-canal (RIC) hearing aid. The RIC aid has become a popular style of aid for individuals with hearing loss ranging from mild to severe.

In-the-Ear Aids

All components of an **in-the-ear (ITE) aid** are built into a custom-made mold (see Figure 15–10) that fits snugly in the bowl of the outer ear. The mold is normally made to be similar to the color of one's skin. The ITE hearing aid can be used by people who have mild-to-severe hearing losses. This aid is not recommended for individuals who have a severe-to-profound hearing loss, or problems with finger or hand dexterity that make manipulating small controls difficult.

In-the-Canal Aids

The **in-the-canal (ITC) aid** is custom designed, smaller in size than the ITE aid, and fits partly in

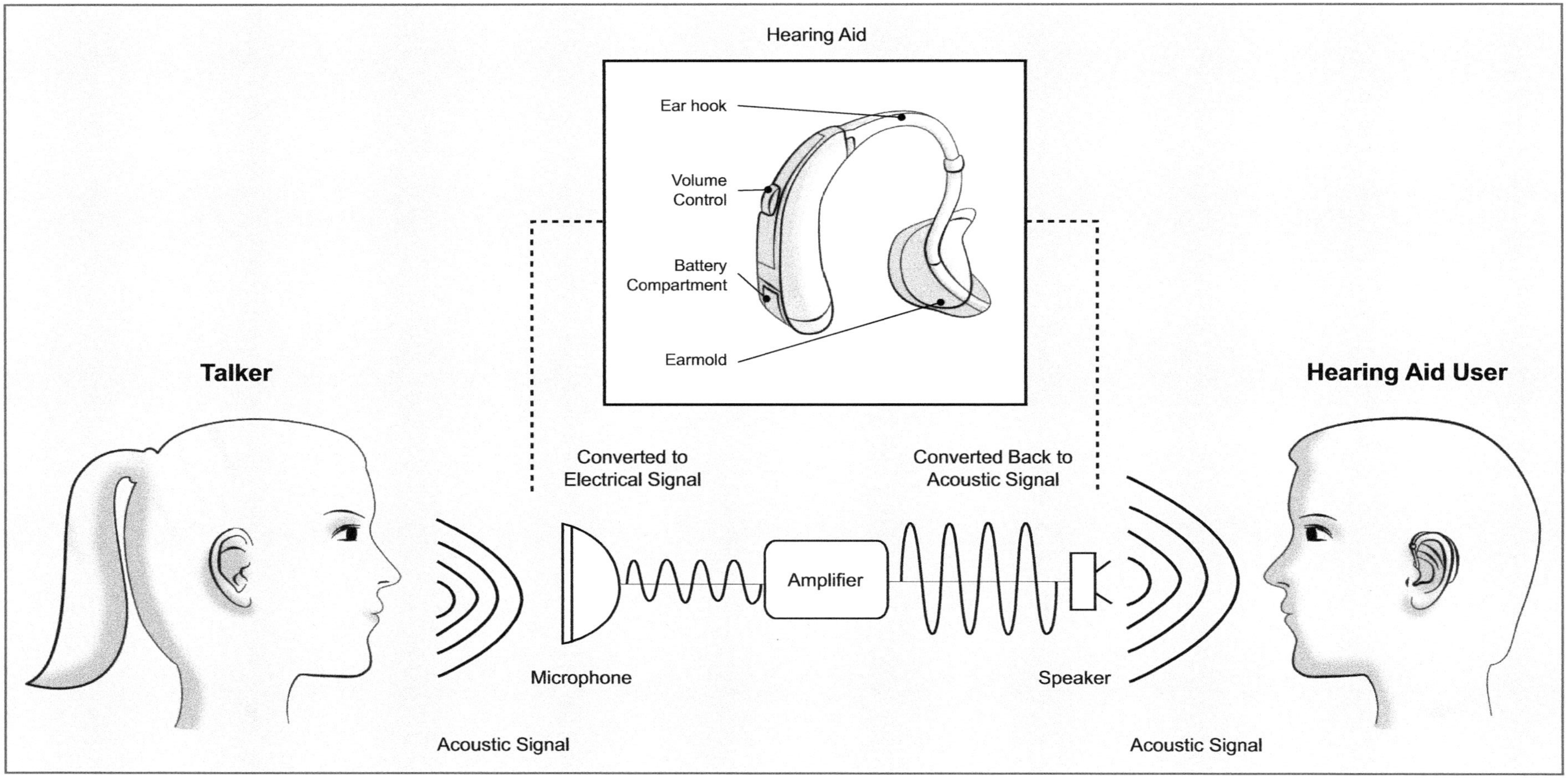

FIGURE 15–9. The transmission of sound between a speaker and a hearing aid user.

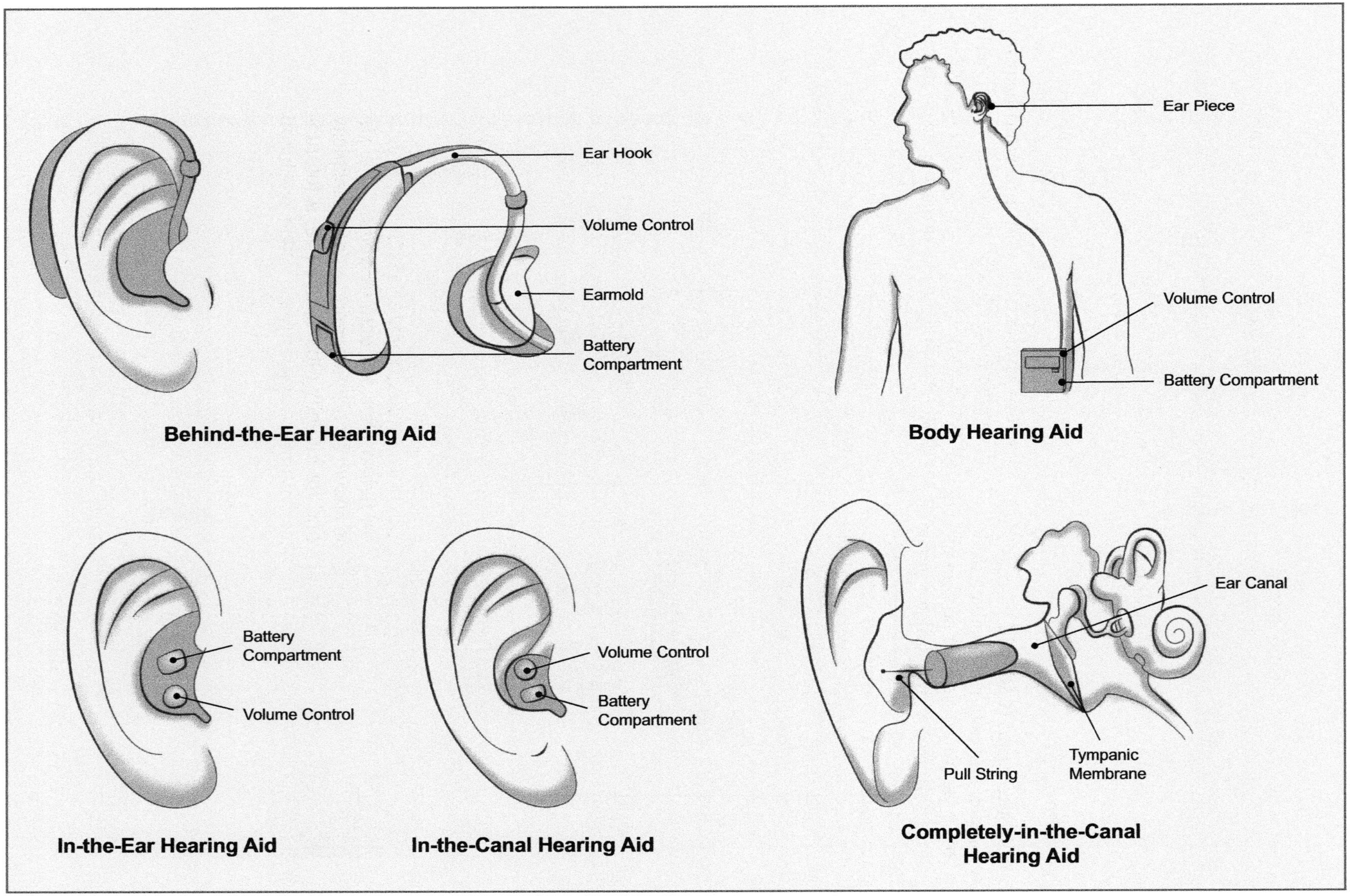

FIGURE 15–10. The various types of hearing aids currently available to individuals with varying degrees of hearing loss. Volume controls on hearing aids are becoming more rare with advances in wireless technology for controlling hearing aids.

the ear canal (see Figure 15–10). It has a wide cosmetic appeal because it is less visible than ITE aids. Like the ITE, all components are housed within a single plastic shell. Because they are smaller in size, ITC aids are particularly good for management of mild-to-moderate hearing losses. People with this aid find it convenient for telephone and cell phone use.

Completely-in-the-Canal Aids

A **completely-in-the-canal (CIC) aid** is small, fits inside the ear canal, and is barely visible (see Figure 15–10). This type of aid has the advantage of sitting very close to the eardrum, which improves sound quality and reduces wind noise and the "echo" sensation sometimes found in larger aids. The size of the CIC aid makes it very appealing from a cosmetic standpoint. The small size, however, also has some disadvantages, such as a short battery life because the batteries are so small. Some people may not be good candidates for a CIC aid if they have unusually shaped ear canals or if they have a severe hearing loss. A slight variation on the CIC aid is called the **invisible-in-the-canal (IIC) aid** and is placed deep in the ear canal. The IIC aid is designed for people with very active lives.

Body-Worn Aids

The earliest forms of modern hearing aids were body worn. This type of aid may seem outdated but is still in use today. These aids can be clearly distinguished from other hearing aids because they require a battery pack and amplifier that is worn in a harness on the body (or situated in a shirt pocket; see Figure 15–10). They are much less bulky than the older body aids and are more attractively designed. These days, **body aids** are used by individuals with profound hearing loss because they are likely to provide the highest level of sound amplification. They also are prescribed for some individuals who do not have the manual dexterity to operate a BTE aid, as they are simple to operate with large controls and switches that are easy to handle. Finally, the cost of body aids tends to be substantially less than BTE-style aids.

Over-the-Counter Hearing Aids

The typical process of obtaining a hearing aid involves an assessment by an audiologist who prescribes a specific type of hearing aid (such as the various types listed earlier). Hearing aids are known to be pricey, and for some individuals, the cost is prohibitive. However, over-the-counter

FYI

Count Alessandro Volta (1745–1827) was an Italian physicist born in Como, Italy. He is known for his pioneering work in electricity and for inventing the voltaic pile, a forerunner of the electric battery, which produced a steady stream of electricity. The electrical unit known as the volt was named in his honor. Volta was also the first to note that the auditory system could be stimulated electrically. He inserted an electrical current into his ears via two metal rods. He reported a sensation that was like a "boom within the head" followed by a sound similar to that of "boiling of thick soup."

(OTC) hearing aids are an option, especially for those with mild-to-moderate hearing loss. These include BTE and ITE styles of hearing aids that are sold directly from the manufacturer. No in-person visit to the audiologist is required. The person simply buys the device and begins using it immediately. The OTC hearing aids can be either self-fitting or not self-fitting. A self-fitting aid allows the user to adjust settings to suit their hearing needs. A non-self-fitting aid comes with a volume control and a few predetermined settings. Both types cost less than prescription hearing aids. It is still advisable for individuals with hearing loss to seek the advice of an audiologist when considering the purchase of a hearing aid.

Assistive Listening Devices

The hearing needs of some individuals cannot be successfully addressed with hearing aids alone. In these cases, devices have been created that are used to facilitate listening in various environments, especially those with excessive noise. Some **assistive listening devices** are designed to be used with hearing aids, whereas others are designed for independent use. Assistive listening devices can amplify a sound, but their primary purpose is to separate background (distracting) sounds from speech sounds. They improve what is known as the **signal-to-noise ratio**, which is the difference in level between the signal of interest and the background noise. Examples of assistive listening devices include (a) a telecoil, (b) soundfield amplification, and (c) captioning. A helpful feature of most hearing aids is called the telecoil, or "t-switch." A telecoil is used when speaking and listening on a telephone. A hearing aid uses a microphone to pick up sound and send it into the ear canal. When the telecoil switch is activated, the hearing aid also can detect a magnetic signal transmitted through the actual telephone device. This magnetic signal serves to further enhance the signal-to-noise ratio allowing for better listening over the telephone. **Soundfield amplification** systems typically are found in classroom settings and are designed to amplify and broadcast the teacher's voice through loudspeakers. The system consists of a microphone/FM transmitter, amplifier, and one or more loudspeakers. **Captioning (closed)** is a form of assistive listening device, in which words that are said on a television show are embedded in the signal and become visible with a special decoder. The decoder lets hard-of-hearing individuals see captions at the bottom of the screen that tell them what is being spoken in the television program. Most televisions have a built-in option to display closed captioning of broadcasts; however, this feature will work only if the specific television program has been captioned beforehand. These days, captioning can also be found on many 24-hour news channels, without the need for a decoder. These television stations provide a seemingly endless stream of text information in addition to what is being spoken.

FYI

Emerson Romero (1900–1972) was a silent film actor who was deaf. The advent of talking movies ended his career and impacted filmgoers who were hearing impaired. He is credited with introducing early methods of film captioning that made Hollywood movies accessible to the deaf.

Auditory Implants

An auditory implant provides a new mechanism for hearing when use of a traditional hearing aid alone is insufficient. An auditory implant is very different from a traditional hearing device.

Hearing aids amplify sound, whereas auditory implants compensate for damaged or nonworking parts of the auditory system. There are four principal types of auditory implants: (a) bone-anchored hearing aid, (b) cochlear implant, (c) auditory brainstem implant, and (d) middle ear implant.

Bone-Anchored Hearing Aid

We typically think of hearing as a process of air conduction. That is, sound is transmitted through the air, which travels down the ear canal toward the eardrum, middle ear ossicles, and the inner ear. However, sound is also transmitted through bone conduction via the bones in the head that bypass the outer and middle ear going straight to the inner ear (see also Chapter 14). Conventional hearing aids sit in the ear canal and transmit sound via air conduction. Some people cannot use conventional hearing aids due to chronic outer or middle ear infection problems or lack of a functioning ear canal (e.g., atresia). A **bone-anchored hearing aid (BAHA)** is an auditory implant for people with hearing loss who cannot receive benefit from a normal hearing aid. The BAHA works **percutaneously** (i.e., through the skin) by vibrating the skull directly through a small titanium fixture that is implanted in the skull behind the ear (Figure 15–11). The device works by taking the sound from the outside and transmitting it to the inner ear through the temporal bone, thereby bypassing the ear canal and the middle ear. The BAHA was first used in Europe in 1977 and has been approved for use in the United States since 1996 for conductive and mixed hearing losses.

Cochlear Implant

One of the most groundbreaking biomedical achievements in the last 30 years was the cochlear implant. Prior to 1978, the primary aural rehabilitation device for profoundly deaf or severely hard-of-hearing children and adults was a BTE hearing aid. An ideal candidate for a cochlear implant (child or adult) is an individual with (a) a severe-to-profound sensorineural hearing loss in both ears, (b) receiving little or no benefit from hearing aids, and (c) having access to an education and (re)habilitation follow-up program. The major components of a cochlear implant are located outside as well as inside the head. The components located outside the head are a microphone that picks up sounds in the environment and a sound processor that arranges the sounds

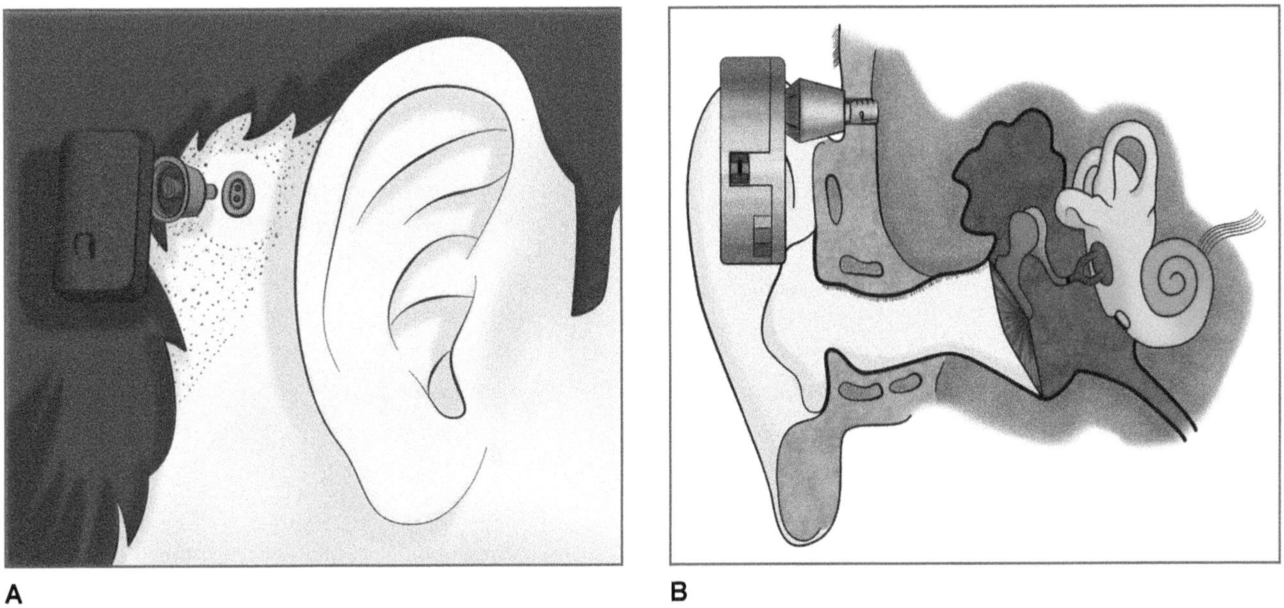

A B

FIGURE 15–11. A bone-anchored hearing aid (BAHA). **A.** The BAHA is attached to a small titanium implant behind the ear. **B.** The sound travels via the bones of the skull to the inner ear.

FYI

Source: Smallworldsocial, CC BY-SA 4.0 <https://creativecommons.org/licenses/by-sa/4.0>, via Wikimedia Commons.

Professor Graeme Clark is credited with inventing the first multichannel cochlear implant. The prototype of currently used cochlear implants was implanted in the first adult at the Royal Victorian Eye and Ear hospital in Melbourne, Australia, in 1978. The early term used for a cochlear implant was a *bionic ear.*

into an electrical signal that is transmitted through the skull. The transmitted signal sent through the skull is picked up by a receiver located inside the head. This receiver sends the electrical impulses to an array of 22 electrodes that stimulate different regions of the cochlea (Figure 15–12). A cochlear implant does not restore normal hearing. Instead, it can give a severely hard-of-hearing person a useful representation of sounds in the environment to assist with the understanding of speech. Although sound quality is sometimes described as mechanical, the cochlear implant provides users with the ability to sense sound that they could not otherwise hear. As of January 2022, approximately 1,000,000 individuals in more than 120 countries have received a cochlear implant. In the United States, roughly 130,000 adults and 75,000 children have received a cochlear implant.

Auditory Brainstem Implant

An **auditory brainstem implant (ABI)** is the first device specifically designed to bypass the cochlea and the auditory nerve to transmit sound directly to the brainstem. Because it bypasses the auditory nerve, the device is most useful for people who have lost or will lose their hearing in both ears following the removal of an auditory nerve

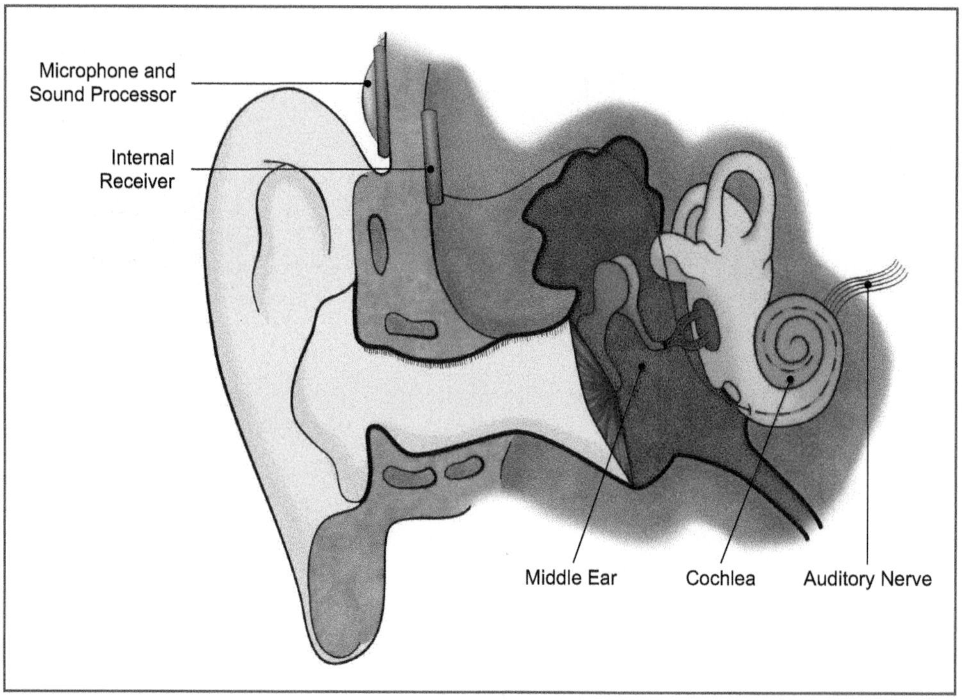

FIGURE 15–12. A cochlear implant.

tumor. Similar to a cochlear implant, the device involves components located outside and inside the head. The ABI device consists of a tiny microphone positioned by the ear, a sound processor, and an array of 21 electrodes implanted directly on a nerve center at the base of the brainstem, called the cochlear nucleus. The microphone picks up sounds from the environment and transmits them to a receiver inside the skull. This receiver stimulates the brainstem electrodes, allowing for electrical impulses of sound to be transmitted to the brain (Figure 15–13). Most ABI recipients benefit from the device through increased sound awareness. Most patients can hear noises like a telephone ringing or horn honking, but the degree of hearing usefulness can vary greatly. Few ABI recipients are able to understand speech without lip reading, but this may improve in the future. However, the environmental and speech sounds that patients receive through the ABI help to significantly improve their communication and quality of life.

Middle Ear Implant

The newest type of implant to be developed is specific to the middle ear. This **middle ear implant** is not a hearing aid (i.e., the device does not amplify sounds). Instead, this implant is designed to convert sound into mechanical vibrations that are then delivered to the inner ear. Similar to a cochlear implant and ABI, a middle ear implant involves components located outside and inside the head. The external component receives sounds that are then delivered to a transducer implanted in the middle ear that causes the ossicles to vibrate. A middle ear implant can be used to treat individuals with conductive, mixed, or sensorineural losses. The implant is ideal for individuals who cannot tolerate a traditional type of hearing aid that is inserted into the ear canal.

Auditory Training

The fitting of a hearing aid alone may not be sufficient to compensate for a hearing loss. Individuals may still experience difficulties with their overall communication. Research has shown that auditory training can significantly improve communication and overall satisfaction with a hearing aid (Nkyekyer et al., 2019). Auditory training is a process of improving one's listening skills using a variety of activities. These activities include listening and recalling words and sentences of

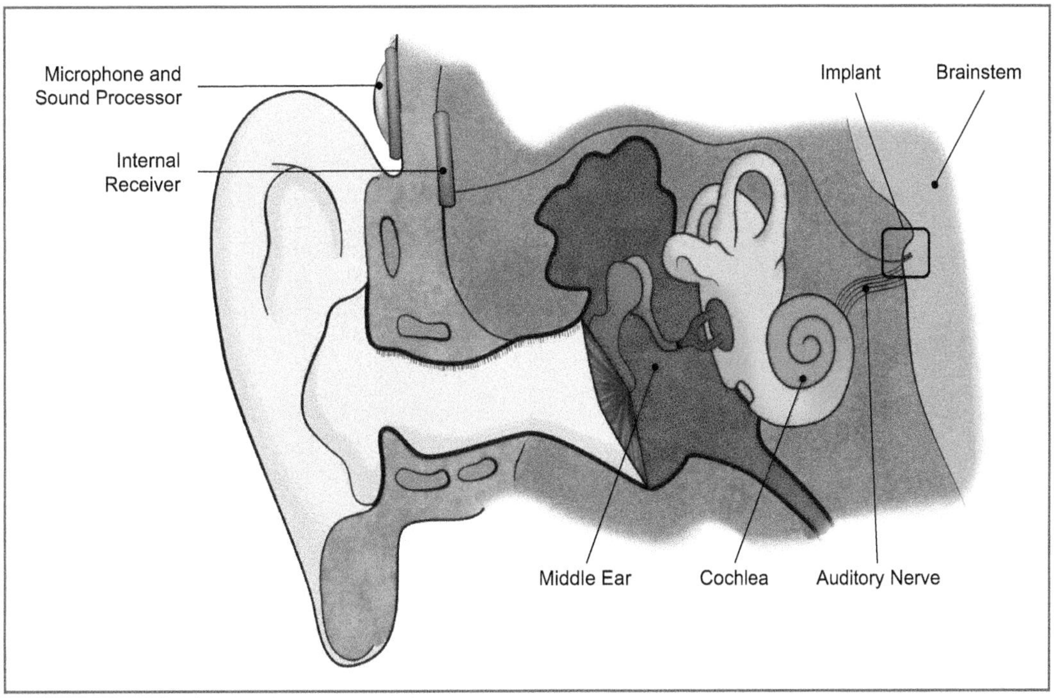

FIGURE 15–13. An auditory brainstem implant.

FYI

Source: DataBase Center for Life Science (DBCLS), CC BY 4.0 <https://creativecommons.org/licenses/by/4.0>, via Wikimedia Commons.

The tiny fly known as *Ormia ochracea* has developed a unique and powerful set of ears that allow it to locate the exact location of singing crickets. Scientists are examining how the tiny ears of this creature function and are attempting to use this as a model for designing miniature microphones for hearing aids.

varying length and under varying listening conditions. A variety of smartphone apps and computer programs are now available to hearing aid users that provide interactive auditory training activities. Learning new ways of listening coupled with wearing a hearing aid can greatly benefit real-world listening abilities in both children and adults.

TREATMENT APPROACHES: SPEECH AND LANGUAGE REHABILITATION

Another aspect of aural rehabilitation concerns treatment of the speech and language abnormalities that may accompany a hearing loss. Generally, the earlier the hearing loss occurs (e.g., congenital, prelingual) and the more severe the hearing loss (e.g., severe, profound), the greater is its impact on speech and language. The presence of a severe hearing loss during the critical periods of speech and language development deprives a child of the opportunities to hear language and can thus affect a child's ability to develop the features of normal communication (i.e., form, content, and use). Some of the primary speech and language disorders that result from a severe hearing loss are provided in Table 15–1. A summary of these features is provided next followed by an assortment of treatment approaches.

Speech and Language Characteristics

Phonology

A child with a severe hearing loss is likely to show a speech sound disorder. The child's ability to accurately produce consonants and vowels is influenced by two variables: (a) speech **sound visibility** and (b) **acoustic characteristics**. Some speech sounds are more easily perceived on the face of a speaker compared with others. For a severely hard-of-hearing child, this visual information can assist in learning to produce speech sounds accurately. For example, the /f/ sound is highly visible compared with the /k/ sound. Not surprising, low-visibility sounds such as /k/ are likely to be misarticulated more often than highly visible sounds.

All consonants and vowels have unique acoustic characteristics that are differentiated from one another in terms of duration (sec), loudness (dB), and frequency (Hz). Depending on the configuration of a person's hearing loss, some sounds are less likely to be perceived clearly compared with others, and this can lead to inaccurate speech sound production. For example, assuming a child has a high-frequency hearing loss, sounds that are naturally produced with a high acoustic frequency (e.g., /s/, /sh/) are less likely to be perceived and produced clearly compared with sounds that have a low acoustic frequency (e.g., /m/, /z/). The general acoustic characteristics of speech sounds are shown in Figure 15–14. A hearing loss that falls outside the range of the acoustic characteristics for various speech sounds would presumably be problematic for a hard-of-hearing individual to perceive. In turn, the same sounds may be difficult to produce accurately.

Voice

Voice disorders are often found in the severely hard-of-hearing and deaf populations. Foremost

Table 15–1. Characteristics of Speech and Language Found in Deaf and Severely Hard of Hearing Individuals

Feature	*Characteristics*
Phonology	Consonant and vowel omissions, substitutions and distortions Less visible phonemes more likely to be misarticulated Acoustic features of phonemes that can influence perception and production
Semantics	Vocabulary can range from normal to severely impaired
Syntax	Short and simple sentences Incorrect word order and sentence constructions
Pragmatics	Limited understanding of figurative language, idioms, metaphors Restricted range of communicative intents such as conversational skills
Voice	Quality is impaired, likely to be hypernasal Pitch is likely to be high Regulation of loudness may be impaired
Suprasegmental features	Slow speaking rate Impaired speech intonation and phrasing

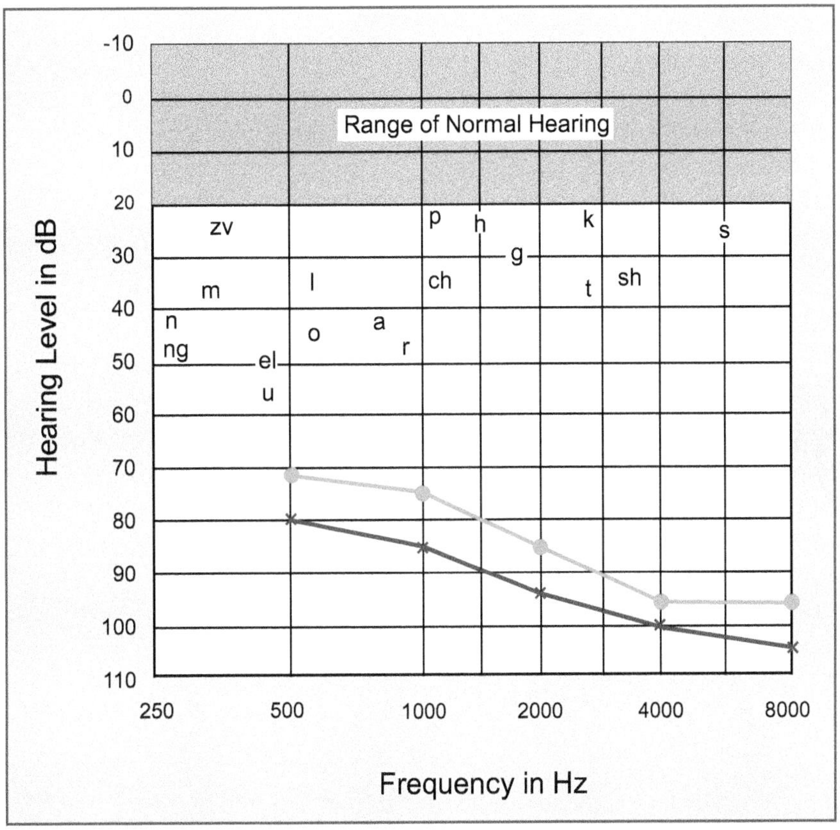

FIGURE 15–14. Acoustic features of various consonants and vowels overlaid on an audiogram. In the case of an individual with a severe bilateral hearing loss, it is unlikely these sounds would be audible.

among these voice problems is the production of **hypernasal speech**. This excessive nasality is thought to occur due to a lack of auditory feedback during speaking. We tend to take for granted that we produce most speech sound by closing off the nasal cavity. Without auditory feedback, a deaf speaker may not learn the motor routines needed to separate the oral and nasal cavities, resulting in inadequate velopharyngeal closure and subsequent speech nasality. A second feature of voice found to be impaired is voice pitch, particularly among individuals with deafness. Attempts to produce voice, without being able to hear one's own voice, tend to result in excessive tension in the region of the larynx. This results in abnormally tense vocal fold vibration that lead to the production of a high-pitched voice.

Language

Deaf children acquire language in the same developmental stages as a child with normal hearing; however, deaf children generally develop language at a slower pace. The primary deficit is in the area of language **syntax** and includes problems with grammatical markers, articles, and word endings. The deficit likely results from a combination of factors. The syntactic structure of English is both complex and subtle, with several inconsistencies. For example, consider these three sentences: (a) "I am going home," (b) "I am going to school," and (c) "I am going to the store." It is not surprising to find an individual with hearing impairment unable to grasp the subtleties of these differences and say something like, "I am going to home" or "I am going school" (Schow & Nerbonne, 2017). Another factor influencing an individual's correct use of syntax may stem from the mismatch between the language systems used by deaf and hearing individuals. For example, the language structure of American Sign Language is quite different from Standard English. For a deaf child who first learned American Sign Language, the later acquisition of Standard English may prove challenging.

Speaking Rate

There is considerable research confirming that hard-of-hearing individuals speak more slowly than normal hearing speakers. Prelingual deaf children speak at one fourth the rate of normally hearing children and adults. And even after practice, the deaf child's speaking rate is still one half that of normally hearing children and adults (Dwyer et al., 2009).

> *FYI*
>
> A 2015 study from Harvard University found that women and men talk differently about their hearing loss. Women were more than twice as likely as men to disclose a loss of hearing and to offer helpful suggestions about how to talk to them. In contrast, men who disclosed the existence of a hearing loss did not offer strategies to the listener about how best to communicate with them.

Rehabilitation Approaches

Speech Reading

For people with deafness, use of their eyes rather than ears provides a critical link with the world. One way of taking advantage of this visual link for communication is the act of speech reading. **Speech reading**, sometimes called lip reading, involves the decoding of language spoken by an individual by paying close attention to the speaker 's mouth. The speech reader will also use the speaker's facial expressions, gestures, and hand movements as visual cues. All this decoding is performed without being able to hear the speaker's voice. Even under optimal conditions, speech reading involves a great deal of guesswork. When we speak English, only 30% of the consonants and vowels are clearly visible on the mouth. For example, compare the highly visible "f" and "th" sounds with the nearly invisible "t" and "k" sounds (Figure 15–15). The speech reader needs to become adept at filling in the gaps between visible and invisible sounds to read words and phrases. People with deafness who are experienced speech readers can decode approximately 40% of single words. Speech reading is not normally used as the sole means of aural rehabilitation. Speech read-

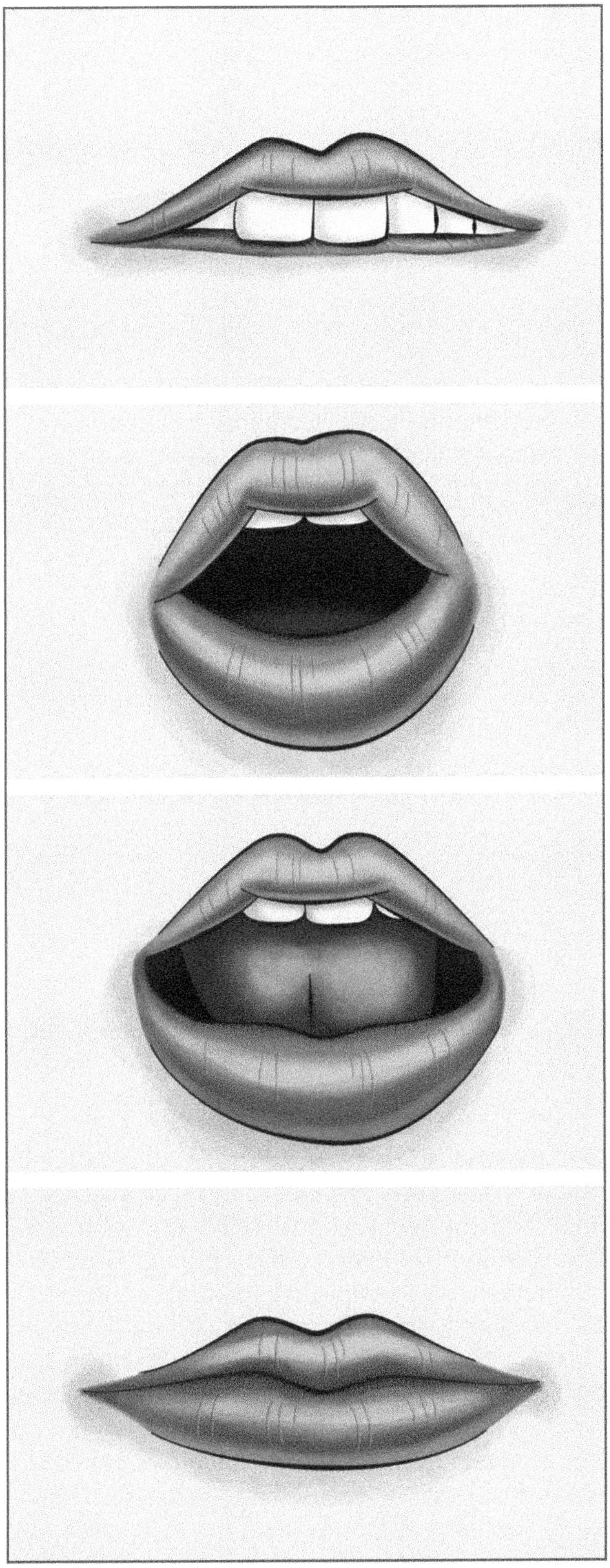

FIGURE 15–15. Various mouth shapes that can be seen during speech reading. Can you identify the sounds being produced by this speaker?

> FYI
>
> A speech reader's poem by Grace Cleys (1997):
>
> *You, who have good hearing*
> *Are mystified, it's true*
> *To watch a group of people*
> *Try to lipread, as we do.*
>
> *It's exciting, quiet enchanting*
> *And a thrill amid some fears*
> *As we slowly try to listen*
> *With our eyes instead of ears.*
>
> *At times it can be tricky*
> *And often just plain fun*
> *Success means lots of practice*
> *Perfection's seldom won.*
>
> *We share each other's troubles*
> *And laugh at our mistakes*
> *It takes a load of practice*
> *And lots of give and takes.*

ing is a strategy that is used in combination with other assistive listening devices to communicate effectively.

Cued Speech

Cued speech was created as a means of helping to solve the decoding problems related to speech reading. Some speech sounds are not readily visible (e.g., "t," "k"), and some speech sounds look almost identical. Consider the differences between the sounds "m," "b," and "p." All of these sounds are produced with the lips closed and could easily be confused by the speech reader when trying to distinguish the words "my," "buy," or "pie." Cued speech is a supplement to spoken language in which the speaker uses a set of sound-related hand shapes while talking to a severely hard-of-hearing individual. These hand shapes are intended to remove the guesswork from speech reading. It is a phonemically based system that uses eight hand shapes in four locations near the face. A total of 36 different cues are used to clarify 44 different sounds in English (Figure 15–16).

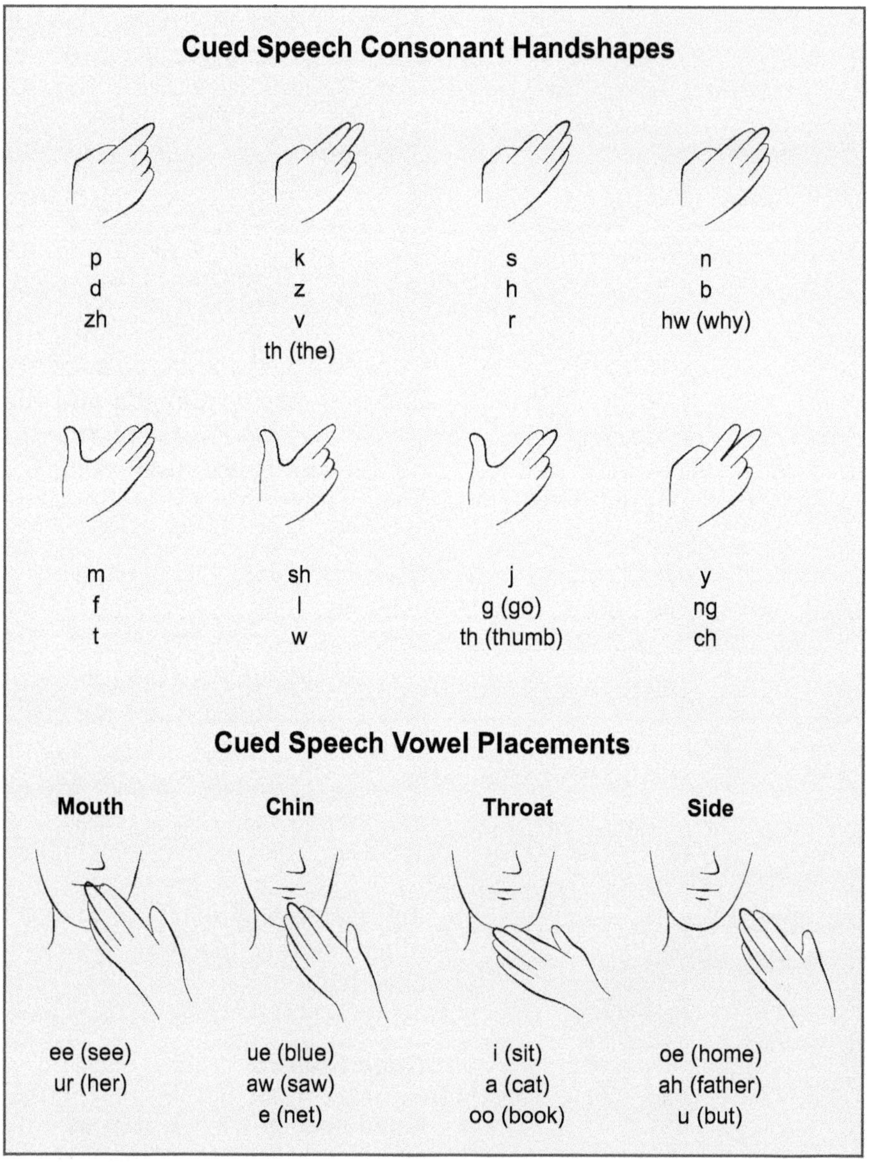

FIGURE 15–16. The hand symbols used for cued speech.

Cued speech has not been used widely as a rehabilitation technique. The major limitation is that the system is not applicable to everyday communication situations. Both the speaker and the speech reader need to be familiar with the cued speech system of communication.

Oral/Aural Approach

The terms **oral** and **aural** refer to the mouth and ear, respectively. Thus, the oral/aural approach to speech and language rehabilitation focuses on improving both speech and hearing abilities. This method stresses the use of speech articulation, hearing aids, and speech reading skills. A primary objective is to develop clear spoken language abilities to enable the person to function in a hearing society. People using this method are discouraged from relying exclusively on visual cues (such as sign language). Use of various biofeedback devices can be helpful in the development of oral skills. For example, the **nasometer** (see Chapter 6) is designed to measure both oral and nasal airflow during speech. The device provides a visual display of both types of flow that can be used by the speaker as a form of feedback to subsequently modify excessive nasality. An instrument known as a **Visi-Pitch** can be useful in helping to reduce a high-pitched voice. The device provides a visual display of fundamental frequency (i.e., pitch) during speaking activities. The severely hard-of-hearing individual learns to associate the visual display with the feeling of tension in the throat linked to loudness and pitch of voice. This has been referred to as *muscle memory*.

Manual Approach

Manual communication is often thought of as exclusive use of **sign language**. In reality, manual communication involves movement of the hands, body, face, and head as the primary mode of communication. Advocates of the manual communication approach believe that knowledge and understanding of language are more important than the ability to speak clearly. Because deaf and severely hard-of-hearing individuals use the visual mode more readily, communicating through the visual mode is a natural form of expression. Two examples of manual communication are **finger spelling** and sign language. Finger spelling is the process of creating words using a finger alphabet and is generally used alongside sign language to spell out names, places, and unusual words that do not have their own distinct sign. The finger alphabet used in Canada and the United States is based on hand shapes formed using one hand. The finger alphabet used in the United Kingdom, Australia, and New Zealand uses two hands (Figure 15–17). Sign language is the process of forming

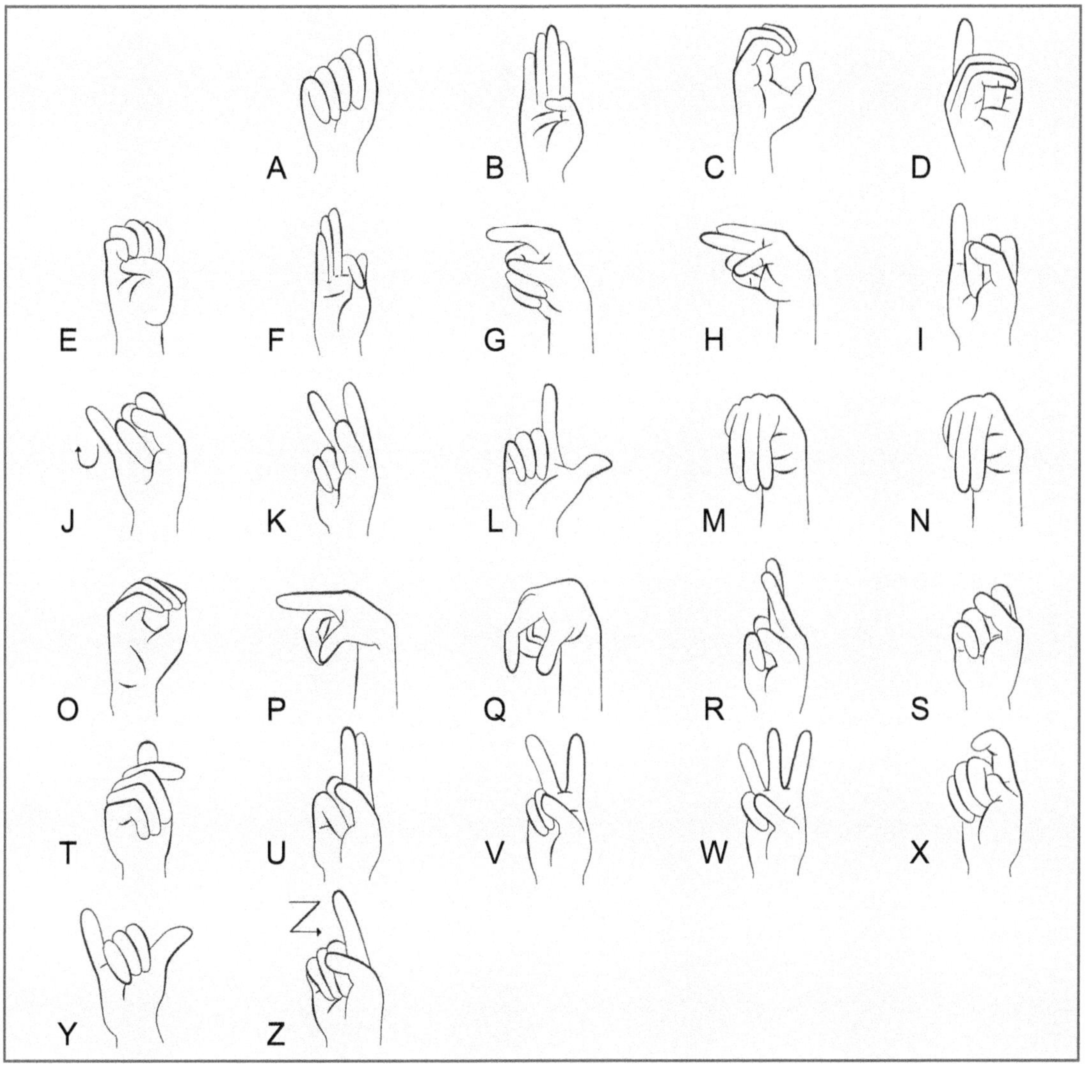

A

FIGURE 15–17. **A.** Manual finger spelling alphabet used in America.. *continues*

B

FIGURE 13–17. *continued* **B.** Manual finger spelling alphabet used in the United Kingdom.

sentences using various hand shapes that reflect specific words. American Sign Language is the visual/gestural language used by many people in the Deaf community in the United States, Canada, and parts of Mexico, although it originated in Europe. It is considered a distinct language and not just a visual representation of English. American Sign Language has its own grammar and syntax and does not follow the word order we would normally use when speaking English. British Sign Language is the sign language used in the United Kingdom and is quite distinct from American Sign Language in the hand shapes for various words, as well as grammar and syntax. The Australian and New Zealand sign language systems have evolved from British Sign Language.

FYI

In April 2006, the New Zealand government officially declared New Zealand sign language as one of three official languages in the country. The two other official languages of the country are English and Maori. Other countries that have made a similar declaration concerning sign language include Sweden, Denmark, Finland, Norway, Switzerland, Ireland, Scotland, Portugal, and Greece.

Simultaneous Communication Approach

Simultaneous communication (SimCom) is an aural rehabilitation approach that encourages all possible modes of communication to help a hearing-impaired individual communicate effectively. The various modes of communication include using a combination of spoken language, sign language, finger spelling, speech reading, amplification, writing, and gestures. SimCom is a common form of communication used in educational settings for deaf children. Advocates of this approach believe that individuals can learn and use language in a way best suited to their needs, while developing communication skills to function in the hearing world.

Counseling

Once a person is fit with a hearing aid and receives training in use of the aid, problems may persist related to experiencing a hearing loss. Among these experiences is a feeling of negativity related to hearing impairment. The provision of emotional and psychological counseling support can be an important feature of aural rehabilitation. Tye-Murray (2020) emphasized two forms of counseling that are relevant: **informational counseling** and **personal adjustment counseling** (Figure 15–18). During informational counseling, the audiologist engages in a dialogue with the patient to go over the steps of the aural rehabilitation plan, including use of the hearing aid, and the availability of aural rehabilitation classes. Personal adjustment counseling is directed toward the patient's self-image and the openness to accept hearing loss as a permanent

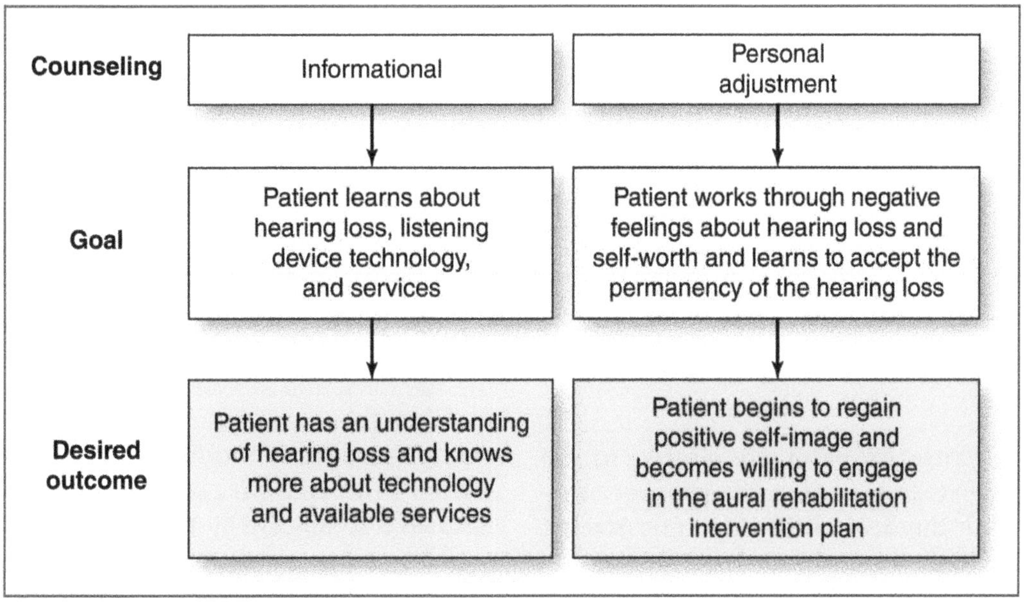

FIGURE 15–18. Two types of counseling provided in an aural rehabilitation setting. (*Source:* From *Foundations of Aural Rehabilitation: Children, Adults, and Their Family Members* [6th ed.], by N. Tye-Murray. Copyright © 2024 Plural Publishing, Inc. All rights reserved.)

condition while continuing to lead a fulfilled and productive life (Tye-Murray, 2020).

The Deaf and Blind Person

A critical feature of most aural rehabilitation programs is to capitalize on an individual's existing communication skills. This includes using sound amplification and visual cues such as speech, reading, and sign language. Alternatively, an individual with blindness relies primarily on auditory cues to communicate effectively. In the case of an individual who has lost vision and hearing, aural rehabilitation is particularly challenging. **Deaf-blindness** is defined as a combination of both auditory and visual disabilities that can contribute to severe disorders of development, learning, and communication. The prevalence of deaf-blindness is approximately 1 per 10,000 individuals. For the profoundly deaf and blind individual, the primary means by which they experience the outside world is through touch. The National Federation of the Blind lists several methods of communication that are available to the deaf-blind person. These include (a) manual alphabet, (b) print-in-palm, (c) Braille, and (d) the Tadoma method.

Manual Alphabet

The use of a manual alphabet involves the speaker (encoder) forming a series of hand motions that depict letters of the alphabet. The deaf-blind person then decodes these symbols into words by placing their hand over the hand of the person making the letters. The manual alphabet can be one of the quickest and most versatile communication methods for a deaf-blind person.

Print-in-Palm

The basics of **print-in-palm** are similar to the manual alphabet. In this case, the speaker communicates with the deaf-blind person by tracing the shapes of block (capital) letters on the palm of their hand with an index finger. Using this system does not involve learning a unique manual alphabet but rather simply the letters making up the standard alphabet.

Braille

Braille is a tactile reading and writing system that was developed by the Frenchman **Louis Braille** (1809–1852) who also happened to be blind. Based on a system of six raised dots that occur in different patterns, an entire alphabet, including punctuation, can be coded. The user learns to sequence the patterns and translate them into words and language.

Tadoma Method

The **Tadoma method** was developed in Sweden in the 1920s and named after two children (Tad and Oma) who were deaf and blind. The method requires the deaf-blind individual to place a thumb on a speaker's lips and spread their remaining fingers along the speaker's face and neck (Figure 15–19). Communication is transmitted through vibrations, motions of the jaw, and facial expressions of the speaker. Although the Tadoma method is very difficult and time-consuming to learn, it has proven successful, allowing fluent Tadoma users the ability to comprehend as well as produce spoken language.

CULTURAL CONSIDERATIONS AND AURAL REHABILITATION

Culture is defined as a system of values, attitudes, beliefs, and learned behaviors shared by a population. Culture is shaped by factors such as geographic location, education, age, and sex. A person's hearing abilities can also be a defining feature of one's culture. For example, cultural differences can be found in the United States regarding the form and style of sign language exhibited by Black/African American users compared to White/European American users. This can include signs that are reflective of the Black/African American lexicon (e.g., "My bad" or "Girl, please") as well as using a large plane of space for signing (Hyter & Salas-Provance, 2023) (Figure 15–20).

Individuals with deafness comprise a unique group of people who do not rely on hearing as part of their way of life. Sociologists have identified

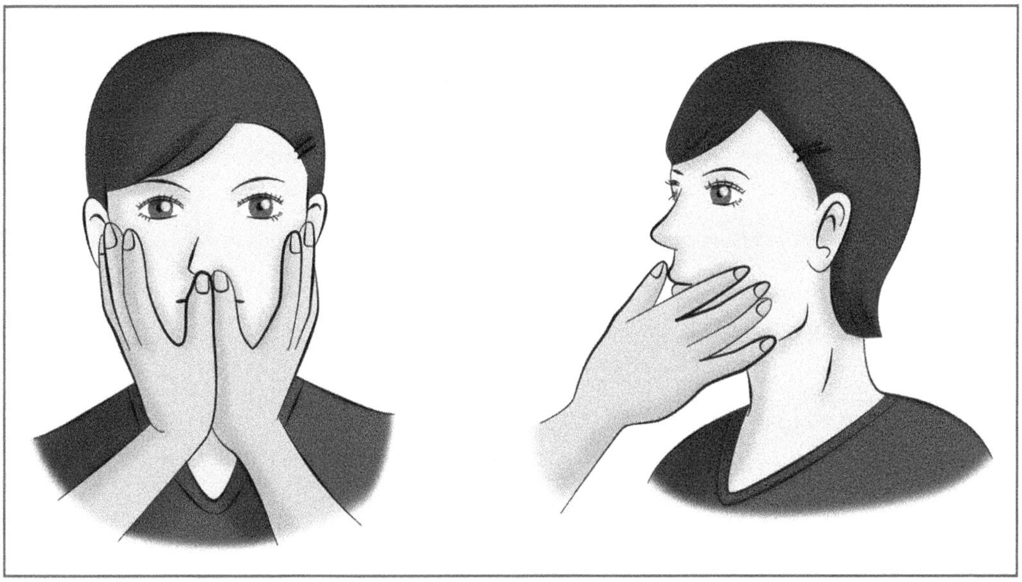

FIGURE 15–19. The Tadoma method used by individuals with deaf-blindness to comprehend spoken language.

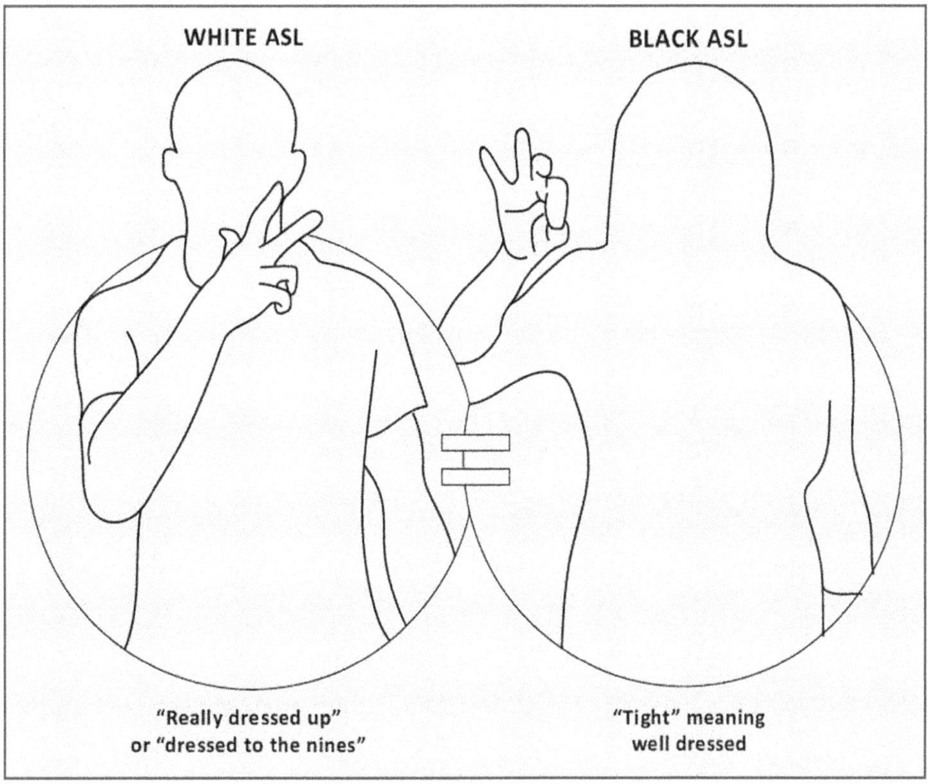

FIGURE 15–20. Side-by-side comparison of a White/European American person and a Black/African American person using American Sign Language for the same concept "dressed up." (*Source*: From *Culturally Responsive Practices in Speech, Language, and Hearing Sciences* [2nd ed.], by Y. D. Hyter and M. B. Salas-Provance. Copyright © 2023 Plural Publishing, Inc. All rights reserved.)

two opposing perspectives on culture and deafness, which are referred to as the medical model and the cultural model. In the **medical model**, deafness is viewed as an illness and disability. Indeed, the term *hearing impaired* can be construed as reflective of the medical model. The disability can be repaired by surgery and/or prosthetic devices such as a cochlear implant or hearing aid. The condition can also be treated by allied health professionals, including audiologists and speech-language pathologists. The medical model discourages separatism from the hearing world; instead, emphasis is placed on encouraging deaf people to acquire oral language skills. The use of sign language is discouraged. In the **cultural model**, deaf people are seen as nondefective individuals who are members of a minority culture. Deafness is not an illness or impairment but a difference, so there is no need for surgical intervention. Deaf and hard-of-hearing people are disabled only by barriers created by other people trying to make them fit into the hearing world. The cultural model sees the Deaf community as having its own unique culture. Evidence of Deaf culture is found in several areas. Deaf and hard-of-hearing people produce plays, books, artwork, magazines, and movies targeted at deaf and hard-of-hearing audiences. Socialization in the Deaf community takes many forms. A particularly popular means of socialization is meeting at a restaurant, which has come to be known as a *signing supper* or American Sign Language dinner. Another popular social vehicle is the *Deaf coffee*, a meeting at a local café to chat. The Deaf community also has its own online dating sites.

There are cultural assumptions in regard to the manner in which the word deaf is written. The term *deaf*, as written with a lower case "d," is used to refer to people who are profoundly hearing impaired and choose to use oral communication as their first language of communication. The term *Deaf*, as written with a capital "D," is used to describe people who are profoundly hearing impaired and do not view their hearing loss as an illness or disability. Sign language is likely to be their major mode of communication. Capital "D" deafness denotes the social, political, and cultural strands of members belonging to the Deaf community.

FYI

There is a bit of debate as to whether chronic snoring can cause a noise-induced hearing loss. The noise generated by a person snoring can sometimes exceed 70 dB (comparable with the loudness of a vacuum cleaner), so it is no wonder its relationship to hearing loss is being explored.

SUMMARY OF CHAPTER

Aural rehabilitation involves techniques used with people who are hearing impaired to improve their ability to communicate, which includes both listening and speaking. Several devices to improve hearing and various forms of treatment have been developed to assist individuals with a diagnosed hearing loss. One component of aural rehabilitation is the direct treatment of hearing loss that can be accomplished via (a) surgery, (b) hearing aid fitting, and/or (c) auditory implants. Another aspect of aural rehabilitation concerns treatment of the speech and language abnormalities that accompany a hearing loss. As a rule, the earlier the hearing loss occurs and the more severe the hearing loss (e.g., severe, profound), the greater is its impact on speech and language. Deaf-blindness is defined as a combination of both auditory and visual disabilities that can contribute to severe disorders of development, learning, and communication.

AURAL REHABILITATION ON THE WORLD WIDE WEB

Following are websites that provide further information on the topic of aural rehabilitation. At the time of publication, each website was freely accessible.

Better Hearing Institute
http://www.betterhearing.org

Hearnet.Com Public Service Announcements
https://www.hearnet.com/features/feature_PSA.shtml

Oral Deaf Education Video
https://www.youtube.com/watch?v=-5RmCyGgtAY

Hearing Aid and Implant Video
http://www.medel.com

Deaf-Blind Resource
https://nfb.org

Hellen Keller Videos
http://www.youtube.com/watch?v=Gv1uLfF35Uw

http://www.youtube.com/watch?v=8ch_H8pt9M8

STUDY QUESTIONS

1. What are the various types of hearing aids that are currently available?
2. What are the four principal types of auditory implants?
3. What are the possible communication characteristics of a profoundly hard-of-hearing person?
4. What are the types of rehabilitation approaches to working with a profoundly hard-of-hearing person?
5. What are the various forms of communication available to the deaf-blind person?

REFERENCES

Cleys, G. (1997). *A lip readers poem.*

Dwyer, C., Robb, M., O'Beirne, G., & Gilbert, H. (2009). The influence of speaking rate on nasality in the speech of hearing-impaired individuals. *Journal of Speech, Language, and Hearing Research, 52*, 1321–1333.

Hyter, Y., & Salas-Provance, M. (2023). *Culturally responsive practices in speech, language, and hearing sciences* (2nd ed.). Plural Publishing.

Nkyekyer, J., Meyer, D., Pipingas, A., & Reed, N. S. (2019). The cognitive and psychosocial effects of auditory training and hearing aids in adults with hearing loss. *Clinical Interventions in Aging, 14*, 123–135.

Schow, R., & Nerbonne, M. (2017). *Introduction to audiologic rehabilitation* (7th ed.). Pearson Education.

Tye-Murray, N. (2020). *Foundations of aural rehabilitation: Children, adults, and their family members* (5th ed.). Plural Publishing.

GLOSSARY

60-60 rule Hearing prevention rule that translates to a listening level of 60% of the maximum volume for no more than 60 min.

abducted To move away from the midline position. Vocal fold opening is a form of abduction.

abductor-type spasmodic dysphonia Severe voice disorder resulting from an inability to normally open the vocal folds to create a speaking voice.

accent Characteristic of speech pronunciation as determined by regional or social background.

acid reflux Regurgitation of stomach acid into the esophagus.

acoustic characteristics Features of speech sounds that are described according to the domains of amplitude, frequency, and time.

acoustic neuroma Benign tumor located on the eighth cranial nerve that may affect hearing and balance.

acoustic reflex Involuntary muscle contraction that occurs in the middle year as a result of sudden loudness in sound.

acquired disorder Communication impairment that results after a period of normal communication. A traumatic brain injury is a form of acquired disorder.

acrocentric chromosome Chromosome with its centromere located near the end of the chromosome.

active muscular process Contraction of muscles for a specified movement. Breath inhalation involves an active muscular process.

acute care hospital Hospital that provides short-term and highly specialized patient care.

addition Type of speech sound misarticulation in which one or more consonants or vowels are included in the target word production.

adducted To move toward the midline position. Vocal fold closing is a form of adduction.

adductor-type spasmodic dysphonia Severe voice disorder resulting from an inability to normally close the vocal folds to create a speaking voice.

adenoids Pairs of lymphoid tissue located in the various regions in the back of the pharynx that serve to filter out debris from inhaled air. A related term is tonsils.

adenosine triphosphate (ATP) Adrenaline nucleotide that is used during muscle contraction. ATP is thought to provide natural protection from acquiring a noise-induced hearing loss.

adult-centered therapy Form of speech and language therapy in which the adult plays a dominant and directive role in a child's therapy session.

adventitious deafness Form of acquired communication disorder, where a hearing loss occurred after a period of normal hearing. An acoustic neuroma could result in an adventitious hearing loss.

affricates Category of consonants classified according to the manner in which they are articulated in the vocal tract. The consonant /ch/ is an example of an affricate.

age of mastery Approach to determining a child's acquisition of speech sounds. Each sound is expected to be acquired (mastered) by a particular age.

age of suppression Approach to determining a child's suppression of phonological processes. Each process (e.g., final consonant deletion) is expected to disappear by a particular age.

aided alternative or augmentative communication Use of an external device to support augmentative and alternative communication.

air conduction testing Form of hearing test where sounds are presented through earphones directly into the ear canal.

alaryngeal speech Unique form of speaking in the absence of a larynx. Removal of the larynx is often a result of cancer.

alcohol-related neurodevelopmental disorder Condition under the umbrella of fetal alcohol spectrum disorder resulting in a range of developmental disabilities due to alcohol consumption during pregnancy.

alphabet Standard set of letters used to display spoken language. Each symbol generally assumes a sound (phoneme) of the language.

altered auditory feedback Collective term for masking, delayed auditory feedback, and frequency-altered feedback. These forms of feedback are used in the treatment of stuttering.

alternative communication Communication system that is an alternative to natural speech or writing.

alveolar ridge Gum ridge of the upper jaw (maxilla) located directly behind the teeth.

alveoli Final branches of the respiratory tree in the lungs; function to exchange gas between the lungs and the bloodstream.

Alzheimer, Alois German psychiatrist who was the first to identify the unique brain disease related to cell death.

Alzheimer disease Most common form of dementia characterized by progressive memory loss and intellectual abilities.

amniocentesis Medical procedure used in the prenatal diagnosis of chromosomal and fetal abnormalities.

amplifier Key feature of a hearing aid, designed to boost the loudness level of incoming sound before entering the ear canal.

amplitude Height of a sound wave. Related terms are intensity and loudness.

amyotrophic lateral sclerosis Progressive and fatal neurodegenerative disease; also known as motor neuron disease or Lou Gehrig disease.

anatomy Science concerning the structure of the body.

anencephaly Condition present at birth that affects the formation of the brain and the skull bones that surround the head.

ankyloglossia Condition caused by an abnormally short lingual frenulum. The condition is commonly referred to as "tongue tie."

anomic aphasia Expressive language disorder characterized by a severe problem with recalling words.

anthropometry Science that relates to the measurement of body dimensions.

aphasia Disorder that results from damage to the regions of the brain that are responsible for language. A similar term is dysphasia.

aphonia Medical term used to describe a condition in which a person is unable to speak, or has lost their voice.

apical Relating to the tip or apex.

apoplexy Rupture and bleeding of an internal organ.

applied behavior analysis Type of interpersonal therapy designed to improve social skills; based on principles of learning theory.

approximates Classification of consonant sounds that have articulatory and acoustic qualities that fall somewhere between true consonants and vowels. Examples include /w/ and /r/.

apraxia Neurological disorder characterized by an inability to perform purposeful movements on command. Apraxia of speech is a unique form of speech sound disorder.

Aristotle Greek philosopher who made significant contributions to science and logic.

Aronson, Arnold American researcher and clinician who made contributions to treatment of speech apraxia and voice disorders.

articulation Location at which two structures make contact. Speech articulation concerns the manner in which various anatomical structures work together to create speech sounds.

articulation approach Treatment for speech sound disorders that focuses on the motoric aspects of speech production.

articulation disorder Mispronunciation of speech sounds.

articulatory system Anatomical structures used for creating the sounds of speech, which include cavities, muscles, and bone.
arytenoid cartilages Pair of triangular-shaped cartilages within the larynx that serve as points of attachment for the vocal folds.
Asperger, Hans Austrian pediatrician and child psychiatrist who was the first to describe "autistic psychopathology," which was later named Asperger syndrome.
aspiration Inhalation of foreign material such as food or fluids in the lungs.
aspiration pneumonia Entrance of food or fluids into the trachea that leads to the eventual development of harmful bacteria that forms in the lungs or bronchial tubes.
assistive listening device Any type of device that helps an individual to function better in their daily communication. Closed captioning on a television is a form of an assistive listening device.
assistive technology Any device that is used to improve functional abilities for people with disabilities.
asymmetrical hearing loss Hearing loss in both ears; however, the degree and configuration of hearing loss are not identical.
atresia Absence or incomplete development of the ear canal.
audiogram Graph used to depict an individual's hearing.
audiologist Professional who specializes in the diagnosis and management of disorders of the auditory and vestibular portions of the ear.
audiology Branch of science that is concerned with balance, hearing, and related disorders.
audiometer Machine (typically a computer) that is used for measuring hearing sensitivity.
audition Act of hearing.
auditory brainstem implant Device designed to bypass the cochlea and the auditory nerve to transmit sound directly to the brainstem.
auditory brainstem response Electrical signal evoked from the brainstem in response to an auditory signal. This response is often used as a test of hearing in infants.
auditory communication Use and perception of sound that forms the basis of communication.
auditory cortex Region of the brain responsible for the processing of auditory (sound) information; also called Heschl gyrus, which is located in the temporal lobes.
auditory nerve Nerve that carries auditory and balance information from the inner ear to the brainstem; also known as the cochlear nerve or the eighth cranial nerve.
auditory processing disorder Broad term used to describe a variety of problems with the brain that can interfere with the understanding of auditory information.
augmentative and alternative communication (AAC) Unique form of communication to assist people with severe expressive communication difficulties.
augmentative communication Communication approach that is a supplement to existing normal communication.
aural Relating to the ear or to the sense of hearing.
aural habilitation Management of hearing loss for an individual born with a hearing impairment.
aural rehabilitation Management of hearing loss for an individual who originally had normal hearing.
auricle Outer ear; also known as the pinna.
autism A bio-neurological developmental disability that generally appears before 3 years of age.
autism spectrum disorder Group of autistic conditions with similar features that may vary in symptoms and severity.
autonomic nerves Portion of the nervous system that regulates involuntary physiologic processes.
babbling Repeated production of the same or nearly similar syllable strings. A common type of vocalization produced by children during the period of 4 to 10 months of age.
bacterial meningitis Inflammation of the meninges due to bacterial infection.
barium Soft metallic element that is silvery white in its purest form. If swallowed, the substance is clearly visible during x-ray examination.
basal Relating to, or forming, the base.
basilar membrane Located within the cochlea and separates the cochlear duct from the scala tympani.
behaviorist theory Theory based on the assumption that a child's speech and language

development is shaped by individuals and events in the child's environment.

behind-the-ear (BTE) aid Type of hearing aid where the primary components of the aid are situated and fit behind the ear.

Bell, Alexander Graham Inventor of the telephone.

Bell, Alexander Melville Scientist with interests in speech and deafness. Father of Alexander Graham Bell.

beneficence Act of doing good or being charitable.

Bertillon, Alphonse French police officer credited with applying methods of anthropometry to describe suspected criminals.

between-word disfluencies Speech disfluencies that occur across words, such as a phrase repetition or an interjection.

bilabial Class of consonants categorized according to the place of articulation in the vocal tract. Examples of bilabial consonants are /b/ and /m/.

bilateral cleft lip Cleft that involves separation of the lip on both sides of the mouth, often shown as a large open gap.

bilateral hearing loss Impairment of hearing that occurs in both ears.

bilingualism Ability to communicate in two languages, which may include speaking, listening, reading, and writing.

biofeedback Teaching a client to control various functions of the body through relaxation, visualization, and cognitive control processes.

birth defect Abnormality of structure, function, or body chemistry usually present at birth that can result in physical or intellectual disability.

Blackwell, Elizabeth First woman in the United States to graduate from medical school and practice medicine.

Bleuler, Eugen Swiss psychiatrist that was one of the first individuals to use the term autism to describe a withdrawn self-absorbed patient.

Bliss, Charles Created a universal picture language known as Blissymbolics.

blocks Type of speech disfluency characterized by a complete, momentary stoppage in the forward flow of speech.

Bloom, Lois Professor of speech-language pathology who developed the framework of form-content-use to define communicative competency.

bodily movements Features of stuttering whereby certain body parts, such as the head and eyes, move during moments of stuttering.

body aid Type of hearing aid that involves a battery pack and amplifier worn in a harness that delivers sound to the ears. A very powerful hearing aid.

body language Form of nonverbal communication that involves use of various parts of the body.

bolus Food that has been chewed and mixed in the mouth with saliva.

bone-anchored hearing aid (BAHA) Surgical implant for the treatment of hearing loss that works through bone conduction.

bone conduction testing Test of hearing that bypasses the outer and middle ear by sending sound vibrations through the skull bones toward the cochlea.

Borg, Pär Aron Swedish teacher who developed the first manual sign language alphabet.

bound morpheme Morpheme that cannot stand alone as an independent word while carrying lexical meaning when attached to another morpheme.

brachycephaly Condition in which the head is disproportionately wide (or flattened).

bradykinesia Abnormal slowness in the execution of movement.

braille Tactile reading and writing system based on a series of raised dots.

Braille, Louis Frenchman who developed a reading and writing system based on a series of six raised dots that occur in varying patterns.

brainstem nuclei Cluster of sensory or motor nuclei located in the brainstem.

breathy voice Quality of voice production where excessive air accompanies the voice.

Bridgman, Laura First deaf-blind child in the United States to gain a formal education.

Broca's aphasia Expressive language disorder where a person is able to comprehend language but has difficulty executing the motor movements to produce words. A form of nonfluent aphasia.

Broca's area Region of the left cerebral temporal lobe that plays a role in the expression of speech and language.

Broca, Paul French neurosurgeon responsible for naming the region in the left frontal lobe responsible for speech production (Broca area).

Brodmann areas Series of 52 distinct regions of the cerebral cortex that are identified according to cellular structure and function.

Brodmann, Korbinian German neurologist who mapped the cerebral cortex into 52 distinct functional areas.

Brodnitz, Friedrich Well-known medical specialist in the treatment of vocal disorders, particularly those associated with singing.

bronchial tubes Series of subdivided tubes that carry air to and from the mouth and the lungs. The smallest of these tubes are called bronchioles.

bronchioles Smallest air passageways comprising the lungs.

bronchitis Inflammation of the bronchial tubes.

Brown, Hallie Quinn Daughter of former slaves who was a black civil rights leader, teacher, and elocutionist.

Brown, Roger American psychologist who developed the mean length of utterance measure to chart morphological development.

Bryngelson, Bryng Pioneer in the speech-language pathology profession in the United States. He had a particular interest in the area of stuttering.

Butler, Margaret F. Pioneer in the area of otolaryngology.

captioning (closed) Assistive listening device that provides a visual display of text on a television.

Carhart, Raymond "Father of modern-day audiology in the United States."

Carter, Henry Vandyke Individual responsible for drawing all of the anatomical illustrations in the famous textbook, *Gray's Anatomy.*

case history Detailed account of facts gathered about an individual or family that have analytical value for medical, educational, or psychological conditions.

Casserius, Julio Italian anatomist who made an important contribution to the study of voice.

castrato Adult male with a singing voice equivalent to a soprano that occurs as a result of castration or an endocrine disorder.

cell Basic unit of life.

cellular anatomy and physiology Microscopic study of cells and tissues; also called histology.

central auditory system Portion of the auditory system consisting of the auditory nerve, brainstem, and brain.

central nervous system Portion of the nervous system consisting of the brain, brainstem, and spinal cord.

centromere Region of a chromosome where the arms of a chromosome intersect.

cerebral palsy Nonprogressive disorder that affects muscle tone, movement, and motor skills.

cerebrovascular accident Condition where the blood supply to the brain is disturbed in some way resulting in brain cell death; also called stroke.

cerebrum Largest portion of the brain divided into two hemispheres.

Certificate of Clinical Competency Qualification granted by the American Speech-Language-Hearing Association to audiologists and speech-language pathologists who meet the educational and clinical criteria for independent practice.

cerumen Normally extruded product of the ear canal; also known as earwax.

cervical (neck) auscultation Use of a stethoscope placed on the neck to listen to sounds produced during swallowing.

child-centered therapy Approach to working with a communicatively impaired child where the therapist provides treatment to the child that is geared around the child's naturally occurring play activity.

childhood apraxia of speech Type of speech sound production disorder characterized by inconsistent misarticulations patterns. Considered to be a rare and poorly understood disorder.

Chomsky, Noam American linguist who proposed the nativist theory of early language acquisition.

chorionic villus sampling Medical procedure used in the prenatal diagnosis of chromosomal and fetal abnormalities.

chromosomal syndrome Birth defect resulting from visible changes in the chromosomal structure of the individual.

chromosomes Threadlike strand of DNA and proteins that are found in every cell nucleus of a living organism.

cilia Slender mircoscopic hair-like structure.

circumlocutions Roundabout manner of talking rather than using specific, direct language.

Clark, Eve British linguist who is an expert in the area of first language acquisition.

Clark, Graeme Australian professor of otolaryngology who developed the first multichannel cochlear implant.

Class I malocclusion Normal alignment of the upper and lower jaw, with the exception of some minor dental abnormalities.

Class II malocclusion Abnormal alignment of the upper and lower jaw, indicative of a severe overbite.

Class III malocclusion Abnormal alignment of the upper and lower jaw, indicative of a severe underbite.

cleft lip or palate Lack of fusion of the lip and/or palate during embryonic development.

cleft palate team Team of specialists in various aspects of medical, health, and educational care who work together to assist individuals with a cleft lip/palate.

Clerc, Laurent The "Father of deaf education in the United States."

clinical assessment Common approach to the initial screening of dysphagia that occurs in a clinic setting.

cloning The process of producing a genetically identical organism.

cluttering Fluency disorder characterized by excessively fast speaking rate and word formulation difficulties.

cochlea Snail-shell-shaped structure that serves as the hearing organ of the inner ear.

cochlear implant Surgically implanted device in the cochlea that provides individuals with a sense of sound.

cochlear nucleus Location in the central auditory system where the auditory nerve inserts to the base of the brainstem.

code of ethics Series of broad statements created by a professional body to guide members of the association in their ethical decision-making.

cognitive behavioral therapy Psychotherapy approach that focuses on correcting patterns of thinking that are maladaptive.

cognitive communication disorder Broad term used to describe a wide range of specific communication problems that can result from damage to regions of the brain that control the ability to think.

columella Fleshy portion of skin under the nose that separates the left and right nostrils.

coma State of extreme unresponsiveness in which the individual exhibits no voluntary movement.

communication Process of transferring information from one source to another.

communication act Exchange of thoughts, messages, or information by speech, signals, writing, or behavior.

communication board Low-technology communication device that displays symbols, pictures, or text to convey messages and meaning.

communication disorder Inability to understand or use speech and language to relate to others in society.

communication needs model Approach to assessing the communication needs of an individual being considered for augmentative and alternative communication.

communicative competency Ability to use language in a grammatically correct and socially appropriate manner.

compensatory strategy Ways to use strengths or intact abilities to compensate for weaknesses.

complete cleft lip Complete separation of the lip extending to the nostril.

complete cleft palate Complete separation from the palate extending from the alveolar ridge to the uvula.

completely-in-the-canal (CIC) aid A miniaturized hearing aid that fits entirely into the ear canal. Typically used by individuals with mild to moderate hearing losses.

complex sound Sound that contains more than one frequency component.

comprehensive Complete and all-inclusive coverage.

computed tomography X-ray procedure that combines many x-ray images with the aid of a computer to generate cross-sectional views of various structures of the body. A computed tomography scan is more commonly known as a CT scan.

concussion Direct blow to the head that may result from violent shaking of the head or a whiplash-type injury.

conductive hearing loss Hearing loss associated with a problem in the transmission of sound through either the outer or middle ear.

confidential voice Treatment technique for improving voice quality that involves using a soft, breathy voice.

congenital anomaly Physical, metabolic, or anatomical deviation from the normal pattern of development that is apparent at birth or detected later in life.

congenital deafness Profound hearing loss that is found at birth.

congenital disorder Abnormal condition that is found at birth.

connectionism Theory regarding locations in the cerebrum that are responsible for specific body functions.

connotative Denotes or implies an attribute.

consecutive bilingualism Form of bilingualism in which the primary language was learned first followed by learning of another language.

consonant voicing Classification of consonants based on the presence of vocal fold vibration during articulation of the sound. The sounds /b/ and /z/ are examples of voiced consonants. The sounds /p/ and /s/ are examples of voiceless consonants.

constraints Limitations related to combining speech sounds in a specific language.

continuous phonation Stuttering therapy technique that involves the constant use of vocal fold vibration across words and phrases as a means of maintaining speech fluency.

contrecoup Head injury that involves a secondary injury that is opposite to the primary injury, whereby the brain essentially rocks back and forth.

cooing Early vocal behavior produced by infants that involves use of k-like and g-like sounds during comfort vocalizations; also known as gooing.

Cooper, Herbert K. Physician from Pennsylvania who was a pioneer in the development of cleft palate teams to assist those with a cleft lip or palate.

coregulation Interaction and exchange of information that occurs between individuals.

cortex Surface area of the cerebrum.

Corti, Alfonso Italian anatomist who provided a detailed description of the inner ear, with particular reference to the cochlea. The organ of Corti is named in his honor.

cortical localization Theory that attributes specific functions to different areas of the brain.

covert behavior To conceal or hide a behavior.

covert repair theory Theory of stuttering that attributes the disorder to a temporal impairment in the phonological encoding of words prior to actual speech production.

cranial nerves Series of 12 sensory and motor nerves that emerge directly from the brainstem.

craniectomy Surgical removal of a portion of the cranium.

craniofacial abnormality Congenital disorder that primarily affects the cranium and facial bones.

craniosynostosis Premature fusing of the cranial sutures that results in restricted growth of the skull.

Crick, Francis Nobel Prize winner for discovering the double-helix structure of DNA. His colleague who assisted in the discovery was James Watson.

cricoid cartilage Part of the laryngeal framework; consists of a ring-shaped cartilage that sits on top of the trachea.

Cri du Chat syndrome Syndrome resulting from genetic material missing from chromosome 5.

Crouzon, Louis Octave French neurosurgeon who was the first to describe the craniosynostosis syndrome, later named Crouzon syndrome.

Crouzon syndrome Genetic disorder caused by mutations on the long arm of chromosome 10.

crying Earliest vocal behavior demonstrated by infants.

cued speech Means of communication in which a speaker uses hand signals to clarify ambiguous mouth movements for lip readers.

culturally competent Ability of individuals and systems to work or respond effectively across cultures.
culturally responsive Ability to understand cultural differences and recognize biases.
cultural model Perspective of aural rehabilitation that views deaf people as disabled and members of a minority culture.
culture Set of attitudes, values, beliefs, and goals shared by a group.
Cupid's bow Curve of the upper lip indicated by a slight dip, said to resemble the bow of Cupid, the Roman god of love.
cycle One complete back and forth movement of vibration.
cycles approach Treatment approach for working with severely phonologically disordered children. The approach emphasizes a wide range of sound productions by the child that are addressed in a series of cycles.
cytology Microscopic study of animal and plant cells.
cytomegalovirus Form of the herpesvirus that rarely causes serious illness in healthy adults. However, the disease can have devastating effects on a newborn.
Darwin, Charles English naturalist who laid the foundations of the theory of evolution.
Davis, Hallowell American physiologist who did pioneering work on the physiology of hearing and the inner ear.
Davis, Pauline American researcher who performed the first auditory-evoked test on a human using electroencephalography.
de León, Pedro Ponce Spanish monk who is often credited as being the first teacher of the deaf.
deaf-blindness Condition in which both sound and sight are profoundly impaired.
deafness Minimal hearing or complete loss of hearing.
debate Form of communication that involves engagement in argument by discussing opposing points of view.
decibel scale (dB) Unit of measure for loudness.
decode To extract the underlying meaning of a signal.
dedicated system Augmentative and alternative communication device that is specifically designed for communication.
deep brain stimulation Surgical treatment involving the implantation of a brain pacemaker that sends electrical signals to specific parts of the brain. Used as an approach to the treatment of Parkinson disease.
deglutition Medical term for swallowing.
Déjerine-Klumpke, Augusta Pioneering neurologist known for her contributions to neurology and neuroanatomy.
demands and capacities theory Theory of stuttering that views moments of disfluency as resulting when a child's capacities for fluency are not equal to speech performance demands.
dementia Progressive decline in cognitive function due to damage or disease in the body.
denotative Word that has distinct meaning.
dentition Type, number, and alignment of a set of teeth.
deoxyribonucleic acid (DNA) Genetic material found in the cells of all living organisms.
description Language therapy technique involving labeling by the therapist to call attention to the child about the labels and descriptions of objects and activities.
developmental diagnosis Determination of a developmental disability based on the results of formal and observational testing.
developmental disorder Condition that is assumed to have been present at birth; however, in some cases the manifestation of the disorder is not visible until the child matures.
developmental history Process of documenting the achievement of developmental milestones.
developmental monitoring Also called developmental surveillance; process of recognizing children who may be at risk for developmental delays.
developmental screening More formal approach than developmental monitoring to examining how a child is developing, which can include questionnaires and checklists.
dialect Variety of language that is spoken among a particular group. A dialect is rule-governed and has distinct linguistic features.
dialogue Form of communication that involves a conversation between two or more people.
diaphragm Dome-shaped muscle that sits below the lungs. The muscle is most active during the process of inspiration.

Dieffenbach, Johann Friedrich German surgeon who performed pioneering surgery for maxillofacial disorders.

digitized speech Transformation of human voice that can be stored on a computer.

direct laryngoscopy Procedure in which an otolaryngologist uses an instrument such as a flexible scope to examine the vocal folds.

direct selection Method of selection in which an individual using alternative or augmentative communication uses a body part or prosthesis to indicate choices on a communication device (e.g., touching, eye gazing).

Directions Into Velocities of Articulators (DIVA) Model of speech production that provides an account of the network of brain regions involved in speech acquisition and production.

discourse Type of communication that involves a verbal exchange.

discrete trial training Behavioral treatment for autism that breaks down skills into small "discrete" components.

discussion Formal discourse on a topic.

disfluency Disruption in the forward flow of speech.

disfluency cluster Occurrence of two or more disfluencies on the same word and/or adjacent words.

dissection Process of disassembling and observing an anatomical structure to determine its internal structure.

distortion Type of speech sound misarticulations in which a consonant or vowel is misarticulated to such an extent that the sound produced is unrecognizable.

Down, John Langdon English physician who is best known for his description of what is now called Down syndrome.

Down syndrome Chromosomal disorder caused by the presence of an extra 21st chromosome; also known as trisomy 21.

Downs, Marion American audiologist who pioneered universal newborn hearing screening.

drug therapy Approach to the treatment of disease by the administration of drugs, chemicals, and antibiotics.

Duffy, Joseph American speech-language pathologist who helped define the distinguishing clinical characteristics of dysarthria.

Dutrochet, Henri French physiologist who is credited with identifying the cell.

dysarthria Motor speech disorder characterized by poor speech sound articulation.

dysphagia Medical term for the symptom of difficulty in swallowing.

dysphonation Unusual form of voice production, often characterized by moments of chaotic vocal fold vibration.

early intensive behavioral intervention Treatment approach for autism that involves 20 to 40 hours per week of treatment in children under the age of 5 years.

echolalia Repetition of words or phrases made by another individual; a feature of speaking often associated with autism. The manner of echolalia can be either immediate or delayed.

echolocation Sensory system used by animals such as dolphins and bats using high-pitched sounds to determine the direction and distance of objects; also called biosonar.

edema Medical condition in which abnormally large volumes of fluid enter muscle tissue.

efficiency Peak level of performance by using minimal effort or resources.

effortful swallowing Dysphagia treatment technique that involves the deliberate and forceful act of swallowing.

elective therapy Form of speech-language therapy that is based on helping an individual improve their communication abilities, although there is no diagnosed communication disorder. A person who speaks English as a second language may see elective therapy to help reduce their accent.

electroencephalography Recording of electrical activity along the scalp produced by the firing of neurons within the brain.

electrolarynx Device that is intended to reproduce the role of the vocal folds in patients who have had their larynx removed. A handheld device that produces audible vibrations is placed against the neck, and the person mouths speech sounds.

electromyography Technique for testing and recording the electrical activity of muscles.

electronic devices Category of instruments used to help diminish moments of stuttering.

electropalatograph Device that records the timing and location of tongue contact with the hard palate during speaking activities; also called a palatometer.

embolism Obstruction in a blood vessel due to a blot clot.

embryo Organism in its early stages of development, especially before it reaches a recognizable form.

embryology Branch of biology that deals with the formation and early development of living organisms.

Empedocles Greek philosopher who speculated on the origins of life and human development.

encode Process of creating a message into code.

endolymph Thick fluid that fills the cochlear duct of the inner ear.

endolymphatic hydrops Overaccumulation of endolymph in the inner ear. Often found to be a cause of Ménière disease.

English as a second language (ESL) Person who first acquired a language other than English.

enteral tubes Tube used for the delivery of nutrition that bypasses normal ingestion of food through the mouth.

epidemiology Branch of medicine that deals with the causes, distribution, and control of disease within a population.

epiglottis Leaf-shaped flap of cartilage that covers the trachea during moments of swallowing.

esophageal dysphagia Disorder of swallowing that is due to abnormal function in the esophagus.

esophageal speech Alternative approach to producing speech without using the vocal folds. A form of speaking used by people having undergone a laryngectomy.

esophageal stage Third and final stage in the process of swallowing.

esophagitis Inflammation of the lining of the esophagus.

esophagus Muscular tube that connects the throat to the stomach. Commonly known as the gullet.

ethical behavior Behavior that conforms to accepted professional standards of conduct.

ethnicity Social groups with a shared sense of identity, geography, culture, and history.

ethology Study of animal behavior with special interest in genetically programmed behaviors known as instincts.

etiology Study of causation.

Eulenberg, John Computer scientist and linguist with interest in augmentative and alternative communication.

Eustachi, Bartolomeo Italian anatomist who described structures of the human body including the eustachian tube of the ear.

Eustachian tube Hollow structure of bone and cartilage extending from the middle ear to the rear of the throat (pharynx).

evidence-based practice Decision-making process that is based on considering the best available research. In medicine, it is used to help make informed, clinical decisions for patient care.

executive functioning disorder Disorder of the cognitive processes that help regulate, control, and manage thoughts and actions.

exhalation phase Outward flow of air composing one phase of the breathing cycle.

external auditory meatus Cartilaginous and bony tube that runs from the outer ear to the tympanic membrane; also called the ear canal.

Fairbanks, Grant Professor in the field of communication disorders who made major contributions to the area of treatment of speech sound disorders.

falsetto Voice register of males that is above (higher than) the normal speaking range.

family-centered practice Approach to intervention that involves partnering with family members.

fast mapping Mental process whereby a new concept can be learned based on a single exposure to the concept.

feedback loops Information about the result of an event or action is sent back to the original input of the system. In the case of communication, the speaker obtains feedback from the listener regarding the original message uttered.

feeding tube Medical device used to provide nutrition to a person who is unable to obtain nutrition through swallowing.

Ferrein, Antoine French anatomist known for his work concerning the physiology of the voice. He is credited with coining the term vocal cords.

fetal alcohol spectrum disorder Umbrella term for a range of disorders associated with alcohol consumption during pregnancy.

fetal alcohol syndrome Severe form of fetal alcohol spectrum disorder that affects physical and cognitive development resulting from mothers who consumed alcohol during pregnancy.

fetus Unborn child, spanning the period from 8 weeks following conception to the moment of birth.

fiberoptic endoscopic evaluation of swallowing Procedure for evaluating the oral stage of swallowing based on examination of the oral/pharyngeal cavity with the use of a fiberoptic endoscope.

finger spelling Representation of letters and numbers of a writing system with the use of one or two hands. A system of communication commonly used by individuals with severe and profound hearing loss.

fissure Long narrow opening. Fissures along the cerebral cortex provide points of demarcation for the various lobes of the brain.

fistula Narrow opening or passageway caused by disease or injury.

fixed articulators Speech articulators that have no movable action. Examples of fixed articulators include the teeth and hard palate.

fluctuating hearing loss Condition in which a person's hearing may improve or worsen from one day to the next.

fluency Effortless flow of speech that includes proper use of rhythm, rate, pausing, and language formulation.

fluency disorder Disruption in the forward flow of speech.

fluency shaping Comprehensive therapy for the treatment of stuttering that focuses on changing all speaking behavior, not just moments of stuttering.

fluent aphasia Language disorder in which a person has difficulty comprehending spoken and written language, although their ability to speak seems to remain relatively intact.

form Shape or structure of an item that provides distinctive character.

formal communication Style of communication that follows a specific code for particular settings.

Fox, Michael J. American actor with a form of Parkinson disease referred to as early-onset parkinsonism.

FOXP2 Gene located on chromosome 7 that has been implicated in the development of normal speech and language skills.

Fragile X syndrome Most common form of inherited intellectual disability that results in a mutation of a gene located on the X chromosome.

Franco, Pierre Sixteenth-century Swiss surgeon known as the "Father of cleft palate surgery."

free morpheme Smallest unit of language that can occur by itself.

frequency Number of vibrations that occur per second.

frequency transposition Technique used in the programming of hearing aids that extends the audibility of higher frequency sounds for people who cannot receive this information from a conventional hearing aid.

Freud, Sigmund Austrian neurologist who is considered the founding father of psychoanalysis.

fricatives Category of consonant sounds classified according to the manner in which they are articulated in the vocal tract. The /s/ and /f/ consonants are examples of fricatives.

frontal lobes Front of the cerebral cortex, primarily involved in the execution of motor movement as well as mental reasoning.

front-back confusion Impairment in the ability to perceive the origin (direction) of a sound source.

functional disorder Disorder that results in the absence of a known anatomical, physiological, or neurological cause.

functional dysphagia Form of dysphagia that has no identifiable organic cause.

fundamental frequency Lowest frequency component of a complex sound.

Gage, Phineas One of the earliest documented cases of a severe brain injury and its impact on mental function following recovery.

Galen, Claudius Second-century physiologist who is often considered the founder of laryngology and voice science.
Gall, Franz Joseph German anatomist and pioneer in the study of brain functions who developed a system for studying the brain by noting the shape of the skull, called phrenology.
Gallaudet, Thomas Hopkins American educator and founder of the first American school for the deaf.
García, Manuel Spaniard who developed the laryngeal mirror.
gastroesophageal reflux disease Chronic condition in which stomach acid is regurgitated resulting in heartburn and indigestion.
gastronomy tube Feeding tube used in situations when a person is unable to swallow normally. The tube is placed directly into the stomach and is used to deliver nutrition to the body; also called a percutaneous endoscopic gastrostomy (PEG) tube.
gaze coupling Early form of communicative exchange between a young infant and parent where the infant turns toward the speaker and gains eye contact.
gene mutation Permanent change in the DNA that makes up a gene.
gene splicing Form of genetic engineering where specific genes are inserted into the genome of a different organism.
genes Hereditary unit that occupies a specific location on a chromosome and determines a particular characteristic in an organism.
genetic counseling Service that is designed to help families who may be at risk for an inherited disease or abnormal pregnancy outcome, and to discuss the chances of having children who are affected.
genetic syndrome Disorder caused by abnormalities in one or more genes.
genetics Branch of biology that deals with heredity and the transmission of characteristics among organisms; relating to genes or heredity.
genome Total DNA sequence that characterizes a species, including humans.
genotype Genetic makeup of an organism.
geographic dialects Variations in the style of speaking according to geographic region. A New England dialect is an example of a geographic dialect.
geographic region Demarcated areas of the world. Some disease conditions vary in regard to geographic region.
Glasgow Coma Scale Scoring system used to describe the level of consciousness in a person following a brain injury.
glides Category of consonant sounds classified according to the manner in which they are articulated in the vocal tract. The /w/ is an example of a glide.
global aphasia Most severe form of aphasia that affects all modalities of language expression and comprehension.
globus Sensation of a lump in the throat.
glossectomy Surgical removal of the tongue.
glottal Location in the vocal tract that is just above the vocal folds (glottis).
glottal stop /ʔ/ Speech sound produced by a momentary complete closure of the glottis followed by an explosive release.
glottis Space between the open vocal folds.
Grandin, Temple Professor of animal science who is a person with autism spectrum disorder.
graphic cuing Language treatment technique for individuals with brain injury that involves providing familiar photographs to facilitate communication.
Gray, Henry Nineteenth-century English anatomist whose classic publication regarding human anatomy is still used today.
grommet See pressure equalization tube.
gross anatomy Study of organs, parts, and structures of a body that are visible to the naked eye.
Gutzmann, Hermann German physician who studied speech disorders from a medical point of view.
gyri Bump or ridge like those found along the surface of the cerebral cortex.
habitual pitch Speaking voice that is most commonly used.
hair cells Sensory receptors that are found in the inner ear (cochlea and vestibular apparatus).
hard-of-hearing Person who has any level of hearing impairment other than deafness.
hard palate Bony roof of the mouth that separates the nasal cavity from the oral cavity.

Hawk, Sara Stinchfield First individual in the United States to obtain a doctorate in speech-language pathology.
head pointer Adaptive device that can be used for direct alternative or augmentative communication symbol selection. It may be affixed to an individual's head, usually with a band or helmet.
hearing aid Device that can amplify sound waves in order to help a hard-of-hearing person perceive sounds more clearly.
helicotrema Opening at the apical end of the cochlea that connects the scala vestibuli canal with the scala tympani canal.
helix Cartilaginous rim of the outer ear.
hemiparesis Body weakness or paralysis occurring on one side of the body only.
hemispatial neglect Syndrome characterized by reduce awareness or failure to attend to the opposite side of space.
hemispheres Two halves of a circle. The cerebrum (brain) is divided into a left and right hemisphere.
hemorrhage Excessive loss of blood from blood vessels.
heredity Genetic transmission of characteristics from parent to offspring.
Hertz, Heinrich German physicist who was the first to send and receive radio waves.
hertz (Hz) scale Notation used to refer to frequency, or the number of vibrations per second. Developed in honor of Heinrich Hertz.
hieratic Cursive form of Egyptian hieroglyphics.
hieroglyphics System of writing using pictorial symbols to represent sounds or meanings.
high-frequency hearing loss Configuration of hearing loss where a person is unable to clearly perceive sounds that are in excess of 1000 to 2000 Hz.
high technology Alternative or augmentative communication device that has synthesized speech and print output as well as programming/editing capabilities.
Hippocrates Greek physician who described the importance of the lungs, trachea, lips, and tongue in phonation in the early fifth century BC.
Hirano, Minoru Japanese researcher known for his contributions to vocal fold anatomy and physiology.
hoarse voice Voice quality, involving an unusually low-pitched voice.
holism theory Theory that views brain functioning as a single, nonlocalized organ.
Hooke, Robert English philosopher who coined the term *cell* to refer to the basic unit of life.
Human Genome Project International scientific undertaking to determine the complete structure of the human genetic material known as DNA.
human papillomavirus Viral infection that commonly causes skin or mucous membrane growth (warts).
Hunt, James Nineteenth-century speech therapist from England with expertise in stuttering.
Husson, Raoul Developed one of the earliest modern theories of normal voice production known as the neurochronaxic theory.
Hutchinson, Miller Reese American electrical engineer who developed the first electrical hearing aid.
hyoid bone Horseshoe-shaped bone that is located high in the neck. The most superior portion of the laryngeal framework.
hyperfunctional voice Speaking with excessive muscular effort and force resulting in a tense, high-pitched voice. A form of spasmodic dysphonia.
hyperlexia Acquiring the ability to read at an early age and at a high level.
hypernasal speech Abnormal speech and voice characterized by the excess flow of sound through the nasal cavity.
hyponasal voice Abnormal speech and voice characterized by too little flow of sound through the nasal cavity.
hypnotherapy Approach to the treatment of a variety of health conditions by hypnotism or by inducing prolonged sleep.
hypofunctional voice Refers to inadequate muscle tone of the laryngeal mechanism during the production of voice often resulting in weak, low-pitched voice that may also sound breathy. Found in some conditions associated with muscle weakness such as amyotrophic lateral sclerosis.
hypotonia Decrease of normal muscle tone or tension.
hypertelorism Abnormally increased distance between the eyes.

idioglossia Unique, specialized language thought to be indicative of the early speech spoken by twins.
idioms Words or phrases that cannot be taken literally.
idiopathic Condition that is of unknown origin.
immittance testing Form of audiological testing that provides information regarding eardrum mobility and eardrum function; often called tympanometry.
in-the-canal (ITC) aid Type of hearing aid where all components of the aid are situated directly within the ear canal.
in-the-ear (ITE) aid Type of hearing aid where all components of the aid are situated within the entrance of the ear canal.
incidence Number of new cases that occur during a particular period of time.
incomplete cleft lip Cleft that does not penetrate the nostrils.
incomplete cleft palate Cleft that does not encompass the entire hard and soft palate structure, only a portion is affected.
incus Middle bone of the three small bones (ossicles) of the middle ear, also known as the anvil to reflect its unique shape.
indirect laryngoscopy Procedure in which an otolaryngologist uses an instrument, such as a mirror, to examine the vocal folds.
indirect selection An alternative or augmentative approach to accessing symbols that does not involve direct physical pointing.
infant Child under the age of 12 months. Derived from the Latin word meaning "without speech."
infant mortality Death of a child less than 1 year of age. Often used as a barometer of the social well-being of a country.
informal communication Specific code of communication that allows for a varied manner of speaking.
informational counseling Educating patients and families about test results and the consequences of untreated hearing loss.
ingestion Consumption of food or drink by an organism.
inhalation phase Inward flow of air composing one phase of a breathing cycle.
inhibiting Inability to suppress emotions. Some individuals with brain injury may show difficulty with inhibiting.
initial assessment First phase in the diagnosis of aphasia where the speech-language pathologist meets with the patient while still in the hospital.
intelligence quotient (IQ) Measure used to estimate intellect, usually calculated by examining the ratio of a person's mental age compared with their chronological age.
intelligibility Term used to describe the clarity of a person's speech sound productions.
intensity Maximum disturbance of a sound wave. Also referred to as amplitude.
interactionist theory Theory of language development whereby children acquire their language through a combination of behavioral and nativist processes.
International Classification of Functioning. Disability, and Health (ICF) Framework developed by the World Health Organization that classifies health according to a number of domains.
International Phonetic Alphabet (IPA) System of phonetic notation developed by the International Phonetic Association that can be used to represent the sounds of any language.
interpersonal communication Form of communication that occurs between two or more people.
invisible-in-the-canal (IIC) aid Miniature hearing aid that sits deep in the ear canal.
Iowa Scale for Rating the Severity of Stuttering Scale used for determining the severity of speech disfluency based on noting the number and type of speech disfluencies occurring within a conversational speech sample.
Itard, Jean-Marc Gaspard French physician known for his work with deaf and intellectually impaired individuals, particularly Victor, the wild boy of Aveyron.
itinerant speech-language pathologist Speech-language pathologist who works in a number of settings. Speech-language pathologists who work for a school system tend to work in more than one school setting.
Jackson, Huglings Considered the father of British neurology for his work in epilepsy and aphasia.
Janssen, Zaccharias Dutch spectacle-maker who is believed to be the inventor of the microscope.

Jean, Andre French physiologist who studied the role of the brainstem in the process of swallowing.

Johnson, Wendell American speech-language pathologist known for his work in stuttering.

Kanner, Leo Austrian psychiatrist known for his work in autism.

karyotype Arrangement of chromosomes within a cell.

Keller, Helen First deaf-blind person to achieve a university education; later became an advocate for individuals with disabilities.

King Louis II King of France during the period of 843–879 who was also known to stutter.

Klumpke palsy Form of paralysis resulting from injury to spinal nerves.

L1 Abbreviation used to designate the first or dominant language.

L2 Abbreviation used to designate the second or less dominant language.

labio-dental Class of consonants that are categorized according to their place of articulation within the vocal tract. Examples of labio-dental consonants are /f/ and /v/.

laceration Wound or cut that involves direct tearing of tissue.

Lahey, Margaret Developed a framework for describing the various strands of language, according to form, content, and use.

Lashley, Karl First individual to define autism, based on examination of 11 self-absorbed children who had autistic disturbances of affect contact.

lalophobia Fear of speaking

language Expression of human communication through which information can be experienced, explained, and shared.

language acquisition device Proposed by Noam Chomsky as a special biological brain mechanism that humans are born with that enables them to learn language.

language content Aspect of language that concerns meanings of individual words and words in combination. Another name for language content is semantics.

language delay Language disorder indicating that the child's language system is similar to younger, nondisordered children.

language deviance Language disorder whereby the child is exhibiting a linguistic system that is unlike that of younger nondisordered children.

language difference Situation in which the language features of a community differ from the majority. The rules are normal for the smaller community.

language expansions Language therapy approach in which the therapist restates the child's utterance using a fuller and grammatically correct language model.

language form Aspect of language that concerns the features of phonology, morphology, and syntax.

language sampling Feature of a language assessment in which a representative sample of the child's typical expressive language behavior is collected and later analyzed.

language use Aspect of language in a social context. Another name for language use is pragmatics.

Larsen, George L. American speech-language pathologist who was one of the first individuals to develop specific treatment techniques for individuals with dysphagia.

laryngeal prominence Protrusion in the human neck formed by the thyroid cartilages. Also known as the Adam's apple.

laryngeal system Anatomical structures that comprise the larynx, which include cartilages, muscles, and bone.

laryngectomy Partial or complete removal of the larynx, including the vocal folds. The most common form of surgery to treat laryngeal cancer.

laryngitis Inflammation of the vocal folds, associated with symptoms of sore throat and swallowing difficulty.

larynx Structure that consists of a number of muscles and cartilages that work cooperatively to produce voice.

late talker Children between the ages of 16 and 30 months who are slow in acquiring their first 50 words.

Lee Silverman Voice Treatment (LSVT) Structured programmatic approach to voice therapy. The premise of the approach is to encourage a full, loud speaking voice to improve overall voice quality as well as speech clarity.

left neglect Situation in which a person who experiences a right hemisphere stroke no longer acknowledges the left side of their body.

Lejeune, Jerome French geneticist who discovered the chromosome abnormalies in humans that causes Down syndrome, as well as Cri du Chat syndrome.

Levi-Montalcine, Rita Italian neurologist who discovered a protein that causes developing cells to grow. Her research has implications for helping to restore hearing.

Lidcombe Program Stuttering treatment program developed in Australia for children younger than 6 years of age.

Liepmann, Hugo German neurologist who distinguished various types of apraxia.

Light, Janice Speech-language pathologist who has made significant contributions in the area of augmentative and alternative communication.

limbic system Region deep within the cerebrum that includes part of or most of the other lobes (i.e., frontal, parietal, and temporal). The limbic system is involved in affective behaviors such as emotion and motivation.

lingua-alveolar Class of consonants categorized according to their place of articulation within the vocal tract. Examples of lingua-alveolar consonants are /t/ and /s/.

lingua-dental Class of consonants categorized according to their place of articulation within the vocal tract. An example of a lingua-dental consonant is /th/.

lingual frenulum Tendon that extends from the floor of the mouth to the underside of the tongue.

lingua-palatal Class of consonants categorized according to their place of articulation within the vocal tract. An example of a lingua-palatal consonant is /sh/.

lingua-velar Class of consonants categorized according to their place of articulation within the vocal tract. Examples of lingua-velar consonants are /k/ and /g/.

linguistics Scientific study of the structure and function of language.

lips Two bands of muscular tissue.

liquids Class of consonant sounds organized according to the manner in which they are articulated in the vocal tract. The consonants /r/ and /l/ are examples of liquids.

lobule Anatomical extension such as that found at the base of the outer ear.

localism theory Theory of brain functioning that assigns specific functions of the brain to specific regions of the brain.

Logemann, Jeri A. American speech-language pathologist who is a pioneer in the assessment and treatment of dysphagia.

logopedics Commonly used term in Europe to refer to the study and treatment of communication disorders.

Lotter, Victor American psychologist who published the book *Infantile Autism* that focused on neurogenic and environmental causes of autism.

loudness Psychological perception of the intensity of an acoustic signal.

low technology Augmentative and alternative communication device that does not involve a power source.

lower respiratory tract Cavities of the body that include the trachea, bronchial tubes, and lungs.

lungs Two spongy organs that function to remove carbon dioxide from the body and provide it with oxygen.

magnetic resonance imaging (MRI) Test that uses a magnetic field and pulses of radio wave energy to make a picture of organs and structures inside the body.

maintenance Type of swallow used to remove natural buildup of saliva in the oral cavitiy.

Maling, Reginald Created an electronic alternative or augmentative communication device known as the patient-operated selector mechanism (POSM).

malingerer Someone who intentionally fakes or exaggerates a psychological or physical condition for personal gain.

malleus Outermost of the three small bones (ossicles) of the middle ear, also known as the hammer to reflect its unique shape.

malocclusion Uneven alignment between the upper and lower teeth.

mandible Anatomical name for the lower jaw.

manner of articulation Classification of consonant sounds in regard to how they are articulated in the vocal tract.

manual communication Use of hand gestures to transfer information between individuals.

Manzolini, Anna Morandi Anatomist and wax modeler with a special interest in the anatomy of the eye and ear.
Masako Maneuver Swallowing exercise where the tongue is protruded and held in place by biting down the anterior portion of the tongue during the process of swallowing.
mass communication Exchange of information to a large public audience through some sort of medium, such as radio, television, or the internet.
mastication Act of chewing.
Maudsley, Henry British psychiatrist who made some of the earliest observations of children who appeared to be autistic.
maximal contrast approach Treatment approach for phonological disorders that is designed to enact widespread change. Rather than targeting early developing sounds, later developing sounds are the focus of therapy.
McNaughton, Shirley One of the first individuals to use Bliss symbols as a form of augmentative and alternative communication.
mean length of utterance (MLU) Measure that examines a child's increasing ability to combine words and produce complex utterances by noting the average length of utterances according to grammatical morphemes.
medical model Approach to the identification of disorders on the basis of an identifiable physical cause.
memory Person's ability to remember things.
Mendel, Gregor Austrian botanist who is known as the "Father of modern genetics" based on his work with pea plants.
Ménière disease Disorder of the inner ear that can affect balance and hearing.
Ménière, Prosper French otolaryngologist who was the first to describe a form of vertigo (dizziness) that is now known as Ménière disease.
meningitis Infection of the fluid that surrounds the brain and spinal cord. The condition is caused by either viral or bacterial infection.
metacentric chromosome Chromosome with a centrally placed centromere that divides the chromosome into two arms having approximately equal length.
metalinguistic awareness Ability to reflect consciously on the nature and properties of language.
microcephaly Abnormal smallness of the head.
microform cleft Rare anomaly that can appear as a small scar on the lip.
micrognathia Condition of abnormal smallness of the upper and lower jaws, usually the mandible.
microphone Transducer that is designed to transform acoustic energy into an equivalent electrical representation.
middle ear implant Surgical procedure designed to stimulate movement of the ossicles of the middle ear to incoming sound as a means of improving hearing.
minimal pair Situation where two words differ in pronunciation by only one sound, and the change in sound results in a change in word meaning. The words "dear" and "gear" are examples of minimal pairs.
misarticulation Any deviation, great or small, in the pronunciation of consonant or vowel phonemes.
mixed (or global) aphasia Communication disorder that involves impairment in both comprehension and production of language; generally considered the most severe form of aphasia.
mixed dysarthria Nonpure form of dysarthria involving a combination of two or more types.
mixed hearing loss Simultaneous occurrence of both a conductive hearing loss and sensorineural hearing loss.
modal register Middle register of one's speaking voice.
model Academic term used to refer to an abstract idea.
modified barium swallow Radiological imaging procedure that is used for the evaluation and treatment of swallowing disorders.
monotonic voice Lack of natural melodic voice inflection. A condition associated with the speaking voice of individuals with Parkinson disease.
Montessori-based intervention Language treatment technique using structured activities that take place in the context of social interaction.
Morgan, Thomas Hunt Pioneer in the area of genetics. Received the Nobel Prize for his work on hereditary traits of fruit flies.
morphology Smallest meaningful units of language.

mosaicism Condition in which the cells composing an organism are not identical, having differing genotypes.

motor learning Ability to perform a motor sill as a result of practice and experience.

motor nerves Portion of the nervous system that sends messages from the brain to the body.

motor speech disorders Impaired speech sound production ability resulting from motor pathway damage affecting the muscles responsible for producing speech.

mouth breathing Process of inhalation and exhalation through the oral cavity rather than the nasal cavity.

movable articulators Anatomical structures involved in speech production that are capable of moving. Examples of movable articulators include the lips, tongue, and soft palate.

multifactorial Cause of a communication disorder attributed to more than one variable.

multilingualism Individual who has knowledge of two or more languages. This knowledge may include the ability to speak, understand, read, or write more than one language.

multimodal communication Use of unaided and aided modes of augmentative and alternative communication.

multiple sclerosis Disease in which the nerves of the central nervous system degenerate causing an impairment of movement, sensation, and body functions.

Mutual Recognition of Credentials Agreement Pact signed by various speech-language pathology professional organizations worldwide that provides a framework for professionals from one country to practice as therapists in another country.

myelin sheath Insulating envelope that surrounds the core of a nerve fiber (axon) to facilitate the transmission of nerve impulses.

myoelastic aerodynamic theory of phonation Well-accepted theory of voice production that involves coordination of muscle tension and breath pressure.

myringotomy Surgical incision into the tympanic membrane (eardrum) that is usually performed to relieve pressure or fluid buildup in the middle ear.

nares External openings of the nose; also called nostrils.

nasal cavity Cavity lying between the floor of the cranium and the roof of the mouth and extending from the nostrils to the pharynx.

nasals Class of consonant sounds categorized according to the manner in which they are articulated in the vocal tract. The consonants /m/ and /n/ are examples of nasal consonants.

nasogastric tube (NG tube) Type of feeding tube used on a short-term basis and involves passing a tube through the nose, pharynx, and esophagus directly into the stomach.

nasometer Commercially available instrument designed to measure both oral and nasal airflow emitted during speech production.

naturalistic developmental behavioral intervention Management of individuals with austism spectrum disorder that is implemented in natural settings.

National Institute on Deafness and Other Communication Disorders U.S. government agency that supports research on normal and disordered communication.

nativist theory Theory of normal language acquisition proposed by Noam Chomsky, which suggests that humans are born with the biological makeup to learn language.

natural theory Theory of phonological development proposed by David Stampe based on the natural occurrence and suppression of phonological patterns (or processes).

near-infrared spectroscopy Noninvasive instrument that measures changes in blood flow in the front part of the brain.

Negus, Sir Victor British laryngologist who was a pioneer in detailing the anatomy of the human and animal larynx.

neural plasticity Refers to the ability of the brain and/or certain parts of the nervous system to change in order to adapt to new conditions, such as an injury.

neural tube defects Congenital abnormality of the brain and spinal cord resulting from incomplete closing of the neural tube during embryonic development. Spina bifida is an example of a neural tube defect.

neurochronaxic theory Theory proposed in 1950 that viewed the frequency of vocal fold vibration as being dependent on excitation of nerve cells from the laryngeal nerve.

neurogenic Having its origin or starting with the nervous system.

neurogenic stuttering Form of stuttering characterized by a high number of involuntary repetitions or prolongations of speech that do not seem to be a result of poor (hesitant) language formulation difficulties or of psychiatric problems. A condition sometimes found in Parkinson disease.

neurological Relating to nerves and the nervous system.

neuromonics Treatment for tinnitus that combines the use of a novel approach to acoustic stimulation with a structured program of counseling and support by a clinician.

neuromuscular electrical stimulation (E-Stim) Electrical current used to stimulate the same electrical impulses that are activated during normal exercise. By passively activating the muscle, the body responds in much the same way as during normal exercise.

neuroplasticity Brain's ability to reorganize itself by forming new neural connections throughout life

neuroprosthetics Design and manufacture of neural prosthetics that can serve as a substitute for a motor or sensory modality that may have been damaged. A cochlear implant is a form of a neuroprosthetic device.

neuropsycholinguistic theory Theory of stuttering based on the assumption that producing fluent speech involves sophisticated timing between the formulation of language and the actual motor execution of speech movement. Stuttering results in a situation where there is a disruption in the timing (integration) of linguistic formulation and speech movement.

neurotypical Someone who thinks, perceives, and behaves in ways that are normal within their culture.

noise Acoustic sound wave that has random variations in amplitude and frequency. A lack of periodicity (back and forth vibration).

noise-induced hearing loss Hearing impairment that results from exposure to excessively loud sounds.

nonbehavioral tests Form of audiology testing that does not require the person to push a button or raise their hand in response to sounds. Rather, the tests are designed to measure natural physiological responses to sounds. The auditory brainstem response is a nonbehavioral test.

nonfluent aphasia Language disorder in which an individual has difficulty expressing themself when speaking or writing, although their ability to understand language seems to remain relatively intact.

nonmaleficence Ethical principle in health sciences and public health practice in which the professional strives to do no harm to the patient.

nonstandardized testing Form of assessment in which there is no consistent or standardized manner to perform the assessment. This form of assessment generally provides the examiner with more flexibility. The collection and subsequent analysis of a language sample is a common form of nonstandardized testing.

nonverbal communication Form of communication in which the exchange of information occurs without the use of spoken words. The use of eye contact is a form of nonverbal communication.

norms Standard, model, or pattern regarded as typical. Norms are often used to assess individuals who are suspected of having a communication disorder.

nucleus Central part of a cell that contains hereditary material.

objective assessment Approach to evaluating a communication disorder using commercially available test instruments.

obstruction Obstacle or blockage that impedes progress. A common disorder of the outer ear involves an obstruction of the ear canal.

obturator Prosthetic device serving to close an opening in the body, such as a cleft palate.

occipital lobes Posterior lobe of each cerebral hemisphere that contains the visual centers of the brain.

occlusion Fitting together of the upper and lower teeth.

odynophagia Pain associated with the act of swallowing.

omission Pattern of speech misarticulations whereby the intended speech sound is deleted.

onomatopoeia Use of sounds to signify a word based on the sound associated with the particular word. For example, beep-beep would be a form of onomatopoeia to signify the word *car*.

onset To start or begin. The onset of stuttering typically occurs at 3 years of age.

open system Augmentative and alternative communication device that has multiple functions, one of which is for communication.

Operation Smile International charity program for treating facial deformities such as cleft lip and palate.

optimality theory Theoretical approach to describing the structure of grammar in a given language.

optimum pitch Level at which we can produce our strongest voice.

oral Relating to the mouth.

oral cavity Space inside the mouth that runs from the inside of the lips to the back of the throat.

oral stage First stage in the three-stage process of swallowing.

Organ of Corti Specialized structure located within the scala media of the cochlea. The organ contains hair cells that assist in the transfer of sound through the auditory system.

organic disorder Medical or health condition with a known physical cause.

oro-facial examination Routine assessment of the structure and function of the mouth and face in regard to their influence on speech sound production.

oropharyngeal dysphagia Most common form of dysphagia that reflects an impairment in the transfer of liquid or food from the mouth and pharynx to the opening of the esophagus.

orthognathic surgery Procedure that is designed to correct conditions of the jaws and face related to structure and growth.

orthographic transcription Type of annotation system used for detailing a sample of spoken language. The standard alphabet is used to write every word that is spoken.

Orton, Samuel American physician who was interested in the area of learning disabilities, particularly those associated with reading.

ossicular chain Three tiny bones that compose the middle ear, consisting of the malleus, incus, and stapes.

other disfluencies Class of speech disfluencies that are found to occur in people who do not stutter as well as those who do stutter. An example of an other disfluency is a phrase repetition.

otitis externa Infection of the ear canal, often associated with persistent exposure to water. Also called swimmer's ear.

otitis media Infection of the middle ear space behind the eardrum. The duration of a bout of otitis media can range from acute to subacute, or chronic.

otitis media with effusion Form of otitis media characterized by buildup of fluid in the middle ear space; also called glue ear.

otoacoustic emissions Tiny sounds that emerge from the inner ear either spontaneously or shortly after the ear is exposed to an external sound. A screening test for newborn hearing.

otolaryngologist Surgeon who specializes in the diagnosis and treatment of disorders of the ear, nose, or throat; also called an ENT.

otosclerosis Hereditary disorder that results in abnormal growth in the middle ear that causes hearing loss.

otoscope Instrument consisting of a light and magnifying lens that is used for examining the external auditory meatus (ear canal) and tympanic membrane (eardrum).

ototoxic hearing loss Hearing impairment (both temporary and permanent) that can result from high doses of certain drugs.

overt behavior Openly visible behavior.

pagoclone Antianxiety drug that is currently being evaluated as a treatment for stuttering.

papilloma Benign wart-like tumors that form over muscle tissue. Papillomas have been found to form on the vocal folds.

paralanguage Nonverbal features that accompany speech and help convey meaning.

parallel talk Language therapy approach in which the therapist describes out loud what the child is seeing, hearing, or thinking during the play activity.

Pare, Ambroise French surgeon in the 16th century.

parent-directed therapy Feature of speech and language therapy in which parents are an active and integral part of the child's therapy program.

parenteral tube Feeding tube in which nutrition is delivered to the body intravenously; also called an IV tube.

parietal lobes Lobes located at the top of the cerebral cortex that are largely responsible for sensation.

Parkinson disease Degenerative neurological syndrome of the central nervous system that is characterized by rhythmical muscular tremors.

Parkinson, James English surgeon who first described a neurological syndrome later referred to as Parkinson disease.

participation model Augmentative and alternative communication assessment and treatment approach that emphasizes the individual's daily functional communication needs.

particulate theories Early theories of genetics that posited that information from each part of the parent had to be communicated to create the corresponding body part in the offspring.

Passavant, Philip Gustav German surgeon who was one of the first to propose a series of surgical solutions to help reduce hypernasal speech in cleft lip and palate.

passive muscular process Relaxation of muscles for a specified movement. Breath exhalation involves a passive muscular process.

pediatric dysphagia Swallowing disorder in children.

pediatric feeding disorder Impaired oral intake that is not age appropriate and is associated with medical, nutritional, feeding skill, and/or psychosocial dysfunction.

Penfield, Wilder Famous brain surgeon who made contributions in mapping brain function.

per oral Through or by way of the mouth.

percentage of consonants correct Measure used to determine the severity of an individual's speech sound disorder. The percentage is calculated by examining the total number of consonants composing a speech sample in comparison with the number of consonants produced accurately by the speaker.

percutaneously Any surgical procedure that involves an opening through the skin.

perforated eardrum Puncture in the tympanic membrane.

perilymph Fluid that is found in scala vestibuli and scala media ducts of the cochlea.

peripheral auditory system Portion of the hearing anatomy that consists of the outer, middle, and inner ear structures.

peripheral nervous system Portion of the nervous system that lies outside the brain and spinal cord.

peristalsis Rippling, wavelike muscle contractions that occur when food is digested.

person-centered approach Approach to treatment where the client is placed at the center of services and treated as a person first.

personal adjustment counseling Form of counselling that helps patients and families cope with the physiological and emotional impact of a communication disorder.

personality and emotional adjustment theory Theory that considers an individual's personality and subsequent behavioral patterns in the development of a voice disorder.

pervasive developmental disorder Group of disorders characterized by delays in development of social, language, motor, and/or cognitive skills.

pharyngeal cavity See definition for *pharynx*.

pharyngeal flap Surgical procedure designed to reduce hypernasality. A flap of skin creates a bridge between the back of the throat and the soft palate.

pharyngeal fricative /ʕ/ Unique consonant that is articulated with the root of the tongue against the pharynx.

pharyngeal stage Second stage in the three-stage process of normal swallowing, where the tongue transports material toward the back of the throat.

pharyngoplasty Form of surgery to reduce nasality in speech by narrowing the pharynx.

pharynx Hollow muscular tube that runs from the back of the nose to the top of the trachea (windpipe) and esophagus (food tube); also called the throat.

phenotype Observable physical characteristics of an organism.

phenylketonuria Genetic disorder that is characterized by an inability of the body to utilize the amino acid phenylalanine, which is essential for delivering protein to the body.

philtrum Shallow groove or depression running down the center of the outer surface of the upper lip.

phonation Sound made by the vibration of the vocal folds and modified by the resonance of the vocal tract.

phonatory disorder Abnormality in the ability to produce one's voice.

phonemes Consonant and vowel sounds spoken in a language.

phonetic inventory List of speech sounds that a person is able to accurately articulate.

phonetic-motoric disorder Theory of speech apraxia where the disorder is attributed to difficulty with the linguistic/phonetic organization and motoric execution of speech.

phoniatrics Medical research and treatment of organs involved in speech production.

phonophobia Fear of loud sounds

phonological approach Form of treating phonological disorders based on a linguistic (as opposed to motoric) approach.

phonological awareness Understanding of the sounds of words and word parts, including the ability to identify and manipulate larger parts of the spoken language such as words, syllables, and rhyme.

phonological difference Pattern of speaking found in bilingual speakers where the individual's dominant language affects the pronunciation of the less dominant language. The patterns are predictable based on the phonological features of the dominant language and therefore not considered to reflect a phonological disorder.

phonological disorder Impairment in the accurate production of speech sounds.

phonological interference Pattern of speech sound production found in bilingual speakers, where the phonological patterns of one language affect (interfere with) the pronunciation patterns in another language.

phonological processes Systematic pattern of speech sound production that affects an entire class of speech sounds. Stopping of fricatives is an example of a phonological process.

phonology Study of the speech sounds of a language.

phonomicrosurgery Surgical treatment of voice pathology using a microscope and micro-instruments.

phonosurgery Medical operation designed to repair damage to the vocal folds.

phonotrauma Any form of abuse to the vocal folds.

phrenology Study of the shape of the skull that was thought to reveal a person's character and mental capacity.

physical appearance Form of communication that is transmitted based on physical features of the individual.

physiology Biological study of the function of living organisms and their parts.

Piaget, Jean Swiss psychologist known for his study of the intellectual growth of children.

pica Craving and chewing substances that have no nutritional value.

picture-naming task Common method of sampling a person's speech sound production skills in which a person is asked to name a picture containing specific consonant and vowel sounds.

pinna Most visible portion of the outer ear; also known as the auricle.

pipe speech Manner of speaking where the upper and lower jaws are immobilized. This effect can be achieved by biting the end of a pipe and speaking at the same time.

pitch Perceptual impression of the vocal fundamental frequency of an individual's speaking voice.

pivotal response training Behavioral treatment for autism that is play-based and initiated by the child.

place of articulation Description of consonant sounds in regard to the location in the vocal tract where the sound was articulated.

positron emission tomography (PET) scan Method of body scanning in which a small amount of radiolabeled compound is injected or inhaled in the tissue to be studied.

postauricular muscle response Electrophysiological method of testing hearing sensitivity based on detecting muscular activity located behind the outer ear in response to sound.

postlingual deafness Profound hearing loss that occurred after a person learned to talk.

Prader-Willi syndrome Disorder caused by a genetic deletion of portions of chromosome 15.

pragmatics Study of language as it is used in a social context.

prelingual deafness Profound hearing loss that was present before a child learned to talk.

prelinguistic Vocal behaviors a child demonstrates prior to producing first words (language). The production of babbling is a prelinguistic vocal behavior.

premorbid state Individual's health status before the occurrence of a physical disease or emotional illness.

prenatal causes Factors which contribute to disability that occur prior to birth.

prenatal diagnosis Process of assessing the health status of a fetus prior to birth.

presbycusis Type of hearing loss that gradually occurs as people grow older.

pressure equalization tube Small tube that is inserted through the tympanic membrane (eardrum) to provide ventilation to the middle ear, also known as a grommet.

prevalence Total number of cases of a disease in a given population at a specific time.

primary assessment Full assessment of language expression and comprehension in an individual with suspected aphasia.

primary auditory center Region in the temporal lobe of the brain that is responsible for the sensation of sound, also called Heschl gyrus.

primary characteristics Core features. The primary characteristics of stuttering are the moments of stuttering that occur while speaking.

print-in-palm Approach used to communicate with a deaf-blind person by tracing the shapes of block letters on the palm of their hand with an index finger.

progressive hearing loss Hearing loss that gets worse over time. Persistent exposure to loud noise can result in a progressive hearing loss.

proteomics Branch of genetics that studies the proteins expressed by the genome of an organism.

proxemics Study of cultural, behavioral, and sociological aspects of spatial distance between individuals.

psychogenic disorder Disorder that stems from mental or emotional problems as opposed to having a known physiological cause.

psychogenic stuttering Type of stuttering that is thought to be caused by emotional trauma or problems with thought or reasoning.

psychological disturbance Disorder of the mind involving thoughts, behaviors, and emotions that cause either self or others significant distress.

psychosocial behavior Mental and physical reactions that occur when an individual is placed in an environmental setting.

puberphonia Unusually high-pitched speaking voice that persists beyond puberty.

pulse register Lowest range of speaking voice; also known as vocal fry register.

pure tone Sound composed of a single frequency.

pure-tone audiometry Use of single-frequency sounds (tones) in the evaluation of a person's hearing sensitivity.

qualitative Evaluation based on description of attributes, characteristics, and properties without the use of numbers.

quantitative Evaluation based on numeric description of attributes, characteristics, and properties.

race Group of people classified on the basis of common history, nationality, geographic distribution, or genetically transmitted physical characteristics.

range of motion Description of movement in regard to maximal and minimal movement.

Raph, Jane Beasley American professor of speech-language pathology who developed a social interaction approach to treating speech sound disorders in children.

rate of movement Description of movement in regard to the speed at which the movement is performed.

reciprocity Mutual agreement or dependence. Professional reciprocity refers to an agreement between associations regarding the qualifications to practice as an audiologist or speech-language pathologist in another state or country.

reflux Flowing back of fluid, often associated with the human digestive system and the reflux of gastric juices.

register of voice Range of voice produced by humans including low-, medium-, and high-pitched sounds.

rehabilitation hospital Hospital that is devoted to providing rehabilitation care to patients with various neurological or orthopedic conditions on an inpatient basis.

residual errors Pattern of speech sound misarticulations that involve either a fricative or liquid consonant.

respiratory cycle One complete breath, including an inspiratory and expiratory phase.

respiratory training Treatment approach to improving voice quality that involves focus on proper breathing techniques.

retrocochlear pathology Abnormality of the auditory system that occurs beyond the cochlea, most often seen as tumor of the auditory nerve or brainstem.

reverse swallow See definition for *tongue thrust*.

rib cage Twelve sets of bones that enclose the lungs and heart.

right hemisphere syndrome Acquired brain injury that results in language and cognitive impairments.

right hemisphere theory of recovery Theory related to left hemisphere brain damage where the right hemisphere takes over all functions that would have normally occurred in the left hemisphere.

Rimland, Bernard American psychologist who was influential in the field of autism.

Roe, F. Hall Individual with severe expressive language difficulty who used a communication board.

Romero, Emerson Cuban-American silent film actor who developed an early form of close captioning.

Roux, Philibert Joseph French surgeon who is credited as performing one of the first repairs of a cleft palate.

Rustin, Lena British speech-language pathologist who was an expert clinician in the area of stuttering management.

S * T = P Abbreviation for the source-filter theory of phonation.

SALT (systematic analysis of language transcripts) Computer software program designed to provide a detailed grammatical analysis of a sample of spoken (and transcribed) English.

Sarno, Martha Taylor American researcher in the field of neurogenic communication disorders.

savant Scholar or learned person.

scala media Middle chamber of the cochlea located between the scala tympani and scala media. The chamber is filled with endolymph. Also called the cochlear duct.

scala tympani Lower chamber of the cochlea that is filled with perilymph.

scala vestibuli Upper chamber of the cochlea that is filled with perilymph.

scanning Message selection technique in which items are presented sequentially.

schisis Medical term for opening, which is used to describe an orofacial cleft.

Schuell, Hildred American speech-language pathologist who devoted her career to the evaluation and treatment of aphasia.

Schulthess, Rudolf Swiss scientist who theorized that stuttering was due to spasms of the larynx.

Scripture, Edward Wheeler One of the first Americans trained in the field of psychology who developed skills in hearing measurement such as threshold testing and magnitude estimation. He was interested in various aspects of disordered speech production.

Seashore, Carl American psychologist interested in music, voice, and hearing. He built the first audiometer.

secondary characteristics Features that are not part of the primary form. Secondary characteristics of stuttering are those behaviors that occur in addition to the primary moment of stuttering.

self-talk Internal dialogue we use to view the world, explain situations, and communicate to ourselves.

semantics Study or science of meaning in language.

semicircular canals Three tiny circular tubes of the inner ear that are positioned at right angles to each other. They serve as the body's balance organ.

semiotics Theory and study of signs and symbols, especially as they relate to communication.

sensorineural hearing loss Most common type of hearing loss resulting from damage to the inner ear or regions of the central auditory system.

sensory nerves Portion of the nervous system that sends messages from the body to the brain.

severity Term used to describe degrees of hearing loss ranging from mild to profound.

severity scale Approach to estimate the severity of communication using a fixed numeric scale, such as 1 to 9, with 1 = low severity and 10 = high severity.

sign language Language that uses a system of manual, facial, and other body movements as a means of communication.

signal-to-noise ratio Measure of signal strength relative to background noise. The ratio is usually measured in decibels (dB).

simultaneous bilingualism Individual who has acquired two or more languages with equal skill in both.

simultaneous communication (SimCom) Combined use of sign language and speech to communicate.

single words Earliest identifiable language productions produced by children, usually by the age of 12 months.

Skinner, Burrhus Frederic (B. F.) American psychologist who published significant scientific works in the analysis of behavior.

Smile Train International charity that provides cleft lip and palate surgery to children in need, as well as provides medical training to doctors.

social media Network of friends, colleagues, and other personal contacts.

socioeconomic dialect Manner of speaking that is associated with an individual's financial and/or social status.

socioeconomic status Measure based on financial and social indicators.

SODA Acronym that describes the notation of disordered speech patterns, *S* = substitution, *O* = omission, *D* = distortion, *A* = addition.

soft palate Soft tissue that composes the back of the roof of the mouth, also known as the velum.

sound Vibrations that are transmitted through a medium. Sound can be described according to its duration, amplitude, and frequency of vibration.

sound sequencing Therapy approach for speech apraxia where the sounds of a word are first produced individually before producing the word in its entirety.

sound visibility Notion that some speech sounds are more readily visible on a talker's face compared with others. For example, the /f/ sound is high visibility, whereas the /h/ sound has low visibility.

sound wave Pressure wave that is propagated through air (or other media) that is generally audible to the human ear.

soundfield amplification System often used in classrooms for hearing-impaired children, whereby the teacher's voice is transmitted through a microphone and loudspeaker.

sound-to-symbol relationship Relationship between a specific speech sound and the corresponding letter in the alphabet for that sound. In general, the English language has a poor sound–symbol relationship. The phonetic alphabet provides an exact sound–symbol relationship.

source Point of origin. For the generation of speech, the source is the respiratory system.

spasmodic dysphonia Voice disorder caused by involuntary muscle movements in the vocal folds.

speaker One of two individuals required for successful communication. Another name for a speaker is encoder. The term is also a component of a hearing aid that delivers an acoustic signal to the ear.

speaking rate Speed at which a person speaks. Speaking rate is typically reported according to the number of words (or syllables) spoken per minute.

specific language impairment (SLI) Preschool child who shows difficulty with language that is not caused by a known neurological, sensory, intellectual, or emotional deficit.

speech chain The sequence of events in communication between the mind of the speaker to the mind of the listener.

speech communication Discipline concerned with the act of speaking.

speech delay Communication disorder in which the speaking behavior demonstrated by the individual is quantitatively (as opposed to qualitatively) different from normal.

speech-generating device Feature of augmentative and alternative communication systems that provides digitized or synthesized speech output.

speech intelligibility Characterization of the clarity of speech sound production.

speech-language pathologist Professional educated in the field of speech-language pathology.

speech-language pathology Study of disorders that affect a person's speech, language, and swallowing behavior, including methods of assessment, treatment, and prevention.

speech reading Deciphering of spoken language on the basis of visual cues provided by the speaker, also known as lip reading.

speech sound disorder Deviation in the production of consonants and/or vowels.

speech spontaneity Aspect of speech sampling that requires the person to either speak freely or name specific words.

spina bifida Serious birth abnormality in which the spinal cord is malformed during fetal development. The spinal cord lacks its usual protective skeletal and soft tissue covering.

spinal nerves Collection of 31 pairs of nerves that enter and exit the spinal cord. The nerves provide motor, sensory, or combined input to various parts of the body.

spontaneous recovery Natural reappearance of function following a period of lessened response. A concept associated with the recovery of communication skills shortly after a stroke.

spoonerism Unintentional transposition of sounds within or across words that occurs when speaking.

stammering See definition for stuttering.

Stampe, David American linguist who created the theory of natural phonology.

standardized testing Form of assessment in which a test is administered and scored in a consistent manner.

stapedectomy Surgical removal of the stapes bone within the middle ear as a means of improving hearing.

stapedius Smallest skeletal muscle of the human body whose purpose is to stabilize the stapes bone that is inserted into the oval window of the cochlea.

stapes Innermost of the three small bones (ossicles) of the middle ear, also known as the stirrup to reflect its unique shape.

statistical learning theory Theory that focuses on the statistical aspects of learning such as that related to the acquisition of language.

Steer, Max American speech-language pathologist who developed the speech-language pathology educational program at Purdue University.

Steinthal, Heymann German philosopher and linguist who first used the term apraxia.

stem cell Unspecialized cell that gives rise to a specialized cell, such as a blood cell.

Stevens, Nettie Maria American biologist and geneticist who discovered that chromosomes determine the sex of a species.

stimulation Aphasia treatment approach that encourages the patient to use all modalities of communication.

stoma Surgically created opening in the surface of the body.

stops Group of consonants that are organized according to their manner of articulation, namely the complete obstruction of forward airflow followed by a sudden release of air. The consonants /p/, /t/, and /k/ are examples of stops.

strength State, property, or act of being strong.

stroke Injury to the blood vessels of the brain, usually in the form of a clot or hemorrhage.

structural Speech sound disorders that result from abnormalities of the mouth and vocal tract.

structure Aspect of speech sampling that requires the person to produce speech in either a natural (home) or unnatural (clinic) environmental setting.

stuttering Disorder in which the flow of speech is disrupted by involuntary repetitions and prolongations of sounds, syllables, words or phrases, and involuntary silent pauses or blocks; also known as stammering.

stuttering-like disfluencies Speech disfluencies that are most indicative of a stuttering disorder. Examples of a stuttering-like disorder include a syllable repetition and a sound prolongation.

stuttering modification Treatment technique in which the main goal is to stutter more easily as opposed to speaking more fluently.

stuttering severity instrument Standardized test used to evaluate the severity of stuttering exhibited by children and adults.

subjective assessment Approach to evaluating a communication disorder using methods of observation and questioning.

submetacentric chromosome Chromosome whose centromere lies between its middle and its end but slightly closer to the middle.
submucous cleft Condition in which a cleft of the palate is not visible as a result of the cleft being covered by a mucous membrane lining.
substitutions Pattern of speech misarticulation whereby the intended speech sound is replaced (substituted) by another speech sound.
Sukhareva, Grunya Russian clinical psychiatrist who is credited with identifying some of the primary features of autism.
sulcus Deep, narrow groove in tissue. Various landmarks of the cerebral cortex are demarcated on the basis of sulci.
Sullivan, Anne Teacher and friend of Helen Keller.
swallowing center Region in the brainstem that is involved in the coordination and regulation of essential swallowing activity.
Sweet, Henry English linguist who made a significant contribution to the field of phonetics.
switch Device used in alternative or augmentative communication to assist with the selection of symbols.
symbol Visual display that represents object actions, events, or concepts.
symmetrical hearing loss Hearing loss of both areas in which the configuration and severity of the loss are identical.
syndrome Group of symptoms that collectively characterize an abnormal condition or disease.
syntax Study of the form of language such as grammatical rules.
synthesized speech Artificial computer-generated version of human speech.
syrinx Vocal organ of a bird.
tactile communication Form of nonverbal communication in which touching (e.g., handshaking, kissing) conveys a message from sender to receiver.
Tadoma method Form of communication used by deaf-blind individuals to assist with comprehension of speech. The method involves placement of the hands on the speaker's face to decipher facial movements.
Taylor, Orlando American professor who identified and described the rule-governed speech and language characteristics of Black/African American English.
technology Application of science, math, engineering, art, and other fields of knowledge to create tools and implementations deemed useful by a society.
teeth Hard bonelike structures aligned in a row along the base of the jaw that are used for biting and chewing.
telecoil Hearing aid device that can amplify sound waves transmitted through a telephone.
telehealth Use of digital technology to deliver and access health care without an in-person office visit.
temperament Manner in which a person thinks, behaves, and reacts.
Templin, Mildred American pioneer in speech-language pathology. Known for her research in the area of phonological development.
temporal bone Bone that forms the sides and base of the skull.
temporal lobes Side regions of the cerebral cortex that are primarily involved in the processing of sensory input.
temporomandibular joint Joint that connects the mandible (lower jaw) to the temporal bone of the skull.
tensor tympani Small muscle located in the middle ear that influences the mobility of the tympanic membrane (eardrum).
teratogenic Relating to, or causing, a malformation of an embryo or fetus.
Thelwall, John Best known as the radical orator during the movement for parliamentary reform in Britain in the late 18th century.
theory of mind Capacity to understand other people by ascribing mental states to them.
Thome, A German scholar who believed stuttering was caused by spasms of the respiratory system.
Threats, Travis American professor who pioneered using the International Classification of Functioning, Disability, and Health framework for clinical practice in speech-language pathology.
threshold Point that must be exceeded in order to elicit a response. A person's hearing threshold represents the lowest level of loudness necessary to perceive a sound.

thrombosis Formation of a blood clot inside a blood vessel that obstructs blood flow.
Thunberg, Greta Swedish environmental activist who is self-reported to be on the autism spectrum.
thyroarytenoid muscle Anatomical name for the vocal folds.
thyroid cartilage Largest of the cartilages composing the framework of the larynx. A landmark of the thyroid cartilage is a notch, also known as the Adam's apple.
tinnitus Perception of ringing in the ears without an external cause.
Titze, Ingo Voice scientist who has made significant contributions to vocal fold physiology and voice rehabilitation.
tongue Fleshy movable, muscular organ attached to the floor of the mouth. The primary organ for taste, swallowing, and speech production.
tongue advancement (or tongue carriage) Categorization of vowels according to the horizontal location of the tongue within the oral cavity.
tongue elevation (or tongue height) Categorization of vowels according to the vertical location of the tongue within the oral cavity.
tongue thrust Forward movement of the tongue, especially in the initial stage of swallowing. An infantile swallowing pattern that should diminish with age.
tonotopic organization Cellular structure of the inner ear whereby the frequencies represented in the cochlea are organized from high to low.
trachea Tube-like cartilaginous structure that is a portion of the respiratory tract; also called the windpipe.
tracheoesophageal speech Technique for speaking following laryngectomy. Air is diverted to the esophagus causing it to vibrate and create sound.
tract Anatomical area consisting of a series of related structures.
traditional approach Method of treating speech sound disorders. The approach begins with teaching the sound at an isolated level and gradually progressing to the production of the same sound in conversational speech.
tragus Projection of skin-covered cartilage in front of the ear canal.
transcranial magnetic stimulation Brain stimulation technique that induces a low electrical current between two electrodes placed on the scalp.
transducer Device that takes one form of energy and converts it into another type of energy.
transfer function Transformation that is used to describe the output of a device as a function of the input of the device. Speech production involves the transformation of the original source (vocal folds) into a specific sound resulting from changes in vocal tract configuration.
transmission model Conceptualization of communication that involves encoding (a speaker) and decoding (a listener).
traumatic brain injury Injury that occurs when a sudden outside force causes damage to the brain.
Travis, Lee Edward "Father of speech-language pathology in the United States." He was particularly interested in the area of stuttering.
triad of impairments A diagnosis of autism based on difficulties in three areas, social interaction, communication, and imagination.
Turner, Henry American physician who was the first to describe a genetic condition in women caused by the absence of one of the X sex chromosomes.
Turner syndrome Medical disorder in females as a result of an absent X (sex) chromosome.
two-word combinations Early language utterances produce by children at approximately 2 years of age.
tympanic membrane Thin concave-shaped membrane that separates the outer ear canal from the middle ear; also called the eardrum.
tympanogram Graphic display of sound reflected back from the eardrum during a tympanometry test.
tympanometer Instrument used to measure the compliance (sometimes called admittance) of the tympanic membrane. The results of the test are displayed on a graph called a tympanogram.
tympanometry Test performed to evaluate eardrum (tympanic membrane) mobility and middle ear functioning.

tympanoplasty Microsurgical procedure to repair a damaged tympanic membrane.

ultrasound Use of high-frequency sound waves to create an image of internal body structures.

unaided alternative or augmentative communication Use of nonverbal means of natural communication without the need for an external device.

unilateral cleft lip During fetal development, failure of the lip to form on one side of the nose.

unilateral hearing loss Type of hearing loss where one ear has normal hearing, and the other ear is impaired.

universal newborn screening Approach to the screening of hearing in newborn infants whereby all children in a setting (country, county, etc.) are evaluated.

upper respiratory tract Cavities of the body that include the nose, mouth, and throat.

uvula Small fleshy mass of tissue that suspends from the back of the soft palate.

validation therapy Treatment technique used to confirm, through words and gestures, what the person with dementia says.

Van den Berg, Janwillem Dutch scientist who proposed the myoelastic-aerodynamic theory of phonation.

Van Gogh, Vincent Dutch painter during the 19th century.

Van Riper, Charles American pioneer in the field of speech-language pathology. He made significant contributions to the areas of stuttering and speech sound disorders.

Vanderheiden, Gregg Engineer who made significant contributions to device technology used for augmentative and alternative communication.

velopharyngeal closure Contact between the soft palate (velum) and the back of the throat (pharynx) that normally occurs during swallowing and the production of speech.

velopharyngeal inadequacy Malfunctioning of the physiological relationship between the soft palate (velum) and the back of the throat (pharynx), in which a lack of contact between the two structures occurs.

ventilation tube Small tube inserted through the tympanic membrane to ventilate the middle ear and prevent fluid from accumulating. Also called a pressure equalization tube or grommet.

ventriloquism Art of projecting voice to give the illusion of it coming from another source, such as a dummy or doll figure.

verbal communication Basis of expressive (vocal) communication that is one way for people to communicate face-to-face.

verbalizations Production of vocal sounds that express meaning.

vermilion border Region of redness that surrounds the lips.

vestibular apparatus Region of the inner ear that is important for maintaining balance and spatial orientation. Consists of the utricle, saccule, and semicircular canals.

Vicker, Beverly Speech-language pathologist who performed clinical work in the 1960s and 1970s using communication boards for severely disabled individuals.

videofluoroscopy Motion x-ray of the body that combines traditional fluoroscopy (x-ray) with video technology.

videofluoroscopic swallowing study Use of motion x-ray to visualize swallowing.

viral meningitis Infection of the protective membranes surrounding the brain or spinal cord that results from a virus. This form of meningitis is quite common and is a relatively mild illness compared with bacterial meningitis.

virgules Diagonal (/) mark that serves as a form of pronunciation. The individual phonemes of a language are usually depicted using virgules (e.g., /t/, /m/, /f/, etc.).

Visi-Pitch Commercially available instrument designed to measure and display the vocal fundamental frequency (pitch) of spoken voice.

visible speech Phonetic system developed by Melville Belle to represent the position of speech articulators for individual consonants and vowels.

visual communication Transfer of information between individuals on the basis of vision.

vocal abuse Any behavior that strains or injures the vocal folds, thus affecting their normal functioning.

vocal folds Two muscular bands located within the framework of the larynx that protect the trachea from the entrance of foreign matter. These muscular bands also vibrate for the generation of voice; also known as the vocal cords.

vocal function exercise Treatment approach to improving voice production involving increased strength and coordination of the laryngeal musculature.

vocal hygiene Science of vocal health and steps taken to ensure proper care of the vocal mechanism.

vocal misuse Improper speaking behavior that can lead to temporary or permanent changes to one's speaking voice.

vocal nodules Small inflammatory or fibrous growth that develops on the vocal folds.

vocal polyp Small swelling in the mucous membranes covering the vocal folds; also known as Reinke edema or polypoid degeneration.

vocal tract Anatomical cavity in animals where sound is produced.

vocalizations Any sound produced through the action of a vocal apparatus.

vocology Science and practice of voice rehabilitation.

voice banking Process by which large portions of a person's voice are recorded and then uploaded to a speech-generating computer system.

voice disorder Condition in which the natural generation of voice and voice resonance is impaired.

voice feminization Voice therapy procedure that involves the change of voice from masculine to feminine, usually as a result of gender transformation.

voice masculinization Voice therapy procedure that involves the change of voice from feminine to masculine, usually as a result of gender transformation.

voice quality Subjective aspect of voice that is perceived by listeners.

voice rest Therapy procedure that involves complete cessation of speaking (including whispering) as a means of healing the vocal folds.

voiced consonant Consonant that is produced with vocal fold vibration such as the /z/ sound.

voiceless consonant Consonant that is produced without vocal fold vibration, such as the /s/ sound.

Volta, Alessandro Italian physicist who invented the voltalic pile, a forerunner of the electric battery.

von Békésy, Georg Hungarian physiologist who received the Nobel Prize for his research on the functioning of the inner ear.

von Graefe, Karl Ferdinand Pioneer of plastic and reconstructive surgery.

von Helmholtz, Hermann German physicist who made important contributions in acoustics and optics.

von Kölliker, Albert Swiss histologist who was a pioneer in the study of cellular embryology.

von Langenbeck, Bernard Skilled surgeon who developed a procedure for the closure of the hard palate.

von Leden, Hans Otolaryngologist who coined the term *phonosurgery* to refer to the restoration of voice using surgical techniques.

von Siebold, Carl Casper One of the first surgeons to recognize the importance of speech therapy for individuals with cleft lip and palate.

Waldeyer, Wilhelm German anatomist who identified the material residing within a cell nucleus that he termed *chromosome*.

Wallace, Alfred Nineteenth-century anthropologist who, together with Charles Darwin, supported the concept of natural selection.

Watson, James Nobel Prize winner for discovering the double-helix structure of DNA. His colleague who assisted in the discovery was Francis Crick.

waveform Graph obtained by plotting the characteristics of a sound wave against time.

weak central cohesion theory Perceptual-cognitive style indicating a limited ability to understand social context or to "see the forest through the trees."

Weiss, Deso Hungarian psychiatrist and speech-language pathologist who made research and clinical contributions to the area of speech fluency, notably cluttering.

Wernicke's aphasia Language disorder that impacts the comprehension of spoken and written language, resulting from damage to the left temporal lobe (Wernicke's area) region of the brain; also known as a form of fluent aphasia.

Wernicke's area Region of the left cerebral temporal lobe that plays an important role in the understanding of speech and language.

Wernicke, Karl German neurologist who deduced that the left temporal lobe region of the brain was localized for understanding language. This region became known as Wernicke area.

whistle register Highest register of the human voice; also known as flageolet register.

whole genome sequencing Laboratory process whereby the genome of an individual's entire DNA is obtained.

wild boy of Aveyron Feral child, known as Victor, who was found wandering in the woods in France. His lack of speech provided early insight to the role of the environment in learning language.

Williams Syndrome Genetic condition characteristed by intellectual disability or learning problems.

Wilson, Matthew American Revolutionary War minister and physician who wrote a compendium of medicine called the *Therapeutic Alphabet*.

Wing, Lorna British psychiatrist who recognized that autism could be considered along a spectrum, having many different causes.

within-word disfluencies Disruptions in the forward flow of speech that occur within the boundary of a single word. Examples include the repetition or prolongation of a consonant at the beginning of a word.

World Health Organization Branch of the United Nations that is concerned with public health.

written language Form of communication based on the representation of language by means of a writing system.

Wundt, Wilhelm German physiologist and psychologist who has been referred to as the "Father of experimental psychology."

Yearsley, James British surgeon who advocated removal of the tonsils as a form of treatment for stuttering.

Yoder, David Speech-language pathologist who made significant research and clinical contributions in the area of augmentative and alternative communication.

Yoshinaga-Itano, Christine American professor who emphasized the importance of early identification of hearing loss on a child's academic and communication success.

Young, Edna Hill American speech-language pathologist known for developing the moto-kinesthetic method of speech therapy for children with cleft lip and palate.

Yperman, Jehan Medieval surgeon who developed a variety of procedures for repair of facial defects.

Zemlin, Willard R. American speech-language pathologist who was interested in the basic anatomy and physiology of the speech and hearing mechanisms.

Zwaardemaker, Hendrik Dutch otolaryngologist who coined the term *presbycusis*.

zygote Cell (organism) that results from fertilization.

INDEX

Note: Page numbers in **bold** reference non-text information.

C

D

E

F

G

H

J

K

L

M

N

O

P

Q

R

S

T

V